John Tetlow

A Progressive Series of Inductive Lessons in Latin

Based on Material Drawn From Classical Sources, Especially from Cæsar's

Commentaries

John Tetlow

A Progressive Series of Inductive Lessons in Latin
Based on Material Drawn From Classical Sources, Especially from Cæsar's Commentaries

ISBN/EAN: 9783337178796

Printed in Europe, USA, Canada, Australia, Japan

Cover: Foto ©Paul-Georg Meister /pixelio.de

More available books at **www.hansebooks.com**

A

PROGRESSIVE SERIES

OF

INDUCTIVE LESSONS

IN

LATIN,

BASED ON MATERIAL DRAWN FROM CLASSICAL
SOURCES, ESPECIALLY FROM CAESAR'S
COMMENTARIES.

BY

JOHN TETLOW, A.M.,

MASTER OF THE GIRLS' LATIN SCHOOL, BOSTON.

The mind should be introduced to principles through the medium of examples, and so should be led from the particular to the general — from the concrete to the abstract. . . .

Children should be led to make their own investigations, to draw their own inferences. — HERBERT SPENCER'S ESSAY ON EDUCATION.

BOSTON:
PUBLISHED BY GINN, HEATH, & CO.
1884.

Entered, according to Act of Congress, in the year 1884, by

JOHN TETLOW,

in the Office of the Librarian of Congress at Washington.

J. S. CUSHING & CO., PRINTERS, BOSTON

PREFACE.

THIS manual is the result of an attempt to apply the inductive method to elementary instruction in Latin. The value of this method as an instrument for developing and strengthening the mental faculties has long been recognized and will probably not be questioned. As applied to Latin, it brings the pupil into immediate contact with classical examples, teaching him to view these, rather than the rules of the grammarian, as the original sources of knowledge and the final test of correctness; and it leads him, through the observation and study of such examples, to the discovery of the syntactic laws which underlie them. In a word, it trains the pupil in the methods required for original investigation.

But, while the value of the inductive method will not be denied, there will probably be various opinions as to what constitutes a successful application of it, and equally various standards by which a given application of it will be judged. Practical teachers, who know from daily experience in the class-room that the undeveloped powers of youth are extremely feeble, are inclined to view with distrust any method of instruction which undertakes to make the pupil a discoverer rather than a learner; while, on the other hand, the mere theorist demands that the pupil be told nothing, but that he be led to discover everything. It will not be necessary for me to state in detail the principles which have guided me in determining how much or how little the pupil should be aided in the work of discovering and formulating rules from examples; these principles may be readily inferred from an examination of the method of exposition adopted in any one of the lessons, taken at random, in which the laws or usages of the language are treated. I have striven to keep constantly in view the mental immaturity of the pupils for whom these lessons are intended, and the limitations as to time by which their teachers are necessarily restricted. Keeping these in view, I have felt that it would be safer to err on the side of affording too much rather than too little help.

From the character of the material used in the exercises and reading lessons of this manual, it will be seen that I do not agree with those who think that the pupil should be introduced to the study of Latin through the medium of entertaining stories written by modern Latinists. On the contrary, that method seems to me the best which takes the pupil by the shortest road into the domain of classical antiquity, and which, by bringing him into direct contact with the subject-matter, the modes of thought, the forms of expression, and the choice and arrangement of words peculiar to the classical writers, most thoroughly equips him for the intelligent study of the acknowledged masterpieces of Latin literature. Accordingly, I have drawn not merely the examples used for purposes of exposition, but also the short sentences supplied for practice on forms and constructions, and the longer passages selected for connected translation, from classical sources.

The short sentences supplied for practice on forms and constructions are arranged in separate sets entitled respectively "Exercises" and "Supplementary Exercises." Of these two sets, the Exercises will probably in most cases furnish ample material for the grammatical work of the first year; the Supplementary Exercises, which are somewhat more difficult, may be drawn upon for additional practice or for periodical reviews, or they may be reserved for the second year, to be studied as progressive exercises in Latin composition in connection with the first author read.

The material provided for connected translation consists of easy anecdotes from Cicero, and of those passages from Caesar in which the usages of the Druids and the manners and customs of the Gauls and Germans are described. The latter, owing to their intrinsic value and interest, and to their comparative freedom from the constructions of indirect discourse, seem especially suited to the needs of the beginner. The plan of the book also contemplates the early introduction of the study of the simpler modes of word-formation as an aid to the development of power to read at sight. Special suggestions relating to the lessons on word-formation and the anecdotes from Cicero will be found in the notes introduced at pages 74 and 224.

In the special vocabularies of the earlier lessons, in the lessons on word-formation, and in the general Latin-English vocabulary, English words or parts of words that are *cognate* with the Latin forms under which they appear are printed in SMALL CAPITALS; whereas English words or parts of words that are *borrowed* (directly or indirectly) from the Latin forms under which they appear are printed in *Gothic Italic*. This distinction, the use of which was suggested to me by a similar distinction in Professor White's excellent *Greek Lessons*, I have tried to render as serviceable as possible by confining the differences in type just mentioned to those letters of the English word which alone mark its relationship to the Latin. Thus, cōnsulātus is translated *consulship*, and peditātus, FOOT-*soldiers*. I have not, of course, meant to imply by this method of printing that the exhaustive study of the origin and history of English words should form a part of the first year's work in Latin; but rather to supply material for occasional excursions in this direction. For example, the connection between the Latin veniō and the English COME is not so obvious that it can easily be made clear to beginners; and, unless some bright boy or girl whose curiosity has been excited by the silent suggestion of the change in type should ask for an explanation, the teacher should pass over this word without comment. On the other hand, the operation of Grimm's law in such words as pater, FATHER, frāter, BROTHER, and māter, MOTHER, is so interesting, and at the same time so easily made clear, that the teacher may profitably use these and similar examples as a means of leading the pupil to a recognition of the general law which they illustrate.

As it was a part of my plan to introduce a few simple lessons on word-formation, and, in the etymological part of the general vocabulary, to trace complete words to the stems from which they are formed, it seemed desirable that, in dealing with the several declensions in substantives and adjectives, I should devote some attention to stems. Accordingly, besides pointing out the stems of the several paradigms of declension, I have also called upon the pupil to explain the formation of the nominative, referring him to the grammar for the necessary information and guidance. The paragraphs in which these references to the grammar occur are, of course, comparatively unimportant for the beginner, and they may, at the discretion of the teacher, be postponed or omitted. They are numbered as follows: **121, 162, 188, 195, 197, 250, 266**.

It will be seen that, in giving the principal parts of verbs, I have taken the liberty to deviate slightly from established usage. In place of the *supine* in **-um**, which is generally given as the fourth of the principal parts, I have substituted the *perfect participle*. The necessity of a reform in this direction was first recognized and pointed out by Professor Lane, who introduced this substitution many years ago in his teaching, and has also incorporated it in the Latin grammar which he is preparing for publication. When word-formation was so little understood that the supine was thought to be the source from which the perfect and future participles, and primitives in **-tor, -tiō, -tus,** and **-tūra** were derived, there was an obvious propriety in recognizing the supine as one of the principal parts of the verb. Clipped of final **-um, it** yielded a base — the so-called supine stem — which was seen to be common to all these forms. As, moreover, identity of base was supposed to indicate community of origin, the forms just enumerated were naturally viewed as offshoots from this parent stem. As a matter of fact, however, the perfect and future participles, primitives in **-tor,** -tiō, -tus, and -tūra, and the supines in **-tum** and **-tū** are all simply parallel formations from the root or from the verb stem. Thus, the participles cultus and cultūrus, and the primitive substantives cultor, cultūra, cultus, and cultiō, are formed directly from the root col-, *till;* in like manner, the participles audītus and audītūrus, and the substantives audītor, audītus, and audītiō, are formed directly from audī-, *hear,* the stem of audiō. While then there is, in a restricted sense, a *real* supine stem ending in -tu-, which lies at the foundation of two verbal forms, the former and the latter supine, the *so-called* supine stem ending in -t-, euphonically -s-, is purely a figment of the grammarians.

Again, although our dictionaries, in giving the principal parts of verbs, record more than 2500 supines in -um, Richter has shown, in his contributions to the study of this form of the verb, that only 236 such supines are to be found in the texts of the Latin writers from the time of Plautus to the early Christian centuries.

It is clear then that the supine, instead of being a principal part of the verb, is a very insignificant part. On the other hand, the perfect participle is found in all the passive tenses for completed action; it is, indeed, in these tenses the only essential part, for the auxiliary is often omitted. Moreover, if a mechanical base must be recognized as an artificial **help** to the pupil while he is committing to memory those forms of the verb that have certain letters in common, the perfect participle yields this base as readily as the supine. A reference to sections **136** and **137 will** show that the treatment of the perfect participle as **one of the** principal parts of the verb renders easy and natural **the application** of the inductive method to a subject which must otherwise **be left** unexplained.

It has been the prevailing **practice** in Latin dictionaries and special vocabularies to **account for the** form **and** meaning of words whose etymology is given, by referring them to other complete words from which they are not directly formed, but with which they are merely connected in formation. This loose and inaccurate way of explaining the derivation and meaning of words must soon give place to a sounder method. One special vocabulary[1] has already appeared in this country in which the subject of etymology is differently treated, and other works founded on the same principles are in preparation. In harmony with this tendency, and **in** the hope of developing right habits of thought in the pupil from the outset, I have been careful to **refer** the words whose etymology is explained in the general vocabulary, directly to the roots or stems from which they are formed.[2] Lest this **mode** of presentation should seem obscure to the learner, who **in his actual reading meets** not stems, but complete words, **I have thought it best, in the** case of formation from stems, **to add in parenthesis the** complete word to which the stem belongs.

The vocabulary of an introductory book does not call for much in the way of pictorial illustration; but what it does call for, it **calls** for imperatively. Such words, for example, as **scūtum** and **signa militāria** cannot be understood by the pupil without the aid of a picture. Expressions of this kind, therefore, for which illustrations from the antique were available — eleven in number — I have thought it best to illustrate. The cuts used for this purpose have been taken from Rich's *Dictionary of Antiquities* and Guhl and Koner's *Leben der Griechen und Römer*.

In conclusion, I desire to express my grateful sense of obligation

---

[1] Greenough's *Vocabulary to* **Virgil**.

[2] This statement does not, of course, apply to those instances in which a word is said to be merely "connected with" another word in formation.

to the friends who have kindly **read and** criticized this book as it has **been** sent to them **in** sheets from the press. I am especially indebted **to Professor** George M. Lane of Harvard University, who has not **only placed at** my disposal such of his manuscript **and** printed collections **as would be** of service **to** me, but has critically examined **the proof-sheets, and** aided me by corrections and suggestions that **have** added to **the** value of **the book** in every part. I am **also under** special obligations to **William C.** Collar, A.M., Head-master of the Roxbury Latin School, for valuable notes and criticisms.

Mr. J. S. Cushing, **under** whose supervision this book has been printed, has, by **his** unfailing patience **and** courtesy, and by his suggestive skill, materially lightened the **labor of** carrying the sheets through the press.

JOHN TETLOW.

BOSTON, May 1, 1884.

CONTENTS.

LESSONS.		PAGES.
INTRODUCTORY:	Alphabet, Syllabication, Quantity, Accent....	1–7
I.	The Four Conjugations	7–8
II.–III.	Present Indicative Active: Conjugations I.–IV.	9–12
IV.	Substantives: First Declension	12–13
V.–VI.	Ablative with Prepositions. — Subject Nominative. — Accusative of Direct Object	13–16
VII.	Substantives: Second Declension	16–17
VIII.	The **Preposition In.** — Genitives: Possessive, Subjective, Objective	18–20
IX.	Adjectives: **First** and Second Declensions	21–23
X.	Adjectives: Attributive and Predicate. — Dative with Adjectives	23–26
XI.–XII.	Present, Imperfect, and Future Indicative of **Both** Voices	26–28
XIII.	**Ablatives:** Means or Instrument and Voluntary Agent,	29–31
XIV.	Substantives of the Third Declension: Mute Stems..	**31–33**
XV.–XVI.	Perfect, Pluperfect, **and** Future Perfect **of Both** Voices. — **Principal** Parts.....................	33–37
XVII.–XVIII.	Agreement of the Participle in Compound Tenses. — Dative of Indirect Object	38–42
XIX.	Substantives of the Third Declension: Liquid and -s- Stems	43–44
XX.–XXI.	Imperatives of Both **Voices.** — The Vocative.........	45–49
XXII.	Substantives of the **Third** Declension: Vowel Stems,	49–51
XXIII.	Adjectives of the Third Declension: Vowel Stems ..	51–53
XXIV.–XXV.	Apposition. — Predicate Agreement. — Accusative with Prepositions	53–57
XXVI.	Substantives of the Third Declension: Stems Apparently Consonant. — Adjectives of One Termination. — Present Participle.....................	57–60
XXVII.	Ablative of Specification. — Ablative of Time When,	60–63
XXVIII.	Third Declension: Gender......................	63–66
XXIX.	Substantives: Fourth Declension.................	67–69
XXX.	Adjectives: Regular Comparison	69–71

INDUCTIVE LATIN LESSONS.

INTRODUCTORY.

NOTE.— The Latin alphabet, which for the vowels is phonetic, is here introduced for the convenience of those teachers who aim to secure a correct quantitative pronunciation. As success in this direction depends on a right beginning, it is recommended that the pupil be taught the Latin names of the single letters and diphthongs at the outset, and that, until right habits have been established, these Latin names be used in occasional exercises in oral spelling.

I.

1. LATIN ALPHABET.

	CHARACTER.	NAME.	PRONUNCIATION OF NAME.
	a	a	$ăh$
	$ā$	$ā$	$āh^1$
	b	be	bay^2
	c	ce	kay^2
	d	de	day^2
	e	e	$ĕ$ (as in *met*)
	$ē$	$ē$	foregoing sound prolonged.[1]
	f	ef	*ef*
	g	ge	gay^2
	h	ha	*hah*
Vowel:	i	i	$ĕĕ$
	$ī$	$ī$	$ēe^1$
Consonant:	j	i	ee^3
	k	ka	*kah*
	l	el	*el*
	m	em	*em*
	n	en	*en*

Character.	Name.	Pronunciation of Name.
o	o	ŏ (as sometimes heard in *whole, i.e.,* the continental short *o*, **not so** broad as the *o* in *not*)
ō	ō	foregoing sound prolonged.[1]
p	pe	*pay*[2]
q	qu	*koo*
r	er	*e* as in *met* ; *r* trilled.
s	es	*ess*
t	te	*tay*[2]
Vowel: u	u	*ŏo*
ū	ū	*ōo*[1]
Consonant: v	u	*oo*[4]
x	ix	*eeks*
[y	ü	like French *u* or German *ü*]
[z	zēta	as in Greek]

2. Latin Diphthongs.

ae	ae	*ai*[1] (as in *aisle*)
au	au	*ou*[1] (as in *house*)
oe	oe	*oi*[1] (as in *toil*)
ui	ui	*oo–ee*[1] (rapidly uttered)
eu	eu	*eh–oo*[1] (rapidly uttered)

[1] The diphthongs and long vowels should occupy twice as much time in utterance as the short vowels.

[2] The sound here represented by *-ay* is approximate only; the true sound of Latin "e" has no *ee*-vanish.

[3] *ee* here represents the pronunciation of the letter "j" used by itself; *e.g.*, in oral spelling. In combination with other letters, "j" has the power of "y" in *yes*.

[4] *oo* here represents the pronunciation of the letter "v" used by itself; *e.g.*, in oral spelling. In combination with other letters, "v" has the power of "w" in *we*.

II.

SYLLABICATION.

3.   EXAMPLES.

1. Au'-di-ŏ,[1] *I hear.*   3. Proe'-li-um, *battle.*
2. Ge'-ner, *son-in-law.*   4. A-mī-ci'-ti-a, *friendship.*

4. OBSERVATION AND INFERENCE: Note that in each of the foregoing examples a *single consonant* stands between two vowels (see: d, Ex. 1; n, Ex. 2; l, Ex. 3; m, c, and t, Ex. 4). To which vowel is it joined in writing? Frame a rule for Syllabication in such cases.

5.   EXAMPLES.

1. An'-nus, *year.*   3. Bel'-lum, *war.*
2. Mit'-tō, *I send.*   4. Ag'-ger, *mound.*

6. OBSERVATION AND INFERENCE: Note that in each of the foregoing examples a *consonant is doubled* between two vowels (see: n-n, Ex. 1; t-t, Ex. 2; l-l, Ex. 3; g-g, Ex. 4). To which vowel is each consonant joined in writing? Frame a rule for Syllabication in such cases.

7.   EXAMPLES.

1. A'-sper, *rough.*   5. Bel'-gae, *the Belgae.*
2. Frā'-trēs, *brothers.*   6. Am'-plus, *ample.*
3. Jū-stus, *just.*   7. Lin'-gua, *tongue.*
4. Rŏ-strum, *beak.*   8. Ar'-ma, *arms.*

8. OBSERVATION AND INFERENCE: Note that in the foregoing examples *two or more consonants* stand between two vowels (see: sp, Ex. 1; tr, Ex. 2; st, Ex. 3; str, Ex. 4; l-g, Ex. 5; m-pl, Ex. 6; n-gu, Ex. 7; r-m, Ex. 8). Note, further, that such of these groups of consonants as can *begin a word* belong to the *second* vowel, and so begin a syllable (see Exs. 1–4); whereas, such of these groups as *cannot begin a word* are *divided* (see Exs. 5–8). Frame a rule for Syllabication in such cases.

9.   **EXAMPLES.**

1. **Ab'-e-ŏ** (ab, *away;* **eŏ,** *I go*), *I go away.*
2. **In-ī'-quus** (in-, *not;* aequus, *fair*), *unfair.*
3. **Ab'-est** (ab, *away;* **est,** *he is*), *he is away.*
4. **Red'-i-mŏ** (red-, *back;* emŏ, *I buy*), *I buy back.*

10. OBSERVATION: Note that the foregoing examples are *compounds*, and that, in syllabication, the *parts* of each compound are treated as *separate words*. Frame a rule for the Syllabication of Compounds.

11.   **EXERCISE.**

Spell, syllabicate, and pronounce the following words: —

[2] **dēleō,** *I destroy.*
[3] **impedīmentum,** *impediment.*
[4] **injūria,** *injury.*
[4] **prōvincia,** *province.*
[4] **inūtilis,**[5] *unprofitable.*
[4] **jūstitia,** *justice.*
[2] **oppĭdum,** *town.*

[2] **littera,** *letter.*
[2] **māgnus,**[6] *great.*
[2] **occupō,** *I seize.*
[4] **officium,** *duty.*
[2] **redeō,**[7] *I return.*
[2] **adeō,**[8] *I go to.*
[2] **dīxit,**[9] *he said.*

---

[1] The accented syllable of Latin words will be marked until the subject of accentuation has been treated.
  [2] Accent the first syllable.
  [3] Accent the fourth syllable.
  [4] Accent the second syllable.
  [5] **inūtilis** (compound) = in-, *not*, ūtilis, *useful.*

[6] The combination gn can begin a word.
  [7] **redeō** (compound) = red-, *back;* eō, *I go.*
  [8] **adeō** (compound) = ad, *to;* eō, *I go.*
  [9] x, though a double consonant (= c + s), is treated as a single consonant in syllabication.

III.

QUANTITY.

12.   EXAMPLES.

1. Recū'sat, *he refuses.*   4. *Lau*'dat, *he commends.*
2. Tī*mēs*, *you fear.*   5. *Proe*'lium, *battle.*
3. *Jū*'stus, *just.*   6. *Ae*'vum, *age.*

13. OBSERVATION AND INFERENCE: Note that **the** italicized syllable in **each of** the foregoing examples contains a *long vowel* (see Exs. 1-3) **or a** *diphthong* (see Exs. 4-6). Such a syllable is *long*. Frame **a** rule for the Quantity of a Syllable containing a Long Vowel or Diphthong.

Note that the syllables *not italicized* in the foregoing examples contain a *short vowel*. Such syllables are *short*. Frame a rule for the Quantity of a Syllable containing a Short Vowel.

NOTE: For an exception to the rule implied in the last paragraph, see 15 below.

14.   EXAMPLES.

1. *An*'nus, *year.*   4. *Jū*'stus, *just.*
2. *Bel*'gae, *the Belgae.*   5. *Val*'lum, *wall.*
3. *Lin*'gua, *tongue.*   6. *Dux*, *leader.*

15. OBSERVATION AND INFERENCE: Note that the *vowel* of the italicized syllable in each of the foregoing examples is *followed by two consonants* (see Exs. 1-5) or by a *double consonant* (see *x*,[1] Ex. 6). The *vowel* so placed may be long (see Exs. 4 and 5) or short (see Exs. 1, 2, 3, and 6), but the *syllable* is *long*. Frame a rule for the Quantity of a Syllable whose Vowel is followed by Two Consonants or a Double Consonant.

NOTE: For an exception to the foregoing, see A. & G. 18, *e*; H. 10, III.; G. 11.

16. **EXAMPLES.**

1. Amĭci′tia, *friendship.*
2. Ha′beō, *I have.*
3. Proe′lium, *battle.*
4. Vi′ae, *ways.*

17. OBSERVATION AND INFERENCE: Note that the *vowel* of the italicized syllable in each of the foregoing examples is *followed by* another *vowel* (see Exs. 1–3) or by a *diphthong* (see Ex. 4). Both the *vowel* so placed and the *syllable* containing it are *short.* Frame a rule for the Quantity of a Syllable whose Vowel is followed by another Vowel or by a Diphthong.

$$^1 x = c + s \text{ or } g + s.$$

IV.

ACCENT.

18. **EXAMPLES.**

1. An′nus, *year.*
2. Lau′dō, *I commend.*
3. Jū′stus, *just.*
4. Lin′gua, *tongue.*

19. OBSERVATION AND INFERENCE: Note that the foregoing examples are words of *two syllables.* Which syllable is *accented?* Frame a rule for the Accent of Latin Words of Two Syllables.

20. **EXAMPLES.**

1. Habē′mus, *we have.*
2. Recūsā′mus, *we refuse.*
3. Cōnfir′mō, *I establish.*
4. Trānspor′tō, *I transport.*
5. Ha′beō, *I have.*
6. Amīci′tia, *friendship.*
7. Op′pidum, *town.*
8. Po′pulus, *people.*

21. OBSERVATION AND INFERENCE: Note **(1)** that the foregoing examples are words of *more than two syllables,* (2) that in Exs. 1–4 the *penult*[1] is *long,* and (3) that in Exs. 5–8 the *penult* is *short.* Which syllable is *accented* when the *penult* is *long* (see Exs. 1–4)? Which syllable is *accented* when the *penult* is *short* (see Exs. 5–8)? Frame a rule for the **Accent of Latin Words of More than Two Syllables.**

THE FOUR CONJUGATIONS.

22.   **EXERCISE.**

Spell each of the following words, syllable by syllable; give the Quantity of each syllable when you have spelled it; then Pronounce the complete word; thus, **r-e, re,** *short;* **c-ū, cū,** *long;* **s-ā, sā,** *long;* **m-u-s, mus,** *short;* **recūsā′mus.**

amō, *I love.*
cōn-firmās,[2] *you* (sing.) *establish.*
laudat, *he commends.*
recūsāmus, *we refuse.*
probātis, *you* (pl.) *approve.*
trāns-portant,[2] *they transport.*

moneō, *I warn.*
habēs, *you* (sing.) *have.*
manet, *he remains.*
pārēmus, *we obey.*
tenētis, *you* (pl.) **hold.**
timent, *they fear.*

[1] The Penult is the last syllable **but** one; **the** Antepenult, the last but **two.**
[2] Compound; in **the** vocabularies of this book the parts of compound words will be separated by the hyphen.

LESSON I.

THE FOUR CONJUGATIONS.

NOTE: It is assumed that the pupil is already familiar with the parts of speech and their properties (as person, number, gender, mood, **tense,** etc.), or, failing this, that the teacher will explain and illustrate them as occasion requires.

The long vowels are marked throughout this book; vowels not marked are to be pronounced short. As a practical aid in the observance of quantity, it is recommended that the pupil be required, in written exercises, to mark the long vowels.

23.   **EXAMPLES.**

1. Amō, *I love;* amāre, *to love.*
2. Moneō, *I warn;* monēre, *to warn.*
3. Tegō, *I cover;* tegere, *to cover.*
4. Audiō, *I hear;* audīre, *to hear.*

24. EXPLANATION: The foregoing examples show that in Latin the *present infinitive* **active** is formed, not as in English by placing the preposition *to* before the simple form of the verb, but by adding -re. Moreover, some verbs (as **amō**) have a characteristic vowel -ā- before this infinitive ending, others (as **moneō**) have -ē-, others (as **tegō**) have -e-, and others (as **audiō**) have -ī-. Accordingly,

THE FOUR CONJUGATIONS.

25. Latin verbs are divided into four groups called

CONJUGATIONS.

1. The First Conjugation includes all verbs whose present infinitive active has the characteristic vowel **-ā-** before the ending **-re**; as: amā-re, *to love.*

2. The Second Conjugation includes all verbs whose present infinitive active has the characteristic vowel **-ē-** before the ending **-re**; as: monē-re, *to warn.*

3. The Third Conjugation includes all verbs whose present infinitive active has the characteristic vowel **-e-** before the ending **-re**; as: tege-re, *to cover.*

4. The Fourth Conjugation includes all verbs whose present infinitive active has the characteristic vowel **-ī-** before the ending **-re**; as: audī-re, *to hear.*

26. Learn, with meanings, the Present Indicative and Infinitive of the following verbs, and tell to which Conjugation each belongs:—

VOCABULARY.

cōn-firmō,[1] **-āre,**[2] *establish.*
dē-leō, -ēre,[2] [3]*destroy.*
dūcō, -ere, *lead.*
emō, -ere, *buy.*
habeō, -ēre, *have.*
impediō, -īre, *hinder.*
laudō, -āre, *commend.*
maneō, -ēre, *remain.*[3]
mūniō, -īre, *fortify.*
probō, -āre, *approve.*[3]

pūniō, -īre,[3] *punish.*
quaerō, -ere, *inquire.*[3]
re-cūsō, -āre,[3] *refuse.*
regō, -ere, [3]*rule.*
tegō, -ere, *cover.*
teneō, -ēre, *hold.*
timeō, -ēre, *fear.*
trāns-portō, -āre, *transport.*[3]
veniō, -īre, COME.[3]
vestiō, -īre, *clothe.*

---

[1] In translating the indicative, supply the pronoun *I.*

[2] To be read: **cōnfirmāre, dēlēre,** &c.

[3] English words or parts of words that are **borrowed** from the Latin are printed in the vocabularies of this book in *this type;* English words or parts of words that are *cognate* with Latin words are printed in SMALL CAPITALS.

LESSON II.

THE PRESENT INDICATIVE ACTIVE: CONJUGATIONS I. AND II.

27. Learn the inflection, with meanings, of the Present Indicative Active of **amō**: A. & G. p. 76, also § 194, *a*; H. p. 86, also § 446; G. p. 54, also § 198.

28. Inflect (like **amō**) the Present Indicative Active of **cōnfirmō,** *I establish ;* **laudō,** *I commend ;* **probō,** *I approve ;* **recūsō,** *I refuse ;* **trānsportō,** *I transport.*

29. Learn the inflection, with meanings, of the Present Indicative Active of **moneō** (or **dēleō**) : A. & G. p. 80 ; H. p. 90 ; G. p. 58.

30. Inflect (like **moneō** or **dēleō**) the Present Indicative Active of **habeō,** *I have ;* **maneō,** *I remain ;* **pāreō,** *I obey ;* **teneō,** *I hold ;* **timeō,** *I fear.*

31.   EXAMPLES.

Monet, *he warns,* or *he is warning.*
Nōn monent, *they do not warn,* or *they are not warning.*

32.   EXERCISES.

I. 1. Cōnfirmō. 2. Laudat. 3. Probātis. 4. Nōn recūsāmus. 5. Trānsportant. 6. Cōnfirmās. **7.** Nōn probāmus. **8.** Laudātis. 9. Habeō. 10. Manet. 11. Pārent. 12. Tenēs. **13.** Nōn timēmus. 14. Manēs. **15.** Manētis. 16. Nōn pāret. 17. Recūsant. 18. Timeō. 19. Trānsportat. 20. Habēmus. 21. Tenētis. 22. Laudās. 23. Nōn cōnfirmant. 24. Recūsō. 25. Nōn pārēs.

II. 1. I approve. 2. He transports. 3. We commend. 4. They do not refuse. 5. You (pl.) establish. 6. You (sing.) do not commend. 7. They approve. 8. He refuses. 9. You (sing.) have. 10. We are not obeying. 11. I am holding. 12. He does not fear. 13. You (pl.) fear. 14. They are not remaining. 15. He has. 16. You (sing.) are remaining. 17. He does not commend. 18. I obey. 19. We transport. 20. I am remaining. 21. You (sing.) do not obey. 22. He establishes. 23. We do not approve. 24. You (pl.) have. 25. They are establishing.

33.   Supplementary Exercises.

I. 1. Probat. 2. Pārēmus. 3. Nōn laudant. 4. Recūsātis. 5. Maneō. 6. Timēs. 7. Cōnfirmāmus. 8. Habētis. 9. Nōn tenet. 10. Recūsās. 11. Pāreō. 12. Probant. 13. Trānsportātis. 14. Nōn probō. 15. Manēmus.

II. 1. He holds. 2. They do not commend. 3. You (sing.) approve. 4. He does not obey. 5. We are remaining. 6. You (sing.) fear. 7. I am establishing. 8. You (pl.) approve. 9. They transport. 10. We do not have. 11. You (pl.) hold. 12. You (sing.) refuse. 13. They obey. 14. I do not fear. 15. I am commending.

LESSON III.

The Present Indicative Active: Conjugations III. and IV.

34. Learn the inflection, with meanings, of the Present Indicative Active of **tegō** (**regō** or **emō**): A. & G. p. 82; H. p. 94; G. p. 64.

35. Inflect (like **tegō, regō,** or **emō**) the Present Indicative Active of **dīcō,** *I say;* **dūcō,** *I lead;* **mittō,** *I send;* **pōnō,** *I place;* **quaerō,** *I inquire.*

36. Learn the inflection, with meanings, of the Present Indicative Active of **audiō**: A. & G. p. 86; H. p. 98; **G.** p. 68.

37. Inflect (like **audiō**) the Present Indicative Active of **mūniō**, *I fortify;* **pūniō**, *I punish;* **veniō**, *I come;* **vestiō**, *I clothe;* **impediō**, *I hinder.*

38. Learn the inflection, with meanings, of the Present Indicative of **sum**: A. & **G.** p. 68; H. p. 84; G. p. 50. Inflect the Present Indicative of **absum**,[1] *I am away.*

39. EXERCISES.

I. 1. Dīcit. 2. Dūcimus. 3. Mittis. 4. Pōnunt. 5. Quaerō. 6. Dīcitis. 7. Mūniunt. 8. Nōn pūnīmus. 9. Veniō. 10. Vestīs. 11. Impedit. 12. Mūnītis. 13. Es. 14. Absunt.[1] 15. Nōn laudāmus. 16. Mittimus. 17. Timet. 18. Impediō. 19. Sumus. 20. **Nōn ha**bent. 21. Cōnfirmat. 22. Abestis. 23. Dūcis. 24. **Nōn** pōnō. 25. Timētis. 26. Venīmus. 27. **Abes**. 28. Vestiunt. 29. Nōn quaerit. 30. Sum.

II. 1. We say. 2. He is not leading. 3. I am placing. 4. You (sing.) inquire. 5. They do not send. 6. You (pl.) lead. 7. I do not punish. 8. They are fortifying. 9. He hinders. 10. We are coming. 11. You (sing.) clothe. 12. You (pl.) **are** fortifying. 13. You (pl.) are. 14. He approves. 15. They are away. 16. We do not inquire. 17. I have. 18. You (sing.) punish. 19. We **are**. 20. You (pl.) **do not** obey. 21. I refuse. 22. He is away. 23. They say. 24. You (sing.) send. 25. We do not fear. 26. They punish. 27. You (sing.) are away. 28. You (pl.) do not come. 29. I am hindering. 30. He is.

40.   Supplementary Exercises.

I. 1. Dicis. 2. Pūnit. 3. Absumus.[1] 4. Nōn laudātis. 5. Sunt. 6. Nōn dūcō. 7. Manent. 8. Impedīmus. 9. Quaeritis. 10. Absum.[1] 11. Mūnīs. 12. Nōn probās. 13. Estis. 14. Mittunt. 15. Tenēmus. 16. **Venit.**

II. 1. You (sing.) are. 2. You (pl.) do not refuse. 3. We are away. 4. I am fortifying. 5. He sends. 6. I am not away. 7. He inquires. 8. You (pl.) are hindering. 9. They do not have. 10. You (sing.) lead. 11. We obey. 12. They are. 13. We are sending. 14. We establish. 15. He does not come. 16. You (pl.) clothe.

[1] *b* before *s* is sounded like *p*; hence, pronounce *apsum, apsumus, apsunt.*

LESSON IV.

Substantives: First Declension.

Note: It is assumed that the teacher will here prepare the way by oral instruction for the **declension** of a Latin **noun** with the translation of its cases. For suggestions, see A. & G. § 31.

41. Learn the declension, with meanings, of **stella** (A. & G. 35) or **mēnsa** (H. 48; G. 27).

42. Define *Stem*, and give the stem[1] of **stella** (A. & G. 21, coarse type) or **mēnsa** (H. 46; G. 24).

43. Observe the *gender* of the substantives in the vocabulary of this lesson; then learn the Rule for Gender: A. & G. 35, to the second period; H. 48; G. 28.

44. Decline, giving stem, gender, and meanings, the substantives in the following

VOCABULARY.[2]

amicitia, -ae, F., *friendship.*
Aquitānia, -ae, F., *Aquitania.*[3]
Belgae,[4] -arum, M., *the **Belgae**[3]* (or *Belg*ians).
causa, -ae, F., *cause.*
cōpia, -ae, F., *abundance;* in pl., *forces, troops.*

contrōversia, -ae, F., *dispute.*
Galba,[5] -ae, M., ***Galba.***[3]
injūria, -ae, F., *injury.*
patria, -ae, F., *native country.*
porta, -ae, F., *gate.*
prōvincia, -ae, F., *province.*
sententia, -ae, F., *opinion.*

---

[1] The stem vowel of the first declension will be treated as -ā- in this book, the long quantity being original. **Stellā- and mēnsā-** will therefore be considered **the stems of stella** and mēnsa respectively. The teaching of the grammars on this point is not uniform.

[2] The pupil should remember that the only object for which he is required to learn declensions is, that he may become so familiar with the forms as to be able to give the English equivalent of a Latin form, or the Latin equivalent of an English form, *on the instant.* In preparing this vocabulary, therefore, he should not content himself with being able merely to name the cases of each substantive in their order, but should practise such exercises as the following: Express in Latin, *of friendship, the Belgians', by disputes, to the gate,* &c.; express in English, **Aquītāniae, causārum, injūriā, sententiās,** &c.

[3] For fuller information, see the general vocabulary.

[4] Omit the singular in declining.

[5] Read A. & G. 75, 1; H. 130, I, 1).

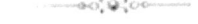

LESSON V.

ABLATIVE WITH PREPOSITIONS. — SUBJECT-NOMINATIVE. — ACCUSATIVE OF DIRECT OBJECT.

NOTE: It is assumed that the **pupil is** familiar with the structure of the simple sentence, **or,** failing this, that the teacher will orally explain such terms as *subject, predicate, object,* etc.

45. EXAMPLES.[1]

1. **Ab injūriā (1, 31,** 16)[2], *from injury.*
2. **Ā prōvinciā** (1, 33, 4), (away) *from **the**[3] province.*
3. **Cum cōpiīs** (4, 21, 3), *with the forces.*
4. **Dē injūriīs** (1, 14, 6), *for injuries.*
5. **Ex** (or **ē**) **prōvinciā** (7, 65, 1), *from* (out of) *the province*
6. **Prō patriā** (Cic. *Tusc.* 4, 19, 43), *in **behalf** of* [one's] *country.*
7. **Sine causā** (1, 14, 2), *without cause.*

46. Observation and Inference:[1] Note (1) the *prepositions* in the foregoing examples, and (2) the *case* of the *substantives* with which they are used. Frame a **rule for** the Case of Substantives used with the foregoing Prepositions.

47. References for Verification:[1] A. & G. 152, *b*; H. 434; G. 418.

48.   **EXAMPLES.**

1. **Aquītānia pertinet** (1, 1, 7), *Aquitania extends.*
2. **Contrōversia est** (6, 13, 5), *there is a*[3] *dispute.*
3. **Belgae pertinent** (1, 1, 6), *the Belgians extend.*
4. **Patent portae** (Cic. *Cat.* 1, 5, 10), *the gates* **are open.**[4]
5. **Praestat amīcitia** (Cic. *Lael.* 5, 19), *friendship* **takes precedence.**[4]

49. Observation and Inference: Note (1) the *number, person* and *case* of the *substantives*, (2) the *number* and *person* of the *verbs*, and (3) the *order of the words* in the foregoing examples. What is the usual order of *subject* and *predicate* (see Exs. 1–3)? What seems to be the effect when **this order is reversed** (see Exs. 4 and 5)? Frame rules (1) for the Case of the Subject of the sentence in Latin, (2) for the Number and Person of the Verb, and (3) for the Position of Subject and Predicate.

50. References for Verification: A. & G. 173, 204, 343, 344, *a*; H. 368, 460, 560, 561, I.; G. 194, 202, 676, 675, 1, 1.

51.   **EXAMPLES.**

1. **Causam probant** (6, 23, 7), *they approve the cause.*
2. **Sententiam laudant** (Sall. *Cat.* 53, 1), *they commend the opinion.*
3. **Amīcitiam cōnfirmāre** (1, 3, 1), *to establish friendship.*
4. **Sententiās dīcere** (Caes. *B. C.* 1, 1, 2), *to express opinions.*
5. **Laudāmus dīvitiās** (Sall. *Cat.* 52, 22), *we commend* **riches.**[4]

52. Observation and Inference: Note (1) the *class* (*i.e.*, whether *transitive* or *intransitive*) to which the verbs belong, (2) the *case* of the *substantives* construed with them, and (3) the *order of the words* in the foregoing examples. Frame rules for the Case and Position of the Direct Object of a transitive verb in Latin.

VOCABULARY AND EXERCISES. 15

53. REFERENCES FOR VERIFICATION: A. &. G. 237; H. 371; G. 327. For the order of the words, see the references in **50**; also H. **561,** II.

¹ The pupil should first study carefully the examples in connection with the paragraph designated "Observation and Inference," and should commit the examples to memory. Before consulting the sections in the grammar referred to under the heading "References for Verification," he should strive to discover for himself the principles which the examples illustrate, and to frame independently the rule for construction. When he has framed such a rule **to** the best of his ability, he **may consult** the grammar for the purpose **of** verifying **or** correcting his inferences **or** his phraseology. The references, or their equivalent in grammatical English, should then be fixed in the memory for use in the exercises which follow.

² **Citations** given without name **are** from Caesar's Gallic War

³ There is no article in Latin. In translation from Latin into English, the article must be supplied wherever the English usage requires it; in translation from English into Latin, the article must be disregarded.

⁴ *This type* in the English translation denotes emphasis.

LESSON VI.

VOCABULARY AND EXERCISES.

54. VOCABULARY,¹

ab, ā,² prep. w. abl., *away from, from*.
cum, prep. w. abl., *with*.
dē, prep. w. abl., *from, about*.
ē-dūcō, -ere, *lead out*.
ex, ē,³ prep. w. abl., *out of, from*.
Gallia, -ae, F., *Gaul*.
Genāva, -ae, F., *Geneva*.

longē, adv., *far*.
prō, prep. w. abl., *in front of, in behalf of*, FOR.
pūgnō, -āre, *fight*.
red-dō, -ere, *return* (trans.), *restore*.
sine, prep. w. abl., *without*.
Tolōsa, -ae, F., *Toulouse*.
vīta, -ae, F., *life*.

55. EXERCISES.

I. **1.** Galba dūcit. 2. Galba cōpiās dūcit. 3. Galba cōpiās ex Galliā dūcit. 4. Amīcitiam cōnfirmant. 5. Cum Belgīs amīcitiam cōnfirmant. 6. Belgae timent. 7. Belgae sine causā timent. 8. Genāva abest. **9.** Genāva longē abest. 10. Genāva ā Tolōsā longē abest. 11. Dē injūriīs quaerit. 12. Vītam prō vītā reddunt.

II. 1. The Belgians lead-out.[4] 2. The Belgians lead-out their[5] forces. 3. We are leading-out our[5] forces from the province. 4. They are inquiring about the forces. 5. He establishes friendship. 6. We are establishing friendship with the Belgians. 7. You (sing.) fear without cause. 8. He leads his forces out-of Italy. 9. They are fighting for their[5] country.

56.   **Supplementary Exercises.**

I. 1. Cōpiās ex prōvinciā ēdūcunt. 2. Dē pūgnā cōgnōscit. 3. Galliam ab injūriā dēfendit. 4. Messālla lacrimās nōn tenet. 5. Amīcitiam recūsāmus, nōn appetimus.

II. 1. Toulouse is at a great distance (is-distant far) from Geneva. 2. They learn about the injuries. 3. Galba is transporting his[5] forces from (out-of) Gaul. 4. We do not keep-back our[5] tears. 5. You reject friendships, you do not seek after [them].[6]

---

[1] This vocabulary and subsequent special vocabularies will contain the words of the "Exercises" only; the words of the "Supplementary Exercises" will be found in the general vocabulary at the end of the book. Words once given in a special vocabulary will not be repeated in subsequent special vocabularies.

[2] Use ab before words beginning with a vowel; use ā before words beginning with a consonant. For fuller information, see general vocabulary

[3] Use ex before words beginning with a vowel; use ex or ē before words beginning with a consonant.

[4] Words connected by a hyphen are to be treated in translation as a single expression.

[5] Omit the possessive here. See A. & G. 197, c; H. 447; G. 299.

[6] Words in brackets are to be omitted in translation.

LESSON VII.

SUBSTANTIVES: SECOND DECLENSION.

57. Learn the declension, with gender and meanings, of **servus** (or **hortus**), **puer, ager, vir, bellum** (or **templum**): A. & G. 38; H. 51; G. 29, 31.

58. Give the *stem* of each of the substantives in the foregoing paragraph, and explain the formation of the *nominative* from the stem. For this purpose read: A. & G., first paragraph of the note preceding 38, and first sentence of the second paragraph; H. 51, 1, 2, 1), 2), 4), 5); G. 29, 31, 32[3].

59. Observe the *gender* of the substantives in the vocabulary of this lesson; then learn the Rule for Gender: A. & G. 39; H. 51; G. 30.

60. Decline, **giving stem,** gender, and meanings, the substantives in the following

VOCABULARY.[1]

ager, -gri, M., *land, field;* in pl., also *country districts.*
castra, -ōrum,[2] N., *camp.*
conloquium, -ii, N., *conference.*
frūmentum, -i, N., *grain* (usually of harvested grain); in pl., *grain* (especially of standing grain).
Gallī,[2] **-ōrum,** M., *the Gauls.*
gener, -erī, M., *son-in-law.*
Helvētiī,[2] **-ōrum,** M., *the Helvetians.*
hīberna,[2] **-ōrum,** N., *winter-quarters.*
impedīmentum, -ī, N., *hindrance;* in pl., *baggage.*

imperium, -iī, N., *command, control.*
Labiēnus,[3] **-ī,** M., *Labienus.*[4]
lēgātus, -ī, M., *ambassador; lieutenant.*
mūrus, -ī, M., *wall.*
oppidum, -ī, N., *town* (viewed as stronghold).
populus, -ī, M., *people, race.*
proelium, -iī, N., *battle.*
puer, -erī, M., *child, boy.*
studium, -iī, N., *zeal; devotion; pursuit.*
vīcus, -ī, M., *village.*
vir, virī, M., *man.*

---

[1] See foot-note 2, Lesson IV.
[2] Omit the singular in declining.
[3] See foot-note 5, Lesson IV.

[4] For fuller information, see general vocabulary.

LESSON VIII.

The Preposition **In**. — Genitives: Possessive, Subjective, Objective.

61. EXAMPLES.

1. **In Galliam contendit** (1, 7, 1), *he hastens into Gaul.*
2. **In conloquium venīre** (1, 35, 2), *to come to a conference.*
3. **Frūmenta ex agrīs in oppida comportant** (3, 9, 8), *they collect the grain from the country districts* [and convey it] *into the towns.*
4. **In vīcō hiemāre** (3, 1, 4), *to pass the winter in the village.*
5. **In mūrō** (2, 6, 3), *on the wall.*
6. **In Galliā in hībernīs** (2, 1, 1), *in winter-quarters in Gaul.*

62. Observation and Inference: Note that in the first three of the foregoing examples **in** means *into* or *to*, and therefore answers the question *whither?*; note, on the other hand, that in the last three examples **in** means *in* or *on*, and answers the question *where?*. Note, further, the *case* of the *substantives* construed with **in** in the two sets of examples. With what cases, then, may **in** be used, and with what difference of meaning? Frame a rule for the Case of Substantives used with **in**.

63. References for Verification: A. & G. 152, *c*, last two lines; H. 435, n. 1; G. 419.

64. EXAMPLES.

1. **In castrīs Helvētiōrum** (1, 29, 1), *in the camp of* (i.e., belonging to) *the Helvetians.*
2. **Oppidum Rēmōrum** (2, 6, 1), *a town of* (i.e., belonging to) *the Remi.*
3. **Divitiacī studium** (1, 19, 2), *the devotion of Divitiacus* (Divitiacus manifests the devotion).
4. **Fuga Gallōrum** (1, 40, 8), *the flight of the Gauls* (the Gauls flee).
5. **Prō injūriīs populī** (1, 30, 2), *in return for the injuries of* (i.e., done to) *the people.*
6. **Britanniae imperium** (2, 4, 7), *authority over* (i.e., exercised towards) *Britain.*

65. OBSERVATION AND INFERENCE: Note (1) that the *genitive* in each of the foregoing examples limits a *substantive*, (2) that the genitive denotes a *different person* or *thing* from that **denoted** by the limited substantive, and (3) that the relation of the genitive to the limited substantive is (in most of the examples) expressed in English by the preposition *of*. Frame a rule for these **and similar** Genitives.

66. REFERENCES FOR VERIFICATION: A. & G. 213; H. 393, 395.

67. OBSERVATION AND INFERENCE: Note the *order of the words* in the examples just considered. What seems to be the **usual** position **of** the **genitive with** reference to the substantive **which** it limits?

68. REFERENCES FOR VERIFICATION: H. 565; G. 678.

69. OBSERVATION: Note further (1) that in Exs. 1 and 2 **the** genitive expresses *possession*, and may therefore be called a *Possessive Genitive*; (2) that in Exs. 3 and 4 the genitive expresses the *subject* of the feeling or action denoted by the limited substantive, and may therefore be called a *Subjective* **Genitive**; (3) that in **Exs.** 5 and 6 the genitive expresses the *object* **of the action denoted by** the limited substantive, and **may** therefore **be called an** *Objective Genitive*.

70. REFERENCES: A. & G. 214, 217; H. 396, I., II., III.; G. 360, 361, 1, 2.

71. VOCABULARY.

ad-ministrō, -āre, *execute.*
Aeduī,[1] -ōrum, M., *the Aeduans.*
ap-petō, -ere, *strive to secure.*
bellum, -i, N., *war.*
beneficium, -ii, N., **benefit.**
Britannia,[2] -ae, F., *Britain.*
con-locō, -āre, *place.*
dē-pōnō, -ere, *put aside.*
Divitiacus,[2] -i, M., *Divitiacus.*[3]
in, prep., w. acc., INto (opp. **ex**); w. abl., IN, **ON**.

memoria, -ae, F., *remembrance.*
mittō, -ere, *send.*
neg-legō, -ere, *disregard, neglect.*
ob-tineō, -ēre, *hold.*
oc-cidō, -ere, *kill, slay.*
postulō, -āre, *demand.*
Rōmānī,[1] -ōrum, M., *the Romans.*
saxum, -i, N., *stone.*
socer, -eri, M., *father-in-law.*
vastō, -āre, *lay waste.*

72.   **EXERCISES.**

I. 1. Labiēnus est in Galliā in hībernīs. 2. In Galliam lēgātum mittit. 3. Beneficiōrum memoriam nōn dēpōnimus. 4. Aeduōrum agrōs vastant. 5. Gener socerum occīdit. 6. Ab castrīs oppidum Aeduōrum longē abest. 7. Divitiacus Britanniae imperium obtinet. 8. Saxa in mūrō conlocant. 9. In castra cum impedīmentīs veniunt. 10. Studium Galbae nōn neglegit.

II. 1. They send ambassadors into the town. 2. We do not demand control of the war. 3. He strives-to-secure the **friendship of the Romans**. 4. The Romans are in winter-quarters. 5. The fathers-in-law kill their sons-in-law. 6. They execute the orders (imperium) of the lieutenant. 7. We do not disregard the wrongs (injūria) of the Aeduans. 8. The baggage is in the camp. 9. They come into camp without their baggage.

73.   **Supplementary Exercises.**

I. 1. Frūmentum in prōvinciam portant. 2. Sunt frūmenta in agrīs Aeduōrum. 3. Aeduōrum injūriās nōn neglegit. 4. Fuga Gallōrum Rōmānōs commovet.

II. 1. He puts-aside the remembrance of his injuries. 2. The fields of the Aedui are at a great distance (are-distant far) from the camp. 3. They carry the baggage into the camp. 4. [There] are stones on the wall.

---

[1] Omit the singular in declining.
[2] See foot-note 5, Lesson IV.
[3] For fuller information, see general vocabulary.

LESSON IX.

ADJECTIVES: FIRST AND SECOND DECLENSIONS.

74. EXAMPLES.
   SINGULAR.
M. Vir bonus (Cic. *Off.* 3, 15, 61), *a* **good** *man.*
F. Vīllam bonam (Cic. *Off.* 3, 13, 55), *a* good *country-house.*
N. Solō bonō (Cat. *R. R.* 1), *by* good *soil.*

   PLURAL.
M. Virōs bonōs (Cic. *Tusc.* 5, 10, 28), good *men.*
F. Bonās hōrās (Mart. 1, 113), good (*i.e.*, valuable, precious) *hours.*
N. Verbōrum bonōrum (Cic. *Brut.* 66, 233), *of* good (*i.e.*, well-chosen) *expressions.*

75. OBSERVATION AND INFERENCE: Note (1) the *number, gender,* and *case* of the *substantives* in each of the foregoing examples, and (2) the *form* of the *adjective* associated with it. Does the Latin adjective, like the English, remain unchanged **in form, or is** it varied to suit **the number, gender, and case of the substantive to** which it belongs? Are Latin **adjectives, then, declined?**

76. REFERENCES FOR **VERIFICATION: A.** & G. **186;** H. 438; G. 285.

77. Learn the declension, with stems, of **bonus: A.** & G. 81; H. 147, 148; G. 33.

78. Learn the declension, with stems, of **miser** (or **līber**) and **niger** (**aeger** or **piger**): A. & G. 82; H. 149, 150; G. 34.

79. Decline, giving stems, the *adjectives* in the following

VOCABULARY.

ad-scendō, -ere, *ascend.*
aeger, -gra, -grum, adj., *ill, sick.*

asper, **-era,** -erum, adj., *rough, rugged.*

dīvidō, -ere, *separate.*
im-plōrō, -āre, *implore.*
jugum, -ī, N., YOKE,(mount.)*ridge.*
lacrima, -ae, F., TEAR.
līber, -era, -erum, *free.*
māgnus, -a, -um, adj., *great.*
multus, -a, -um, adj., *much;* in pl., *many.*
noster, -tra, -trum, adj., *our.*
numerus, -ī, M., *number.*

perīculum, -ī, N., *danger, peril.*
prae-cēdō, -ere, *excel.*
re-linquō, -ere, *leave behind.*
reliquus, -a, -um, adj., *remaining.*
Rhodanus, -ī, M., *the Rhone.*
Rōmānus, -a, -um, adj., *Roman.*
Sēquanī, -ōrum, M., *the Sequani.*
servus, -ī, M., *slave.*
superō, -āre, *conquer, defeat.*

80. OBSERVATION AND INFERENCE: Note the *order of the words* in the examples of 74. What seems to be the usual position of the adjective with respect to its substantive?

81. REFERENCES FOR VERIFICATION: A. & G. 343, *c*; H. 565, with 1; G. 678.

82. Decline together, with meanings: **puer aeger,** *a sick child;* **jugum asperum,** *a rugged ridge;* **populus Rōmānus** (in sing.), *the Roman people;* **reliquae cōpiae** (in pl.), *the remaining forces.*

83. EXERCISES.

I. 1. Populī Rōmānī amīcitiam recūsat. 2. Līberōs Galliae populōs superat. 3. Multōs puerōs aegrōs relinquunt. 4. Multīs dē[1] causīs[2] Helvētiī reliquōs Gallōs praecēdunt. 5. Māgnum servōrum numerum habet. 6. Rhodanus prōvinciam nostram ab Helvētiīs dīvidit.

II. 1. The Rhone separates the Sequani from our province. 2. Our forces are ascending the rugged ridge. 3. The sick **children** are in[1] great danger. 4. He implores with[1] many **tears**. 5. He leads-out the **remaining forces of** the Helvetians.

84. Supplementary **Exercises.**

I. 1. Auxilium ā populō Rōmānō implōrant. 2. Dīvitiacī **māgnum in**[3] populum Rōmānum studium cōgnōscit. 3. Multīs dē causīs in jugō asperō lēgātum relinquit. 4. Lēgātum magnō cum perīculō in Galliam mittō.

II. 1. For[4] many **reasons** our forces excel the **Helvetians.** 2. The sick child implores aid with many **tears.** 3. The free races of Gaul refuse the friendship of our lieutenant.

[1] A. & G. 345, a; G. 680, 2. [3] Translate: *to.*
[2] Translate: *for many reasons.* [4] See 83, I., sent. 4.

LESSON X.

Adjectives: Attributive and Predicate. — Dative with Adjectives.

85. EXAMPLES.

1. Amīcitia numquam molesta est (Cic. Lael. 6, 22), *friendship is never troublesome.*
2. **Vērae amīcitiae** sempiternae sunt (Cic. Lael. 9, 32), *true friendships are everlasting.*
3. Fortūna caeca est (Cic. Lael. 15, 54), *Fortune is blind.*
4. Imbēcilla **est nātūra** (Cic. Lael. 17, 63), *nature is weak.*[1]
5. **Tanta est** stultitiae incōnstantia (Cic. Cat. Maj. 2, 4), *such is the inconsistency*[1] *of folly.*
6. Sumus ōtiōsī (Cic. Lael. 5, 17), *we are at-leisure.*[1]
7. At[2] sunt mōrōsī, et anxiī, **et** īrācundī senēs[3] (Cic. Cat. Maj. 18, 65), *but, you will say,*[2] *the old are full-of-whims, uneasy, and irritable.*[1]

86. OBSERVATION: Compare the foregoing examples with those of **74.** Note that in the latter the adjectives simply qualify their substantives *without the intervention of a verb,* whereas in the examples **of 85** the adjectives are connected **with their** substantives by some form **of** the verb **sum.** The adjectives of 74 merely designate an *attribute* or quality, and are called *Attributive Adjectives;* the adjectives of **85** unite with the verb to form the *predicate,* and are called *Predicate Adjectives.* Note, further, that the predicate adjective, like the attributive, **agrees**[4] with its substantive in *gender, number,* and *case.*

87. REFERENCES: A. & G. 186, *a, b*; H. 438, 2; G. 284, I., 285, 202[2].

88. OBSERVATION AND INFERENCE: Note the *order of the words* in the examples of **85.** Does the predicate adjective appear regularly *to follow* or *to precede* the verb (see Exs. 1–5)? What appears to be the effect when this order is *reversed* (see Exs. 6, 7)? Why is the subject placed *last* in Ex. 5? Why does **Imbēcilla est** stand at the *beginning* of the sentence in Ex. 4?

89. REFERENCES FOR VERIFICATION: A. & G. 343, with *a*, 344, *a*; H. 560, 561, I., II.; G. 676, 1, 2, 3, 675, 1, 1.

90. EXAMPLES.

1. Maurō cārus (Sall. *Jug.* 108, 1), *dear to the Moor.*
2. Populō Rōmānō **perīculōsum** (1, 33, 3), *dangerous to the Roman people.*
3. Castrīs idōneum (1, 40, 1), *suitable for a camp.*
4. Helvētiīs amīcus (1, 9, 3), *friendly to the Helvetians.*
5. Cupidīs[5] odiōsum et molestum (Cic. *Cat. Maj.* 14, 47), *vexatious and annoying to* [those who are] *desirous.*
6. **Fīnitimī Belgīs** (2, 2, 3), *adjacent to the Belgians.*
7. Inimīcum **Pompējō** (Sall. *Cat.* 19, 1), *hostile to Pompey.*

91. OBSERVATION AND INFERENCE: Note (1) the *meaning* of the *adjectives* in the foregoing examples, and (2) the *case* of the *substantives* construed with them. Frame a rule for the Case of Substantives construed with such Adjectives as the foregoing.

92. REFERENCES FOR VERIFICATION: A. & G. 234, *a*; H. 391, I.; G. 356.

93. OBSERVATION AND INFERENCE: Note the *order of the words* in the examples of **90.** Does the dative appear regularly *to follow* or *to precede* the adjective (see Exs. 1–5)?

VOCABULARY AND EXERCISES.

94. VOCABULARY.

adversus, -a, -um, adj., *unsuccessful, adverse.*
aedificium, -ī, n., *building.*
amīcus, -a, -um, adj., *friendly, favorably-disposed.*
bellicōsus, -a, -um, adj., *warlike.*
cārus, -a, -um, adj., *dear.*
crēber, -bra, **-brum,** adj., *frequent, numerous.*
discipulus, -ī, m., *pupil.*
equus, -ī, m., *horse.*
fīnitimus, **-a,** -um, adj., *bordering on, adjacent.*
Germānī, -ōrum, m., *the Germans.*
grātus, **-a, -um,** adj., *pleasant, agreeable.*

jūstus, -a, -um, adj., *just, founded in right.*
magister, -trī, m., *master; teacher.*
miser, -era, -erum, adj., *wretched.*
numquam, adv., *never.*
perīculōsus, -a, **-um,** adj., *dangerous, perilous.*
perniciōsus, -a, -um, adj., *destructive, ruinous.*
pulcher, **-chra,** -chrum, adj., *beautiful.*
socius, -iī, m., *ally.*
supplicium, -iī, n., *punishment.*
templum, -ī, n., *temple.*
victōria, -ae, f., *victory.*

95. EXERCISES.

I. 1. Lēgātum māgnō cum perīculō **mittit.** 2. Victōria Germānōrum populō Rōmānō perīculōsa est. 3. Multī sociī aegrī in castrīs manent. 4. Germānī **asperī** et **bellicōsī** sunt. 5. Supplicium **socerī** generō nōn est grātum. 6. Helvētiī sunt līberī. 7. **Magister** discipulīs cārus est, discipulī[6] magistrō. 8. In Britanniā sunt crēbra aedificia.

II. 1. The Romans have beautiful temples. 2. Divitiacus is favorably-disposed to the Helvetians. 3. The horses of our lieutenant are beautiful. 4. The authority (**imperium**) of the Roman people in **Gaul** is founded-in-right. 5. Aquitania is adjacent to the Roman province. 6. The life of slaves is wretched. 7. **An** unsuccessful battle is ruinous **to** the Romans. 8. Free men are never wretched.

96. Supplementary Exercises.

I. 1. Victōriae cōpiārum nostrārum virīs bonīs grātae sunt. 2. Divitiacus multīs cum lacrimīs obsecrat. 3. Reliquōs Belgās in officiō continet. 4. Diligentia discipulōrum magistrīs grāta est. 5. Divitiaci māgnum in **populum** Rōmānum studium cōgnōscit. 6. Nostrī equī nōn sunt nigrī, sed rubrī.

II. 1. The idleness of pupils **is** annoying **to** their teachers. 2. The Belgians **are free**. 3. Ariovistus is savage, passionate, [and] headstrong. 4. He selects **a place** suitable for a camp. 5. He **carries-on** war for (**dē**) many reasons. 6. The Helvetians excel the rest-of-the (*i.e.*, remaining) Gauls.

---

[1] See foot-note 4, Lesson V.
[2] **At** here introduces an objection which the speaker supposes will suggest itself to the minds of his hearers.
[3] **senēs**, *the old*, belongs to the third declension, which will be treated later.

[4] **ōtiōsī** in Ex. 6 agrees with **nōs**, *we*, the omitted subject of **sumus**.
[5] A. & G. 188; H. 441, 1; G. 195, 1.
[6] sc. cārī sunt.

LESSON XI.

Verbs: Present, Imperfect, and Future Indicative of Both Voices.

97. Learn the inflection and synopsis, with meanings,[1] of the Present, Imperfect, and Future Indicative of **sum**: A. & G. p. 68; H. p. 84; G. p. 50.

98. Inflect (like **sum**) in the same tenses: **absum**; also learn the synopsis.

99. Learn the inflection and synopsis, with meanings,[1] of the Present, Imperfect, and Future Indicative, Active and Passive, of **amō**: A. & G. pp. 76, 78; H. pp. 86, 88; G. pp. 54, 56.

100. Inflect (like **amō**) in the same **tenses of both** voices: **cōnfirmō, laudō, probō**; also learn the synopsis of these verbs.

EXERCISES ON THE INDICATIVE: 27

101. Learn (as in **99**) the inflection and synopsis **of moneō** (or **dēleō**): A. & G. p. 80; H. pp. 90, 92; **G.** pp. 58, 60.

102. Inflect (like **moneō** or **dēleō**): **habeō, teneō,** timeō; also learn the synopsis of these verbs.

103. Learn (as in **99**) **the inflection and** synopsis of **tegō** (**regō** or **emō**): A. & G. p. **82**; H. pp. 94, 96; G. pp. 64, 66.

104. Inflect (like **tegō, regō,** or **emō**): **dūcō, mittō, pōnō; also learn** the synopsis of these verbs.

105. Learn (as in **99**) the inflection and synopsis of **audiō**: A. & G. p. 86; H. pp. 98, 100; G. pp. 68, **70.**

106. Inflect (like **audiō**): **impediō, pūniō, vestiō;** also learn the synopsis of these verbs.

---

[1] The teacher will make such oral explanations on the Latin **use** of the tenses here considered as may **be** needed to lead the pupil to a correct and **(for** present purposes) adequate translation of the paradigms. See A. & G. 276, 277, 278; H. 466, 467, I., II., 468, 469, I., II., 470; G. 218, 222, 234.

LESSON XII.

EXERCISES ON THE PRESENT, IMPERFECT, AND FUTURE INDICATIVE OF BOTH VOICES.

107.   EXERCISES.

I. 1. Abestis. 2. Laudāmur. 3. Cōnfirmābās. 4. Habēbō. 5. Tenēbuntur. 6. Dūcētur. 7. Mittēbantur. 8. Mūniēbātis. 9. Vestiēbāmur. **10.** Aberat. 11. Recūsās.

12. Probābis. 13. Habēris. 14. Dūcēminī. 15. Erimus. 16. Nōn pūniunt. 17. Pōnitur. 18. Impediēbāris. 19. Manet. 20. Nōn timēbunt. 21. Erāmus. 22. Vestīre. 23. Tenēbātur. 24. Laudābor. 25. Nōn dīcimus. 26. Quaerēbam. 27. Pūniēbar. 28. Nōn veniētis. 29. Aberis. 30. Trānsportantur.

II. 1. I do not obey. 2. I am led. 3. We shall be commended. 4. They were saying. 5. You (pl.) were not feared. 6. He will obey. 7. We were establishing. 8. They were sent. 9. We shall inquire. 10. I was coming. 11. I shall be away. 12. We are feared. 13. The camp will be fortified. 14. They do not refuse. 15. He will be clothed. 16. You (sing.) were hindered. 17. We were. 18. They will remain. 19. I am held. 20. You will be sent. 21. He was led. 22. They were coming. 23. It is-in-process-of-**fortification**.[1] 24. We do not approve. 25. He will have. 26. You (sing.) punished. 27. You were not obeying. 28. We were hindered. 29. You (pl.) will transport. 30. I shall be feared.

108.   Supplementary Exercises.

I. 1. Nōn manēbant. 2. Dūciminī. 3. Vestiēre. 4. Impediēbar. 5. Trānsportātur. 6. Nōn recūsābis. 7. Tenēbāminī. 8. Mittēmur. 9. Dīcitis. 10. Eram. 11. Aberātis. 12. Pōnuntur. 13. Probābuntur. 14. Cōnfirmābis. 15. Mūnient. 16. Pūniēminī. 17. Nōn timēbantur. 18. Recūsābās. 19. Manēbant. 20. Mittitur.

II. 1. We shall obey. 2. We were not commended. 3. You (pl.) were **coming**. 4. You (sing.) will be hindered. 5. We were away. 6. We are led. 7. You do not have. 8. He will be punished. 9. They were inquiring. 10. He will be. 11. He will say. 12. It was-in-process-of-fortification.[2] 13. You (sing.) were praised. 14. I shall be away. 15. We shall be clothed. 16. You were held. 17. They do not approve. 18. You (sing.) are not feared. 19. I am sent. 20. I shall be punished.

[1] Present passive of **mūniō**.   [2] Imperfect passive of **mūniō**.

LESSON XIII.

Ablatives: Means or Instrument and Voluntary Agent.

109. **EXAMPLES.**

1. Frūmentō juvāre (2, 3, 3), *to aid* [him] *with grain.*
2. Ut fūmō **sīgnificābātur** (2, 7, 4), *as was made evident by the smoke.*
3. **Armīs contendere** (2, 13, 2), *to contend with arms.*
4. **Copulīs continēbantur** (3, 13, 8), *they were held fast by means of grapnel-hooks.*
5. **Castra vāllō fossāque mūnīre** (2, 5, 6), *to fortify the camp with a rampart and a ditch.*

110. Observation and Inference: Note, in the foregoing examples, that the substantives which designate the *means* or *instrument by which* the action expressed by the **verb is performed, are in the** *ablative.* Frame a rule for the Case **of Substantives denoting** Means or Instrument.

111. References for Verification: A. & G. 248; H. 420; G. 403[1].

112. EXAMPLES.

1. **Ab Suēbīs premēbantur** (4, 1, 2), *they were harassed by the Suebi.*
2. **Sī postulātur ā populō** (Cic. *Off.* 2, 17, 58), *if the people demand it* (lit., if it is demanded by the people).
3. **Ab Arvernīs Sēquanīsque** ... (1, 31, 4), [invited] *by the Arverni and Sequani.*
4. **Ab Divitiacō** ... (1, 32, 1), [delivered] *by Divitiacus.*
5. **Ā Labiēnō** ... (1, 22, 1), [held] *by Labienus.*

113. Observation and Inference: Compare the *ablatives* in the foregoing examples with those of **109.** Note that the ablatives in **109** designate *things* used as *instruments*, and that they are not accompanied by a preposition; but that the ablatives in **112** designate *persons* acting as *voluntary agents*, and that they are accompanied by the preposition **ā** or **ab**. How, then, is the Agent, as distinguished from the Instrument, to be expressed in Latin?

114. REFERENCES FOR VERIFICATION: A. & G. 246; II. 415, I.; G. 403[2].

115. VOCABULARY.

ac-cūsō, -āre, *call to account.*
aqua, -ae, F., *water.*
Ariovistus, -ī, M., *Ariovistus.*[1]
com-moveō, -ēre, *disturb, disquiet.*
com-pleō, -ēre, FILL.
concilium, -iī, N., *council.*
con-vocō, -āre, *call together, convoke.*
dīcō, -ere, *say, express.*
et,[2] conj., *and.*
ex-citō, -āre, *stimulate, excite.*
ex-pellō, -ere, *drive out, expel.*

fossa, -ae, F., *ditch, moat.*
fuga, -ae, F., *flight.*
fūmus, -ī, M., *smoke.*
pateō, -ēre, *lie open, extend.*
praemium, -iī, N., *reward.*
-que,[2] conj., *and.*
sarmenta, -ōrum, N. (usu. pl.), *light branches.*
sīgnificō, -āre, *show, make evident.*
tribūnus, -ī, M., *tribune.*[1]
vāllum, -ī, N., *wall, rampart.*

116. EXERCISES.

I. 1. Fossam aquā complent. 2. Ab Aeduīs accūsātur. 3. Castra vāllō fossāque mūniēbant. 4. Concilium ā Belgīs convocābitur. 5. Sarmentīs fossās Rōmānōrum complēbimus. 6. Sententiae ā tribūnīs dīcēbantur. 7. Rōmānī adversō proeliō et fugā Gallōrum commoventur. 8. Superābuntur Belgae, expellentur Germānī.

II. 1. The Germans will be defeated by the Gauls. 2. I shall fortify the camp with a rampart. 3. The forces of the Gauls are defeated by Ariovistus. 4. The Helvetians were adjacent to the Roman province. 5. He will stimulate the tribunes by great rewards. 6. The camp, as (ut) was made evident by the smoke, extended over-a-wide-space (lātē, adv.[3]). 7. The baggage was held by our-men.[4] 8. The ditches will be filled with water.

117. Supplementary Exercises.

I. 1. Oppidum nātūrā locī mūniēbātur. 2. Concilium ab lēgātō convocātur. 3. Frūmenta in agrīs mātūra nōn **erant**. 4. Castrīs idōneum **locum** dēligēs. 5. Increpitantur **atque incūsantur** reliquī Belgae **ā Nerviīs**. 6. Undique **locī nātūrā Helvētiī** continentur.

II. 1. The camp will be defended **by our-men**.[4] 2. A place suitable for a camp is selected. 3. The **towns were** fortified, and the grain was conveyed from the country **districts** into the towns. 4. The lieutenant will be harassed with difficulties by the Veneti. 5. **You (pl.)** will **recompense the** lieutenant **with a** great reward.

---

[1] See the general vocabulary.
[2] et, *and*, simply connects; -que, *and*, implies close connection and is enclitic (appended to the second member); atque (āc), *and also*, gives emphasis to the second member: A. & G. 156, *a*; H. 554, I., 2; G. 477, 478, 479.
[3] Place the adverb before the verb: A. & G. 343; H. 567; G. 676 with Rem.
[4] See foot-note 5, Lesson X.

LESSON XIV.

Substantives of the Third Declension: Mute Stems.

118. **Learn the** paradigms of declension given in the following sections of the grammar: A. & G. 46; H. 57, 58, 59; G. 54.

119. Decline:[1] **prīnceps, -ipis**, M., *chief;* **rēx, -gis**, M., *king;* **dux, -cis**, C.,[2] *leader;* **mīles, -itis**, M., *soldier;* **caput, -itis**, N., *head;* **jūdex, -icis**, C.,[2] *judge;* **rādīx, -īcis**, F., *root;* **lapis, -idis**, M., *stone;* **custōs, -ōdis**, C.,[2] *guard*.

120. Note that the *stems* of the foregoing nouns are: **prīncip-, rēg-, duc-, mīlit-, capit-, jūdic-, rādīc-, lapid-, custōd-**.

121. Explain the formation, from the stem, of the *nominatives* in **119**: A. & G. 44, 45, *a* (first sentence), *b* (first two sentences), *c* (entire); H. 57, 2, 58, 1, 2), 3), 5), 59, 1, 3); G. 51 (entire).

122. Decline together, with meanings:[1] **dux Rōmānus,** *a Roman leader;* lēx dūra, *a harsh law;* **eques noster,** *our horseman;* caput magnum, *a large head;* **vōx lībera,** *free speech;* jūdex jūstus, *a just judge.*

123. VOCABULARY.[3]

cadō, -ere, *fall.*
in-fluō, -ere, *flow* INTO, *flow.*
Juba, -ae, M., *Juba.*[4]
Ōceanus, -ī, M., *ocean.*
paucī, -ae, -a, adj.(sing. rare), FEW.
pedes, -itis, M., FOOT-*soldier.*
per-turbō, -āre, *disturb.*

Prōcillus, -ī, M., *Procillus.*[4]
Rhēnus, -ī, M., *the Rhine.*
trā-dūcō, -ere, *lead across.*
trahō, -ere, *draw, drag.*
vitium, -iī, N., *fault.*
vōx, vōcis, F., *voice; speech; utterance, outcry.*

124. EXERCISES.

I. 1. Lēgēs reddit. 2. Rēx Germānōrum est in Galliā. 3. Equitēs ex oppidō peditēsque mittuntur ā rēge Jubā. 4. Ducēs cōpiās trādūcēbant. 5. Ducis vitium mīlitibus perniciōsum est. 6. Peditum **vōcibus** equitēs perturbābantur. 7. **Paucī** dē **nostrīs** equitibus cadunt. 8. Mīlitēs **lapidibus** pūgnant. 9. Prōcillus ā custōdibus īn fugā trahēbātur. 10. Rhēnus **multīs capitibus**[5] in Ōceanum īnfluit.

II. 1. The laws will be restored. 2. The Rhine has many sources (heads). 3. King Juba sends many horsemen from the town. 4. The guards were dragging Prōcillus in their flight. 5. The forces of the leaders will be led across. 6. The outcries of the soldiers disturbed the leader. 7. The flight of the horsemen was fraught-with-danger (**perīculōsus,** adj.) to the foot-soldiers.

125.   Supplementary Exercises.

I. 1. Contrōversiae rēgum compōnentur.   2. In pūgnā mīlitis officia praestābat.   3. Sēquanī caput dēmittunt.   4. Mīlitēs **ab** signīs discēdent.   5. Dux in vāllō custōdēs dispōnit.   **6.** Etiam mīlitum vōcibus carpēbātur.

II. 1. The judges will settle the disputes.   **2.** The foot-soldiers were forsaking (withdrawing from) their standards.   **3.** I shall perform the duties of a **leader in the fight.**   4. Guards were placed at intervals on the wall by the leader.   5. Even the common-soldiers (**mīles**) were reviling **the leader with** outcries.

¹ See foot-note **2, Lesson IV.**   ³ See also, for vocab., **119** and **122.**
² Common **gender, i.e., masculine or** feminine.   ⁴ See general vocabulary.
                                                        ⁵ Translate: *mouths.*

LESSON XV.

VERBS: PERFECT, PLUPERFECT, AND FUTURE PERFECT OF BOTH VOICES. — PRINCIPAL PARTS.

126. Learn **the inflection and** synopsis, **with** meanings,[1] **of** the Perfect, Pluperfect, and Future Perfect Indicative **of sum: A. & G. pp. 68, 69;** H. p. 84; G. pp. 50, 51.

127. Learn, as in **126,** the inflection and synopsis of absum.[2]

128. Learn the inflection and synopsis, with meanings,[1] of the Perfect, Pluperfect, and Future Perfect Indicative, Active and Passive, of **amō:** A. **& G.** pp. 76, 78; H. pp. 86, 88; G. pp. 55, 57.

129. Inflect (like **amō**) in the foregoing tenses **of** both voices: **cōnfīrmō,** *establish;* **laudō,** *commend;* also learn the synopsis of these verbs.

130. Learn, as in **128**, the inflection and synopsis of **moneō** (or **dēleō**): A. & G. p. 80; H. pp. 90, 92; G. pp. 59, 61.

131. Inflect (like **moneō** or **dēleō**) in the foregoing tenses of both voices: habeō,³ *have, hold;* compleō,⁴ *fill;* also learn the synopsis of these verbs.

132. Learn, as in **128**, the inflection and synopsis of **tegō** (**regō** or **emō**): A. & G. p. 82; H. pp. 94, 96; G. pp. 65, 67.

133. Inflect (like **tegō, regō,** or **emō**) in the foregoing tenses of both voices: dūcō,⁵ *lead;* mittō,⁶ *send;* also learn the synopsis of these verbs.

134. Learn, as in **128**, the inflection and synopsis of audiō: A. & G. p. 86; H. pp. 98, 100; G. pp. 69, 71.

135. Inflect (like **audiō**) in the foregoing tenses of both voices: pūniō, *punish;* vestiō, *clothe.*

136. OBSERVATION: In committing to memory the forms of the verbs thus far introduced, the learner may have observed the following facts: —

1. The Present, Imperfect, and Future tenses, Active and Passive, in the several conjugations, have a common stem. This stem may be obtained by cutting off the syllable -re from the *Present Infinitive Active,* and is called the *Present Stem.* Thus the present stem of amō is **amā-**; the present stem of moneō (dēleō) is monē- (dēlē-); of **tegō** (**regō,** emō) is tege- (rege-, eme-); of audiō is audī-. Again, the *Present Infinitive Active* shows to which conjugation the verb belongs.

2. The Perfect, Pluperfect, **and Future Perfect** tenses of the **Active Voice,** in the several conjugations, have a **common stem.** This stem may be obtained by cutting off the person-ending -t

from the **third** person singular of the *Perfect Indicative Active*, and is called the *Perfect Stem*. Thus the **perfect** stem of amō is amāvī-; the perfect stem of moneō (dēleō) is monuī- (dēlēvī-); of tegō (regō, emō) is tēxī- (rēxī-, ēmī-); **of audiō is** audīvī-.

3. The Perfect, Pluperfect, and Future Perfect **tenses of the** Passive Voice, in the several conjugations, are made **up of the forms** of sum in combination with the *Perfect Participle*.

137. INFERENCE: In view **of the foregoing** observed facts, what parts **of** the **verb, besides the** *Present Indicative Active*, are, from their **importance, entitled to be called the** *Principal Parts?*

138. VERIFICATION: **The** principal parts of **amō,** *love*, **moneō,** *warn*, **dēleō,** *destroy*, **tegō,** *cover*, **regō,** *rule*, **emō,** *buy*, **audiō,** *hear*, are :

PRES. IND. ACT.	PRES. INF. ACT.	PERF. INDIC. ACT.	PERF. PART. PASS.
amō	amāre	amāvī	amātus
moneō	monēre	monuī	monitus
dēleō	dēlēre	dēlēvī	dēlētus
tegō	tegere	**tēxī**	**tectus**
regō	**regere**	rēxī	**rēctus**
emō	**emere**	ēmī	ēmptus
audiō	**audīre**	audīvī	audītus

---

[1] **The teacher** will make such oral explanations on the Latin use of the tenses here considered as may be needed to lead the pupil to a correct and (for present purposes) adequate translation of the paradigms. The two meanings **of** the Latin perfect, and the distinction between the imperfect and the historical **perfect,** should receive special notice. See **A. & G. 277, 279,** 280, 281, also 115, *b*, *c* ; **H. 468, 469,** I., II., 471, I., II., 6, 472, **473; G. 222, 223, 226,** 227, 231, 232, 233, 236.

[2] The perf. indic. of **absum** is **āfuī.**
[3] The perf. indic. act. of **habeō** is **habuī**; the perf. participle is **habitus.**
[4] The perf. indic. act. of **compleō** is **complēvī**; the perf. participle is **complētus.**
[5] The perf. indic. act. of **dūcō** is **dūxī**; the perf. participle is **ductus.**
[6] The perf. indic. act. of **mittō** is **mīsī**; the perf. participle is **missus.**

LESSON XVI.

Vocabulary and Exercises.

139. Learn from the general vocabulary (at the end of the book) the Principal Parts of the verbs in the following

VOCABULARY.

ab-dūcō, *lead away.*
con-veniō, COME *together.*
con-vocō, *call together.*
ē-nūntiō, *divulge.*
frangō, BREAK, *crush.*
per-moveō, *move deeply.*

pōnō, *place.*
postulō, **demand.**
mūniō, *fortify.*
teneō, *hold.*
trā-dō, *surrender.*

140.   EXERCISES.

I. 1. Cōnfirmāvī.   2. Cōnfirmābam.   3. Audītus erās. 4. Ēnūntiāverō.   5. Vestītus eris.   6. Convocātī estis. 7. Convocābāminī.   8. Postulāverat.   9. Mūnītī erant. 10. Habitus es.   11. Frēgeritis.   12. Vestītī erunt. 13. Convēnimus.   14. Conveniēbāmus.   15. Posueram. 16. Missī sunt. 17. Mittēbantur. 18. Āfuerant. 19. Nōn habuerimus. 20. **Complēvistī.** 21. Complēbās. 22. Permōtus est. 23. Fuerāmus. 24. Trāditus eram. 25. Permōtus erit. 26. **Nōn** pūnīvit. 27. **Nōn** pūniēbat. 28. Convocātī erātis. 29. Āfuerit. 30. Ductī eritis. 31. Posuērunt. 32. Pōnēbant. 33. Laudātī sumus. 34. Laudābāmur. 35. Complēverās.   36. Nōn convēnerint.   37. Audītī erāmus. 38. Frēgistī.   39. Frangēbās.   40. Fuistī. 41. Erātis.   42. Fuērunt.

II. 1. I was clothed.   2. I was (habitually) clothed. 3. You (sing.) had been surrendered.   4. We shall have been called together.   5. You (pl.) will have come together. 6. He had heard.   7. He has filled.   8. They will have been led **away**. 9. **You** (pl.) had been deeply moved. 10. You **(sing.)** were sent. 11. You (sing.) were (habitually) sent. 12. I shall have held. 13. I had fortified. 14. **You** (pl.) clothed. 15. You (pl.) used **to clothe**. 16. **You** (pl.) were clothing. 17. You (sing.) have divulged. 18. **You** (pl.) had been. 19. He had been led. 20. You (sing.) will have been commended. 21. **They** demanded. 22. They were demanding. 23. They **were wont** to commend. 24. You (pl.) were **away**. 25. He was wont to be deeply moved. 26. **You** (pl.) had held. 27. We shall not have been **led**. 28. We shall have broken. 29. He will have been. 30. I was in the habit of punishing. 31. **You (sing.) have not been** away. 32. We were not heard. 33. You (pl.) used to hear. 34. They fortified the camp. 35. They were fortifying the camp. 36. The camp was in process of fortification. 37. You (sing.) **will have** divulged. 38. They have not been. 39. You (sing.) have not punished. 40. They had led away. 41. **We had** commended. 42. He will have held.

141. Supplementary Exercises.

I. 1. Permōtī **erāmus.** 2. **Abductus est.** 3. Complēverit. 4. Trādiderātis. 5. Tenuērunt. 6. **Missī** erimus. 7. Nōn habuerās. 8. Āfuistis. 9. Fuit. 10. Erat. 11. Cōnfirmāverint. 12. Positī erant. 13. Missus sum. 14. Mittēbar. 15. Pūnītus eram. 16. Pūniēbantur. 17. Frēgerant. 18. Abductus erat. 19. Posuimus. 20. Pōnēbāmus.

II. 1. We divulged. 2. They had been placed. 3. They have been crushed. 4. **You** (sing.) will have been led away. 5. We had demanded. 6. He will have had. 7. You (sing.) will have **been.** 8. I shall have fortified. 9. I shall have been clothed. 10. I led. 11. We did not lead. 12. You (pl.) were not leading. 13. You were wont to be led. 14. They had come together. 15. **He** had been away. 16. You (pl.) had been called together. 17. They will have been filled. 18. I shall have established. 19. You (sing.) had been. 30. They were away.

LESSON XVII.

Agreement of the Participle in Compound Tenses. — Dative of Indirect Object.

142. EXAMPLES.

1. **Mūrus nūdātus est** (2, 6, 2), *the wall was stripped*.
2. **Gallia posita** est (1, 16, 2), *Gaul is situated*.
3. **Proelium restitūtum est** (1, 53, 1), *the battle was renewed*.
4. **Repertī** sunt equitēs Rōmānī (Cic. Cat. 1, 4, 9), *Roman knights were found*.
5. **Tabulae repertae sunt** (1, 29, 1), *lists were found*.
6. **Castra** posita erant (2, 8, 3), *the camp had been pitched*.

143. Observation and Inference: Note the *gender*, *number*, and *case* of the *participle* and of the *substantive* in each of the foregoing examples. Does the **participle**, like the adjective, agree with its substantive? Frame a rule for the Gender, Number, and Case of the Participle[1] in the tenses for completed action.

144. References for Verification: A. & G. 186; H. 438, 1.

145. EXAMPLES.

1. **Umbrēnō negōtium dat** (Sall. *Cat.* 40, 1), *he assigns the work to Umbrenus*.
2. **Dumnorigī custōdēs** pōnit (1, 20, 6), *he puts guards over Dumnorix*.
3. **Neque nostrīs cēdēbant** (Caes. *B. C.* 1, 57, 3), *nor did they yield to our men*.
4. **Labiēnō timēbat** (7, 56, 2), *he feared for* [the safety of] *Labienus*.
5. **Patriae cōnsulere** (Nep. *Epam.* 10, 1), *to take thought for* [the welfare of] *one's country*.
6. **Praeterita Divitiacō condōnāre** (1, 20, 6) *to overlook the past* [out of regard] *for Divitiacus*.

DATIVE OF INDIRECT OBJECT.

7. **Favēre Helvētiīs** (1, 18, 8), *to favor the Helvetians.*
8. **Lēgātīs imperat** (5, 1, 1), *he gives orders to the lieutenants.*
9. **Vercingetorigī pārent.** (7, 63, 9), *they obey (i.e., yield obedience to) Vercingetorix.*
10. **Lacedaemoniīs servīre** (Nep. Alc. 9, 4), *to be enslaved to the Lacedaemonians.*
11. **Semper cīvitātī indulserat** (7, 40, 1), *he had always been partial to the community.*
12. **Persuādent Rauricīs** (1, 5, 4), *they prevail upon the Raurici.*
13. **Fāmae suae pepercit** (Sall. Cat. 52, 32), *he has spared his own reputation.*
14. **Miserīs succurrere** (Verg. Aen. 1, 630), *to succor* (lit., run under) *the wretched.*
15. **Invidēre bonīs** (Sall. Cat. 51, 38), *to envy* (lit., look askance at) *the good.*
16. **Dux suīs aderat** (7, 62, 5), *the leader stood by (i.e., supported) his men.*
17. **Negōtiō praefuerant** (5, 2, 3), *they had been in charge of* (lit., had been before) *the work.*
18. **Cōnsiliīs obstitit** (Nep. Con. 2, 3), *he opposed* (lit., stood against) *the plans.*

146. OBSERVATION AND INFERENCE: Note that the *datives* in the foregoing examples express the person *to* or *for whom*, or the thing *to* or *for which*, something is done; in other words, these datives denote the *object indirectly affected* by the action expressed by the verb. Frame a rule for the Case of the Indirect Object.

Note, further, the *order of the words* in the foregoing examples. Does the indirect object usually *follow* or *precede* the verb? What appears to be the effect **when** this order is reversed (see Exs. **7**, 12, and 15)?

147. REFERENCES FOR VERIFICATION: A. & G. 224, 343, 344; H. 382, 567, 1; G. 343, 676, 2, 3, 675, 1, 1.

148. OBSERVATION: Note that the verbs in Exs. 1, 2, and 6, are *transitive;* and that they take, besides the dative of the indirect

object, an *accusative* of the *direct object*. Note also the *order of the words* in these examples. Does the indirect object usually *follow* or *precede* the direct (see Exs. 1 and 2)? What appears to be the effect when this order is reversed (see Ex. 6)?

149. REFERENCES: A. & G. 225; H. 384, II., 567, 3; G. 344, 676, Rem., 2, 3.

150. OBSERVATION: Note that the verbs in the remaining examples are *intransitive*, and that they take the dative of indirect object **only**.

151. REFERENCES: A. & G. 226; H. 384, I.

152. OBSERVATION AND INFERENCE: Note that in Exs. 7–13, the dative is used with verbs of *favoring* (favēre, 7), *commanding* (imperat, 8), *obeying* (pārent, 9), *serving* (servīre, 10), *indulging* (indulserat, 11), *persuading* (**persuādent, 12**), *sparing* (pepercit, 13). Frame a rule for the Case of the Substantive construed with these and similar verbs.

153. REFERENCES FOR VERIFICATION: A. & G. 227; H. 385, I., II.; G. 345.

154. OBSERVATION AND INFERENCE: Note that the verbs in Exs. 14–18 are *compounded* with the *prepositions* **sub** (suc-currere, 14), **in** (in-vidēre, 15), **ad** (ad-erat, 16), **prae** (prae-fuerant, 17), and **ob** (ob-stitit, 18) respectively. Note further that, in the compounds given **above**, the force of the *preposition* is felt *independently* of the *verb*.[2] Frame a rule for the Case of the Substantive construed with such Compounds.

155. REFERENCES FOR VERIFICATION: A. & G. 228; H. 386; G. 346.

---

[1] Participles in -us, -a, -um, are declined like adjectives in **-us, -a, -um**.

[2] The learner must not infer that *all* verbs compounded with these prepositions take the **dative**.

LESSON XVIII.

Vocabulary and Exercises.

156.   VOCABULARY.

commodum, -ī, N., *advantage*.
con-dōnō, -āre, -āvī, -ātus, *overlook*.
cōnsilium, -iī, N., *plan*.
cōnsulō, -ere, -luī, -ltus, *take thought, have regard, consult*.
Dumnorix, -igis, M., *Dumnorix*.
fāma, -ae, F., *reputation*.
faveō, -ēre, fāvī, fautum,[1] *favor*.
fortūna, -ae, F., *fortune*.
im-pellō, -ere, -pulī, -pulsus, *urge on, impel*.
im-perō, -āre, -āvī, -ātus, *command; demand*.
indulgeō, -ēre, -sī, -tus, *indulge*.
inter-sum, -esse, -fuī, *take part in*.
in-videō, -ēre, -vīdī, -vīsus, *envy*.
īra, -ae, F., *anger, passion*.
līberī,[2] -ōrum, M., *children*.
meus, -a, -um, poss. pron., MY.

obses, -idis, C., *hostage*.
ob-stō, -āre, -stitī, STAnd *against, oppose*.
Orgetorix, -igis, M., *Orgetorix*.
pāreō, -ēre, -uī, *obey*.
pāx, pācis, F., *peace*.
per-suādeō, -ēre, -suāsī, -suāsus, *persuade*.
precēs,[3] -um, F., *entreaties*.
prō-videō, -ēre, -vīdī, -vīsus, *provide*.
servitūs, -ūtis, F., *slavery, servitude*.
sub-veniō, -īre, -vēnī, -ventum,[1] COME *to the support of*.
sūmō, -ere, sūmpsī, sūmptus, *take*, (of punishment) *inflict*.
vester, -tra, -trum, poss. pron., *your* (pl.).
virtūs, -ūtis, F., *manliness, valor, virtue*.

157.   EXERCISES.

I. 1. Virtūtī nostrae fortūna invidet. 2. Magis (*rather*) fāmae vestrae quam (*than*) īrae cōnsulitis. 3. Prōvinciae māgnum mīlitum numerum imperat. 4. Cūr (*why?*) meīs commodīs obstās? 5. Celeriter (*quickly*) sociīs subvēnērunt. 6. Pāx cōnfirmāta est. 7. Oppidum mūnītum **erat**. 8. Līberī Aeduōrum in servitūtem abductī **erant**. 9. **Aeduīs** obsidēs reddit. 10. Haec (nom. pl. neut., *these things*) sī (*if*) ēnūntiāta erunt, dē obsidibus supplicium sūmet. 11. Ariovistus mīlitēs **in** servitūtem Rōmānīs **nōn** trādiderat.

12. Dumnorix favēbat Helvētiīs.   13. Cōnsulēmus miserīs.
14. Ā reliquīs obsidēs trāditī sunt.

II. 1. Orgetorix persuaded the Helvetians.   2. The Gauls have been defeated by the Romans.   3. He overlooked the injury [out of regard] for the entreaties of Divitiacus.   4. He has placed guards over[4] Orgetorix.   5. The plan was approved by the leaders.   6. Expressions[5] were heard.   7. The leader had demanded of the Gauls[6] a great number of hostages.   8. Labienus had provided grain for the soldiers.   9. The leader indulges the soldiers, but (sed) the soldiers do not obey the leader.   10. The horsemen had not taken part in the battle.   11. The leader will quickly (celeriter) come to the support of the soldiers.   12. The Gauls have been urged on by their chiefs.

158.   Supplementary Exercises.

I. 1. Juventūs Catilīnae inceptīs favēbat.   2. Divitiacus cōnsiliīs Dumnorigis obstābat.   3. Ariovistus Rōmānīs salūtem nōn committit.   4. Ab **Arvernīs Sēquanīsque** Germānī mercēde arcessītī erant.   5. Arma Gallōrum ex oppidō trādita erant.   6. In castrīs Helvētiōrum tabulae repertae erunt.   7. Dux Gallōrum suīs aderat.   8. Equitibus celeriter subveniunt peditēs.

II. 1. I shall not restore the hostages to the Aeduans.   2. He had given the boy a beautiful book.   3. Many hostages had been given by the rest.   4. They will prefer friendship to many advantages.   5. We shall take thought for the safety of the unfortunate soldiers.   6. Dumnorix envied Divitiacus and did not[7] yield obedience to the Roman people.   7. The ditches have been filled with light branches.   8. The beautiful temples had been destroyed by the Roman soldiers.

---

[1] Verbs that are *invariably* intransitive have the perfect participle in the neuter gender only; accordingly, in the principal parts of such verbs, the neuter form of the participle will be given.

[2] līberī, *children*, with reference to their parents; puerī, *children*, as a class.

[3] Usually plural.
[4] Sign of dative.
[5] vōx, vōcis; see 123.
[6] Use the dative.
[7] And not, neque.

LESSON XIX.

SUBSTANTIVES OF THE THIRD DECLENSION: LIQUID AND -S-STEMS.

159. Learn the paradigms of declension given in **the** following sections of the grammar: A. & G. 49; H. 60, 61; G. 40, 43, 46, 49.

160. Decline: cōnsul, -is, M., *consul;* contentiō, -ōnis, F., *contention;* **homo, -inis,** C., *man;* flūmen, -inis, N., *river;* latus, **-eris,** N., *side;* pater, -tris, M., *father;* tempus, -oris, N., *time;* timor, -ōris, M., *fear.*

161. Note that the *stems* of the foregoing nouns are: cōnsul-, contentiōn-, homin-, flūmin-, lates-,[1] **patr-,** tempos-,[1] timōr-.

162. Explain the formation, from **the stem, of the** *nominatives* in **160**: A. & G. 48, *a, b, c, d*; H. 60, 1, 1), 2), 3), 61, 1, 1), 2), **3), 4)**; G. 42, 48.

163. Decline together, with meanings: **cōnsul dēsignātus,** *consul elect;* **contentiō nostra,** *our contention;* **homo miser,** *wretched man;* **flūmen lātum,** *broad river;* **latus sinistrum,** *left side;* **pater vester,** *your father;* **tempus aliēnum,** *an unfavorable time;* **timor māgnus,** *great fear.*

164. VOCABULARY.[1]

altus, -a, -um, adj., *high, tall.*
arbor, -oris, F., *tree.*
Caesar, -aris, M., *Caesar.*
com-mittō, -ere, -mīsi, -missus, *engage in.*

com-pōnō, -ere, -posui, **-positus,** *set at rest, settle.*
con-tineō, **-ēre,** -tinui, **-tentus,** *hem in.*
corpus, -oris, N., *body.*

ex-erceō, -ēre, -cui, -citus, *exercise, train.*
honōs or honor, -ōris, m., *honor.*
legiō, -ōnis, f., *legion.*³
nōmen, -inis, n., NAME.
occupō, -āre, -āvī, -ātus, *seize; employ.*

opus, -eris, n., *work.*
parcō, -ere, pepercī (parsī), SPARE.
per-veniō, -īre, -vēnī, -ventum, *arrive,* COME.
tribuō, -ere, -uī, -ūtus, *award.*

165.   EXERCISES.

I. 1. Cōnsulem dēsīgnātum accūsant. 2. Contentiōnēs nostrae compositae sunt. 3. Hominī miserō parcēs. 4. Flūmine lātō continentur. 5. Tempore⁴ aliēnō proelium commīsit. 6. Māgnum in timōrem hominēs pervēnerant. 7. Arborēs sunt altae. 8. Caesarī honōrem tribuit. 9. Mīlitēs in opere occupātī erant. 10. Nōmen Caesaris legiōnibus est cārum.

II. 1. The consuls elect have been called to account. 2. Honors will be awarded to Caesar. 3. Caesar's honors are acceptable⁵ to the legions. 4. The wretched men obeyed the consuls. 5. The legions engage in battle at an unfavorable time.⁶ 6. A broad river hems in the Helvetians. 7. The contentions of the wretched men will be set at rest. 8. The horsemen trained their bodies.

166.   Supplementary Exercises.

I. 1. Latus sinistrum castrōrum flūmine mūniēbātur. 2. Virginī pulchrae parcēmus. 3. Legiōnēs ab opere dēductae erant. 4. Gallī nōmen Caesaris timēbant. Patrēs vestrī magis (*rather*) virtūte quam (*than*) dolō contendēbant.

II. 1. Rivers protected the sides of the camp. 2. The fear of the legions is disquieting to Caesar. 3. The commander will recall his men from the work. 4. The beautiful maidens will obey their fathers.

---

¹ s in the oblique cases between two vowels becomes r: A. & G. 11, *a*; H. 31, 1; G. 48².
² See also, for vocab., 160 and 163.
³ See also general vocabulary.

⁴ Ablative of *time when;* use preposition *at* in translating: A. & G. 256; H. 429; G. 392.
⁵ grātus, -a, -um, adj.
⁶ See 165, I., sent. 5.

LESSON XX.

VERBS: IMPERATIVES OF BOTH VOICES. — THE VOCATIVE.

167. Learn the **inflection,** with meanings, of the Imperatives, Present and Future, of **sum**: A. & G. p. 69; H. p. 85; G. p. 51.

168. Learn, as in **167**, the inflection of **absum**.

169. Learn the inflection, with meanings, of the Imperatives, Present and Future, Active and Passive, of **amō**: A. & G. pp. 77, 79; H. pp. 87, 89; G. pp. 54, 56.

170. Inflect (like **amō**) in the foregoing tenses of both voices: **cōnfirmō,** *establish;* **laudō,** *commend.*

171. Learn, as in **169**, the inflection of **moneō** (or **dēleō**): A. & G. p. 81; H. pp. 91, 93; G. pp. 58, 60.

172. Inflect (like **moneō** or **dēleō**) in the foregoing tenses of both voices: **habeō,** *have, hold;* **compleō,** *fill.*

173. Learn, as in **169**, the inflection of **tegō** (**regō** or **emō**): A. & G. p. 83; H. pp. 95, 97; G. pp. 64, 66.

174. Inflect (like **tegō, regō, or emō**) in the foregoing tenses of both voices: **dūcō,** *lead;* **mittō,** *send.*

175. Learn, as in **169**, the inflection of **audiō**: A. & G. p. 87; H. pp. 99, 101; G. pp. 68, 70.

176. Inflect (like **audiō**) in the foregoing tenses of both voices: **pūniō,** *punish;* **vestiō,** *clothe.*

IMPERATIVES. — THE VOCATIVE.

177. EXERCISES.

I. 1. Cōnfirmā. 2. Tenēminī. 3. Vestīre. 4. Pōnite. 5. Tenētor. 6. Mittitōte. 7. Convocantor. 8. Vestītor. 9. Habētō. 10. Mūnītō. 11. Mittuntō. 12. Es. 13. Abeste. 14. Laudāminī. 15. Nē[1] dūcuntor. 16. Complēte. 17. Conveniuntō. 18. Este. 19. Cōnfirmātō. 20. Abestōte. 21. Mittere. 22. Estō. 23. Pōne. 24. Nē[1] habentō. 25. Dūcitor.

II. 1. Be (thou) established. 2. Be (ye) sent. 3. You (ye) shall hold. 4. Fortify (ye). 5. Thou shalt establish. 6. They shall be clothed. 7. It shall be placed. 8. Fortify (thou). 9. He shall send. 10. It shall be had. 11. They shall not[1] be called together. 12. Be it [so] (fut.). 13. They shall not[1] be. 14. Come (ye) together. 15. Thou shalt be praised. 16. Thou shalt fill. 17. He shall not[1] be clothed. 18. Be (ye) away. 19. Commend (thou). 20. Be (thou) clothed. 21. Thou shalt not[1] be established. 22. Be ye led. 23. Thou shalt hold. 24. They shall lead. 25. Ye shall be.

178. Supplementary Exercises.

I. 1. Vestīminī. 2. Habēre. 3. Nē cōnfirmātōte. 4. Mitte. 5. Convocāte. 6. Nē pōnuntor. 7. Laudāre. 8. Dūciminī. 9. Abestō. 10. Suntō. 11. Mūnītōte.

II. 1. Hold (ye). 2. Be (ye) called together. 3. Be (thou) placed. 4. You (ye) shall clothe. 5. Have (thou). 6. They shall not be called together. 7. He shall not be. 8. Be (thou) away. 9. Call (ye) together. 10. Have (ye).

179. EXAMPLES.

1. **Dēsilīte, mīlitēs** (4, 25, 3), *jump overboard, my men* (lit., soldiers)!
2. **Sīc exīstimō, patrēs cōnscrīptī** (Sall. Cat. 51, 15), *this is my opinion* (I think thus), *conscript fathers*.
3. **Est** ut dīcis, **Catō** (Cic. Cat. Maj. 3, 8), *it is as you say, Cato*.
4. **Tū**[2] vērō perge, **Laelī**[3]! (Cic. Lael. 9, 32) *pray go on, Laelius!*
5. **Tē**[4] hortor,[5] mī[6] **Cicerō** (Cic. Off. 1, 3), *I exhort you, my [dear] Cicero*.

VOCABULARY. 47

180. OBSERVATION AND INFERENCE: Note (1) that the *substantive* **in each** of the foregoing examples represents the *person addressed*, (2) that this substantive is in the *vocative*, and (3) that it stands, **not** at the beginning of the sentence, but after one or more words. Frame a rule for the Case and Position of the substantive used in Direct Address.

181. REFERENCES FOR VERIFICATION: **A. & G.** 241; H. 369, 569, VI.; G. 194, Rem. 3 with fine-print note.

---

¹ Use **nē** (not **nōn**) when the *future* imperative is negatived; the *present* imperative does not take a negative in prose.
² **Tū**, pron. **2d** pers. nom. sing, *thou, you.*
³ See **A. & G.** 40, *c*; H. 51, 5; G. 29, Rem. **2.**

⁴ **Tē**, pron. 2d pers. acc. sing., *thee, you.*
⁵ **hortor** has a passive form, but an active meaning; such verbs are called *deponent*, and will be treated later.
⁶ See A. & G. 40, *c*; H. 185, note 1; G. 29, Rem. 2.

LESSON XXI.

VOCABULARY AND EXERCISES.

182. VOCABULARY.

agō, -ere, ēgī, āctus, *do.*
animōsus, -a, -um, adj., *full of courage.*
bonus, -a, -um, adj., *good.*
Catilīna, -ae, M., *Catiline.*
C.¹ Fannius,² -lī, M., *Gajus Fannius.*
C.¹ Laelius,² -lī, M., *Gajus Laelius.*
cōnscrīptus,³ -a, -um, *enrolled, conscript.*
custōdia, -ae, F., *guardianship;* in pl., *guards.*
dē-fendō, -ere, **-fendī, -fēusus,** *defend.*

facultās, -ātis, F., *opportunity.*
fīlius,² -lī, M., *son.*
M. Tullius,² -lī, M., *Marcus Tullius.*
prae-stō, -āre, -itī, -ātus or -itus, *exhibit.*
pūrgō, -āre, -āvī, -ātus, *cleanse, purge.*
Rōma, -ae, F., *Rome.*
sē-cernō, -ere, -crēvī, -crētus, *separate.*
tectum, -ī, N., *dwelling.*
vigilia, -ae, F., WAKE*fulness;* in pl., WATCHmen.

183.   EXERCISES.

I. 1. Habētis, mīlitēs, facultātem[4]; praestāte virtūtem.[4]
2. Pūrgā[4] Rōmam, Catilīna.   3. Jam diū (*for a long time*), patrēs cōnscrīptī,[3] in perīculīs sumus.[5]   4. Audī, mī[6] fīlī.
5. Multīs proeliīs, mīlitēs, exercēminī.   6. M. Tullī,[7] quid (neut. sing. acc. interrog. pron., *what*) agis?

II. 1. In battle (battles), soldiers, you are to be (fut. imper.) full of courage.   2. Many do,[8] indeed (quidem[9]), inquire, Gajus Laelius, as (ut) has been said[10] by Fannius.
3. Separate yourself (tē), Catiline, from the good.   4. Defend your dwellings by guards and watchmen.   5. Thou shalt be defended, consul, by [means of] guards and watchmen.   6. Very well (vērō[11]), you shall hear, my son.

184.   Supplementary Exercises.

I. 1. Quoniam (*Seeing that*) supplicātiō dēcrēta est, celebrātōte illōs diēs (acc. pl., *those days*) cum conjugibus āc līberīs vestrīs.
2. Vōs,[12] Quirītēs,[13] in vestra tecta discēdite.   3. Tū,[14] Fannī, nōn rēctē (*rightly*) jūdicās dē Catōne.   4. Memoria vestra, discipulī, vocābulīs Latīnīs exercētor.   5. Virtūs, virtūs, inquam,[15] C. Fannī, et conciliat amīcitiās et cōnservat.

II. 1. Therefore,[16] conscript fathers, take thought for yourselves;[17] preserve[18] yourselves,[19] [your] wives, [your] children, and your[20] fortunes; defend[21] the name and safety of the Roman people.   2. You were, then,[22] at Laeca's,[23] Catiline.   3. Lay aside your favorable disposition towards me,[24] conscript fathers, and think of (dē) your children.   4. Ye shall stand by the unfortunate, praetors!

---

[1] C had originally the sound of g-hard. This sound it retained (even after the introduction of the character G) when used as an abbreviation for the name **Gājus**.

[2] See foot-note 3 at the end of the preceding lesson.

[3] See cōnscrīptus in the general vocabulary.

[4] Note the emphatic position.

[5] Translate: *have been*, and see A. & G. 276, *a*; H. 467, 2; G. 221.

[6] See foot-note 6, Lesson XX.

[7] Note the exceptional position of the vocative, due to the excitement of the speaker.

[8] Express the emphasis denoted in English by "do," by placing the verb first.

⁹ Place **quidem** after the verb, and let the vocative **follow** before the subject.
¹⁰ The participle must be neuter.
¹¹ Place **vērō** after the verb.
¹² **Vōs**, pron. 2d pers. nom. pl. *you.*
¹³ From **Quirīs, -ītis**; in the plural, applied to the Romans when acting in a civil capacity. Translate: *fellow citizens.*
¹⁴ See foot-note 2, Lesson XX.
¹⁵ *I say;* **inquam** is a defective verb, *i.e.,* it lacks most of its parts.

¹⁶ **Quā rē.**
¹⁷ **vōbīs.**
¹⁸ Place the verb before its objects.
¹⁹ **vōs.**
²⁰ For gender, see A. & G. 187; H. 439, 1; G. 286.
²¹ Place the verb after its objects; see A. & G. 344, *f*; H. 562; G. 684.
²² **igitur.**
²³ **apud** (prep.) **Laecam.**
²⁴ Arrange thus: *your towards* **me** (**ergā mē**) *favorable disposition.*

LESSON XXII.

Substantives of the Third Declension: Vowel Stems.

185. Learn the paradigms of declension given in the following sections of the grammar: A. & G. 52; H. 62, 63; G. 59.

186. Decline: **collis**,¹ **-is**, M., *hill;* **hostis**,¹ **-is**, C., *enemy;* **īgnis**,² **-is**, M., *fire;* **nāvis**,³ **-is**, F., *ship;* **puppis**,³ **-is**, F., *stern;* **rūpēs, -is**, F., *rock;* **īnsīgne, -is**, N., *badge;* **vectīgal, -ālis**, N., *revenue.*

187. Note that the *stems* of the foregoing nouns are: **colli-, hosti-, īgni-, nāvi-, puppi-, rūpi-, īnsīgni-, vectīgāli-.**

188. Explain the formation, from the stem, of the *nominatives* in **186**: A. & G. 51, *a, c*; H. 63, 1, 1); G. 58 (first three paragraphs).

189. Decline together, with meanings: **collis asper**, *a rugged hill;* **hostis noster**, *our enemy;* **īgnis clārus**, *a bright fire;* **nāvis longa**, *a ship of war* (lit., *long ship*); **puppis alta**, *a high stern;* **rūpēs sinistra**, *a rock on the left;* **īnsīgne pulchrum**, *a beautiful badge;* **māgnum vectīgal**, *a large revenue.*

190. VOCABULARY.

ac-commodō, -āre, -āvī, -ātus, *adjust.*
altitūdō, -inis, F., *height.*
augeō, -ēre, auxī, auctus, *increase.*
barbarus, -a, -um, adj., *rude;* used subst., *barbarian.*
clāssis, -is, F., *fleet.*
com-pellō, -ere, -pulī, -pulsus, *drive in a body, drive.*
cremō, -āre, -āvī, -ātus, *burn.*
figūra, -ae, F., *shape.*
fīnis, -is, M. (sometimes F. in sing.), *boundary;* in pl., also *territories.*
mare, -is, N., *sea.*
op-pūgnō, -āre, -āvī, -ātus, *assault.*
prae-mittō, -ere, -mīsī, -missus, *send forward.*
prae-sum, -esse, -fuī, *be in command of.*
silva, -ae, F., *wood, forest.*
terra, -ae, F., *earth, land.*
turris, -is, F., **tower.**

191. EXERCISES.

I. 1. In fīnēs Helvētiōrum pervēnērunt. 2. Ab hostibus ignī corpora sunt cremāta. 3. Lēgātum cum nāvī longā praemittit. 4. Caesar clāssī praeerat. 5. Nāvium figūrā permōtī sunt barbarī. 6. Nostrī hostīs in silvās collīsque compulērunt. 7. Insīgnia accommodāta erant. 8. Oppidum oppūgnat terrā[5] marīque.[5]

II. 1. They had persuaded the enemy.[6] 2. The height of the sterns exceeded[7] [that of] the towers. 3. The bodies of the enemy will be burned.[8] 4. The lieutenant has arrived with ships of war.[9] 5. The shape of the ships alarmed[10] the barbarians. 6. The enemy[6] will be driven by our men into the hills. 7. The revenues have been increased by Caesar.

192. Supplementary Exercises.

I. 1. Māgna hostium multitūdō sitī cōnsūmēbātur. 2. Nāvēs longae aedificantur in flūmine. 3. Gallī animālia immolant. 4. Neque terrā neque marī effugium dabātur hostibus. 5. Turrīs altās excitant.

II. 1. They were **building** ships of war on the river. 2. Living creatures are sacrificed by the Gauls. 3. The enemy erect a high tower on the hill. 4. A lieutenant was in command of the enemy's fleet.

¹ Decline **collis** and **hostis** with only **-em in** the accusative, and only **-e** in the ablative; otherwise like **turris**. (The rare instances in which **collis** has -ī in the ablative may be disregarded.)
² Decline **īgnis** with only **-em** in the accusative; otherwise like **turris**.
³ Decline **nāvis** and **puppis** throughout like **turris**.
⁴ See also, for vocab., 186 **and 189.**
⁵ Ablative of *place where;* use preposition *by* in translating.
⁶ Use the plural.
⁷ **superō, -āre, -āvī, -ātus.**
⁸ Translate: *will be burned by fire.*
⁹ "Ships **of war**" = *long ships.*
¹⁰ **per-moveō, -ēre, -mōvī, -mōtus.**

LESSON XXIII.

ADJECTIVES OF THE THIRD DECLENSION: VOWEL STEMS.

193. Learn the declension of the adjectives **levis (trīstis** or **facilis)** and **ācer**: A. & G. 84; H. 153, 154; G. 82.

194. Decline (like **levis, trīstis,** or **facilis**): **omnis,** *all, every;* **fortis,** *brave;* **mīlitāris,** *military;* **dēclīvis,** *sloping;* **humilis,** *low.*

195. Note that the *stems* of the foregoing adjectives are: **omni-, forti-, mīlitāri-, dēclīvi-, humili-**; explain the formation, from the stem, of the *nominative forms:* cf. A. & G. 51, *c;* G. 81.

196. Decline (like **ācer**): **alacer,** *eager;* **equester,** *pertaining to cavalry;* **pedester,** *pertaining to infantry;* also: **celer,**¹ **celeris, celere,** *swift.*

197. Note that the *stems* of the foregoing adjectives are: **alacri-, equestri-, pedestri-, celeri-**; explain the formation, from the stem, of the *nominative forms:* cf. A. & **G. 51,** *b, c;* H. **p.** 59, foot-note 6; G. 81, 82.

198. Decline together, with meanings : **proelium equestre,** *a cavalry engagement;* **īnsīgne mīlitāre,** *a military badge;* **omne animal,** *every animal;* **animus alacer,** *an eager spirit;* **turris humilis,** *a low tower;* **nāvis celeris,**[1] *a swift ship;* **collis dēclīvis,** *a sloping hill;* **cōpiae pedestrēs,** *infantry;* **hostis fortis,** *a brave enemy.*

199. VOCABULARY.[2]

ad, prep. w. acc., *to, for.*
com-būrō, -ere, -ussī, -ustus, *burn up.*
con-tendō, -ere, -dī, -tus, *contend.*
dē-dūcō, -ere, -dūxī, -ductus, *withdraw, recall.*
ex-spectō, -āre, -āvī, -ātus, *look for.*

ex-citō, -āre, -āvī, -ātus, *erect.*
in-cendō, -ere, -cendī, -cēnsus, *set fire to, burn.*
in-struō, -ere, -strūxī, -strūctus, *draw up.*
pūgna, -ae, F., *fight.*
sus-tineō, -ēre, -uī, -tentus, *sustain.*

200. EXERCISES.

I. 1. Īnsīgnia mīlitāria relinquunt. 2. Hostēs equestribus proeliīs contendunt. 3. Caesar pedestrīs cōpiās dēdūxit. 4. Oppida omnia incendunt, frūmentum omne combūrunt. 5. Mīlitēs ad pūgnam alacrēs erunt. 6. Mīlitēs nostrī omnia[3] fortī sustinēbant animō.[4] 7. Gallī celerem[5] victōriam exspectābant.

II. 1. They erect a low tower. 2. He drew up his forces on[6] a sloping hill. 3. A speedy[7] victory had been looked for by the Gauls. 4. Caesar's infantry has been recalled. 5. All the legions were eager for the fight. 6. Caesar favored the infantry.

201. Supplementary Exercises.

I. 1. Ariovistus equestribus proeliīs cottīdiē (*daily*) contendit. 2. Omnēs hostēs terga vertērunt. 3. Nerviī pedestribus valent cōpiīs.[8] 4. Dumnorix reliqua omnia Aeduōrum vectīgālia parvō pretiō[9] redēmit. 5. Nam (*for*) ut[10] Gallōrum alacer est animus, sīc[10] mollis mēns est.

II. 1. Caesar hastened thither (eō) with[11] his infantry. 2. They **first (prīmum)** joined battle with their cavalry,[12] [and] then (de'inde) suddenly displayed their infantry. 3. Ariovistus will inflict severe punishment on (dē)[13] all the hostages. 4. The embassy was intrusted to Orgetorix by general vote.

[1] celer has celerum in the genitive plural; but as this form is found only as a substantive, it should be omitted in declining.
[2] For vocab., see also 194, 196, 198.
[3] Used substantively. A. & G. 188; H. 441, 1; G. 195, Rem. 2.
[4] Ablative of *manner*; use prep. *with* in translating. **See A.** & G. 248, Rem.; H. 419, III.; G. **401**.
[5] *speedy*.
[6] **in**.
[7] **See sent. 7** of the preceding exercise.

[8] Ablative of *cause:* A. & G. 245; H. 416; G. 407.
[9] Ablative of *price:* A. & G. 252; H. 422; G. 404.
[10] **ut ... sīc,** *as* ... *so, although ... yet.*
[11] Omit **cum :** A. & G. 248, *a*; H. 419, I., 1, 1), **(1);** G. 391, Rem. 1.
[12] Translate: *they first began* (committō) *a cavalry battle.*
[13] "inflict punishment on" = *take* (sūmō) *punishment from* (dē).

LESSON XXIV.

Apposition. — Predicate Agreement. — Accusative with Prepositions.

202. EXAMPLES.

1. **Dīvitiacus Aeduus respondit** (1, 32, 3), *Divitiacus the Aeduan replied.*
2. **Dīvitiacī frātris studium** (1, 19, 2), *the devotion of Divitiacus,* [his] *brother.*
3. **Praeterita Dīvitiacō frātrī condōnāre** (1, 20, 6), *to overlook the past* [out of regard] *for Divitiacus,* [his] *brother.*
4. **Flaccum** et Pomptīnum praetōrēs vocāvī (Cic. Cat. **3, 2, 5**), *I summoned Flaccus and Pomptinus, the praetors.*
5. **In flūmen Rhodanum īnfluit** (1, 8, 1), *it flows into the river Rhone.*
6. **Ā Bibracte, oppidō Aeduōrum** (1, 23, 1), *from Bibracte, a town of the Aeduans.*

203. OBSERVATION AND INFERENCE: Note, in the foregoing examples, that Aeduus, frātris, frātrī, praetōrēs, flūmen, and oppidō denote the *same person* or *thing* as Divitiacus, Divitiacī, Divitiacō, Flaccum et Pomptīnum, Rhodanum, and Bibracte, respectively; and that the former are added to the latter for *further description* merely. A substantive thus added for further description is called an *Appositive,* and the usage is called *Apposition.* Does the Appositive differ from the principal substantive in *case,* or agree with it? Does it usually agree in *gender* and *number* (see Exs. 1–4)? Does it *invariably* agree in *gender* (see Ex. 5)? Does the Appositive appear regularly *to precede* or *to follow* the principal substantive? Frame a rule for the Case of the Appositive.

204. REFERENCES FOR VERIFICATION: A. & G. 183, 184, *b*; H. 363, 1; G. 319.

205.   EXAMPLES.

1. **Lēgātiōnis Divicō prīnceps fuit** (1, 13, 2), *Divico was the leader of the embassy.*
2. **Testis est Ītalia** (Cic. *Manil.* 11, 30), *Italy is a witness.*
3. **Pausaniās Lacedaemonius māgnus homo fuit** (Nep. *Paus.* 1, 1), *Pausanias, the Lacedaemonian, was a great man.*
4. **[Casticī] pater populī Rōmānī amīcus appellātus erat** (1, 3, 4), *the father of Casticus had been called the friend of the Roman people.*
5. **Audācia fortitūdō vocātur** (Sall. *Cat.* 52, 11), *audacity is called fortitude.*

206. OBSERVATION AND INFERENCE: Note, in the foregoing examples, that prīnceps, testis, homo, amīcus, and fortitūdō, denote the *same person* or *thing* as Divicō, Ītalia, Pausaniās, pater, and audācia, respectively; and that the **former are added to** the latter for *further description.* Note, however, that the descriptive substantives here illustrated are *not,* like those of 202, **merely** *appended* to the principal substantive, but that they are connected with it by the *verb;* also that they unite with the verb to **form** the *predicate* of the sentence. As they thus form a part **of the** predicate, they **are called** *Predicate Substantives.* Does the

Predicate Substantive differ from the *subject* in *case*, or agree with it? Does the Predicate Substantive appear regularly *to follow* or *to precede* the *verb*? Frame a rule for the Case **of the Predicate** Substantive.

207. REFERENCES FOR VERIFICATION: A. & G. 183, 185; H. 362, 1; G. 324.

208.   **EXAMPLES.**

1. **Ad Caesarem revertērunt** (1, 31, 1), *they returned to Caesar.*
2. **Ante oppidum** (2, 32, 4), *before the town.*
3. **Apud Sēquanōs** (1, 9, 3), *among the Sequani.*
4. **Contrā populum Rōmānum** (2, 13, 2), *against the Roman people.*
5. **Inter fīnēs** Helvētiōrum et Allobrogum (1, 6, 2), *between the boundaries of the Helvetians and Allobroges.*
6. **Per fīnēs Aeduōrum** (1, 12, 1), *through the territory of the Aeduans.*
7. **Post tergum** (4, 15, 1), *behind [one's] back.*
8. **Propter timōrem** (Caes. B. C. 2, 35, 5), *because of fear.*
9. **Trāns Rhodanum** (1, 10, 5), *across the Rhone.*

209. OBSERVATION AND **INFERENCE**: Note (1) the *prepositions* in the foregoing examples, and (2) **the** *case* **of** the substantives with which they are used. Frame a rule **for the** Case of Substantives construed **with the foregoing** Prepositions.

210. REFERENCES FOR VERIFICATION: A. & G. 152, a; H. 433; G. 417.

LESSON XXV.

VOCABULARY AND EXERCISES.

211.   VOCABULARY.

Aeduus, -i, M., *an Aeduan.*
Allobrogēs, -um, M., *the Allobroges.*
amīcus, -i, M., *friend.*
appellō, -āre, -āvi, -ātus, *call, entitle.*

apud, prep. w. acc., *among*.
Athēniēnsis, -is, c., *an Athenian*.
atque,¹ conj., *and also, and*.
avus, -i, M., *grandfather*.
cōnsanguinei, -ōrum, M., *blood-relations, kinsmen*.
eques, -itis, M., *knight*.²
extrā, prep. w. acc., *beyond*.
frāter, -tris, M., BROTHER.
frīgus, -oris, N., *cold, frost*.
Gallicus, -a, -um, adj., *Gallic*.
honestus, -a, -um, adj., *honorable*.
iter, itineris, N., *way; journey, march*.

lingua, -ae, F., TONGUE, *language*.
L. Pīsō, -ōnis, M., *Lucius Piso*.³
mātūrus, -a, -um, *ripe*.
nam,⁴ conj., *for*.
propter, prep. w. acc., *on account of, owing to*.
scientia, -ae, F., *knowledge, skill*.
Sēquanus, -i, M., *a Sequanian*
trāns, prep. w. acc., *across*.
vergō, -ere, *incline*.
vergobretus, -ī, M., *vergobret* (see also general vocabulary).

212. EXERCISES.

I. 1. Orgetorix in itinere persuādet Casticō,⁵ Catamantaloedis⁶ fīliō, Sēquanō. 2. Ariovistus rēx atque amīcus ā senātū (*senate*) appellātus est. 3. Procillum³ propter linguae Gallicae scientiam ad Ariovistum mīsit. 4. Collis aequāliter (*uniformly*) dēclīvis ad flūmen Sabim⁷ vergēbat. 5. Divicō⁸ dux Helvētiōrum fuerat. 6. Thrasybūlus,⁵ Lyceī⁵ fīlius, Athēniēnsis.⁹ 7. Apud Aeduōs summus magistrātus (*the chief magistrate*) vergobretus appellātur.

II. 1. The Roman knights, honorable and good men, approve. 2. They send ambassadors to Dumnorix the Aeduan. 3. For, owing to the frosts, the grain was not ripe in the fields. 4. Lucius Piso the lieutenant was the grandfather of Lucius Piso, Caesar's father-in-law. 5. Geneva is a town of the Allobroges. 6. The Segūsiāvī⁵ are beyond the province, across the Rhone. 7. The Aeduans have oftentimes¹⁰ been called brothers and kinsmen by the senate.¹¹

213. Supplementary Exercises.

I. 1. Trāns Sabim flūmen omnēs Nerviī cōnsēderant. 2. Iter Caesaris per fugitīvōs hostibus nūntiātur. 3. Omnēs Belgae contrā populum Rōmānum conjūrāvērunt obsidēsque inter sē (acc. pl.

themselves) dedērunt. 4. C. Valerius Procillus, familiāris Caesaris, habēbātur princeps Galliae prōvinciae. *5. Ējus rěi (*of this fact*) **populus** Rōmānus est testis. 6. Is (*this*) pāgus appellābātur Tigurīnus.

II. 1. Titus Labienus, an experienced leader, **has been appointed lieutenant.** 2. The reputation of the Treveri for **valor** (gen.) is unparalleled among the Gauls. 3. The river Arar flows through the territory of the **Aeduans and** Sequanians into the Rhone. 4. Dumnorix **was** the **brother of Divitiacus.** 5. The village of the Veragri **is called Octodurus.** 6. **You** have attacked Cicero, the consul elect, **Catiline.** 7. **The tenth** legion, through the military tribunes (tribunes of the soldiers), returned thanks to Caesar. 8. **And he also persuades** Dumnorix the Aeduan, the **brother of Divitiacus.**

---

¹ See foot-note 2, Lesson XIII.
² See **eques** in the general vocabulary.
³ See **Pīsō** in the general vocabulary.
⁴ **Nam**, *for*, should be placed at the beginning of the sentence.
⁵ The English form is the same as the Latin nominative.

⁶ **Catamantaloedēs**, -is, M., *Catamantaloedes* (a ruler of the Sequani).
⁷ **Sabis**, -is, M., *the Sabis* (modern *Sambre*, a river in Belgic Gaul).
⁸ **Divicō**, -ōnis, M., **Divico** (a prominent Helvetian).
⁹ sc. **fuit.**
¹⁰ **saepenumerō.**
¹¹ See 212, I., **second sentence.**

LESSON XXVI.

SUBSTANTIVES OF THE THIRD DECLENSION: STEMS APPARENTLY CONSONANT. — ADJECTIVES OF ONE TERMINATION. — PRESENT PARTICIPLE.

214. Learn the paradigms of declension in the following **sections** of the grammar: A. & G. 54; H. 64. In G. read **54**, Rem. (first six lines), **59**, Rem. 3, **and** 60, 1.

215. Decline: **pars, -tis,** F., *part;* **cīvitās, -ātis,** F., *community;* **cohors, -tis,** F., *cohort;* **adulēscēns, -entis,** C., *youth;* **mēns, mentis,** F., *mind.*

216. Decline together, with meanings: **sinistra pars,** *the left side* (part); **fīnitima cīvitās,** *the neighboring community;* **reliqua cohors,** *the remaining cohort;* **adulēscēns fortis,** *a brave youth;* **mēns mollis,** *a yielding disposition.*

217. Learn the declension of the adjectives **atrōx** (**audāx** or **fēlīx**) and **egēns** (or **prūdēns**): A. & G. 85, *a*; H. 155, 156, 157; G. 83.

218. Decline **vēlōx, -ōcis,** *swift;* **ferāx, -ācis,** *fertile;* **ingēns, -entis,** *huge;* **potēns, -entis,** *powerful.*

219. Decline together, with meanings: **pedes** vēlōx, *a swift foot-soldier;* **ager ferāx,** *fertile land;* **ingēns īnsula,** *a huge island;* **rēx potēns,** *a powerful king.*

220. Learn, with meanings, the present participles of **amō, moneō** (or **dēleō**), **tegō** (**regō** or **emō**), **audiō**: A. & G. 113, *a* with pp. 77, 81, 83, 87; H. pp. 87, 91, 95, 99; G. pp. 54, 58, 64, 68.

221. Decline the present participles: **amāns, monēns,** (or **dēlēns**), **tegēns** (**regēns** or **emēns**), **audiēns**: A. & G. 85, *a* (**egēns**), 87, *a*; H. 157 (**amāns**) with note; G. 83 (**prūdēns**), 85, 2 (second paragraph).

222. Decline together, with meanings: **mulier flēns,** *the woman weeping;* **labōrantēs nostrī,** *our men struggling against odds;* **cīvitās flōrēns,** *a flourishing community;* **continēns silva,** *an uninterrupted forest.*

223. Learn the declension of **vetus**; A. & G. 85, *b*; H. 158; G. 83.

224. Decline together, with meanings: **vetus injūria**, *a former injury.*

225. VOCABULARY.[1]

animus, -i, M., *mind; heart.*
con-locō, -āre, -āvi, -ātus, *place; give in marriage.*
cōn-sistō, -ere, -stiti, *take position;* STAND.
Crassus, -i, M., *Crassus.*
decimus, -a, -um, adj., TENth.
dē-ligō, -ere, -lēgi, -lēctus, *select.*
homo, -inis, c. (always M. when it refers to a male), *man.*

lātus, -a, -um, adj., *broad, extensive.*
māter, -tris, F., MOTHER.
petō, -ere, -ivi or -ii, -itus, *ask for.*
poena, -ae, F., *satisfaction; punishment.*
re-petō, -ere, -ivi, or -ii, -itus, *demand back, demand.*
Suessiōnēs, -um, M., *the Suessiones.*
timor, -ōris, M., *fear.*

226. EXERCISES.

I. 1. Legiōnis decimae mīlitēs **in sinistrā parte** cōnstiterant. 2. **Crassum** adulēscentem fortem praemittet. 3. Timor omnium **mentīs** animōsque perturbābat. 4. Peditēs vēlōcēs āc[2] fortēs dēliguntur. 5. In flūmine Rhēnō sunt multae ingentēsque **īnsulae.** 6. Equitēs labōrantibus nostrīs subveniunt. 7. Caesar prō veteribus Helvētiōrum[3] injūriīs **populī**[3] Rōmānī poenās repetit.

II. 1. They establish friendship with the neighboring communities. 2. The lands of the Suessiones are extensive and fertile. 3. He gives his mother in marriage to a powerful man. 4. The women weeping ask for peace. 5. Crassus, a brave youth, came to the support of the horsemen [who were] struggling against odds.

227. Supplementary Exercises.

I. 1. Ā[4] fronte et ab[4] sinistrā parte nūdāta erant castra. 2. Equitēs recentī proeliō[5] perterritī erant. 3. Lēgātīs pācem atque amicitiam petentibus līberāliter respondit. 4. Auxiliārēs opīniōnem pūgnantium⁶ praebēbant.⁷ 5. Rhēnus multās ingentīsque īnsulās efficit.⁸ 6. In dēclīvī āc **praecipitī locō equōs sustinent.**

II. 1. Nearly (**ferē**) all the centurions of the remaining cohorts were either (**aut**) **wounded** or (**aut**) slain. 2. The Suessiones possessed extensive **and fertile** lands. 3. He comes-upon⁹ the soldiers fighting. 4. The Morini had uninterrupted woods and marshes. 5. **Can I**¹⁰ lay aside the remembrance of recent injuries? 6. **They put** (**conjēcērunt**) **to** (in w. acc.) flight the enemy [who were] again offering resistance.

---

¹ For **vocabulary**, see also **215, 216, 219, 222, 224.**
² See foot-note 2, Lesson XIII.
³ What kind of genitive? See **64** and **69.**
⁴ In Latin the place *at which* an action occurred is often viewed as the point *from which* it proceeded, and so **ab** or **ex** is used where the English idiom requires *in* or *on*. Translate *in front* **and** *on the left side.*

⁵ A. & G. 259 *a*; H. 425, 1, 1); G. 387.
⁶ Used substantively: A. & G. 113, *f*; H. 441; G. 438.
⁷ **opīniōnem praebēbant**, *produced the impression.*
⁸ Pres. indic. 3d. sing. of **efficiō**.
⁹ **occurrō**; see **154** and **155.**
¹⁰ **Num possum** (*am I able*) with infinitive. Read: A. & G. 210, c (last sentence); H. 351, 1, **note** 3; G. 458.

LESSON XXVII.

ABLATIVE OF SPECIFICATION. — ABLATIVE OF TIME WHEN.

228. EXAMPLES.

1. **Helvētiī reliquōs Gallōs virtūte praecēdunt** (1, 1, 4), *the Helvetians surpass the remaining Gauls in valor.*
2. **Oppida sua omnia, numerō ad duodecim, incendunt** (1, 5, 2), *they burn all their towns, about twelve in number.*
3. **Suēba nātiōne** (1, 53, 4), *Swabian by birth.*
4. **Nervius nōmine Verticō** (5, 45, 2), *a Nervian named Vertico* (lit., Vertico by name).
5. **Cīvitās hominum multitūdine praestābat** (2, 15, 1), *the community took the lead in population* (in number of inhabitants).

ABLATIVE OF TIME WHEN.

229. OBSERVATION AND INFERENCE: Note, in the foregoing examples, that **virtūte, numerō, nātiōne, nōmine,** and **multitūdine** show *in what particular* or *in respect to what* the statement (made or implied) is true. In what *case* **are these** substantives? Frame a rule for the Case of Substantives thus used.

230. REFERENCES FOR VERIFICATION: A. & G. 253; H. 424; G. 398.

231. EXAMPLES.

1. Tertiā vigiliā **solvit** (4, 23, 1), *he set sail at the third watch.*
2. Hōrā quartā **Britanniam attigit** (4, 23, 2), *he reached Britain at the fourth hour.*
3. **Ūnō tempore** accidit (Caes. *B. C.* 3, 15, 4), *on one occasion it happened.*
4. **Omnī tempore** (1, 11, 3), *at all times* (lit., at every time).
5. **Paucīs annīs** (1, 31, 11), *within a few years.*
6. **Nocte ad Nerviōs pervēnērunt** (2, 17, 2), *they came by night to the Nervii.*

232. OBSERVATION AND INFERENCE: Note, in the foregoing examples, that vigiliā, **hōrā, tempore** (Exs. 3 and 4), annīs, and nocte express *time at which* or *time within which*. In what *case* are these substantives? Frame a **rule for the** Case of Substantives denoting *time when* or *within which.*

233. REFERENCES FOR VERIFICATION: A. & G. 256 (to the semicolon); H. 429; G. 392.

234. VOCABULARY.

Aquitāni, -ōrum, M., *the Aquitani* or *Aquitanians.*
Celtae, -ārum, M., *the Celts (Kelts).*
com-memorō, -āre, -āvī, -ātus, *recount.*
etiam, conj., *also, even.*
ex-īstimō, -āre, -āvī, -ātus, *reckon, consider.*

initium, -ī, N., *beginning.*
institūtum, -ī, N., *institution.*
lātitūdō, -inis, F., *breadth, extent.*
lēx, lēgis, F., LAW.
multitūdō, -inis, F., *multitude, number.*
nox, noctis, F., NIGHT.

opportūnus, -a, -um, adj., *fit, opportune.*
ōrātiō, -ōnis, f., *speech, address.*
prae-stō, -āre, -itī, -ātus or -itus, *excel.*
regiō, -ōnis, f., *territory.*

suus, -a, -um, *his, her, its, their.*
tempestās, -ātis, f., *time.*
tertius, -a, -um, THIRD.
ūnus, -a, -um, ONE.
videō, -ēre, vīdī, vīsus, *see.*

235.   **EXERCISES.**

I. 1. Helvētiī virtūte omnibus Gallīs **praestābant.** 2. Caesar initiō ōrātiōnis sua in Ariovistum beneficia **commemorāvit.** 3. Aquītānia et regiōnum lātitūdine et multitūdine hominum tertia pars Galliae exīstimātur. 4. Ā castrīs oppidum Rēmōrum[1] nōmine Bibrax[2] longē aberat. 5. Paene[3] ūnō tempore et ad[4] silvās et īn flūmine hostēs vīsī sunt. 6. Multā nocte[5] sē[6] in castra recēpit.[6]

II. 1. The Belgians, Aquitanians, [and] Celts differ[7] from one another[8] in language, institutions, [and] laws. 2. Among the Suessiones, even within our-own remembrance, Divitiacus has been king. 3. The Suessiones have towns to the number of twelve[9] (twelve in number). 4. Caesar arrived at an opportune moment (time). 5. [There] was at this[10] time at Rome[11] a Numidian[12] named Massiva.[13]

236.   **Supplementary Exercises.**

I. 1. Populī Rōmānī sociī atque amīcī grātiā, dignitāte, honōre auctiōrēs (*increased, made richer*) sunt. 2. Ūnā nocte omnēs hermae[14] dējectī sunt.[15] 3. Intempestā nocte[16] conjūrātiōnis prīncipēs convocat per M. Porcium Laecam. 4. Duae[17] fuērunt Ariovistī uxōrēs, ūna Suēba nātiōne, altera Nōrica. 5. Catō cum modestō pudōre, cum innocente abstinentiā certābat. 6. Tertiā vigiliā omnibus cōpiīs[18] ex oppidō ērūpērunt.

II. 1. Our fleet **excelled the** ships of the Veneti in speed. 2. Accordingly in the beginning kings trained, some[19] the mind, others the body. 3. There **was, not far** from the road, a town of the Numidians named Vaga. 4. You were, then, at Laeca's on **that** (illā) night, Catiline. 5. The Bellovaci were foremost[20] among the Belgians in valor, in influence, and in population (number of inhabitants). 6. Nor in **the last**[21] war with (obj. gen.) the Allobroges did the Aeduans render[22] assistance to the Romans.

[1] The English form is the same as the Latin nominative.
[2] **Bibrax, -actis, F.,** *Bibrax* (mod. *Bièvre*).
[3] paene, adv., *almost.*
[4] ad, prep., *close by, at.*
[5] multā nocte, *late at night.*
[6] sē recēpit (perf. of recipiō, **take back**), *returned.*
[7] differunt.
[8] *from one another,* inter sē (lit., *among themselves*).
[9] duodecim, indecl. adj.
[10] eā (fem. sing. to agree with the proper **case of** tempestās).
[11] Use the locative form: A. & G. 36, c; H. 48, 4; G. 27, 2.
[12] Numida, -ae, M.

[13] **Massīva, -ae,** M.; see 228, Ex. 4.
[14] **Hermēs** (or **Herma**), -ae, M., *Hermes-pillar* (see general vocabulary); for declension, see A. & G. 37; H. 50; G. 72.
[15] Perf. pass. of dēiciō, *throw down.*
[16] intempestā nocte, *at an unseasonable hour of the night.*
[17] Nom. pl. fem., *two.*
[18] A. & G. 248, *a,* H. 419, I., 1, 1), (1); G. 391, Rem. 1.
[19] pars (in apposition w. "kings").
[20] *were foremost,* plūrimum valēbant.
[21] proximus, -a, -um, adj.
[22] *did render,* tulērunt, perfect of ferō.

LESSON XXVIII.

THIRD DECLENSION: GENDER.[1]

237. EXAMPLES.

1. Caesar, M., *Caesar.*
2. vir, M., *man.*
3. rēx, M., *king.*
4. Semprōnia, F., *Sempronia.*
5. mulier, F., *woman.*
6. rēgīna, F., *queen.*
7. cīvis, C., *citizen.*
8. hostis, C., *enemy.*
9. cūstōs, C., *guard.*

238. OBSERVATION AND INFERENCE: Note **(1)** that Exs. 1–3 designate *males*, and that they are of the *masculine gender;* **(2)** that Exs. 4–6 designate *females*, and that they are of the *feminine gender;* **(3)** that Exs. 7–9 designate *either males or females,* and that they are of the *common* (masc. or fem.) **gender.** Frame a general rule for the Gender of Substantives, of whatever declension, whose Gender is determined by their Signification.

239. EXAMPLES.

1. mucrō, M., *sharp point.*
2. pulmō, M., *lung.*
3. sermō, M., *conversation.*
4. dolor, M., *pain.*
5. honor, M., *honor.*
6. timor, M., *fear.*
7. caespes, **-itis**, M., *turf.*
8. gurges, **-itis**, M., *whirlpool.*
9. trāmes, **-itis**, M., *path.*

240. OBSERVATION AND INFERENCE: Note the *gender* of the foregoing substantives, observing at the same time the *nominative endings* printed in **bold-face type**. Frame a rule for the Gender of Substantives of the Third Declension whose Nominative ends in: **-ō, -or, -es** (gen. -itis).

241. EXAMPLES.

1. aet**ās**, F., *age.*
2. cīvit**ās**, F., *community.*
3. volunt**ās**, F., *pleasure.*
4. nūb**ēs**, -is, F., *cloud.*
5. rūp**ēs**, -is, F., *rock.*
6. vall**ēs**, -is, F., *valley.*
7. class**is**, F., *fleet.*
8. nāv**is**, F., *ship.*
9. turr**is**, F., *tower.*
10. mē**ns**, F., *mind.*
11. pa**rs**, F., *part.*
12. ur**bs**, F., *city.*
13. no**x**, F., *night.*
14. vō**x**, F., *voice.*
15. pā**x**, F., *peace.*
16. fortitū**dō**, **-inis**, F., *fortitude.*
17. māgnitū**dō**, **-inis**, F., *size.*
18. multitū**dō**, **-inis**, F., *multitude.*
19. ferrū**gō**, **-inis**, F., *iron-rust.*
20. imā**gō**, **-inis**, F., *image.*
21. orī**gō**, **-inis**, F., *source.*
22. sal**ūs**, -ūtis, F., *safety.*
23. senect**ūs**, -ūtis, F., *old age.*
24. virt**ūs**, -ūtis, F., *virtue.*
25. contempt**iō**, F., *contempt.*
26. leg**iō**, F., *legion.*
27. ōrāt**iō**, F., *speech.*

242. OBSERVATION AND INFERENCE: Note the *gender* of the foregoing substantives, **observing at the** same time the *nominative endings* printed in **bold-face type**. Frame a rule for the Gender of Substantives of the Third Declension whose Nominative ends in: **-ās, -ēs** (gen. -is), **-is, -s** preceded by a consonant, **-x, -dō** (gen. **-dinis**), **-gō** (gen. **-ginis**), **-ūs** (gen. **-ūtis**), **-iō** (abstract and collective).

243.   EXAMPLES.

1. insīgne, N., *badge.*
2. mare, N., *sea.*
3. rēte, N., *net.*
4. agmen, N., *train, army.*
5. flūmen, N., *river.*
6. nōmen, N., *name.*
7. corpus, -oris, N., *body.*
8. frīgus, -oris, N., *cold.*
9. tempus, -oris, N., *time.*
10. genus, -eris, N., *class.*
11. latus, **-eris, N.,** *side.*
12. opus, **-eris, N.,** *work.*

244. OBSERVATION AND INFERENCE: Note the *gender* of the foregoing nouns, observing at the same time the *nominative endings* printed in **bold-face type.** Frame a rule for the Gender of Substantives of the Third **Declension** whose Nominative ends in: **-e, -men, -us** (gen. -oris, -eris).

245.   VOCABULARY.

audāx, -ācis, adj., *bold.*
altus, -a, -um, adj., *high, deep.*
ingēns, -entis, adj., *huge.*
longus, -a, -um, adj., *long.*
magnus, -a, -um, adj., *great.*

noster, -tra, -trum, adj., *our.*
pulcher, -chra, -chrum, **adj.,** *beautiful.*
turpis, -e, adj., *base.*

246.   EXERCISE.

Determine the gender of the following substantives by the rules framed in connection **with** this lesson; indicate **the** gender thus determined by attaching to each substantive an appropriate adjective selected from the vocabulary in **245.**

aestās, -ātis, *summer.*
altitūdō, -inis, *height.*
amor, -ōris, *love.*
arx, arcis, *citadel.*
auris, -is, *ear.*
avis, -is, *bird.*
cālīgō, -inis, *mist.*
carmen, -inis, *song.*
clādēs, -is, *disaster.*
clāmor, -ōris, *shout.*

cohors, -rtis, *cohort.*
cōnsul, -is, *consul.*
contentiō, -ōnis, *contention.*
crīmen, -inis, *charge.*
cubīle, -is, *couch.*
cunctātiō, -ōnis, *delay.*
custōs, -ōdis, *guard.*
Dumnorix, -igis, *Dumnorix.*
dux, ducis, *leader.*
eques, **-itis,** *horseman.*

THIRD DECLENSION: GENDER.

facultās, -ātis, *opportunity.*
familiāritās, -ātis, *intimacy.*
flūmen, -inis, *river.*
foedus, -eris, *treaty.*
furor, -ōris, *rage.*
gēns, gentis, *race.*
homo, -inis, *man* (including woman).
insīgne, -is, *badge.*
juventūs, -ūtis, *youth.*
lātitūdō, -inis, *breadth.*
latrō, -ōnis, *robber.*
levitās, -ātis, *lightness.*
leō, -ōnis, *lion.*
litus, -oris, *shore.*
longitūdō, -inis, *length.*
lūx, lūcis, *light.*
miles, -itis, *soldier.*
mors, mortis, *death.*
nemus, -oris, *grove.*
obses, -idis, *hostage.*
opīnio, -ōnis, *opinion, notion.*

ovīle, **-is,** *sheep-fold.*
palmes, **-itis,** *vine-shoot.*
pater, **-tris,** *father.*
pāvō, -ōnis, *peacock.*
pectus, -oris, *breast.*
pedes, -itis, *foot-soldier.*
prōlēs, -is, *offspring.*
puppis, -is, *stern.*
rādix, **-īcis,** *root.*
regiō, -ōnis, **direction.**
scelus, -eris, *crime.*
sēdēs, -is, *seat.*
sedīle, -is, *seat* (poetic).
sēmen, -inis, *seed.*
servitūs, -ūtis, *servitude.*
sīdus, **-eris,** *constellation.*
stīpes, **-itis,** *stock* (of a tree).
suspīciō, **-ōnis,** *suspicion.*
tēmō, -ōnis, *carriage-pole.*
umbō, -ōnis, *boss* (of a shield).
virgō, -inis, *virgin.*

247. Note the gender of each of the following substantives,[2] and fix its gender in the memory by associating it with an appropriate adjective selected from **245.**

animal, -ālis, N., *animal.*
arbor, -oris, F., *tree.*
caput, -itis, N., *head.*
collis, -is, M., *hill.*

ignis, -is, M., *fire.*
iter, itineris, N., *journey.*
lapis, -idis, M., *stone.*
vectigal, -ālis, N., *revenue.*

---

[1] The rules for gender suggested in this lesson are deemed sufficient as practical aids to the memory. The gender of substantives of the third declension not here provided for, should be learned by observation and practice in reading and writing Latin.

[2] These substantives have already appeared in special vocabularies; they are introduced here because their gender is not provided for in the rules of this lesson.

LESSON XXIX.

Substantives: Fourth Declension.

248. Learn the paradigms of declension given in the following sections of the grammar: **A. & G.** 68; H. 116; G. 67.

249. Decline: **frūctus, -ūs,** M., *fruit;* **exercitus, -ūs,** M., *army;* **manus, -ūs,** F., *hand;* **cornū, -ūs,** N., *horn.*

250. Explain the formation, from the stem, of the *nominative singular* and *dative plural* of the foregoing substantives: A. & G. note preceding 68; H. 116, 1, **2**; G. 67.

251. Note the *gender* of the substantives in **249**, and frame **a** Rule **for the** Gender of substantives of the fourth declension. For verification, see **A. & G.** 69, *a* (first sentence), *b*; H. 116; **G. 68.**

252. Decline together, with meanings: **vetus exercitus,** *veteran army;* **omnis frūctus,** *all the fruit;* **manus sinistra,** *left hand;* **dextrum cornū,** *right wing* (lit., *horn*).

253. VOCABULARY.[1]

ā-mittō, -ere, -misi, -missus, *lose.*
cōgō, -ere, coēgi, coāctus, *collect.*
cōnspectus, -ūs, M., *sight.*
cōnsulātus, -ūs, M., *consulship.*
dē-dūcō, -ere, -dūxi, -ductus, *carry off.*[2]
dē-sistō, **-ere,** -stiti, *desist, cease.*

equitātus, -ūs, M., *cavalry.*
impetus, -ūs, M., *attack, onset.*
locus, -i, M., *place;* pl. (usually) loca, -ōrum, N., *places.*
manus, -ūs, F., *hand;* **art;** *band.*
nātūra, -ae, F., *nature.*
occāsus, -ūs, M., *setting.*

peditātus, -ūs, M., FOOT-*soldiers*, *infantry*.
pellō, -ere, pepulī, pulsus, *beat*.
re-moveō, -ēre, -mōvī, -**mōtus**, *remove*.

senātus, -ūs, M., *senate*.
sōl, -is, M., *sun*.
sub,³ prep. w. acc. and abl., *under*; sub occāsum, *towards the setting*.

254.   EXERCISES.

I. 1. Hostēs ā⁴ sinistrō cornū pulsī erant. 2. Sub occāsum **sōlis** dēstitērunt. 3. Nam equitātuī Dumnorix praeerat. 4. Manūs ā Belgīs cōgēbantur. 5. Oppidum et **nātūrā** locī et manū mūnītum erat. 6. Gallī māgnās peditātūs equitātūsque cōpiās cōgunt. 7. Ariovistus in cōnsulātū meō rēx atque **amīcus ā** senātū appellātus est.

II. 1. The **horses of all** have been removed from sight. 2. Caesar began **the battle** on⁵ the right wing. 3. All the fruits had been **lost**. 4. The cavalry sustains the attack of the enemy. 5. Almost (**paene**) **in sight of** our army the children of the Aeduans were carried off into slavery. 6. Crassus is in command **of all the cavalry**. 7. The Aeduans had lost all their **senate** [and] all their cavalry.

255.   Supplementary Exercises.

I. 1. Tertiā ex⁴ parte lacū Lemannō et flūmine Rhodanō Helvētiī continentur. 2. Dumnorix māgnum numerum equitātūs suō sūmptū semper alit. 3. Manūs cōguntur, exercitus in ūnum locum condūcitur. 4. **Caesar** ab decimae legiōnis cohortātiōne ad dextrum cornū **vēnit.** 5. Helvētiī **tamen nōn** parēs sunt nostrō exercituī. 6. **Sōlis** occāsū suās cōpiās **in** castra redūxit. 7. Paene ūnō **tempore et ad silvās et** in flūmine et **jam in** manibus nostrīs hostēs vīsī sunt.

II. 1. The enemy **could**⁶ not withstand **the** onsets of our men. 2. The twelfth legion **had** taken position on⁷ the right wing. 3. Caesar opened the engagement on⁵ the **right** wing. 4. Thence he leads his army into **the country**⁸ of the Allobroges. 5. Towards sunset⁹ they ceased 6. **The** forces (bands) of the enemy were **kept** apart. 7. Gradually those (eī, nom. pl.) who (**quī**, nom. pl.) **were in** command of the cavalry were disquieted.

¹ See also, for vocabulary, 252.
² See also 199.
³ A. & G. 152, c ; H. 435, note 1.
⁴ Translate on, and see foot-note 4, Lesson XXVI.
⁵ See 254, I., sent. 1.

⁶ *were not* **able (nōn poterant)** *to withstand.*
⁷ **in**; why not **ā** as in the next sentence?
⁸ **fīnēs**, plural.
⁹ *setting of the sun.*

LESSON XXX.

Adjectives: Regular Comparison.

256.   **EXAMPLES.**

1. Positive: **altus (st. alto-),** *high, deep.*
   Comparative: **altior, M. & F., -ius, N.,** *higher, deeper.*
   Superlative: **altissimus, -a, -um,** *highest, deepest.*

2. Positive: **fortis (st. forti-),** *brave.*
   Comparative: **fortior, M. & F., -ius, N.,** *braver.*
   Superlative: **fortissimus, -a, -um,** *bravest.*

3. Positive: **prūdēns (st. prūdent-),** *sagacious.*
   Comparative: **prūdentior, M. & F., -ius, N.,** *more sagacious.*
   Superlative: **prūdentissimus, -a, -um,** *most sagacious.*

4. Positive: **fēlix (st. fēlici-),** *happy.*
   Comparative: **fēlicior, M. & F., -ius, N.,** *happier.*
   Superlative: **fēlicissimus, -a, -um,** *happiest.*

257. Observation and Inference: Note, in the foregoing examples, (1) that the *nominative* of the *comparative* and *superlative* is formed by the addition of **-ior** (N. **-ius**) and **-issimus** (**-a, -um**),¹ respectively, to the *stem* of the *positive;* and (2) that in *vowel-stems* the *final vowel* of the stem *disappears* before these endings. Frame a rule for the Comparison of Adjectives.

258. References for Verification: A. & G. 89; H. 162; G. 86.

259. Learn the declension of the comparative **melior (trīstior or altior): A. & G. 86;** H. 154; G. 87.

260. Compare: (like **altus**) **lātus**, *broad*, **longus**, *long;* (like **fortis**) **levis**, *light*, **gravis**, *heavy;* (like **prūdēns**) **potēns**, *powerful*, **sapiēns**, *wise;* (like **fēlīx**) **vēlōx**, *swift*, **ferāx**, *fertile;* also decline their Comparatives.

261. Decline together, with meanings: **mōns** altior, *higher mountain;* gravior fortūna, *harder lot;* longius iter, *longer road.*

262.   VOCABULARY.[2]

aetās, -ātis, f., *age.*
circum-dūcō, -ere, -dūxī, -ductus, *lead around.*
cīvitās, -ātis, f., *community, state.*
com-mittō, -ere, -mīsī, -missus, *commit, intrust.*
fīlia,[3] -ae, f., *daughter.*
gravis, -e, adj., *heavy; severe, hard.*
nōbilis, -e, adj., *high-born, noble.*

rēgnum, -ī, n., *kingdom; sovereignty.*
re-sistō, -ere, -stitī, *resist.*
salūs, -ūtis, f., *safety.*
semper, adv., *always.*
Sēquanī, -ōrum, m., *the Sequani* or *Sequanians.*
vulgō, adv., *commonly.*

263.   EXERCISES.

I. 1. Dē obsidibus gravius[4] supplicium sūmet. 2. Oppidum ex[5] omnibus partibus altissimās[4] rūpēs habēbat. 3. Omnium fortissimī sunt Belgae. 4. Fīliam hominī nōbilissimō conlocat. 5. Resiste, mīles fortissime. 6. Omnēs graviōris aetātis[6] convēnerant. 7. Peditum fortissimōrum salūtem equitātuī nōn committam. 8. In Galliā ā potentiōribus vulgō rēgna[7] occupābantur. 9. Cohortēs longiōre itinere[8] circumductae erant.

II. 1. The swiftest foot-soldiers are not always the bravest. 2. The Helvetians were hemmed in by a broader and deeper river. 3. They send the noblest men in[9] the state. 4. The punishment of the Sequani is too severe.[4] 5. The lands of the Suessiones were very extensive[4] and (very) fertile. 6. On[5] one side the Helvetians are hemmed in by the river Rhine [which is] exceedingly broad and (exceedingly) deep.

ADJECTIVES: REGULAR COMPARISON. 71

264.   **Supplementary Exercises.**

I. 1. **Carinae** plāniōrēs sunt quam[10] nostrārum nāvium. 2. Ubī dē Caesaris adventū Helvētiī certiōrēs[11] factī sunt,[12] lēgātōs mittunt nōbilissimōs cīvitātis.[13] 3. Est gravior **fortūna** Sēquanōrum quam[14] reliquōrum. 4. Suessiōnēs lātissimōs **ferācissimōsque** agrōs possident. 5. Locus ex omnī Galliā opportūnissimus āc frūctuōsissimus jūdicātus est.

II. 1. Ariovistus will inflict the severest punishment on[15] **all the hostages**. 2. The Romans will be more **faint-hearted** (of feebler courage[16]). 3. Nor **according to Swabian notions** (according to the customs[17] **of the** Suebi) is anything[18] esteemed baser or more spiritless. 4. **Among the** Helvetians Orgetorix was by **far the** most-exalted-in-rank.[19] 5. The **Morini** were-making-for **the denser woods**. 6. **Dumnorix**, for-the-sake[20] of [extending **his**] political power, gave his mother [in marriage] to a man of-very-high-rank[19] and of-very-great-influence.[21]

---

[1] Superlatives, therefore, are adjectives of the first and second declensions, and are declined like **bonus**.

[2] For vocabulary, see also 256, 260, 261.

[3] For irregularity in the declension of the plural, see A. & G. 36, e; H. 49, 4; G. 27, 3.

[4] The Latin comparative and superlative admit of other translations than those given in 256. Thus, **gravior** may mean *severer, rather severe* (i.e., severer than usual), *too severe* (i.e., severer than is fitting); **gravissimus** may mean *severest* or *very* (*exceedingly*) *severe*.

[5] See foot-note 4, Lesson XXVI.

[6] *All* [who were] *of advanced age*, i.e., *all the elders*. For the genitive **aetātis**, see A. & G. 215; H. 396, V. n 1; G. 364.

[7] Translate by the singular, *sovereignty* or *royal power*; the plural is used in the Latin because repeated instances are referred to.

[8] A. & G. 258, g; H. 429, 1, 3); G. 387.

[9] "In the state" = *of the state*.

[10] sc. **carīnae**.

[11] Predicate adjective with the passive verb **factī sunt** and limiting **Helvētiī**.

[12] **factī sunt**, perf. pass. of **faciō**, *make*; **certiōrēs** factī sunt, (were made more certain, and so) *were informed*.

[13] See 263, II., **sent. 3**.

[14] sc. **fortūna**.

[15] See 263, I., sent. 1.

[16] *of feebler courage*, **īnfirmiōre animō**; A. & G. 251; H. 419, II.; G. 402.

[17] Express "according to" by putting the word for "customs" in the ablative: A. & G. 253; H. 416; G. 398.

[18] **quicquam**, nominative neuter singular.

[19] Superlative of **nōbilis**.

[20] **causā**; **causā** follows the genitive that limits it.

[21] Superlative of **potēns**.

LESSON XXXI.

Substantives: Fifth Declension.

265. Learn the declension of rēs, F., *thing;* diēs, M.,[1] *day;* fidēs, F., *faith;* spēs, F., *hope;* aciēs, F., *edge, line of battle, line:* A. & G. 72, 74, *d*; H. 120, 122, 1, 2; G. 69, Rem. 1.

266. Explain the formation, from the stem, of the *nominatives* in **265**: A. & G. note preceding 72; H. 120, 1; G. 69.

267. Note the *gender* of the substantives in **265**, and frame a general Rule for the Gender of substantives of the fifth declension. For verification, see A. & G. 73; H. 123; G. 70.

268. Decline together, with meanings: in sing., **rēs mīlitāris,** *the military art;* in pl., **multae rēs,** *many things;* in sing., **diēs septimus,** *the seventh day;* in pl., **paucī diēs,** *a few days;* in sing., **māgna fidēs,** *great confidence;* in sing. and in nom. and acc. pl. **spēs asperior,** *a more discouraging prospect;* in sing., **aciēs triplex,** *triple line of battle.*

269. VOCABULARY.[2]

ac-cīdō, -ere, -cīdī, *happen, occur.*
cōn-stituō, -ere, -uī, -ūtus, *station, post.*
dī-mittō, -ere, -mīsī, -missus, *dismiss; lose.*
dolus, -ī, M., *treachery.*
frūmentārius, -a, -um, *pertaining to grain;* rēs frūmentāria, *provisions.*

juventūs, -ūtis, F., YOUTH.
medius, -a, -um, adj., MIDD*le*, MID*dle part of.*[3]
occāsiō, -ōnis, F., *occasion, chance.*
*posterus,[4] -a, -um, adj., *following.*
premō, -ere, pressī, pressus, *press hard, distress.*
quaerō, -ere, -sīvī or -iī, -ītus, *seek; inquire.*

SUBSTANTIVES: FIFTH DECLENSION. 73

secundus, -a, -um, adj., *second*.
servō, -āre, -āvī, -ātus, *keep*; fidem servāre, *to keep one's word*.
trā-dō, -ere, -didi, -ditus, *surrender; impart*.
trigintā, indecl. num. adj., THIRTY.
ūsus, -ūs, M., *experience*.

270. EXERCISES.

I. 1. Diē septimō pervēnit. 2. Hostēs sine fidē tempus atque occāsiōnem dolī quaerunt. 3. Diērum trīgintā habēbant frūmentum. 4. In ūnā⁵ virtūte omnem spem salūtis pōnunt. 5. Multa dē rērum nātūrā juventūtī trādunt. 6. In colle mediō³ triplicem **aciem īnstrūxit**. 7. Omnem reī frūmentāriae spem dīmīserant. 8. Reliquās legiōnēs prō castrīs **in aciē cōnstituit**.

II. 1. The army⁶ of the enemy had been beaten on the left wing. 2. A very opportune incident⁷ occurred. 3. On the following day he inquired about the remaining matters.⁷ 4. Caesar will keep his word as-to⁸ the number of days. 5. The remaining legions take position in line of **battle on the middle of the** hill. 6. The soldiers of the **second line** were distressed for provisions.⁹ 7. The tribunes had no great experience in military **affairs**.¹⁰

---

¹ diēs is sometimes **feminine in the singular**.
² See also 265, 268.
³ medius in agreement with a substantive usually denotes *the middle of*; thus, in colle mediō, *on the middle of the hill*; see A. & G. 193; H. 440, notes 1 and 2; G. 287, Rem.
⁴ The asterisk (*) indicates **that the** form to which it is attached is **not in use**.

⁵ *alone*.
⁶ **exercitus** = *army* (generic term); **agmen** = *army* (on the march); **aciēs** = *army* (drawn up in battle array). Which is to be preferred here?
⁷ rēs.
⁸ dē.
⁹ Use the ablative.
¹⁰ rēs in the singular.

LESSON XXXII.

Adjectives: Peculiarities of Comparison.

NOTE: As the four conjugations in verbs, and the several declensions in substantives and adjectives, have now been treated, the special vocabularies hitherto printed in connection with the exercises will be discontinued. The pupil will henceforth be obliged to depend wholly, therefore, on the general vocabularies at the end of the book. In consulting the Latin-English vocabulary for the meaning of a word whose formation or composition is given, he should study carefully what is printed in brackets, so as to be able to trace the meaning of the complete word from the meaning of the parts which enter into its formation. Right habits formed at this stage will greatly facilitate the acquisition of power to translate at sight.

At this point also, or a little later at the discretion of the teacher, the pupil may with profit begin to take occasional short lessons on the formation of words (see lessons beginning p. 209), and to translate and commit to memory passages from the anecdotes introduced at p. 224. The lessons on formation and the anecdotes should be completed before the continuous extracts from Caesar (p. 234) are begun.

271. Compare, with meanings: **ācer**, *sharp*; **celer**, *swift*; **miser**, *wretched*; **pulcher**, *beautiful*: A. & G. 89, *a*; H. 163, 1; G. 88, 1.

272. Compare, with meanings: **facilis**, *easy*; **difficilis**, *difficult*; **similis**, *like*; **humilis**, *low*: A. & G. 89, *b*; H. 163, 2; G. 88, 2.

273. Compare, with meanings: **bonus**, *good*; **malus**, *bad*; **māgnus**, *great*; **parvus**, *small*; **multus**, *much*: A. & G. 90; H. 165; G. 89.

274. Compare, with meanings: **citerior**, *hither, on this side*; **interior**, *inner*; **prior**, *former*; **propior**, *nearer*; **ulterior**, *farther*: A. & G. 91; H. 166; G. 89, Rem. 2.

275. Compare, with meanings: **exterus**, *on the outside*; **inferus**, *below*; ***posterus**, *coming after*; **superus**, *above*: A. & G. 91, *a*; H. 163, 3; G. 89, Rem. 1.

PECULIARITIES OF COMPARISON. 75

276.   **EXERCISES.**

I. **1.** Pulcherrimam tōtīus[1] Galliae urbem suīs manibus succendunt. **2.** Inter novissimum[2] hostium agmen et nostrum prīmum, longum spatium intererat. **3.** Cum proximīs cīvitātibus pācem et amīcitiam cōnfirmant. **4.** Tamen humillimus homo dē plēbe ope[3] dīgnus **est**. **5.** Mājōrī tamen partī placuit castra dēfendere. **6.** In Galliam ulteriōrem contendit. **7.** Mājōrēs nātū[4] lēgātōs ad Caesarem mīsērunt. **8.** Quam[5] māximīs potest[6] itineribus contendit. **9.** Sed Sēquanīs pējus accidit. **10.** Trāductī sunt plūrēs.[7] **11.** Summae virtūtis difficillima **est via.**

II. **1.** *Genera*[8] is the *last*[8] town of the Allobroges and nearest to the territories of the Helvetians. **2.** [There] was but[9] one legion in farther Gaul. **3.** At night-fall[10] they will hasten to the Rhine. **4.** They had the greatest abundance of ships. **5.** He had stationed the legions **on** the summit-of[11] the ridge. **6.** The bravest soldiers **had been** posted[12] in the upper line. **7.** They collect as **many ships** as they possibly can.[13] **8.** The lot of the Sequani was most pitiable.

277.   **Supplementary Exercises.**

I. **1.** Caesar Procillo[14] summam omnium rērum fidem habēbat. **2.** Belgae ab extrēmīs Galliae fīnibus oriuntur,[15] pertinent ad īnferiōrem partem flūminis Rhēnī. **3.** Proximō diē Caesar ē castrīs cōpiās suās ēdūxit. **4.** Multō[16] mājor alacritās studiumque mājus exercituī injectum est.[17] **5.** Deī Mercuriī sunt plūrima simulācra. **6.** Plūra[7] Gallōrum **scūta** ūnō **ictū** pīlōrum trānsfīxa et conligāta sunt. **7.** Nostrī mājōrēs[18] exemplum posterīs[19] prōdidērunt pulcherrimum.[20] **8.** Collis īnfimus[21] apertus erat, ab superiōre parte silvestris.

II. **1.** The Sequanian land is the best in[22] **all**[1] Gaul. **2.** He hastens by forced marches[23] into farther Gaul and arrives at (**ad**) Geneva. **3.** Caesar treats with Ariovistus on matters of-the-highest-importance.[24] **4.** At night-fall[10] they hastened to the Rhine and the marches²⁵ of the Germans. 5. He stationed all the auxiliaries in front of the smaller camp in sight of the enemy. 6. In that place was the shortest route into farther Gaul. 7. The river Axona is in the remotest [part of the]²³ territories of the Remi. 8. The lot of the **Sequani is more pitiable and** grievous than [that] of the rest.

---

¹ Genitive feminine of **tōtus, -a, -um**, *all, whole*; see A. & G. 83; H. 151, 1; G. 35.

² **novissimum agmen**, *the rear;* for comparison, see A. & G. 91, c, 2; H. 167, 2; G. 89, 3.

³ Ablative with **dīgnus**: A. & G. 245, *a* (first line), H. 421, III.; **G. 373, Rem. 3.**

⁴ **mājōrēs nātū**, [those who are] *greater by birth*, i.e., *the elders.*

⁵ **quam** strengthens the superlative **māximīs**; read A. & G. 93, *b*; H. 170, 2, (2); G. 317.

⁶ **Pres. indic. 3d sing.** of **possum**, *be able, can;* translate: *by the greatest possible marches*, *by forced marches.* **potest** might have been omitted.

⁷ *More* (than one, *i.e.*) *several.* For declension, see A. & G. 86; H. 165, note 1; G. 89.

⁸ Put the word for **"last"** at the beginning, and the word for **"Geneva"** at the end. What is the effect of this arrangement?

⁹ **Erat omnīnō.**

¹⁰ "At night-fall" = *at the first part of the night* = **prīmā nocte**; see A. & G. 193; H. 440, notes 1 and 2; G. 287, Rem.

¹¹ Superlative **of superus** in agreement with substantive; **see** preceding references.

¹² "had been posted" = *had taken position;* use **cōnsistō.**

¹³ **possunt**, 3d pl. pres. indic. of **possum**; imitate 276, I., sent. 8.

¹⁴ **Procillō** (dat.) **habēbat**, *reposed in Procillus.*

¹⁵ *begin;* **oriuntur** has a passive form, but an active meaning.

¹⁶ *greater by much*, i.e., *far greater;* for the ablative, see A. & G. 250; H. 423; G. 400.

¹⁷ **injectum est**, perf. pass. of **inicio**: *was infused.*

¹⁸ Comparative of **māgnus** used substantively: *ancestors.*

¹⁹ Plural of *posterus used substantively: *posterity.*

²⁰ Note the emphatic position of **pulcherrimum.**

²¹ *at the bottom.*

²² cf. foot-note 9, Lesson XXX.

²³ Imitate 276, I., sent. 8.

²⁴ Superlative of **superus.**

²⁵ "marches" = *borders, frontiers;* use the plural of **fīnis.**

²⁶ Superlative of **externus** in agreement with substantive; cf. foot-note 10.

LESSON XXXIII.

NUMERALS: CARDINALS.

278. Learn, with meanings, the cardinal numerals: A. & G. 94; H. 174; G. 93.

279. Learn the declension of: **ūnus** (A. & G. 83, a; H. 175; G. 35), **duo** (A. & G. 94, b; H. 175; G. 92), **trēs** (A. & G. 94, c; H. 175; G. 92), **ducentī** (A. & G. 94, d; H. 177).

280. Decline together: **duae legiōnēs**, *two legions;* **itinera duo**, *two roads;* **trēs senātōrēs**, *three senators;* **passūs ducentī**, *two hundred paces.*

281. Decline together, **with** meanings: in the sing., **ūnum iter**, *one route;* in the sing., **ūna spēs**, *the only hope;* in the pl., **ūnī Suēbī**, *the Suebi alone;* in the pl., **ūna castra**, *one camp.* See A. & G. 94, a; H. 175, n. **1**; G. 95, Rem. 2 (second line).

282.   EXAMPLES.

1. **Equitēs mīlle** (Cic. *Fam.* 10, 9, 3), *a thousand horsemen.*
2. **Equitum mīlle** (Caes. *B. C.* 3, 84, 4), *a thousand **horsemen** (lit., a thousand of horsemen).*
3. **Mīlia passuum tria** (1, 22, 5), ***three** miles (lit., three thousands of paces).*

283. OBSERVATION: Note (1) that **mīlle** (Ex. 1) is an *indeclinable adjective;* (2) that **mīlle** (Ex. 2) **is** a *substantive* in the *singular number* limited by the *genitive* **equitum**;[1] (3) that **mīlia** (Ex. 3) is a *substantive* in the *plural number* limited by the *genitive* **passuum**.[1]

284. REFERENCES: **Read carefully:** A. & G. 94, e with note (to the semicolon); H. 178 with **note** (to the **semicolon**); G. 308.

285. Decline together: **diēs quīndecim**, *fifteen days;* **mīlia sexāgintā tria**, *sixty-three thousand.* See A. & G. 94, c (second sentence); H. 176; G. 92.

286.   EXERCISES.

I. 1. Factiōnēs sunt duae. 2. Mīlia hominum vīgintī quattuor[2] ad Ariovistum vēnērunt. 3. Vīcōs quadringentōs

incendunt.   4. Cum duābus legiōnibus jugum adscendit.
5. Gallia est dīvīsa in partēs trēs.   6. Caesar scūtum ab novissimīs ūnī mīlitī³ dētraxit.   7. Oppida sua omnia, numerō ad⁴ duodecim, vīcōs ad quadringentōs, incendunt.
8. Quīndecim mīlia Atrebatēs pollicentur,⁵ Ambiānī decem mīlia, Morinī vīgintī quīnque² mīlia, Menapiī septem mīlia, Aduātucī decem et novem² mīlia.

II. 1. The place was six hundred paces⁶ distant.   2. There were only two routes.   3. The Belgians inhabit one part.
4. The Nervii were reduced from six hundred senators to three.⁷   5. Six thousand men hastened to the Rhine.
6. The Nervii were reduced from sixty thousand men to barely⁸ five hundred.   7. He stationed two legions on the topmost ridge.   8. The sum total⁹ was¹⁰ about⁴ three hundred sixty-eight thousand.

287.   Supplementary Exercises.

I. 1. Omnium rērum summa erat capitum Helvētiōrum mīlia ducenta et sexāgintā tria, Tulingōrum mīlia trīgintā sex, Latovicōrum quattuordecim, Rauricōrum vīgintī tria, Bōjōrum trīgintā duo.   2. Ex litterīs Caesaris diērum¹¹ vigintī supplicātiō ā senātū dēcrēta est.

II. 1. In twenty-five days they raised an embankment three hundred and thirty feet⁶ broad [and] eighty feet⁶ high.   2. He pitches his camp three miles⁶ from the camp of the enemy.   3. The Helvetians with five hundred horse had routed a great force of cavalry.

---

¹ It will be enough for the pupil at present to note that the *substantives* mīlle and mīlia are followed by the genitive; the *kind* of genitive used after these substantives will be discussed in the next lesson.

² What other form of expression is possible?

³ ūnī mīlitī, *from a soldier*, dat. of ind. obj. after dētraxit; in the Latin expression, the soldier is viewed as the person *to* whom the action is done. See A. & G. 229; H. 385, 2; G. 344, Rem. 2.

⁴ ad with numerals = *about*.

⁵ pollicentur, *promise*, has a passive form with active meaning.

⁶ Use the accusative; this use of the accusative will be discussed in the next lesson.

⁷ Express: *from six hundred to three senators*.

⁸ Express: *barely to*.

⁹ "sum total" = *sum of all*.

¹⁰ *was*, fuērunt. See A. & G. 204, b; H. 462; G. 202, Rem. 1, 3).

¹¹ cf. Lesson XXX., foot-note 6.

LESSON XXXIV.

PARTITIVE GENITIVE. — ACCUSATIVE OF DURATION
OF TIME AND EXTENT OF SPACE.

288. EXAMPLES.

1. **Māgna est corporis pars aperta** (4, 1, 10), *a great part of the body is exposed.*
2. **Impedīmentōrum māgnum numerum** (2, 17, 2), *a great quantity of baggage.*
3. **Nihil vīnī** (2, 15, 4), *no wine* (lit., nothing of wine).
4. **Mīlia hominum vīgintī quattuor** (1, 31, 10), *twenty-four thousand men.*
5. **Omnium fortissimī sunt Belgae** (1, 1, 3), *the Belgians are the bravest of all.*
6. **Nōbilissimōs cīvitātis** (1, 7, 3), *the men of highest rank in the community.*
7. **Multum aestātis** (5, 22, 4), *a considerable part of the summer.*
8. **Satis ēloquentiae, sapientiae parum** (Sall. Cat. 5, 4), *enough eloquence,* [but] *not enough discretion.*

289. OBSERVATION AND INFERENCE: Note, in each of the foregoing examples, **that** the *genitive* designates **the** *whole*, and that the word **which the** genitive limits designates a *part*. The genitive thus used is called the *Partitive Genitive*. Frame a rule for the Partitive Genitive.

290. REFERENCES FOR VERIFICATION: A. & G. 216; H. 397; G. 366.

291. OBSERVATION: What part of speech is the *partitive word* in Exs. 1–4? in Exs. 5–7? in Ex. 8? Read A. & G. 216, a, 1, 2, 3, 4; H. 397, 1, 2, 3, 4; G. 367, 368, 369, 370, 371, Rem. 4.

292. EXAMPLES.

1. **Diēs continuōs quīnque Caesar prō castrīs suās cōpiās prōdūxit** (1, 48, 3), *for five days in succession Caesar led out his forces* [and arrayed them] *in front of the camp.*

2. **[Casticī] pater rēgnum** in Sēquanīs multōs annōs obtinuerat (1, 3, 4), *the father of Casticus had held regal power among the Sequani for many years.*

3. Repūgnantēs diem **noctemque obsident** (7, 42, 6), *they besiege day and night those that resist.*

4. Oppidum aberat mīlia passuum **octō** (2, 6, 1), *the town was eight miles distant.*

5. Duās fossās quīndecim pedēs lātās perdūxit (7, 72, 3), *he made* (carried) *two trenches fifteen feet wide.*

6. Hercyniae silvae lātitūdō novem diērum iter patet (6, 25, 1), *the breadth of the Hercynian forest extends over nine days' journey.*

293. OBSERVATION AND INFERENCE: Note, in Exs. 1–3, that diēs, annōs, **diem**, and noctem answer the question *how long?* In what *case* are they? Note, in Exs. 4–6, that mīlia, pedēs, and iter answer the question *how far?* In what *case* are they? Frame a rule for the Case of Substantives denoting Duration of Time or Extent of Space.

294. REFERENCES FOR VERIFICATION: A. & G. 256 (last part), 257; H. 379; G. 335, 2, 336, 337.

295.   **EXERCISES.**

I. 1. Magistrātūs **Aeduōrum** antīquitus[1] rēgiam potestātem annuum obtinēre cōnsuērant.[2]   2. Ā castrīs oppidum Rēmōrum nōmine **Bibrax** aberat mīlia passuum octō. 3. **Suēbōrum gēns est** longē māxima et bellicōsissima Germānōrum omnium.   4. Mīlitēs aggerem lātum pedēs trecentōs trīgintā, altum pedēs octōgintā exstrūxērunt.   5. Paucōs diēs ad Vesontiōnem reī frūmentāriae causā[3] morātur.[4]

II. 1. Night **lasts** (is) thirty days together[5] at the winter season.[6]   2. Nor **was** there left much time before (to) sunset.   3. The territories of the Helvetians extended **two** hundred and forty miles in[7] length, [and] a hundred and eighty in[7] breadth.   4. He selected a place suitable for a camp about six hundred **paces from** the Germans. 5. After the destruction of the Cimbri, **they had been for many years** harassed by their neighbors.

296.   Supplementary Exercises.

I. 1. Prima legiō **in castra** vēnerat, **reliquaeque** legiōnēs magnum spatium aberant.   2. Explōrātōrēs hostium omnī flūminis parte[8] erant dispositī.   3. Aeduī et Arvernī dē potentātū inter sē[9] multōs annōs contendunt.[10]   4. Frūmenta tantā multitūdine jūmentōrum atque **hominum cōnsūmēbantur**.   5. Ā lacū Lemannō ad montem Jūram **mīlia passuum decem novem** mūrum **perdūcit**.   6. Ariovistus multōs mēnsēs castrīs[11] sē[12] āc palūdibus[11] tenuerat.

II. 1. He was distant a few days'[13] march from the Germans. 2. The enemy not only[14] blockades the roads, but also[14] leaves behind a strong enough garrison[15] for the camp.   3. Storms ensued[16] several days in succession.[17]   4. The place was distant about six hundred paces from the enemy.   5. There was the **greatest** abundance of everything in the town.   6. For several years **he has** farmed[18] **the revenues** of **the Aedui**.

---

[1] **antīquitus,** *in former times.*
[2] **cōnsuērant,** contracted from **cōnsuēverant:** A. & G. 128, *a*; H. 235; G. 151, 1.
[3] See Lesson XXX., foot-note 20.
[4] **morātur,** *he delays,* has a passive form with reflexive meaning.
[5] "thirty days together" = *thirty successive days.*
[6] *at the winter season,* sub **brūmā.**
[7] **in** with accusative.
[8] Ablative of *place where* with preposition omitted; read A. & G. 258, *f*; H. 425, 2; G. 386.
[9] **inter sē,** *among themselves, with each other.*
[10] **contendunt,** *have been contending:* A. & G. 276, *a*; H. 467, 2; **G. 221.**

[11] **As the ablative** of *place where* in **this instance** expresses also *means by which,* **the** preposition **in** is omitted: H. 425, 1, 1); G. 387.
[12] *himself,* accusative singular.
[13] "a few days' march" = *a march of a few days;* cf. 287, I., sent. 2 and foot-note.
[14] *not only . . . but also,* et . . . . et.
[15] "a strong enough garrison" = *enough of garrison.*
[16] **secūtae sunt** (passive form **with** active meaning).
[17] "in succession" = *successive.*
[18] "has farmed the revenues" = *has the revenues farmed. Farmed,* **redēmptus, -a, -um.**

LESSON XXXV.

NUMERALS: ORDINALS. — ADJECTIVES: GENITIVE IN -īus, DATIVE IN -ī.

297. Learn, with meanings, the first twenty-five ordinal numerals: A. & G. 94; H. 174; G. 93.

298. Study the following table of alternative expressions:

thirteenth, **tertius decimus** or **decimus et tertius** (similarly 14–17).
eighteenth, **duodēvīcēsimus** or **octāvus decimus** (similarly 19).
twenty-first, **vīcēsimus prīmus** or **ūnus et vīcesimus.**
twenty-second, **vīcēsimus secundus** or **altér et vīcēsimus.**
twenty-third, **vīcēsimus tertius** or **tertius et vīcēsimus** (similarly 24 and 25).

299. Decline[1] together: in the sing., **legiō decima,** *the tenth legion;* **cēnsōrēs vīcēsimī sextī,** *the twenty-sixth censors.*

300. Learn the declension of: **alius,** *other;* **nūllus,** *not any, no;* **sōlus,** *alone;* **tōtus,** *whole;* **ūllus,** *any;* **ūnus,** *one;* **alter,** *other* (of two); **uter,** *which* (of two); **neuter,** *neither:* A. & G. 83 with *a* and *b*; H. 151, 1; G. 35 with Rem. (end).

301. Decline together: **aliud iter,** *another road;* **nūlla vōx,** *not a word;* **ūllum perīculum,** *any danger at all.*

302. Decline together, in the sing.: **prōvincia tōta,** *the whole province;* **altera pars,** *the other side;* **utra pars,** *which part* (of two)?

GENITIVE IN -īus, DATIVE IN -ī.   83

303.   **EXERCISES.**

I. 1. **Diē** sextō decimō pervēnit. 2. Aliud iter habent nūllum.² 3. Annō ūndēvīcēsimō³ post cōnsulis **mortem,** urbs expūgnāta est. 4. Prīma et secunda aciēs⁴ hostibus⁵ **resistit.** 5. Diērum⁶ vīgintī supplicātiō acciderat **nūllī.**² 6. Sēquanī sōlī **auxilium** nōn implōrant. 7. **Cēnsōrēs** vīcēsimī sextī³ ā prīmīs cēnsōribus **fuērunt.** 8. Galliae tōtīus factiōnēs sunt duae. 9. **Alter alterī**⁷ ūtilis est. 10. Dē quartā vigiliā summum **jugum montis** adscendit. 11. Cum legiōne duodecimā **contendit.** 12. Uter utrī anteferendus⁸ est? 13. Potestās erat neutrī.⁹

II. 1. The soldiers of the **ninth** and **tenth** legions¹⁰ arrived. 2. **Some resisted the enemy**⁵ in one quarter, others in another.¹¹ 3. He left behind the fourteenth legion. 4. There he places the baggage of the entire army. 5. In the twenty-sixth year the town was taken by assault. 6. Some¹² hastened to the mountain, the others¹² **to the** baggage. 7. He waited until¹³ the ninth hour.¹⁴ 8. Neither-party¹⁵ makes¹⁶ a beginning. 9. He will arrive at about the **fourth hour**¹⁴ of the day. 10. They do **not govern according-to**¹⁷ the dictates¹⁸ **of** another. 11. **[It] was the eighteenth** purificatory sacrifice. 12. **He makes a requisition on**¹⁹ **the** whole province.

304.   Supplementary Exercises.

I. 1. Aliud aliī²¹ nātūra iter ostendit. 2. Alterīus factiōnis prīncipātum tenent Aeduī, alterīus Arvernī. 3. Annum jam tertium et vīcēsimum⁸ rēgnat.²¹ 4. Prīma et secunda aciēs⁴ victīs āc summōtīs resistēbat, tertia venientēs sustinēbat. 5. Post sex legiōnēs **tōtīus** exercitūs impedīmenta conlocārat;²² inde duae legiōnēs tōtum agmen claudēbant. 6. Legiōnis¹⁹ nōnae et decimae mīlitēs Atrebatēs celeriter ex locō superiōre in flūmen compulērunt. 7. Alter alterī²³ inimīcus erat.

II. 1. He makes a requisition on¹⁹ the entire province [for] the **greatest possible** number **of soldiers.** 2. He sent Galba with the twelfth legion and a part of the cavalry against[24] the Veragri. 3. They ask of one another[25] the cause of the tumult. 4. The first and second lines[4] are under[26] arms, the third is fortifying the camp. 5. The Helvetians go in quest of another dwelling place, other habitations. 6. Lysander conquered the Athenians when they had been carrying on war twenty-six years.[27]

---

[1] Ordinals are of the first and second declensions, and are declined like bonus.
[2] Note the emphatic position.
[3] What is the alternative expression?
[4] Note the difference between the Latin idiom and the English; aciēs is here singular, but must be translated plural.
[5] A. & G. 227; H. 385, I.; G. 345.
[6] cf. 287, I., sent. 2 and foot-note.
[7] Translate: *They are useful to each other* (the one is useful to the other): A. & G. 203.
[8] *is to be preferred.*
[9] Trans.: *Neither had power* (power was to neither). For the dative, see A. & G. 231; H. 387; G. 349.
[10] cf. foot-note 4.
[11] Translate as if the entire sentence were. *Others resisted the enemy in another part.* See A. & G. 203, c; H. 450, 1; G. 306 (illustrations).
[12] *Some ... the others,* alterī ... alterī.

[13] ad.
[14] See hōra in the general vocabulary.
[15] Use the plural of neuter.
[16] faciunt, 3d pl. of faciō.
[17] ad.
[18] *dictates* (pl.), praescrīptum, ·I, N. (sing.).
[19] "on" is here a sign of the dative of indirect object.
[20] See references under foot-note 11.
[21] *He has been reigning these twenty-three years;* cf. Lesson XXXIV., foot-note 10.
[22] conlocārat = conlocāverat; cf. Lesson XXXIV., foot-note 2.
[23] cf. foot-note 7.
[24] in with accusative.
[25] *Another asks from another;* cf. foot-note 7.
[26] in with ablative.
[27] Translate *Lysander conquered the Athenians carrying on war in the twenty-sixth year.*

LESSON XXXVI.

Ablative Absolute.

305.   EXAMPLES.

I. Time.

1. Caesar necessāriīs rēbus imperātīs, ad legiōnem dēvēnit (2, 21, 1), *Caesar,* WHEN HE HAD ISSUED THE NECESSARY ORDERS (the necessary things having been ordered), *came to the legion.*

ABLATIVE ABSOLUTE. 85

2. **Māgnā multitūdine peditātūs coāctā**, ad castra vēnērunt (4, 34, 5), HAVING COLLECTED A LARGE FORCE OF INFANTRY (a large force having been collected), *they came to the camp*.

3. [Orgetorix], **M. Messāllā et M. Pīsōne cōnsulibus, cīvitāti persuāsit** (1, 2, 1), *Orgetorix*, IN THE CONSULSHIP OF MARCUS MESSALLA AND MARCUS PISO (Marcus Messalla and Marcus Piso being consuls), *persuaded his countrymen*.

4. **Cōgnitō Caesaris adventū, Ariovistus lēgātōs mittit** (1, 42, 1), ON LEARNING THE ARRIVAL OF CAESAR (the arrival having been learned), *Ariovistus sent ambassadors*.

5. **Scūtō dētractō, prōcēssit** (2, 25, 2), *he* SNATCHED A SHIELD AND (a shield having been snatched, he) *went forward*.

II. CAUSE.

6. **Germānī reliquā** fugā dēspērātā, sē in flūmen praecipitāvērunt (4, 15, 2), *the Germans*, DESPAIRING OF FURTHER FLIGHT (further flight having been despaired of), *cast themselves into the river*.

7. **Petentibus Rēmīs**, impetrant (2, 12, 5), AT THE INTERCESSION OF THE REMI (the Remi asking), *they obtain* [their request].

III. CONCESSION.

8. **Paucīs dēfendentibus**, expūgnāre nōn potuit (2, 12, 2), THOUGH BUT FEW DEFENDED (few defending) [it], *he could not take* [it].

IV. MEANS.

9. Militēs, **pīlīs missīs**, hostium phalangem perfrēgērunt (1, 25, 2), *the soldiers*, BY THROWING THEIR HEAVY JAVELINS (javelins having been thrown), *broke through the enemy's phalanx*.

V. CONDITION.

10. Nihil decet repūgnante **nātūrā** (Cic. Off. 1, 31, 110), *nothing is becoming* IF NATURE OPPOSES (nature opposing).

11. **Sēquanīs invītīs**, ire nōn poterant (1, 9, 1), IF THE SEQUANI WITHHELD CONSENT (the Sequani [being] unwilling) *they could not proceed*.

306. OBSERVATION AND INFERENCE: Note that the *ablative expressions* printed in **boldface type** in the foregoing examples might be omitted without injury to the construction. In other words, they are *grammatically independent.* Ablatives which are thus grammatically independent of the remaining parts of the sentence are called *Ablatives Absolute* (*i.e.*, independent ablatives).

Note, further, that all the examples, except 3 and 11, contain a *substantive* in the ablative absolute with a *participle*, whereas, in Ex. 3, *both ablatives* are *substantives*, and, in Ex. 11, the *second ablative* is an *adjective* (**invītīs**).

Note, again, that the ablatives absolute express: in 1–5, *time;* in 6 and 7, *cause;* in 8, *concession;* in 9, *means;* in 10 and 11, *condition.*

Note, finally, that the literal construction of the words is frequently disregarded in the English translation. Thus, in Exs. 1, 8, 10, and 11, the ablative absolute is translated by a *subordinate clause;* in Exs. 2, 4, 6, and 9, a *passive participle* is translated by an *active;* in Exs. 3, 4, 7, and 9, a *preposition with a substantive* is used in translation; and in Ex. 5, the participle is translated by a *verb* connected with the main verb by a *coördinate conjunction.*

Frame rules embodying the foregoing observations.

307. REFERENCES FOR VERIFICATION: A. & G. 255, *a*; H. 431, 1, 2, 4; G. 408, 409.

308.   **EXERCISES.**

I. 1. **Nūllō** hoste prohibente, legiōnem in Allobrogēs perdūxit. 2. Conloquium, interpositā **causā**, tollit. 3. Nōnnūllī ab novissimīs, **dēsertō proeliō,**[1] excēdēbant. 4. Propter lātitūdinem fossae mūrīque altitūdinem, paucīs dēfendentibus, expūgnāre nōn potuit.[2] 5. Mulierēs, **passīs manibus**, flentēs auxilium implōrābant. 6. Repūgnante **nātūrā**, frūstrā contendimus. 7. L. Tullō M'. Lepidō cōnsulibus, **P. Autrōnius et P.** Sūlla, dēsīgnātī cōnsulēs, poenās dederant.

II. 1. They had **not** given battle the-day-before, *although they had seized the higher places.*[3]   2. *Having made this*[4] *address*, he dismissed the council.   3. *At the intercession of*

Dumnorix, they obtain their **request of**[5] **the** Sequani. 4. The women and children **on**[6] **the wall,** *with hands outstretched according to*[7] their wont, besought peace of[5] the Romans. 5. The Caturiges *seize the higher places and*[1] impede the army's **march.**[8] 6. *In Caesar's consulship*, Ariovistus had sought the friendship of the Roman people. 7. The Helvetians, *if Caesar withhold consent*,[9] will endeavor to force a passage[10] through the province.

309.   **Supplementary Exercises.**

I. 1. Secundiōre equitum **proeliō** hostibus, Caesar **suōs in** castra redūxit. 2. Nocte intermissā, **circiter hominum** mīlia sex ad Rhēnum **contendērunt.** 3. Male rē gestā, fortūna dēfuit imperātōrī. 4. Aequātō omnium perīculō, spem fugae tollit. 5. Commūtātō cōnsiliō atque itinere conversō nostrōs ā novissimō agmine lacessunt.

II. 1. Labienus having seized the mountain, awaited **our men.** 2. Although two cohorts were sent by Caesar as-a-reënforcement,[11] the enemy, inasmuch as our men were overcome with terror, broke boldly through the midst [of them]. 3. In the consulship of Cotta and Torquatus, a great many objects on the **Capitol** were struck[12] by lightning.[13] 4. On hearing the **shouting, they all** broke ranks[1] **and hastened to** seek safety in flight.[14]

---

[1] **Imitate 305, Ex. 5.**
[2] nōn potuit, *he was not able.*
[3] Passages in this exercise printed in Italics are to be translated by the ablative absolute.
[4] hāc, abl. sing. fem.
[5] ā, ab.
[6] ex.
[7] cf. foot-note 17, Lesson XXX.
[8] Translate: *restrain the army from the march;* A. & G. 243; H. 413; G. **388.**
[9] See 305, Ex. 11.
[10] Translate: *will attempt a passage through force* (**per vim**). For declension of vīs, *force*, see A. & G. 61; H. 66.
[11] subsidiō (dat.).
[12] percussae sunt (perf. pass. **of** percutiō).
[13] *by lightning*, dē caelō (from heaven).
[14] Ablative of means.

LESSON XXXVII.

Periphrastic Conjugations: Active and Passive.

310. Review the present active and perfect passive participles of amō, moneō (or dēleō), **tegō (regō** or **emō), audio**; and learn, with meanings, the future active participle and the gerundive: A. & G. pp. 77, 79, 81, 83, 87; H. pp. 87, 89, 91, 93, 95, 97, 99, 101; G. pp. 54, 57, 58, 61, 64, 67, 68, 71. Learn also the future participle of **sum:** A. & G. p. 69; H. p. 85; G. p. 51.

311. Observation and Inference: Note, in the foregoing forms, the following facts:—

1. The *present active participle* is formed by the addition of -nt-,[1] nom. -ns,[1] to the *present stem*,[2] and the *gerundive* by the addition of -ndo-,[3] nom. -ndus, to the *same stem*.

2. The *future active participle* is formed by the addition of -tūro-, nom. -tūrus, to the *verb stem* as it appears in the *perfect passive participle*.[4]

Frame rules for the formation of the Present Active Participle, the Gerundive, and the Future Active Participle in the several conjugations.

312. Form and translate the Present and Future Active Participles, and the Gerundive, of:—

ā-mittō, -ere, -mīsī, -missus,[4] *lose.*
cōgō, -ere, coēgī, coāctus, *compel.*
com-moveō, -ēre, -mōvī, -mōtus, *alarm.*
dō, dare, dedī, datus, *give.*

ex-istimō, -āre, -āvī, -ātus, *reckon, think.*
habeō, -ēre, -uī, -itus, *have.*
mūniō, -īre, -īvī or -iī, -ītus, *fortify.*
reperiō, -īre, repperī, repertus, *find.*

313. Learn, with meanings, the Indicative forms of the First (Active) Periphrastic Conjugation[5] of **amō**: A. & G. 129; H. 233; G. 149.

314. Learn, with meanings, the Indicative forms of the Second (Passive) Periphrastic Conjugation[5] of **amō**: A. & G. 129; H. 234; G. 150.

315.   **EXERCISES.**

I. 1. Populī **Rōmānī grātiam repudiātūrus est.** 2. Aquītānia tertia **pars Galliae est exīstimanda.** 3. **Obsidēs** datūrī erant. 4. **Aeduōrum** auctōritātem apud omnēs Belgās **amplificātūrus erit.** 5. Bellum gerendum erit. 6. Neque obsidēs repetītūrī neque auxilium ā populō Rōmānō implōrātūrī fuērunt. 7. Omnia ūnō tempore erant agenda. 8. Mīlitēs ab opere sunt revocandī. 9. Iter **per** prōvinciam per vim tentātūrī sunt.

II. 1. They had been on-the-point-of-restoring **the hostages.** 2. They **were about-to-compel the Allobroges.** 3. The opportunity **must not be lost.** 4. The [soil] of the Gauls[6] **was not to-be-compared with that**[7] **of the Germans.** 5. **The signal will have-to-be-given with** the trumpet. 6. Neither **will men of** hostile disposition[8] be likely-to-refrain from injury and mischief. 7. He had been on-the-point-of-obtaining control of his own state. 8. The force of the enemy will have-to-be-kept-asunder.

316.   Supplementary Exercises.

I. 1. Allobrogibus vel persuāsūrī sumus **vel** vī[9] coāctūrī. 2. Omnia ūnō tempore erant agenda: vēxillum prōpōnendum,[10] signum tubā dandum,[10] ab opere revocandī[11] mīlitēs, aciēs īnstruenda.[10] 3. Aeduōrum injūriās nōn neglēctūrus erit. 4. **Occāsiō** negōtiī bene gerendī[12] āmittenda **nōn** est. 5. Nōs[13] neque lēgātōs missūrī neque ūllam condiciōnem pācis acceptūrī[14] sumus. 6. Uter utrī anteferendus est?

II. 1. The Germans' mode of life is not to be compared with [that] of the Gauls.⁶ 2. Ariovistus is not¹⁵ likely to reject either¹⁵ my good will or¹⁵ the Roman people's. 3. The authority of the Aeduans ought to have been increased among all the Belgians. 4. They were on the point of sacrificing an opportunity of bringing the matter to a successful issue.¹³ 5. The **wrongs of** the Aeduans ought not to be neglected. 6. The enemy **will** not be likely, if an opportunity is afforded [them],¹⁷ to refrain **from** mischief.

---

¹ Note that the vowel of the present participle is short before -nt- and long **before** -ns.

² The present stem may be obtained by **dropping** -re of the present infinitive active; see 136, 1. Note, however, that the **present** stem of verbs of the **fourth** conjugation (as, audiō) **ends in -ie-** (as, audie-) in the **present** participle and gerundive.

³ Note that the vowel **preceding -nd-** is short.

⁴ If the perfect participle ends in **-sus**, the future participle ends in -sūrus.

⁵ Note, in studying the forms of this conjugation, that the *tense* is determined by the form of **sum** used.

⁶ **Gallicus, -a, -um,** adj.

⁷ Use ager here, and **omit it at the** beginning.

⁸ Use the ablative; cf. foot-note 16, Lesson XXX.

⁹ For declension, see references under foot-note 10, Lesson XXXVI.

¹⁰ sc. **erat.**

¹¹ sc. **erant.**

¹² Opportunity of the matter to be well **conducted =** *opportunity of bringing the matter to a successful issue.*

¹³ *We.*

¹⁴ **Fut. act. part. of accipiō.**

¹⁵ not ... either ... or = *neither* ... *nor* = neque ... neque.

¹⁶ See sentence 4 of the **preceding exercise** with accompanying **foot-note.**

¹⁷ Ablative absolute.

LESSON XXXVIII.

Dative of Agent. — Descriptive Genitive. — Descriptive Ablative.

317. EXAMPLES.

1. **Caesarī omnia ūnō tempore erant agenda** (2, 20, 1), *Caesar had to do everything at once* (lit., all things were to **Caesar** to be done).

2. **Nostrīs nāvibus cāsus erat extimēscendus** (3, 13, 9), *the risk was greatly to be dreaded by our ships.*

DESCRIPTIVE GENITIVE. 91

3. **Mīlitibus** cum hostibus erat pūgnandum (4, 24, 2), *the soldiers had to fight with the enemy* (lit., the necessity of fighting was to the soldiers).

4. Cum luxuriā nōbīs¹ certandum est (Cic. Cat. 2, 5, 11), *we have to contend with dissipation* (lit., the necessity of contending is to us).

318. OBSERVATION AND INFERENCE: Note that with the *gerundive*, in the foregoing examples, **the person** *upon whom the necessity rests*, or *by whom the* **work is to be** *done*, **is** expressed by the *dative* (see **Caesarī**, **nāvibus**, **mīlitibus**, **nōbīs**). Frame a rule for such Datives.

319. REFERENCES FOR VERIFICATION: A. & G. 232; H. 388; G. 353.

320. OBSERVATION AND INFERENCE: Note further, that (1) the verbs in Exs. 1 and 2 are *transitive*, and the periphrastic forms have a *subject* expressed, with which they agree in *person*, *number*, and *gender*; whereas (2) in Exs. 3 and 4 the verbs are *intransitive*, the periphrastic forms have *no subject*, but are of **the** *third person singular*, and the *gerundive* is *neuter*. In the **latter case the verb is** said to **be used** *impersonally*. State the second of the foregoing observed **facts in** the **form of a General Rule.**

321. REFERENCES FOR VERIFICATION: A. & G. 146, c; H. 301, 1, 2; G. 199, Rem. 1.

322.   **EXAMPLES.**

1. Volusēnus, vir cōnsiliī māgnī (3, 5, 2), *Volusenus, a man of great sagacity*.

2. Paucōrum diērum iter (4, 7, 2), *a few days' march*.

3. Castra **in** altitūdinem pedum duodecim vāllō mūnīre (2, 5, 6), *to fortify the camp with a wall* (of) *twelve feet high* (in height).

4. Omnēs Britannī capillō sunt prōmissō (5, 14, 2), *all the Britons have* (are of) *flowing hair*.

5. [Thūȳs] barbā erat prōmissā (Nep. Dat. 3, 1), *Thuȳs wore* (was of) *a flowing beard*.

6. **[Catō]** singulārī fuit industriā (Nep. *Cat.* 3, 1), *Cato was* [a man] *of unexampled industry.*

323. OBSERVATION AND INFERENCE: Note, in Exs. 1-3, that the substantives added for description (see **cōnsiliī, diērum, pedum**) are in the *genitive*, and that this genitive is limited by an *adjective* (see **māgnī, paucōrum, duodecim**). A genitive thus added to a substantive for further description is called a *Descriptive Genitive* or a *Genitive of Quality*. **Frame a** rule for the Descriptive Genitive.

324. REFERENCES FOR VERIFICATION: A. & G. 215; II. 396, V., Note 1; G. 364.

325. OBSERVATION AND INFERENCE: Note, in Exs. 4-6, that the substantives added for description (see **capillō, barbā, industriā**), are in the *ablative*, and that this ablative is limited by an *adjective* (see **prōmissō, prōmissā, singulārī**). An ablative thus added to a substantive for further description is called a *Descriptive Ablative* or an **Ablative of Quality**. Frame a rule for the Ablative of Quality.

326. REFERENCES FOR VERIFICATION: A. & G. 251; II. 419, II.; G. 402.

327. OBSERVATION AND INFERENCE: Note that the descriptive expressions in Exs. 2 and 3 denote *measure;* does the ablative, or the genitive, appear to be **preferred for this kind** of description?

Note, further, that **the** descriptive expressions in Exs. 4 and 5 denote *physical characteristics;* which of the two cases appears to be preferred for this kind of description?

Compare Ex. 1 with Ex. **6;** does there appear to be any difference between the genitive **and** ablative in these examples?

328. REFERENCES FOR VERIFICATION: A. & G. 215, *b*, 251, *a*; H. 419, II., 2, 1), 2), 3); G. 402, Rem. 1.

---

[1] Dative plural of **nōs**, *we.*

LESSON XXXIX.

329. Illustrative Exercises on the Foregoing Constructions.

I. 1. Aduātucī Caesarī sunt cōnservandī. 2. Tum māgnī ponderis **saxa in** mūrō conlocābant. 3. Ingentī māgnitūdine **corporum Germānī, incrēdibilī** virtūte atque exercitātiōne in **armīs sunt.** 4. **Nōn** omittendum est Nerviīs cōnsilium. 5. **Flūminis erat** altitūdō circiter pedum **trium.** 6. Procillum, summā virtūte et hūmānitāte adulēscentem, **ad** Ariovistum mittit. 7. Num hominēs tantulae statūrae tantī oneris turrim movēre possunt?[1] 8. Cum tantā multitūdine hostium lēgātō nōn est dīmicandum.

II. 1. Sabinus will have to keep[2] the forces **of the enemy** asunder. 2. Our horsemen and light armed[3] foot-soldiers again **sought** flight in[4] another direction. 3. A mountain of **great** height bounds the remaining space. 4. The commander **must** exercise[2] no slight diligence. 5. Protected [as they **were**] by a rampart (of) fifteen miles in **circuit,** they kept themselves[5] within the town.[6] 6. Iccius the Reman, [a man] of the highest rank and influence among his [countrymen], sent a messenger to Caesar. 7. Neither ought the Romans to have feared[7] without cause. 8. The Romans move forward with remarkable speed[8] engines of great height.

330. Supplementary Exercises.

I. 1. Volusēnus, tribūnus mīlitum, vir et cōnsiliī māgnī et virtūtis, ad Galbam accurrit. 2. Mīlitibus autem, impedītīs manibus, simul et dē nāvibus dēsiliendum et in flūctibus cōnsistendum et cum hostibus erat pūgnandum. 3. Cīvitās erat māgnā inter Belgās auctōritāte. 4. Ab utrōque[9] latere collis trānsversam fossam obdūxit **circiter** passuum quadringentōrum.   5. Sēquanīs **vērō** omnēs cruciātūs erant **perferendī**.   6. Ūrī sunt speciē et colōre et figūrā taurī.[10]

II. 1. Agesilaus was of small stature and spare figure. 2. [It is] not in vain [that] men of such valor ven**ture** to cross a very broad river. 3. Caesar will have to inflict **punishment** on the Veneti. 4. The general should distribute his army more-widely.[11] 5. The Britons have all parts of the body shaved[12] except the head and the upper lip.

---

[1] *are able, can.*
[2] cf. 317, Ex. 1.
[3] Translate *foot-soldiers of light armor.*
[4] **in with accusative.**
[5] sēsē (acc. pl.).
[6] Ablative without prepositio.; cf. **296**, I., sent. 6, with foot-note.
[7] cf. Ex. 3 in **317**; see also **320** (2).

[8] cf. foot-note 4, Lesson XXIII.
[9] uterque, -traque, -trumque, *each* (of two).
[10] The descriptive ablative here takes a genitive instead of an adjective.
[11] lātius.
[12] Translate *are of every part of the body shaved.*

LESSON XL.

NUMERALS: DISTRIBUTIVE.

331. Learn, with meanings, the distributive numerals from *one* to *twelve:* A. & G. 95; H. 174; G. 95.

332. Decline together: **bīnae nāvēs,** *ships* [taken] *two and two;* **duodēna mīlia,** *twelve thousand apiece:* A. & G. 95; H. 179.

333.   EXAMPLES.

1. Prīncipēs singulōs (5, 6, 4), *the chiefs one at a time.*
2. Singulī singulōs dēlēgerant (1, 48, 5), *they had each selected one.*
3. Bīnae āc ternae **nāvēs** (3, 15, 1), *ships in groups of two and three.*
4. Quaternae cohortēs **ex** quīnque legiōnibus (Caes. B. C. 1, 83, 2), *four cohorts from each of the five legions.*

NUMERALS: DISTRIBUTIVE.

5. **Ūna¹ castra** (Caes. *B. C.* 1, 71, 4), *one camp.*
6. **Bīna¹ castra** (Caes. *B. C.* 3, 19, 1), *two camps.*
7. **Trīnīs¹** castrīs (7, 66, 2), *in three camps.*

334.   EXERCISES.

I. 1. Singulās bīnae āc ternae nāvēs circumsteterant. 2. Imperant Sēquanīs duodēna mīlia. 3. Ternās² cohortēs ex quattuor legiōnibus relīquit. 4. Inter bīna¹ castra Pompēī³ atque Caesaris ūnum flūmen **intererat Apsus.** 5. Ibī turrēs cum ternīs tabulātīs ērigēbat. 6. Circiter mīlia passuum decem ab Rōmānīs, **trīnīs⁴** castrīs Vercingetorix cōnsēdit.

II. 1. Caesar and Ariovistus brought ten [soldiers] each **to the conference.** 2. Soldiers in groups of five⁵ and six **surrounded** single [soldiers]. 3. The floats he made fast **by** means of four² anchors at⁶ each of the four corners. 4. He resolved to spend the winter with three legions in three¹ camps. 5. He erected towers of **two stories each.**

335.   Supplementary Exercises.

I. 1. Caesar singulīs legiōnibus singulōs **lēgātōs** praefēcit.⁷ 2. Imperant Morinīs quīna mīlia. 3. Bīnīs⁸ cohortibus relictīs, reliquum exercitum in cōpiōsissimōs **agrōs** Biturīgum indūcit. 4. Prīmam aciem quaternae cohortēs ex quīnque legiōnibus tenēbant.

II. 1. And-so with equal courage they matched⁹ [their ships] one by one against the ships of the enemy [taken] two and two. 2. One camp seemed now to-have-been-formed¹⁰ out of two.

---

¹ A. & G. 95, *b*; H. 174, 2, 3); G. 95, Rem. 2.
² cf. 333, Ex. 4.
³ Genitive of **Pompējus.**
⁴ Would **ternīs** be admissible here? See foot-note 1.
⁵ cf. 333, Ex. 3.
⁶ "at" = *from;* cf. foot-note 4, Lesson XXVI.
⁷ Perfect indicative of **praeficiō.**
⁸ The distributive shows that *two* from *each legion* is meant.
⁹ **obiciēbant** (pronounced: objiciēbant), imperf. indic. of **obiciō** (pronounced: **objiciō**).
¹⁰ **facta.**

LESSON XLI.

Pronouns: Personal and Reflexive.

336. Learn, with meanings, the declension of the Personal Pronouns: A. & G. 98; H. 184; G. 98, 99.

337.   **EXAMPLES.**

1. **Audīte Rōmānōs mīlitēs** (7, 20, 8), *listen to* [these] *Roman soldiers.*
2. **Est** ut dīcis, Catō (Cic. *Cat. Maj.* 3, 8), *it is as you say, Cato.*
3. **Nōs, nōs cōnsulēs dēsumus** (Cic. *Cat.* 1, 1, 3), *we, we the consuls are remiss.*
4. **Vōsne**[1] **Domitium, an vōs Domitium** dēseruit (Caes. *B. C.* 2, 32, 8), *did you desert Domitius, or did Domitius desert you?*

338. OBSERVATION AND INFERENCE: Note that, in Exs. 1 and 2, the *personal pronouns* **vōs** and **tū**, subjects of **audīte** and **dīcis**, are *not expressed*; whereas, in Exs. 3 and 4, **nōs** and **vōs** *are expressed*. What appears to be the reason of this difference? Frame a rule for the Nominative of the Personal Pronoun.

339. REFERENCES FOR VERIFICATION: A. & G. 194, *a*; H. 446; G. 198.

340.   **EXAMPLES.**

1. **Habētis** ducem memorem vestrī (Cic. *Cat.* 4, 9, 19), *you have a leader* [who is] *thoughtful of you.*
2. Grāta mihī vehementer **est memoria nostrī tua** (Cic. *Fam.* 12, 17, 1), *your remembrance of us is exceedingly gratifying to me.*
3. Dēsīgnat ad caedem ūnum quemque[2] **nostrūm** (Cic. *Cat.* 1, 1, 2), *he marks each one of us for slaughter.*
4. **Minus habeō vīrium** quam vestrūm utervīs[3] (Cic. *Cat. Maj.* 10, 32), *I have less strength than either of you.*

341. OBSERVATION AND INFERENCE: Of the *two forms* of genitive in the plural of the personal pronouns, which appears from the foregoing examples to be preferred for the *objective genitive?* which for the *partitive genitive?*

342. REFERENCES FOR VERIFICATION: A. & G. 194, *b*; H. 446, n. 3; G. 99, Rem. 1.

343. Learn, with meanings, the declension of the Reflexive Pronoun: A. & G. 98, *c*; H. 184 with 2; G. 100.

344.   EXAMPLES.

1. **Ariovistus tantōs sibī spīritūs sūmpserat** (1, 33, 5), *Ariovistus had taken upon himself such airs.*
2. **Reliquī sēsē fugae mandārunt** (1, 12, 3), *the rest fled* (gave themselves up to flight).
3. **Duo dē prīncipātū inter sē contendēbant** (5, 3, 2), *two were contending with each other* (between themselves) *for supremacy.*
4. **Inter sē differunt** (1, 1, 2), *they differ from one another* **(among themselves).**
5. **Dē mē pauca dīcam** (Cic. *Cat.* 4, 10, 20), *I will* **speak** *briefly of myself.*
6. **Tū tē in custōdiam dedistī** (Cic. *Cat.* 1, 8, 10), *you offered to give yourself into custody.*

345. OBSERVATION AND INFERENCE: Note (1) that the foregoing examples are *simple sentences*, and that the *reflexive pronoun* refers to the *subject;* (2) that the preposition **inter** with the reflexive, in Exs. 3 and 4, gives the latter a *reciprocal* force (*each other, one another*); (3) that in Exs. 5 and 6, where the subject of the sentence is of the *first* or *second person* the *personal pronoun* (see **mē** and **tē**) performs the office of the *reflexive.* Frame rules embodying the foregoing observations.

346. REFERENCES FOR VERIFICATION: A. & G. 196, *f*, 98, *a*; H. 448 with note, 449; G. 295, 212.

347. **EXAMPLES.**

1. [Patria] **tēcum,** Catilīna, sīc agit (Cic. *Cat.* 1, 7, 18), *your country, Catiline, thus remonstrates with you.*
2. **Haec**[5] **vōbīscum ūnā cōnsul agam** (Sall. *Cat.* 20, 17), *these* [measures] *I shall as consul carry out in conjunction with you.*
3. ... sēcum habēbat (3, 18, 1), *he kept about his person* (had with himself).

348. OBSERVATION AND INFERENCE: Note, in the foregoing examples, that **tēcum, vōbīscum, sēcum** are used in place of **cum tē, cum vōbīs, cum sē.** Frame a rule for the Position of **cum** used with the Ablative of the Personal Pronouns.

349. REFERENCES FOR VERIFICATION: A. & G. 99, *e*; H. 184, 6; G. 414, Rem. 1.

---

[1] -ne is here an interrogative particle introducing the first part of the double question; the second part is introduced by an: A. & G. 211; H. 353, 1; G. 460.
[2] Acc. masc. sing. of quisque, *each*.
[3] This pronoun is made up of **uter** (*whichever of the two*) and **vīs** (*you wish* or *you please*); the first part is declined, the second remains unchanged.
[4] Contracted from mandāvērunt; cf. Lesson XXXIV., foot-note 2.
[5] Acc. neut. pl. of **hīc,** *this*.

LESSON XLII.

ILLUSTRATIVE EXERCISES ON THE PERSONAL AND REFLEXIVE PRONOUNS.

350. EXERCISES.

I. 1. Ego vigilō ad salūtem, tū ad perniciem reī pūblicae. 2. Ab exercitū meō tē removeō. 3. Orgetorix sibī mortem cōnscīvit. 4. Habētis ducem memorem vestrī,[1] oblītum suī.[1] 5. Tū, C.[2] Aviēne, mihi reīque pūblicae inūtilis fuistī. 6. Catilīna sēcum suōs ēdūcet. 7. Obsidēs inter sēsē dant. 8. Nūllum ego ā vōbīs praemium virtūtis postulō. 9. Utrīque[3] nostrūm grātum est. 10. Nimium mihi sūmam. 11. Equitēs vōbīscum dē amōre reī pūblicae certant.

II. 1. Which-one[4] **of us does not know?** 2. Your fellow citizens all **fear you.** 3. **We seek** the safety, **you** (pl.) the destruction **of** our common country. 4. The **citizens will** vie with **us in**[5] patriotism (love of the commonwealth). 5. The Aedui and Arverni had been contending[6] with each other many years. 6. To you our common country **commits herself.** 7. **No** one has [ever] **contended** with me without [effecting] his own destruction. 8. I do not myself[7] commend myself. 9. It will be gratifying to you both.[8] 10. It is with difficulty[9] that **I** keep from[10] **you the** hands of your countrymen. 11. **Review with me [the** events of] the night before.[11]

351.   Supplementary Exercises.

I. 1. Vōbīs supplex manūs tendit patria commūnis, vōbīs sē, vōbīs vītam omnium cīvium commendat. 2. Equitum Rōmānōrum ego vix abs[10] tē jam diū manūs āc tēla contineō.[12] 3. Ego meīs cōpiīs meōque exercitū vōbīs rēgna conciliābō. 4. Belgae, Aquītānī, Gallī lēgibus inter sē differunt. 5. Gallōs auxiliī causā **sēcum** habēbat. 6. Cicerō amantissimus utriusque nostrŭm est.

II. 1. I, I the consul, am remiss. 2. **Lead out**[13] **with** you, **too,** all your [associates]. 3. Dismiss **your kind** solicitude for[14] **me,** and think of yourselves **and** your **children.** 4. The Belgians **unite in** a sworn league against the Roman people and exchange[15] hostages. 5. **Your** house and mine[16] are building[17] rapidly. 6. And-so they surrendered themselves and all their [effects] to Caesar.

---

[1] **vestrī** is in the objective genitive after **memorem**; **suī** is in the same construction after **oblītum.**

[2] **C.** is here an abbreviation for **Gāī,** vocative of **Gājus;** see Lesson XXI., foot-note 1.

[3] **each** (of two), *both;* decline like **uter,** appending **-que** throughout.

[4] **Quis?**

[5] **dē.**

[6] A. & G. 277, *b*; H. 469, 2; G. 225.

[7] **ipse,** nom. singular masculine.

[8] cf. sent. 9 of the preceding exercise.

[9] Translate: *I with difficulty keep.*

[10] **abs** may be used for **ā** before **tē.**

[11] Translate: *the preceding night.*

[12] cf. Lesson XXI., foot-note 5.

[13] **ēdūc'** (accent the final syllable): A. & G. 128, *c*; H. 238, n. 2; G. 151, 4.

[14] Arrange: *your for* **me (ergā mē)** *kind solicitude.*

[15] Translate: *give among themselves.*

[16] Translate: *the house of each of us.*

[17] Present passive.

LESSON XLIII.

GENITIVE WITH ADJECTIVES. — THE GERUND.

352. **EXAMPLES.**

1. **[Plēbēs]** cupida rērum novārum bellō favēbat (Sall. *Cat.* 48, 1), *the commons, desirous of a change* (of new things), *favored war.*
2. **[Cōnsidius]** reī mīlitāris perītissimus habēbātur (1, 21, 4), *Considius was accounted very well versed in the military art.*
3. **Bellī haud īgnārus** (Sall. *Jug.* 28, 5), *not unacquainted with war.*
4. **Habētis ducem** memorem vestrī, oblītum suī (Cic. *Cat.* 4, 9, 10), *you have a leader* [who is] *thoughtful of you, forgetful of himself.*
5. Plēna erant **omnia** timōris (Caes. *B. C.* 2, 41, 8), *all* (lit., all things) *were filled with fear.*
6. Erant complūrēs cōnsilī[1] participēs **nōbilēs** (Sall. *Cat.* 17, 5), *there were a great many nobles concerned in the plot.*
7. Flaccum et Pomptīnum, amantissimōs reī pūblicae **virōs**, ad mē vocāvī (Cic. *Cat.* 3, 2, 5), *I summoned . Flaccus and Pomptinus, men warmly attached to the commonwealth.*
8. **Corpus** [Catilīnae] patiēns inediae [fuit] (Sall. *Cat.* 5, 3), *Catiline's constitution was capable of enduring abstinence from food.*

353. OBSERVATION AND INFERENCE: Note, in the foregoing examples, (1) that the *adjectives* **cupida, perītissimus, īgnārus, memorem, oblītum, plēna, participēs, amantissimōs, patiēns,** from the nature of their signification, require an *object of reference* to complete their meaning; and (2) that the *substantive* added in each instance to complete the meaning of the adjective **is** in the *genitive case* (see rērum, reī, bellī, vestrī, suī, timōris, cōnsilī, reī pūblicae, inediae). Also, after noting carefully the *meaning* of the adjectives that **govern** the genitive in the foregoing examples, frame a rule stating what Classes of Adjectives take **a** Genitive to complete **their meaning.**

354. REFERENCES FOR VERIFICATION: A. & G. 218, *a, b*; H. 399, I., 1, 2, 3, II.; G. 373, 374.

355. Learn, with meanings, the gerunds of amō, moneō (or dēleō), tegō (regō or emō), audiō: A. & G. pp. 77, 81, 83, 87; H. pp. 87, 91, 95, 99; G. pp. 55, 59, 65, 69.

356. EXAMPLES.

1. Jūs vocandī **senātum** (Liv. 3, 38, 10), *authority to convene* (of convening) *the senate*.
2. **Hominēs** bellandī cupidī (1, 2, 4), *men fond of fighting*.
3. **Dē rēbus pertinentibus ad beātē** vīvendum (Cic. Off. 1, 6, 19), *concerning matters which contribute to a happy life* (to living happily).
4. Ōrātōrem aptum ad dīcendum (Cic. Tusc. 1, 3, 5), *an orator with aptitude for speaking*.
5. **Mōrēs [puerōrum] sē inter lūdendum dētegunt** (Quint. 1, 3, 11), *the moral traits of children reveal themselves in play* (amid playing).
6. **Hominis mēns discendō alitur** (Cic. Off. 1, 30, 105), *the mind of man is strengthened by study* (by studying).
7. Reperiēbat in quaerendō Caesar (1, 18, 10), *Caesar learned on making inquiry*.

357. OBSERVATION AND INFERENCE: Note, in Ex. 1, that the *gerund* **vocandī** *governs* the *accusative* of *direct object* (see **senātum**); and, in Ex. 3, that the *gerund* **vīvendum** *is modified* by the *adverb* **beātē**. In view of these facts, what *part of speech* does the Gerund appear to be?

What is the *case*, and what the *construction*, in the foregoing examples, of the gerunds **vocandī, bellandī, vīvendum, dīcendum, lūdendum, discendō, quaerendō**. In view of the several constructions here illustrated, what *part of speech* does the Gerund appear to be?

The Gerund, then, shares the nature of what *two* parts of speech? In what constructions may it be used?[2]

358. References for Verification: A. & G. 295, 297³, 298 (to the semicolon), 300, 301; H. 541, 542, I., III., IV.; G. 427, 429³, 433³, 432³, 434³.

---

¹ A. & G. 40, b; H. 51, 5; G. 29, Rem. 1.
² The Gerund may be in the *genitive after a substantive*, as in Ex. **1**; in the *genitive after an adjective*, as in Ex. 2, etc.
³ Omit, **for the** present, in reading, the reference to the Gerundive.

LESSON XLIV.

Illustrative Exercises on the Foregoing Constructions.

359.   **EXERCISES.**

I. 1. Cōnsulī¹ jūs est vocandī **senātum**. 2. Diēs prōlātandō māgnās opportūnitātēs corrumpunt. 3. **Nōn sōlum** ad discendum prōpēnsī sumus, vērum etiam **ad docendum**. 4. Dumnorix est cupidus rērum novārum. 5. Diem ad dēlīberandum sūmam. 6. Mīlitēs praedae sunt participēs. 7. Nōn ego tam barbarus neque tam imperītus rērum. 8. **Summa erat difficultās nāvigandī**. 9. Prohibenda est īra in pūniendō. 10. Titus equitandī perītissimus fuit.

II. 1. They strengthen the conspiracy by not believing [in its existence]. 2. In the free towns there are less [adequate] resources for defence.² 3. Private citizens have³ no authority to convene⁴ the senate. 4. Catiline was covetous of others' [property],⁵ lavish of his own. 5. Epaminondas was skilled in war, brave in action,⁶ of very great courage, devoted to the truth. 6. Epaminondas was a **good** listener.⁷ 7. In deliberating, the mind⁸ is often drawn into contradictory opinions. 8. The soldiers of Sulla, recalling⁹ **former** victory, ardently-desired civil war.

360.   **Supplementary Exercises.**

I. 1. Ea[10] facta commemorandō, mīlitum animōs accendēbat. 2. Hostium parātus erat ad dīmicandum animus. 3. Carthāgō fuit aemula imperī[11] Rōmānī. 4. Spatium pīla in hostēs coniciendī[12] nōn dabātur. 5. Sagittāriōrum adventū Rēmīs studium prōpūgnandī accēssit. 6. Dumnorix fuit cupidus rērum novārum, cupidus imperiī, māgnī animī, māgnae inter Gallōs auctōritātis.

II. 1. No one was able to maintain his position[13] on the wall. 2. Our consul was inured to toil,[8] **of penetrating** intellect, not unacquainted with war, and utterly[14] **unmoved** in the face of dangers. 3. Caesar acquired[15] **glory by giving, by** relieving, [and] by pardoning.   4. **The barbarians are very fond** of cattle.

---

[1] cf. **Lesson XXXV.**, foot-note 9.
[2] " for defence " = *for defending*.
[3] **Translate: no** *authority is to private citizens;* see foot-note 1.
[4] " to convene " = *of convening*.
[5] **aliēnus**, -a, -um, in neuter singular, used substantively.
[6] **manus**; cf. **229** and **230**.
[7] Translate: *fond of listening*.
[8] Use the plural.
[9] **memor** with genitive.
[10] **ea**, accusative neuter plural, *these*.
[11] See foot-note 1, preceding lesson.
[12] Pronounce: **conjiciendī**.
[13] Translate: *power was to no one of maintaining*, etc.; see foot-note **1**.
[14] Sign of superlative
[15] **adeptus est.**

LESSON XLV.

DEMONSTRATIVES: **Hīc, Iste, Ille.**

361. Learn the declension of the demonstratives: **hīc**, *this*; **iste**, *that* (of yours); **ille**, *that*. A. & G. p. 52 (including the first sentence **of** *a*); H. 186, I., II., III.; G. 102, I., II., III.

362. Decline together: **haec legiō**, *this legion*; **hōc respōnsum**, *this answer*; **ista mēns**, *that purpose of yours*; **gladiātor iste**, *that* [worthless] *gladiator*; **illud tempus**, *that time*; **Sōcraticus**[1] **ille**, *the famous disciple of Socrates*.

363. EXAMPLES.

1. **Senātus haec intellegit: hīc tamen vīvit** (Cic. *Cat.* 1, 1, 2), *the senate knows these things* (just referred to by the speaker); *yet this man* (in sight of the speaker, and perhaps designated by a gesture) *lives*.

2. **Huic legiōnī Caesar indulserat praecipuē** (1, 40, 15), *Caesar had especially favored this* (just referred to) *legion*.

3. **Mūtā istam mentem** (Cic. *Cat.* 1, 3, 6), *change that purpose of yours*.

4. **Nēmō est istōrum tam misericors** (Cic. *Cat.* 2, 7, 16), *there is no one of those men* (with a touch of contempt) *so compassionate* . . .

5. **At ille diem noctemque nāvem** tenuit in ancorīs (Nep. *Th.* 8. 7), *yet he kept his vessel at* anchor a day and a night.

6. **Illō** tempore (Caes. *B. C.* 1, 7, 5), *at that time*.

7. **Ille mānsuētūdine clārus factus**[2]; **huic sevēritās dīgnitātem addiderat** (Sall. *Cat.* 54, 2), *the former became illustrious through his clemency; to the latter austerity gave*[3] *dignity*.

8. **Mēdēa illa** (Cic. *Manil.* 9, 22), *the famous Medea*.

364. OBSERVATION AND INFERENCE: Are the *demonstratives* in Exs. 1, 4, 5, 7 used *substantively* or *adjectively?* Answer the same question for Exs. 2, 3, 6, 8. Does the demonstrative, when used *adjectively*, appear regularly *to follow* or *to precede* its substantive? Which of these demonstratives may appropriately be called the *demonstrative* of the *first person?* Which the *demonstrative* of the *second person?* Which of the *third?* What other distinctions or peculiarities in the use of these pronouns do the translations of the foregoing examples reveal?

365. REFERENCES FOR VERIFICATION: A. & G. 101, 102, *a, b, c,* 343, *d*; H. 450, 2, 4, 569, I., 1; G. 290, 291, 292, 2, Rem. 1, 678, Rem. 2.

366. EXERCISES.

I. 1. Sī deerit hōc remedium, ad illud[4] dēclīnandum est.
2. Xenophōn, Sōcraticus[1] ille, scrīpsit historiam. 3. Nōs

DEMONSTRATIVES. 105

autem,⁵ **virī** fortēs, istīus⁶ furōrem āc tēla vītāmus. 4. Vītam istam fugae sōlitūdinīque mandā. 5. Ille per mē crēvit. 6. Illīus facilitās, hūjus cōnstantia laudābātur. 7. Illō tempore rēgnum obtinēbat. 8. Ad hās suspīciōnēs certissimae rēs accēdunt. 9. Māgna huic Jovī⁷ habenda est grātia. 10. Gladiātōrī **istī** nihil dabō.

II. 1. Of all these, the Belgians are the bravest. 2. The beauty of the former,⁸ the virtue of the **latter**,⁸ was commended. 3. Two Roman knights relieved you of that⁹ anxiety. 4. Indeed,¹⁰ **I suppose, that**¹¹ **centurion** Manlius declared war in his **own name.**¹² 5. Having given this **answer,**¹³ he withdrew. 6. How long will that insane folly **of yours mock us**? 7. Swords are drawn both by those and by our party. 8. He, yonder¹⁴ Jupiter, resisted [them]. He [preserved] the Capitol, he [preserved] these temples, he preserved the whole¹⁵ city.

---

¹ **Sōcraticus, -a, -um,** *belonging to Socrates* ; **hence, used** substantively, *disciple of Socrates.*
² sc. est ; perfect passive of **faciō.**
³ Lit., *had added.*
⁴ **Ille** (especially the neuter **illud**) often, as here, means *the following.*
⁵ Conjunction, *however, but* ; for position, see. A. & G. 345, *b*; H. 569, III.; G. 486, Rem.
⁶ Contemptuous ; translate : *that madman* or *that wretch.*

⁷ See **Jūppiter** in general vocabulary.
⁸ See 363, Ex. 7.
⁹ See 363, Ex. 3.
¹⁰ **Etenim** (at the beginning).
¹¹ Contemptuous.
¹² Ablative of *manner.*
¹³ What construction? cf. 305, Ex. 2.
¹⁴ " yonder " = *that.*
¹⁵ **cūnctus, -a, -um**; see **cūnctus** in general vocabulary.

LESSON XLVI.

DEMONSTRATIVES (DETERMINATIVES): **Is, Ipse, Īdem.**

367. Learn the declension of the demonstratives (determinatives): **is,** *he, this, that;* **ipse,** *self;* **īdem,** *the same:* A. & G. 101; H. 186, IV., V., VI.; G. 101.

368. Decline together: **ea mūnītiō,** *that fortification;* **id iter,** *that journey;* **hōc ipsum tempus,** *this very time;* **eadem** fortūna, *the same fortune;* **īdem prīnceps,** *the same chief.*

369.   EXAMPLES.

1. **Id hōc facilius eīs persuāsit** (1, 2, 3), *he persuaded them to it* (persuaded it to them) *more easily because-of-the-following-fact* (hōc).
2. **In eō itinere persuādet Casticō** (1, 3, 4), *on this journey he prevails upon Casticus.*
3. **Dīxī ego īdem īn senātū** (Cic. *Cat.* 1, 3, 7), *I also* (I the same) *said in the senate.*
4. **Haec** eadem centuriōnibus mandābant (7, 17, 8), *they delivered these same* [assurances] *to the centurions.*
5. **Eōdem tempore equitēs fugam petēbant** (2, 24, 1), *at the same time the cavalry took to flight.*
6. **Ipse eōdem itinere ad eōs contendit** (1, 21, 3), *he hastened in person to them* (he himself hastened, etc.) *by the same route.*
7. **Ipse** sibī inimīcus est (Cic. *Fin.* 5, 10, 28), *he is an enemy to himself* (i.e., he is his own enemy).
8. **Ipsō terrōre** equōrum ōrdinēs perturbant (4, 33, 1), *by the mere fright* (fright itself) *of the horses, they throw the ranks into confusion.*
9. **Hōc ipsō tempore** (6, 37, 1), *at this very time.*

370. OBSERVATION: Compare **id** (Ex. 1) with **eō** (Ex. 2); which is used *substantively?* which *adjectively?* Note that **eīs** (Ex. 1) and **eōs** (Ex. 6) are used as *personal* **pronouns.** Compare **īdem** (Ex. 3) and **eadem** (Ex. 4) with **eōdem** (Ex. 5) and **eōdem** (Ex. 6); which are used *substantively?* which *adjectively?* Note that **īdem** (Ex. 3) is translated *also.* Note that **ipse** is translated, in Ex. 6, *in person;* in Ex. 8, *mere;* and in Ex. 9, *very.* Note that **ipse** (Ex. 7) does not, as the English translation might lead us to expect, agree with **sibī**, but with the *subject* of **the** sentence.

371. REFERENCES: A. & G. 195, *e*, *f*, *l*; H. 451, 3, 452, 1, 2; G. 100, 296, 297, **298.**

372.   EXERCISES.

I. **1. Māgna**[1] huic ipsī Jovī habenda est grātia.[1]   2. Eōdem tempore lēgātī ab Aeduīs veniēbant.   3. Initium ējus[2] fugae factum est[3] ā Dumnorige atque ējus[4] equitibus.   4. Id ab ipsīs per eōrum nūntiōs comperī.   5. Ipse sibī mortem cōnscīvit.   6. Atrebatēs eandem bellī fortūnam experiuntur.[5]   7. Hōc idem in reliquīs fit[6] cīvitātibus.   8. Pompējus eadem illa agit.   9. Ipsōrum linguā Celtae, nóstrā Gallī appellantur.   10. Ob eās causās eī mūnītiōnī T. Labiēnum lēgātum praefēcit;[7] ipse in Ītaliam contendit.   11. Ipse ad eōs contendit equitātumque omnem ante sē[8] mittit.

II. 1. From Pontus also[9] the famous Medea once fled.[10]   2. For[11] this reason Caesar hastened into Gaul.   3. With equal[12] speed they hastened to our camp.   4. Learn these [facts] from the very [persons] who[13] have escaped[14] from the massacre itself.   5. All [men] love themselves.   6. The Germans came in-great-numbers to him in[15] camp.   7. Having called[16] together their chiefs, he takes them severely to task.   8. Divitiacus the Aeduan again[17] responded.   9. He, in the consulship[18] of Marcus Messalla and Marcus Piso, persuaded his countrymen.   10. This district was called the Tigurine.   11. On the following day they move their camp **from** that place. Caesar does[18] the same.

[1] Note the emphasis produced by the separation of the adjective from its substantive.
[2] Used adjectively, *this*.
[3] Perfect passive of **faciō**, *make*.
[4] Used as a personal pronoun, *his*.
[5] From **experior**, which has a passive form with active meaning.
[6] 3d sing. pres. of **fīō**, *be done*.
[7] 3d sing. perf. indic. of **praeficiō**.
[8] Could **eum** be substituted for **sē**? See A. & G. 196; H. 449, 1); G. 295.
[9] cf. 369, Ex. 3.
[10] **profūgit**, perf. of **profugiō**.
[11] cf. 372, sent. 10.
[12] Translate: *the same*.
[13] **quī**, nominative plural masculine.
[14] **fūgērunt**, perf. of **fugiō**.
[15] Note the difference of idiom: "to him in camp" = *to him into camp*.
[16] What **construction** must be used?
[17] Translate: *the same Divitiacus*.
[18] **facit**, 3d sing. pres. indic. of **faciō**.

373. Supplementary Exercises on Lessons XLV. and XLVI.

I. 1. Hīc testāmentō, ille proximitāte nītitur.[1] 2. Ipsō terrōre equōrum et strepitū rotārum ōrdinēs plērumque perturbant. 3. Māgna[2] dīs[3] immortālibus habenda est atque huic ipsī Jovī **Statōrī**, antīquissimō custōdī hūjus urbis, grātia.[2] 4. Exclūsī eōs quōs (*whom*) tū ad **mē mīserās**. 5. **Īdem**[4] **prīncipēs** cīvitātum ad Caesarem revertērunt. 6. Ego ūnīus ūsūram **hōrae** gladiātōrī istī ad vīvendum nōn dabō. 7. Id hōc facilius eīs persuāsit, quod undique locī nātūrā Helvētiī continentur. 8. Helvētiī ferē cottidiānīs proeliīs cum Germānīs contendunt, cum (*when*) aut **suīs**[5] fīnibus eōs[6] prohibent aut ipsī in eōrum[7] fīnibus bellum gerunt.

II. 1. That which[8] *they*[9] had accomplished[10] in twenty days, *he* had done in one day. 2. He was the only one to be feared[11] **out of all that-crew.**[12] 3. **You gave yourself into custody.** 4. On your arrival those benches [near you] were cleared.[13] 5. **The Suessiones** enjoy[14] the same constitution and the same laws. 6. This [part of] Gaul is my province just as[15] that is yours.

[1] *relies, depends*; this verb is passive in form, but active in meaning, and is construed with the ablative.
[2] cf. 372, foot-note 1.
[3] From **deus**; for declension, see A. & G. 40, *f*; H. 51, 6; G. 29, 5.
[4] Nom. pl. masc. of **īdem**.
[5] See references under foot-note 8, Lesson XLVI.; also G. 294. What change of meaning would result if **eōrum** were substituted for **suīs**?
[6] What would be the meaning if **sē** were substituted for **eōs**?
[7] What would **suīs** mean here?
[8] **quod**, neuter singular accusative.
[9] Use the proper form of **ipse**.
[10] **cōnfēcerant**, from **cōnficiō**.
[11] Translate: *he alone* (**ūnus**) *was to be feared* (pass. periphrastic).
[12] Use the plural of **iste**.
[13] **vacuēfacta sunt**, perfect passive of **vacuēfaciō**.
[14] **ūtuntur**; this verb has a passive form with active meaning, and is construed with the ablative.
[15] **sīcut**.

LESSON XLVII.

The Gerundive Construction. — The Two Supines.

374. EXAMPLES.

1.
   a. **Jūs vocandī senātum** (Liv. 3, 38, 10), *right of convening the senate.*
   b. **Jūs vocandī senātūs**, *right of the senate to be convened.*

   } *authority to convene the senate.*

2.
   a. **Cupiditās bellum gerendī**, *desire of carrying on war.*
   b. **Cupiditās bellī gerendī** (1, 41, 1), *desire of war to be carried on.*

   } *eagerness to fight.*

3.
   a. **Diēs prōlātandō** (Sall. Cat. 43, 3), *by putting off the days.*
   b. **Diēbus prōlātandīs**, *by the days to be put off.*

   } *by postponing the day [of execution].*

4.
   a. **Male gerendō negōtium**, *by managing business badly.*
   b. **Male gerendō negōtiō** (Cic. Cat. 2, 10, 21), *by business to be managed badly.*

   } *through bad management of business.*

375. Observation and Inference: Note that, in the examples marked *a*, the *gerund* is used with a *direct object*; whereas, in the examples marked *b*, the *gerundive* is used *in agreement with the substantive which was formerly the direct object*, and the *latter* has the same construction which the *gerund* formerly had. Note, further, that the two forms of expression have the *same meaning.* The examples marked *a* illustrate the *Gerund Construction*; those marked *b* illustrate the *Gerundive Construction.* Frame a rule for changing the Gerund Construction to the Gerundive.[1]

376. References for Verification: A. & G. 296; H. 544, 1; G. 428.

377. Restore the gerund construction to the gerundive in the following examples:

1. Exercitum Ariovistum opprimendī causā habet, *he has an army for the purpose of crushing Ariovistus.*
2. Ea facta commemorandō, mīlitum animōs accendēbat, *by recalling these exploits, he fired the hearts of the soldiers.*

378 Learn the following supines:[2]

1st Conjugation.
1. rogātum, *to ask.*
2. memorātū, *in relating.*

2d Conjugation.
1. vīsum, *to see.*
2. monitū, *in reminding.*

3d Conjugation.
1. perditum, *to ruin.*
2. dictū, *in saying.*

4th Conjugation.
1. audītum, *to hear.*
2. audītū, *in hearing.*

379. Observation: It has been seen (Lesson XLIII.) that the *gerund* is a verbal *substantive* of the *second declension*, used in four cases. The *supine* is also a verbal *substantive;* of what *declension* is it, and in what *cases* is it used?

380. EXAMPLES.

1. Lēgātōs mittunt rogātum auxilium (1, 11, 2), *they send ambassadors to ask assistance.*
2. Ad senātum vēnisse[3] auxilium postulātum (1, 31, 9), *to have come to the senate to petition for assistance.*
3. Incrēdibile memorātū est (Sall. Cat. 6, 2), *it is incredible to relate* (in the relating).
4. Difficile dictū est (Cic. Lael. 3, 12), *it is difficult to speak* (in the speaking).

381. Observation and Inference: Note, in the first two of the foregoing examples (1) that the *supines* rogātum and postulātum are construed with *verbs of motion* (mittunt and vēnisse); and (2) that they express *purpose.* Frame a rule for the use of the Supine in -um.

382. References for Verification: A. & G. 302; H. 546; G. 436.

383. OBSERVATION AND INFERENCE: Note, in Exs. 3 and 4, (1) that the *supines* **memorātū** and **dictū**, are used with *adjectives;* and (2) that they answer the question *in what respect?* or *from what point of view?* Frame a rule for the use of Supines in -ū.

384. REFERENCES FOR VERIFICATION: A. & G. 303; H. 547; G. 437.

---

[1] The gerundive construction is generally preferred to the gerund construction; and, in connection with a preposition, the gerundive construction is always to be taken.

[2] **amō, dēleō, tegō, regō,** and **emō**, which have heretofore served as paradigms, have no supine.

[3] Perf. act. infin. of **veniō.**

LESSON XLVIII.

ILLUSTRATIVE EXERCISES ON THE GERUND, GERUNDIVE, AND SUPINES.

385.   EXERCISES.

I. 1. Gallī legiōnis opprimendae cōnsilium cēpērunt.[1] 2. Diēs prōlātandō māgnās opportūnitātēs corrumpunt. 3. Vix iīs rēbus administrandīs tempus **dabātur.** 4. Ex cīvitāte profūgī et **ad** senātum vēnī auxilium postulātum. 5. Perfacile factū[2] est cōnāta perficere.[3] 6. Ariovistus cum suīs omnibus cōpiīs ad occupandum Vesontiōnem contendit. 7. Propīnquās suās nūptum **in** aliās cīvitātēs Dumnorix conlocārat.[4] 8. Nec hōc est dictū mīrābile. 9. Dē expūgnandō oppidō spēs hostēs fefellit. 10. Sum cupidus tē audiendī. 11. Nōn modo ad īnsīgnia accommodanda, sed etiam **ad galeās** induendās tempus dēfuit. 12. Frontō **vir** movendārum lacrimārum perītissimus fuit.

II. 1. You had sent two knights to me to pay their respects. 2. The best [thing] to do[2] is to declare war. 3. *He* was more earnest to restore[5] me **than** [he had been] to retain me. 4. Caesar gave the signal for the battle to begin.⁶ 5. He gives his daughter in marriage⁷ to Manilius. 6. You have been able not merely to set at defiance the laws, but even to destroy⁸ them. 7. Of this kind of death it is difficult to speak. 8. In recounting the disaster of the community, they said . . . 9. They are seeking⁹ to destroy themselves and the commonwealth. 10. Orgetorix is selected to accomplish¹⁰ these things.

386. Supplementary Exercises.

I. 1. **Caesar** exercitum in Galliā Ariovistī opprimendī **causā** habēbat. 2. **Mīlitēs in** quaerendīs suīs¹¹ pūgnandī tempus **dīmittēbant.** 3. **Ea dē** rē difficile dictū est. 4. Exclūsī eōs quōs¹² tū ad mē salūtātum mīserās. 5. Ipse in citeriōrem Galliam ad **conventūs agendōs** profectus est.¹³ 6. Tōtīus ferē Galliae lēgātī, prīncipēs cīvitātum, ad **Caesarem grātulātum¹⁴ convēnērunt.**

II. 1. They squander their wealth in levelling **mountains.** 2. One legion had **been** sent to forage.¹⁵ 3. **The** best **thing to do**² is to cut off¹⁶ **the** Romans from grain **and supplies.** 4. All the morally bad, then, [are] slaves: nor **is** this so wonderful in-point-of-fact¹⁷ as in the form of statement.¹⁸ 5. Suddenly the Gauls formed¹ the design of renewing the war and crushing the legion. 6. You live, and you live not to forsake,¹⁹ but to **persevere in**¹⁹ your shameless course.

---

¹ **cēpērunt,** *formed,* perf. indic. of capiō.
² **factū,** supine in -ū of **faciō,** *do.*
³ Pres. infin. of **perficiō,** *accomplish.*
⁴ See Lesson XXXV., foot-note 22.
⁵ Translate: *desirous of restoring.*
⁶ Translate: *of the battle to be begun.*
⁷ cf. 385, I., sent. 7.
⁸ "have been able to destroy" = *have availed for destroying.* cf. 385, I., sent. 11.
⁹ **eunt,** 3d person plural of **eō,** *go.*
¹⁰ The gerundive of **cōnficiō,** *accomplish,* is **cōnficiendus, -a, -um.**

¹¹ sc. **sīgnīs.**
¹² *whom.*
¹³ Perf. indic. of **proficīscor,** *set out.*
¹⁴ Sup. of **grātulor,** *congratulate;* this verb has a pass. form with act. meaning.
¹⁵ **frūmentātum,** sup. of **frūmentor,** which has a pass. form with act. meaning.
¹⁶ **prohibeō** with abl.
¹⁷ rē.
¹⁸ Translate: *in saying.*
¹⁹ cf. 386, I., sent. 5.

LESSON XLIX.

VERBS IN -iō OF THE THIRD CONJUGATION. — THE RELATIVE **PRONOUN**.

387. Learn, with meanings, the inflection and synopsis of **capiō**, *take*, in the Indicative and Imperative moods, Active and Passive; also the Participles, Gerunds, and Supines: A. & G. p. 83; H. pp. 106–108; G. pp. 72, 73.

388. Using **capiō** as a model, form the same parts of: rapiō, *snatch*; jaciō, *throw*; ēiciō,[1] *expel*.

389. Learn the declension of the relative pronoun **quī**, *who, which, that, what:* A. & G. 103; H. 187; G. **103**.

390. EXAMPLES.

1. In fīnēs Ambiānōrum pervēnit, quī sē sine morā dēdidērunt (2, 15, 2), *he came into the territories of the Ambiani, who surrendered without delay.*
2. Gallia est **omnis** dīvīsa in partēs trēs, quārum ūnam incolunt Belgae (1, 1, 1), *all Gaul is divided into three parts, one of which the Belgians inhabit.*
3. Illī, cum iīs quae retinuerant et cēlāverant armīs, ēruptiōnem fēcērunt (2, 33, 2), *they, with those arms which they had withheld and concealed, made a sortie.*
4. Longē sunt hūmānissimī, **quī** Cantium incolunt (5, 14, 1), *[those] who inhabit Kent are by far the most highly civilized.*

391. OBSERVATION AND INFERENCE: Note, in Exs. 1–3, that the *relatives* quī, quārum, and quae refer to Ambiānōrum, partēs, and armīs respectively; and that they agree with these substantives in *number* and *gender*. **The** substantive **to** which a relative thus refers is called the *Antecedent*.

In what *construction* is **quī** (Ex. 1)? **quārum** (Ex. 2)? **quae** (Ex. 3)? Is the *case* of the Relative, then, determined by that of the Antecedent?

Frame a rule for the Gender, Number, and Case of the Relative.

392. REFERENCES FOR VERIFICATION: A. & G. 198; H. 445; G. 615, **616**.

393. OBSERVATION: Note that, in Ex. 4, the antecedent of **quī** (**eī**, *those*) is omitted.

394. REFERENCES: A. & G. 200, *c*; H. 445, 6; G. 620, 621.

---

[1] **ēiciō** (= ex + jaciō) is to be pronounced as if it were written **ējiciō**; so also all compounds of **jaciō** with monosyllabic prepositions: as, **abiciō** (pronounced: **abjiciō**), **coniciō** (pronounced: **conjiciō**), etc. For the principal parts of **ēiciō**, see the general vocabulary.

LESSON L.

ILLUSTRATIVE EXERCISES ON THE RELATIVE PRONOUN.

395.   **EXERCISES.**

I. 1. Id quod ipsī diēbus vīgintī cōnfēcerant, ille ūnō diē fēcit. 2. **Belgae** proximī sunt Germānīs, **quī** trāns Rhēnum incolunt, quibuscum[1] continenter bellum gerunt. 3. In castrīs Helvētiōrum tabulae repertae sunt, quibus in **tabulīs** ratiō cōnfecta **erat**. 4. **Quī**[2] omnibus hominibus crēdit, saepe dēcipitur. 5. Legiōnem cui Galba praeerat, mīsit. 6. Sūlla cum magnō equitātū in castra vēnit, quōs[3] ex Latiō et ā sociīs coēgerat. 7. Helvētiī lēgātōs ad **eum** mittunt; cūjus lēgātiōnis Divicō prīnceps fuit. 8. Egō[4] quī tē cōnfirmō,[4] ipse mē nōn possum.[5]

II. 1. Those will be visited with punishment[6] by whom **arms shall be taken.**[7] 2. Catiline, whom the consul has expelled, **is fleeing.** **3. These are** [the things] which **I** demand. **4. He** sends[8] reënforcements **to** the support of[8] **our** men **who are in** retreat.[9] 5. He hastened to convey his army across. . . . This[10] movement made one side of his camp secure. 6. The nature of the site which our men had selected for a camp was as follows.[11] 7. We often despise those with whom and among whom we live. **8. Here** am [I] who did[4] [the deed].

396. Supplementary Exercises.

I. 1. Convocātīs Aeduōrum principibus, quōrum māgnam cōpiam in castrīs habēbat, in hīs Liscō, quī summō magistrātuī praeerat, graviter eōs accūsat. 2. Ultrā eum locum quō in locō Germānī cōnsēderant, castra posuit. 3. Ūnus ex eō numerō quī[8] ad caedem parātī erant, Massīvam obtruncat. 4. Tum dēmum Liscus, ōrātiōne Caesaris adductus, quod anteā tacuerat prōpōnit. 5. Nāvium quod[12] fuerat ūnum in locum coēgerant; quibus[13] āmissīs, sē Caesarī dēdidērunt.

II. 1. He persuades Casticus, whose father had held sovereign power among the Sequani for many years. 2. The Helvetians send ambassadors to Caesar . . . Of this[14] embassy, Divico, who had been the leader of the Helvetians, was the head. 3. Meanwhile, by means of that legion which he had with him and the soldiers who had assembled from the province, he extends a wall from Lake Geneva, which flows into the river Rhone, to mount Jura, which separates the territory of the Sequani from [that of] the Helvetii.

---

[1] A. & G. 304, e; H. 187, 2; G. **414.** Rem. 1.; cf. **348** and **349.**
[2] Account for the omission of the antecedent.
[3] Read: A. & G. 199, b; H. 445, 5; G. 616, 3, I.
[4] Note that the verb of the relative clause agrees in person **with** the antecedent (expressed or understood).
[5] *am able, can;* sc. **cōnfirmāre.**
[6] Use the plural.
[7] Translate: *shall have been taken.*

[8] **submittō** with dative.
[9] "who are in retreat" = *fleeing.*
[10] "This movement" = *which thing.* In Latin the relative is often used where the English idiom requires a demonstrative.
[11] "as follows" = *this.*
[12] **nāvium quod fuerat,** *all their ships* (lit., what of ships there had been).
[13] Translate *these;* cf. foot-note 10.
[14] See **395,** I., sent. 7; cf. foot-note 10.

LESSON LI.

Two Accusatives: Same Person or Thing.
— With Compounds.

397.   EXAMPLES.

1. **[Casticī] patrem** senātus **amīcum** appellāverat, *the senate had called the father of Casticus friend.*
2. **[Casticī] pater** ā senātū **amīcus** appellātus erat (1, 3, 4), *the father of Casticus had been called friend by the senate.*
3. Hunc **[montem]** mūrus circumdatus **arcem** efficit (1, 38, 6), *a wall built round it makes this mountain a citadel.*
4. Ancum Mārcium **rēgem** populus creāvit (Liv. 1, 32, 1), *the people chose Ancus Marcius king.*
5. Tē sapientem et **appellant et exīstimant** (Cic. *Lael.* 2, 6), *you they both call and think wise.*

398. OBSERVATION AND INFERENCE: Note, in Exs. 1 and 3–5, that the verbs are followed by *two accusatives* denoting the *same person* or *thing*. What *classes* of verbs (*i.e.*, verbs of what meaning) admit this double construction? Frame a rule for the Two Accusatives here illustrated.

399. REFERENCES FOR VERIFICATION: A. & G. 239, *a*; H. 373; G. 334.

400. OBSERVATION: Note, in Ex. 1, that the senate did not *call* the father of Casticus, but *called* him *friend;* and that, therefore, the complete predicate is not **appellāverat**, but **amīcum appellāverat**. As **amīcum** forms an essential part of the *predicate*, it may be called the *Predicate Accusative* in distinction from **patrem**, which is the *Direct Object*. What are the Predicate Accusatives in Exs. 3–5? What are the Direct Objects?

401. OBSERVATION: Note that, in Ex. 2, the *passive construction* is illustrated. What has the Predicate Accusative of the

TWO ACCUSATIVES.

Active Construction become in the Passive? What has the Direct Object become? Change Exs. 3–5 into the Passive Construction.

402. REFERENCES: H. 373, 1, 2; G. 197 (second paragraph).

403.   EXAMPLES.

1. **Hibērum cōpiās trājēcit** (Liv. 21, 23, 1), *he threw his forces* **across** *the Ebro.*
2. **Duodecim mīlia equitum Hibērum trādūxit** (Liv. 21, 23, 1), *he led twelve thousand horse across the Ebro.*
3. **Id animum advertit** (1, 24, 1), *he directed his attention to this.*

404. OBSERVATION AND INFERENCE: Note that the verbs in the foregoing examples are *compounds*, being made up of a *simple verb* and a *preposition*. Is the *simple verb* in each instance *transitive* or *intransitive*? What *case*, then, would it take if it stood alone? What *case* would the *preposition* take if it stood alone? How, then, are the *two accusatives* to be accounted for? Frame a rule for the Two Accusatives here illustrated.

405. REFERENCES FOR VERIFICATION: A. & G. 239, *b*; H. 376; G. 330, **Rem. 1.**

406.   EXERCISES.

I. 1. Ariovistus in cōnsulātū **meō rēx** atque amīcus ā senātū appellātus est. 2. **Suā** cunctātiōne hostēs nostrōs mīlitēs alacriōrēs ad pūgnandum **effēcerant.** 3. Omnēs cōpiās Rhēnum trādūxerant. 4. Hostis apud mājōrēs nostrōs is dīcēbātur quem nunc peregrīnum dīcimus. 5. Hāc igitur mente Hellēspontum **cōpiās** trājēcit. 6. Caesarem certiōrem faciunt.

II. 1. Spurius Cassius was made master of the horse. 2. In this **council** he proclaimed Cingetorix a public enemy. 3. On![1] veterans, conduct a new army and a new leader across the Ebro! 4. The full moon rendered the tides **very** high. 5. Caesar, having been informed by Titurius, led **all** his cavalry and light armed[2] Numidians across **the bridge.**

---

[1] **Agite,** 2d pl. imper. of **agō,** *lead.*   [2] cf. Lesson XXXIX., foot-note 3.

LESSON LII.

Two Accusatives: Person and Thing.

407.　　　　　　　EXAMPLES.

1. Racilius **mē sententiam rogāvit** (Cic. Q. Fr. 2, 1, 3), *Racilius asked me my opinion.*
2. **Is enim** est prīmus rogātus sententiam (Liv. 37, 14), *for he was asked his opinion first.*
3. Juventūtem mala facinora ēdocēbat (Sall. Cat. 16, 1), *the youth he trained to* (taught thoroughly) *acts of lawlessness* (evil deeds).
4. Cicerō per lēgātōs **cūncta ēdoctus** [est] (Sall. Cat. 45, 1), *Cicero received detailed information of* (was thoroughly taught) *everything through the envoys.*

408. Observation and Inference: Note, in Exs. 1 and 3, that the verbs are **in** the *active* and are **followed by** *two accusatives*, **one** of the *person*, the other of the *thing*.' Note that, in Exs. 2 and 4, the same verbs are used in the *passive*. What does the Accusative of the Person become in the passive construction? the **Accusative of the** Thing? What *classes* of verbs (*i.e.*, verbs of **what** meaning) admit this double construction?[1] Frame a rule for the constructions here illustrated.

409. References for Verification: A. & G. 239, *c*, Rem. (first two lines); H. 374, 1; G. 333, Rem. 1.

410.　　　　　　　EXAMPLES.

1. **Quaerit ex perfugīs causam** (7, 44, 2), *he asks the deserters for an explanation* (an explanation from **the** deserters).
2. **Mulierēs pācem ab Rōmānīs petiērunt** (2, 13, 3), *the women besought the Romans for peace* (asked peace from the Romans).
3. Ab **Lentulō** postulant jūsjūrandum (Sall. Cat. 44, 1), *they demand of Lentulus an oath.*

ILLUSTRATIVE EXERCISES. 119

411. OBSERVATION AND INFERENCE: Do the foregoing **verbs** of asking and demanding conform to the rule already established (**407** and **408**)? How is the *person* expressed with **quaerō, petō,** and **postulō**? Frame a rule for the construction to be used with these verbs.

412. REFERENCES FOR VERIFICATION: **A.** & **G.** 239, Rem. (second paragraph); H. 374, n. 4; G. 333, 2.

413.   **EXERCISES.**

I. 1. Caesar sententiam ā cōnsule rogātus est. 2. Celeriter concilium dīmittit, Liscum retinet; quaerit ex sōlō ea quae in conventū dīxerat. 3. Cicerōnem lēgātī cūncta ēdocuērunt. 4. **Quod ab** alterō postulant, in sē recūsant. 5. Hōs ego dē rē pūblicā sententiam rogō. 6. Ad haec **quae** interrogātus es, respondē.

II. 1. Cato, on being appealed to for[2] **his opinion,** delivered **the** following address. 2. We must **ask Caesar** for **peace.**[3] 3. Cicero, thoroughly-informed-of everything through the envoys, directed the praetors . . . 4. The **Ubii** earnestly pressed Caesar for aid. 5. You taught us this **art.** 6. Cicero asked Silanus his opinion first, because **he** was consul elect.

---

[1] The learner should be careful to distinguish the two accusatives here considered from those illustrated **in 397.** In the examples under 397 **the two** accusatives denote the *same* person or thing; whereas, of the two accusatives illustrated **in 407,** one denotes the per**son,** the other the thing.
[2] Translate: *having been asked.*
[3] cf. Exs. in 317.

414.   Supplementary Exercises on Lessons LI. and LII.

I. 1. **Liscus** summō magistrātuī praeerat, **quem** vergobretum appellant Aeduī, quī creātur annuus. 2. Licet vōbīs **in** Ubiōrum fīnibus cōnsīdere, quōrum sunt lēgātī apud mē et ā mē auxilium petunt. 3. Caesar rogātus sententiam ā cōnsule, haec **verba** locūtus est.[1] 4. Trēs jam partēs cōpiārum Helvētiī id flūmen trādūxerant. 5. Sed juventūtem, quam, ut suprā dīximus, inlēxerat, multīs modīs[2] mala facinora ēdocēbat.

II. 1. Having armed the soldiers whom he thought suitable for this enterprise, he came to the town. 2. There-is-a-panic[3] throughout the camp,[4] and they ask of one another[5] the cause of the confusion. 3. When[6] the Helvetians had been informed[6] of his arrival, they sent ambassadors to him. 4. In this struggle,[7] the **Germans** whom Caesar had led across the Rhine ignominiously fled. 5. Dionysius taught Epaminondas music. 6. Under the tuition of Hannibal[8] he had been thoroughly-trained-in all the arts of war.

---

[1] *spoke;* perf. indic. of **loquor**, which has a pass. form with act. meaning.
[2] cf. Lesson XXIII., foot-note 4.
[3] trepidātur: A. & G. 146, c; H. 301, 1; G. 199, Rem. 1.
[4] Translate: *in the entire camp;* cf. Lesson XXXIV., foot-note 8.
[5] cf. Lesson XXXV., foot-note 25.
[6] Use **ubī** with the perfect indicative.
[7] cf. Lesson XXVI., foot-note 5.
[8] Translate: *under Hannibal* [as] *master.*

LESSON LIII.

Interrogative Pronouns. — Interrogative Particles: -ne, Nōnne, Num.

415. Learn the declension of the interrogatives: **quis** (subst.), *who?* **quid** (subst.), *what?* and **quī** (adj.), *which, what?*: A. & G. 104; H. 188, I., II.; G. 104 and Rem.

416. Decline together: **quī mīles,** *what soldier?* **quae urbs,** *what city?* **quod genus,** *what class?*

417.   EXAMPLES.

1. **Quis tē ex hāc tantā frequentiā salūtāvit?** (Cic. *Cat.* 1, 7, 16), *who in* (lit., out of) *this* (so) *great concourse greeted you?*
2. **Quid tandem tē impedit? Mōsne majōrum?** (Cic. *Cat.* 1, 11, 28), *what, pray, hinders you? Is it the practice of the fathers?*

3. **Nōnne [vōs] prōjēcit ille?** (Caes. *B. C.* 2, 32, 8), *did not he cast you off?*

4. **Num negāre audēs? Quid tacēs?** (Convincam, sī negās) (Cic. *Cat.* 1, 4, 8), *do you dare to deny it? Why are you silent? I will prove it, if you deny it.*

418. OBSERVATION AND INFERENCE: Note, in the foregoing interrogative sentences, that the question in each **case** is indicated not by a change in the order of the words, but by the introduction of some interrogative word. Note, further, that **the** interrogative word is a *pronoun* in Ex. 1 (see **Quis**), and in the first question of Ex. 2 (see **Quid**); whereas, **in the** second question of Ex. 2 (see -ne in **Mōsne**), in Ex. 3 (see **Nōnne**), and in the first question of Ex. 4 (see **Num**), it is an *interrogative particle*. Does the question containing **the appended** interrogative particle -ne (Ex. 2) suggest the answer *yes*, **the** answer *no*, or does it simply ask for information? What answer does **Nōnne** (Ex. 3) suggest? **Num** (Ex. 4)?

419. REFERENCES FOR VERIFICATION: A. & G. **210**, *a*, *c*; H. 351, 1, Notes 1, 2, and 3, also 2; G. 456, 457, 458.

420. EXERCISES.

I. 1. Quid proximā, quid superiōre nocte ēgīstī? 2. Ubī proximā nocte fuīstī, **quōs conv**ocāvīstī? 3. Quam rem pūblicam habēmus? 4. **In** quā urbe vīvimus? 5. Nōnne sibī salūtem fugā petīvit? 6. Num dubitās id imperante mē facere quod jam tuā **sponte** faciēbās?[1] 7. Numquamne familia nostra quiēta erit? 8. Quibus[2] gaudiīs[3] exsultābis! 9. Cui est Āpūlia attribūta? 10. Quō tandem[4] animō[5] hōc tibī ferendum est? 11. Potestne[5] tibī haec lūx, **Catilīna**, aut hūjus caelī spīritus esse[5] jūcundus? 12. Nōnne **etiam** aliō incrēdibilī scelere hōc scelus cumulāstī?[6]

II. 1. What plan[7] will **they** adopt? 2. **What and** how-great states are in arms? 3. In[8] **what** direction **is the** enemy marching? 4. **Whom** did you **leave at** Rome,[9] whom did you take[10] with **you**? 5. To whom has the Picene district been assigned? 6. [When] betrayed by[11] him, were you not preserved by Caesar's generosity? 7. "Do you see, soldiers?" says he.[12] 8. In-what-way did they defend their towns? 9. Can [there] be[5] peace or amity between[13] purposes so opposed? 10. Do you not seem[14] to see with your eyes these [things] which you have heard?

421. **Supplementary Exercises.**

I. 1. Autrōniō nōnne sodālēs, nōnne conlēgae suī, nōn veterēs amīcī dēfuērunt? 2. Quanta est īnsulae māgnitūdō? quae aut quantae nātiōnēs incolunt? quem ūsum bellī habent? quī sunt idōneī portūs? 3. Quae in conciliō Gallōrum dē Dumnorīge sunt dicta? 4. Num mē fefellit, Catilīna, diēs?

II. 1. Shall I stand in arms[15] against Caesar, my general? 2. Did not all these who are foremost in the commonwealth desert Autronius? 3. Did, then, the shipwreck of so-many leaders do-away-with the art of steering? 4. From what classes of men are those [contemptible][16] **forces obtained**? 5. From what regions do they come, and what [things] have they learned there?

---

[1] **tuā sponte faciēbās,** *you were going to do of your own free will.*
[2] The interrogatives are used in exclamations.
[3] cf. foot-note 4, Lesson XXIII.
[4] **tandem,** *pray* (exclamation).
[5] potest, 3d sing. of possum; **esse,** pres. infin. of sum; potest esse, *can be.*
[6] cumulāstī = cumulāvistī; cf. foot-note 2, Lesson XXXIV.
[7] "what plan" = *what* **(subst.)** *of plan* (part. gen.)?
[8] Translate: *into what part?*
[9] See Lesson XXVII., foot-note 11.
[10] "take" = *lead out.*
[11] per.
[12] inquit (def.), *says he,* is placed after one or more words of a direct quotation.
[13] in with ablative.
[14] Translate: *Do you not seem to yourselves?* For *seem,* use the passive of videō.
[15] "in arms" = *armed.*
[16] Which of the demonstratives must be used here?

LESSON LIV.

Verbs: Subjunctive Mood.

422. Learn, without meanings, the inflection and synopsis of the Subjunctive Tenses of **sum**: A. & G. pp. 68, 69; H. p. 85; G. p. 50.

423. Inflect **(like sum)** in the same tenses: **absum**; **also** learn the synopsis.

424. Learn, without meanings, the inflection **and** synopsis **of the** Subjunctive Tenses, Active and Passive (including **the** Periphrastic Conjugations), of **amō**: A. & G. pp. 76, 77, 78; H. 87, 89, 115; G. pp. 54–57, **82.**

425. Inflect (like **amō**) in the **foregoing** Tenses **of** both Voices: **cōnfirmō, laudō**; **also learn the** synopsis of these verbs.

426. Learn (as in **424**) the inflection and synopsis of **moneō** (or **dēleō**): A. & G. p. 80; H. pp. 91, 93; G. pp. 58–61.

427. Inflect (like **moneō** or **dēleō**): **habeō, compleō**; also learn the synopsis of these verbs.

428. Learn (as in **424**) the inflection and synopsis **of tegō (regō** or **emō**): A. & G. p. 82; **H.** pp. 95, **97;** G. pp. 64–67.

429. Inflect (like **tegō, regō,** or **emō**): **dūcō, mittō**; also learn the synopsis of these verbs.

430. Learn (as in **424**) the inflection and synopsis of **capiō**: A. & G. p. 83; H. pp. 106, 108; G. pp. 72, 73.

431. Inflect (like **capiō**): **rapiō, jaciō**; also learn the synopsis of these verbs.

432. Learn (as in **424**) the inflection and synopsis of **audiō**: A. & G. p. 86; H. pp. 99, 101; G. pp. 68–71.

433. Inflect (like **audiō**): **pūniō, vestiō**; also learn the synopsis of these verbs.

LESSON LV.

SUBJUNCTIVE IN INDIRECT QUESTIONS. — SEQUENCE OF TENSES.

434. EXAMPLES.

1. **Quis habet Etrūriam?** *who has Etruria in charge?*
2. **Videō quis habeat Etrūriam** (Cic. *Cat.* 2, 3, 6), *I see who has Etruria in charge.*
3. **Cui est Āpūlia attribūta?** *to whom has Apulia been assigned?*
4. **Videō cui sit Āpūlia attribūta** (Cic. *Cat.* 2, 3, 6), *I see to whom Apulia has been assigned.*

435. OBSERVATION AND INFERENCE: Note that the questions contained in Exs. 1 and 3 invite a *direct answer*, and that the verb is in the *indicative mood*. Note, further, that in Exs. 2 and 4 these questions have been made the *direct object* of **videō**, and that they *no longer invite an answer*. The questions of Exs. 1 and 3 are called *Direct* or *Independent;* those of Exs. 2 and 4 are called *Indirect* or *Dependent*. What *mood* in the Indirect Question has taken the place of the *indicative* in the Direct? Does any change of mood take place in English? Frame a rule for the Mood to be used in Indirect Questions.

SEQUENCE OF TENSES. 125

436. REFERENCES FOR VERIFICATION: A. & G. 334; H. 529, I.; G. 469.

437. What are the Primary or Principal Tenses of the verb? the Secondary or Historical Tenses? See A. & G. 285, 1, 2; H. 198, I., 1, 2, 3, 4, II., 1, 2, 3; G. 216.

438.   EXAMPLES.

1. Videō quis habeat **Etrūriam** (Cic. Cat. 2, 3, 6), *I see who has Etruria in charge.*
2. Vidēbō quis habeat **Etrūriam**, *I shall see who has Etruria in charge.*
3. Vīderō **quis habeat** Etrūriam, *I shall have seen who has Etruria in charge.*
4. **Videō quis habuerit** Etrūriam, *I see who had* (has had) *Etruria in charge.*
5. Vidēbō quis habuerit Etrūriam, *I shall see who had* (has had) *Etruria in charge.*
6. Vīderō quis habuerit Etrūriam, *I shall have seen who had* (has had) *Etruria in charge.*
7. Vidēbam quis habēret **Etrūriam**, *I saw who had Etruria in charge.*
8. Vīdī quis habēret **Etrūriam**, *I saw who had Etruria in charge.*
9. Vīderam quis **habēret Etrūriam**, *I had seen who had Etruria in charge.*
10. **Vidēbam quis habuisset** Etrūriam, *I saw who had had Etruria in charge.*
11. Vīdī quis habuisset Etrūriam, *I saw who had had Etruria in charge.*
12. Vīderam quis habuisset Etrūriam, *I had seen who had had Etruria in charge.*

439. OBSERVATION AND INFERENCE: Is **the** verb **of** the *leading clause*, in Exs. 1–6, in a *primary* or a *secondary tense?* Answer the same question for the *subjunctive* of the *dependent clause* in the same examples. Is the verb of the *leading clause*, in Exs. 7–12, in a *primary* or a *secondary tense?* Answer the same question for the *subjunctive* of the *dependent clause* in the same examples. Does the subjunctive of a dependent clause, then, adapt its tense to that of the verb in the leading clause? Frame a general rule for the Tense of the Subjunctive in Dependent Clauses.

440. REFERENCES FOR VERIFICATION: A. & G. 286; H. 490, 491; G. 510 (first paragraph).

441. OBSERVATION AND INFERENCE: Note that the action denoted by the *subjunctive*, in Exs. 1–3 and 7–9, is represented as *continued*, or *incomplete*, with reference to the action denoted by the *leading verb*. Which *tense* of the *subjunctive* is used to express this continuance or incompleteness when the leading verb is in a *primary tense* (see Exs. 1–3)? when the leading verb is in a *secondary tense* (see Exs. 7–9)?

Note that the action denoted by the *subjunctive*, in Exs. 4–6 and 10–12, is represented as *completed* with reference to the action denoted by the *leading verb.* Which *tense* of the *subjunctive* is used to express this completeness when the leading verb is in a *primary tense* (see Exs. 4–6)? when the leading verb is in a *secondary tense* (see Exs. 10–12)?

Frame special rules for the Tense of the Subjunctive in Dependent Clauses.

442. REFERENCES FOR VERIFICATION: A. & G. 286, Rem.; H. 492, 1, 2, 493, 1, 2; G. 510.

LESSON LVI.

ILLUSTRATIVE EXERCISES ON THE FOREGOING PRINCIPLES.

443. EXERCISES.

I. 1. Quid proximā, quid superiōre nocte ēgerīs, **quis** nostrŭm[1] īgnōrat? 2. Expōnam enim vōbīs, Quirītēs, **ex** quibus generibus hominum istae[2] **cōpiae comparentur.**

3. Quid **eā nocte** ēgisset, quid in proximam cōnstituisset, ēdocuī. 4. Quid hostēs cōnsiliī caperent, exspectābat. 5. Quae in Trēverīs gererentur, ostendit. 6. Videō quanta tempestās invidiae nōbīs impendeat. 7. Intellegō quantō id cum perīculō fēcerim. 8. Docēbat etiam quae senātūs **cōnsulta**, quotiēns, quamque honōrifica in Aeduōs facta essent. 9. **Quibus angustiīs** ipse Caesar ā Venetīs **premātur, docet.**

II. 1. Who among us[3] does not know **where** you were last night? 2. He understood at what risk[4] he **had** done this. 3. Caesar **knew for**[5] what reason these **things** were said. 4. I will recount what cities, fortified by nature, the Roman people took in war.[6] 5. Caesar inquired of the captives wherefore Ariovistus did not come to an engagement.[7] 6. They compel merchants to declare from what districts they come, and what (pl.) they have learned there. 7. **Nor** was it altogether clear in what direction the enemy **had** marched. 8. He made known what he disapproved **in him**. 9. **He set forth to the** citizens **what the senate had decreed** the-day-before.

444. Supplementary Exercises.

I. 1. Dumnorigem ad sē vocat; quae in eō reprehendat, ostendit. 2. Neque **quanta esset** īnsulae māgnitūdō, neque quae **aut** quantae nātiōnēs **incolerent**, neque quem ūsum bellī habērent, reperiēbat. 3. **Et** viātōrēs etiam invītōs cōnsistere cōgunt et quid quisque eōrum audierit aut cōgnōverit, quaerunt. 4. Memorāvit quibus in locīs māximae hostium cōpiae ā populō Rōmānō parvā manū fūsae essent. 5. Vidētē quās in partēs hostēs iter faciant.

II. 1. **At** the same time he-called-his-attention-to what **had** been said in his own presence[8] in the council of the Gauls about Dumnorix. 2. He had not-yet perceived for **w**hat reason they were withdrawing. 3. Who among[3] us does not know what (pl.) was done last night, what the night before? 4. The consul pointed out from what classes of men Catiline's forces had been collected.   5. Ascertain what⁹ is the nature of the mountain and what⁹ the ascent by a circuitous path.¹⁰

¹ Why not **nostrī**?
² Contemptuous.
³ "who among us" = *who of us.*
⁴ Trans. *with how-great risk.*
⁵ **dē.**
⁶ "in war" = *by fighting.*
⁷ "to come to an engagement" = *to contend in battle* = **proeliō dēcertāre.**
⁸ Trans.: *himself present* (abl. abs.).
⁹ **quālis, -e,** adjective.
¹⁰ Trans.: *in circuit.*

LESSON LVII.

INDEFINITES.

445. Learn the declension of the indefinites: **quis,** *any one;* **quī,** *any;* **quīdam,**¹ *a, a certain, some one;* **quīvīs,** *any you please, any one you please;* **aliquis,** *some, some one;* **quisque,** *every, each, every one, each one:* A. & G. 104, 105, *c, d* (first four lines and paradigm), *e* (first three lines); H. 190, 1, 2, 1), 2), Notes 1 and 2; G. 105, 1, 2, 5, 6.

446. Decline together: **sī quis,** *if any one;* **sī qua rēs,** *if anything;* **spēs aliqua,** *some hope;* **quīdam**¹ **homo,** *a man;* **quodcumque**² **bellum,** *whatever war;* **nōbilissimus quisque,** *all the nobility;*³ **quaevīs vīs,**⁴ *any force whatever.*

447.   EXERCISES.

I. 1. Nāvēs tōtae (*throughout*) factae erant ex rōbore ad quamvīs vim⁴ et contumēliam perferendam.   2. Nam omnēs in quibus aliquid dīgnitātis fuit, eō convēnerant. 3. Ubī cuique locus silvestris spem salūtis aliquam offerēbat, cōnsēderat.   4. Haec castra silvam quandam¹ contingēbant. 5. Errant sī quicquam⁵ ab hīs praesidiī spērant.   6. Quaecumque² bella gerentur sine ūllō perīculō tuō cōnficientur. 7. Obsidēs nōbilissimī cūjusque³ līberōs poscit et in eōs

INDEFINITES.

omnia exempla cruciātūsque ēdit, sī **qua rēs nōn** ad voluntātem ējus **facta est.**

II. 1. They are conscious[6] of [having done] **some wrong.**
2. It-is-better for us to-submit-to[7] any fortune whatever.
3. He hears these [tidings] from some (**quĭdam**) deserters belonging-to-the-town.   **4.** Nor do **they** have any[8] clothing except skins.   **5.** Unless some help[9] **comes from**[10] Caesar, the same thing will have to be done by[11] all the Gauls.
6. Caesar summons[12] **the foremost men of** each community.
7. Whoever shall **be in authority over**[13] **the** province, shall defend the Aedui.   **8.** And so they dare **to** attack[14] any number whatever.

448.   Supplementary Exercises.

I. 1. Alicūjus injūriae sibī cōnscius est.   **2.** Idōneum **quendam** hominem dēlēgit, Gallum, ex iīs quōs auxiliī causā **sēcum** habēbat.   **3.** Neque eōrum mōribus turpius quicquam[5] habētur.
4. At Caesar, prīncipibus cūjusque cīvitātis ad sē ēvocātīs, māgnam partem Galliae in officiō tenuit.

II. 1. By [holding out] great **rewards, he prevailed upon** one (**quĭdam**) of[15] the Gallic horsemen.   **2. I shall** send to you some one of[15] my [followers].   **3. And so they dare,** however few [they may be], to attack[14] **any number whatever of** horsemen.
4. There is timber of **every** description **except** beech and fir.
5. If any crime has **been** committed, these-same-persons[16] determine the rewards and the penalties.

---

[1] n is used for m before d, e.g., **quendam** (acc. sing.) and **quōrundam** (gen. pl.).
[2] A. & G. 105, a.
[3] Lit., every noblest [man]; decline in singular only; note that **quisque** follows the superlative.
[4] For declension of **vīs**, see A. & G. 61; H. 66; G. 76, D.
[5] **quisquam,** anyone, has **quicquam** or **quidquam,** anything, in the nominative and accusative neuter singular; it lacks the feminine singular and the entire plural. For use of quisquam, see A. & G. 202, c; H. 457; G. 304.

[6] Translate: they are conscious to themselves.
[7] **patī,** pres. infin. pass. with act. meaning.
[8] Translate: anything of clothing; see foot-note 5.
[9] "some help" = something of help.
[10] Translate shall be in Caesar.
[11] What construction must be **used?**
[12] to summon = ad sē ēvocāre.
[13] Use obtineō with accusative.
[14] to attack, adīre ad.
[15] "of" = from.
[16] **īdem,** nom. pl. masc.

LESSON LVIII.

DATIVE OF POSSESSION. — DATIVE OF SERVICE.

449. EXAMPLES.

1. **Hīs erat inter sē dē prīncipātū contentiō** (7, 39, 2), *these had a struggle with each other for precedence* (lit., there was to these a struggle, etc.).
2. **At Catōnī studium modestiae, decoris erat** (Sall. Cat. 54, 5), *Cato, on the other hand, had a preference for sobriety and dignity of behavior* (lit., there was to Cato a preference, etc.).
3. **Est igitur hominī cum deō similitūdō** (Cic. Leg. 1, 8, 25), *man has, then, a likeness to God* (lit., there is to man a likeness, etc.).

450. OBSERVATION AND INFERENCE. With what *case* is the verb **sum** construed in the foregoing examples? By what English verb is it translated? How, then, may Possession be expressed in Latin? Frame a rule for the construction here illustrated.

451. REFERENCES FOR VERIFICATION: A. & G. 231; H. 387; G. 349.

452. EXAMPLES.

1. **Caesar equitātum suīs auxiliō mīsit** (4, 37, 2), *Caesar sent the cavalry to the assistance of his men* (to his for assistance).
2. **Tulingī, quī novissimīs praesidiō erant** (1, 25, 6), *the Tulingi, who served as a guard to the rear* (were to the rear for protection).
3. **Quibus corpus voluptātī, anima onerī fuit** (Sall. Cat. 2, 8), *to these the body* [served] *for pleasure,* [and] *thought was a bore* (the soul was for a burden).
4. **Eāsdem cōpiās praesidiō nāvibus relīquit** (5, 11, 7), *he left the same forces to guard the ships* (to the ships for protection).

DATIVES: POSSESSION AND SERVICE.

453. OBSERVATION AND INFERENCE: With how many *datives* are the verbs in the foregoing examples construed? What do these datives respectively denote? Note that the *transitive verbs* (see **mīsit, Ex.** 1, and **relīquit,** Ex. 4) take, besides the dative, an *accusative* also. Frame a rule embodying your observations.

454. REFERENCES FOR VERIFICATION: A. & G. 233; H. 390, I., II.; G. 350.

455.   **EXERCISES.**

I. 1. Quid in meā **Galliā Caesarī negōtiī est?** 2. Multīs corpus voluptātī, **anima onerī est.** 3. **Lēgātum** minōribus castrīs praesidiō relīquerat. 4. Familiāritās mihi cum eō est. 5. Q. Caepiōnī fortūna bellī crīminī, invidia populī calamitātī fuit. 6. In hāc īnsulā est fōns aquae dulcis cui nōmen Arethūsa **est.** 7. Tertiam legiōnem nostrīs subsidiō mīsit.

II. 1. Traders have no access to them. 2. The friendship of the Roman people is a protection to me. 3. Two legions served as a guard to the baggage. 4. Our diminutive stature excites the contempt[1] of the Gauls. 5. **No one** could maintain his position[2] **on the wall.** 6. He sent the third line to the relief of **our men [who** were] struggling against odds.[3]

456.   Supplementary Exercises.

I. 1. At nōbīs est domī[4] inopia, forīs aes aliēnum. 2. Mihi autem mīrum vidētur quid in meā Galliā aut Caesarī aut omnīnō populō Rōmānō negōtiī sit.[5] 3. Mīlitēs sibī ipsī ad pūgnam erant impedimentō. 4. Ea rēs māgnō ūsuī nostrīs fuit.

II. 1. These [matters] are my business.[6] 2. He reminded many, to whom this had been a source of booty, of the victory[7] of Sulla. 3. The associates of Catiline had all sorts of[8] miseries in abundance, but no[9] favorable condition or[9] prospect.

---

[1] Trans.: *is to the Gauls for contempt.*
[2] cf. Lesson XLIV., foot-note 13.
[3] Present participle of **labōrō.**
[4] Locative form, *at home;* for declension, see: A. & G. 70, *f;* H. 119, 1; G. 67, Rem. 2.
[5] Account for **mood and tense.**
[6] Trans.: *are to me for a care.*
[7] Use the genitive.
[8] "all sorts of" = *all.*
[9] "no ... or" = *neither any ... nor.*

LESSON LIX.

The Infinitive with Subject Accusative as Object. — Tense of the Infinitive.

457. Learn, with meanings, the Infinitives of **sum**: A. & G. p. 69; H. p. 85; G. p. 51.

458. Learn, with meanings, the Infinitives, Active and Passive, of **amō**: A. & G. pp. 77, 79; H. pp. 87, 89; G. pp. 55, 56. Form the Infinitives of **cōnfirmō** and **laudō**.

459. Learn (as in **458**) the Infinitives of **moneō** (or dēleō): A. & G. p. 81; H. pp. 91, 93; G. pp. 59, 61. Form the Infinitives of **habeō** and **compleō**.

460. Learn (as in **458**) the Infinitives of **tegō** (regō or emō): A. & G. p. 83; H. pp. 95, 97; G. pp. 65, 67. Form the Infinitives of **dūcō** and **mittō**.

461. Learn (as in **458**) the Infinitives of **capiō**: A. & G. p. 83; H. pp. 107, 108; G. pp. 72, 73. Form the Infinitives of **rapiō** and **jaciō**.

462. Learn (as in **458**) the Infinitives of **audiō**: A. & G. p. 87; H. pp. 99, 101; G. 69, 71. Form the Infinitives of **pūniō** and **vestiō**.

463. EXAMPLES.

1. **Nostrōs nōn esse īnferiōrēs intellēxit** (2, 8, 3), *he knew that our men were not inferior* (lit., our men not to be inferior).

TENSE OF THE INFINITIVE. 133

2. **Neque hominēs temperātūrōs**[1] exīstimābat (1, 7, 4), *nor did he think that the men would refrain* (lit., **the** men to be about to refrain).
3. Divicō **respondit ita** Helvētiōs īnstitūtōs esse (1, 14, 7), *Divico replied that the Helvetians had been so trained* (lit., **the** Helvetians to have been so trained).
4. Caesar Dumnorigem dēsignārī **sentiēbat** (1, 18, 1), *Caesar perceived that Dumnorix was* **meant** (lit., Dumnorix to be meant).

464. OBSERVATION AND INFERENCE: Note **that,** in each of the foregoing examples, the leading verb has, for its object, a clause whose *verb* is in the *infinitive* and whose *subject* is in the *accusative*. Note, further, that **intellēxit** is a verb of *knowing*, exīstimābat a verb of *thinking*, **respondit** a verb of *telling*, and sentiēbat a verb of *perceiving*. What *classes* of verbs, then, take the Infinitive with Subject Accusative as Object? Frame a rule for this construction.

465. REFERENCES FOR VERIFICATION: A. & **G. 272; H. 535,** I. (read also 1, 2, 3); G. 527.

466. OBSERVATION AND INFERENCE: Note that the *present infinitives* **esse** (Ex. 1) and **dēsignārī** (Ex. 4) are translated by the *past tense;* and that they denote, therefore, the same time as the verbs (**intellēxit** and **sentiēbat**) on which they depend. In other words, these **present** infinitives represent the time of the action not as present absolutely, but as present relatively to **the** time denoted by the principal verb. How does the *future infinitive* **temperātūrōs** (Ex. 2) represent the time of the action? Answer the same question for the *perfect infinitive* **īnstitūtōs esse** (Ex. 3). Frame a rule for the use of the Infinitive Tenses.

467. REFERENCES FOR VERIFICATION: A. & G. 288; **H. 537;** G. 529, 530.

[1] sc. esse; the auxiliary of the **fut. infin.** act. is often omitted.

LESSON LX.

Illustrative Exercises on the Foregoing Constructions.

468.   EXERCISES.

I. 1. Dīxit pējus victōribus Sēquanīs quam **Aeduīs victīs** accidisse.   2. Lēgātum sēsē māgnō cum perīculō ad eum missūrum[1] exīstimābat.   3. Reperiēbat initium fugae factum[2] ā Dumnorige.   4. Ex perfugīs quibusdam oppidānīs audit .Saburram Uticae appropīnquāre.   5. Divitiacus respondit scīre sē illa esse vēra.   6. Summum in cruciātum sē ventūrōs[1] vidēbant.

II. 1. Caesar remembered[3] that the army had been beaten by the **Helvetians and sent under the yoke**.   2. They said that the Aedui had lost all their **nobility, all their senate,** [and] all their **cavalry**.   3. He said that our plans were reported to the enemy.   4. Caesar learned that by these means (things) Dumnorix was increasing his private resources.   5. Caesar answered that he would make peace with them.   6. He knew that it would be [attended] with great danger to the province.[4]

469.   Supplementary Exercises.

I. 1. Reperiēbat etiam in quaerendō initium fugae factum ā Dumnorige atque ējus equitibus; eōrum fugā reliquum esse equitātum perterritum.   2. Sē suīs cōpiīs suōque exercitū illīs rēgna[5] conciliātūrum cōnfirmat.   3. Negāvit **aut** cōnferendum esse Gallicum cum Germānōrum **agrō**, aut hanc cōnsuētūdinem **victūs cum illā** comparandam.

II. 1. They knew **that** he had done **in one day what** *they*[6] had accomplished with-the-utmost-difficulty in twenty days.   2. They **supposed** that they should either persuade the Allobroges or con-

COMPLEMENTARY INFINITIVE. 135

strain them **by force**. 3. He said that he had **fled from the state** and come **to the** senate to solicit[7] aid.

[1] cf. Lesson LIX., foot-note 1.
[2] sc. esse.
[3] "remembered" = *held by memory*.
[4] Use the genitive.
[5] The plural is used here because sovereign power in two states is thought of; use the singular in translation.
[6] Use the proper form of *ipse*.
[7] cf. **380**, Ex. **2**.

LESSON LXI.

COMPLEMENTARY INFINITIVE. — INFINITIVE AS SUBJECT.

470. EXAMPLES.

1. **Neque fugere dēstitērunt** (1, 53, 1), *nor did they cease to flee*.
2. **Helvētiī nostrōs lacessere coepērunt** (1, 15, 3), *the Helvetians began to attack our men*.
3. **... quod accidere solēbat** (6, 15, 1), *which was wont to happen*.

471. OBSERVATION AND INFERENCE: **Note that** the infinitives fugere (Ex. 1), lacessere (Ex. 2), **and** accidere (Ex. 3), are *without subject accusative*. Note, **further,** that the verbs on which these infinitives depend (**dēstitērunt, coepērunt, solēbat**), are verbs of *incomplete meaning*. As the infinitive in these cases is added to *complete* the meaning of the verb on which it depends, **it is** called the *Complementary Infinitive*. After what *class* of verbs, **then,** is the Complementary Infinitive used? Frame a rule for this construction.

472. REFERENCES FOR VERIFICATION: A. & G. 271 with note; H. 533, I., 1, 2; G. 424.

473. EXAMPLES.

1. **Mea facta** mihī dīcere licet (Sall. *Jug.* 85, 24), *I have the right to speak of my own deeds* (to speak is lawful for me).
2. **[Mihī]** nōn placuit reticēre (Sall. *Jug.* 85, 26), *I am resolved not to remain silent* (to remain silent has not seemed good to me).

3. Tē prōvidēre decet (Sall. *Jug.* 10, 7), *it is proper for* **you to see to** *it* (for.you to see to it is becoming).

4. **Pulchrum est bene** facere rēī pūblicae (Sall. *Cat.* 3, 1), *to serve the commonwealth by deeds* (to do well for the commonwealth) *is honorable*.

474. OBSERVATION AND INFERENCE: Note that the verbs licet (Ex. 1), **placuit** (Ex. 2), and decet (Ex. 3), are *impersonal;* and that they have as *subject* an *infinitive*, either *without* subject accusative (see dīcere, Ex. 1, and reticēre, Ex. 2), or *with* subject accusative (see **tē** prōvidēre, Ex. 3). Note also that the verb est (Ex. 4) has an *infinitive* (**facere**) as *subject*. With what *classes* of verbs, then, is the Infinitive used as Subject? Frame a rule for this construction.

475. REFERENCES FOR VERIFICATION: A. & G. 270, *a*; H. 538, 1; G. 423.

476. EXERCISES.

I. 1. Līberī eōrum īn servitūtem **abdūcī nōn dēbent.**[1] 2. Hīs rēbus coercērī mīlitēs solent. 3. Nōn oportet[1] mē ā populō Rōmānō in meō jūre impedīrī. 4. Nōbīs est in animō sine ūllō maleficiō per prōvinciam iter facere. 5. Nōbīs praestat quamvīs fortūnam ā populō Rōmānō patī[2] quam ā **Gallīs per** cruciātum interficī. 6. Cōnstituērunt jūmentōrum quam[3] māximum numerum coëmere. 7. In- īquum est dē stīpendiō recūsāre.

II. 1. It-was-generally-understood that Caesar would first carry on war in Venetia. 2. Still, the majority were in favor of defending[4] the **camp**. 3. They decided to establish friendship with the neighboring **states**. 4. The Helvetians began[5] to maintain their ground more **boldly**.[6] 5. Priority of time ought not in every instance to **be regarded**.[7] 6. We are at liberty[8] to do this. 7. Their lands ought[9] not to be laid waste.

DEPONENT VERBS.

477. **Supplementary Exercises.**

I. 1. Ariovistus respondit amīcitiam populī Rōmānī sibī praesidiō, **nōn** dētrīmentō esse oportēre. 2. Helvētiī audācius⁶ subsistere et proeliō nostrōs lacessere coepērunt. 3. Sī antīquissimum quodque tempus¹⁾ spectārī oportet, populī Rōmānī jūstissimum **est** in Galliā imperium.

II. 1. It is the intention of¹¹ the Helvetians to march through the country of the Sequani and Aedui. 2. It is reported to Caesar that the Helvetians intend to march **through the** country of the Sequani **and** Aedui. 3. If the decision of **the senate** has a claim to be respected,¹² **Gaul ought⁹ to be free.**

---

¹ **dēbeō** is **personal; oportet** is **impersonal.** Both express moral obligation, or a necessity founded on duty.
² See **foot-note 7**, Lesson LVII.
³ cf. **foot-note 5**, Lesson XXXII.
⁴ Trans.: *it seemed good* (**placuit**) *to the greater part to defend.*
⁵ **coepērunt.**
⁶ **audācius**, *more boldly.*

⁷ Translate: *it is not right* (oportet) [for] *each earliest time to be regarded.* For order, cf. Lesson LVII., foot-note 3.
⁸ Trans.: *it is permitted to us.*
⁹ Use **dēbeō.**
¹⁰ See sent. 5 in the preceding exercise.
¹¹ Imitate 476, I., sent. 4.
¹² Translate: *if it is proper* [for] *the decision of the senate to be respected.*

LESSON LXII.

DEPONENT VERBS. — ABLATIVE WITH Ūtor, Fruor, ETC.

478. EXAMPLES.

1. **Tabulās pīctās mīrārī** (Sall. *Cat.* 11, 6), *to admire paintings.*
2. **Hostem verērī** (1, 39, 6), *to fear the enemy.*
3. **Hostēs** sequitur (1, 22, 5), *he pursues the enemy.*
4. **Oppidō** potitur (7, 11, 8), *he gets possession of the town.*
5. **Ad Vesontiōnem morātur** (1, 39, 1), *he tarries (i.e., detains himself) at Vesontio.*

479. OBSERVATION: Note, in the foregoing examples, that the verbs have a *passive form*, but an *active* (Exs. 1–4) or *reflexive*

(Ex. 5) *meaning*. Such verbs are called *Deponent* (from dē-pōnō, *lay aside*) because they have laid aside their passive meaning.

480. REFERENCES: A. & G. 135; H. 231; G. 211.

481. Learn the inflection **and synopsis** of one deponent verb under each conjugation: A. & G. 135, *a, c*; H. 231, 1, 3, 232 (see note); G. pp. 74–81.

482. EXAMPLES.

1. **Māteriā** ūtēbātur (4, 31, 2), *he used the timber*.
2. **Vīta** quā fruimur brevis est (Sall. Cat. 1, 3), *the life which we enjoy is short*.
3. . . . **quōrum māgna** multitūdō servōrum mūnere fungitur (Nep. Paus. 3, 6), *large numbers of whom discharge the duty of slaves*.
4. Numidae lacte **et carne vescēbantur** (Sall. Jug. 89, 7), *the Numidians subsisted on milk and meat*.
5. Caesar oppidō potītur (7, 11, 8), *Caesar obtains possession of the town*.

483. OBSERVATION AND INFERENCE: With what *case*, in the foregoing examples, are the following verbs construed: ūtēbātur (Ex. 1), fruimur (Ex. 2), fungitur (Ex. 3), vescēbantur (Ex. 4), potītur (Ex. 5)? Frame a rule for the Case of Substantives used with these verbs:

484. REFERENCES FOR VERIFICATION: A. & G. 249; H. 421, I.; G. 405.

485. EXERCISES.

I. 1. Linguā Gallicā multā jam Ariovistus longinquā cōnsuētūdine[1] ūtēbātur. 2. Equitēs officiō fūnctī renūntiant paucōs in aedificiīs **esse** inventōs. 3. Lacte, cāseō, carne[2] vescor. 4. Tūtius esse arbitrābantur, commeātū interclūsō, sine ūllō vulnere victōriā potīrī. 5. Quae agat,[3] quibuscum loquātur,[3] sciō. 6. Is mihī vīvere atque fruī animā vidētur,

ILLUSTRATIVE EXERCISES. 139

quī praeclārī facinoris aut artis bonae fāmam quaerit.
7. Partiendum[4] sibī exercitum putāvit.   8. Vercingetorix ex arce suōs cōnspicātus ex oppidō ēgreditur.

II. 1. Our men obtained possession of the baggage **and camp**. 2. Wondering[5] what **was**[3] **the cause of this** behavior, he inquired of them personally. 3. They **share**[6] with their **leaders** all advantages in life. 4. The [territories of the] Belgians begin at the extreme **confines of** Gaul [and] extend towards the north-east.[7]   5. It is very easy to obtain[8] control of all Gaul. 6. Adopting[5] the same policy, they burn their towns and villages, and set out together with the Helvetians. 7. And I do not know whether[9] this is[3] **to be wondered at.**

486.   Supplementary Exercises.

I. 1. Est genus quoddam hominum, quod Hīlōtae vocātur, quōrum māgna multitūdō agrōs Lacedaemoniōrum colit servōrumque mūnere fungitur. 2. Rōmānōs pulsōs[10] superātōsque,[11] castris impedīmentisque eōrum hostēs **potītōs**[10] renūntiāvērunt. 3. In suis fīnibus dēcertābunt et domesticis cōpiis reī frūmentāriae ūtentur.

I. 1. One of those who stood next[11] stepped over[12] this [man] as he lay prostrate[13] and discharged[12] the same office. 2. The soldiers will subsist chiefly on milk, cheese, and game. 5. How long, pray, Catiline, will you abuse our patience?

---

[1] cf. Lesson XXIII., foot-note 8.
[2] carō, carnis, f., *flesh, meat*.
[3] Account for mood and tense.
[4] A. & G. 135, *d*; H. 231, 2; sc. *esse*.
[5] Use perf. part.
[6] Trans.: **enjoy** *together with their leaders*.
[7] Trans.: *north and rising sun*.
[8] Use **potior**.
[9] Express *whether* by appending -ne to the gerundive.
[10] sc. *esse*.
[11] Trans.: *one from the nearest*.
[12] "stepped over and discharged" = having stepped over, discharged.
[13] Trans.: *this* [man] *lying*.

LESSON LXIII.

INDEPENDENT USES OF THE SUBJUNCTIVE: HORTATORY, OPTATIVE, DUBITATIVE.

HORTATORY SUBJUNCTIVE.

487. EXAMPLES.

1. **Persequāmur eōrum mortem** (7, 38, 8), *let us avenge their death.*
2. **Discēdant in Ītaliā omnēs ab armīs** (Caes. *B. C.* 1, 9, 5), *let all throughout Italy lay down their arms* (withdraw from arms).
3. **Quaesierit sānē** (Cic. *Mil.* 17, 46), *suppose, if you will* (sānē), *that he did make inquiry.*

488. OBSERVATION AND INFERENCE: Note that the *subjunctive* **persequāmur** (Ex. 1) expresses *exhortation,* that **discēdant** (Ex. 2) expresses *command,* and that **quaesierit** (Ex. 3) expresses *concession.* Are the clauses containing these subjunctives *dependent* or *independent?* Frame a rule for these and similar Subjunctives.

489. REFERENCES FOR VERIFICATION: A. & G. 266; H 483, 484, II., III., IV.; G. 256, 1, 3, 257.

OPTATIVE SUBJUNCTIVE.

490. EXAMPLES.

1. **Stet haec urbs praeclāra** (Cic. *Mil.* 34, 93), *may this illustrious city abide!*
2. **Utinam P. Clōdius vīveret** (Cic. *Mil.* 38, 103), *would that Publius Clodius were alive!*
3. **Utinam ille omnēs sēcum cōpiās suās ēdūxisset** (Cic. *Cat.* 2, 2, 4), *would that he had taken with him all his forces!*

491. OBSERVATION AND INFERENCE: Note that the *subjunctives* in the foregoing examples express *wish.* Are the clauses containing them *dependent* or *independent?* In what *tense* is the subjunctive in Ex. 1? Does the wish in this example relate to *present, past,* or *future time?* Is the wish conceived of as *possible* or *impossible* of *fulfillment?* In what *tense* is the subjunctive in Ex. 2? To what *time* does it relate? Does it represent the wish as *fulfilled* or *unfulfilled?* Answer the last three questions for the subjunctive in Ex. 3. What *particle* accompanies the subjunctive in Exs. 2 and 3? Frame rules for Mood and Tense in Expressions of Wishing.

492. REFERENCES FOR VERIFICATION: **A. & G. 267, b; H. 484, I., 483, 1, 2; G. 253, 254.**

DUBITATIVE SUBJUNCTIVE.

493.   **EXAMPLES.**

1. **Ēloquar an sileam** (Verg. *Aen.* 3, 39), *shall I speak out, or hold my peace?*
2. **Hunc ego nōn admīrer** (Cic. *Arch.* 8, 18), *can I help admiring* (should I not admire) *this man?*
3. **Nam quid dē Cȳrō nūntiāret** (Cic. *Mil.* 18, 48), *pray, what need had he to bring news of Cyrus?*

494. OBSERVATION AND INFERENCE: Note (1) that the *subjunctives* in Ex. 1 are in a *question* expressing *doubt*, (2) that the *subjunctive* in Ex. 2 is in a *question* expressing *indignation*, (3) that the *subjunctive* in Ex. 3 is in a *question* expressing *impossibility*. Are the questions containing these subjunctives **dependent** or **independent?** Frame a rule for these and similar Subjunctives.

495. REFERENCES FOR **VERIFICATION:** A. & G. 268; H. 484, V., 486, II.; G. 258, 251.

LESSON LXIV.

ILLUSTRATIVE EXERCISES ON THE HORTATORY, OPTATIVE, AND DUBITATIVE SUBJUNCTIVES.

496.   EXERCISES.

I. 1. Discēdat uterque **ab** armīs exercitūsque dīmittat. 2. Valeant, valeant, cīvēs **meī**; sint incolumēs, sint flōrentēs, sint beātī; **stet** haec urbs praeclāra mihique patria cārissima! 3. **Nam** quid ea memorem, quae, nisi eīs quī vidēre, nēminī crēdibilia sunt? 4. Tranquillā rē **pūblicā** meī cīvēs perfruantur! 5. Proficiscantur, nē[1] patiantur dēsīderiō[2] suī Catilīnam miserum tābēscere. 6. Hunc **ego nōn dīligam, nōn admīrer**? nōn omnī ratiōne dēfendendum putem? 7. **Utinam exstārent** illa **carmina!** 8. Mihī salvā rē pūblicā vōbīscum perfruī liceat! 9. Hōc utinam ā prīncipiō tibī placuisset!

II. 1. Let Marius have eternal glory;[3] let Pompey be **preferred** to all. 2. Would that my fellow **citizens had** been uninjured, had been prosperous, had been happy! 3. But **who** could suppose that the Teucri would come[4] to **the shores of Hesperia?** 4. May I but (**modo**) accomplish **my endeavors!** 5. Why should I speak of Gabinius? 6. If they remain **in the** city, let them look for what[5] they deserve. 7. If they **cannot**[6] stand, let them fall. 8. Who could hesitate to release himself **from fear,**[7] and the commonwealth from peril?[7]

497. Supplementary Exercises.

I. 1. Utinam P. Clōdius nōn modo vīveret, sed etiam praetor, cōnsul, dictātor esset potius[8] quam hōc spectāculum vidērem! 2. **Sit Scīpiō clārus** ille, cūjus virtūte Hannibal ex Ītaliā dēcēdere **coāctus est; habeātur** vir ēgregius Paullus ille, cūjus currum rēx potentissimus et nōbilissimus Persēs honestāvit. 3. Cūr dē vestrā **virtūte aut dē meā dīligentiā dēspērētis?**

II. 1. Therefore **let** the reprobates go; let them separate themselves from the good. 2. Would that this which I am saying were not[1] true![9] 3. Why should I allow soldiers to be wounded who have done their best to serve me?[10]

---

[1] nē is the regular negative with the hortatory and optative subjunctives.
[2] cf. Lesson XXIII., foot-note 8.
[3] Translate: *be of eternal glory*.
[4] In what mood? See 463, Ex. 2.
[5] "**what**" = *those* [things] *which*.
[6] **nōn** possunt.

[7] Ablative without preposition.
[8] *rather*.
[9] **Translate:** *would that I were not saying **this** truly*.
[10] "who have . . . me" = *having deserved best* (**optimē**) *from* (**dē**) *me*.

LESSON LXV.

ADVERBS: FORMATION AND COMPARISON.

498.	EXAMPLES.

POSITIVE.

ADJECTIVES.

1. jūstus (st. jūsto-);
2. līber (st. lībero-);
3. pulcher (st. pulchro-);
4. ācer (st. ācri-);
5. fortis (st. **forti-**);
6. audāx **(st. audāci-)**;
7. **sapiēns (st.** sapient-);

ADVERBS.

jūstē, *justly*.
līberē, *freely*.
pulchrē, *beautifully*.
ācriter, *sharply*.
fortiter, *bravely*.
audācter (audāciter), *boldly*.
sapienter, *wisely*.

COMPARATIVE.

8. jūstior, *juster;*
9. līberior, *freer;*
10. pulchrior, *more beautiful;*
11. ācrior, *sharper;*
12. fortior, *braver;*
13. audācior, *bolder,*
14. sapientior, *wiser;*

jūstius, *more justly*.
līberius, *more freely*.
pulchrius, **more beautifully**.
ācrius, *more sharply*.
fortius, *more bravely*.
audācius, *more boldly*.
sapientius, *more wisely*.

SUPERLATIVE.

15. jūstissimus (st. jūstissimo-);
16. līberrimus (st. līberrimo-);
17. pulcherrimus (st. pulcherrimo-);
18. ācerrimus (st. ācerrimo-);
19. fortissimus (st. fortissimo-);
20. audācissimus (st. audācissimo-);
21. sapientissimus (st. sapientissimo-);

jūstissimē, *most justly*.
līberrimē, *most freely*.
pulcherrimē, *most beautifully*.
ācerrimē, *most sharply*.
fortissimē, **most** *bravely*.
audācissimē, *most boldly*.
sapientissimē, **most** *wisely*.

144 ADVERBS: FORMATION AND COMPARISON.

499. Observation and Inference: Note that the *adverbs* formed from *adjectives* of the *second* and *first declensions* (Exs. 1-3, positive, and Exs. 15-21, superlative) end in -ē; and that these adverbs may be formed from the *stem* of the *adjective* by changing the *final stem vowel* to -ē.[1]

Note, further, that adverbs formed from the *positive* of *adjectives* of the *third declension* (see Exs. 4-7) may be obtained by adding the suffix -ter to the *stem* of the *adjective*.[2]

Note, finally, that the *comparative* of an adverb formed from an adjective (see Exs. 8-14) is the *neuter singular accusative* of the *comparative* of the *adjective* used adverbially.

Frame rules for forming the Positive, Comparative, and Superlative of Adverbs from the corresponding Adjectives.

500. References for Verification: A. & G. 148, *a, b, d*; H. 304, II., 2, IV., 306; G. 90, 1, 2, 4.

501. Form adverbs from the following adjectives and compare them: **indīgnus,** *unworthy;* studiōsus, *eager;* miser, *wretched;* **celer,** *quick, swift;* gravis, *heavy;* brevis, *brief;* vehemēns, *violent;* **prūdēns,** *sagacious;* fēlīx, *happy.*

502. Account for the form of the following adverbs: facile, *easily;* multum, *much;* plūrimum, *very much, exceedingly;* postrēmum, *finally;* crēbrō, *frequently;* paulō, *by a little, a little;* ūnā, *in company, together;* quā, *where:* A. & G. 148, *d, e*; H. 304, I., II.; G. 90, 3, 4.

503. Compare: **diū,** *long* (in time); **saepe,** *often;* bene, *well;* male, *ill:* A. & G. 92; H. 306, 2, 4; G. 91.

504.   EXERCISES.

I. 1. Celeriter concilium dīmittit, Liscum retinet; quaerit ex sōlō ea quae in conventū dīxerat; dīcit līberius atque audācius. 2. Persequāmur eōrum mortem quī indīgnissimē interiērunt.³ **3.** Belgae ā cultū atque hūmānitāte prōvinciae longissimē absunt, minimēque ad eōs mercātōrēs saepe commeant. **4.** Omnēs ācerrimē fortissimēque pūgnābant. 5. Omnia quae absunt vehementius hominum mentēs **perturbant.**

II. 1. They were able⁴ to use their swords more easily. **2.** Galba was-not-disposed⁵ to try fortune further.⁶ 3. Having assembled the leaders of the Aedui, he took them severely to task. 4. They knew that he had done in a single day what⁷ they had accomplished with the utmost difficulty in twenty days. 5. The-battle-was-carried-on⁸ with the greatest energy. 6. The enemy broke through the midst [of **them]** with the greatest boldness. 7. The army must **be more widely** distributed.

505. Supplementary Exercises.

I. 1. Caesar amīcissimē dē vōbīs et illī gravissimē jūdicāvērunt. 2. Lēgātī dīxērunt Aeduōs omnī tempore dē populō Rōmānō bene meritōs esse. 3. Equitēs cupidius novissimum agmen insecūtī sunt. 4. Pūblicē māximam putan**t esse** laudem quam lātissimē ā suīs fīnibus vacāre agrōs.

II. 1. Darts could⁴ not be thrown very easily⁹ from the lower position, and [those] cast by **the** Gauls fell with greater force.¹⁰ 2. Dumnorix was especially popular with¹¹ the common people.

---

¹ Adverbs in -ē were originally ablative forms.
² But stems in -nt- drop -t- before -ter.
³ Perf. Indic. 3d pl. of **intereō**, *perish*.
⁴ **poterant**.
⁵ **nōlēbat**.
⁶ Comparative of **saepe**.
⁷ " what " = *that which*.
⁸ **pūgnābātur**.
⁹ **satis commodē**.
¹⁰ Translate: *more heavily*.
¹¹ " popular with " = *acceptable to*.

LESSON LXVI.

ABLATIVE: SEPARATION AND WANT.

506.　　　　　　**EXAMPLES.**

1. [Marius] bis Italiam **obsidiōne līberāvit** (Cic. *Cat.* 4, 10, 21), *Marius twice relieved Italy from siege.*
2. Vōs Sulpicium vītā prīvāstis (Cic. *Phil.* 9, **4**, **8**), [it is] *you* [who] *have deprived Sulpicius of life.*
3. Eō errōre careō (Cic. *Lael.* 3, 10), *I am free from that error.*
4. Sed nōn egeō medicīnā (Cic. *Lael.* 3, 10), *but I need no medicine.*
5. Iter ab Arare Helvētiī āverterant (1, 16, 3), *the Helvetians had turned their line of march away from the Arar.*
6. Proeliō abstinēbat (1, 22, 3), *he held off from battle.*
7. **Hannibal ex Italiā dēcēdere** coāctus est (Cic. *Cat.* 4, 10, 21), *Hannibal was forced to withdraw from Italy.*
8. Helvētiī **hōc cōnātū dēstitērunt** (1. 8, 4), *the Helvetians desisted from this attempt.*
9. Ēgredere ex urbe (Cic. *Cat.* 1, 8, 20), *depart from the city.*
10. Hostēs proeliō excēdēbant (3, 4, 3), *the enemy withdrew from the fight.*

507. OBSERVATION AND INFERENCE: Note that each of the foregoing illustrations contains a verb expressing *separation*, and that this verb is construed with the *ablative*.

Is the ablative in Exs. 1–4, used *with* or *without* a *preposition?* With what **classes of** verbs, then, does the Ablative of Separation omit the preposition?

With what prepositions are the verbs of separation in Exs. 5–10 compounded? Note that the *ablatives* construed with these compound verbs in Exs. 5, 7, and 9 *have a preposition;* whereas the *ablatives* in Exs. 6, 8, and 10 *have no preposition.* What explanation of this difference can you suggest?

Frame rules for the use or the omission of the Preposition with the Ablative of Separation.

508. REFERENCES FOR VERIFICATION: A. & G. 243, *a, b*; H. 414, I., 413, n. 3; G. 388 (both paragraphs).

ABLATIVE: SEPARATION AND WANT. 147

509. EXAMPLES.

1. **Gubernātōre** opus est (Liv. 24, 8), *there is need of a pilot.*
2. **Auctōritāte** tuā nōbīs opus est (Cic. Fam. 9, 25, 3), *we have need* (there is to us need) *of your authority.*
3. **Factō** opus est (Sall. Cat. 1, 6), *there is need of action.*
4. **Mātūrātō** opus est (Liv. 8, 13, 17), *there is need of hastening.*

510. OBSERVATION AND INFERENCE: By what *case* is the *person* or *thing needed* expressed with **opus** in the foregoing examples (see **gubernātōre, auctōritāte, factō,** and **mātūrātō**)? By what *case* is the *person needing* expressed (see **nōbīs** in Ex. 2)? Note that the *thing needed* is expressed in Exs. 3 and 4 by the *perfect passive participle* (see **factō** and **mātūrātō**). What constructions, then, are used with **opus**?

511. REFERENCES FOR VERIFICATION: A. & G. 243, *e*; H. 414, IV., n. 2, n. 3; G. 390.

512. EXERCISES.

I. 1. Flūmen Rhodanus prōvinciam nostram ab Helvētiīs dīvidit. 2. Ēgredere **ex** urbe, Catilīna, līberā rem pūblicam metū. 3. Huic trādita urbs est, nūda praesidiō.[1] 4. Magistrātibus igitur opus est, sine quōrum **prūdentiā esse** cīvitās **nōn** potest. 5. Factō, nōn cōnsultō, in tālī perīculō opus est. 6. Helvētiī, eā spē dējectī, hōc cōnātū dēstitērunt. 7. Complūrēs diēs frūmentō mīlitēs carent.[2] 8. Ūna centuria facta est immūnis mīlitiā.[1] 9. Hunc ā tuīs ārīs arcēbis.

II. 1. The charioteers, meanwhile, gradually withdrew from the battle. 2. We shall live without anxiety and fear, and shall free mind and body from trouble. 3. The orator has need of a mind [that **is**] free[1] from envy and all vices. 4. **They threatened Caesar** with the **sword** [as he was] coming **out** from the senate. 5. It is a great undertaking **and** requires no (**nōn**) slight practice. 6. There is no need **of** deliberation.[3]

---

[1] A. & G. 243, *d*; H. 414, III.; G. 388 (end).
[2] cf. Lesson XXI., foot-note 5.
[3] cf. sent. 5, preceding exercise.

LESSON LXVII.

Ablatives: Source and Cause.

Ablative of Source.

513. EXAMPLES.

1. **Pīsō amplissimō genere nātus** (4, 12, 4), *Piso, born of a very illustrious family.*
2. **Eā familiā ortum** (Sall. *Cat.* 31, 7), *descended from such a family.*
3. **Is Ascanius, quācumque mātre genitus** (Liv. 1, 3, 3), *this Ascanius, of whatever mother born* . . .

514. OBSERVATION AND INFERENCE: Note that the *perfect participles* in the foregoing illustrations express *birth* or *origin*. How is *source* denoted in connection with these participles? Frame a rule for this construction.

515. REFERENCES FOR VERIFICATION: **A. & G. 244, a;** H. 415, II.; G. 395.

Ablative of Cause.

516. EXAMPLES.

1. **Caesar beneficiīs māgnus habēbātur** (Sall. *Cat.* 54, 2), *Caesar was considered great because of his benefactions.*
2. **Ipsā vacuitāte omnis molestiae gaudēmus** (Cic. *Fin.* 1, 11, 37), *we take pleasure in the mere absence of all annoyance.*

517. OBSERVATION AND INFERENCE: What do the *ablatives* in the foregoing examples express? Frame a rule for these and similar Ablatives.

518. REFERENCES FOR VERIFICATION: A. & G. 245; H. 416; G. 407.

519. EXERCISES.

I. 1. Mithridātēn[1] rēgiō genere ortum, rēgem cōnstituit.
2. Helvētiī suā victōriā īnsolenter glōriābantur.   3. Alter

est Cotus, antīquissimā familiā **nātus atque** ipse homo **summae** potentiae. 4. **Eārum rērum memoriā** māgnam sibī auctōritātem in rē mīlitārī sūmēbant. 5. Reperiēbat plērōsque Belgās esse ortōs ab[2] Germānīs. 6. Gubernātōris **ars** ūtilitāte laudātur.

II. 1. Catiline made a boast of his vices. 2. Lycomedes, descended from a royal race, laid claim to this priestly dignity. 3. He had said this at the bidding of his master. 4. Lucius Catiline, [who was] **born of a noble** family, was **of** great vigor both of mind and **of body.** 5. Cato was commended for his steadfastness. 6. **This** happened because of the inexperience of the enemy, and the valor of the soldiers.

---

[1] **Greek accusative of** Mithridātēs, -is, m., *Mithridates.*

[2] A. & G. 244, *a*, Rem.; H. 415, II., note; G. 395 (end).

520. Supplementary Exercises on Lessons LXVI. and LXVII.

I. 1. Pars castrōrum nūdāta dēfēnsōribus **premī** vidēbātur. 2. Ex essedīs dēsiliunt et pedibus proeliantur. 3. Quid[1] mihī aut vītā aut cīvitāte opus est,[1] quam **beneficiō** Caesaris habēre vidēbor? 4. Omnium rērum nātūrā cōgnitā levāmur superstitiōne, līberāmur mortis metū. 5. Tantummodo inceptō opus est.

II. 1. Among these was Piso, an Aquitanian, born of a very illustrious family. 2. Why should anybody suppose[2] that this [man] will withdraw from his allegiance? 3. When a violent tempest arises,[3] then there is need of a man and a pilot. 4. Catiline withdrew **from the** city because of his fear of the consul. 5. Labienus, having **seized** the mountain, was waiting for our men and holding **off** from battle.

---

[1] **Quid** (adv. acc.) **mihī opus est,** *what need have I?*

[2] What mood? See **493,** Ex. 3.

[3] Use the perfect tense.

LESSON LXVIII.

IRREGULAR VERB: **Possum.** — IMPERSONAL USE OF INTRANSITIVE VERBS IN THE PASSIVE.

521. Learn the composition, inflection, and synopsis of **possum**, *be able, can:* A. & G. 120, *b*; H. 290, II., notes 1, 2, 1), 2), 3); G. 115.

522. EXAMPLES.

1. **Ācriter pūgnātum est** (1, 50, 2), *the fight was vigorously maintained.*
2. **Dictō pārētur** (Liv. 9, 32, 4), *the order is obeyed* (obedience is rendered to the order).
3. **Huic reī subventum est ā nōbīs** (Cic. *Att.* 1, 17, 9), *I supported this proposition* (to this thing support was given by us).
4. **Hūc concurritur** (7, 84, 2), *they make for this point in a body* (a general rush is made).

523. OBSERVATION AND INFERENCE: Note that the verbs in the foregoing illustrations are *intransitive*, i.e., they do not take a direct object in the active voice. How are they used in the *passive?* **What**, then, is the *gender* of the *participle* in the compound tenses of the passive (see Exs. 1 and 3; cf. also **317**, Exs. 3 and 4)? In **the case** of intransitive verbs that govern the *dative* (*e.g.*, **pāreō**, **obey**, **subveniō**, *support*), is this dative *changed* in the passive, or is it *retained* (see Exs. 2 and 3)? Frame a rule for the use of Intransitive Verbs in the Passive.

524. REFERENCES FOR VERIFICATION: A. & G. 146, *c*; H. 301, 1; G. 199, Rem. 1, 208.

525. EXERCISES.

I. 1. Tōtīus Galliae[1] plūrimum Helvētiī possunt. 2. Sed Caesar, ubī ad eum ventum est, haec verba locūtus est. 3. Quam māximīs **potest** itineribus in Galliam ūlteriōrem contendit. 4. Labiēnus, ut erat ēī praeceptum ā Caesare, **proeliō** abstinēbat. 5. Hīs persuādēre **nōn** poterant. 6. Hīs persuādērī nōn poterat. 7. Neque **hostibus** nocētur. 8. Mihī profectō poterit īgnōscī. 9. Nōbīs parum crēdēbātur. 10. Intellegēs quid invictī Germānī virtūte possint.[2] 11. Quid hostis virtūte posset,[2] perīclitābātur.

II. 1. He demands of the **whole province** the largest possible[3] number of soldiers. 2. **He says that** he cannot[4] grant any one a passage **through the province.** 3. He had very little influence[5] **owing to his youth.** 4. I am believed. 5. Why am **I** envied? 6. **I am** convinced that he will not reject my friendship. 7. The ships of the enemy could **not** be injured.[6] 8. He shows what the discipline **and resources** of the Roman people have been able [to effect]. 9. Those with whom they had come up[7] made a stand.

526.   Supplementary Exercises.

I. 1. Pūgnātur ūnō tempore omnibus locīs; **quae minimē vīsa** pars firma est, hūc concurritur. 2. Caesar intellēxit **neque hostium** fugam reprimī neque iīs nocērī **posse.** 3. Sēsē nē vultum[8] quidem Germānōrum dīcēbant ferre[9] **potuisse.** 4. Id oppidum ex itinere oppūgnāre cōnātus, propter **mūrī** altitūdinem expūgnāre nōn potuit.

II. 1. He inquired of them **what** communities were in arms, and what was their strength[10] in **war.** 2. For they had learned that the enemy's ships could not be damaged[11] by the beak. 3. A rush was made to-that-point[12] from the nearest redoubts, and the fight was maintained desperately by the enemy.

---

[1] A. & G. 216, a, 2; H. 307, 3; G. 371.
[2] Account for **mood and** tense.
[3] cf. sent. 3 **of the** preceding exercise.
[4] "He, says **that** he cannot" = he denies that he can.
[5] Translate: was able very little.
[6] cf. sent. 6, preceding exercise.
[7] Translate: Those to whom it **had** been come.

[8] Note that with nē ... quidem the emphatic word is placed **between nē** and quidem.
[9] Present infinitive of ferō.
[10] "what was their strength" = what they could.
[11] cf. preceding **exercise, sent.** 2.
[12] eō.

LESSON LXIX.

IRREGULAR VERBS: **Volō, Nōlō, Mālō.** — SUBJUNCTIVE IN FINAL CLAUSES (CLAUSES OF PURPOSE).

527. Learn the inflection and synopsis of **volō**, *wish, be willing;* **nōlō**, *be unwilling;* **mālō**, *wish rather:* A. & G. 138, 1, 2, 3; H. 293 with note 2; G. 189.

528. EXAMPLES.

1. Nōnnūllī, ut suspīciōnem vītārent, remanēbant (1, 39, 3), *some stayed to escape* (that they might escape) *suspicion.*
2. **Nē exīre posset**, valvās obstrūxērunt (Nep. Paus. 5, 2), *they barricaded the doors that he might not get out.*
3. **Virgultīs conlēctīs, quibus fossās compleant**, pergunt (3, 18, 8), *having gathered brushwood with which to fill* (that with it they may fill) *the trenches, they proceed.*
4. Praesidia dispōnit, quō facilius [Helvētiōs] **prohibēre possit** (1, 8, 2), *he establishes garrisons at intervals, that* (thereby) *he may the more easily keep off the Helvetians.*

529. OBSERVATION AND INFERENCE: Note that the dependent clauses in the foregoing examples express *purpose.* Clauses expressing purpose are called *Final Clauses.* What *mood* is used in final clauses? Is the final clause in Ex. 1 *affirmative* or *negative?* What *particle* introduces it? Answer the same questions for the final clause in Ex. 2. Note that the final clause in Ex. 3 is introduced by the *relative pronoun* **quibus**, and that **quibus** is equivalent in meaning to **ut eīs**. Note that the final clause in Ex. 4 contains a *comparative* (**facilius**); by what word is this final clause introduced? Frame rules (1) for the Mood and (2) for the Introductory Word to be used in Final Clauses.

530. REFERENCES FOR VERIFICATION: A. & G. 317, *b*; H. 497, I., II., 1 (first sentence), 2 (first sentence); G. 543, 1 (first sentence), 2, 545, 1, 2, 3.

NOTE: The sequence of tenses in dependent subjunctive clauses has already been illustrated and explained (see Lesson LV.).

FINAL CLAUSES.

531.   EXERCISES.

I. 1. Sī pāce ūtī vultis, inīquum est dē stīpendiō recūsāre.
2. Caesar omnium ex cōnspectū remōvit equōs, **ut spem fugae
tolleret.**   3. Nōlī exīstimāre hunc esse exercitum.   4. Nē
commeātū prohibērētur, ūltrā eum locum castrīs idōneum
locum dēlēgit.   5. Praestō erat ille, quī fugientīs exciperet.
6. Ab hīs quaerēbat cūr **bellum** quam pācem māluissent.
7. Quō barbarōs facilius **repellerent,** classēs aedificārunt[1]
exercitūsque comparārunt.[1]

II. 1. What **do you mean ?**[2]   2. **Cato chooses** rather
to submit than **to fight.**   3. **On** (in) making inquiry, he
learned for **(dē) what reasons** Ariovistus was unwilling to
treat with Caesar.   4. They sent[3] envoys to Dumnorix,
that at **his** intercession[4] they might obtain[5] their request
from **the** Sequani.   5. He was at hand to effect a junction[6]
with the leaders in-the-city.   6. He endeavored to keep **the
forces of the enemy apart, that it might not be necessary to
fight**[7] with so great a multitude at **once.**   7. **In order to
retard**[8] Caesar's attack more effectually, **he** barricaded[3] **the
gates.**

532.   **Supplementary Exercises.**

I. 1. Equitātum **omnem** praemittit, quī[8] videant[5] quās in partēs
hostēs iter faciant.[5]   2. Nōluit **eum** locum vacāre.   3. Quae
vellet ostendit.   4. **Omnia** permiscērī māvultis quam exercitūs
dīmittere.   5. Omnīs ālāriōs in cōnspectū hostium cōnstituit, ut
ad speciem ūterētur.   6. Quāle praemium Miltiadī sit tribūtum
docēbō, **quō** facilius intellegī possit quae omnium cīvitātum sit
nātūra.   7. Ille etiam grave tum vulnus accēpit, nē quid dē
summā rē pūblicā dēminuerētur.

II. 1. Do not force these [men] to do without your aid.[9]   2. **He**
wishes to discuss[10] with you matters of the highest interest to
[you] both.[11]   3. He ordered **them** to open **the maniples,** that
they might more easily use their swords.   4. **Caesar** places in
command of the legion a lieutenant, that the individual soldiers[12]

may have him as a witness of their valor.   5. He explained why Cato had chosen rather to submit than to fight.   6. They sent[3] envoys to him to say[5] that it was their intention[13] to march without [committing any] depredation.   7. He barricaded[8] the gates that the soldiers might not break[5] into the town.

---

[1] cf. Lesson XXXIV., foot-note 2.
[2] " What do you mean? " = *what do you wish for yourself?*
[3] Use the historical present, see: A. & G. 276, *d*; H. 467, III.; G. 220.
[4] **Translate:** *he* [being] *intercessor.*
[5] For tense, see: A. & G. 287, *e*; H. 495, II.; G. 511, Rem. 1.
[6] " to effect a junction " = *who should unite himself.*
[7] Use cōnflīgō impersonally in the **passive** periphrastic conjugation.

[8] cf. Lesson L., foot-note 3.
[9] Translate · *Be unwilling* (cf. 531, I., sent. 3) *to rob these of your aid.*
[10] agere dē.
[11] " matters of the highest interest to you both " = *the greatest things of each.*
[12] " the individual **soldiers** " = *each one.*
[13] " that it was their intention " = *that it was to themselves in mind.*

LESSON LXX.

Irregular Verbs: Ferō, Eō. — Complementary Final Clauses.

533. Learn the inflection and synopsis of ferō, *bear*, and eō, *go:* A. & G. 139, 141; H. 292, 2, 295; G. 186, 185.

534.   EXAMPLES.

1. **Persuādent Rauricīs utī ūnā cum iīs proficiscantur** (1, 5, 4), *they persuade the Raurici to go with them.*

2. **Ariovistus postulāvit nē quem peditem addūceret** (1, 42, 4), *Ariovistus demanded that he should not bring a single foot-soldier.*

3. **Veritus ut impetum** sustinēre posset, litterās Caesarī remittit (5, 47, 4), *fearing that he might not be able to sustain the attack, he sent back a dispatch to Caesar.*

4. **Nē Divitiacī animum offenderet, verēbātur** (1, 19, 2), *he feared that he might wound the feelings of Divitiacus.*

535. OBSERVATION AND INFERENCE: Note that **the final clauses** in the **foregoing** examples **are** the *direct objects* of the verbs on which they depend, and that they therefore express **purpose** somewhat less obviously than those of the preceding lesson. As they complete the meaning of the verbs whose objects they are, they are called *Complementary Final Clauses*. Note, further, that the verbs on which they depend (see **persuādent**, 1, **postulāvit**, 2, **veritus**, 3, **verēbātur**, 4) denote an *action directed towards the future*. What *class of verbs*, then, do Complementary Final Clauses follow? What Mood do they require? **Frame a rule** for Complementary Final Clauses.

536. REFERENCES **FOR VERIFICATION:** A. & G. 331; H. 498, I., II., III.; G. 546.

537. OBSERVATION AND INFERENCE: Note that, in Exs. 3 and 4. the complementary final clause follows a verb of *fearing* (**veritus**, Ex. 3, **verēbātur**, Ex. 4). How is **ut** (Ex. 3) translated? Is this its *usual* meaning? How is **nē** (Ex. 4) translated? Is this its *usual* meaning? Frame a rule for the use of the Particle after Expressions of Fearing.

538. REFERENCES FOR VERIFICA**TION:** A. & G. 331, *f*; H. 498, III., note 1; G. 552⁵.

539.   **EXERCISES.**

I. 1. Fer mihi **auxilium.** 2. Servitūtem perferre mālunt. 3. In **tabulīs** nōminātim ratiō cōnfecta erat quī numerus domō[1] exīsset[2] eōrum, quī arma ferre possent. **4. Neutrī trānseundī** initium faciunt. 5. Hīs mandāvit ut quae dīceret Ariovistus cōgnōscerent et ad sē referrent. 6. Mulierēs mīlitēs implōrābant nē sē in servitūtem Rōmānīs trāderent. 7. Timēbant nē ab hoste circumvenīrentur. 8. Rem[3] frūmentāriam, ut satis commodē supportārī posset, timēbant. 9. Nōnnūllī Caesarī nūntiārant[2] nōn propter timōrem sīgna lātūrōs mīlitēs. 10. Ego enim ab ineunte aetāte incēnsus sum studiō utrīusque vestrūm.

II. 1. At one time[4] they waged war against [others], at

another⁴ they repelled [it when] waged against [themselves]. 2. One must often incur enmity⁵ for the public welfare. 3. He went away at the beginning of summer.⁶ 4. He warns him to avoid⁷ all grounds of suspicion. 5. They feared that our army might be led against⁸ them. 6. Take care to attach to yourself the aid⁹ **of all** [classes]. 7. He persuades this [man] to go over to the enemy. 8. Caesar thought that he ought to take special precautions¹⁰ lest this should happen. 9. "Lay the matter before the senate," **you say:** I shall not.¹¹ 10. I must return. 11. Go hence!

540. Supplementary Exercises.

I. 1. Rōmānī conversa sīgna bipartītō intulērunt. 2. Is Amūlium rēgem interēmisse fertur. 3. Respondit in eam partem itūrōs atque ibī **futūrōs Helvētiōs.** 4. Sīc eat quaecumque Rōmāna **lūgēbit hostem!**¹² 5. **Allobrogibus imperāvit** ut Helvētiīs frūmentī cōpiam facerent. 6. Eō cōnsiliō domōs¹ suās Helvētiī reliquērunt, **utī tōtī Galliae** bellum īnferrent imperiōque **potīrentur.**¹³ 7. Caesar postulāvit nē Helvētiōs frūmentō nēve aliā rē juvārent.

II. 1. Would **that the** soldiers had passed through without [committing any] depredation! 2. I do not know through whose territory they have **gone.** 3. They betook themselves to the town. 4. They suffer no wine¹⁴ **to** be imported. 5. It is your [duty] to see **that** they do not injure me. 6. They demanded of Ariovistus that **he** should select some place for a conference. 7. There-was-reason-to-fear¹⁵ that they might seem to have been cruel.

---

¹ For declension, see: A. & G. 70, *f*; H. 119, 1; G. 67, Rem. 2.
² A. & G. 128, *a*; H. 235; G. 151, 1.
³ **Rem frūmentāriam, ut ... posset** = Ut rēs frūmentāria ... **posset.** The construction used in the text gives special emphasis to **rem frūmentāriam.**
⁴ **aliās ... aliās,** *at one time ... at another.*
⁵ "One must often incur enmity" = *enmities must often be incurred.*
⁶ Trans.: *summer beginning.*
⁷ In this and similar cases occurring later, the English infinitive is to be translated by *ut* with the subjunctive.
⁸ **addūcō ad.**
⁹ Use the plural.
¹⁰ Use **the** passive impersonally.
¹¹ Trans.: *I shall not lay the matter.*
¹² The **exclamation** of Horatius as he slew his sister: Liv. 1, 26, 4.
¹³ Note that this final clause is in apposition with **eō cōnsiliō.**
¹⁴ "no wine" = *nothing of wine.*
¹⁵ Passive periphrastic.

LESSON LXXI.

IRREGULAR VERB: Fīō. — ABLATIVE OF COMPARISON. — ABLATIVE OF DIFFERENCE.

541. Learn the inflection and synopsis of **fīō**, *be made, become:* A. & G. 142; H. 294; G. 188.

542.   EXAMPLES.

1. { *a.* Quis est **enim quam ego mītior?**
   { *b.* Quis **est enim mē mītior?** (Cic. *Cat.* 4, 6, 11),   } *for who is milder than I?*

2. { *a.* **Docet sē** nihil amplius scīre quam lēgātōs (Sall. *Cat.* 47, 1),
   { *b.* Docet sē nihil amplius scīre lēgātīs,   } *he declares that he knows no more than the envoys.*

3. **Lūce sunt** clāriōra nōbīs tua cōnsilia (Cic. *Cat.* 1, 3, 6), *your schemes are clearer to us than the light.*

4. Celerius omnī opīniōne (2, 3, 1), *more quickly than any one had thought possible* (than all opinion).

543. OBSERVATION AND INFERENCE: Note, in Ex. 1, *a*, that **quam** is *expressed* with the *comparative* mītior, and that ego is in the *nominative;* whereas, in Ex. 1, *b*, quam is *omitted*, and the *nominative* ego **has been** changed to the *ablative* mē. Compare Ex. 2, *a* with Ex. 2, *b;* how has the omission of **quam** affected the *accusative* lēgātōs? Note, further, that **quam** is omitted after the comparative in Exs. 3 and 4; in what *case* are lūce (Ex. 3) and opīniōne (Ex. 4)? By what Case, then, is the Comparative followed **when** quam is omitted? Frame a rule for **this** construction.

544. REFERENCES FOR VERIFICATION: A. & G. 247; H. 417; G. 399.

545.   EXAMPLES.

1. **Hibernia dīmidiō** minor [est] quam Britannia (5, 13, 2), *Ireland is smaller by half than Britain.*

2. **[Patria] mihī vītā meā multō est cārior** (Cic. *Cat.* 1, 11, 27), *my country is far* (by much) *dearer to me than my life*.

3. **Paucīs ante diēbus** (1, 18, 10), *a few days before* (before by a few days).

4. **Quō minus petēbat glōriam, eō magis illa sequēbātur** (Sall. *Cat.* 54, 5), *the less he paid court to glory, the more she followed* [him] (lit., by **what less, by that** more).

546. OBSERVATION AND INFERENCE: Note, in Ex. 1, that the *ablative* **dīmidiō** tells *by how much* Ireland is smaller **than** Britain; in other words, it expresses the *degree of difference* **denoted** by the *comparative* **minor.** Point out the words in the remaining examples which express degree of difference. In what case are they? By what case, then, is Degree of Difference denoted after Comparative expressions? **Frame a** rule for this construction.

547. REFERENCES FOR VERIFICATION: A. & G. 250; H. 423; G. 400.

548.   **EXERCISES.**

I. 1. Dē Caesaris adventū Helvētiī certiōrēs fīunt. 2. Quid fierī velit, ēdocet. 3. Proelium adversum paucīs ante diēbus erat factum. 4. Semprōniae cāriōra omnia quam[1] pudīcitia fuit.[2] 5. Celerius opīniōne exercitum addūcit. 6. Nēmō Rōmānōrum fuit ēloquentior[3] Cicerōne. 7. Multō ego vigilō ācrius ad salūtem quam tū ad perniciem reī pūblicae. 8. Quārē in hostēs impetus nōn fieret, nōndum perspexerat. 9. Quantō vōs attentius ea agētis, tantō illīs animus īnfirmior erit. 10. Fēstīnandō plūs timōris quam perīculī effēcerant.

II. 1. **This** was **at** that time easily **done.** 2. Would that **an attack on**[4] the enemy were in progress. 3. He holds all his **[friends] dear**; me indeed[5] [he holds] dearer than himself.[6] 4. These are under **(in)** arms the year after, those remain at home.[7] 5. The greater the fault is, the severer is the mortification. 6. There-was-in this

DEFECTIVE VERBS: **Ōdī, Coepī, Meminī.** 159

man **no less vanity than** recklessness.⁸   7. He showed what
he **wished** to have done.⁹   8. He accomplished less than
he **had** anticipated.¹⁰   9. That is much more to be feared.

549.   Supplementary Exercises.

I. 1. Crēbrī ad eum rūmōrēs adferēbantur, litterīsque item Labiēnī certior fīēbat. 2. In cōnspectum hostium celerius opiniōne eōrum exercitum addūcit. 3. Eārum rērum ā nostrīs fīet nihil. 4. Bellī spolia māgnifica magis quam¹ ōrātiō mea vōs hortantur. 5. Carīnae **aliquantō** plāniōrēs sunt quam nostrārum nāvium. 6. Quō **dēlīctum mājus est, eō poena** est tardior.

II. 1. **These [reports] which are talked of** are less [important] than is generally **supposed.**¹¹ 2. [Those] who had advanced a little **too far for the purpose of** seeking [materials for] an embankment,¹² had¹³ **to** be sent for. 3. The immortal gods seemed to foreshadow these things which are now taking place. 4. The **safety** of my fellow citizens has always been dearer to me than **my** own life.⁸ 5. He has not yet learned what is in progress.

---

¹ Rewrite this sent. omitting **quam.**
² **tuit** here follows the number of the nearer substantive **pudīcitia** rather than that of the more remote **omnia.**
³ Rewrite this sent. introducing **quam.**
⁴ **In** with accusative.
⁵ **quidem;** it follows the **word which** it emphasizes.
⁶ Use the reflexive **sē** with **ipse.**
⁷ *at home,* **domī.**
⁸ Express in two **ways.**
⁹ cf. 548, I., sent. **2.**
¹⁰ *less than his own expectation.*
¹¹ **Translate:** *less than opinion.*
¹² cf. **386,** I., sent. 1.
¹³ cf. examples in **317.**

LESSON LXXII.

DEFECTIVE VERBS: Ōdī, Coepī, Meminī. — VERBS OF MEMORY.

550. Learn the inflection and synopsis, with meanings, of **coepī,** *I began;* **ōdī,** *I hate;* meminī, *I remember:* A. & G. 143, *a, b, c,* **note;** H. 297, 1., 2; G. 190, 5.

551.   **EXAMPLES.**

1. Vīvŏrum meminī (Cic. *Fin.* 5, 1, 3), *I keep the living in mind.*
2. Meminī, neque **unquam** oblīviscar **noctis** illīus (Cic. *Planc.* 42, 101), *I remember, nor shall I ever forget that night.*
3. Aliī, reminiscentēs veteris fāmae (Nep. *Phoc.* 4, 1), *others, recalling his early fame.*
4. Recordor nōn L. Brūtum sed legiōnēs **nostrās** (Cic. *Cat. Maj.* 20, 74), *I call to mind not Lucius Brutus, but our legions.*
5. Omnia meminērunt (Cic. *Cat. Maj.* 7, 21), *they remember everything.*
6. **Num** illa oblītus est (Cic. *Ac.* 2, 33, 106), *did he forget those things?*
7. **Ea reminiscere** (Cic. *Fam.* 4, 5, 5), *recall these things.*
8. **Id saepe sum** recordātus (Cic. *Att.* 8, 12, 5), *I have often recalled it.*

552. OBSERVATION AND INFERENCE: By what *cases* may verbs of *remembering* and *forgetting* be followed (see foregoing examples)? What seems to be the *regular* construction with **recordor** (see Exs. 4 and 8)? What case regularly follows verbs of remembering and forgetting when the thing remembered or forgotten is expressed by a *neuter adjective* or *pronoun* (see Exs. 5–8)? What seems to be the construction after **meminī, oblīviscor**, and **reminiscor** when the object remembered is *not* expressed by a *neuter adjective* or *pronoun* (see Exs. 1–3)? Frame rules embodying these observations.

553. REFERENCES FOR VERIFICATION: A. & G. 219 and Rem. (last sentence); H. 406, II., 407, note 1; G. 375, Rem. 2.

554.   **EXERCISES.**

I. 1. Semper in cīvitāte quibus[1] opēs nūllae sunt vetera ōdēre, nova exoptant. 2. Helvētiī proeliō nostrōs lacessere coepērunt. 3. Mementō meī. 4. Reminiscere veteris incommodī populī Rōmānī. 5. Plērīque mortālēs, sceleris oblītī, dē poenā disserunt. 6. Eās rēs reminiscī et recordārī videntur. 7. In mūrum lapidēs jacī coeptī sunt.[2] 8. Intellegēbat **omnēs** hominēs condiciōnem servitūtis ōdisse. 9. Quam multa meminērunt augurēs! 10. Probātūrus sum vōbīs dēfēnsiōnem meam sī id memineritis, quod oblīvisci

ILLUSTRATIVE EXERCISES.

nōn potestis. 11. Mēns mea pueritiae memoriam **recordātur** ūltimam. 12. Cōnstantiae tuae meminī.

II. 1. I entreat you to remember these **things**. 2. It is not becoming either[3] to exercise partiality or[3] to cherish hatred. 3. They began to follow and **attack our men** in (ā) the rear. 4. A great quantity **of** dust began[2] **to be** seen. 5. Remember (pl.) us. 6. I cannot forget the old indignity. 7. Recall to **mind** the ancient valor of the Helvetians. 8. When I **reflect on** all the stages of your life, I do not see at what **period you learned** those things. 9. He favors the **Helvetians,** [but] hates Caesar. 10. Turn your thoughts from[4] slaughter and conflagrations. 11. He forgets nothing but[5] injuries. 12. He recalled the bitter experience of an earlier time. 13. I call to mind[6] not the two Decii, not the two Scipios, — but our own legions.

555.   Supplementary Exercises.

I. 1. Eundem Achillam,[7] cūjus suprā meminimus, **omnibus** cōpiīs praefēcit. 2. Atque ego, quī omnia officiō mētior, recordor tamen tua cōnsilia. 3. Cum aliquō **dolōre flāgitiōrum**[8] suōrum recordābitur. 4. Plērīque mortālēs **postrēma** meminēre, et in hominibus impiīs sceleris **eōrum** oblītī dē **poenā** disserunt, sī ea paulō sevērior fuit. 5. **Parum** ōdisse malōs cīvēs vidētur.

II. 1. I forget for-the-moment[9] your injuries, Clodia. 2. The mind remembers the past, sees the present, foresees the future. 3. He exhorted the Aeduans to forget disputes and disagreement. 4. They began by putting to death[10] all the worst[11] without trial.

---

[1] cf. 393 and 394.
[2] A. & G. 143, a (second line); H. 297, 1; G. 190, 5 (end).
[3] Trans. *it is becoming neither . . . nor*.
[4] "turn your thoughts from" = *forget*.
[5] "nothing but" = *nothing unless*.
[6] **recordor**.

[7] For declension, see **Aenēās (or Leōnidās)**: A. & G. 37; H. 50; G. 72.
[8] Is this the *usual* construction **with** recordor?
[9] jam.
[10] Trans. *They at first began to put to death*.
[11] "all the worst" = *each worst*; cf. Lesson LVII., foot-note 3.

LESSON LXXIII.

Subjunctive in Consecutive Clauses (Clauses of Result).

556. EXAMPLES.

1. Ita mē gessī ut omnēs cōnservārēminī (Cic. *Cat.* 3, 10, 25), *I so conducted my administration that you were all saved.*
2. Ita repente prōcurrērunt ut spatium nōn darētur (1, 52, 3), *they ran forward so suddenly that no time was allowed.*
3. **Quis** est tam lyncēus quī in tantīs tenebrīs nihil offendat (Cic. *Fam.* 9, 2, 2), *who is so sharp-sighted as not to stumble amid such darkness* (that he would not stumble, etc.).
4. Quae rēs, commeātūs **ut ad eum** portārī possent, efficiēbat (2, 5, 5), *this movement rendered it possible for supplies to be brought to him* (brought it about that supplies could, etc.).
5. Eādem nocte accidit ut **esset lūna plēna** (4, 29, 1), *on the same night it chanced that it was full moon.*

557. Observation and Inference: Note that the dependent clauses in Exs. 1–3 express *consequence* or *result*. Such clauses are called *Consecutive Clauses*, or *Clauses of Result*. What *mood* is used in consecutive clauses? Is the consecutive clause in Ex. 1 *affirmative* or *negative?* What *particle* introduces it? Answer the same questions for the consecutive clause in Ex. 2. Is the negative particle of the consecutive clause the same as that of the *final clause* (see **528, Ex.** 2)? Note that the consecutive clause in Ex. 3 is introduced by the *relative pronoun* (quī), and that quī is here equivalent in meaning to **ut is**. Frame a rule for the Mood and the **Introductory Word to be used in** Consecutive Clauses.

558. References for Verification A. & G. 319 and *a* (first sentence); **II.** 500, I., II., G. 554.

559. Observation and Inference: Note that the consecutive clause of Ex. 4 is the *direct object* of the verb (**efficiēbat**) on which it depends, and that the latter is a verb denoting the *accom-*

plishment of an effort. What *class* of verbs, then, do Object Clauses of Result follow? What Mood do they require? Frame **a** rule for Object Clauses of Result.

560. REFERENCES FOR VERIFICATION: A. & G. 332; H. 501, II., 1; G. 557.

561. OBSERVATION AND INFERENCE: Note that the consecutive clause of Ex. 5 is the *subject* of the *impersonal verb* **accidit.** With what *class* of verbs, **then,** are Subject Clauses of Result found? What Mood do they require? Frame a rule for Subject Clauses of Result.

562. REFERENCES **FOR** VERIFICATION: A. & G. 332, *a*; H. 501, I., 1; G. **558.**

563.   EXERCISES.

I. 1. Quis potest esse tam āversus ā vērō quī neget haec omnia quae vidēmus? 2. Tantus timor exercitum occupāvit ut omnium mentēs animōsque perturbāret. 3. Fīēbat **ut** minus facile fīnitimīs bellum īnferre possent. 4. Nōn **tam** imperītus sum rērum ut nōn sciam Aeduōs Rōmānīs auxilium nōn tulisse. 5. Verbōrum obscūritās facit ut nōn intellegātur **rēs.** 6. Fortūna vestra facit ut īrae meae temperem. 7. Illae tamen omnēs dissēnsiōnēs erant ējusmodī[1] quae nōn ad dēlendam, sed commūtandam rem pūblicam pertinērent. 8. Aliquot dē causīs acciderat ut Gallī bellī renovandī cōnsilium caperent. 9. Tanta rērum commūtātiō est facta ut nostrī proelium redintegrārent.

II. 1. Sabinus gave ground for so-strong-a[2] suspicion of his cowardice that the enemy dared to come **up** even[3] to **the** rampart **of** the camp. 2. Nor am I so iron-hearted as not to be affected.[4] 3. Ariovistus had assumed such arrogance that he seemed insufferable.[5] 4. The-result-will-be[6] **that** the enemy will escape danger by their swiftness. 5. The obscurity of the subject[7] causes the language not to be understood.[8] 6. So stealthily did they glance at one another[9]

that they seemed to betray themselves by-their-own-actions.[10]
7. The Aeduans have deserved so [well] of (dē) the Roman people that their towns ought not to be assaulted.

564. **Supplementary Exercises.**

I. 1. Ējusmodī[1] sunt tempestātēs cōnsecūtae utī sub pellibus mīlitēs continērī nōn possent. 2. Nēmō enim est tam senex quī sē annum nōn putet posse vīvere. 3. Hostēs tantam virtūtem praestitērunt ut ex jacentium corporibus pūgnārent.

II. 1. And it so happened that out of so large[2] a number not a single ship[11] was missing.[12] 2. We are not **persons of such incredulity that**[13] **nothing** seems to us[13] true. 3. And so, although twelve ships had been lost,[14] he rendered it possible for the voyage to be made[15] **well enough with the rest.**

---

[1] *of such a kind, such:* A. & G. 215, a; H. 396, V., n. 1; G. 364.
[2] **tantus.**
[3] **jam.**
[4] Translate: *that I am not affected.*
[5] Translate: *did not seem sufferable.*
[6] cf. 563, I., sent. 3.
[7] Use rēs in plural.
[8] Translate: *causes that the language is not understood.*
[9] Translate: *among themselves.*
[10] Use **ipse** in app. with the subject.
[11] "not a single ship" = *no ship at all.*
[12] "was missing" = *was missed.*
[13] "persons of such incredulity that to us" = *those to whom.*
[14] Ablative absolute.
[15] Translate: *caused that it could be sailed;* use **nāvigō** impersonally in the passive.

LESSON LXXIV.

Subjunctive in Clauses Introduced by Quōminus and Quīn.

565. **EXAMPLES.**

1. Tē īnfirmitās valētūdinis tuae tenuit **quō minus venīrēs** (Cic. *Fam.* 7, 1, 1), *the feebleness of your health kept you from coming* (so that thereby [quō = ut eō] you came less)
2. Neque **illīs superbia** obstābat quō minus aliēna īnstitūta imitārentur (Sall. *Cat.* 51, 37), *neither did pride prevent them from imitating foreign institutions.*

566. OBSERVATION AND INFERENCE: Note that the dependent clauses in the foregoing examples are introduced by **quō minus**. What mood do they take (see **venīrēs**, Ex. 1, and **imitārentur**, Ex. 2)? Note also that the verbs on which these clauses depend (**tenuit**, Ex. 1, and **obstābat**, Ex. 2) are verbs of *hindering*. Frame a rule for the Mood to be used in clauses like the foregoing.

567. REFERENCES FOR VERIFICATION: A. & G. 319, *c*; H. 505, II., 1; G. 549.

568. EXAMPLES.

1. Nēmō est tam fortis **quīn reī novitāte** perturbētur (6, 39, 3), *no one is so brave as not to be disconcerted by the unexpectedness of the situation.*
2. **Quis est quīn** contendat (Sall. Jug. 4, 7), *who is there who does not contend?*
3. Retinērī nōn potuerant quīn tēla conicerent (1, 47, 2), *it had not been possible to restrain them from throwing darts* (lit., they had not been able to be restrained, etc.).
4. Nōn dubitābat quīn summissiōrēs essent futūrae (8, 31, 2), *he had no doubt that they would be more submissive.*
5. Nūllum tempus intermīsērunt quīn lēgātōs mitterent (5, 55, 1), *they let no occasion pass without sending ambassadors.*
6. Facere nōn possum **quīn** cottīdiē ad tē mittam (Cic. Att. 12, 27, 2), *I cannot help writing to you every day.*

569. OBSERVATION AND INFERENCE: Note that the consecutive clauses in the foregoing examples are introduced by **quīn**, and that the leading clause in each example contains a *negative expression*. Note, further, that the *negative expression* of the leading clause is: a *general negative* (**nēmō**) in Ex. 1; an *interrogative implying a negative* in Ex. 2 (quis est = nēmō est); a negative expression of *hindering* (retinērī nōn potuerant) in Ex. 3; a negative expression of *doubting* (nōn dubitābat) in Ex. 4; **and** a negative expression of *omitting* or *refraining* (nūllum ... intermīsērunt and facere nōn possum) in Exs. 5 and 6. Frame a rule, or rules, for the use of **quīn** with the Subjunctive in Consecutive **Clauses.**

570. References for Verification: A. & G. 319, *d*; H. 504; G. 550, 551.

571.   **EXERCISES.**

I. 1. Nēmō est quīn ubivīs quam ibī ubī est esse mālit. 2. Sed custōdiīs quō[1] **id sine** perīculō minus[1] facerēmus impediēbāmur.   3. Nōn est dubium **quīn** tōtīus Galliae[2] plūrimum Helvētiī possint.   4. **Nōn possunt** mīlitēs continērī quīn in urbem irrumpant urbem**que dēleant.**   5. Neque **abest** suspīciō quīn ipse sibī mortem cōnscīverit. 6. Quis est quīn cernat quanta vīs sit in sēnsibus? 7. **Prohibērī** nōn possumus quō minus cottīdiē aquam petāmus.   8. **Nōn dubitō** quīn probātūrus sim vōbīs **dēfēnsiōnem meam.**   9. Ego nihil praetermīsī quīn Pompējum ā Caesaris conjūnctiōne āvocārem.   10. Nāvēs ventō tenēbantur quō minus in eundem portum venīre possent.

II. 1. **The** enemy endeavored to hinder our men from fleeing for refuge to their camp.   2. We have not[3] **been able** to deter even[3] the Suessiones from conspiring with the **Belgians.**   3. We do not doubt that he will inflict the severest punishment on all the hostages.   4. Nothing is so difficult that it cannot be found out by searching.   5. There is no doubt[4] that the Romans will deprive the Aeduans of freedom.[5] 6. **Nor did he** refuse **to** submit to the penalty of the law. 7. I cannot help[6] declaring to you my opinion.   8. **Who then can doubt**[7] **that [true] wealth** consists in virtue?

572.   **Supplementary Exercises.**

I. 1. Quis est omnium quīn dīvitiīs et sūmptibus, nōn probitāte neque industriā cum mājōribus suīs contendat?   2. Tum vērō dubitandum nōn exīstimāvit quīn ad eōs proficiscerētur 3. Itaque dēterritus nōn est quō minus, prīmā aciē prō vallō instrūctā, reliqua pars exercitūs opus faceret.

II. 1. Rest assured[8] **that** the Romans will wrest liberty from **the Aeduans.**   2. Parmenio wished to deter him from drinking

the drug. 3. Nor do we refuse to remain⁹ forever under your **sway.** 4. **No one** might¹⁰ withdraw from the line of march **without** being cut off by Caesar's cavalry.

---

¹ quō may be separated from minus **by the** intervention of other words.
² See foot-note 1, Lesson LXVIII.
³ See Lesson LXVIII., foot-note 8.
⁴ cf. 571, I., sent. 3.
⁵ Translate: *wrest freedom from* (lit., to) *the Aéduans* (dat.).
⁶ See 568, Ex. 6.
⁷ What mood? See 493, Ex. 3.
⁸ Translate: *be unwilling to doubt*.
⁹ " remain " = *be*.
¹⁰ **Nūllī licēbat.**

LESSON LXXV.

Subjunctive in Relative Clauses of Characteristic.

573. EXAMPLES.

1. Secūtae sunt tempestātēs quae nostrōs in castrīs **continērent** (4, 34, 4), *there ensued storms which* (of such severity that they) *kept our men in camp.*
2. Hōc quī postulāret reperiēbātur nēmō (Caes. B. C. 3, 20, 4), *no one was found who* (so unreasonable that he) *demanded this.*
3. Fuēre quī crēderent (Sal. Cat. 17, 7), *there were some who believed.*
4. Rem idōneam dē quā quaerātur, et hominēs dīgnōs quibuscum disserātur putant (Cic. Ac. 2, 6, 18), *they consider the subject suitable to be inquired into, and the men worthy of being argued with.*

574. OBSERVATION AND INFERENCE: Note that the relative clauses of result in the foregoing examples express some *characteristic* of the antecedent. Thus the relative clause quae ... continuērent (Ex. 1) describes the severity of the storms by saying **that** they kept the men in camp. Note, further, that the relative clause of characteristic follows a *general negative* (nēmō) in Ex. 2, **an** *indefinite* (omitted) *antecedent* in Ex. 3, an antecedent limited by idōneam in Ex. 4, and an antecedent limited by dīgnōs in Ex. 4. In what *mood* **is the verb** of a Relative Clause of Characteristic?

168 RELATIVE CLAUSES OF CHARACTERISTIC.

With what Antecedents are Relative Clauses of Characteristic especially used? Frame a rule embodying these observations.

575. REFERENCES FOR VERIFICATION: A. & G. 320, *a, f*; H. 503, I., II., 2; G. 633, 634.

576. **EXERCISES.**

I. 1. Erant omnīnō itinera duo quibus itineribus domō[1] **exīre** possent. 2. Erant eō tempore quī exīstimārent **indicium** illud ā P. Autrōniō māchinātum.[2] 3. Indignī vōs **estis** quī in meō exercitū ōrdinēs dūcātis. 4. Voluptās est sōla[3] quae nōs vocet ad sē. 5. Neque is sum quī mortis **perīculō terrear.** 6. Repertī sunt mīlitēs quī scūta manibus **revellerent et** dēsuper vulnerārent. 7. Hunc Caesar **idōneum** jūdicāverat quem cum mandātīs mitteret.

II. 1. **Storms followed which prevented the** enemy from fighting. 2. [There] are [persons] here who urge you **to** revolt[4] from us. 3. **He deems Procillus a suitable** [person] to send[5] to Ariovistus. 4. **He** seems to be worthy to command. 5. Nor has any one been found[6] up to this **time** who refused[6] to die. 6. There were [some] who said that Catiline had passed round blood in sacrificial dishes.

577. Supplementary Exercises.

I. 1. **Quī** sē ūltrō mortī offerant facilius reperiuntur quam quī dolōrem patienter ferant. 2. **Morinī** Menapiīque supererant quī in armīs essent neque ad eum lēgātōs dē pāce mīsissent. 3. Quis **servus libertāte**[7] dignus **fuit cui** nostra salūs cāra nōn esset?

II. 1. [He] who quietly obeys seems to be worthy to command. 2. In the camp of Pompey it was possible to see many things which betokened confident expectation of victory. 3. Nor is there any one who asserts that he has penetrated to the beginning of that forest. 4. There are [those] who say that Catiline has been driven into exile by me.

---

[1] See foot-note 1, Lesson LXX.
[2] sc. esse.
[3] A. & G. 320, *b*; H. 503, II., 1.
[4] Translate: *urge that you* **revolt.**
[5] cf. sent. **7, foregoing** exercise.
[6] A. & G. **287,** *a*; H. 495, 1; G. 511, Rem. 2.
[7] cf Lesson XXXII., foot-note 3.

LESSON LXXVI.

CONSTRUCTIONS USED WITH VERBS OF FEELING.

578.   EXAMPLES.

1. **Miserēminī sociōrum** (Cic. *Verr.* 2, 1, 28, 72), *pity [our] allies.*
2. **Miserēscite rēgis** (Verg. *Aen.* 8, 573), *take pity on the king.*
3. **Commūne perīculum miserābantur** (1, 30, 4), *they bewailed the common danger.*

579. OBSERVATION AND INFERENCE: Note that **miserēminī** (Ex. 1) and **miserēscite** (Ex. 2) are *intransitive*, and mean '*feel* pity'; what *case* follows them? Note, on the other hand, that **miserābantur** is *transitive* and means '*express* pity for,' 'lament,' 'bewail'; what *case* follows it? Frame a rule for the construction to be used with these verbs?

580. REFERENCES FOR VERIFICATION: A. & G. 221, *a*; H. 406, I.; G. 376 (first line).

581.   EXAMPLES.

1. **Tuī mē miseret, meī piget** (Enn. ap. Cic. *Div.* 1, 31, 66), *I pity thee, I loathe myself* (it pities me of thee, it loathes me of myself).
2. **Taedet omnīnō eōs vītae** (Cic. *Att.* 5, 16, 2), *they are utterly weary of life* (it wearies them of life).
3. **Mē meōrum factōrum nunquam paenitēbit** (Cic. *Cat.* 4, 10, 20), *I shall never regret my acts* (it will never repent me of my acts).
4. **Pudet mē nōn tuī quidem, sed Chrysippī** (Cic. *Div.* 2, 15, 35), *I am not ashamed of you indeed, but of Chrysippus.*

582. OBSERVATION AND INFERENCE: Note that **miseret** (Ex. 1), **piget** (Ex. 1), **taedet** (Ex. 2), **paenitēbit** (Ex. 3), and **pudet** (Ex. 4) are *impersonal verbs* of *feeling* or *emotion*. By what case is the *person experiencing the feeling* expressed? (See **mē**, Ex. 1, **eōs**, Ex. 2, **mē**, Ex. 3, **mē**, Ex. 4.) By what case is the *object exciting the feeling* expressed? (See **tuī** and **meī**, Ex. 1, **vītae**, Ex. 2, **factōrum**, Ex. 3, **tuī** and **Chrysippī**, Ex. 4.) Frame a rule for the constructions to be used with the foregoing Impersonals.

583. REFERENCES FOR VERIFICATION: A. & G. 221, *b*; H. 409, III.; G. 376.

584. **EXAMPLES.**

1. Quid illīus interest **ubī sīs** (Cic. *Att.* 10, 4, 10), *what matters it to him where you are?*
2. Docet quantō opere commūnis salūtis intersit manūs hostium distinērī (2, 5, 2), *he shows how important it is for the general safety that the forces of the enemy be kept apart.*
3. **Meā** māgnī interest tē ut videam (Cic. *Att.* 11, 22, 2), *it is of great importance to me to see you.*
4. **Tuā māximē interest tē valēre** (Cic. *Fam.* 16, 4, 4), *it is of the greatest importance to you that you keep your health.*

585. OBSERVATION AND INFERENCE: Note that with the *impersonal* **interest** the *person* or *thing affected* is expressed by the *genitive* in Exs. 1 and 2 (see **illīus**, Ex. 1, and salūtis, Ex. 2). Note, however, that in Exs. 3 and 4 the person interested is expressed *not* by the genitive of the personal pronoun, **as might have been expected**, but by the *ablative feminine* of **the** *possessive* (see meā, Ex. 3, and tuā, Ex. 4). Frame **a** rule **for** the constructions to be used with the Impersonal **interest**, to express the Person **or** Thing Affected.

586. REFERENCES FOR VERIFICATION: A. & G. 222, *a*; H. 408, I., 1, 2; G. 381 (both paragraphs).

587. **EXERCISES.**

I. 1. Mē meōrum cōnsiliōrum nunquam paenitēbit. 2. Misereor vestrī. 3. Miseret tē aliōrum, tuī tē nec miseret nec pudet.[1] 4. Sunt hominēs quōs īnfāmiae suae neque pudeat neque taedeat. 5. Māgnī[2] interest Cicerōnis, vel meā potius, vel mehercule utriusque. 6. Quis est hodiē cūjus intersit istam lēgem manēre? 7. Māgnī[2] interest tuā et mea. 8. Allobrogēs Umbrēnum ōrābant ut suī **miserērētur**. 9. Miserantur commūnem Galliae fortūnam. 10. Dē summīs saepe rēbus cōnsilia ineunt, quōrum eōs in vestīgiō paenitēre necesse est.   **11.** Mē cīvitātis mōrum piget taedetque.

II. **1.** You are neither sorry for nor ashamed of yourself. **2.** It concerns the general safety for me to have a conference with Ariovistus.   **3.** The women bewailed their little children. **4.** I have not been dissatisfied with my soldiers, nor you with your leader.   **5.** It is highly[2] important **to me** for **us** to be together.   **6.** They are **neither** ashamed of their infamy nor weary [of it].   **7. It is** of more[3] importance to them than to me.   **8. He demands** that they have compassion on him.[4]   **9. Can any one pity us?**

588.   Supplementary Exercises.

I. **1.** Nōn tam meā quam reī pūblicae interest utī salvus sim. **2.** Plērīque eōrum quī ante mē sententiās dīxēre, cāsum reī pūblicae miserātī sunt.   **3.** Eōrum nōs magis miseret quī nostram misericordiam nōn requīrunt, quam quī illam efflāgitant.   **4.** Hūjus post mortem, populum jūdiciī suī paenitēbat.

II. **1.** It matters very little[5] to **me**.   **2.** Caesar **used** to say that it was not so important for himself[6] **as for** the state that he should be preserved.   **3.** Do you not **feel** that you dishonor[7] this temple, the city,[8] life,[8] light[8]?   **4.** I pity the misfortunes of Jugurtha.   **5.** Every one is dissatisfied with his own lot.

---

[1] For the arrangement of the words in this sentence, see references under Lesson XXI., foot-note 21.
[2] A. & G. 252, a; H. 408, III.; G. 382, 1.
[3] magis.
[4] A. & G. 196, a; H. 449, 1; G. **521.**

[5] minimē.
[6] Proper form of suus.
[7] "Do you not feel that you dishonor this temple?" = *does it not shame you of this temple?*
[8] Repeat "**not**" with each substantive.

LESSON LXXVII.

CONDITIONAL SENTENCES: PRESENT AND PAST SUPPOSITIONS.

PRESENT AND PAST SUPPOSITIONS, PROTASIS INDETERMINATE.

589. EXAMPLES.
1. **Sī** mē cōnsulis, suādeō (Cic. *Cat.* 1, 5, 13), *if you ask my advice, I recommend* [it].
2. **Sī** quisquam fuit unquam remōtus ab inānī laude, ego profectō is sum (Cic. *Fam.* 15, 4, 13), *if there ever was any one indifferent to empty applause, I assuredly am the man.*
3. **Sīn autem servīre meae** glōriae māvīs, ēgredere (Cic. *Cat.* 1, 9, 23), *if, however, you prefer to minister to my glory, depart.*
4. **Sī stāre nōn possunt, corruant** (Cic. *Cat.* 2, 10, 21), *if they cannot stand, let them fall.*

590. EXPLANATION OF TERMS: Sentences like the foregoing, containing a clause introduced by **sī**, *if*, or one of its compounds (see **sīn**, Ex. 3), are called *Conditional Sentences*. The clause expressing the *condition* (sī ... cōnsulis, Ex. 1, sī ... laude, Ex. 2, sīn ... māvīs, Ex. 3, sī ... possunt, Ex. 4) is called the *Protasis;* the clause expressing the *conclusion* (suādeō, Ex. 1, ego ... sum, Ex. 2, ēgredere, Ex. 3, corruant, Ex. 4) is called the *Apodosis*.

591. OBSERVATION AND INFERENCE: Note that the *Protasis* in the foregoing examples *simply states* a supposed case, without implying either that it is *true* or that it is *false*. Thus, sī mē cōnsulis, *if you ask my advice* (Ex. 1), does not imply that the person addressed either *does* or *does not* ask the advice of the speaker. Note, further, that the Protasis expresses a *present* supposition in Exs. 1, 3, and 4; and a *past* supposition in Ex. 2. In what *mood* is the verb of the Protasis in each of these examples (see cōnsulis, Ex. 1; **fuit**, Ex. 2; māvīs, Ex. 3; possunt, Ex. 4)? Is there a like uniformity as to mood in the verbs of the Apodosis (see **suādeō**, Ex. 1; sum, Ex. 2; ēgredere, Ex. 3; **corruant**, Ex. 4)? Frame a rule for the use of Moods in Conditional Sentences like the foregoing.

592. REFERENCES FOR VERIFICATION: A. & G. 306; H. 508 and 4; G. 597.

PRESENT AND PAST SUPPOSITIONS, PROTASIS FALSE.

593.   EXAMPLES.

1. **Servī meī sī mē metuerent, domum meam relinquendam putārem** (Cic. Cat. 1, 7, 17), *if my slaves feared me, I should think that I ought to leave house and home.*
2. **[Vītam] sī ēripuisset, multās animī atque corporis poenās adēmisset** (Cic. Cat. 4, 4, 8), *if he had taken away life, he would have relieved* [them] *of many torments of mind and body.*
3. **Magis id dīcerēs, sī adfuissēs** (Cic. Lael. 7, 25), *you would say so all the more, if you had been there.*
4. **Sī interfectus esset, quid dīcerent** (Cic. Cat. 2, 7, 15), *what would they say, if he had been put to death?*

594. OBSERVATION AND INFERENCE: Note that the Protasis in each of the foregoing examples states the supposed case in such a way as to imply its *falsity*. Thus, **servī meī sī mē metuerent**, *if my slaves feared me* (Ex. 1), implies that the **speaker's slaves** *do not* fear him; and **sī ... adfuissēs**, *if you had been there* (Ex. 3), implies that the person addressed *was not* there.

Note, further, that the Protasis expresses a *present* supposition in Ex. 1, and a *past* supposition in Exs. 2, 3, and 4; also, that the verb of the Apodosis refers to *present* time in Exs. 1, 3, and 4, and to *past* time in Ex. 2.

What *mood* is used in both Protasis and Apodosis in these examples? What *tense* is used for *present* time? for *past* time? Frame a rule for the use of Mood and Tense in Conditional Sentences like the foregoing.

595. REFERENCES FOR VERIFICATION: A. & G. 308; H. 510 and n. 1; G. 599.

596.   EXERCISES.

I. 1. Sī iterum experīrī volunt, ego iterum parātus sum dēcertāre.   2. Sī Catilīna in urbe remānsisset, numquam nōs rem pūblicam līberāssēmus.   3. Parcite dignitātī Lentulī sī ipse famae suae unquam pepercit. 4. Sī quid mihī ā Caesare opus esset, ego ad eum vēnissem. 5. Id ego sī verbō adsequī possem, istōs ipsōs ēicerem. 6. Sī et in urbe et in eādem mente permanent, ea quae merentur exspectent. 7. Mihī sī haec condiciō cōnsulātūs data est, feram nōn sōlum fortiter vērum etiam libenter. 8. Sī in hunc animadvertissem, crūdēliter fēcissem.

II. 1. If they wish to enjoy peace, it is unfair [for them] to refuse [to pay][1] the tribute. 2. Bring back the men if you wish to be free from suspicion in-my-eyes.[2] 3. If there were room for error, I should readily permit [it]. 4. If he had been conscious[3] of [having done] any wrong, it would not have been difficult [for him] to be on his guard. 5. Pardon the young[4] Cethegus[4] if he has not a second time made war on his country. 6. Still, if it is your pleasure, let it be voted. 7. Nor would you, if you were an Athenian, ever have been illustrious. 8. Would[5] he,[6] then, if he had lived to be a hundred years[7] old, regret[6] his old age?

597.   Supplementary Exercises.

I. 1. Huic facinorī sī paucōs putātis adfīnēs esse, vehementer errātis. 2. Sī quid ille mē vult, illum ad mē venīre oportet. 3. Sī hōc idem huic adulēscentī optimō P. Sēstiō dīxissem, jam mihī senātus vim et manūs intulisset. 4. Sī id culpā senectūtis accideret, eadem mihī ūsū venīrent.

II. 1. If you cannot die contentedly, do you hesitate to consign your life to flight and solitude? 2. If your parents hated you, you would, as I think, withdraw to some place out of their sight.[8] 3. If Catiline had come off conqueror, doubtless great bloodshed and disaster would have overwhelmed the country.

---

[1] recūsāre dē.
[2] mihī.
[3] Translate: *conscious to himself.*
[4] Translate: *the youth of Cethegus.*
[5] What inter. particle? cf. 417, Ex. 4.
[6] cf. 581, Ex. 3.
[7] had lived to the hundredth year.
[8] ab eōrum oculīs.

LESSON LXXVIII.

CONDITIONAL SENTENCES: FUTURE SUPPOSITIONS.

598. EXAMPLES.

1. **Nunquam lābēre sī tē audiēs** (Cic. *Fam.* 2, 7, 1), *you will never err if you* (shall) *follow your own convictions* (hear yourself).
2. **Sī iste ūnus tollētur, perīculum residebit** (Cic. *Cat.* 1, 13, 31), *if he alone* (shall) *be removed, the danger will remain.*
3. **Vix feram sermōnēs hominum sī id fēceris** (Cic. *Cat.* 1, 9, 23), *it will be hard for me to endure men's criticisms if you do* (shall **have** done) *this.*

599. OBSERVATION AND INFERENCE: Note that the Protasis in each of the foregoing examples states a supposed *future case* with *vividness*, though without implying either that it will **or that** it will not be fulfilled. What *mood* and what *tenses* are used **in** both Protasis and Apodosis in this form **of conditional** sentence? Note that, in Ex. 3, the action **expressed by** the verb of the Protasis (**fēceris**) is represented **as** *completed* **at the time** denoted by the verb of the Apodosis (**feram**); what *tense* is used **to** express this completeness? Note, further, **that the verbs** of the Protasis in the foregoing examples are rendered by the *present* tense in the English translation; in such cases, which language is the more exact, the Latin or the English? Frame a rule for the use of Mood and Tenses in Conditional Sentences like the foregoing.

600. REFERENCES FOR VERIFICATION: A. & G. 307 (to the semicolon), ***a, c*** (omit what follows the comma in the third line); H. 508 and **2**; G. 597.

601. EXAMPLES.

1. **Sī quis deus mihī largiātur ut repuerāscam, valdē recūsem** (Cic. *Cat. Maj.* 23, 83), *if some god should freely grant me the privilege of becoming* **a** *child again, I should stoutly refuse it.*

2. **Ego sī Scīpiōnis dēsīderiō mē movērī negem, mentiar** (Cic. *Lael.* 3, 10), *if I should say that I am* not affected *with grief at the loss of Scipio, I should speak falsely.*

3. **Sī gladium** quis apud tē sānā mente dēposuerit, repetat īnsāniēns, reddere peccātum sit (Cic. *Off.* 3, 25, 94), *if a man should deposit* (should have deposited) *with you a sword* [when] *in his right mind, and should* **ask it back** *again* [when] *insane, it would* **be** *wrong to restore it.*

602. OBSERVATION AND INFERENCE: Note that the Protasis in the foregoing examples states the supposed future case with *less vividness* than in the examples of **598**, and thereby represents the fulfillment of the supposed case as somewhat less probable. What *mood* and what *tenses* are used in both Protasis and Apodosis in this form of conditional sentence? Note that, in Ex. 3, the action expressed by the verb of the first Protasis (**dēposuerit**) is represented as *completed* at the time denoted by the verb of the Apodosis (**sit**); what *tense* is used to express this completeness? Frame a rule for the use of Mood and Tenses in Conditional Sentences like the foregoing.

603. REFERENCES FOR VERIFICATION: A. & G. 307, *b, c*; H. 509 and n. 1; G. 598.

604. EXERCISES.

I. 1. Nisi dēcēdēs, ego tē prō hoste habēbō. 2. Sī discēsseris, māgnō ego tē praemiō remūnerābor. 3. Haec sī tēcum patria loquātur, nōnne impetrāre dēbeat? 4. Sī quis deus tē interroget, quid respondeās? 5. Sī poterimus, castellum expūgnābimus; sī minus potuerimus, agrōs Rēmōrum populābimur. 6. Sī vim facere cōnābiminī, prohibēbō. 7. Sī tē interfēcerō, multīs ego nōbilibus grātum faciam.

II. 1. **If we can,**[1] we shall destroy the bridge; **if we cannot,**[1] we shall cut off the Romans from supplies. 2. I could not go away if I should wish [to]. 3. If you give satisfaction **to** the Aeduans **for** (**dē**) the injuries [you have done

ILLUSTRATIVE EXERCISES.   177

them], **I shall make peace with you.**   4. Ought not[2] the **country to** obtain her request, even if she should not be **able to apply** force?   5. If this (pl.) is reported[3] to **Ariovistus**, he will inflict punishment on (dē) the hostages.   6. If you do[3] this, there will be lasting friendship between you and the Roman people.[4]

605.   Supplementary Exercises.

I. 1. Etiam sī hominum studia dēficiant, **dī**[5] ipsī immortālēs cōgant tanta vitia superārī.   2. Sī sē ējēcerit, sēcumque suōs ēdūxerit, exstinguētur atque dēlēbitur stirps āc sēmen malōrum omnium.   3. **Si quis** pater **familiās,**[6] līberīs suīs ā servō interfectīs, supplicium **dē** servō nōn sūmpserit, utrum[7] is clēmēns an crūdēlissimus esse videātur?   4. Nisi dēcēdēs atque exercitum dēdūcēs ex hīs regiōnibus, ego tē nōn prō amīcō sed hoste habēbō.   5. Pietāte **adversus deōs sublātā,**[8] fidēs etiam et jūstitia tollātur.

II. 1. If they should remain in Rome,[9] they would be rescued by a hired mob.   2. If this takes place it will be [attended] with great danger to the province.[10]   3. If any [punishment] of undue severity is inflicted upon him[11] by Caesar, no one will suppose that it was not done at[12] **my desire.**

---

[1] cf. sent. 5, preceding exercise.
[2] cf. 604, sent. 3.
[3] cf. sent. 2, preceding exercise.
[4] Translate: *to the Roman people with you.*
[5] See 373, foot-note 3.
[6] A. & G. 36, b; H. 49, 1; G. 27, Rem. 1.
[7] Omit in translation.
[8] Trans. by a conditional clause. Expand the abl. abs. into the ordinary form of protasis.
[9] cf. Lesson XXVII., foot-note 11.
[10] Use the genitive.
[11] Translate: *if anything too-severe shall have happened to him from Caesar.*
[12] Use ablative of cause.

LESSON LXXIX.

CONCESSIVE CLAUSES. — CLAUSES OF PROVISO.

606. **EXAMPLES.**

1. Quamquam premēbantur, tamen **omnia** fortissimō sustinēbant animō (8, 42, 3), *although they were hard pressed, still they endured everything with the bravest spirit.*
2. Senectūs, quamvīs nōn sit gravis, tamen aufert viriditātem (Cic. *Lael.* 3, 11), *old age, though it be not burdensome, yet takes away one's vigor.*
3. Etsī mātūrae sunt hiemēs, tamen contendit (4, 20, 1), *although the winters set in early, he hastened notwithstanding.*
4. **Nōnne impetrāre** dēbeat, etiamsī vim adhibēre nōn possit (Cic. *Cat.* 1, 8, 19), *ought she not to obtain her request, even though she should not be able to employ force?*

607. OBSERVATION AND INFERENCE: Note that the clauses in the foregoing examples **introduced by quamquam** (Ex. 1), quamvīs (Ex. 2), **etsī** (Ex. 3), and **etiamsī** (Ex. 4) express something granted or *conceded.* For this reason they are called *Concessive* **Clauses.** Note that the Concessive **Clause** introduced by **quamquam** (Ex. 1), unlike that introduced by quamvīs (Ex. 2), concedes an *admitted fact,* and therefore takes the *indicative mood* (see **premēbantur**). What *mood* does the Concessive Clause introduced by **quamvīs** take (see **sit**, Ex. 2)? Note that **etsī** (Ex. 3) and **etiamsī** (Ex. 4) are compounds of **sī**, and that, like **sī**, they take the *indicative or subjunctive* as already explained (Lessons LXXVII.-VIII.). Frame rules for the Mood of the verb in Concessive Clauses.

608. REFERENCES FOR VERIFICATION: A. & G. 313, *a, c, e*; H. 515, I., II., III. ; G. 605, 1-3, 606, 607, 608.

609. **EXAMPLES.**

1. Dum locus pūgnandī darētur, singulās bīnīs nāvibus obiciēbant (Caes. *B. C.* 1, 58, 4), *provided an opportunity of fighting presented itself, they matched one ship against two.*

2. **Manent ingenia senibus, modo permaneat** industria (Cic. *Cat. Maj.* 7, 22), *the old retain their mental powers* (powers remain to the old), *if only industry hold out*.

3. **Māgnō mē metū līberābis, dum modo inter mē atque tē mūrus intersit** (Cic. *Cat.* 1, 5, 10), *you will free me from great fear, if only there be a wall between you and me*.

610. OBSERVATION AND INFERENCE: Note that the clauses in the foregoing examples introduced by **dum** (Ex. 1), **modo** (Ex. 2), and **dum modo** (Ex. 3) express a *proviso* or *condition*; what mood do they take (see **darētur**, Ex. 1, **permaneat**, Ex. 2, and **intersit**, Ex. 3)? Frame a rule **for the Mood to** be used in clauses like the foregoing.

611. REFERENCES FOR VERIFICATION: A. & G. 314; H. 513, I.; G. 575.

612.   EXERCISES.

I. 1. Sed est tantī[1] dum modo ista reī pūblicae perīculīs sējungātur calamitās. 2. Quamquam crēbrō audiēbat Labiēnum ab inimīcīs suīs sollicitārī, tamen **nōn crēdidit**. 3. Etiamsī Catilīna perierit, in rē pūblicā **sēminārium** Catilīnārum **erit**. 4. **Nōn igitur potestās est cōnservandae reī** pūblicae, quamvīs ea premātur **perīculīs**. 5. Neque, dum sibī rēgnum parāret, quicquam **pēnsī** habēbat.[2] 6. Illa, quamquam ferenda nōn fuērunt, tamen tulī. 7. Hominēs, quamvīs in turbidīs rēbus sint, tamen interdum animīs relaxantur.[3]

II. 1. Even though he receives the injury, he yet seems to commit [it]. 2. You at any rate assented to[4] my departure, provided I should be at Rome[5] on the first[6] of January. 3. The Romans, although they were weary of marching[7] and fighting,[7] yet eagerly[8] advanced to meet [him]. 4. And yet[9] that flattery, pernicious though[10] it be, can nevertheless injure no one but[11] him who is pleased by it. 5. He spared neither expense nor his own honor, if only he might make them faithful to himself.

613.   **Supplementary Exercises.**

I. 1. Sed quamquam haec tālia sunt, tamen obviam **īre inimīcis meīs animus mē subigit.**   2. Ista vēritās etiamsī jūcunda[12] nōn est, mihī tamen grāta[12] est.   3. Nihil tam difficile est quod nōn cupidissimē factūrī **simus, dum** ea rēs cīvitātem aere aliēnō līberet.   4. **Quamvīs nōn fueris suāsor et** impulsor profectiōnis meae, approbātor certē fuistī.

II. 1. Life is short, though it extend beyond a thousand years.   2. But Sulla, although he held the same opinion,[13] nevertheless protected the Moor from injury.   3. They will shrink from no **peril,** provided the province be restored to Caesar through their efforts.[14]

[1] **est tantī,** *it is worth such a price:* A. & G. 252, *a*; H. 404, n. 1; G. 379.
[2] **Neque quicquam pēnsī habēbat,** *nor did he have any scruple.*
[3] **animīs relaxantur,** *unbend.*
[4] *you were approver of.*
[5] cf. foot-note 11, Lesson XXVII.
[6] "first" = *Kalends.*
[7] Ablative.
[8] **intentus** (adj.) in agreement with subject.
[9] A. & G. 313, f; H. 515, n. 2; G. 607, Rem. 2.
[10] cf. 606, Ex. 2.
[11] "no one but" = *no one unless.*
[12] **jūcundus,** *agreeable,* because to one's taste; **grātus,** *welcome,* **because** valuable in itself.
[13] *to hold the same opinion,* **eadem exīstimāre.**
[14] Translate: *through themselves.*

LESSON LXXX.

SPECIAL CONSTRUCTIONS: GENITIVE WITH VERBS OF CONDEMNING, ETC. — **Egeō** AND **Indigeō.** DATIVE WITH **Ēripiō,** ETC.

614.   EXAMPLES.

1. **Prīncipēs cīvitātis īnsimulātī [sunt] prōditiōnis** (7, 38, 2), *the foremost men in the state have been charged with treachery.*

2. **Prōditiōnis damnātus est** (Nep. *Th.* 8, 2), *he was condemned for treason.*

3. **Videō tē** absolūtum esse improbitātis (Cic. *Verr.* 2, 1, 28, 72), *I see that you were acquitted of wrong doing.*

615. OBSERVATION AND INFERENCE: Note that **īnsimulātī sunt** (Ex. 1), **damnātus est** (Ex. 2), and **absolūtum esse** (Ex. 3) are verbs of *accusing, condemning,* and *acquitting* respectively. By what *case* is the *charge* expressed with these verbs (see **prōditiōnis**, Ex. 1, **prōditiōnis**, Ex. 2, **improbitātis**, Ex. 3)? Frame a rule for the construction to be used with these and similar verbs.

616. REFERENCES FOR VERIFICATION: A. & G. 220; H. 409, II. and n. 2; G. 377.

617.   **EXAMPLES.**

1. **Nīl attigit nisi** arma, quōrum indigēbat (Nep. *Thr.* 2, 6), *he touched nothing but arms, and of these he stood in need.*
2. **[Eōs], quibus** rēbus indiguērunt, **adjūvit** (Nep. *Att.* 9, 3), *he aided them with those things of which they stood in need.*
3. **Neque cōnsilī neque audāciae eguēre** (Sall. *Cat.* 51, 37), *they lacked neither caution nor boldness.*
4. **Alterum alterīus auxiliō eget** (Sall. *Cat.* 1, 7), *each (of these two things) needs the aid of the other.*

618. OBSERVATION AND INFERENCE: It has already been shown that verbs denoting *want* regularly take the *ablative* (Lesson LXVI.). With what *cases* is **indigeō** construed in the foregoing examples (see **quōrum**, Ex. 1, and **rēbus**, Ex. 2)? What *cases* may be used with **egeō** (see **cōnsilī** and **audāciae**, Ex. 3, and **auxiliō**, Ex. 4)? Frame a special rule for these two verbs.

619. REFERENCES FOR VERIFICATION: A. & G. 223; H. 410, V., 1; G. 389, Rem. 2.

620.   **EXAMPLES.**

1. **Id mihī tū abstulistī** (Cic. *Div. in Caecil.* 5, 19), *you have robbed me of that* (have taken that away to my hurt).
2. **Haec illī dētrahenda auxilia exīstimābat** (6, 6, 5), *he thought that these allies ought to be detached from him* (withdrawn to his injury).

3. **Mihī timōrem** ēripe (Cic. *Cat.* 1, 7, 18), *free me from fear* (take **away** fear as a favor to me).

621. OBSERVATION AND INFERENCE: It has already been shown that verbs of *separation* usually take the *ablative* (Lesson LXVI.). Note, however, that, in the foregoing examples, **abstulistī** (Ex. 1), **dētrahenda** (Ex. 2), and **ēripe** (Ex. 3) are construed with the *dative* (see: mihī, Ex. 1, illī, Ex. 2, and mihī, Ex. 3). Note, further, that the dative in these examples designates the *person*, and that the action expressed by the verb of separation is viewed as something done *to* or *for* the person affected. Frame a rule for this use of the Dative.

622. REFERENCES FOR VERIFICATION: A. & G. 229; H. 386, 2; G. 346 (end).

623.   EXERCISES.

I. 1. Nōnnūllōs ambitūs Pompējā lēge damnātōs in integrum restituit. 2. Tuāsne injūriās persequar ipse auxilī egēns? 3. Populī Rōmānī beneficium mihī per contumēliam ab inimīcīs extorquētur. 4. Sī ille nōn **fuisset**,[1] Agēsilāus Asiam rēgī ēripuisset. 5. Accūsātus capitis absolvitur, multātur tamen pecūniā. 6. Sī quis opis ējus indigēbat, habēbat quod statim daret.

II. 1. Unless you return,[2] we shall condemn you to death. 2. **No one of** (ex) the common people lacked aid against [an enemy] more powerful [than himself]. 3. You **have** been deprived of life before your time.[3] 4. He seized a shield from a[4] soldier in the rear.[5] 5. And, by Hercules, Sulla, before I knew you,[6] I needed no one.[7] 6. What [punishment] is too severe for[8] men convicted of so heinous a crime?

624.   Supplementary Exercises.

I. 1. Sīn autem vītam mihī fors adēmerit, hi omnia tibī prō mē persolvent. 2. Summae inīquitātis condemnārī dēbeō nisi vestram vītam meā salūte habeō cāriōrem. 3. Ptolomaeum aliēnārum opum indigentem recēperat. 4. Multī praetereā capitis damnātī exsulēsque convēnerant.

TEMPORAL CLAUSES WITH Postquam, ETC.

II. 1. All are at liberty[9] to lay down their arms[10] without risk of injury except [those] condemned[9] for capital offences. 2. This **man's** army should have been taken from him.[11] 3. This town **lacked** nothing [that was] serviceable.[12]

---

[1] *If it had not been for him.*
[2] cf. 598, Exs. 1 and 2.
[3] Translate: *Life has been taken away from you before-your-time* (**immātūrus**).
[4] Use the proper form of **ūnus.**
[5] **ab novissimīs.**
[6] Translate: *before you known.*

[7] In the genitive and ablative, **nūllus** (not **nēmō**) must be used for *no one.*
[8] Use in with accusative.
[9] Translate: *it is permitted to all except to* [those] *condemned.*
[10] Translate: *to withdraw from arms.*
[11] Translate: *From this man* [his] *army was to be taken* (pass. periphr.).
[12] Translate: *no serviceable thing.*

LESSON LXXXI.

TEMPORAL CLAUSES: Postquam, Ubī, Ut, Simul Atque; Cum (Temporal).

625. EXAMPLES.

1. **Postquam cōpiās venīre vīdit, flūmen exercitum trādūcere mātūrāvit** (2, 5, 4), *when he saw that the forces were advancing, he hastened to convey his army across the river.*

2. **Ubī sē parātōs esse arbitrātī sunt, oppida incendunt** (1, 5, 2), *when they thought that they were ready, they burnt the towns.*

3. **Sed Pompējus, ut equitātum suum pulsum vīdit, sē in castra equō contulit** (Caes. B. C. 3, 94, 5), *but Pompey, when he had seen his cavalry routed, spurred into camp.*

4. **Simul atque sīgna nostra vīdērunt, portās aperuērunt** (Caes. B. C. 1, 18, 2), *as soon as they beheld our standards, they opened their gates.*

626. OBSERVATION AND INFERENCE: Note that the *temporal clauses* in the foregoing examples refer to a *definite point of past time*, and that they are introduced by **postquam** (Ex. 1), **ubī** (Ex. 2), **ut** (Ex. 3), and **simul atque** (Ex. 4), respectively. In what *mood* and *tense* are the verbs of these temporal clauses (see: **vīdit,** Ex. 1, **arbitrātī sunt,** Ex. 2, **vīdit,** Ex. 3, and **vīdērunt,** Ex. 4)? Note, further, that the verb of the temporal clause may be translated by the *pluperfect* (see *had seen*, Ex. 3). Frame a rule for the Mood and Tense **of the Verb in Temporal** Clauses like **the** foregoing.

627. EXAMPLES.

1. Cum cīvitās armīs jūs suum **exsequī** cōnārētur, Orgetorix mortuus est (1, 4, 3), *when the state undertook to maintain its authority by force of arms, Orgetorix died.*
2. Haec cum flēns ā Caesare peteret, Caesar ējus dextram prēndit (1, 20, 5), *as he in tears was urging these requests on Caesar, Caesar grasped his hand.*
3. Diū cum esset pūgnātum, castrīs nostrī potītī **sunt** (1, 26, 4), *after a long struggle* (when the battle had been fought a long time), *our men got possession of the camp.*
4. **Cum** trīduum iter fēcisset, inveniēbat ex captīvīs ... (2, 16, 1), *after marching three days, he learned from prisoners ...*

628. OBSERVATION AND INFERENCE: Note that the *temporal clauses* in the foregoing examples, like **those of 625, refer to** *past time*, but that they are introduced by **cum.** Note, further, that in the present examples **the** attention of **the** writer is fixed on **the** *main action*, and that the temporal clause merely marks in an *incidental* way the time of its occurrence. What *mood* and what *tenses* are used in the foregoing temporal clauses (see **cōnārētur,** Ex. 1, peteret, Ex. 2, esset pūgnātum, Ex. 3, and fēcisset, Ex. 4)? Which of these tenses denotes the *same time* as the leading verb? which *time prior?* Frame a rule for the Mood and Tense to be **used** with **cum** in Temporal Clauses of Narration.

629. REFERENCES FOR VERIFICATION of Rules framed under **626** and **628**: A. & G. 323, 324, 325; H. 518, n. 1, 521, II., 2; G. 563, 586.

630. EXERCISES.

I. 1. Quōrum dē nātūrā mōribusque Caesar cum quaereret, sīc reperiēbat. 2. Ubi lēgātī **ad eum** revertērunt, negat[1] sē posse iter ūllī per prōvinciam dare. 3. Quō cum Catilīna vēnisset, quis eum senātor appellāvit? 4. Caesar, postquam in Trēverōs vēnit, duābus dē **causīs** Rhēnum trānsīre cōnstituit. 5. **Cum haesitāret,** cum tenērētur, **quaesīvī quid**[2] dubitāret proficiscī. 6. Quō ut ventum est, **Alexandrīnī** trepidantēs in omnēs partēs castrōrum discurrere **coepērunt.** 7. Quō cum vēnisset,[3] cōgnōscit[1] missum in Hispāniam ā Pompējō Vībullium Rūfum. 8. Simul atque oppidānī in **spem** auxiliī vēnērunt, clāmōre sublātō, arma capere, portās claudere, mūrum complēre coepērunt.

II. 1. When (**ubī**) the **Helvetians had** been informed[4] **of** his arrival, they sent ambassadors to him. 2. Having noted[5] these [facts], he called an assembly[6] [and] severely upbraided them. 3. Caesar on perceiving[7] this withdrew his forces to the nearest hill. 4. When (**cum**) these [ships] were drawing near to Britain, and were in sight[8] from the camp, **a storm** suddenly arose. 5. As soon as they had recovered[4] from flight, they sent envoys for (**dē**) peace. 6. Having said[5] these things, he swore that he would not return to camp except (**nisi**) [as] victor. 7. On returning[9] thence, he followed the camp of Gajus **Claudius Nero.**

631. Supplementary Exercises.

I. 1. Ubī sē diūtius dūcī intellēxit, convocātīs eōrum prīncipibus, graviter eōs accūsat.[1] 2. Cum advesperāsceret, occultē ad pontem Mulvium pervēnērunt. 3. Quod postquam barbarī fierī animadvertērunt, fugā salūtem petere contendērunt. 4. Caesarī cum id nūntiātum esset,[3] mātūrat[1] **ab** urbe proficiscī.

II. 1. **When he** inquired what communities were in arms, he learned as follows. 2. When Caesar arrived there (**eō**), he demanded hostages, arms, [and] slaves. 3. On his departure for Italy, Caesar dispatched Servius Galba with the twelfth legion to (**in**) the Nantuates. 4. In this community two were contending with each other[10] for (**dē**) supremacy; of whom one,[11] as soon as intelligence-was-received[12] **of** Caesar's arrival, came to him.

---

[1] See refs. Lesson LXIX., foot-note 3.
[2] *why* (adv. acc.).
[3] See refs. Lesson LXIX., foot-note 5.
[4] For tense, cf. 625, Ex. 3.
[5] Use **cum** with temporal clause.
[6] Ablative **absolute.**
[7] Use **postquam.**
[8] "were in sight " = *were seen.*
[9] Use **ut** with temporal clause.
[10] Translate: *between themselves.*
[11] **alter.**
[12] Use **cōgnōscō** impersonally.

LESSON LXXXII.

Cum with the Indicative in Temporal Clauses.

632. EXAMPLES.

1. **Cum** Caesar in Galliam vēnit, alterīus factiōnis prīncipēs erant Aeduī (6, 12, 1), *at the time when Caesar came into Gaul, the Aedui were at the head of one party.*
2. **Tum** cum ex urbe Catilīnam ēiciēbam ... putābam ... (Cic. Cat. 3, 2, 3), *at the time when I was striving to drive Catiline out of the city ... I supposed ...*
3. **Tum** cum rēs māgnās permultī āmīserant, scīmus fidem concidisse (Cic. Manil. 7, 19), *at the time when a great many had lost large fortunes, we know that there was a financial panic* (credit fell prostrate).
4. Cum tū haec legēs, illum **Rōmae esse oportēbit** (Cic. Fam. 12, 30, 5), *by the time this letter reaches you, he will be due in Rome.*

633. OBSERVATION AND INFERENCE: Note that the temporal clauses introduced by **cum** in the foregoing examples, unlike those of **627**, mark the time of the main action *with definiteness and precision*. What mood does **cum** take under these circumstances (see vēnit, Ex. 1, ēiciēbam, Ex. 2, āmīserant, Ex. 3, legēs, Ex. 4)? Frame a rule for the Mood to be used in Temporal Clauses like the foregoing.

634. EXAMPLES.

1. **Factum** perīculum patrum nostrōrum memoriā, cum laudem exercitus meritus vidēbātur (1, 40, 5), *a trial was made within the memory of our fathers, on which occasion* (= and on that occasion) *the army appeared to have merited praise.*
2. Hōc facere apparābant, cum mātrēsfamiliae repente prōcurrērunt (7, 26, 3), *they were getting ready to do this, when suddenly the matrons rushed forth.*
3. **Vix** agmen novissimum prōcesserat, cum Gallī flūmen trānsīre nōn dubitant (6, 8, 1), *scarcely had the rear advanced, when the Gauls without hesitation crossed the river.*

Cum WITH THE INDICATIVE. 187

635. OBSERVATION AND INFERENCE: Note that the temporal clauses introduced by **cum** in the foregoing examples express the *main statement;* in other words, that the temporal clause, although subordinate in *form* (grammatically), is *principal in thought* (logically). What *mood* does **cum** take under these circumstances (see: **vidēbātur**, Ex. 1, **prōcurrērunt**, Ex. 2, **dubitant**, Ex. 3)? Frame a rule for the Mood to be used with **cum** in Temporal Clauses like the foregoing.

636.   EXAMPLES.

1. **Cum singulās bīnae nāvēs circumsteterant, mīlitēs summā vī contendēbant** (3, 15, 1), *whenever* (*i.e.,* if in any case) *two ships had been brought to bear on one, the soldiers would struggle with all their might.*

2. **Cum sē inter** turmās **īnsinuāvērunt, dēsiliunt** (4, 33, 1), *whenever* (*i.e.,* if in any case) *they have worked their way into the squadrons, they leap down.*

637. OBSERVATION AND INFERENCE: Note that **cum** in the foregoing examples means *whenever,* and that the temporal clause is equivalent to the *protasis of a general supposition.* What *mood* does **cum** take under these circumstances (see: **circumsteterant**, Ex. 1, **īnsinuāvērunt**, Ex. 2)? Frame a rule for the Mood to be used with **cum** in Temporal Clauses like the foregoing.

638. CAUTION: It has been shown in the preceding lesson (**627, 628, 629**) that in *temporal clauses* of *narration,* **cum** with the *imperfect* or *pluperfect tense* commonly takes the *subjunctive;* is this true of the temporal clauses illustrated in the present lesson (see: **ēiciēbam, 632,** Ex. 2; **āmīserant, 632,** Ex. 3; **vidēbātur, 634,** Ex. 1; **circumsteterant, 636,** Ex. 1)?

639. REFERENCES FOR VERIFICATION of **Rules** framed under **633, 635, 637**: A. & G. 325, *a, b, c,* 309, c; H. 521, I., II., 1; G. 582, 585.

640.   EXERCISES.

I. 1. Sed tum cum illum extermināri volēbam, eōs infirmōs sine illō fore[1] putābam.   2. Neque vērō, cum aliquid mandārat, cōnfectum **putābat**. 3. Dumnacus īnstruit aciem, quae suīs **esset**[2] **equitibus** praesidiō, cum repente legiōnēs in cōnspectum veniunt. 4. Haec cum facta sunt in conciliō, māgnā spē et laetitiā omnium discēssum **est**.[3] 5. Ad equōs sē celeriter, cum ūsus est, recipiunt. 6. Repentīnā ruīnā pars ējus **turris concidit, cum hostēs** inermēs sē ūniversī prōripiunt.

II. 1. The legions were a mile distant, **when** Scipio, fearing that[4] he should lose the town, led out all his forces. 2. Whenever our cavalry made-a-raid[5] on the fields, he would-let-loose[6] his chariot men. 3. When I was-striving-to-expel[7] him from the city, I had this in view. 4. O glorious day,[8] when I shall depart to join[9] that divine company of **spirits!** 5. But whenever the supply of this class fails,[10] they have recourse to the **sacrifice of** the innocent. 6. And now Sulla was marking out the **camp, when the horsemen** announced that Jugurtha had encamped.

641. Supplementary Exercises.

I. 1. Cum quaepiam cohors impetum fēcerat, hostēs vēlōcissimē refugiēbant. 2. Jamque ā Labiēnō nōn longē aberant, cum duās vēnisse legiōnēs cōgnōscunt. 3. Ō praeclārum diem, cum ex hāc turbā et conluviōne discēdám!

II. 1. [He] **who does not ward** off injury from his [friends] whenever he can, acts unjustly. 2. He had shaken the enemy at the first attack, when suddenly a new army bursts into view. 3. **In other** matters, loss is experienced at-the-moment (**tum**) when disaster comes.

---

[1] **fore** = **futūrōs esse**.
[2] Account for mood and **tense**.
[3] *the assembly dispersed;* cf. Exs., 522.
[4] cf. 534, Ex. 4.
[5] Use the pluperfect.
[6] For **tense**, cf. 636, Ex. 1.
[7] For **tense**, cf. 632, Ex. 2.
[8] Use the accusative.
[9] Express "to join" by **in** with accusative.
[10] Use the **perfect tense**.

LESSON LXXXIII.

Cum in Causal and Concessive Clauses.
Accusative in Exclamations.

642.   **EXAMPLES.**

1. **Aeduī, cum sē dēfendere** nōn possent, lēgātōs ad Caesarem mittunt (1, 11, 2), *the Aedui, since they could not defend themselves, sent envoys to Caesar.*

2. Quae cum ita **sint, vestra** tecta dēfendite (Cic. Cat. 2, 12, 26), *this being the case (since these things are thus), defend your dwellings.*

3. **Cum prīmō** impudenter respondēre coepisset, ad extrēmum nihil negāvit (Cic. Cat. 3, 5, 12), *although at first he had begun to reply defiantly, at the end he denied nothing.*

643. OBSERVATION AND INFERENCE: Note that the clauses introduced by **cum** in Exs. 1 and 2 express *cause;* what *mood* do they take (see **possent,** Ex. 1, and **sint,** Ex. 2)? Note that the clause introduced by **cum** in Ex. 3 expresses *concession;* what *mood* does it take (see **coepisset**)? Frame a rule for the Mood to be used with **cum** in clauses denoting Cause or Concession.

644. REFERENCES FOR VERIFICATION: A. & G. 326; H. 515, III., 517; G. 581, III., 1, 2.

645.   **EXAMPLES.**

1. **Ō terram illam beātam** quae hunc virum excēperit (Cic. Mil. 38, 105), *O happy the land which shall receive (shall have received) this man!*

2. **Ō praeclārum diem** cum in illud dīvīnum animōrum concilium proficiscar (Cic. Cat. Maj. 23, 84), *O glorious day, when I shall depart to join that divine company of spirits!*

646. OBSERVATION AND INFERENCE: Note that **terram** (Ex. 1) and **diem** (Ex. 2) are used in *exclamations;* in what *case* are they? Frame a rule for the Case of Substantives used in Exclamations.

647. References for Verification: A. & G. 240, *d*; H. 381; G. 340.

648. EXERCISES.

I. 1. Quae cum **ita sint, patrēs** cōnscrīptī, vōbīs populī Rōmānī praesidia nōn dēsunt. 2. Ō tempora! Ō mōrēs! senātus haec intellegit, cōnsul **videt:** hīc tamen vīvit. 3. Mīlitēs, **cum** frīgore et adsiduīs **imbribus** tardārentur, **tamen** continentī labōre omnia haec superāvērunt. 4. Ō mē miserum, ō mē īnfēlīcem! revocāre tū mē in patriam **potuistī,** ego tē in patriā retinēre nōn poterō? 5. Hī **cum** per **sē** minus valērent, Germānōs atque Ariovistum sibī **adjūnxerant.** 6. Cum prīmī ōrdinēs hostium concidissent, **tamen** ācerrimē reliquī resistēbant.

II. 1. Notwithstanding this,[1] I shall nevertheless make peace with you **if you make reparation**[2] to the Aedui for (**dē**) injuries. 2. Verily, if this **man's** comrades follow him,[3] [how] happy [shall] we [be], [how] fortunate the commonwealth! 3. It is a very easy matter,[4] as (**cum**) we excel all in valor, to obtain control of all Gaul. 4. Not being able[5] to sustain the assaults of our men, they betook themselves to their baggage and wagons. 5. O wretched lot! 6. Although **the Suebi had not been** able to drive out the Ubii, they nevertheless **compelled** them to pay tribute.[6]

649. Supplementary Exercises.

I. 1. Illī, cum neque vī contendere neque clam trānsīre possent, **revertī** sē in suās sēdēs simulāvērunt. 2. At hostēs, cum ipsī **nōn** amplius octingentōs equitēs[7] **habērent,** celeriter nostrōs perturbāvērunt. 3. O praeclārum mūnus aetātis, sī quidem id aufert ā nōbīs quod est in adulēscentiā vitiōsissimum!

II. 1. The Helvetians, **because (cum)** they knew that he had crossed the river in a single day, **sent ambassadors** to him. 2. Caesar, although **there** was no doubt whatever[8] about the purpose of his adversaries, sent back the legion to Pompey. 3. O wretched old man, in-that-he[9] did not see that death ought to be disregarded!

[1] *although these* [things] *are so.*
[2] cf. 598, Ex. 1.
[3] Trans.: *if his comrades shall have followed this* [man].
[4] Translate: *it is very easy.*
[5] Translate: *since they were not able.*
[6] "Compelled them to pay tribute" = *made them tributary to themselves.*
[7] A. & G. 247, c; H. 417, n. 2.
[8] Translate: *it was by no means* (minimē) *doubtful.*
[9] quī (= cum is) with subjunctive.

LESSON LXXXIV.

Temporal Clauses with Priusquam and Antequam.

650. EXAMPLES.

1. **Priusquam quicquam cōnārētur, Divitiacum ad sē vocārī jubet** (1, 19, 3), *before taking any action, he gave orders for Divitiacus to be summoned before him.*
2. **Nec prius**[1] **sunt vīsī quam**[1] **castrīs appropinquārent** (6, 37, 2), *and they were not seen until they were close upon the camp.*
3. **Antequam dē meō adventū audīre potuissent, in Macedoniam perrēxī** (Cic. Planc. 41, 98), *before they could hear of my coming, I proceeded to Macedonia.*
4. **Neque prius**[1] **fugere dēstitērunt quam**[1] **ad flūmen pervēnērunt** (1, 53, 1), *nor did they cease to flee until they had reached the river.*
5. **Omnia ante**[1] **facta sunt quam**[1] **iste Ītaliam attigit** (Cic. Verr. 2, 2, 66, 161), *everything was done before he reached Italy.*

651. Observation and Inference: Note that the temporal clauses in the foregoing examples are in *narration* and that they are introduced by **priusquam** (Exs. 1, 2, 4) or **antequam** (Exs. 3, 5). Note that the verb of the temporal clause in Exs. 1–3 is in the *imperfect* or *pluperfect tense;* in what *mood* is it (see: **cōnārētur**, Ex. 1, **appropinquārent**, Ex. 2, **potuissent**, Ex. 3)? What other temporal particle takes the same mood with these tenses in narration (see Exs. in **627**)? Note that the temporal clauses in Exs. 4 and 5 mark the time of the main action with *definiteness* and *precision*, what *mood* do they take (see **pervēnērunt**, Ex. 4, and **attigit**, Ex. 5)? What other temporal particle takes the same mood under the same circumstances (see **632**, Ex. 1)? Frame a rule for the Moods to be used with **priusquam** and **antequam** in Narration.

652.   EXAMPLES.

1. **Ante** quam prō L. Mūrēnā dīcere **īnstituō**, prō mē ipsō pauca dīcam (Cic. *Mur.* 1, 2), *before I undertake to speak in behalf of Lucius Murena, I shall say a few words in my own behalf.*

2. **Nunquam conquiēscam ante quam illōrum ratiōnēs percēperō** (Cic. *de Orat.* 3, 36, 145), *I shall never rest until I have learned their methods.*

3. **Is vidēlicet ante quam veniat in Pontum**, lītterās ad Pompējum mittet (Cic. *Agr.* 2, 20, 53), *doubtless before going to Pontus (i.e., that he may the more* **effectually** *accomplish his purpose* in going to Pontus) *he will send a letter to Pompey.*

653. OBSERVATION AND INFERENCE: Note that the temporal clauses in the foregoing examples refer to the *future*; what *moods* and *tenses* may **priusquam** and **antequam** take under these circumstances (see: **īnstituō**, Ex. 1, **percēperō**, Ex. 2, **veniat**, Ex. 3)? Frame a rule for the Moods and Tenses to be used with **priusquam** and **antequam** in Temporal Clauses referring to the Future.

654. REFERENCES FOR VERIFICATION of Rules framed under **651** and **653**: A. & G. 327, *a*; H. 520, I., 1, 2, II.; G. 576, 579.

655.   EXERCISES.

I. 1. Nec prius ille est vacuus relīctus locus quam fīnis est pūgnandī factus. 2. Prius ad hostium castra pervēnit quam quid agerētur Germānī sentīre possent. 3. Prius quam dē cēterīs rēbus respondeō, dē amīcitiā pauca dīcam. 4. Caesar priusquam eōdem est profectus, lūna vīsa est. 5. Ducentīs annīs **antequam Rōmam** caperent, in Italiam

Gallī dēscendērunt. 6. Nōn dēfatīgābor ante **quam illōrum ancipitēs viās percēperō.**

II. 1. **Nor** did they cease to pursue[2] until they drew near to the gates. 2. He arrived before Pompey could be aware of [it]. 3. For the purpose of getting information on these points[3] before making[4] the trial, he sent forward Volusenus with a ship of war. 4. Before I come back to the main question, I will say a few [words] about myself. 5. A few [words] must be said **by** way of explanation[5] **before I begin.**[6] 6. Nor was there **an** end of butchering. 7.**The Sulla** had sated all his [followers] with riches.

656. **Supplementary** Exercises.

I. 1. Nāvibus eōrum occupātīs, priusquam ea pars Menapiōrum quae citrā Rhēnum erat certior fieret, flūmen trānsiērunt. 2. Nōn prius vīdit turmās Juliānās quam suōs caedī sēnsit. 3. Ante quam dē rē pūblicā dīcam ea quae dīcenda[7] hōc tempore arbitror, expōnam vōbīs breviter cōnsilium et profectiōnis et re-versiōnis meae.

II. 1. They begged Caesar **to send them aid** before **the** king should collect a force. 2. **I shall make a** point of coming[8] to you before I pass quite out of your recollection. 3. The ambassadors did not depart until they had seen[9] the soldiers embarked on [board] the ships.

---

[1] The parts of **priusquam** and **antequam** may be separated by the intervention of other words.
[2] Trans.: *make an end of pursuing.*
[3] **Translate**: *for these* [things] *to be ascertained.*
[4] cf. 650, Ex. 1.
[5] Translate: *a few* [things] *must be made clear.*
[6] *i.e.*, in order that I may begin satisfactorily; cf. 652, Ex. 3.
[7] sc. **esse.**
[8] Translate: *I shall bestow pains that I may* **come.**
[9] cf. 650, Ex. 4.

LESSON LXXXV.

TEMPORAL CLAUSES WITH **Dum** AND **Quoad**.—PRICE.

657. EXAMPLES.

1. **Dum** Caesar morātur, ad eum lēgātī vēnērunt (4, 22, 1), *while Caesar was delaying, envoys came to him.*
2. **Quoad** vīvēs, nunquam tibī redditam grātiam putāverīs (Sall. *Jug.* 110, 4), *as long as you* (shall) *live, never consider yourself fully requited* (that requital has been rendered to you).
3. [**Ferrum**] retinuit quoad renūntiātum est vīcisse Boeōtōs (Nep. *Epam.* 9, 3), *he kept the sword in place until it was reported that the Boeotians were victorious* (had conquered).
4. **Dum** nāvēs eō **convenīrent**, exspectāvit (4, 23, 4), *he waited for* (until) *the ships to come* (should come) *up* (*i.e.*, that the ships might come up before he attempted a landing).
5. Exercēbātur ad eum fīnem quoad **complectī posset** atque **contendere** (Nep. *Epam.* 2, 4), *he trained himself to the end that he might be able* (until he should be able) *to grapple and fight.*

658. OBSERVATION AND INFERENCE: Note that, in Exs. 1–3, the temporal clauses introduced by **dum** (Ex. 1) and **quoad** (Exs. 2 and 3) express *time merely;* what *mood* do they take (see: morātur, Ex. 1, **vīvēs**, Ex. 2, renūntiātum est, Ex. 3)? Note that, in Exs. 4 and 5, the temporal clauses introduced by these particles express *purpose* as well as time; what *mood* do they take (see: convenīrent, Ex. 4, and posset, Ex. 5)? Frame a rule for the Moods to be used with **dum** and **quoad**.

659. REFERENCES FOR VERIFICATION: A. & G. 328 (to the period); H. 519, I., II., 1, 2; G. 571, 573, 574.

660. OBSERVATION: Note that, in Ex. 1, **dum** is used with the present indicative (see **morātur**) although *past time* is referred to.

661. REFERENCES: A. & G. 276, *e*; H. 467, 4; G. 572.

662.   EXAMPLES.

1. Vīgintī talentīs ūnam ōrātiōnem Īsocratēs vēndidit (Plin.
  N. H. 7, 31), *Isocrates sold a single oration for twenty talents*.
2. Emāmus vel māgnō (Cic. Att. 13, 29, 3), *let us buy even* [if we
  have to buy] *at a high price*.
3. Līs aestimātur centum talentīs (Nep. Tim. 3, 5), *the fine is
  fixed at a hundred talents*.
4. Nēmō nisi vīctor pāce bellum mūtāvit¹ (Sall. Cat. 58, 15), *none
  but the victor exchanges war for peace*.

663. OBSERVATION AND INFERENCE: Note that vēndidit (Ex. 1) is a verb of *selling*, emāmus (Ex. 2), a verb of *buying*, aestimātur (Ex. 3), a verb of *valuing*, and mūtāvit (Ex. 4), a verb of *exchanging;* by what *case* is the *price* denoted (see: talentīs, Ex. 1, māgnō, Ex. 2, talentīs, Ex. 3, pāce, Ex. 4)? Frame a rule for the Case of words denoting Price.

664. REFERENCES FOR VERIFICATION: A. & G. 252; H. 422; G. 404.

665.   EXAMPLES.

1. Ēmit tantī quantī Pȳthius voluit (Cic. **Off. 3, 14, 59**), *he bought at Pythius's own price* (for as much as Pythius wished).
2. Vēndō nōn plūris, fortasse etiam minōris (Cic. Off. 3, 12, 51), *I sell no dearer, perhaps even cheaper*.

666. OBSERVATION AND INFERENCE: Note that ēmit (Ex. 1) and vēndō (Ex. 2) are verbs of *buying* and *selling* respectively; and that the *price* is here expressed by tantī (Ex. 1), quantī (Ex. 1), plūris (Ex. 2), and minōris (Ex. 2). In what *case* are these words? Frame a special rule for the constructions here illustrated.

667. REFERENCES FOR VERIFICATION: A. & G. 252, d; H. 405; G. 380.

668.   EXERCISES.

I. 1. Dum ea geruntur, iī quī prō portīs castrōrum in statiōne erant, Caesarī nūntiāvērunt pulverem vidērī. 2. Ipse intereā, quoad legiōnēs conlocātās cōgnōvisset, in Galliā morārī cōnstituit.   3. Dīcit quantī cūjusque agrī decumās vēndiderit. 4. Quot minīs eam ēmit? Quadrāgintā minīs. 5. Ipse, equō vulnerātō, dējectus, quoad potuit fortissimē restitit. 6. Quod nōn opus est, asse cārum. 7. **Vēndō** meum minōris **quam** ille. 8. Sīc deinceps omne opus contexitur dum jūsta mūrī altitūdō expleātur. 9. Dum haec geruntur, nūntiātum est equitēs accēdere.

II. 1. Nor did they **cease to pursue**[2] until the horsemen had utterly routed the enemy.[3] 2. **But to wait until the forces of** the enemy should be augmented, he thought was the height of folly.[4] 3. For how much **did he buy** her? Cheap.[5] 4. Would a good man buy[6] for a denarius[7] what is worth **a** thousand denarii[8]? 5. While he was delaying a few days near (**ad**) Vesontio, great alarm suddenly took possession of the army. 6. That sufficient time might intervene for the soldiers to assemble,[9] he answered the envoys ... 7. We cannot buy for less. 8. This penalty was fixed at fifty talents.

669. Supplementary Exercises.

I. 1. Caesar nōn exspectandum sibī statuit dum in Santonōs Helvētii pervenīant. 2. Quae tribuerat beneficia tam diū meminerat quoad ille grātus erat quī accēperat. 3. Hōc nōn minōris **aestimāmus quam quemlibet** amplissimum triumphum. 4. **Eōrum salūtem** cīvitās levī mōmentō aestimāre **nōn potest.**

II. 1. Wait until you can know what you have to do.[10] 2. While they were getting[11] these things together,[11] about six thousand men made haste to [reach] the Rhine. 3. I did my utmost[12] to dispose of[13] the tithes at the highest possible price.

---

[1] The **perfect is here used to express** a general **truth, and must be translated** by the present.
[2] Trans. *make an end of pursuing.*
[3] Trans.: *drove the enemy headlong.*
[4] Translate: *he thought to be of the greatest folly.*
[5] vīlī (sc. **pretiō**), *at a low rate.*
[6] **Ēmatne?**
[7] See **dēnārius**, Latin-English vocab.

[8] Translate *what is of a thousand denarii;* for form of genitive (**dēnāriūm**), see: A. & G. 40, *e*, H. 52, 3; G. 29, 3; **for mood of** verb, see Exs. in 573.
[9] cf. 657, Ex. 4.
[10] cf. 317, Ex. 1.
[11] Express passively.
[12] Translate: *Effort was bestowed by me with the greatest energy.*
[13] **ut** with subjunctive.

LESSON LXXXVI.

PLACE FROM WHICH. — PLACE TO WHICH. — PLACE WHERE.

670. EXAMPLES.

1. **Ab urbe** proficiscī (1, 7, 1), *to set out from the city.*
2. Cīvitātī persuāsit **ut dē** fīnibus **suīs** exīrent (1, 2, 1), *he persuaded his countrymen to emigrate.*
3. **Ex** prōvinciā convēnerant (1, 8, 1), *they had come together from the province.*
4. Brundisiō veniēbant (Caes. B. C. 3, 25, 1), *they came from Brundisium.*
5. **Athēnīs** vēnimus (Cic. Att. 5, 12, 1), *we came from Athens.*
6. **Domō** dūxerat (1, 53, 4), *he had brought from home.*
7. **Rūre** [redīre] (Ter. Eun. 3, 5, 63), *to return from the country.*

671. OBSERVATION AND INFERENCE: Note that, in Exs. 1–3, which illustrate the common usage, *place from which* is denoted by the *ablative with a preposition* (see: **ab urbe**, Ex. 1, **dē fīnibus**, Ex. 2, **ex prōvinciā**, Ex. 3). Note, however, that in Exs. 4 and 5, where the substantive denoting 'place from which' is the name of a *town*, the ablative *without a preposition* is used (see: **Brundisiō**, Ex. 4, and **Athēnīs**, Ex. 5). Note, further, that **domus** and **rūs**, like names of towns, *have no preposition* (see: **domō**, Ex. 6, and **rūre**, Ex. 7). Frame a rule for the **expression** of Place From Which.

672. REFERENCES FOR VERIFICATION: A. & G. 258, *a*; H. 412, I., II., 1; G. 411, Rem. 1².

673. EXAMPLES.

1. **Ad eum locum** vēnit (1, 49, 1), *he came to that place.*
2. **In Galliam** contendit (1, 7, 1), *he hastens into Gaul.*
3. **Rōmam** profectus (6, 12, 5), *having set out for Rome.*
4. **Corfīnium** pervenit (Caes. B. C. 1, 15, 6), *he comes to Corfinium.*
5. **Domum** revertērunt (2, 29, 1), *they returned home.*
6. **Domōs suās** invītant (Sall. Jug. 66, 3), *they invite to their homes.*
7. Abī **rūs** (Pl. Most. 1, 1, 63), *go into the country.*

674. Observation and Inference: Note that in Exs. 1 and 2, which illustrate the common usage, *place to which* is denoted by the *accusative with a preposition* (see : ad locum, Ex. 1, and in Galliam, Ex. 2). Note, however, that in Exs. 3 and 4, where the substantive denoting 'place to which' is the name of a *town*, the accusative *without a preposition* is used (see : **Rōmam**, Ex. 3, and **Corfīnium**, Ex. 4). Note, further, that **domus** and **rūs**, like names of towns, *have no preposition* (see: domum, Ex. 5, **domōs**, Ex. 6, rūs, Ex. 7). Frame a rule for the expression of Place To Which.

675. References for Verification: A. & G. 258, *b*; H. 380, I., II., 2, 1) ; G. 410.

676. EXAMPLES.

1. **In eōrum fīnibus** (1, 1, 4), *in their territories.*
2. **Erat in Galliā legiō ūna** (1, 7, 2), *there was in Gaul one legion.*
3. **Ut Rōmae cōnsulēs, sīc Carthāginī rēgēs** (Nep. *Hann.* 7, 4), *as at Rome consuls, so at Carthage kings.*
4. **Remanēre Brundisiī** (Caes. *B. C.* 1, 25, 2), *to stay at Brundisium.*
5. **Tum māximum magistrātum Thēbīs obtinēbat** (Nep. *Pel.* 3, 2), *at that time he held the highest magistracy at Thebes.*
6. **Domī mīlitiaeque, marī atque terrā** (Sall. *Cat.* 53, 2), *at home and abroad, on land and sea.*
7. **Bellī domīque** (Sall. *Jug.* 41, 7), *in war and in peace.*
8. **Locus humī dēpressus** (Sall. *Cat.* 55, 3), *a place underground* (sunk in the ground).
9. **An rūrī cēnsēs tē esse** (Pl. *Most.* 1, 1, 7), *do you think you're in the country?*

677. Observation and Inference: Note that, in Exs. 1 and 2, which illustrate the common usage, *place where* is denoted by the *ablative with a preposition* (see In fīnibus, Ex. 1, and in Galliā, Ex. 2). Note, however, that in Exs. 3–5, where the substantive denoting place is the name of a *town*, a *locative* form is used *without a preposition* (see : **Rōmae** and **Carthāginī**, Ex. 3, **Brundisiī**, Ex. 4, and **Thēbīs**, Ex. 5). Note, further, that in the first and second declensions singular, this *locative* is the same in form as the *genitive* (see **Rōmae**, Ex. 3, and **Brundisiī**, Ex. 4); and that, in the third declension and in the plural, it is the same as the *dative* or *ablative* (see **Carthāginī**, Ex. 3, and **Thēbīs**, Ex. 5). Note, further, that the *preposition is not used* with the *ablatives* **marī** and **terrā** (Ex. 6); also with the *locatives* **domī** (Exs. 6 and 7), **mīlitiae** (Ex. 6), **bellī** (Ex. 7), **humī** (Ex. 8), and **rūrī** (Ex. 9). Frame a rule for the expression of Place Where.

678. REFERENCES FOR VERIFICATION: A. & G. 258, *c*, *d*; H. 425, I., II., 426, 2; G. 412, Rem. 1.

LESSON LXXXVII.

ILLUSTRATIVE EXERCISES ON THE FOREGOING CONSTRUCTIONS.

679. EXERCISES.

I. 1. Ab Allobrogibus in Segūsiāvōs exercitum dūcit. 2. Lēgātī Carthāginiēnsēs Rōmam vēnērunt. 3. Interim Diōn Syrācūsīs interfectus est. 4. In Galliā morārī cōnstituit. 5. Id nōs faciēmus, cum tū domō proficīscēns vēneris Lemnum.[1] 6. Dionȳsius **tyrannus** Syrācūsīs expulsus Corinthī puerōs docēbat. 7. Nūllam partem Germānōrum domum **remittere possum**. 8. Reliquī, quī domī mānsērunt, **sē atque illōs alunt**. 9. Celeriter ad eās quās dīximus mūnītiōnēs pervēnērunt. 10. Diem quō Rōmā sīs exitūrus, cūrā ut sciam. 11. Armōrum māgnā multitūdine dē mūrō in fossam jactā, pāce sunt ūsī. 12. Nunc rūs abībō. 13. Illī erat animus bellī ingēns, domī modicus. 14. Xerxēs terrā marīque bellum intulit Graeciae. 15. Vārus venientem Uticam Tūberōnem portū atque oppidō prohibet. 16. Jacet humī. 17. Rēs ipsa hortārī vidētur paucīs[2] īnstitūta mājōrum domī mīlitiaeque disserere. 18. Rūre **hūc** advenit.

II. 1. Having gone out **from** the camp, they hastened **to** the Rhine. 2. Caesar came to Brundisium. 3. When this battle had been reported[3] across the Rhine, the Suebi began to return home. 4. He thinks he's in the country. 5. Complete control of public affairs,[4] both civil[5] and military,[5] was intrusted to Alcibiades. 6. Oedipus was born at Thebes. 7. A certain Demaratus fled from Corinth to Tarquinii. 8. His services in the battle before (apud) Sena were highly[6] valued. 9. There were but two routes by which they could go out from home. 10. Neither by land nor by sea had the enemy been able to prove a match[7] [for them]. 11. The archers came from Crete[1] and Lacedaemon. 12. When (cum) his arms had been seized[8] at Capua and his slaves seen at Naples, he abandoned his design. 13. The Allobroges are on their way home. 14. Eporedorix had very great influence[9] at home.

680. Supplementary Exercises.

I. 1. Uxōrem domō sēcum dūxerat. 2. Multa populus Rōmānus domī mīlitiaeque, marī atque terrā, praeclāra facinora fēcit. 3. Sed is nātus et omnem pueritiam Arpīnī altus est. 4. Arcem Syrācūsīs quam mūnierat Dionȳsius ad urbem obsidendam, ā fundāmentīs disjēcit. 5. Eōrum quī domum rediērunt cēnsus habitus est. 6. Quibus rēbus Rōmam nūntiātīs, tantus repente terror invāsit ut cōnsul ex urbe profugeret. 7. Athēnīs profectus est.

II. 1. I am able to sleep on the ground. 2. He learns that the envoys have been sent home in advance. 3. A letter was brought from Athens for Archias,[10] who held the chief magistracy in Thebes. 4. In the consulship of Marcus Claudius and Lucius Furius,[3] envoys came from Rome to Carthage. 5. A list had been made out [showing] how many[11] of them had left their homes.[12] 6. The-people-of-Zama meantime sent envoys to Caesar at Utica.[13] 7. He is very powerful at home.

---

[1] The names of small islands have the same construction as the names of towns.
[2] briefly.
[3] Ablative absolute.
[4] tōta rēs pūblica.
[5] Translate: at home and in war.
[6] A. & G. 252, a; H. 404; G. 379.
[7] "to prove a match" = to be equal.
[8] In what mood? cf. Exs. under 627.
[9] Translate: was of very great influence.
[10] See Lesson LXXII., foot-note 7.
[11] "how many" = what number.
[12] Trans.: had gone out from home.
[13] Trans.: to Caesar to Utica.

LESSON LXXXVIII.

Indirect Discourse: Declaratory and Imperative Sentences.

681.   **EXAMPLES.**

1.
   - *a.* **Mōns tenētur**, *the mountain is held.*
   - *b.* Cōnsidius dīcit **montem tenērī** (1, 22, 2), *Cōnsidius says that the mountain is held.*

2.
   - *a.* [**Nōs**] **parātī sumus**, *we are ready.*
   - *b.* **Sē parātōs esse** arbitrātī sunt (1, 5, 2), *they thought that they were ready.*

3.
   - *a.* **Helvētiī castra mōvērunt**, *the Helvetians have broken up their camp.*
   - *b.* Caesar cōgnōvit **Helvētiōs castra mōvisse** (1, 22, 4), *Caesar learned that the Helvetians had broken up their camp.*

4.
   - *a.* **Ego id quod in Nerviīs fēcī faciam**, *I shall do what I did in the case of the Nervii.*
   - *b.* Caesar respondit **sē id** quod in Nerviīs **fēcisset factūrum** (2, 32, 2), *Caesar replied that he should do what he had done in the case of the Nervii.*

682. Observation and Inference: Note that the examples marked *a* in the foregoing illustrations, give the *exact language* of the *original speaker* as it came from his lips (see Exs. 1 and 4), as it passed through his mind without being actually spoken (see Ex. 2), or as it was communicated through messengers or letters (see Ex. 3). Note, further, that the examples marked *b* show the *transformations* which the language of the original speaker undergoes when it is *reported*. The examples marked *a* illustrate what is called *Direct Discourse;* the examples marked *b* illustrate what is called *Indirect Discourse.* Define Direct Discourse. Define Indirect Discourse.

683. References for Verification: A. & G. 335; H. 522, 1; G. 651.

681. EXAMPLES.

1.
- a. **Mōns tenētur**, *the mountain is held.*
- b. Cōnsidius dīcit **montem tenērī** (1, 22, 2), *Considius says that the mountain is held.*

2.
- a. [**Nōs**] **parātī sumus**, *we are ready.*
- b. **Sē parātōs esse** arbitrātī sunt (1, 5, 2), *they thought that they were ready.*

3.
- a. **Helvētiī castra mōvērunt**, *the Helvetians have broken up their camp.*
- b. Caesar cōgnōvit **Helvētiōs castra mōvisse** (1, 22, 4), *Caesar learned that the Helvetians had broken up their camp.*

4.
- a. **Ego id quod in Nerviīs fēcī faciam**, *I shall do what I did in the case of the Nervii.*
- b. Caesar respondit **sē id quod in Nerviīs fēcisset factūrum** (2, 32, 2), *Caesar replied that he should do what he had done in the case of the Nervii.*

684. OBSERVATION AND INFERENCE: Note that the examples marked *a* illustrate *declaratory sentences* in which the principal *verb* is in the *indicative mood* (see: **tenētur**, Ex. 1, *a*; **sumus**, Ex. 2, *a*; **mōvērunt**, Ex. 3, *a*; **faciam**, Ex. 4, *a*) and its *subject* in the *nominative case* (see: **mōns**, Ex. 1, *a*; **nōs**, Ex. 2, *a*; **Helvētiī**, Ex. 3, *a*; **ego**, Ex. 4, *a*).

Note, further, that, in the corresponding examples of Indirect Discourse marked *b*, the *indicative* has been changed to the *infinitive* (see: **tenērī**, Ex. 1, *b*; **esse**, Ex. 2, *b*; **mōvisse**, Ex. 3, *b*; **factūrum**, Ex. 4, *b*), and that the *nominative* has been changed to the *accusative* (see: **montem**, Ex. 1, *b*; **sē**, Ex. 2, *b*; **Helvētiōs**, Ex. 3, *b*; **sē**, Ex. 4, *b*).

Note, finally, in **Ex. 4**, that the verb of the *subordinate* clause has been changed from the *indicative* of the Direct Discourse (see **fēcī**, Ex. 4, *a*) to the *subjunctive* in the Indirect (see **fēcisset**, Ex. 4, *b*).

Frame a rule for the constructions to be used in Declaratory Sentences of Indirect Discourse.

685. REFERENCES FOR VERIFICATION: A. & G. 336; H. 523, I., 524; G. 653.

686. **EXAMPLES.**

1.
- *a.* **Adī cīvitātēs,** *visit the communities.*
- *b.* Huic imperat **adeat cīvitātēs** (4, 21, 8), *he ordered this man to visit the communities.*

2.
- *a.* **Nōlī hostis populō Rōmānō fierī,** *do not become an enemy to the Roman people.*
- *b.* Lēgātōs ad Bocchum mittit postulātum **nē hostis populō Rōmānō fieret** (Sall. Jug. 83, 1), *he sent ambassadors to Bocchus to urge him not to become an enemy to the Roman people.*

687. OBSERVATION AND INFERENCE: Note that the examples marked *a* in the foregoing illustrations contain *imperative* expressions (see: **adī**, Ex. 1, *a*, and **nōlī fierī**, Ex. 2, *a*). Note, in the corresponding examples of Indirect Discourse marked *b*, that these imperative expressions are denoted by the *subjunctive* (see: **adeat**, Ex. 1, *b*, and **nē fieret**, Ex. 2, *b*). Frame a rule for Imperative Expressions in Indirect Discourse.

688. REFERENCES FOR VERIFICATION: A. & G. 339; H. 523, III.; G. 655.

689. NOTE: The Tenses of the Infinitive in Indirect Discourse follow the rules already framed for dependent infinitives (see **466** and **467**, Lesson LIX.); the Tenses of the Subjunctive in Indirect Discourse follow the rules already framed for dependent subjunctives (see **439-442**, Lesson LV.). But see, also: H. 525, 1; G. 657.

LESSON LXXXIX.

Illustrative Exercises on the Foregoing Principles.

690. **EXERCISES.**

I. 1. Aeduīs ego obsidēs nōn reddam. 2. Ariovistus respondit: Aeduīs sē obsidēs redditūrum nōn esse. 3. Mihī ea rēs cūrae erit. 4. Caesar pollicitus est sibī eam rem cūrae futūram. 5. Allobrogibus sēsē persuāsūrōs[1] exīstimābant. 6. Intellegimus eam rem nōn minus ex ūsū terrae Galliae quam populī Rōmānī accidisse. 7. Lēgātī ad Caesarem grātulātum[2] convēnērunt: intellegere sēsē eam rem nōn minus ex ūsū terrae Galliae quam populī Rōmānī accidisse. 8. Hōc[3] est gravior fortūna Sēquanōrum, quod sōlī nē in occultō[4] quidem querī audent. 9. Dīvitiacus respondit: hōc esse graviōrem fortūnam Sēquanōrum, quod sōlī nē in occultō quidem querī audērent. 10. Cum volēs, congredere. 11. Ariovistus respondit: cum vellet, congrederētur. 12. Ariovistus respondit: sē nōn sine exercitū in eās partēs Galliae venīre audēre quās Caesar possidēret.

II. 1. No one has [ever] contended with me without [meeting] his own destruction. 2. Ariovistus made answer that no one had [ever] contended with him without [meeting] his own destruction. 3. I shall wage war neither against[5] the Aeduī nor against their allies. 4. Ariovistus made answer that he should wage war neither against the Aeduī nor against their allies. 5. Caesar observed that the Sēquanī were gazing on the ground. 6. What business[6] has Caesar in my Gaul, which I conquered in war?[7] 7. I am at a loss to understand[8] what business Caesar has in my Gaul, which I conquered in war. 8. Ariovistus answered that he was at a loss to understand what business

Caesar had in **his Gaul, which he** had conquered in war.
9. Restore the hostages which you have [received] from the
Aedui.   10. Caesar sent ambassadors to him [who were
authorized to demand] that he should restore the hostages
which he had [received] from the Aedui.

691.   Supplementary Exercises.

NOTE: In the following sentences, restore to the direct form the passages in indirect discourse.

I. 1. Animadvertit Caesar Sēquanōs nihil eārum rērum facere quās cēterī facerent.   2. Lēgātī **ab** Aeduīs veniēbant questum[2]: sēsē nē obsidibus[4] quidem datīs pācem redimere potuisse.   3. Caesar honōris Dīvitiācī causā sēsē eōs in fidem receptūrum et cōnservātūrum dīxit.   4. Ad haec Q. Mārcius respondit: ab armīs discēdant,[9] Rōmam supplicēs proficīscantur.[9]   5. Aduātucī lēgātōs ad Caesarem mīsērunt, quī ad hunc modum locūtī: nē sē armīs dēspoliāret; sibī omnēs ferē finitimōs esse inimīcōs; ā quibus sē dēfendere trāditīs armīs nōn possent.

II. 1. Ariovistus answered that the Aedui, inasmuch **as they had been** defeated, had become subject to him.   2. **Caesar sent** ambassadors to Ariovistus [who were commissioned to demand] that he should bring no more men[10] across the Rhine into Gaul.
3. Nor did they think that men of hostile disposition would refrain from injury.

---

[1] sc. **esse.**
[2] cf. **381.**
[3] Ablative of cause.
[4] See Lesson LXVIII., foot-note 8.
[5] **bellum īnferre** with dative.
[6] cf. Lesson LIII., foot-note **7.**
[7] "**in** war" = *by means of war.*

[8] Translate: *it seems strange to me.*
[9] The subjunctive is here in a primary tense, although the leading verb **respondit** is in a secondary tense; this frequently happens in indirect discourse.
[10] Trans.: *not any* (**nē quam**) *multitude of men more* (**amplius**).

LESSON XC.

Conditional Sentences in Indirect Discourse.

692. EXAMPLES.

1.
   a. **Sī quid ille mē vult, illum ad mē venīre oportet**, *if that man wants anything of me, he ought to come to me.*
   b. Ariovistus respondit: **sī quid ille sē velit,**[1] **illum ad sē venīre oportēre** (1, 34, 2), *Ariovistus replied that, if that man wanted anything of him, he ought to come to him.*

2.
   a. **Sī quid petere vultis, ab armīs discēdite**, *if you wish to ask for anything, lay down your arms.*
   b. Mārcius respondit: **sī** quid **petere** velint,[1] ab armīs **discēdant**[1] (Sall. *Cat.* 34, 1), *Marcius replied that, if they wished to ask for anything, they must lay down their arms.*

3.
   a. **Sī quid mihī opus esset, ego vēnissem,** *if I were in need of anything, I should have come myself.*
   b. Ariovistus respondit: **sī** quid ipsī opus esset, sēsē **ventūrum fuisse** (1, 34, 2), *Ariovistus replied that, if he were in need of anything, he should have come himself.*

4.
   a. **Id sī fīet, māgnō cum perīculō erit,** *if this happens* (shall happen), *it will be attended with great danger.*
   b. **Id sī fieret,** intellegēbat māgnō cum perīculō futūrum (1, 10, 2), *he saw clearly that, if this should happen, it would be attended with great danger.*

5.
   a. **Sī id ita fēceris, populō Rōmānō amīcitia tēcum erit,** *if you do* (shall have done) *this, you will have the friendship of the Roman people.*
   b. Ad eum Caesar lēgātōs cum hīs mandātīs mittit: **sī id ita fēcisset, populō Rōmānō amīcitiam cum eō futūram** (1, 35, 1 and 4), *Caesar sent ambassadors to him, who were commissioned to say that, if he should do this, he would have the friendship of the Roman people.*

CONDITIONAL SENTENCES.

a. **Voluptās quidem, sī ipsa prō sē loquātur, concēdat dīgnitātī,** *indeed, if Pleasure herself were to speak in her own behalf, she would yield precedence to Worth.*

b. **Voluptātem quidem, sī ipsa prō sē loquātur, concēssūram** arbitror **dīgnitātī** (Cic. *Fin.* 3, 1, 1), *indeed, I think that, if Pleasure herself were to speak in her own behalf, she would yield precedence to Worth.*

693. NOTE: The foregoing examples involve no new principles; they merely illustrate the application of the principles of Indirect Discourse **to Conditional Sentences.**

694.   **EXERCISES.**

I. 1. **Sī iterum** experīrī vultis, ego iterum parātus sum dēcertāre.   2. **Ariovistus** respondit: sī iterum experīrī velint,[1] sē iterum parātum esse dēcertāre.   3. Nōlī proelium committere nisi meae cōpiae prope hostium castra vīsae erunt.   4. Labiēnō erat praeceptum ā Caesare: nē proelium committeret nisi ipsīus cōpiae prope hostium castra vīsae essent.[2]   5. Caesar profectus est in Ītaliam; **neque** aliter Carnūtēs interficiendī Tasgetiī cōnsilium cēpissent, neque Eburōnēs, sī ille adesset, tantā contemptiōne nostrī **ad** castra venīrent.   6. Titūrius clāmitābat: Caesarem profectum in Ītaliam; neque aliter Carnūtēs interficiendī Tasgetiī cōnsilium fuisse captūrōs, neque Eburōnēs, sī ille adesset, tantā contemptiōne nostrī ad castra ventūrōs esse.   7. Aeduīs ego bellum nōn īnferam, sī in eō manēbunt quod convēnit.   8. Ariovistus respondit: Aeduīs sē bellum inlātūrum nōn **esse, sī in eō** manērent quod convēnisset.   9. Ariovistus ad Caesarem lēgātōs mittit: velle sē agere cum eō; utī aut conloquiō diem cōnstitueret aut, sī id minus vellet, ē suīs aliquem ad sē mitteret.

II. 1. If Hamilcar had lived longer, the Carthaginians would have carried their arms **into**[3] Italy.   2. It was evident that, if Hamilcar had lived longer, the Carthaginians would have carried[4] their arms into Italy.   3. Unless you withdraw[5] **your army from** these regions, I shall regard **you** as (prō) an enemy. 4. Ariovistus answered that, **unless Caesar** should withdraw his army from these regions, he should regard him as an enemy. 5. If you wish to enjoy peace, it is unreasonable to object to the tribute. 6. Ariovistus answered that, if they wished to enjoy peace, **it** was unreasonable to **object** to the tribute. 7. If **you** want anything, return on the thirteenth of **April**.[6] 8. He told the ambassadors in reply,[7] to return **on the** thirteenth of April if they wanted anything.

695.   Supplementary Exercises.

NOTE: In the following sentences, restore to the direct form the **passages in indirect discourse.**

I. 1. Caesar respondit: sī jūdicium senātūs observārī oportēret, līberam dēbēre esse Galliam. 2. Ariovistus respondit: sī discēssisset[8] **Caesar, māgnō** sē illum **praemiō** remūnerātūrum, et quaecumque bella gerī vellet **sine ūllō ējus labōre** et perīculō cōnfectūrum. 3. Nisi eō ipsō **tempore nūntiī dē Caesaris** victōriā essent adlātī, exīstimābant plērīque **futūrum fuisse ut**[9] **oppidum** āmitterētur.

II. 1. If the flight of the Gauls disquiets any, these can learn, if they take the trouble to inquire,[10] that Ariovistus conquered more by craft than by valor. 2. Caesar took them severely to task [saying that] if the flight of the Gauls disquieted any, these could learn, **if they should take** the trouble to inquire, that Ariovistus had conquered more by craft than by valor. 3. Most people think **that** Hamilcar, if he had lived longer, would have carried[4] his arms into Italy.

---

[1] cf. foot-note 9, preceding lesson.
[2] Note that, in accordance with **the** law of sequence **of tenses, the future perfect vīsae erunt (sent. 3) has** become the pluperfect subjunctive **vīsae essent** after the secondary tense **erat praeceptum**: II. 525, 2.
[3] **arma īnferre** with dative.
[4] cf. **fuisse captūrōs,** sent. 6, **preceding exercise.**
[5] cf. 692, Ex. 4.
[6] **ad Īdūs Aprīlīs or ad Īd. Aprīl.**

See **Īdūs** in the general vocab. Note that **Aprīlīs** is here an adjective in the accusative plural agreeing with **Īdūs.**
[7] **Lēgātīs respondit.**
[8] cf. foot-note 2.
[9] **futūrum fuisse ut āmitterētur** is a periphrastic expression for the fut. pass. infin. of **āmittō**; translate: *a great many thought that the town would have been lost.*
[10] Translate: *if they shall inquire.*

LESSON XCI.

NOTE: In this and the following lessons on formation, attention is confined to such modes of formation as are easily understood, and are copiously illustrated in the vocabulary of this book.

FORMATION: SUBSTANTIVES.

I. NAMES OF AGENTS.

696. EXAMPLES.

I. ROOTS OR VERB STEMS.	II. SUFFIX.	III. STEMS.	IV. NAMES OF AGENTS.
1. ¹√duc-, *lead*,	+ -tŏr-	= ductŏr-, st. of	ductor, *leader.*
2. √vĭc-, *conquer*,	+ -tŏr-	= victŏr-, st. of	victor, *conqueror.*
3. ōrā-(st. of ōrō), *speak*,	+ -tŏr-	= ōrātŏr-, st. of	ōrātor, *speaker.*
4. imperā- (st. of imperō), *command*,	+ -tŏr-	= imperātŏr-, st. of	imperātor, *commander.*

697. OBSERVATION AND INFERENCE: Note that the substantives in column IV. denote the *agent* (doer) of the *action* expressed by the corresponding *root* or ***verb stem*** in column I. Thus **ductor** from √**duc-**, *lead*, means 'he who leads' or 'leader.' Hence these substantives are called *Names of Agents*. Note that these names of agents are formed by adding to *roots* (see Exs. 1 and 2) or to *verb stems* (see Exs. 3 and 4) the *suffix* -tŏr-, nom. -tor. Frame a rule for the formation of Names of Agents.

698. Form, as in the foregoing examples, Names of Agents **from** the following —

1. ROOTS: √doc-, TEACH; √lĕg-,² *read*; √pĭg-,² *paint*; √sta-, STAY (= *make* STAND); √suād-,³ (*make* SWEET, and so) *advise*, *urge.*

2. VERB STEMS: **approbā-,** *approve;* **dēprecā-,** *intercede;* dictā-, *dictate;* **explōrā-,** *explore;* mercā-, *trade.*

3. COMPOUNDS ENDING IN A ROOT: dē-√ser-, *desert;* **im-√pol-,**[4] *impel;* in-√ven-, COME UPON, *discover;* prae-√i,[5] *go* BEFORE; prō-√dā-,[6] *give away, betray.*

II. ABSTRACTS DENOTING STATE.

699.   EXAMPLES.

I. ROOTS OR BASES TREATED AS ROOTS.	II. SUFFIX.	III. STEMS.	IV. ABSTRACTS DENOTING STATE.
1. √**dol-,** TEAR, *rend,*	+ -ōr-	= dolōr-, st. of	dolor, *pain.*
2. √fur-, *rage,*	+ -ōr-	= furōr-, st. of	furor, *fury.*
3. Base am- (in **amō**), *love,*	+ -ōr-	= amōr-, st. of	amor, *love.*
4. Base pud- (in **pu-det**), *shame,*	+ -ōr-	= pudōr-, st. of	pudor, *modesty.*

700. OBSERVATION AND INFERENCE: Note that the substantives in column IV. are *abstracts* denoting the *state* suggested by the corresponding roots or bases in column I. Thus **furor** from √fur-, *rage,* means 'a state of rage' or 'fury.' Note that these abstracts are formed by adding to *roots* or to *bases treated as roots* the *suffix* -ōr-, nom. -or. Frame a rule for the formation of Abstracts denoting State.

701. Form Abstracts denoting State from the following —

1. ROOTS: √**ang-,** *squeeze,* √**lab-,** *lay hold of;* √**ters-,**[7] *tremble;* √**tim-,** *choke, be breathless.*

2. BASES TREATED AS ROOTS: rūm-, *sound;* **clām-,** *call, call out.*

---

[1] Roots are denoted by the sign √. Thus √**duc-** is to be read 'root duc-.'
[2] -g- and -gu- become -c- before -t-.
[3] -dt- becomes -s-.
[4] -o- of the root is here weakened to -n-, and -t- of the suffix becomes -s-.
[5] prae -i- is contracted to prae-.
[6] -a- of the root is here weakened to -i-.
[7] -s- of the root becomes -r-.

LESSON XCII.

FORMATION: SUBSTANTIVES (*continued*).

III. ABSTRACTS DENOTING ACTION.

702.   EXAMPLES.

I. Roots or Verb Stems.	II. Suffixes.	III. Stems.	IV. Abstracts denoting Action.
1. √sta-, STA*nd*,	+ -tiōn-	= statiōn-, st. of	statiō, STA*nding*; *a post* or **station**.
2. √gnā-, *be born*,	+ -tiōn-	= ¹(g)nātiōn-, st. of	nātiō, *being born*; *a race* or **nation**.
3. ōrā- (st. of ōrō), *speak*,	+ -tiōn-	= ōrātiōn-, st. of	ōrātiō, *speaking*; *an address*.
4. lēgā- (st. of lēgō), *de-pute*,	+ -tiōn-	= lēgātiōn-, st. of	lēgātiō, *deputing*; *a deputation* or **embassy**.
5. √ic-, *hit*,	+ -tu-	= ictu-, st. of	ictus, *hitting*; *a blow*.
6. √or-, *rise*,	+ -tu-	= ortu-, st. of	ortus, *rising*; *origin*.
7. cōnā- (st. of cōnor), *en-deavor*,	+ -tu-	= cōnātu-, st. of	cōnātus, *endeavoring*; *an effort* or *undertaking*.
8. equitā- (st. of equitō), *ride*,	+ -tu-	= equitātu-, st. of	equitātus, *riding*; *cavalry*.

703. OBSERVATION AND INFERENCE: Note that the substantives in column IV. are *abstracts* denoting the *action* suggested by the corresponding roots or verb stems in column I. Note further, however, that these abstracts may become *concrete* and assume other than their literal meanings. Thus **ōrātiō**, from the verb-stem **ōrā-**, *speak*, means not only 'speaking,' but 'that which is spoken' or 'an address.'

Note that these abstracts are formed by adding to *roots* or to *verb stems* the *suffixes* **-tiōn-**, nom. -tiō (Exs. 1–4), and **-tu-**, nom. **-tus** (Exs. 5–8). Frame a rule for the formation of Abstracts denoting Action.

704. Form Abstracts in **-tiō** from the following—

1. ROOT: √fac-, DO, *make*.
2. BASE TREATED AS ROOT: quaes-, *inquire*.
3. COMPOUNDS ENDING IN A ROOT: cō-√gnā-, *be born with*; con-√ten-, *stretch vigorously, struggle*; con-√jug-,[2] YOKE *together*; oc-√cād-,[3] *fall towards*; re-√vert-,[4] *turn back*; ē-√rup-, *break forth*; pro-√fac-,[5] *make* FOR*th* or *off*; dē-√fend-,[3] *thrust off*.
4. COMPOUNDS ENDING IN BASES TREATED AS ROOTS: dis-sent-, *think differently*; in-curr-,[6] *rush against*.
5. VERB STEMS: mūnī- (st. of mūniō), *fortify*; aestimā- (st. of aestimō), *value*; perturbā- (st. of perturbō), *throw into confusion*; cunctā- (st. of cunctor), *delay*; conjūrā- (st. of conjūrō), *swear together*; supplicā- (st. of supplicō), *kneel*; cohortā- (st. of cohortor), *exhort*; exercitā-, (st. of exercitō), *exercise repeatedly*; vēnā- (st. of vēnor), *hunt*; commūtā- (st. of commūtō), *change completely*; māchinā- (st. of māchinor), *devise*.

705. Form Abstracts in **-tus** from the following—

1. ROOTS: √vīgu-,[7] *live*; √frūgu-,[7] *enjoy*; √si-, *put*; √cād-,[3] *fall*; √por-, FARE, *go through*; √flūgu-,[7] *flow*; √col-,[8] *till*; √pat-,[9] *spread*.
2. BASES TREATED AS ROOTS: quaes-, *seek*; sent-,[4] *become aware*; ūt-,[4] *enjoy, use*.
3. COMPOUNDS ENDING IN A ROOT: ad-√ī-, *go to, approach*; ad-√ven-, COME *to*; cōn-√spec-, SPY *at a glance*; amb-√ī-, *go about*; con-√ven-, COME *together*; sūm-[10] (for sub-√em-), *spend*; circu-√ī-, *go round*; oc-√cād-,[3] *fall towards* or *down*.

4. VERB STEMS: cruciā- (st. of crucĭō), *torture;* magistrā- (st. of magistrō), *direct, be master;* commeā- (st. of commeō), *go to and fro;* vestī- (st. of vestĭō), *clothe.*

---

[1] **Initial** g- is lost before -n-.
[2] The abstract formed from con-√jug- has -n- before -g- after the analogy of **conjungō**; see also foot-note 2, Lesson XCI.
[3] See foot-note 3, Lesson XCI.
[4] -tt- becomes -s-.
[5] -a- of the root is here weakened to -e-.

[6] One -r- disappears and -t- becomes -s-.
[7] See foot-note 2, Lesson XCI.
[8] -o- is weakened to -n-.
[9] -tt- becomes -ss-.
[10] -p- sometimes (as here) grows up between -m- and -t-.

LESSON XCIII.

FORMATION: SUBSTANTIVES (*continued*).

IV. SUBSTANTIVES DENOTING SUBJECT, MEANS, RESULT.

706.   EXAMPLES.

I.	II.	III.	IV.
ROOTS OR VERB STEMS.	SUFFIXES.	STEMS.	SUBSTANTIVES DENOTING SUBJECT, MEANS, RESULT.
1. √crī-, *sift,*	+ -min-	= crīmin-, st. of	crīmen, *that which* **sifts;** *a judicial decision.*
2. √ag-, *lead,*	+ -min-	= agmin-, st. of	agmen, *that which is led;* **army** (*on* **the** *march*).
3. **impedī-** (st. of impedĭō), *hinder,*	+ -mento-	= impedīmento-, st. of	impedīmentum, *means of hindering;* **impediment.**
4. √frag-, BREAK,	+ -mento-	= fragmento-, st. of	fragmentum, *result of* BREAKING; **fragment.**

707. OBSERVATION AND INFERENCE: Note that the substantives in column IV. denote (1) the *subject* of the action, viewed actively (see Ex. 1) or passively (see Ex. 2); (2) the *means* or *instrument* (see Ex. 3); (3) the *result* (see Ex. 4). Note that these substantives are formed by adding to *roots* or *verb stems* the *suffixes* -min-, nom. -men, and -mento-, nom. -mentum. Frame a rule for the formation of substantives denoting Subject, Means, Result.

708. Form substantives in **-men** from the following —

1. ROOTS: √sē-, *sow*; √vī-, *plait*; √nū-, *nod*; √lūc-,[1] *shine*; √flūgu-,[1] *flow*.
2. VERB STEMS: **certā-**, *struggle*; ōrnā-, *embellish*.

709. Form substantives in **-mentum** from the following —

1. ROOTS: √torqu-,[1] *twist, hurl*; √sarp-,[2] *lop, prune*; √mov-,[3] *push*; √jūg-,[1] YOKE; √frūgu-,[1] *enjoy*.
2. COMPOUND ENDING IN A ROOT: dē-√trī-, *rub away*.
3. VERB STEMS: mūnī-, *fortify*; fundā-, BOTTO*m, make secure*; testā-, *bear witness*.

V. NEUTER ABSTRACTS: PRIMITIVE AND DENOMINATIVE.

710.   EXAMPLES.

I.	II.	III.	IV.
ROOTS, OR COMPOUNDS ENDING IN A ROOT.	SUFFIX.	STEMS.	NEUTER ABSTRACTS: PRIMITIVES.
1. √od-, *hate*,	+ -io- =	**odio-**, st. of	**odium**, *hatred; a grudge*.
2. con-√loqu-, *talk with*,	} + -io- =	**conloquio-**, st. of	**conloquium**, *talking together; a conference*.
3. in-√cand-,[4] *set fire to*,	} + -io- =	**incendio-**, st. of	**incendium**, *setting fire to; a conflagration*.

NOUN STEMS.   NEUTER ABSTRACTS
                                               DENOMINATIVES.

4. arbitro-,[5] (st. of arbiter), *umpire*, } + -io- = arbitrio-, st. of { arbitrium, *being umpire; a decision (of the umpire)*.

5. artific- (st. of artifex), *artificer*, } + -io- = artificio-, st. of { artificium, *artisanship; a trade*.

6. exsul- (st. of ex-sul), *exile*, } + -io- = exsilio-,[6] st. of { exsilium, *being an exile; banishment*.

711. OBSERVATION AND INFERENCE: Note that the substantives in column IV. are *neuter abstracts* which may become *concrete* in meaning. Note that the neuter abstracts in Exs. 1–3 are from *roots* and are therefore called *Primitives*; whereas those in Exs. 4–6 are from *noun stems* and are therefore called *Denominatives*. **Note, further,** that the denominatives denote *office* (see Ex. 4), *employment* (see Ex. 5), *condition* (see Ex. 6). Note, finally, that both primitives and denominatives are formed by the *suffix* **-io-**, nom. **-ium**. Frame a rule for the formation of Primitive and Denominative Neuter Abstracts.

712. Form Primitive Abstracts in **-ium** from the following —

COMPOUNDS ENDING IN A ROOT: prae-√sed-,[7] SIT BEFORE; sub-√sed-,[7] SIT *in support;* in-√gen-, *beget* IN.

713. Form Denominative Abstracts in **-ium** from the following —

NOUN STEMS: convīvā-[5] (st. of convīva), *table companion;* indic- (st. of index), *informer;* jūdic- (st. of jūdex), *judge;* supplic- (st. of supplex), *suppliant;* benefico-[5] (st. of beneficus), *kind, obliging;* malefico-[5] (st. of maleficus), *mischievous;* sacrifico-[5] (st. of sacrificus), *sacrificial;* rēmig- (st. of rēmex), *rower;* aedific- (st. of *aedifex[9]*), *builder*.

[1] Medial -c- (or -qu-) and -g- (or -gu-) are dropped before many consonants (here before -m-).
[2] -p- here disappears before -m-.
[3] -v- becomes -u-, and the resulting diphthong -ou- becomes -ō-.
[4] See foot-note 5, Lesson XCII.
[5] The final vowel of the stem disappears before the initial vowel of the suffix.
[6] -n- of the stem is weakened to -i-.
[7] -e- of the root is here weakened to -i-.
[8] The term 'noun' includes both 'substantive' and 'adjective.'
[9] The asterisk * is used to mark a form which is not found in any classical writer, but which is assumed as affording a rational explanation of existing forms. In the present case, as artifex gave rise to artificium (see 710, Ex. 5), so it is assumed that *aedifex gave rise to aedificium.

LESSON XCIV.

FORMATION: SUBSTANTIVES (*continued*).

VI. FEMININE ABSTRACTS DENOTING QUALITY.

714.   **EXAMPLES.**

I. ADJECTIVE STEMS.	II. SUFFIXES.	III. STEMS.	IV. FEMININE ABSTRACTS DENOTING QUALITY.
1. audāci-[1] (st. of audāx), *bold*,	+ -iā-	= audāciā-, st. of	audācia, *boldness*.
2. īgnāvo-[1] (st. of īgnāvus), *idle*,	+ -iā-	= īgnāviā-, st. of	īgnāvia, *idleness*.
3. trīsti- (st. of trīstis), *sad*,	+ -tiā-	= trīstitiā-, st. of	trīstitia, *sadness*.
4. jūsto-[2] (st. of jūstus), *just*,	+ -tiā-	= jūstitiā-, st. of	jūstitia, *justice*.
5. brevi- (st. of brevis), *short*,	+ -tāt-	= brevitāt-, st. of	brevitās, *shortness*.
6. dīgno-[2] (st. of dīgnus), *worthy*,	+ -tāt-	= dīgnitāt-, st. of	dīgnitās, *worth*.
7. forti- (st. of fortis), *brave*,	+ -tūdin-	= fortitūdin-, st. of	fortitūdō, *bravery*.
8. lāto-[2] (st. of lātus), *broad*,	+ -tūdin-	= lātitūdin-, st. of	lātitūdō, *breadth*.

DENOTING QUALITY. 217

715. OBSERVATION AND INFERENCE: Note that the substantives in column IV. are *feminine abstracts* denoting *quality*, and that they **are formed** from *adjective* **stems** by the addition of the *suffixes:* -iă-, nom. -ia; -tiă-, nom. -tia; -tāt-, nom. -tās; -tūdin-, nom. -tūdō. Note that vowel stems *lose* their *final vowel* **before** the initial vowel of the suffix -iă- (see Exs. 1 and 2); and that the *final vowel* of -o- stems is weakened into -i- before the suffixes -tiă-, -tāt-, and -tūdin- (see Exs. 4, 6, 8). Frame a rule for the formation of Feminine Abstracts denoting Quality.

716. Form Feminine Abstracts in **-ia** from the following —

ADJECTIVE STEMS: adulēscent- (st. of adulēscēns), *young;* dīligent- **(st. of dīligēns)**, *attentive;* grāto- (st. of grātus), *pleasing;* īnfāmi- **(st. of īnfāmis)**, *disreputable;* inopi- (st. of inops), *without resources;* invido- (st. of invidus), *envious;* īnscient- (st. of īnsciēns), *inexperienced;* īrācundo- (st. of īrācundus), *passionate;* misericordi- (st. of misericors), *tender-*HEARTed*;* potent- (st. of potēns), *powerful;* prūdent- (st. of prūdēns), *sagacious;* scient- (st. of sciēns), *knowing;* superbo- **(st. of superbus)**, *proud.*

717. Form, in like manner, Feminine Abstracts in **-ia** from the following —

SUBSTANTIVE STEMS: **custōd-** (st. of custōs), *guard;* mīlit- (st. of mīles), *soldier;* vīctōr- **(st. of vīctor)**, *victor.*

718. Form Feminine Abstracts in **-tia** from the following —

ADJECTIVE STEMS: amīco- (st. of amīcus), *friendly;* dūro- (st. of dūrus), *hard;* inimīco- (st. of inimīcus), UN*friendly;* laeto- (st. of laetus), *joyful;* pudīco- (st. of pudīcus), *modest.*

719. Form, in like manner, a Feminine Abstract in **-tia** from the following —

SUBSTANTIVE STEM: **puero-** (st. **of puer)**, *child.*

720. Form Feminine Abstracts in **-tās** from the following —

ADJECTIVE STEMS: aequo- (st. of aequus), *even;* alacri- (st. of alacer), *eager;* atrōci- (st. of atrōx), *savage;* celeri- (st. of celer), *swift,* crūdēli- (st. of crūdēlis), *cruel;* cupido- (st. of cupidus), *desirous;* familiāri- (st. of familiāris), *intimate;* hūmāno- (st. of hūmānus), *refined;* inīquo- (st. of inīquus), UN*just,* nōbili- (st. of nōbilis), *noble;* obscūro- (st. of obscūrus), *obscure;* **opportūno-** (st. of opportūnus), *convenient;* probo- (st. of **probus**), *upright;* vāno- (st. of **vānus**), *empty;* vĕro- (st. of **vĕrus**), *true.*

721. Form, in like manner, Feminine Abstracts in **-tās** from the following —

SUBSTANTIVE STEMS: cīvi- (st. of cīvis), *citizen;* auctōr-[3] (st. of auctor), *author;* hērēd-[3] (st. of hērēs), *heir.*

722. Form Feminine Abstracts in **-tūdō** from the following —

ADJECTIVE STEMS: alto- (st. of altus), *high;* longo- (st. of longus), LONG; māgno- (st. of māgnus), *great;* multo- (st. of multus), *much;* sōlo- (st. of sōlus), *alone;* cōnsuēto-[4] (st. of cōnsuētus), *accustomed.*

---

[1] See foot-note 5, Lesson **XCIII**.
[2] Final -o- of the stem is here weakened to -i- before the suffix.
[3] The suffix here assumes -i- after the analogy of vowel stems, and becomes -itāt-, nom. -itās.

[4] The syllable -ti- in *cōnsuētitūdō produced a stuttering sound; it therefore disappeared, and the form became cōnsuētūdō.

FORMATION: ADJECTIVES. 219

LESSON XCV.

FORMATION: ADJECTIVES.

I. ADJECTIVES DENOTING BELONGING OR PERTAINING TO.

723. EXAMPLES.

I. SUBSTANTIVE STEMS.	II. SUFFIXES.	III. STEMS.	IV. ADJECTIVES DENOTING BELONGING OR PERTAINING TO.
1. rēg- (st. of rēx), *king*,	+ -āli-	= rēgāli-, st. of	rēgālis, *belonging or pertaining to kings, regal, royal.*
2. nāvi-[1] (st. of nāvis), *ship*,	+ -āli-	= nāvāli-, st. of	nāvālis, *belonging or pertaining to ships, naval.*
3. mīlit- (st. of mīles), *soldier*,	+ -āri-[2]	= mīlitāri-, st. of	mīlitāris, *belonging or pertaining to soldiers, military.*
4. auxilio-[1] (st. of auxilium), *help*,	+ -āri-[2]	= auxiliāri-, st. of	auxiliāris, *belonging or pertaining to help, auxiliary.*
5. cīvi-[1] (st. of cīvis), *citizen*,	+ -īli-	= cīvīli-, st. of	cīvīlis, *belonging or pertaining to citizens, civil.*
6. viro-[1] (st. of vir), *man*,	+ -īli-	= virīli-, st. of	virīlis, *belonging or pertaining to men, manly.*
7. legiōn- (st. of legiō), *legion*,	+ -ārio-	= legiōnārio-, st. of	legiōnārius, *belonging or pertaining to legions, legionary.*
8. ālā-[1] (st. of āla), *wing*,	+ -ārio-	= ālārio-, st. of	ālārius, *belonging or pertaining to the wing.*

724. OBSERVATION AND INFERENCE: Note that the Adjectives in column IV. denote *belonging* or *pertaining to*, and that they are formed from *substantive stems* by the addition of the *suffixes:* -āli-, nom. -ālis; -āri-, nom. -āris; -īli-, nom. -īlis; -ārio-, nom. -ārius. Note that vowel stems (see Exs. 2, 4, 5, 6, 8) *lose* their *final vowel* before the initial vowel of these suffixes. Frame a rule for the formation of Adjectives denoting Belonging or Pertaining to.

725. Form —

1. Adjectives in -ālis from the following Substantive Stems: morti- (st. of mors), *death ;* nātūrā- (st. of nātūra), *nature ;* anno- (st. of annus), *year ;* capit- (st. of caput), HEAD; lībero- (st. of līber), *freeman ;* quo- (st. of some forms of quī), WHAT; to- (st. of tum), THAT.

2. Adjectives in -āris² from the following Substantive Stems: cōnsul- (st. of **cōnsul**), *consul ;* salūt- (st. of salūs), *safety,* populo-, (st. of **populus**), *people ;* familiā- (st. of **familia**), *household.*

3. Adjectives in -īlis from the following Substantive Stems: puero- (st. of **puer**), *child ;* servo- (st. of servus), *slave,* sen- (st. of **senex**, gen. **senis**), *old person ;* aedi-³ (st. of aedis or **aedēs**), *building.*

4. Adjectives in -ārius from the following Substantive Stems: frūmento- (st. of frūmentum), *grain ;* agro- (st. of ager), *land ;* sagittā-⁴ (st. of sagitta), *arrow ;* aes-⁵ (st. of aes), *money ;* sēmin-⁶ (st. of sēmen), SEED.

II. ADJECTIVES DENOTING FULL OF.

726.   EXAMPLES.

I. SUBSTANTIVE STEMS.	II. SUFFIX.	III. STEMS.	IV. ADJECTIVES DENOTING FULL OF.
1. anno-¹ (st. of annus), *year,*	+ -ōso-	= annōso-, st. of	annōsus, *full of years.*
2. crīmin- (st. of crīmen), *reproach,*	+ -ōso-	= crīminōso-, st. of	crīminōsus, *full of reproaches, reproachful.*
3. sūmptu- (st. of sūmptus), *expense,*	+ -ōso-	= sūmptuōso-, st. of	sūmptuōsus, *full of expense, expensive.*

727. OBSERVATION AND INFERENCE : Note that **the** Adjectives in column IV. denote *full of*, and that they are formed from *substantive stems* by the addition of the *suffix* -**ōso**-, nom. -**ōsus**. Note that the vowel stems regularly *lose* their *final vowel* before the initial **vowel** of the suffix (see Ex. 1), but that -u- stems *retain* u (see Ex. 3). Frame a rule for the formation of Adjectives denoting Full of.

728. Form Adjectives in -**ōsus** from the following:—

SUBSTANTIVE STEMS: **aestu-** (st. of **aestus**), *heat;* animo- (st. of animus), *courage;* **cōpiā-** (st. of cōpiae), *wealth;* frūctu- (st. of **frūctus**), *fruit;* perīculo- (st. of perīculum), *peril;* studio- (st. of studium), *zeal;* **vitio-** (st. of vitium), *fault.*

---

[1] See foot-note 5, Lesson XCIII.
[2] Note that the suffix -āli- becomes -āri- when the stem contains the letter l.
[3] The masc. form of the adj. obtained from this stem is used subst., and means 'aedile' (superintendent of public works, etc.).
[4] The masc. form of the adj. obtained from this stem is used subst., and means 'archer.'
[5] Medial -s- between two vowels often (as here) becomes -r-; the neuter form of the adj. obtained from aes- is used subst., and means 'treasury.'
[6] The neuter form of the adj. is **used** subst., and means ' nursery.'

LESSON XCVI.

FORMATION: VERBS: DENOMINATIVES.

729. EXAMPLES.

I.	II.	III.	IV.
NOUN [1] STEMS.	CHARACTERISTIC FORMATIVE VOWELS.	VERB STEMS.	DENOMINATIVE VERBS.
1. **fugā-**[2] (st. of fuga), *flight*,	+ -ā- =	fugā-, st. of	fugō, *put to flight.*
2. **firmo-**[2] (st. of **firmus**), *firm*,	+ -ā- =	firmā-, st. of	firmō, *make* **firm,** *strengthen.*
3. **levi-**[2] (st. of levis), LIGHT (not heavy),	+ -ā- =	levā-, st. of	levō, *make* LIGHT, LIGHTen.

I.	II.	III.	IV.
Noun[1] Stems.	Characteristic Formative Vowels.	Verb Stems.	Denominative Verbs.
4. nŏmin- (st. of nŏmen), NAME,	+ -ā- =	nŏminā-, st. of	nŏminō, *call by* NAME, NAME.
5. clāro-[2] (st. of clārus), *bright*,	+ -ē- =	clārē-, st. of	clāreō, *be bright*.
6. flōs-[3] (st. of flōs), *flower*,	+ -ē- =	flōrē-, st. of	flōreō, *be in flower*.
7. fīni-[2] (st. of fīnis), *end*,	+ -ī- =	fīnī-, st. of	fīniō, *put an end to*.
8. molli-[2] (st. of mollis), *soft*,	+ -ī- =	mollī-, st. of	molliō, *make soft*, *soften*.
9. īnsāno-[2] (st. of īnsānus), *insane*,	+ -ī- =	īnsānī-, st. of	īnsāniō, *be insane*.

730. Observation and Inference: Note that the *stems* of the *verbs* in column IV. **are formed from the** corresponding *noun stems* in column I. by the addition of the *characteristic vowels* **of** the *first* (see Exs. 1-4), *second* (see **Exs.** 5 and 6), and *fourth* **(see** Exs. 7-9) *conjugations.* Because these verbs are formed from *noun stems,* they are called *Denominatives.* Note that the noun stems which end in a *vowel* (see Exs. 1-3, 5, 7-9) *lose* this vowel before **the** characteristic vowels -ā-, -ē-, -ī-. Frame a **rule for the formation of** Denominative Verbs.

731. Form Denominative Verbs of the First Conjugation from the following —

Noun[1] Stems : **loco**- (st. **of locus**), *place ;* cūrā- (st. of cūra), *care ;* nūntio- (st. of nūntius), *messenger ;* pūgnā- (st. of pūgna), *fight ;* honesto- (st. of honestus), *honorable ;* interpret-[4] (st. of interpres), *interpreter ;* labōs-[3] (st. of labor), *labor ;* laud- (st. of laus), *praise ;* **memori-** (st. of memor), *mindful ;* proelio-[4] (st. of proelium), *battle ;* rēgno- (st. of rēgnum), *sovereignty ;* salūt- (st. **of** salūs), *safety ;* celebri- (st. of celeber), *frequented ;* **sacro-** (st. of sacer), *sacred ;* damno- (st. of damnum), *loss ;* equit- **(st.** of eques), *horse-*

VERBS : DENOMINATIVES. 223

man; **glōriā-**[4] (st. of **glōria**), *glory;* **hiem-** (st. of hiems), *winter;* jūdic- (st. of jūdex), *judge;* laeto-[4] (st. of laetus), *joyful,* lībero- (st. **of līber**), *free;* nūdo- **(st.** of nūdus), *bare;* novo- (st. of novus), NEW; integro- (st. of integer), *whole;* vulnes-[3] (st. of vulnus), *wound.*

732. Form Denominative **Verbs of the** Second Conjugation from the following —

NOUN[1] STEMS: albo- (st. of albus), *white;* flāvo- (st. of flāvus), *yellow;* lūc- (st. of lūx), LIGHT.

733. Form **Denominative Verbs of the Fourth** Conjugation from the following —

NOUN[1] STEMS: lēni- (st. of lēnis), *soft;* saevo- (st. of saevus), *fierce;* **siti- (st.** of sitis), *thirst;* custōd- **(st. of** custōs), *guard.*

---

[1] See foot-note 8, Lesson XCIII.
[3] See foot-note 5, Lesson XCIII.
[5] **See foot-note 5, Lesson** XCV.

[4] Make the verb deponent, *i.e.,* give it a passive form with active or reflexive meaning.

ANECDOTES FROM CICERO.

NOTE: The following anecdotes are to be translated by the pupil and afterwards committed to memory. The point at which the several anecdotes may be taken up is indicated in a bracketed note prefixed to each; and the amount and kind of help afforded in the foot-notes is adapted to the needs of the pupil at the stage thus indicated.

734. **Discourtesy Rebuked.**

[To follow Lesson XXXI.]

Memoriae prōditum est, cum[1] Athēnīs[2] lūdīs[3] quīdam in theātrum grandis nātū vēnisset,[4] māgnō cōnsēssū[5] locum nusquam eī[6] datum[7] ā suīs cīvibus. Cum autem ad Lacedaemoniōs accēssisset,[8] quī,[9] lēgātī cum essent,[10] certō in locō cōnsēderant, cōnsurrēxisse[11] omnēs illī[12] dīcuntur et senem sēssum[13] recēpisse.[14] Quibus[15] cum ā cūnctō cōnsēssū plausus esset[16] multiplex datus,[16] dīxisse ex iīs quendam[17] Athēniēnsīs scīre quae[18] rēcta essent,[19] sed facere[20] nōlle.[21]
—[Cic. *Cat. Maj.* XVIII.].

[1] *when.*
[2] A. & G. 258, *c*; H. 425, II.; G. 412.
[3] The reference is to the great **Panathenaic festival** celebrated once in four years at Athens in honor of Athena as protectress of the city, and participated in by the combined population of Attica.
[4] *had come.*
[5] Abl. of *place where* without prep.
[6] *for him.*
[7] sc. esse; datum esse is the perf. pass. infin. of dō, *give;* the subj. of the infin. (here locum) is in the accusative. Translate: *that room was made* (lit., *room to have been made*).
[8] *he had come near.*
[9] *who,* nom. pl. masc.

[10] *they were.*
[11] *to have risen in a body.*
[12] *those* (*i.e.*, the Lacedaemonians), nom. pl. masc.
[13] *to be seated.*
[14] *to have invited.*
[15] *to them* (lit., *to whom*).
[16] *had been given.*
[17] [prōditum est] dīxisse ex iīs quendam, [the story adds] *that one of the Lacedaemonians said* (lit., one from them to have said).
[18] *what,* nom. neut. pl.
[19] *was.*
[20] Pres. infin. of faciō, *do.*
[21] Pres. infin. of nōlō, *be unwilling.* Translate: *lacked the inclination.*

735. Remarkable Instances of Mental Vigor in Extreme Old Age.

[To follow Lesson XXXV.]

1. Plato[1] ūnō et octōgēsimō annō scrībēns est mortuus.[2]

2. Īsocratēs[3] eum[4] librum quī[5] Panathēnāicus[6] īnscrībitur quartō et nōnāgēsimō annō scrīpsisse sē[7] dīcit, vīxitque quīnquennium posteā.

3. Leontīnus[8] Gorgiās[9] centum et septem complēvit annōs, neque umquam īn suō **studiō** atque opere cēssāvit. Quī,[10] **cum ex** eō quaererētur[11] **cūr tam** diū vellet esse[12] in **vītā:** "Nihil habeō,"[13] inquit,[14] "**quod** accūsem[15] senectūtem." **Praeclārum** respōnsum, et doctō homine[15] dīgnum!

—[Cic. *Cat. Maj.* V.].

[1] **Platō**, -ōnis, M., *Plato*, the celebrated Athenian philosopher; died 347 B.C.
[2] **est mortuus**, *died*.
[3] **Īsocratēs**, -is, M., *Isocrates*, a celebrated Athenian rhetorician and orator; died 338 B.C. On the composition and elaboration of the most celebrated of his orations, the "Panegyric," he is said by some to have spent ten years, by others, fifteen.
[4] *that*, acc. sing. masc.
[5] *which*, nom. sing. masc.
[6] **Panathēnāicus**, -ī, M., *the Panathenaic*, an oration pronounced by Isocrates at one of the Panathenaic festivals; see **734**, foot-note 3.
[7] **scrīpsisse sē**, *that he wrote* (lit., himself to have written).
[8] **Leontīnus**, -a, -um, adj., *of Leontini* (a town in Sicily).
[9] **Gorgiās**, -ae, M., *Gorgias*, a celebrated rhetorician and orator of Leontini in Sicily; born about 480 B.C.
[10] *He* (lit., who).
[11] **cum ex eō quaererētur**, *when he was asked* (lit., when it was inquired from him).
[12] **vellet esse**, *he wished to be*.
[13] **Nihil habeō quod accūsem**, *I have no fault to find with* (lit., I have nothing which I may lay to the charge of).
[14] See Lesson LIII., foot-note 12.
[15] See Lesson XXXII., foot-note 3.

---

736. A Tree Known by Its Fruits.

[To follow Lesson XXXIX.]

Sophoclēs[1] ad summam senectūtem tragoediās fēcit.[2] Quod[3] propter studium cum[4] rem neglegere familiārem vidērētur,[4] ā fīliīs in jūdicium vocātus est, ut[5] **eum**[6] quasi dēsipientem ā rē familiārī removērent[6] jūdicēs. Tum senex dīcitur eam[7] fābulam quam[8] in manibus habēbat et proximē scrīpserat, Oedipum⁹ Colōnēum,⁹ recitāsse¹⁰ jūdicibus, quaesisseque¹¹ num illud¹² carmen dēsipientis vidērētur.¹³ Quō¹⁴ recitātō, sententiīs jūdicum est līberātus.

— [Cic. *Cat. Maj.* VII.]

¹ **Sophoclēs, -is,** M., *Sophocles,* the famous Attic tragic poet, born at the village of Colonus, near Athens, 495 B.C.; died 406 B.C.
² Perfect indicative of **faciō,** *make, compose.*
³ *this* (lit., which), acc. neut. sing.
⁴ **cum vidērētur,** *as he was thought.*
⁵ *to the end that.*
⁶ **cum removērent,** *might remove him.*
⁷ **eam, acc.** sing. fem., *that.*
⁸ **quam,** acc. sing. fem., *which.*
⁹ **Oedipūs, -odis** and **-ī,** M., *Oedipus;* **Colōnēus, -a, -um,** adj., *of Colonus.*

The "Oedipus of Colonus," which was the last and finest play of Sophocles, recalls the scenery and the religious associations of the poet's native village (cf. footnote 1). The passage said to have been recited on the occasion here referred to, contains a chorus descriptive of the beauties of Athens.
¹⁰ *to have recited.*
¹¹ *to have asked.*
¹² **illud,** nom. neut. sing., *that.*
¹³ *seemed* [to them].
¹⁴ **Quō,** abl. neut. sing., *this* (lit., which).

---

737.   **Tit for Tat.**

[To follow Lesson XLII.]

Nāsīca¹ cum ad² poētam Ennium³ vēnisset,² eīque⁴ ab ōstiō quaerentī Ennium ancilla dīxisset⁴ 'domī nōn esse,⁵ Nāsīca sēnsit illam⁶ dominī jūssū dīxisse⁶ et illum⁷ intus esse.⁷ Paucīs post diēbus, cum ad Nāsīcam vēnisset Ennius et eum⁸ ā jānuā quaereret,⁸ exclāmat Nāsīca sē⁹ domī nōn esse. Tum Ennius: "Quid?¹⁰ ego nōn cōgnōscō," inquit, "vōcem tuam?" Hīc Nāsīca: "Homo es impudēns. Ego, cum tē quaererem,¹¹ ancillae tuae crēdidī tē⁹ **domī nōn esse; tū mihī nōn crēdis ipsī¹²?"**

— [Cic. *de Orat.* 2, LXVIII.]

¹ **Nāsīca, -ae,** M., *Nasica* (Publius Cornelius Scipio Nasica), a celebrated Roman jurist.
² **ad vēnisset,** *had come to* [call on].
³ **Ennius, -iī,** M., *Ennius* (Quintus), the father of Roman epic poetry; lived 239-169 B.C.
⁴ **eī** (dat.) **dīxisset,** *had told him.*
⁵ **domī esse,** *was* (lit., to be) *at home.*
⁶ **illam dīxisse,** *that she had said* [so].
⁷ **illum esse,** *that his friend was* (lit., him to be).
⁸ **eum quaereret,** *inquired for him.*
⁹ The subject of an infin. (here **esse**) is in the acc.
¹⁰ *What?*
¹¹ *I inquired for.*
¹² **ipsī, dat.** sing., *self.*

738.   The Soul Immortal.

[To follow Lesson XLVI.]

Apud Xenophōntem¹ moriēns Cȳrus² mājor haec dīcit: "Nōlīte arbitrārī,³ ō meī cārissimī fīliī, mē,⁴ cum ā vōbīs discēsserō, nusquam aut nūllum fore.⁵ Nec enim, dum eram vōbīscum, animum meum vidēbātis, sed eum esse in hōc corpore ex iīs rēbus quās⁶ gerēbam intellegēbātis. Eundem⁴ igitur esse crēditōte, etiam sī nūllum vidēbitis.

— [Cic. *Cat. Maj.* XXII.]

¹ The reference is to a passage in Xenophon's *Cyropaedia*, an historical romance founded on the career of Cyrus the elder.
² Cyrus the elder founded the Persian empire 559 B.C.; after a long and prosperous reign, he was killed in battle 529 B.C. Xenophon, however, in the passage here referred to, represents him as dying quietly in bed with his children and friends about him.
³ Nōlīte arbitrārī, *do not suppose* (lit., be unwilling to suppose).
⁴ cf. 737, foot-note 9.
⁵ fore, used as fut. infin. of sum; mē fore, *that I shall be.*
⁶ quās, acc. pl. fem., *which.*

---

739.   Dead Muscle.

[To follow Lesson L.]

Quae¹ vōx potest esse² contemptior quam Milōnis Crotōniātae?³ quī, cum jam senex esset⁴ āthlētāsque sē exercentīs in curriculō vidēret,⁵ adspexisse⁶ lacertōs suōs dīcitur inlacrimānsque dīxisse:⁷ "At hī quidem mortuī jam sunt." Nōn vērō tam istī quam tū ipse, nūgātor! Neque enim ex tē umquam es nōbilitātus, sed ex lateribus et lacertīs tuīs.

— [Cic. *Cat. Maj.* IX.]

¹ Quae, interrog. pron., nom. sing. fem., *what.*
² See Lesson LIII., foot-note 5.
³ Mīlō, -ōnis, *Milo*; Crotōniātēs, -ae, m., *inhabitant of Crotona.* Milo was a famous athlete of Crotona, in Italy; many stories of his extraordinary feats are told by the ancient writers.
⁴ *he was.*
⁵ *saw.*
⁶ *to have looked at.*
⁷ *to have said.*

740. Tertia's Pet Dog.

[To follow Lesson LIV.]

L. Paullus, cōnsul iterum, cum eī bellum ut[1] cum rēge Persē[2] gereret[1] obtigisset, ut eā ipsā diē domum[3] ad vesperum rediit,[4] fīliolam suam Tertiam,[5] quae tum erat admodum parva, ōsculāns[6] animum advertit trīsticulam. "Quid est," inquit,[7] "mea Tertia? quid[8] trīstis es?" "Mī[9] pater," inquit, "Persa[10] periit."[11] Tum ille artius[12] puellam complexus:[13] "Accipiō," inquit, "mea fīlia, ōmen." Erat autem mortuus catellus eō nōmine.[14] — [Cic. *de Div.* 1, XLVI.]

[1] **ut gereret**, *to conduct* (lit., that he should conduct).
[2] See **Persēs** in general vocabulary; for abl. **Persē**, cf. A. & G. 37 (**comētēs**); II. 50 (**pyrītēs**).
[3] Acc. of *place to which* without prep.
[4] See **redeō** in general vocabulary
[5] The English form is the same as the Latin nom.
[6] See **ōsculor** in general vocab.; **ōsculor** has a pass. form with act. meaning.
[7] See Lesson LIII., **foot-note 12**.
[8] Adverbial accusative, *why*.
[9] See Lesson XX., foot-note 6.
[10] Name of a pet dog; also a possible form of the name **Persēs**.
[11] See **pereō** in general vocabulary.
[12] **artius**, adv., *more closely, closer*.
[13] See **complector** in general vocabulary; **complector** has a pass. form with active meaning.
[14] cf. Exs. in **322**.

---

741. Roman Character in the Earlier Days of the Republic.

[To follow Lesson LIX.]

Curiō[1] ad focum[2] sedentī māgnum aurī pondus Samnītēs[3] cum attulissent,[4] repudiātī sunt. Nōn enim aurum habēre praeclārum sibī vidērī dīxit, sed eīs quī habērent aurum imperāre. — [Cic. *Cat. Maj.* XVI.]

[1] Manius Curius Dentātus, consul three times; he is often referred to in Cicero's writings as a noble **example of** the early Roman simplicity.
[2] **focus, -ī**, M., *fire-place, hearth.* The **focus** was a small platform of brick or stone raised a few inches above the ground; it stood in the **ātrium, which** in primitive times served as sitting room, dining room, and kitchen.
[3] **Samnītēs, -ium**, M., *the Samnites.* The incident here narrated belongs to the period (about 273 B.C.) which followed **the great** wars **of** the Romans with the Samnites and Pyrrhus. Curius then retired **to** his farm in the Sabine country, and is said to have been found here by the Samnite ambassadors, sitting at his hearth and roasting turnips.
[4] See **adferō** in general vocabulary.

ANECDOTES FROM CICERO.

742.   **Brain Better than Brawn.**

[To follow Lesson LXI.]

Olympiae[1] per stadium[2] ingressus esse[3] Milō[4] dīcitur cum umerīs sustinēret bovem. Utrum[5] igitur hās corporis an[5] Pȳthagorae[6] tibī mālīs[7] vīrīs[8] ingeniī darī?—[Cic. *Cat. Maj.* X.]

[1] **Olympia, -ae, F.,** *Olympia,* a small plain in Elis, celebrated as the scene of the Olympic games; these games were held at intervals of four years and attracted spectators and participants from all parts of the world inhabited or colonized by Greeks.

[2] **stadium, -iī,** N., *race-course.* The stadium was an **oblong area** having one end straight and **the** other semicircular, and having **its** sides parallel. Around this area rose the seats of the spectators. The stadium was especially designed for the foot-race. The course extended from the straight end (see A, Fig. 1) to a point near the centre of the semicircle at the opposite end (see B, Fig. 1), and was 606¾ feet **long.**

[3] See **ingredior** in **general** vocab.; **ingredior** has a pass. **form** with act. meaning.

[4] See 739, **foot-note** 3.

[5] See references in foot-note 1, Lesson XLI.

[6] **Pȳthagorās, -ae, M.,** *Pythagoras,* a celebrated **Greek** philosopher who taught at **Crotona** in Italy. Three **hundred of his disciples** were formed **into** a brotherhood, partly philosophical, partly religious, and partly political, for the purpose of studying the doctrines of their master, and cultivating the observances which he enjoined. The contrast drawn in the text between Pythagoras and Milo is suggested by the fact that Milo was a member of this brotherhood.

[7] **mālīs,** second sing. pres. subj. **of mālō,** *prefer;* translate: *should you prefer?*

[8] See refs. in foot-note 10, Lesson XXXVI.

Fig. 1.—Ground-plan of **a stadium at** Cibyra in Lycia.

READING LESSONS.

I.

743. Division into Parties a Characteristic Feature of Gallic Society.

In Galliā nōn sōlum in omnibus cīvitātibus atque in omnibus pāgīs partibusque,[1] sed paene etiam in singulīs domibus factiōnēs sunt; eārumque factiōnum prīncipēs sunt quī[2] summam auctōritātem eōrum jūdiciō[3] habēre exīstimantur, quōrum ad arbitrium[4] jūdiciumque[4] summa[5] omnium rērum cōnsiliōrumque redeat.[6] Idque ējus reī causā[7] antīquitus īnstitūtum[8] vidētur, nē quis ex plēbe contrā potentiōrem auxiliī[9] egēret:[10] suōs enim[11] quisque opprimī et circumvenīrī nōn patitur, neque, aliter sī faciat,[12] ūllam inter suōs habet[13] auctōritātem. Haec eadem ratiō est in summā[14] tōtīus Galliae;[15] namque omnēs cīvitātēs in partēs dīvīsae sunt duās.

744. Classification of the Inhabitants of Gaul.

In omnī Galliā eōrum hominum quī aliquō sunt numerō[1] atque honōre,[1] genera sunt duo; nam plēbēs[2] paene servōrum habētur locō,[3] quae[4] nihil audet per sē, nūllō adhibētur cōnsiliō.[5] Plērīque, cum aut aere aliēnō aut māgnitūdine tribūtōrum aut injūriā potentiōrum premuntur, sēsē in servitūtem dicant nōbilibus: in[6] hōs eadem omnia sunt jūra quae dominīs[7] in[6] servōs. Sed dē hīs duōbus generibus[8] alterum est Druidum,[9] alterum equitum.

745. The Druids the Supreme Authority in Religious and Social Matters.

Illī[1] rēbus dīvīnīs intersunt, sacrificia pūblica āc prīvāta prōcūrant, religiōnēs interpretantur. Ad hōs māgnus adulēscentium numerus disciplīnae causā concurrit, māgnōque hī[2] sunt apud eōs honōre. Nam ferē dē omnibus contrōversiīs pūblicīs prīvātīsque cōnstituunt; et sī quod est admissum facinus, **sī** caedēs facta, sī dē hērēditāte, sī dē fīnibus contrōversia est, īdem³ dēcernunt: praemia poenāsque cōnstituunt. Sī quī aut prīvātus aut populus eōrum dēcrētō nōn stetit,⁴ sacrificiīs interdīcunt.⁵ Haec poena apud eōs est gravissima. Quibus ita est interdictum,⁵ hī numerō⁶ impiōrum **āc** scelerātōrum habentur; hīs omnēs dēcēdunt, aditum eōrum sermōnemque dēfugiunt, nē quid ex contāgiōne incommodī accipiant; neque hīs petentibus jūs redditur neque honōs*ūllus commūnicātur.

746. The Government of the Druids; their Annual Meeting; **the** Origin of their System.

Hīs autem omnibus Druidibus praeest ūnus, quī summam inter eōs habet auctōritātem. Hōc mortuō,¹ aut, sī quī² ex reliquīs³ excellit dīgnitāte, succēdit; aut, sī sunt plūrēs parēs, suffrāgiō⁴ Druidum, nōnnunquam etiam armīs, **dē** prīncipātū contendunt. Hī certō annī tempore **in fīnibus** Carnūtum,⁵ quae regiō tōtīus Galliae⁶ media habētur, **cōnsīdunt** in locō cōnsecrātō. Hūc omnēs undique quī contrōversiās habent conveniunt, eōrumque dēcrētīs jūdiciīsque pārent. Disciplīna⁷ in Britanniā reperta atque inde in Galliam trānslāta esse exīstimātur;⁸ et nunc quī⁹ dīligentius¹⁰ eam rem cōgnōscere volunt plērumque illō discendī causā proficīscuntur.

747. Immunities Enjoyed by the Druids; their Doctrines Orally Transmitted.

Druidēs ā bellō abesse cōnsuērunt,¹ neque tribūta ūnā cum reliquīs pendunt; mīlitiae vacātiōnem omniumque rērum habent immūnitātem. Tantīs excitātī praemiīs, et² suā sponte multī in disciplīnam conveniunt³ et ā parentibus **propīnquīsque** mittuntur.⁴ Māgnum ibi numerum versuum ēdiscere⁵ dīcuntur;⁶ itaque annōs nōnnūllī vīcēnōs⁷ in disciplīnā⁸ permanent. Neque fās⁹ esse exīstimant ea litterīs mandāre,[10] cum[11] in reliquīs ferē rēbus, pūblicīs prīvātīsque ratiōnibus, Graecīs litterīs ūtantur.[12] Id[13] mihī duābus dē causīs īnstituisse videntur,[14] quod neque in vulgum disciplīnam efferrī velint,[15] neque eōs quī discunt litterīs[16] cōnfīsōs minus memoriae studēre; quod ferē plērīsque accidit[15] ut praesidiō[17] litterārum dīligentiam in perdiscendō[18] āc memoriam remittant.[19]

748. Teachings of the Druids.

In prīmīs[1] hōc volunt persuādēre,[2] nōn interīre animās, sed ab aliīs[3] post mortem trānsīre ad aliōs,[3] atque hōc[4] maximē ad virtūtem excitārī[5] putant, metū mortis neglēctō. Multa praetereā dē sīderibus atque eōrum mōtū, dē mundī āc terrārum[6] māgnitūdine, dē rērum nātūrā, dē deōrum immortālium vī āc potestāte disputant et juventūtī trādunt.

749. The Knights or Warrior Class.

Alterum genus est equitum.[1] Iī, cum est ūsus atque aliquod[2] bellum incidit (quod ferē ante Caesaris adventum quotannīs accidere solēbat, utī aut ipsī **injūriās īnferrent aut inlātās prōpulsārent**[3]), omnēs in bellō versantur; atque eōrum ut quisque[4] est genere cōpiīsque amplissimus, ita[4] plūrimōs circum sē ambactōs clientēsque habet. Hanc ūnam **grātiam potentiamque** nōvērunt.[5]

750. Human Sacrifices Prevalent among the Gauls.

Nātiō est omnis Gallōrum admodum dēdita religiōnibus,[1] atque ob eam causam quī sunt adfectī graviōribus[2] morbīs quīque in proeliīs perīculīsque versantur,[3] aut prō victimīs hominēs immolant aut sē immolātūrōs vovent, administrīsque[4] ad ea sacrificia Druidibus ūtuntur, **quod, prō vītā hominis nisi hominis vīta reddātur**,[5] nōn posse deōrum immortālium nūmen plācārī arbitrantur, pūblicēque ējusdem generis habent īnstitūta[6] sacrificia. Aliī immānī māgnitūdine simulācra **habent**, quōrum contexta vīminibus membra vīvīs hominibus complent; **quibus** succēnsīs, **circumventī flammā** exanimantur hominēs. Supplicia eōrum quī in fūrtō aut in latrōciniō **aut aliquā noxā** sint comprehēnsī⁷ grātiōra diīs immortālibus esse arbitrantur; sed, cum ējus generis cōpia dēfēcit,⁸ etiam ad innocentium supplicia dēscendunt.

751. The Gods Worshiped by the Gauls.

Deům māximē Mercurium colunt. Hūjus sunt plūrima simulācra; hunc¹ omnium inventōrem¹ artium ferunt, hunc viārum² atque itinerum² ducem, **hunc** ad quaestūs pecūniae mercātūrāsque habēre vim māximam arbitrantur. Post hunc Apollinem³ et Mārtem et Jovem⁴ et Minervam. Dē hīs eandem **ferē quam** reliquae gentēs habent opīniōnem: Apollinem **morbōs** dēpellere, Minervam operum atque artificiōrum⁵ **initia trādere**, Jovem imperium caelestium tenēre, Mārtem **bella regere**. Huic, cum proeliō⁶ dīmicāre cōnstituērunt, **ea** quae bellō⁶ cēperint⁷ plērumque dēvovent; **cum** superāvērunt, animālia capta immolant, reliquās rēs in **ūnum locum** cōnferunt. Multīs in cīvitātibus **hārum** rērum **exstrūctōs** tumulōs locīs⁸ cōnsecrātīs cōnspicārī licet, neque saepe acci**dit**⁹ ut neglēctā quispiam religiōne¹⁰ aut capta apud sē¹¹ occultāre aut posita tollere audēret;¹² gravissimum ēĭ rēī supplicium cum cruciātū cōnstitūtum **est**.

752. Traditional Origin of the Gauls; their Mode of Designating Intervals of Time; the Relation of Children to Parents.

Gallī sē omnēs ab Dīte¹ prōgnātōs praedicant, idque² ab Druidibus prōditum dīcunt. Ob eam causam³ spatia omnis temporis⁴ nōn numerō diērum, sed noctium⁵ fīniunt⁶; diēs nātālēs et mēnsium et annōrum initia sīc observant ut noctem diēs subsequātur.⁷ In reliquīs vītae īnstitūtīs hōc ferē⁸ ab reliquīs differunt,⁹ quod suōs līberōs,¹⁰ **nisi cum**¹¹ adolēvērunt ut mūnus mīlitiae sustinēre possint, palam **ad** sē adīre¹² nōn patiuntur; fīliumque puerīlī aetāte¹³ in pūblicō in cōnspectū patris adsistere turpe dūcunt.

753. Marriage Settlements among the Gauls; Subjection of Wives.

Virī, quantās pecūniās ab uxōribus dōtis nōmine accēpērunt, tantās ex suīs bonīs, aestimātiōne factā, cum dōtibus commūnicant.¹ Hūjus omnis pecūniae conjūnctim² ratiō habētur frūctūsque servantur: uter eōrum vītā³ superārit.⁴ ad eum pars utriusque cum frūctibus superiōrum temporum pervenit. Virī in uxōrēs, sīcutī in līberōs, vītae necisque habent potestātem; et cum pater familiae inlustriōre locō nātus dēcēssit,⁵ ējus propīnquī conveniunt et, dē morte sī rēs īn suspīciōnem vēnit,⁵ dē uxōribus īn servīlem modum⁶ quaestiōnem habent et, sī compertum est,⁷ īgnī atque omnibus tormentīs excruciātās interficiunt.

754. Funeral Rites and Usages.

Fūnera sunt prō cultū¹ Gallōrum magnifica et sūmptuōsa; omniaque quae vīvīs² cordī² fuisse arbitrantur in īgnem īnferunt, etiam animālia: āc paulō³ suprā hanc memoriam⁴ servī et clientēs, quōs ab iīs dīlēctōs esse cōnstābat, jūstīs fūneribus⁵ cōnfectīs, ūnā cremābantur.

755. Free Discussion of Public Questions Forbidden by Law.

Quae cīvitātēs commodius¹ suam rem pūblicam administrāre exīstimantur,² habent lēgibus sānctum,³ sī quis⁴ quid⁴ dē rē pūblicā ā fīnitimīs rūmōre aut fāmā accēperit,⁵ utī ad magistrātum dēferat⁶ nēve⁷ cum quō⁴ aliō commūnicet: quod saepe hominēs temerāriōs atque imperītōs falsīs rūmōribus terrērī et ad facinus impellī et dē summīs rēbus cōnsilium capere⁸ cōgnitum est.⁹ Magistrātūs quae vīsa sunt¹⁰ occultant; quaeque esse ex ūsū jūdicāvērunt, multitūdinī prōdunt. Dē rē pūblicā nisi per concilium¹¹ loquī nōn concēditur.

II.

756. The Worship of the Germans; their Out-of-Door Life.

Germānī multum ab hāc[1] cōnsuētūdine differunt. **Nam neque Druidēs habent quī rēbus dīvīnīs praesint, neque sacrificiīs student.** Deōrum numerō eōs sōlōs dūcunt quōs cernunt et quōrum apertē opibus juvantur, Sōlem et[2] Volcānum[3] et[2] Lūnam: reliquōs nē fāmā[4] quidem accēpērunt. Vīta omnis in vēnātiōnibus[5] atque in studiīs reī mīlitāris[6] cōnsistit; ab parvulīs[7] **labōrī āc dūritiae student.**

757. Means of Subsistence; Annual Change of Abode.

Agricultūrae nōn student; **mājorque** pars eorum vīctūs in lacte, cāseō,[1] carne[1] cōnsistit. Neque quisquam[2] agrī modum **certum** aut fīnēs habet propriōs, sed magistrātūs āc prīncipēs in annōs singulōs[3] gentibus cōgnātiōnibusque hominum quī ūnā coiērunt, quantum et quō locō vīsum est agrī[4] **attribuunt,** atque annō[5] post aliō trānsīre cōgunt.

758. The Reasons Assigned for this Annual Change of Abode.

Ējus reī multās adferunt causās: nē adsiduā cōnsuētūdine captī studium bellī gerendī agricultūrā[1] commūtent; nē lātōs fīnēs parāre studeant potentiōrēsque humiliōrēs possēssiōnibus expellant; **nē** accūrātius ad frīgora atque aestūs vītandōs[2] aedificent; **nē qua**[3] oriātur pecūniae cupiditās, quā ex rē factiōnēs dissēnsiōnēsque nāscuntur; ut animī aequitāte plēbem contineant, cum suās quisque opēs cum potentissimīs aequārī videat.[4]

759. Deserted Frontiers Deemed an **Evidence of Military** Greatness.

Cīvitātibus māxima **laus** est quam lātissimē circum sē vastātīs fīnibus[1] sōlitūdinēs habēre. Hōc[2] proprium[3] virtūtis⁴ exīstimant, expulsōs agrīs fīnitimōs cēdere neque quemquam⁵ prope audēre cōnsistere: simul hōc⁶ sē fore⁷ tūtiōrēs arbitrantur, repentīnae incursiōnis timōre sublātō.⁸

760. Methods of Government in War and in Peace; Predatory Warfare Deemed Honorable.

Cum bellum cīvitās aut inlātum dēfendit aut īnfert, magistrātūs quī eĭ bellō praesint¹ ut vītae necisque habeant² potestātem, dēliguntur. In pāce nūllus est commūnis³ magistrātus, sed prīncipēs regiōnum⁴ atque pāgōrum⁴ inter suōs jūs dīcunt contrōversiāsque minuunt. Latrōcinia nūllam habent⁵ īnfāmiam quae extrā fīnēs cūjusque cīvitātis fīunt; atque ea juventūtis exercendae āc dēsidiae minuendae causā fierī praedicant.

761. Loyalty of the Germans to their Chiefs; Hospitality to Strangers.

Atque ubĭ quis¹ ex prīncipibus² in conciliō dīxit sē ducem fore, quī³ sequī velint⁴ profiteantur,⁵ cōnsurgunt iī quī et causam et hominem probant, suumque auxilium pollicentur atque ab multitūdine conlaudantur; quī³ ex hīs⁶ secūtī nōn sunt, in dēsertōrum āc prōditōrum numerō dūcuntur, omniumque hīs⁷ rērum posteā fidēs dērogātur.⁸ Hospitem violāre fās nōn putant; quī³ quācumque dē causā ad cōs vēnērunt, ab injūriā prohibent, sānctōs⁹ habent, hīsque omnium domūs patent vīctusque commūnicātur.

EXPLANATORY NOTES ON THE PRECEDING READING LESSONS.

743. [1] **pāgīs** refers to the *districts;* **partibus** to the *parts* or *subdivisions* of the districts. — [2] **quī**, *those who;* cf. **393** and **394.** — [3] **eōrum jūdiciō**, *in their* (*i.e.*, the Gauls') *judgment.* — [4] **arbitrium**, *decision* (of the arbitrator); **jūdicium**, *sentence* (of the judge). — [5] **summa redeat**, *the final appeal is to be made.* — [6] **redeat:** for mood, cf. **573**, Ex. 1. — [7] Note the position of **causā**. — [8] **īnstitūtum :** sc. **esse**. — [9] **auxiliī** : A. & G. 223; H. 410, V., 1; G. 389, Rem.2. — [10] **egēret :** for mood, cf. **528**, Ex. 2; note that **egēret** takes its tense from **īnstitūtum (esse)**, not from **vidētur** : A. & G. 287, *a*; H. 495, IV.; G. 518, Exc. — [11] Note that **enim** is postpositive. — [12] **faciat :** for mood and tense, cf. **601, Ex. 1.** — [13] **habet :** H. 511, 1, (1). — [14] **in summā**, *in general.* — [15] **Galliae** : predicate possessive genitive limiting **ratiō** and separated from it by **est :** A. & G. 214, *c*; H. 401; G. 365.

744. [1] **numerō** and **honōre :** cf. **322**, Ex. 6. — [2] **plēbēs :** archaic form of nominative = **plēbs**. — [3] **locō :** for absence of preposition, see A. & G. 258, *f*; H. 425, 2; G. 385, Rem. — [4] **quae :** *and they* (referring to the common people). — [5] **cōnsiliō :** dat., *they are admitted to no council.* — [6] **in :** *over.* — [7] sc. **sunt;** for case of **dominīs**, cf. Exs. in **449**. — [8] Might the partitive genitive have been used in place of **dē . . . generibus**? See A. & G. 216, *c*; H. 397, **n.** 3; G. 371, Rem. 5. Why is it not used? — [9] **Druidum :** A. & G. 214, *c*; H. 401; G. 365.

745. [1] **Illī:** refers to **Druidum** at the end of **744**. — [2] **hī:** refers to the Druids. — [3] **īdem :** nom. pl. — [4] **dēcrētō nōn stetit :** *does not acquiesce in the decision;* note that **stetit** is construed with the ablative (**dēcrētō**); for tense of **stetit** (translated present), see A. & G. 279, *b*; H. 471, 5. — [5] **sacrificiīs interdīcunt** and **Quibus est interdictum :** with **interdīcō**, the thing from which the person is excluded is expressed by the abl. of separation (see **sacrificiīs**); the person on whom the prohibition is laid is expressed by the dat. (see **Quibus**). For the impersonal use of **interdīcō** in the pass., cf. Exs. in **522**. — [6] **numerō :** abl. of place where, without prep.

746. [1] **mortuō :** perf. part. of *morior;* **hōc mortuō**, *at his death.* — [2] **quī :** used subst. = **quis**. — [3] **ex reliquīs :** see refs. in **744**, note 8. — [4] **suffrāgiō :** in the same construction as **armīs**. — [5] **Carnūtum :**

southwest of Paris, between the Seine and Loire. — ⁶ **Galliae**: gen. after **media**; A. & G. 218, a; H. 399, 3; G. 373. — ⁷ **Disciplīna**: *the Druidical system*. — ⁸ Note that Caesar says here: **disciplīna trānslāta esse exīstimātur**, *the system is thought to have been transferred*; might he have said: **disciplīnam trānslātam esse exīstimātur**, *it is thought that the system was transferred?* See A. & G. 330, b; H. 534, n. 1, (2); G. 528. — ⁹ **quī**: cf. **743**, note 2. — ¹⁰ **dīligentius cōgnōscere**: *to gain a more thorough acquaintance with*, or *a more accurate knowledge of*.

747. ¹ **cōnsuērunt**: cf. Lesson XXXIV., foot-note 2. — ² **et**: *both*. — ³ **in disciplīnam conveniunt**: *place themselves under instruction*; hence, *enter the order*. — ⁴ **mittuntur**: sc. **multī**. — ⁵ **ēdiscere**: *to learn by heart*; note the intensive force of the prep. — ⁶ Note that Caesar says: **ēdiscere dīcuntur**; might he have said: **eōs ēdiscere dīcitur?** cf. **746**, note 8. — ⁷ **vīcēnōs**: why not **vīgintī?** — ⁸ **in disciplīnā**: *under training*. — ⁹ **fās**, def. neut., *divine law*; hence, translated adjectively, *right, lawful, proper*. — ¹⁰ **litterīs mandāre**: *to commit to writing*. — ¹¹ **cum**: *although*. — ¹² **ūtantur**: for mood, cf. **642**, Ex. 3. — ¹³ **Id**: *this practice*. — ¹⁴ **videntur**: cf. note 6. — ¹⁵ Note that in **quod . . . velint** the writer is reporting the reason of the Druids; whereas, below, in **quod . . . accidit** he is assigning a reason of his own. For the difference of mood, see A. & G. 321 and a; H. 516, I. and II.; G. 540 and 541. — ¹⁶ **litterīs**: abl. with **cōnfīsōs**, *depending on*. — ¹⁷ **praesidiō**: *through dependence on*. — ¹⁸ **perdiscendō**: note the intensive force of the prep., and cf. note 5. — ¹⁹ **remittant**: translate *relax* with **dīligentiam**, *enfeeble* with **memoriam**; for mood, cf. **556**, Ex. 5.

748. ¹ **In prīmīs**: *among their foremost* [doctrines]; hence, *especially, particularly*. — ² **persuādēre**: *to inculcate*. — ³ **ab aliīs ad aliōs**: *from one body to another*. — ⁴ **hōc**: *by this belief*. — ⁵ **excitārī**: sc. **hominēs**. — ⁶ **terrārum**: *the earth* (as made up of various lands).

749. ¹ **equitum**: cf. **744**, note 9. — ² **aliquod**: why not **aliquid?** See A. & G. 105, d, n.; H. 190, n. 1; G. 105, 1. — ³ **utī . . . īnferrent** and **utī . . . prōpulsārent are subst. clauses of** result in apposition with **quod**; for the subjunctives, cf. Exs. in 556. — ⁴ **ut quisque amplissimus . . . ita plūrimōs**: *the more distinguished . . . the more numerous*. — ⁵ **nōvērunt**: *acknowledge, recognize*.

750. ¹ **religiōnibus**: *superstition*. — ² **graviōribus**: *of unusual severity*; cf. Lesson XXX., foot-note 4. — ³ **versantur**: *are in the midst*

EXPLANATORY NOTES.

of, are encompassed by. — ⁴ **administrīs**: predicate abl. agreeing in case with **Druidibus**; translate: *they employ the Druids as agents.* — ⁵ **reddātur**: A. & G. 336 (last sentence); H. 524; G. 653. The person making the sacrifice thinks (direct discourse): **nisi vita reddētur, nōn potest nūmen plācāri.** — ⁶ **īnstitūta**: predicate participle; translate: *they have sacrifices established* (not *they have established sacrifices*). See A. & G. 292, *c*; H. 388, 1, n.; G. 230. — ⁷ **sint comprehēnsī**: for mood, see refs. under note **5**. — ⁸ **dēfēcit**: *fails*; for tense, see refs. on **stetit, 745**, note 4.

751. ¹ **hunc** and **inventōrem**: for the two accs., cf. Exs. in **397**. — ² **iter** is simply a *road* leading to a place; **via** is *the usual road*, often a *paved street* or *highway*. **Viārum atque itinerum ducem**: *their guide in journeys.* — ³ **Apollinem**, etc.: sc. **colunt.** — ⁴ Jovem: see Jūppiter in general vocabulary. — ⁵ **operum atque artificiōrum**: *manufactures and industrial arts.* — ⁶ **proeliō** and **bellō**: cf. Lesson XXXIV., foot-note 11. — ⁷ **cēperint**: fut. perf. indic. — ⁸ **locīs**: A. & G. 258, *f*; H. 425, 2. — ⁹ **accidit**: is it in the present tense or the perfect? To determine this, observe the tense of the dependent subjunctive **audēret**: A. & G. 287, *a*; H. 495, 1; G. 511, Rem. 2. — ¹⁰ **religiōne**: *sacredness* (of the offering). — ¹¹ **apud sē**: *at his own house.* — ¹² **audēret**: what is the construction of the clause **ut . . . audēret?** cf. **556**, Ex. 5, and **561.**

752. ¹ **Dīte**: *i.e.*, the god of the under world; in other words, the Gauls believed that their ancestors sprang from the soil. — ² **id**: *this tradition.* — ³ **Ob eam causam**: *i.e.*, on account of their descent from the god **of** the realms of darkness. — ⁴ **spatia omnis temporis**: *all their periods of time*; grammatically, however, **omnis** agrees with **temporis.** — ⁵ **noctium**: cf. the English expressions *fortnight* (fourteen nights) and *sennight* (seven nights). — ⁶ **fīniunt**: *compute, reckon.* — ⁷ **ut noctem diēs subsequātur**: according to the reckoning of the Gauls, therefore, the day began at sunset, and the celebration of all anniversaries was entered upon in the evening. Compare our Christmas *Eve.* — ⁸ **hōc ferē**: *chiefly in this.* — ⁹ **differunt**: *differ*; this meaning appears to be confined to the present system. — ¹⁰ **liberōs**: why **not puerōs?** See Lesson XVIII., foot-note 2. — ¹¹ **nisi cum**: *until.* — ¹² **ad sē adīre**: *to appear before them.* — ¹³ **filium puerili aetāte**: *a son who is a minor.*

753. ¹ **quantās pecūniās . . . accēpērunt, tantās ex suīs bonīs cum dōtibus commūnicant**: *they add to the dowries out of their own* *resources as much money as they have received.* — ² **conjūnctim ratiō habētur**: *a joint account is kept.* — ³ **vītā**: cf. Exs. in **228**. — ⁴ **superārit**: fut. perf. indic. — ⁵ **dēcēssit** and **vēnit**: for force of tense, cf. **750**, note 8. — ⁶ **in servīlem modum**: *as in the case of slaves* (*i.e.*, by torture). — ⁷ **sī compertum est**: *if guilt is proved;* cf. also note 5.

754. ¹ **prō cultū**: *considering the* [imperfect] *civilization.* — ² **vīvīs cordī**: cordī esse alicui = *to lie near one's heart, to be dear to one;* for the two datives, cf. **Exs. in 452**. — ³ **paulō**: cf. Exs. in **545**. — ⁴ **suprā hanc memoriam**: *before our time.* — ⁵ **jūstīs fūneribus**: *the funeral rites proper*, i.e., *the regular* or *established funeral rites.*

755. ¹ **commodius**: *more judiciously* (than the rest). — ² **existimantur**: cf. **746**, note 8. — ³ **sānctum** is here a predicate participle belonging to the clause **utī . . . commūnicet**; cf. **750**, note 6. — ⁴ **quis** and **quī** are indefinite after **sī** and **nē**. — ⁵ **accēperit**: perf. subj., not fut. perf. indic.; why? — ⁶ **dēferat**: cf. Exs. in **686**. — ⁷ **nēve**: *and not;* **nēve** (not **neque**) is the regular continuative particle in negative imperative clauses. — ⁸ **capere**: *rashly enter upon.* — ⁹ **cōgnitum est**: *experience has shown;* what is the subject? — ¹⁰ **quae vīsa sunt**: *what they deem proper.* — ¹¹ **per concilium**: *in public council.*

756. ¹ **hāc**: i.e., *of the Gauls.* — ² **et**: for the repetition of the conjunction, see A. & G. **208**, *b* (last part); H. 554, 6 (last part); G. 483, 2. — ³ **Volcānum**: *Vulcan, the fire god;* hence, here, *fire.* — ⁴ **fāmā**: note the position. — ⁵ **vēnātiōnibus**: plural used because of the repeated instances; **translate** by the singular. — ⁶ **in studiīs rēī mīlitāris**: *in military pursuits.* — ⁷ **ab parvulīs**: *from childhood.*

757. ¹ For the omission of the conjunction **et** with **cāseō** and **carne,** see A. & G. **208**, *b* (first sentence); H. 554, 6; G. 483, **2**; cf. **Sōlem** et Volcānum et Lūnam in **756**. — ² Note that the clause in which **quisquam** appears is negative; see refs. in foot-note 5, Lesson LVII. — ³ **in annōs singulōs**: *every year.* — ⁴ **agrī**: construe with **quantum**: A. & G. 216, *a*, 3; H. 397, 3; G. 371; **quantum . . . agrī,** *as much land and in such a place as they think fit.* — ⁵ **annō post**: *the year after;* cf. **545**, Ex. 3.

758. ¹ **agricultūrā**: cf. **662**, Ex. 4. — ² **vītandōs**: *for the purpose of avoiding,* etc.; **note that vītandōs belongs** to **frīgora** as well as to **aestūs,** but that it agrees with the latter: A. & G. 187; H. 439, 1; G. 286. — ³ **nē qua**: see **755**, note 4; for **qua** instead of **quae**, see A. & G. **105**, *d*; H. 190, 1; G. 105, 1. — ⁴ **videat**: cf. **642**, Ex. 2.

759. ¹ vāstātis **finibus**: abl. abs., *by laying waste their frontiers.* — ² **Hōc**: explained by **expulsōs ... cōnsistere.** — ³ **proprium**: *a special proof* (something peculiarly belonging to). — ⁴ **virtūtis**: for the gen. after **proprius** (where the dat. might be looked for), see: A. & G. 218, *d*; H. 391, II., 4, (2); G. 356, Rem. 1. — ⁵ quemquam: see 757, note 2. — ⁶ hōc: abl. of cause. — ⁷ fore: used as fut. infin. of sum. — ⁸ sublātō: see tollō in general vocabulary.

760. ¹ **praesint**: subj. of purpose. — ² **habeant**: subj. of result. — ³ **commūnis**: *common to all, having general jurisdiction.* — ⁴ **regiōnum atque pāgōrum**: *provinces and districts;* regiō, a portion of country of indefinite extent; pāgus, a district having fixed **boundaries.** — ⁵ **habent**: *involve, are attended with.*

761. ¹ **quis: ubi** (whenever) has here the force of **si**; hence quis is indefinite, *anyone.* — ² **ex principibus**: cf. **744**, note 8. — ³ **qui**: *those who*, cf. **743**, note 2. — ⁴ **velint**: for the mood, cf. **750**, note 7. — ⁵ **profiteantur**: cf. Exs. in **686**; translate: *and that those who wish to follow are to give in their names.* Restore to the direct form: sē ducem ... profiteantur. — ⁶ **his**: refers to those who have expressed a willingness to follow the chief; on **ex his**, cf. note 2. — ⁷ **his**: dat. (not abl.); cf. Exs. in **620.** — ⁸ **omnium ... dērogātur**: *all confidence is thereafter withdrawn from them.* — ⁹ **sānctus**, *sacred* in the sense of inviolable; **sacer**, *sacred* in the sense of consecrated to some divinity. Could **sacrōs**, then, be substituted for **sānctōs** in the present passage?

ABBREVIATIONS.

A. & G., Allen and Greenough's Gram.
abbr., abbreviation, abbreviated.
abl., ablative.
    abl. pers., ablative of the person.
abs., absolute, absolutely.
acc., accusative.
    acc. pers., accusative of the person.
    acc. th., accusative of the thing.
act., active.
adj., adjective, adjectively.
adv., adverb, adverbially.
ant., antecedent.
app., apposition, appositive.
C., common (masculine or feminine).
cf. (cōnfer), compare.
cogn., cognate with.
comp., comparative.
conj., conjunction.
conn., connected.
dat., dative.
    dat. pers., dative of the person.
    dat. ref., dative of reference.
    dat. th., dative of the thing.
def., defective.
demonstr., demonstrative.
denom., denominative.
dim., diminutive.
disc., discourse.
distr., distributive.
e. g. (exemplī grātiā), for example.
Ex., example.
exclam., exclamation.
F., fem., feminine.
fm., form.
fr., from.
fut., future.
G., Gildersleeve's Grammar.
gen., genitive.
    gen. pers., genitive of the person.
    gen. th., genitive of the thing.
ger., gerundive.
H., Harkness's Grammar.
hist., historical.
i. e. (id est), that is.
imper., imperative.
impers., impersonal.
indecl., indeclinable.
indef., indefinite.
indic., indicative.
indir., indirect.
infin., infinitive.
intens., intensive.

interj., interjection.
interrog., inter., interrogative.
intr., intransitive.
irreg., irregular.
lit., literal, literally.
loc., locative.
M., masc., masculine.
mod., modern.
N., neuter.
n., note.
neg., negative.
num., numeral.
opp., opposed to.
opt., optative.
ord., ordinal.
orig., original, originally.
p., page.
p. a., participial adjective.
par., paragraph.
part., participle.
part. gen., partitive genitive.
pass., passive.
perf., perfect.
periphr., periphrastic.
pers., person, personal.
pl., plural.
poss., possessive.
pp., pages.
prep., preposition.
pres., present.
pron., pronoun, pronominal.
q. v. (quod vidē), which see.
ref., reference.
reflex., reflexive, reflexively.
rel., relative.
Rem., remark.
sc. (scilicet), supply, understand.
sent., sentence.
sing., singular.
st., stem.
subj., subjunctive.
subst., substantive, substantively.
suff., suffix.
sup., supine.
superl., superlative.
tr., trans., transitive.
Trans., translate.
usu., usually.
vb., verb.
vocab., vocabulary.
w., with.

VOCABULARIES.

I. LATIN-ENGLISH VOCABULARY.

NOTE: The sign '√' signifies 'root'; thus √gen- is to be read 'root gen-.'
For the use of the asterisk (*), see Lesson XCIII., foot-note 9.
The term 'base' is applied to **stems** or parts **of** stems treated as roots; see clāmor.

English words or parts of words **that have been** *borrowed* (directly or indirectly) from the Latin forms under **which** they **appear, are** printed in *this type*; for examples, see: causa, aeternus. English words or parts of words that are cognate with the Latin forms **under** which they appear, are printed in SMALL CAPITALS; for examples, see: **frāter, pedes.**

Roots, stems, or complete words that enter into the formation of the words in this vocabulary, are given, together with their meanings, in brackets; the nominative or **indicative** form of each stem cited is given in parenthesis; the suffix is not given. For examples, see: audītus, agmen, adjungō, amīcitia.

In the resolution of compounds given in brackets, the hyphen is appended to inseparable prefixes to distinguish them from the prepositions, which may stand alone. Thus in- is the inseparable negative prefix, cognate with English UN-; but in is the preposition, cognate with English IN. For examples, see: **impendeō, imperītus, redeō.**

In the principal parts of verbs, the perfect participle usually appears in the masculine form; but in verbs that are *invariably* intransitive the neuter form is given. For examples, see: dūcō, veniō.

The abbreviations used are explained on the preceding page.

ā, ab, abs

ā, ab, abs (ab before vowels and some consonants, ā before consonants only, abs sometimes in the expression abs tē), prep. w. abl., *away from, from; by; in, on, at:* ab sinistrā parte, *on the left side;* or: ab aliquō quaerere, *to inquire of someone; to:* āversus ā, *hostile to, opposed to,* averse *to.*

ab-dūcō, -ere, -dūxī, -ductus [ab, *away;* dūcō, *lead*], *lead away,* carry OFF.

ab-eō, -īre, -īvī or -iī, -itum [ab, *away;* eō, *go*], *go away.*

ab-solvō, -ere, -vī, -ūtus [ab, *from;* solvō, *loose*], **absolve,** *acquit.*

ac-cendō

abstinentia, -ae. F. [abstinent- (st. of abstinēns), *abstaining*], *self-restraint,* abstinence.

abs-tineō, -ēre, -uī [abs, OFF; teneō, *hold*], *hold* OFF. abstain.

ab-sum, abesse. āfuī [ab, *away;* sum, *be*], *be away, be absent, be distant; be wanting;* ā bellō abesse, *to take no part in war.*

āc, see atque.

ac-cēdō, -ere, -cēssī, -cēssus [ad, *to;* cēdō, *go or come*], *go* or *come to;* approach; *be added;* accēdere ad, *to come up to.*

ac-cendō, -ere, -cendī, -cēnsus [ad, *to;* √cand-, *set fire*], *kindle; inflame, fire.*

ac-cĭdō, -ere, -cĭdī [ad, *to ;* cadō, *fall*], *happen, occur ;* (w. dat. pers.) *happen to, befall.*

ac-cĭpĭō, -ere, -cēpī, -ceptus [ad, *to* (one's self); capĭō, *take*], *accept, receive ; receive* (as by transmission from ancestors); *experience ; hear of, hear.*

ac-commŏdō, -āre, -āvī, -ātus [ad, *to ;* commodō, *make suitable*], *adjust.*

accūrātē, adv. [abl. form of accūrātus, *careful*], *carefully, elaborately.*

ac-currō, -ere, -cucurrī *or* -currī, -cursum [ad, *to ;* currō, *run*], *run to, hasten to.*

ac-cūsō, -āre, -āvī, -ātus [ad, *to, against ;* causa, *charge* (through denom. vb. *causō; cf. causor)], *bring a charge against, call to account, take to task, accuse.*

Achillās, -ae, M., *Achillas* (commander of the forces of Ptolemy Dionysus, king of Egypt).

aciēs, -ē and -ēī, F. [**vac***, sharp*], EDGE; *line of battle, line, army* (drawn up in battle array).

ācrĭter, adv. [ācri- (st. of ācer), *sharp*], *sharply, with energy, vigorously, resolutely, valiantly.*

ad, prep. w. acc. (opp. ab), (of motion towards) *to, against ;* (of nearness) AT, *close by ;* (w. num.) *about ; according to ;* (expressing purpose, especially with gerunds or gerundives) *for ;* ad hunc modum, *as follows ;* ad Īd. April. = ad Īdūs Aprīlis, *on the Ides* (thirteenth) *of April.*

ad-dūcō, -ere, -dūxī, -ductus [ad, *to ;* dūcō, *lead*], *lead to, lead, bring to, bring ; lead, prompt, move, incite, influence.*

ad-ĕō, -īre, -iī (-īvī), -ĭtus [ad, *to ;* eō, *go*], *go to, get* AT, *approach, come into the presence of, appear before ; incur.*

ad-fĕrō, adferre, attŭlī, adlātus (allātus) [ad, *to ;* fĕrō, BEAR, BRING], BRING *to,* BRING, *bring forward, advance.*

ad-fĭcĭō, -ere, -fēcī, -fectus [ad, *to ;* facĭō, DO], DO (something) *to, visit with ;* hence, (in good sense) *bestow upon ;* (in bad sense) *inflict upon ;* adfectus morbis, *having diseases, laboring under diseases.*

ad-fīnis, -e, adj. [ad, *near to ;* finis, *boundary*], *having adjacent boundaries, neighboring ; related to ; privy to, implicated in.*

ad-hĭbĕō, -ēre, -uī, -ĭtus [ad, *to, towards ;* habĕō, *hold*], *hold towards, bring to ; summon, invite, admit ; apply ; exercise.*

ad-hūc (accent the final syllable), adv. [ad, *to ;* hūc, *hither*], *hitherto, up to this time.*

ad-ĭmō, -ere, -ēmī, -ēmptus [ad, *to* (one's self); emō, *take*], (take to one's self from another, and so) *take away from, deprive of* (w. acc. th. and dat. pers.).

ădĭtus, -ūs, M. [ad-vi-, *go to*], *a going to, approach, access ; presence.*

ad-jungō, -ere, -jūnxī, -jūnctus [ad, *to ;* jungo, *join*], *join to, join, unite, add to.*

ad-jŭvō, -āre, -jūvī, -jūtus [ad, *to ;* juvō, *give aid*], *give aid to, aid.*

ad-mĭnister, -trī, M. [ad, *near to ;* minister, *servant*], (one who is at hand to serve, and so) *assistant, minister, agent.*

ad-mĭnistrō, -āre, -āvī, -ātus [ad, *near to ;* ministrō, *serve*], (be at hand to serve, and so) *assist, manage, execute, administer, conduct.*

ad-mīror, -ārī, -ātus [ad, AT; mīror, *wonder*], *wonder* AT, *admire.*

ad-mittō, -ere, -mīsī, -missus [ad, *to ;* mittō, *let go*], *let go to, admit ; allow, permit ; commit, perpetrate, perform.*

admŏdum, adv. [ad, *up to ;* modus, MEAsure, *limit*], (to a [great] measure, and so) *excessively, extremely, quite.*

ad-ŏlēscō, -ere, -ēvī, -ultus [ad, *to* (maturity); olēscō, *grow*], *grow or come to maturity, grow up.*

adrogantia, -ae, F. [adrogant-(st. of adrogāns), *arrogant*], *arrogance, presumption*.

ad-scendō, -ere, -scendī, -scēnsus [ad, *to;* scandō, *climb*], *climb to, climb, ascend*.

ad-sequor, -ī, -cūtus [ad, *up to;* sequor, *follow*], *attain to, accomplish*.

adsiduus, -a, -um, adj. [ad-√sed-, SIT *by*], (sitting or staying by, and so) *constant, long-continued, incessant*.

ad-sistō, -ere, -stitī [ad, AT, *by;* sistō, *place*], *place one's self* AT or *by, place one's self,* **STAND**.

ad-speciō, -ere, -spexī, -spectus [ad, *to*, AT; speciō, *look*], *look* AT or *upon, look*.

adsuēfaciō, -ere, -fēcī, -factus [adsuē- (st. in adsuēscō), *be accustomed;* faciō, *make*], *accustom, habituate, train*.

ad-sum, adesse, adfuī [ad, AT, *near;* sum, *be*], *be* AT *hand, be there; be by to assist, stand by*.

Aduātucī, -ōrum, M., *the Aduatuci* (a German tribe in Belgic Gaul between the Meuse and the Scheldt).

adulēscēns, -entis, C. [p. a., used subst., of adolēscō (with change of o to u), *grow up*], *one not yet grown to maturity; young man* or *woman, youth*.

adulēscentia, -ae, F. [adulēscent- (st. of adulēscēns), *young*], *youth, the time of youth*.

ad-veniō, -īre, -vēnī, -ventus [ad, *to;* veniō, COME], COME *to*, COME.

adventus, -ūs, M. [ad-√ven-, COME *to*], COMing *to, arrival*.

adversus, -a, -um [p. a. of advertō, *turn towards*], 1. *turned towards, facing, opposite; unsuccessful,* **adverse**. 2. **adversus**, prep. w. acc., *towards*.

ad-vertō, -ere, -tī, -sus [ad, *to;* vertō, *turn*], *turn to;* animum advertere, *to perceive*.

ad-vesperāscit, -ere, **-āvit**, im-pers. [ad, *on, near;* vesperāscit, *evening is coming*], *evening is coming on, it is getting to be evening*.

aedificium, -iī, N. [aedific- (st. of *aedifex), *builder;* cf. artificium, fr. artific-, st. of artifex], *building*.

aedificō, -āre, -āvī, -ātus [aedific- (st. of *aedifex), *builder*], (act as a builder, and so) *construct a building;* **build**.

aedīlis, -is, M. [aedi- (st. of aedis or aedēs), *building*], (adj. used subst., and so) *officer having to do with* (public) *buildings, superintendent of public works,* **aedile**.

Aeduī, -ōrum, M., *the Aedui* (a tribe in Celtic Gaul between the Loire and the Saône); in sing., **Aeduus**, -ī, M., an *Aeduan*.

aeger, -gra, -grum, adj., *sick, ill, diseased, feeble*.

aegrē, adv. [abl. fm. of **aeger**, q.v.], *with difficulty*.

aemulus, -a, -um, adj., *envious, jealous*.

aequitās, -ātis, F. [aequo- (st. of aequus), *even*], *evenness;* **animi aequitās**, *contented state of mind, content*.

aequō, -āre, **-āvī**, **-ātus** [aequo- (st. of aequus), *level, equal*], *place on a level, put on equality, make equal, equalize*.

aequor, -oris, N. [base aequ- (in aequō and aequus), *level*], (*evenness*, and so) *surface; sea* (as presenting a level surface).

aerārium, -iī, N. [aes- (st. of aes; -s- becomes -r-), *money*], (adj. used subst., and so) *place for depositing money, treasury*.

aes, aeris, N. [cogn. w. Eng. ORE], *copper, bronze; money;* **aes aliēnum**, *another's money,* i.e., *debt*.

aestās, -ātis, F., *summer season*.

aestimātiō, -ōnis, F. [aestimā- (st. of aestimō), *value*], *valuation, appraisement, estimate*.

aestimō, -āre, -āvī, -ātus, *value, estimate, fix; consider, deem*.

aestuōsus, -a, -um, adj [aestu- (st. of aestus), *heat*], *full of heat, burning hot.*

aestus, -ūs, M., *boiling, tossing,* and so (of fire, etc.) *heat;* (of the sea) *swell;* maritimī aestūs, *tides.*

aetās, -ātis, F. [= aevitās, fr. aevo- (st. of aevum), *age*], *time of life, life, age.*

aeternus, -a, -um, adj. [= aeviternus, fr. aevo- (st. of aevum), *eternity, age*], *eternal.*

Āfrīcānus, -ī, M. [Āfrica- (st. of Āfrica), *Africa*], (adj. used subst.) *conqueror of Africa,* **Afrīcanus** (surname of Scipio the elder as conqueror of Hannibal at Zama 202 B.C.; also of Scipio the younger as **destroyer of** Carthage 146 B.C.).

ager, -grī, M. [cogn. w. Eng. ACRE], *land, soil; field; district;* in pl., *fields,* **country districts.**

Agēsi-lāus, -ī, M., *Agesilaus* (king of the Spartans B.C. 398-361).

ag-ger, -eris, M. [ad, *to;* √ges- (-s- becomes -r-), *carry*], (what is carried to, and so) *materials for constructing a mound* (as earth, stone, brushwood, etc.); *mound, embankment; rampart.*

agmen, -inis, N. [√ag-, *put in motion, lead*], (that which is led, and so) *train,* **army (on the march);** novissimum agmen, *rear.*

agō, -ere, ēgī, āctus [√ag-, *put in motion*], *lead, drive;* **do;** (of courts, assizes, etc.) *hold;* agere dē, *to discuss, to talk over;* agere cum, *to treat or confer with;* (imper.) agite, *on!*

agrārius, -a, -um, adj. [agro- (st. of ager), *land*], *pertaining to land.*

agrī cultūra or **agricultūra**, -ae, F. [ager, *soil,* cultūra, *cultivation*], *cultivation of the* **soil**, *agriculture.*

alacer, -cris, -cre, adj., *eager.*

alacrītās, -ātis, F. [alacri- (st. of alacer), *eager*], *eagerness.*

ālārius, -a, -um, adj. [ālā- (st. of āla), *wing*], *belonging to the wing;* subst., **ālāriī**, -ōrum, M., *auxiliaries* (posted on the wings **of the** army).

albeō, -ēre [albo- (st. of **albus**), *white*], *be white.*

Alexandrēa (or -īa), -ae, F., *Alexandria* (capital of Egypt, founded by Alexander B.C. 331).

Alexandrīnī, -ōrum, M., *inhabitants of Alexandria;* see Alexandrēa.

algor, -ōris, M., *cold.*

aliēnus, -a, -um, adj. [alio- (st. of alius), *other*], *belonging to another, another's, foreign; unfavorable.*

allō, adv. [old case form of alius, *other,* used adv.], *to another place,* ELSE*where.*

aliquandō, adv. [ali- (st. of old forms of alius), giving an indefinite meaning, *some;* quandō, WHEN], *at some time; at any time.*

aliquantus, -a, -um, adj. [ali- (st. of old forms of alius), giving an indefinite meaning, *some;* quantus, HOW *much,* WHAT], *somewhat.*

aliquī, -qua, -quod, indef. adj. pron. [ali- (st. of old forms of alius), giving an indefinite meaning, *some, any;* quī, WHICH], *some; any.*

aliquis, -quid, indef. pron. [ali- (st. of old forms of alius), giving an indefinite meaning, *some, any;* quis, WHO], *some one, something;* **any one,** *anything;* occasionally adj., *some; any.*

aliquot, indecl. adj. [ali- (st. of old forms of alius), giving an indefinite meaning, *some;* quot, HOW *many], several.*

aliter, adv. [ali- (st. of old forms of alius), *other*], *otherwise.*

alius, -a, -ud, adj. and subst. [cogn. with English ELse], *other, another;* alius ... alius [*one* ... *one*], *another* ... *another; one* *another;* ab **allis** ad **aliōs,** *from one* [*body*] *to another.*

Allobrogēs, -um, M., *the Allobroges* (a tribe of Celtic Gauls between the Rhone and the Isère).

alō, -ere, aluī, altus[văl-,*nourish*], *nurture,* **rear,** *bring up, support, maintain.*

alter, -tera, -terum, adj. [comparative form of base al- seen in alius; hence alter refers to two objects, or groups of objects], OTHER (of two); alter ... alter, *the one ... the* OTHER, *each* OTHER.

altitūdō, -inis, F. [alto- (st. of altus), *high, deep*], *height; depth.*

altus, -a, -um [p. a. of alō, *nurture;* cogn. w. English OLD], (made great by nurturing, and so) *high, tall; deep.*

amāns, -antis [p. a. of amō, *love*], *loving, fond, friendly.*

ambactus, -ī, M., *vassal.*

Ambiānī, -ōrum, M., *the Ambiani* (a tribe in Belgic Gaul).

ambitus, -ūs, M. [amb-\ī-, *go about*], *going about; corrupt canvassing for votes,* and so *bribery.*

amicē, adv. [abl. form of amīcus, *friendly, kind*], *kindly, favorably.*

amīcitia, -ae, F. [amīco- (st. of amīcus), *friendly*], *friendship, amity.*

amīcus, -a, -um, adj. [conn. w. amō, *love*], *friendly, favorably disposed;* subst., *friend.*

ā-mittō, -ere, -mīsī, -missus [ab, *from;* mittō, *let go*], *lose.*

amor, -ōris, M. [base am- (in amō), *love*], *love.*

amplificō, -āre, -āvī, -ātus [amplifico- (st. of *amplificus), *making large*]. *enlarge,* **increase,** *extend.*

amplus, **-a,** -um, adj., *large,* *ample; illustrious, glorious, distinguished, magnificent;* n. comp. used adv., **amplius,** *more.*

Amūlius, -ī, M., *Amulius* (legendary king of Alba).

an, conj., *or.*

an-ceps, -cipitis, adj. [amb-, *on both sides, double;* capit- (st. **of** caput), HEAD], (with head on both sides, double headed, and **so**) *double; doubtful; treacherous.*

ancilla, -ae, F., *maid-servant, girl.*

ancora, -ae, F., *anchor.*

angor, -ōris, M. [\aug-, *squeeze*], *strangling; anguish.*

angulus, -ī, M., *angle, corner.*

angustiae, -ārum, F. [angusto- (st. of angustus), *strait, narrow*], **straits,** *difficulties, perplexities.*

anima, **-ae,** F., *air;* **breath;** *life;* **soul, spirit, mind.**

animadvertō, -ere, -tī, -versus [**animum,** *mind;* advertō, *turn to*], **turn the mind** *to, perceive, observe,* **notice, note;** (w. in and acc.) *inflict punishment* ON.

animal, -ālis, N. [= animāle, n. adj. used subst., fr. animā- (st. of anima), *breath, life*], (that which has breath or life, and so) *living creature,* **animal.**

animōsus, -a, -um, adj. [animo- (st. of animus), *courage*], *full of courage, spirited.*

animus, -ī, **M.,** *soul, spirit;* disembodied or *departed* **spirit;** *mind;* **heart, feelings;** *disposition;* **courage.**

annālis, -e, adj. [anno- (st. of **annus**), *year*], *pertaining to the* **year.**

annōsus, -a, -um, adj. [anno- (st. of **annus**), *year*], *full of years.*

annus, -ī, M., *year;* **in annōs singulōs,** *each year, every year.*

annuus, -a, -um, adj. [anno- (st. **of** annus), *year*], *yearly, annual;* translated adv., *annually.*

ante, prep. w. acc., *before, in advance of;* adv., *before, earlier.*

anteā, adv. [ante, *before;* acc. pl. n. ea† (orig. eā), *these things*], *before.*

ante-ferō, -ferre, -tulī, -lātus [ante, *before;* ferō, BEAR], BEAR *before; prefer.*

† This is sometimes explained as an abl.; but see Corss. Aussp. I. 760, II. 455.

ante-pōnō, -ere, -posuī, -positus [ante, *before;* pōnō, *place*], *place before, prefer.*

ante quam or **antequam** [ante, *sooner;* quam, *than*], *before; until.*

antīquitus, adv. [antīquo- (st. of antīquus), *ancient*], *anciently, in former times, in early times.*

antīquus, -a, -um, adj. [=antīcus, fr. anti- (st. of ante), *before*], *ancient, of early date, early.*

aperiō, -īre, -eruī, -ertus, *open.*

apertē, adv. [abl. fm. of apertus, *open*], *openly, manifestly, obviously.*

apertus, -a, -um [p. a. of aperiō, *open*], *open, exposed; free from trees.*

Apollō, -inis, M., *Apollo* (son of Jupiter and Latona, and brother of Diana; god of the sun, and of divination, healing, archery, poetry, music, etc.).

ap-pāreō, -ēre, -pāruī [ad, *to, before;* pāreō, *be ready*], *appear; appāret, it is evident.*

appellō, -āre, -āvī, -ātus, *accost, address, greet; entitle, call.*

appetēns, -entis [p. a. of appetō, *seek after*], *desirous; covetous.*

ap-petō, -ere, -īvī or **-iī, -ītus** [ad, *to, towards, after;* petō, *seek*], *seek after, strive to secure.*

approbātor, -ōris, M. [approbā- (st. of approbō), *approve*], *approver;* **approbātor esse,** *to approve.*

ap-propinquō, -āre, -āvī, -ātum [ad, *to;* propinquō, *draw near*], *draw near to, approach.*

Aprīlis, -is, M. [= *Aperīlis, adj. used subst., fr. aperī- (st. of aperiō), *open*], (the month which opens the ground, *i.e.*) *April.*

Apsus, -ī, M., *Apsus* (a river in southern Illyria).

apud, prep. w. acc., (in designations of place) *with, at, near, about, before;* (w. subst. referring to persons) *at the headquarters of, at the house of, in the works of, according to; in the estimation of, in the case of; among.*

Āpūlia, -ae, F., *Apulia* (province in southern Italy).

aqua, -ae, F., *water.*

aquilō, -ōnis, M. [aquilo- (st. of aquilus), *dark*], (the bringer of storms and darkness, and so) *north wind;* (used adj. w. ventus) *north.*

Aquītānī, -ōrum, M., *the Aquitani;* see Aquītānia.

Aquītānia, -ae, F., *Aquitania* (one of the three chief divisions of Transalpine Gaul, between the Garonne river and the Pyrenees mountains).

āra, -ae, F., *altar;* see Fig. 2.

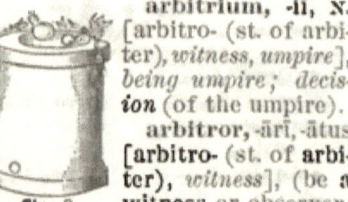

Fig. 2. Altar, from a Pompeian painting.

arbitrium, -iī, N. [arbitro- (st. of arbiter), *witness, umpire*], *being umpire; decision* (of the umpire).

arbitror, -ārī, -ātus [arbitro- (st. of arbiter), *witness*], (be a witness or observer, and so) *be of the opinion, think.*

arbor, -oris, F., *tree.*

arceō, -ēre, -uī [conn. w. arx, *stronghold*], *ward off.*

arcessō, -ere, -īvī, -ītus [intens. fm. of accēdō, *come to,* but with causative meaning; ar = ad], (cause to come to, and so) *invite, summon.*

Arethūsa, -ae, F., *Arethusa* (celebrated fountain near Syracuse, Sicily).

Ariovistus, -ī, M., *Ariovistus* (king of a German tribe in the time of Caesar).

arma, -ōrum, N. [var-, *fit;* cf. ars], (what is fitted to the body, and so) *arms.*

armātūra, -ae, F. [armā- (st. of armō), *equip,* *arm, equipment, armor.*

Arpīnum, -ī, N., *Arpinum* (town in Latium; birthplace of Cicero and Marius).

arrogantia, see adrogantia.

ars, artis, F. [var-, *fit;* cf.

artificium   **Autrōnius**   249

arma], (fitting, skill in fitting, and so) *skill, art; handicraft, occupation, profession*.
   artificium, -iī, N. [artific- (st. of artifex), *artificer*], *artisanship; handicraft, trade ;* in pl., *industrial arts*.
   Arvernī, -ōrum. M., *the Arverni* (a powerful tribe of Celtic Gaul, south of the Aedui).
   arx, arcis, F. [\arc-, *hold fast*], *stronghold, fortress, citadel*.
   ās, assis, M., *as* (copper coin worth about four-fifths of a cent).
   a-scendō, see adscendō.
   Āsia, -ae, F., *Asia* (the continent).
   asper, -era, **-erum,** adj., *rough, rugged; harsh,* **rude,** *fierce*.
   a-spiciō, see adspiciō.
   as-sequor, **see** adsequor.
   assiduus, see adsiduus.
   as-sistō, see adsistō.
   assuēfaciō, see adsuēfaciō.
   at, conj., *but, on the other hand*.
   Athēnae, -ārum, F., *Athens* (capital of Attica).
   Athēniēnsis, -e, adj. [Athēnā- (st. of Athēnae), *Athens*], *Athenian;* used subst., *an Athenian*.
   āthlēta, -ae, M. [borrowed fr. the Greek], *wrestler,* **athlete.**
   atque (before vowels and consonants) *or* **āc** (before consonants only), conj. [ad, *in addition ;* que, *and*], *and also, and*.
   Atrebatēs, -um, M., *the Atrebates* (a tribe in Belgic Gaul).
   atrōcitās, -ātis, F. [atrōci- (st. of atrōx), *fierce*], *ferocity, cruelty, severity*.
   atrōx, -ōcis, adj. [apparently fr. ātro- (st. of āter), *dark*, but w. change of quantity], *dark, hideous,* **atrocious.**
   at-tendō, -ere, -tendī, -tentus [ad, *towards;* tendo, *stretch*], *stretch* or *direct towards; direct the attention to, consider*.
   attentē, adv. [abl. fm. of **attentus,** *intent, attentive*], *attentively, earnestly*.

   Atticus, -ī, M., *Atticus* (surname of Titus Pomponius, friend of Cicero; given to him on account of his long residence in Athens and his familiarity with Greek literature).
   at-tingō, -ere, -tigī [ad, *to;* tangō, *touch*], *touch, come in contact with ; reach, arrive* **AT.**
   at-tribuō, -ere, -uī, -ūtus [ad, *to ;* tribuō, *allot*], *allot to, assign*.
   auctor, -ōris, M. [\aug-, *be strong,* **grow**], (he who **makes** strong or makes grow, and so) *author; adviser*.
   auctōritās, -ātis, F. [auctor- (st. of auctor), *author*], *authority, influence*.
   audācia, -ae, F. [audāci- (st. of audāx), *bold*], *boldness, recklessness,* **audacity.**
   audācter, adv. [audāci- (st. of audāx), *bold*], *boldly, with boldness*. Comp. **audācius,** *more boldly*.
   audāx, -ācis, adj. [**conn. w.** audeō, *dare*], *daring, bold*.
   audeō, -ēre, **ausus** [= *avideō, fr. avido- (**st. of avidus**), *eager*], (be eager, and so) *dare,* **venture.**
   audiō, -īre, -īvī *or* -iī, -ītus [conn. w. auris, EAR], *hear; listen*.
   au-ferō, auferre, abstulī, ablātus [**ab,** *from ;* ferō, BEAR], BEAR or *carry away, remove*.
   augeō, -ēre, **auxī,** auctus[\aug-, *be strong, grow;* **cogn.** w. Eng. WAX], (make **grow, and so)** *augment, increase*.
   augur, -uris, C. [au- = avi- (st. of avis), *bird*], (one whose predictions are founded [in part] on the observation of birds, *i.e.*) *an augur*.
   aurum, -ī, N. [\aus- (-s- becomes -r-), *shine*], (the shining metal, and so) *gold*.
   aut, conj., *either,* **or;** *aut ...* **aut,** *either . . . or*.
   autem, conj. [conn. w. aut], *but, however; moreover, further*.
   Autrōnius, -iī, M., *Publius Autronius Paetus* (one of Catiline's con-

auxiliāris — caelestis

federates in the **conspiracy** of 63 B.C.)
auxiliāris, -e, adj [auxilio- (st. of auxilium), *help*], *belonging* or *pertaining to help, auxiliary*; subst., auxiliārēs, -ium, M., *auxiliary troops, auxiliaries*.
auxilium, -iī, N. [conn. w. augeō, *increase*], *help, aid, assistance*.
āversus, -a, -um [p. a. of āvertō, *turn from*], (turned from, and so) *averse, hostile*; āversus ā, *hostile to*.
ā-vertō, -ere, -vertī, -versus [ā, *from*; vertō, *turn*], *turn from, turn aside*.
Aviēnus, -ī, M., *Gajus Avienus* (a military tribune under Caesar in the African war).
ā-vocō, -āre, -āvī, -ātus [ab, *from*, OFF; vocō, *call*], *call* OFF, *withdraw*.
avus, -ī, M., *grandfather*.

B.

barbarus, -a, -um, adj., *rude, savage*; subst., *barbarian*.
beātus, -a, -um [perf. part. of beō, *make happy, bless*], *happy, blessed*.
Belgae, -ārum, M., *the Belgae* (inhabited northern Gaul between the rivers Seine and Marne and the Rhine).
bellicōsus, -a, -um, adj. [bellico- (st. of bellicus), *pertaining to war*], *warlike*.
bellum, -ī, N. [conn. w. duo, TWO], *war*; belli, *in war*.
bene, adv. [for bone, abl. fm. of bonus, *good*], *well*.
beneficium, -iī, N. [beneficio- (st. of beneficus), *kind, obliging*], *kindness*, **benefit**, *service, favor, generosity*.
Bibrax, -actis, F., *Bibrax* (a town of the Remi in Belgic Gaul).
biduum, -ī, N. [bi- (= dvi-), conn. w. duo, TWO; -duum, conn. w. diēs, *day*], *space of* TWO *days*, TWO *days*.

bīnī, -ae, -a, distr. num. adj. [= *dvīnī, fr. st. of duo, TWO], TWO *and* TWO, *in groups of* TWO, TWO *from each*; (w. substs. pl. in fm., but sing. in meaning) TWO.
bipartītō, adv. [n. abl. of bipartītus, *divided into* TWO *parts*], *in* TWO *parts* or *divisions*.
Biturigēs, -um, M., *the Bituriges* (a tribe in Celtic Gaul, south of the Loire).
Boī or **Bojī,** -ōrum, M., *the Boï* or *Boji* (a Celtic tribe in alliance with the Helvetians).
bonus, -a, -um, adj., *good, honorable*; n. pl. subst., bona, -ōrum, *goods, property, resources*. Comp., melior, -ius, *better*. Superl., optimus, -a, -um, *best; excellent*.
bōs, bovis, C., *ox*.
brevis, -e, adj., *short, brief*.
brevitās, -ātis, F. [brevi- (st. of brevis), *short*], *shortness; diminutive stature*.
breviter, adv. [brevi- (st. of brevis), *short*], *briefly*.
Britannia, -ae, F., *Britain* (including England and Scotland).
Brundisium, -iī, N., *Brundisium* (a town of Calabria on the Adriatic, and the usual port of departure for Greece).

C.

C. 1. abbr. of Gājus, Gāi, M., *Gajus* (a Roman praenōmen or first name). 2. abbr. for centum, HUNDRed.
cadō, -ere, cecidī, cāsum [√cad-, *fall*], *fall*.
caedēs, -is, F. [√caed-, *cut, hew*], *cutting down, slaughter, massacre; assassination, murder*.
caedō, -ere, cecīdī, caesus [√caed-, *cut, hew*], *cut down, cut to pieces; slay, slaughter*.
caelestis, -e, adj. [conn. w. caelum, *heaven*], *pertaining to the heavens, celestial*; n. pl. subst., caelestia, -lum, *heavenly bodies, celestial phenomena*.

caelum   **Celtae**   251

caelum, -ī, N., *sky, heaven;* pl. **caelī,** M., in verse only.

Caepiō, -ōnis, M., *Quintus Servilius Caepio* (as proconsul, fought unsuccessfully with the Cimbri 105 B.C.).

Caesar, -aris, M., *Gajus Julius Caesar* (the famous Roman general and statesman; lived 100–44 B.C.).

calamitās, -ātis, F., *disaster, calamity.*

Campānia, -ae, F., *Campania* (district on the south-west coast of Italy).

capāx, -ācis, adj. [√cap-, *take*], (able to take or hold much, and so) *capacious; capable.*

capillus, -ī, M. [dim. form fr. capit- (st. of caput), HEAD; lit., adj. (sc. crinis, *hair*)], *hair of the HEAD, hair.*

capiō, -ere, cēpī, captus [√cap-, *take*], *take, lay hold of; capture; win, allure, charm, enchain;* (w. cōnsilium) *form, adopt.*

captīvus, -ī, M. [adj. used subst. fr. √cap-, *take*], *captive.*

Capua, -ae, F., *Capua* (chief city of Campania).

caput, -itis, N., HEAD; (w. numerals) *person, soul; capital crime, capital punishment, death; chief city.*

capitālis, -e, adj. [capit- (st. of caput), HEAD], *pertaining to the HEAD or life, capital.*

carcer, -eris, M., *prison.*

careō, -ēre, -uī, *be without.*

carīna, -ae, F., *keel.*

carmen, -inis, N., *song, verse, strain.*

Carnūtēs, -um, M., *the Carnutes* (a tribe of Celtic Gaul on both sides of the Loire).

carō, carnis, F., *flesh, meat.*

carpō, -ere, -psī, -ptus, *pluck; pluck at, carp at, revile.*

carrus, -ī, M., *cart, wagon.*

Carthāgō, -inis, F., *Carthage* (city on the northern coast of Africa; destroyed by Scipio the younger 146 B.C.).

Carthāginiēnsis, -e, adj. [Carthāgin- (st. of Carthāgō), *Carthage*], *Carthaginian;* see *Carthāgō.*

cārus, -a, -um, adj., *dear, precious.*

cāseus, -ī, M., *cheese.*

Cassius, -ī, M., *Lucius Cassius Longinus* (defeated and killed by the Tigurini 107 B.C.).

castellum, -ī, N. dim. [castro- (st. of castrum), *fortified place*], *stronghold.*

Casticus, -ī, M., *Casticus* (a Sequanian, son of Catamantaloedes).

castra, -ōrum, N., *camp.*

cāsus, -ūs, M. [√cād-, *fall*], *falling; chance; misfortune; unfortunate condition.*

Catamantaloedēs, -is, M., *Catamantaloedes* (ruler of the Sequani).

catellus, -ī, M. [dim. fr. catulo- (st. of catulus), *young dog*], *puppy.*

Catilīna, -ae, M., *Catiline* (notorious Roman conspirator; lived 108–62 B.C.).

Catō, -ōnis, M., *Marcus Porcius Cato* (called the elder, or the censor; lived 234–149 B.C.).

causa, -ae, F., *cause, reason; excuse, pretext; enterprise;* **causā** (following its genitive), *for the sake, for the purpose.*

caveō, -ēre, cāvī, cautus, *be on one's guard.*

cēdō, -ere, cēssī, cēssus, *go; withdraw, retire, depart; grant, concede.*

celebrō, -āre, -āvī, -ātus [*celebro-* (presumed original st. of celeber) *frequented*], (make frequented, and so) *throng, frequent; celebrate.*

celer, -eris, -ere, adj., *swift.*

celeritās, -ātis, F. [celeri- (st. of celer), *swift*], *swiftness, speed, celerity.*

celeriter, adv. [celeri- (st. of celer), *swift*], *swiftly, quickly, speedily.*

Celtae, -ārum, M., *Celts* or *Kelts* (name applied by Caesar to the

Gauls who dwelt between the Seine and the Garonne).

cēnseō, -ēre, -suī, -sus, *rate;* (of proceedings in the senate) *vote, decree; think.*

cēnsor, -ōris, M. [base cēns- (in cēnseō), *rate*], (the rating officer, *i.e.*) *censor* (one of two Roman magistrates whose duty it was: 1. **to su**perintend the registration of the citizens and their property; 2. **to** exercise control over the **conduct and** morals of the citizens; 3. to superintend the **administration** of the finances **of** the state).

cēnsus, -ūs, M. [base cēns- (in cēnseō), *rate*], *rating, registration, enumeration, census.*

centum, indecl. num. adj., *a* HUNDred.

centuria, -ae, F. [conn. w. centum, HUNDred], **century** (the century was one-sixtieth **of a legion,** and contained, in **Caesar's time,** about 100 men; see legiō).

centuriō, -ōnis, M. [centuriā- (st. of centuria, *century*], *centurion* (the commanding officer **of** a century; there were sixty centurions in a legion).

Ceraunus (Ptolomaeus), -ī, M., *Ptolemy Ceraunus* (murdered Seleucus and obtained possession of Macedonia 280 B.C.).

cernō, -ere, crēvī, certus [√cer-, *separate*], *separate; distinguish* (by the senses), *perceive, see; decide.*

certāmen, -inis, N. [certā- (st. of certō), *struggle*], (**result of struggling,** and so) *contest.*

certē, adv. [abl. fm. of certus, *certain*], *certainly, assuredly, at any rate.*

certō, -āre, -āvī, -ātus [intens. of cernō, *decide*, fr. certo- (st. of perf. part. certus)], *decide by contest, struggle, vie.*

certus, -a, -um [p. a. **of cernō,** *decide*], *decided, fixed, particular;* ***certain,*** *assured, undoubted;* cer-

tiōrem facere, *to inform;* **certior fieri,** *to be informed.*

cervus, -ī, M. [conn. w. cornū, HORN], (horned animal, and so) *stag.*

cessō, -āre, -āvī, -ātus [intens. of cēdō, *go, retire*], *loiter, abate, cease.*

cēterus, -a, -um, adj., usu. pl., the OTHER, **the remaining, the rest of;* subst., **cēterī,** -ōrum, *the rest.*

Cicerō, -ōnis, M., *Cicero* (the celebrated Roman orator; lived 106-43 B.C.).

circiter, adv. and prep. w. acc. [circo- (st. of circus), *circle*], *round about, about.*

circuitus, -ūs, M. [circu(m)-√i-, *go around*], *going around, circuit.*

circum, adv. and prep. w. acc. [acc. of circus, *circle*], *around, about.*

circum-dō, -are, -dedī, -datus [circum, *around;* dō, *put*], *put around, surround, build around, enclose.*

circum-dūcō, -ere, -dūxī, -ductus [circum, *around;* dūcō, *lead*], *lead around.*

circum-ferō, -ferre, -tulī, -lātus [circum, *around;* ferō, BEAR], *carry round, pass round.*

circum-mūniō, -īre, -īvī, -ītus [circum, *around;* mūniō, *wall*], *wall around, fortify, protect.*

circum-stō, -āre, -stetī [circum, *around;* stō, STAnd], STAnd *around, surround.*

circum-veniō, -īre, -vēnī, -ventus [circum, *around;* veniō, COME], *surround, envelop; surround in a hostile manner, oppress, defraud.*

citerior, -ius, adj. [comp. of citer, **belonging** *to this side*], HITHER, ***on this*** *side.*

citrā, adv. and prep. w. acc. [abl. fem. of citer, *belonging to this side*], *on this side of.*

cīvilis, -e, adj. [cīvi- (st. of cīvis), *citizen*], *pertaining to citizens, civil.*

cīvis, -is, C., *citizen, fellow-citizen.*

cīvitās, -ātis, F. [cīvi- (st. of cīvis), *citizen*], *citizenship; citizens; community, state.*

clam, adv., *secretly, stealthily;* prep. w. abl., *without the knowledge of.*

clāmitō, -āre, -āvī, -ātus [intens. of clāmō, *call*], *cry out, call out.*

clāmor, -ōris, M. [base clām- (in clāmō), *call*], *calling, shout.*

clārēō, -ēre [clāro- (st. of clārus), *bright*], *be bright.*

clārus, -a, -um, adj. [√clā-, **call,** *sound*, conn. w. clāmō, *call out*], *clear-sounding; bright; illustrious, renowned, held in honor.*

classis, -is, F., *fleet.*

claudō, -ere, **-sī, -sus,** *shut, close;* agmen **claudere,** *to bring up the rear.*

clēmēns, -entis, adj., *mild, gentle, forbearing, merciful,* **clement.**

cliēns, -entis, M. [= cluēns, pres. part. of clueō, *hear, obey*, used subst.], (one who hears or obeys, and so) *dependent, retainer, client.*

Clōdius, -iī, M., *Publius* **Clodius** *Pulcher* (opponent of Cicero, whose banishment he procured; killed by Milo 52 B.C.).

Cn. abbr. of **Gnaeus, -ī,** M., *Gnaeus* (a Roman praenōmen or first name).

co-emō, -ere, -ēmī, -ēmptus [co(m)-, *together;* emō, *buy*], *buy up.*

co-eō, -īre, -īvī or -iī, -itus [co(m)-, *together;* eō, *go*], *go together to form a whole, unite,* **combine.**

coepī, coeptus, def., *began.*

co-erceō, -ēre, -cuī, -citus [co(m)-, *completely;* arceō, *shut up*], *enclose, encompass; restrain, confine.*

cōgitō, -āre, -āvī, -ātus [co(m)-, *together;* agitō, *drive*], (drive a matter to and fro in the mind, and so) *weigh carefully, ponder, think, reflect.*

cōgnātiō, -ōnis, F. [co(m)-√gnā-, *be born with*], *being born* **with;** *blood-relationship;* KIN*dred family.*

cō-gnōmen, -inis, N. [co(m)-, *with,* i.e. *in addition to;* (g)nō- men, NAME], *family* NAME, sur- NAME (the third in order of the names of a Roman citizen, being preceded by the praenōmen, or name of the individual, and the nōmen, **or** name of the gens to which the individual belonged; *e.g., Marcus* (praenōmen) *Tullius* (nōmen) *Cicerō* (cōgnōmen).

cō-gnōscō, -ere, -gnōvī, -gnitus [co(m)-, **completely,** *thoroughly;* (g)nōscō, *become acquainted with*], *become thoroughly acquainted with, ascertain, learn;* **recognize;** in perf., KNOW; diligentius cōgnō- scere, *to gain a more thorough acquaintance with, or a more accurate* KNOW*ledge of.*

cōgō, -ere, coēgī, coāctus [co(m)-, *together;* agō, *drive*], *drive together, collect; compel, force, constrain.*

cohors, -rtis, F., **enclosure;** (body of men enclosed, **and so**) *cohort* (the tenth part of a **legion;** it was divided into three maniples and —as each maniple contained two centuries—into six centuries; the number of men in a cohort varied at different periods from 300 to 600, but in Caesar's time the cohort contained about 600 men).

cohortātiō, -ōnis, F. [cohortā- (st. of cohortor), *exhort*], *exhortation, encouragement.*

co-hortor, -ārī, -ātus [co(m)-, intens.; hortor, *exhort*], *exhort, encourage, admonish;* cohortārī inter sē, *to exhort one another.*

col-laudō, see conlaudō.
collēga, see conlēga.
col-ligō, see conligō.
collis, -is, M. HILL.
col-locō, see conlocō.
colloquium, see conloquium.
col-loquor, see conloquor.
colluviō, see conluviō.
colō, -ere, coluī, cultus [√col-,

colōnus   **cōnātus**

till], *till, cultivate;* **honor,** *reverence, worship.*
   colōnus, -ī, M. [**conn.** w. colō, till], *tiller of the soil;* **colonist.**
   color, -ōris, M., **color.**
   com-būrō, -ere, -ūssī, -ūstus [**com-,** *completely;* *būrō, **burn**], **burn** *up, consume.*
   comes, -itis, C. [com-√i-, *go with*], (one who goes with, and so) *comrade,* **companion.**
   commeātus, -ūs, M. [commeā- (st. of commeō), *go to and fro*], *passing* **to** *and fro;* **train,** *convoy;* **supplies.**
   com-memorō, -āre, -āvī, -ātus [com-, *completely;* memorō, *call to mind*], *call to mind in detail, call to mind, mention, recount.*
   com-mendō, -āre, -āvī, **-ātus** [com-, *completely;* mandō, *commit*], **commit** *without reservation,* **commit, intrust.**
   com-meō, -āre, -āvī, -ātus [com-, *habitually;* **meō,** *go,* **pass**], *go to and fro, go.*
   com-minus, adv. [com-, *together;* manus, *hand*], *hand* **to** *hand, at close quarters.*
   com-mittō, -ere, mīsī, -missus [com-, *together;* mittō, *send, make go*], *combine into a whole;* (w. proelium) *join, give, begin, engage in;* **commit, intrust.**
   commode, adv. [abl. **fm. of** commodus, *convenient*], *conveniently,* **easily;** *judiciously, skillfully.*
   commodum, -ī, N. [n. **of adj.** commodus, *convenient,* **used subst.**] *convenience, advantage.*
   com-moveō, -ēre, -mōvī, -mōtus [com-, *completely, thoroughly;* moveō, *move*], *set in violent motion, disturb, disquiet,* **alarm.**
   commūnicō, -āre, **-āvī,** -ātus [conn. w. commūnis, *common*], *share, bestow:* **commūnicāre cum,** *share with, impart* **to; join, unite,** *add:* **cum dōtibus commūnicāre,** *to add to the dowries.*
   com-mūnis, -e, adj. [com-, *mu-*

tually; mūnis, *under obligation.* cf. immūnis], *common, general.*
   commūtātiō, -ōnis, M. [commūtā- (st. of commūtō), *change*], *change, alteration.*
   com-mūtō, -āre, -āvī, -ātus [com-, *completely;* mūtō, *change*], *change completely, alter entirely, change, transform; exchange.*
   com-parō, -āre, -āvī, -ātus [com-, *completely,* and so *carefully;* parō, **prepare**], *prepare* **carefully,** *gather,* **collect.**
   com-parō, -āre, -āvī, -ātus [com-, *together;* parō, *make equal, exchange*], *compare.*
   com-pellō, -ere, -pulī, -pulsus [com-, *together;* pellō, *drive*], *drive in a body.*
   com-periō, -īre, -perī, -pertus [com-√per-, *penetrate completely.* cf. experior], *ascertain with certainty, ascertain, establish by proof, find out.*
   com-plector, -ī, -plexus [com-, *together;* plectō, *braid*], (braid **together, and so)** *en*FOLD, *embrace, clasp; grapple.*
   com-pleō, -ēre, -plēvī, -plētus [com-, *completely;* *pleō, FILL], FILL *completely,* FILL, *complete.*
   com-plūrēs, -a (-ia), gen., -ium, adj. [com-, *together;* plūrēs, *several*], *several.*
   com-pōnō, -ere, -posuī, -positus [com-, *together;* pōnō, *put*], *put together, adjust;* **compose,** *pacify, settle.*
   com-portō, -āre, -āvī, -ātus [com-, *together;* portō, *bring*], *bring together,* **collect.**
   com-prehendō, -ere, -hendī, -hēnsus [com-, *completely;* prehendō, *grasp*], *grasp completely or firmly; take, seize; arrest.*
   cōnāta, -ōrum, N. [n. pl. perf. part. of cōnor, *endeavor,* used subst.], *endeavors, undertaking.*
   cōnātus, -ūs, M. [cōnā- (st. of cōnor), *endeavor*], *endeavoring; effort, undertaking.*

con-cēdō, -ere, -cessī, -cessus [com-, intens.; cēdō, *go, give way*], *yield, submit to,* **comply with** *one's request; grant,* **concede,** *permit.*

con-cīdō, -ere, -cīdī [com-, *together, in a heap;* cadō, *fall*], *fall to the ground, fall.*

concĭlĭō, -āre, -āvī, -ātus [**concĭlĭo-** (st. of concilium), *assembly*], *assemble, bring together;* reconcile; *win, procure.*

concĭlĭum, -ī, N. [**com-****cal-**, *call together*], (calling **together,** and so) *assembly,* **compa***ny;* **coun***cil;* per concilium, *in* **public** *council.*

con-currō, -ere, **-currī** (-cucurrī), -cursum [**com-**, *together;* currō, *run*], **run** *together, rush together,* **hasten in** *a body, flock.*

con-demnō, -āre, -āvī, -ātus [com-, intens.; damnō, **condemn**], **condemn.**

condĭcĭō, -ōnis, F. [com-*dic-*, *say with,* and so *agree together*], *agreement, stipulation,* **condition,** *terms;* **condition,** *lot.*

con-dōnō, -āre, -āvī, -ātus [com-, intens.; dōnō, *give*], *give* **up;** *overlook.*

con-dūcō, -ere, -dūxī, -ductus [com-, *together;* dūcō, *lead*], *lead* or *bring together; collect.*

con-ferō, cōnferre, contulī, conlātus [com-, *together;* ferō, BEAR, BRING], BRING *together,* **col***lect; compare;* BRING *to* BEAR, *apply, bestow upon;* sē cōnferre, *to betake one's self.*

cōn-ficĭō, -ere, **-fēcī**, -fectus [com-, *completely;* **facĭō**, DO], *bring to completion,* **complete**, *finish, bring to an end, accomplish, carry out;* (of a list or register) *make out.*

cōn-fīdō, -ere, -fīsus [com-, *completely;* fīdō, *trust*], *trust fully,* **confide** *in, rely on, depend on.*

cōn-firmō, -āre, -āvī, -ātus [com-, intens.; firmō, *make firm*], *make firm, establish; assure, reassure; assert.*

cōn-flīgō, -ere, -flīxī, -flīctus [com-, *together;* flīgō, *strike*], (strike together, and so) 1. **tr.**, *contrast, oppose;* 2. intr., *contend, fight.*

con-gredior, -gredī, -gressus [com-, *with;* gradior, *step, walk*], *meet with; engage, fight.*

con-icĭō (pronounced: **conjĭcĭō**), -ere, -jēcī, **-jectus** [com-, *together;* **jacĭō**, *throw*], *throw together; throw, cast, hurl; drive;* in fugam **conĭcere**, *to put to flight.*

conjūnctim, adv. [acc. used adv., fr. com-*jug-*, YOKE *together, join*], *jointly,* **together.**

conjūnctĭō, **-ōnis**, F. [com-*jug-*, YOKE *together*], (YOKING *together,* **and so**) *union, intimacy.*

con-jungō, -ere, -jūnxī, -jūnctus [com-, *together;* jungō, *join*], *join, unite.*

con-junx, -jugis, c. [com-, *together;* *jug-, YOKE], (YOKE-fellow, and so) *spouse;* **wife.**

conjūrātĭō, -ōnis, F. [conjūrā-, *swear together*], (swearing **to**gether, and **so**) *conspiracy.*

con-jūrō, **-āre**, -āvī, -ātus [com-, *together;* jūrō, *swear*], **swear to***gether, conspire.*

con-laudō, -āre, **-āvī**, -ātus [com-, intens.; laudō, *commend*], *commend highly, applaud.*

con-lēga, -ae, M. [com-*lēg-*, *depute with*], (fellow-deputy, and so) *colleague, official associate.*

con-lĭgō, -āre, -āvī, -ātus [com-, *together;* lĭgō, *fasten*], *fasten together.*

con-lĭgō, -ere, -lēgī, -lēctus [com-, *together;* legō, *gather*], *gather together, gather,* **collect.**

con-locō, -āre, -āvī, -ātus [com-, *together;* locō, *place*], *place together, place, station, establish, settle; give in marriage.*

conloquium, -ī, N. [com-*loqu-*, *talk with*], *conversation, conference.*

con-loquor, **-ī**, -cūtus [com-, *with;* loquor, *talk*], *converse, confer, have a conference with.*

conluviō, -ōnis, F. [com-√luv-, *wash together*], (collected washings, and so) *dregs, offscourings; turba et conluviō, vile rabble.*

cōnor, -ārī, -ātus, *endeavor, attempt, undertake.*

cōn-sanguineī, -ōrum, M., adj. used subst. [com-, denoting *connection;* sanguineus, *pertaining to blood*], (those connected by blood, and so) *blood-relations, kinsmen.*

cōn-scīscō, -ere, -scīvī or -sciī, -scītus [com-, *together, in* a body; scīscō, *decree*], *decree in a body* or *in common; adjudge; inflict;* **sibī** mortem cōnscīscere, *to commit suicide.*

cōnscius, -a,-um,adj.[com-√sci-, *know with*], *knowing in conjunction with others; conscious.*

cōnscrīptus, -a, -um [perf. part. of cōnscrībō, *enroll*], *enrolled:* patrēs **cōnscrīptī,** *conscript* FATHERS (a title used in formal addresses before the Roman senate. The term *cōnscrīptī* was at first applied to the new senators enrolled from the ranks of the equites in the early days of the republic, and the original form of address was *patrēs et cōnscrīptī.*

cōn-secrō, -āre, -āvī, -ātus [com-, *wholly;* sacrō, *make sacred*], *consecrate, dedicate.*

cōnsēnsus, -ūs, M. [com- sent- (base in sentiō), *perceive* or *feel with* or *in common*], (feeling in common, and so) *consent.*

cōn-sentiō, -īre, -sēnsī, -sēnsus [com-, *together, in common;* sentiō, *feel*], *agree; conspire.*

cōn-sequor, -ī, -cūtus [com-, *close upon;* sequor, *follow*], *follow close upon, follow after, follow, ensue.*

cōn-servō, -āre, -āvī, -ātus [com-, intens.; servō, *keep*], *maintain, preserve, save.*

cōnsessus, -ūs, M. [com-, *together;* √sed-, SIT], (sitting together, and so) *assembly*

cōn-sīdō, -ere, -sēdī, -sessum [com-, *together;* sīdō, SIT], SIT *down together,* SETTLE, *establish one's self; post one's self; encamp.*

cōnsilium, -iī, N. [conn. w. cōnsulō, *deliberate*], *deliberation, counsel; plan, design, purpose, intention, scheme; measure, line of conduct, course, policy; advice; sagacity; council.*

cōn-sistō, -ere, -stitī [com-, intens.; sistō, STAND], *come to a halt,* STOP, *take a position;* STAND, *maintain one's footing or position, make a* STAND*; settle;* (w. in and abl.) *consist* IN or *of.*

cōnspectus, -ūs, M. [com-√spec-, SPY (all parts together, and so) *at a glance*], *sight at a glance, sight; presence.*

cōn-spiciō, -ere, -spexī, -spectus [com-, *together* (all parts being taken in at a glance); speciō, *look at*], *catch sight of, descry, see.*

cōnspicor, -ārī, -ātus [com-√spec- (through presumed noun stem), SPY (all parts together, and so) *at a glance*], *catch sight of, descry, see.*

cōnstantia, -ae, F. [cōnstant- (st. of p. a. cōnstāns), STANDING *firm*], *firmness, constancy.*

cōn-stituō, -ere, -uī, -ūtus [com-, *together,* and so *firmly;* statuō, *set up*], (set up firmly, and so) *station, post; establish, appoint; arrange, fix, settle upon, decide upon; decide, resolve;* dē contrōversiīs cōnstituere, *to settle* or *decide disputes.*

cōn-stō, -āre, -stitī [com-, *with;* stō, STAND], STAND *with; be in agreement with;* impers., *be settled, undisputed, generally understood, well known.*

cōn-suēscō, -ere, -suēvī, -suētus [com-, intens.; suēscō, *become accustomed*], *become accustomed, accustom one's self;* in perf., *be accustomed.*

cōnsuētūdō, -inis, F. [cōnsuē(to)- (st. of cōnsuētus), *accustomed*], *habit, manner, custom, usage, practice.*

cōnsul, -is, M., *consul* (one of the two highest Roman magistrates chosen annually under the republic).

cōnsulāris, -e, adj. [cōnsul- (st. of cōnsul), **consul**], *belonging or pertaining to a consul, consular.*

cōnsulātus, -ūs, M. [cōnsul- (**st. of** cōnsul), **consul**], *consulship.*

cōnsulō, -ere, -uī, -tus, *reflect, deliberate, take counsel;* (w. dat.) *take thought for, have regard for, have an eye to;* (w. acc.) *consult* (for advice).

cōn-sūmō, -ere, -sūmpsī, -sūmptus [com-, *completely;* sūmō, *take*], *take up completely; consume.*

cōn-surgō, -ere, -surrēxī, -surrēctum [com-, *together;* surgō, *rise*], *rise in a body, stand.*

contāgiō, -ōnis, F. [com-√tāg-, *touch together*], *contact.*

contemptiō, -ōnis, F. [com-√tem-, *cut up* (com is intens.)], (cutting treatment, and so) *contempt, scorn, defiance.*

contemptus, -a, -um (p. **a.** of contemnō, *despise*], *contemptible.*

contemptus, -ūs, M. [com-√tem-, *cut up* (com- is intens.)], (cutting treatment, and so) *contempt.*

con-tendō, -ere, -dī, -tus [com-, intens.; tendō, *stretch*], *stretch vigorously, strive; hasten; contend, struggle; vie; contend successfully, prevail.*

contentiō, -ōnis, F. [com-√ten-, *stretch vigorously, struggle*], *struggling, contention, dispute.*

con-texō, -ere, -xuī, -xtus [com-, *together;* texō, *weave*], *weave, join, or put together, frame, construct.*

continēns, -entis [p. **a. of** contineō, *hold together*], *uninterrupted.*

continenter, adv. [continent- (st. of continēns), *uninterrupted*], *uninterruptedly, continuously.*

contineō, -ēre, -tinuī, -tentus [com-, *together;* teneō, *hold*], *hold together, hold, keep; bound, confine; hem in, hold in check, restrain.*

contingō, -ere, -tigī, -tactus [com-, *completely, closely;* tangō, *touch*], *touch, be contiguous to.*

continuus, -a, -um, adj. [com-√ten-, *stretch together*], (stretching or hanging together, and so) *successive, continuous.*

contrā, adv. **and** prep. w. acc., *against.*

contrōversia, -ae, F. [contrōverso- (st. of contrōversus), *opposite*], (opposition, and so) *dispute, controversy.*

contumēlia, -ae, F., *abuse, insult, indignity, reproach :* **per** contumēliam, *by injurious reports, through slanderous accusations; buffeting, violence.*

con-veniō, -īre, -vēnī, -ventus [com-, *together;* veniō, COME], COME *together, assemble;* convenit, *it is agreed upon.*

conventus, -ūs, M. [com-√ven-, COME *together*], *meeting; court.*

con-vertō, -ere, -tī, -sus [com-, intens.; vertō, *turn*], *turn about, change the direction of, reverse :* conversa **signa inferre,** *to face about and advance against.*

convīvium, -iī, N. [convīvā- (st. of convīva), *table companion*], *eating together; banquet.*

con-vocō, -āre, -āvī, -ātus [com-, *together;* vocō, *call*], *call together, call, convoke, assemble.*

cōpia, -ae, F., *abundance, supply;* in pl., *supplies,* **stores,** *wealth, resources, numbers; troops, forces.*

cōpiōsus, -a, -um, adj. [cōpiā- (st. of cōpiae), *wealth*], *abounding in wealth, well supplied, rich.*

cōpula, -ae, F., *grapnel hook* (by which vessels were fastened together in battle).

cor, cordis, N., HEART.

Corinthus, -ī, F., *Corinth* (commercial city of Peloponnesus on the isthmus of Corinth).

cornū, -ūs, N., HORN; (of an army) *wing.*

corpus, -oris, N., *body.*

cor-rumpō, -ere, -rūpī, -ruptus [com-, *completely;* rumpō, *break*], *destroy;* (of an opportunity) *sacrifice.*

cor-ruō, -ere, -uī [com-, *together;* ruō, *fall*], *fall together, fall with a crash, tumble down, fall.*

cottidiānus or **cōtidiānus, -a, -um,** adj. [st. **cottīdi-** (in cottīdiē), *every day*], *belonging to every day, daily.*

cottidiē or **cōtidiē,** adv. [loc. fm. of quot, HOW *many;* loc. or abl. fm. of diēs, *day*], (on as many days as there are, and so) *daily.*

Cotus, -ī, M., *Cotus* (a prominent Aeduan).

Crassus, -ī, M., *Publius Licinius Crassus* (one of **Caesar's** lieutenants).

crēber, -bra, -brum, adj., *frequent, numerous.*

crēbrō, adv. [n. abl. of crēber, *frequent*], *often, frequently, many times.*

crēdibilis, -e, adj. [base **crēd-** (in crēdō), *believe*], *worthy of belief, credible.*

crēdō, -ere, -didī, -ditus (w. acc. and dat.) *intrust;* (w. dat. pers.) *trust, believe, put confidence in, take the advice of;* (w. acc. and inf., or abs.) *believe, suppose.*

cremō, -āre, -āvī, -ātus, *consume by fire, burn.*

creō, -āre, -āvī, -ātus, *make, choose, elect.*

crēscō, -ere, crēvī, crētus [√crē-, *make;* conn. w. creō], (begin to make itself, and so) *come forth, grow, increase, become great.*

Crēta, -ae, F., *Crete* (island in the Mediterranean).

crīmen, -inis, N. [√crī-, *sift*], (that which **sifts,** and so) *judicial decision; accusation, charge, reproach.*

crīminōsus, -a, -um, adj. [**crīmin-** (st. of crīmen), *reproach*], *reproachful.*

cruciātus, -ūs, M.[cruciā- (st. of **cruciō),** *torture*], *torture, torment.*

crūdēlis, -e, adj., *cruel.*

crūdēlitās, -ātis, F. [crūdēli- (st. of crūdēlis), *cruel*], *cruelty.*

crūdēliter, adv. [crūdēli- (st. of crūdēlis), *cruel*], *cruelly.*

culpa, -ae, F., *fault, blame.*

cultus, -ūs, M. [√col-, *till*], *tilling, cultivation, labor; mode of life, condition as to civilization; civilization, culture.*

cum, prep. w. abl., *with;* cum is appended enclitically to the abl. of pers. and rel. prons.; as, **vōbīscum,** *with you.*

cum, conj. [for quom, acc. fm. of pron. st. quo-, WHICH], *at which time, WHEN, WHENever; since, inasmuch as, as; though, although.*

cumulō, -āre, -āvī, -ātus [cumulo- (st. of cumulus), *heap*], *gather into a heap, augment* (by piling up).

cūnctātiō, -ōnis, F. [cūnctā- (st. of cunctor), *delay*], *delaying, delay.*

cūnctus, -a, -um, adj. [contracted fr. conjūnctus, perf. part. of conjungō, YOKE *together*], (all united into one body, and so) *whole, entire, all;* n. pl. used subst., *all things, everything.*

cupidē, adv. [abl. fm. of cupidus, *desirous, eager*], *eagerly, ardently.*

cupiditās, -ātis, F. [cupido- (st. of cupidus), *desirous*], *desire, longing; passionate* or *covetous desire.*

cupidus, -a, -um, adj. [conn. w. cupiō, *desire*], *desirous.*

cupiō, -ere, -īvī (-iī), -ītus, *desire; wish well to.*

cūr, adv. [= old fm. quōr (for *quār), fr. quā rē, *because of which* or WHAt *thing*], WHY, WHEREfore.

cūra, -ae, F., *anxiety, solicitude, care, concern.*

cūrō, -āre, -āvī, -ātus [cūrā- (st. of cūra), *care*], *take care.*

curriculum, -ī, N. [base curr- (in currō), *run*], *running; course.*

currus, -ūs, M. [base curr- (in currō), *run*], (that which runs, and so) *chariot, triumphal car.*

custōdia, -ae, F. [custōd- (st. of custōs), *guard*], *guardianship, protection;* in pl., *guards.*
custōdiō, -īre, -īvī or **-iī, -ītus** [custōd- (st. of custōs), *guard*], *guard, watch over.*
custōs, -ōdis, C., *guard, guardian.*

D.

damnō, -āre, -āvī, -ātus [damno- (st. of damnum), *loss*], *inflict loss upon, harm,* **damage;** *condemn.*
dē, prep. w. abl., (of place) *down from, from,* (of time) *in, during, about:* **dē tertiā vigiliā,** *in the* THIRD WATCH; (of the cause from which a thing proceeds) *for:* **quā dē causā,** *for* WHICH *reason, so;* (of the subject of thought, discussion, etc.) *of, about, concerning, upon, over;* **merēri dē,** *to deserve at the hands of;* **contendere dē,** *to strive* or *contend for.*
dēbeō, -ēre, -buī, -bitus [dē, *from;* habeō, *have*], (have from another, and so) *owe, be under obligation, ought.*
dē-cēdō, -ere, -cessī, -cessum [dē, *from;* cēdō, *go*], *withdraw, depart from, depart; die, decease.*
decem, indecl. num. adj., TEN.
decem et novem or **decem novem,** indecl. num. adj., NINETEEN.
dē-cernō, -ere, -crēvī, -crētus [dē, *from, out;* cernō, *separate, sift*], (sift or separate, as the true from the false, the important from the unimportant, etc., and so) *decide;* (give official expression to one's decision, and so) *vote,* **decree;** *appoint.*
dē-certō, -āre, -āvī, -ātus [dē, intens., and so *to the end, out;* certō, *fight*], *fight it out, fight,* **contend.**
decet, -ēre, -cuit, impers. [√dec-, *esteem;* conn. w. decus, *comeliness,* and dignus, *worthy*], *it is becoming, it is proper.*
decima for **decuma, -ae, F.**(usu. in pl.) [fem. of decimus, TENth

(sc. pars, *part*)], TIthe (tax levied on landholders in the Roman provinces).
decimus, -a, -um, ord. num. adj. [decem, TEN], TENth.
dēcipiō, -ere, -cēpī, -ceptus [dē, giving a bad sense to the verb; capiō, *take* (cf. the English ' take in ')], *deceive.*
dē-clīnō, -āre, -āvī, -ātus [dē, *from;* *clīnō,* **bend**], *turn aside from,* and so *have* **recourse to.**
dēclīvis, -e, adj. [dē-clīvo- (st. of clīvus, *hill*), *down hill*], *sloping.*
dēcrētum, -ī, N. [n. perf. part. of dēcernō, *decide,* **decree**], used subst.], (what has been decided or decreed, and so) *official decision, decree, ordinance.*
decus, -oris, N. [√dec-, *esteem,* conn. w. decet, *it is becoming,* and dignus, *worthy*], *comeliness; ornament; honor;* DIGNIty *of behavior.*
dē-decus, -oris, N. [dē, w. neg. force; decus, *honor*], *dishonor, disgrace, infamy;* **act of baseness,** *deed* **of** *infamy.*
dē-dō, -ere, -didī, -ditus [dē, *from, away, up;* dō, *give*], *give up, surrender, devote.*
dē-dūcō, -ere, -dūxī, -ductus [dē, *from,* **away**; dūcō, *lead*], *lead out,* **withdraw,** *carry off, bring down, bring away, recall.*
dē-fatīgō, -āre, -āvī, -ātus [dē, intens., *utterly, out;* fatīgō, *weary*], *tire out, exhaust.*
dē-fendō, -ere, -fendī, -fēnsus [dē, *from, off;* *fendō, *strike, thrust*], *ward off, repel;* **defend,** *protect.*
dēfēnsiō, -ōnis, F. [dē-√fend-, *thrust off*], (thrusting off assailants, and so) *defence.*
dēfēnsor, -ōris, M. [dē-√fend-, *thrust off*], (thruster off of assailants, and so) *defender.*
dē-ferō, -ferre, -tulī, -lātus [dē, *from;* ferō, **bring**], *bring from, and so report.*

dē-ficiō, -ere, -fēcī, -fectus [dē, *from, off;* faciō, *make*], (make off, break loose from, and so) *forsake, desert, abandon; fail, cease, be wanting.*

dē-fugiō, -ere, -fūgī [dē, *from;* fugiō, *flee*], *flee from, avoid, shun.*

dē-iciō (pronounced : dējiciō), -ere, -jēcī, -jectus [dē, *down;* jaciō, *throw*], *throw down, cast down; unhorse; disappoint.*

dein-ceps, adv. [dein (abridged fm. of deinde), *thereafter, next;* √cap-, *take*], (taking place next, and so) *in succession.*

dē-leō, -ēre, -ēvī, -ētus [dē, *from, out;* *leō, for which, linō, *smear, blot*], *blot out, obliterate; destroy.*

dē-līberō, -āre, -āvī, -ātus [dē, intens., *well, thoroughly;* *līberō (cf. lībrō, *balance*)], *weigh well, weigh, deliberate.*

dēlictum, -ī, N. [u. perf. part. of dēlinquō, *transgress,* used subst.], *transgression, offence.*

dē-ligō, -ere, -lēgī, -lectus [dē, *from, out;* legō, *gather, pick*], *pick out, select, choose.*

dēmentia, -ae, F. [dēmenti- (st. of dēmēns), *out of one's senses, mad*], *madness, folly.*

dē-minuō, -ere, -uī, -ūtus [dē, *from, away;* minuō, *make less, lessen*], *lessen by taking away, diminish, take away.*

dē-mittō, -ere, -mīsī, -missus [dē, *down;* mittō, *cast*], *cast down.*

dēmum, adv. [superl. fm. of dē, *down, from*], (downmost, farthest from, and so) *at last, at length.*

dēnārius, -iī, M. [masc. of adj dēnārius, *containing* TEN (sc. nummus, *coin*)], (coin containing [originally] ten asses) *denarius* (a Roman silver coin equivalent in value to about 16 cents).

dēnsus, -a, -um, adj., *dense.*

dē-pellō, -ere, -pulī, -pulsus [dē, *from, away;* pellō, *drive*], *drive away, avert.*

dē-pōnō, -ere, -posuī, -positus [dē, *away, aside;* pōnō, *place, put*], *put or lay aside, drop.*

dē-populor, -ārī, -ātus [dē, intens., *utterly;* populor, *lay waste*], *lay waste utterly, lay waste, ravage.*

dēprecātor, -ōris, M. [dēprecā- (st. of dēprecor), *pray away, avert by prayer*], (one who averts a threatened evil by entreaty, and so) *intercessor.*

dē-primō, -ere, -pressī, -pressus [dē, *down;* premō, *press*], *press down, depress, sink.*

dē-rogō, -āre, -āvī, -ātus [dē, denoting withdrawal or reversal of action; rogō, (of a law) *propose for enactment*], (withdraw a proposal for enactment, and so) *repeal* (applied to part of a law); *take away, withdraw, withhold.*

dē-scendō, -ere, -scendī, -scēnsus [dē, *down;* scandō, *climb*], *climb down, descend; have recourse, resort.*

dē-scīscō, -ere, -scīvī (-iī), -scītum [dē, denoting withdrawal or reversal of action; scīscō, *approve, assent*], (withhold assent, and so) *withdraw, revolt.*

dē-serō, -ere, -ruī, -rtus [dē, denoting withdrawal or reversal of action; serō, *join*], *desert, abandon.*

dēsertor, -ōris, M. [dē-\ser-, *desert*], *deserter.*

dēsīderium, -iī, N., *longing, regret* (for the absence of something needed).

dēsidia, -ae, F. [dēsid- (st. of *dēses, gen. -idis), *idle*], *idleness, inactivity.*

dēsignātus, -a, -um [perf. part. of dēsignō, *designate, elect*], *elected, elect* (term applied to a person already elected to an office, but not yet inaugurated).

dē-siliō, -īre, -luī [dē, *down;* saliō, *leap*], *leap down.*

dēsipiēns, -entis [p. a. of dēsipiō, *be childish*], *childish, in one's dotage.*

dē-sistō, -ere, -stitī [dē, *from,
off;* sistō, STA*nd*], *desist;* (w.
abl.) *desist* (from). *abandon.*

dē-spērō, -āre, -āvī, -ātus [dē,
w. neg. force; spērō, *hope*], **de-
spair.**

dē-spiciō, -ere, -spexī, -spectus
[dē, *down;* speciō, *look*], *look
down upon,* **despise.**

dē-spoliō, -āre, -āvī, -ātus [dē,
intens.; spoliō, *strip, rob*], *strip,
rob,* **despoil.**

dēstinō, -āre, -āvī, -ātus, *make
fast.*

dē-sum, deesse, dēfuī [dē,
from; sum, *be*], BE *wanting, fail,
desert, abandon.*

dēsuper, adv. [dē, *from;* super,
above], *from* ABOVE.

dē-terreō, -ēre, -uī, -itus [dē,
from, off; terreō, *frighten*], *fright-
en off,* **deter.**

dē-trahō, -ere, -trāxī, -tractus
[dē, *from, off;* trahō, *draw*], *withdraw, take away, seize, snatch.*

dētrīmentum, -ī, N. [dē-√trī-,
rub away], (result of rubbing
away, and so) *loss, damage,* **detri-
ment.**

deus, -ī, M. [conn. w. diēs], *god,
deity.*

dē-voveō, -ēre, -vōvī, -vōtus
[dē, intens.; voveō, *promise solemnly,* **vow**], *solemnly promise to
sacrifice,* **devote, vow.**

dexter, (-tera) -tra, (-terum)
-trum, adj., *right.*

dicō, -āre, -āvī, -ātus [as if fr.
st. dico-, found only in compounds, as vēridicus, *truth-tell-
ing;* conn. w. dīcō], (orig.) *proclaim*, (usu.) *give up, devote,* **dedicate.**

dīcō, -ere, dīxī, dictus [√DĪC-,
point out, show], *say, express,* **give
expression to, tell, talk of, mention; call, name;** jūs dīcere, *to
administer justice;* pauca dīcere,
to speak briefly.

dictātor, -ōris, M. [dictā- (st.
of dictō), *prescribe*, **dictate**], *dictator.*

dictum, -ī, N. [perf. part. of
dīcō, *say*, used subst.], *what is
said, saying; word of command,
order.*

diēs, -ēī (-ēi, -ē), M. (sometimes
F. in sing.) [conn. w. deus], *day;
time.*

dif-ferō, differre, distulī, dīlātus
[dis-, *in different directions;* ferō,
BEAR], *carry in different directions;*
differ (this meaning appears to be
confined to the pres. system).

dif-ficilis, -e, adj. [dis-, w. neg.
force; facilis, *easy*], *hard,* **difficult.**

difficultās, -ātis, F. [difficuli- (st.
of difficul, old form of difficilis),
difficult], **difficulty.**

dignitās, -ātis, F. [digno- (st. of
dignus), *worthy*], *worth,* **dignity;**
standing, position.

dignus, -a, -um, adj., *worthy.*

dīligēns, -entis, adj. [p. a. of
dīligō, *esteem*], (esteeming, and
so) *devoted* (to), *attentive,* **diligent.**

dīligenter, adv. [dīligent- (st.
of dīligēns), *attentive*], *attentively;
thoroughly;* dīligentius cōgnōscere, *to gain a more accurate*
KNOW*ledge of.*

dīligentia, -ae, F. [dīligent- (st.
of dīligēns), *attentive*], *careful-
ness, attentiveness,* **diligence.**

dī-ligō, -ere, -lēxī, -lēctus [dis-,
apart; legō, *choose*], (show one's
esteem for an object by choosing
it in preference to others, and so)
esteem highly, love.

di-micō, -āre, -āvī, -ātum [dis-,
implying TWO contestants, and
so *against;* micō, *dart to and fro*],
(dart to and fro against, and so)
contend.

dīmidium, -lī, N. [n. of adj.
dīmidius, *half*, used subst.; fr.
dis-, *in* TWO and medius, MID*dle*],
half.

di-mittō, -ere, -mīsī, -missus
[dis-, in *different directions*, mittō,
send], (send in different directions, and so) *dismiss, disband,
break up, dissolve; forego, lose.*

Diō or **Diōn**, -ōnis, M., *Dion* (eminent Syracusan, brother-in-law of Dionysius I., and friend of Plato; assassinated B.C. 353).

Dionȳsius, -iī, M., *Dionysius* (1. the elder, tyrant of Syracuse B.C. 405-367; 2. the younger, tyrant of Syracuse B.C. 367-343).

Dīs, -ītis, M. [conn. w. deus and diēs]. *Dis* (the god of the under world), *Pluto*.

dis-cēdō, -ere, -cessī, -cessum [dis-, *apart;* cēdō, *go*], *go apart, withdraw, depart, disperse*: discēdere ab, *desert, abandon*. discēdere ab armīs, *to lay down one's arms*.

disciplīna, -ae, F. [discipulo- (st. of discipulus), *learner*], *instruction, tuition; system* (e.g., the Druidical system), DOC*trines, discipline*.

discipulus, -ī, M. [conn. w. discō, *learn*], *learner, pupil*.

discō, -ere, **didicī** [inceptive fr. √dic-, *point out, show*], (begin to point out, and so) *learn; study, receive instruction*.

dis-currō, -ere, **-currī or -cu**currī, -cursum [dis-, *in different directions;* currō, *run*], *run in different directions, scatter, disperse*.

dis-iciō (pronounced: disjiciō), -ere, -jēcī, -jectum [dis-, *asunder, in pieces;* jaciō, *throw*], *lay in ruins, raze, destroy*.

dis-pōnō, -ere, -posuī, **-positus** [dis-, *apart, at intervals;* pōnō, *place*], *station at intervals*.

dis-putō, -āre, -āvī, -ātus [dis-, *separately, in detail;* putō, *reckon*], *reckon in detail* or *by items; examine,* **discuss**.

dissēnsiō, -ōnis, F. [dis-, *apart, at variance;* base sent-(in sentiō), *perceive, feel*], *disagreement, dissension, discord*.

dis-serō, -ere, -uī, disertus (adj.) [dis-, *at intervals;* serō, *join, bind together*], (arrange words in connected discourse, and so) 1. tr., *discuss;* 2. intr., *discourse, talk*.

dis-tineō, -ēre, -uī, -tentus [dis-, *asunder;* teneō, *keep*], *keep asunder, keep apart*.

diū, adv. [conn. w. diēs, *day, time*], *for a long time, long*. Comp., **diūtius**, *for a longer time, longer; for too long a time, too long*.

dīversus, -a, -um [perf. part. of dīvertō, *turn in different directions*], *opposed*.

Dīvicō, -ōnis, M., *Divico* (a prominent Helvetian; defeated Lucius Cassius Longinus B.C. 107; was ambassador to Caesar B.C. 58).

dīvidō, -ere, -vīsī, **-vīsus,** *divide, separate*.

dīvīnus, -a, -um, adj. [dīvo- (st. of dīvus), *god*], *pertaining to the gods, divine, sacred*.

dīvīsus, -a, -um [perf. part. of dīvidō, *divide*], *divided*.

Dīvitiācus, -ī, M., *Divitiacus* (1. chief of the Aeduans and brother of Dumnorix; 2. chief of the Suessiones).

dīvitiae, -ārum, F [dīvit- (st. of dīves), *rich*], *riches, wealth*.

dō, dare, dedī, datus [√da-, *give*], *give, award, assign, afford, allow, grant*.

doceō, -ēre, -cuī, -ctus [√doc-, *show,* TEACH; conn. w. discō and dīcō], TEACH, *instruct, show, declare, tell, point out*.

doctor, -ōris, M. [√doc-, TEACH], TEACH*er*.

doctus, -a, -um [p. a. of doceō, TEACH], *learned*.

doleō, -ēre, -uī [conn. w. dolor, q. v.], *feel pain; grieve for, be afflicted at*.

dolor, -ōris, M. [√dol-, TEAR, *split;* conn. w. doleō, *feel pain*], *pain; mortification*.

dolus, -ī, M., *deceit, treachery*.

domesticus, -a, -um [conn. w. domus, *house, home*], *domestic, native, private*.

dominus, -ī, M., *master, lord*.

domus, -ūs, F. [√dom-, *build*], (that which is built, and so) *house*, home; family, household; **domī** (loc.), at home, in peace; **domō** (abl.), from home.

dōs, dōtis, F. [√dō-, give], dowry, marriage portion.

Druidēs, -um, M., *Druids* (priests of the Gauls).

dubitō, -āre, -āvī, -ātus [conn. w. dubius, *doubtful*], *doubt; hesitate*.

dubius, -a, -um, adj. [conn. w. duo, TWO], *doubtful*.

ducentī, -ae, -a [st. of duo, TWO; st. of centum, HUNDred], TWO HUNDred.

dūcō, -ere, dūxī, ductus, *lead, bring, take, escort;* **ōrdinem dūcere**, *to command a century, to be a centurion; put off, delay; consider, hold, account, reckon, deem.*

ductor, -ōris, M. [√duc-, *lead*], *leader, commanding officer.*

dulcis, -e, adj., *sweet;* **aqua dulcis**, *fresh water.*

dum, conj., *while, as long as; provided, if only; until.*

dummodo, conj. [dum, *as long as,* provided; modo, *only*], *provided only, if only.*

Dumnacus, -ī, M., *Dumnacus* (leader of the Andes, a tribe in Celtic Gaul, north of the Loire).

Dumnorix, -igis, M., *Dumnorix* (prominent Aeduan, brother of Divitiacus).

duo, -ae, -o, num. adj., TWO.

duodecim, indecl. num. adj. [duo, TWO; decem, TEN], TWELVe.

duodecimus, -a, -um, ord. num. adj. [duodecim, TWELVe], TWELFth.

duodēnī, -ae, -a, distr. num. adj. [duo, TWO; dēnī, TEN *apiece*], TWELVe *apiece.*

dūritia, -ae, F. [dūro- (st. of dūrus), *hard*], *hardness; rigorous mode of life; hardship.*

dux, ducis, C. [√duc-, *lead*], *leader, guide, conductor.*

E.

ē, see ex.

Eburōnēs, -um, M., *the Eburones* (tribe in Belgic Gaul).

ē-discō, -ere, -didicī [ex, *thoroughly*; discō, *learn*], *learn by heart.*

ē-dō, -ere, -didī, -ditus [ex, *forth*; dō, *give, put*], *put forth, bring forth, produce; publish;* (of punishment) *execute, inflict.*

ē-doceō, -ēre, -cuī, -ctus [ex, *thoroughly*; doceō, TEACH], TEACH *thoroughly, inform in detail, train thoroughly in, set forth in detail.*

ē-dūcō, -ere, -dūxī, -ductus [ex, *forth, out*; dūcō, *lead*], *lead out or forth;* (of swords) *draw.*

ef-ferō, efferre, extulī, ēlātus [ex, *forth, out*; ferō, BRING], BRING *forth;* BRING out, *publish.*

ef-ficiō, -ere, -fēcī, -fectus [ex, *out, completely*; faciō, *make*], *work out, accomplish, bring to pass, cause, produce, make, render, form.*

ef-flāgitō, -āre, -āvī, -ātus [ex, intens.; flāgitō, *demand urgently*], *demand with earnestness,* **importune for.**

ef-fugiō, -ere, -fūgī [ex, *forth, away*; fugiō, *flee*], *escape.*

effugium, -iī, N. [ex-√fug-, *flee from, escape*], *flight; means of escape.*

egeō, -ēre, eguī, *lack, need, require.*

ego, gen. meī, pers. pron., I; **mihī** (dat. of ref.) *in* MY *eyes.*

ē-gredior, -ī, -gressus [ex, *forth*; gradior, *step, walk*], *go or come forth or out, withdraw.*

ēgregius, -a, -um, adj. [ē-greg(e) (abl. of grex, *herd*), *out of the herd*], (out of the common herd, and so) *eminent, illustrious.*

ē-iciō (pronounced ējiciō), -ere, -jēcī, -jectus [ex, *forth*; jaciō, *cast*], *cast forth or out, drive out, expel;* **sē ēicere in** (w. acc.), *to make a raid* ON.

ējus modī or **ējusmodī** [is, *that, such;* modus, **manner, kind**] *of such a kind, such.*

ēloquēns, -entis [p. a. of ēloquor, *speak out*], *eloquent.*

ē-mittō, -ere, -mīsī, -missus [ex, *forth, out;* mittō, *send, let go*], *send out, let loose.*

emō, -ere, ēmī, ēmptus [√em-, *take*], (orig. meaning, *take;* cf. adimō and sūmō), *buy.*

Empedoclēs, -is, M., *Empedocles* (natural philosopher of Agrigentum in Sicily; flourished about the middle of the fifth century, B.C.).

enim, conj. [strengthened fm. of nam, *for*] (placed after the first word, or after two or more closely connected words), *indeed, in fact, for.*

Ennius, -iī, M., *Quintus Ennius* (the father of Roman epic poetry; lived 239–169 B.C.).

ē-nūntiō, -āre, -āvī, -ātus [ex, *out, openly;* nūntiō, *declare*], *divulge, report.*

eō, īre, īvī or iī, itum [√ei-, ī-, or i-, *go*], *go, depart; die.*

eō, adv. [case fm. of pron. is, *that*], *to that place, thither.*

eōdem, adv. [case fm. of īdem, *the same;* cf. eō], *to the same place.*

eques, -itis, M. [equo- (st. of equus), *horse*], *horseman;* in pl., *horsemen, horse; knight* (the knights constituted an order in Rome intermediate in rank between the patricians and the plebeians).

equester, -tris, -tre, adj. [equit- (st. of eques), *horseman*], *pertaining to cavalry, cavalry* (adj.).

equitātus, -ūs, M. [equitā- (st. of equitō), *ride*], *riding; cavalry.*

equitō, -āre, -āvī, -ātum [equit- (st. of eques), *horseman*], (be a horseman or act as a horseman, and so) *ride.*

equus, -ī, M., *horse.*

ergā, prep. w. acc., *towards.*

ergō, adv., *therefore, then.*

ē-rigō, -ere, -rēxī, -rēctus [ex, *from below, up;* regō, *make straight*], *erect, raise.*

ē-ripiō, -ere, -ripuī, -reptus [ex, *from, away;* rapiō, *seize*], *take*

away by force, seize, wrest, deprive.

errō, -āre, -āvī, -ātus, *wander; err, be mistaken.*

ē-rumpō, -ere, -rūpī, -ruptus [ex, *forth;* rumpō, *burst, break*], *break forth, make a sally.*

ēruptiō, -ōnis, F. [ē-√rup-, *break forth*], (breaking forth, and so) *sally, sortie.*

essedum, -ī, N. [Celtic word], *two-wheeled war chariot* (used by the Gauls and Britons).

et, conj. (for distinction between et and **other** conjunctions meaning *and,* see 'and' in the English-Latin vocabulary), *and;* et . . . et, *both* . . . *and.*

etiam, conj. [et, *and;* jam, *now, furthermore*], *also, even.*

etiam sī or **etiamsī,** conj. [etiam, *even;* sī, *if*], *even if, even though, although.*

ē-vocō, -āre, -āvī, -ātus [ex, *forth;* vocō, *call*], *call forth, summon.*

ex or **ē,** prep. w. abl. (for distinction between ex and other prepositions meaning *from,* see 'from' in the English-Latin vocabulary), *out of, from;* (by difference of idiom) *on:* ex itinere, *on the march;* (after a superl.) *in;* by reason of, because of, in conformity with.

ex-agitō, -āre, -āvī, -ātus [ex, *forth, out;* agitō, *drive violently*], *drive violently forth; harass, disquiet.*

exanimō, -āre, -āvī, -ātus [ex-animo- (st. of exanimus), *lifeless*], (make lifeless, and so) *deprive of life;* in pass., *perish.*

ex-cēdō, -ere, -cēssī, -cēssus [ex, *forth, out;* cēdō, *go*], *go forth, withdraw, depart.*

ex-cellō, -ere, excelsus (adj.) [ex, *from below, up;* *cellō, *raise*], 1. tr., *raise up;* 2. intr., *rise; be prominent* or *distinguished, excel.*

ex-cipiō, -ere, -cēpī, -ceptus [ex, *from, out;* capiō, *take*], *take out; except; capture; intercept.*

ex-cĭtō, -āre, -āvī, -ātus [ex, forth, out; cĭtō, call], call forth, stimulate, excite, rouse.

ex-clāmō, -āre, -āvī, -ātus [ex, out; clāmō, call], call out.

ex-clūdō, -ere, -sī, -sus [ex, out; claudō, shut], shut out, **exclude**.

ex-crucĭō, -āre, -āvī, -ātus [ex, intens.; crucĭō, torture], torture excessively, torture.

ex-cūsō, -āre, -āvī, -ātus [ex, from; causa, charge (through *causō; cf. causor)], release from a charge, **excuse**; **sē excūsāre**, to apologize.

exemplum, -ī, N. [ex-√em-, take out], (what is taken out to serve as a sample, **and so**) copy, image; **example**, precedent; punishment inflicted by way of warning.

ex-eō, -īre, -iī (-īvī) -ĭtus [ex, out; eō, go], go out, go away, go forth.

ex-erceō, -ēre, -cuī, -cĭtus [ex, forth, on; arceō, drive], drive on, keep busy, **exercise, train**.

exercĭtātĭō, -ōnis, F. [exercĭtā- (st. of exercĭtō), exercise frequently, practise], practice, experience.

exercĭtus, -ūs, M. [exercē- (st. of exerceō), train], (lit., training, and so, used concretely) a trained body of men, an army.

ex-haurĭō, -īre, -hausī, -haustus [ex, out of, off; haurĭō, draw, drain], drain off.

exĭmĭus, -a, -um, adj. [ex-√em-, take out], (taken out of the common herd, and so) **exceptional, extraordinary**, especial.

ex-istĭmō, -āre, -āvī, -ātus [ex, out; aestĭmō, reckon or think], value, reckon; consider, **think**, deem.

ex-optō, -āre, -āvī, -ātus [ex, intens.; optō, desire], desire earnestly, long for.

expedĭō, -īre, -īvī or -iī, -ītus [ex-ped- (st. of pēs, FOOT), FOOT-free], (make foot-free, and so) unfetter, extricate, disentangle, set free; (reflexively) take **care** of itself.

expedītus, -a, -um [p. a. of expedĭō, disentangle], unincumbered, free from obstructions.

ex-pellō, -ere, -pulī, -pulsus [ex, out; pellō, drive], drive out, **expel**, banish.

ex-perĭor, -īrī, -pertus [ex-√per-, penetrate or test thoroughly. cf. comperĭō], test thoroughly, try, make trial of, make trial, measure strength with.

ex-pleō, -ēre, -ēvī, -ētus [ex, completely; *pleō, FILL], FILL up, **complete**.

explōrātor, -ōris, M. [explōrā- (st. of explōrō), search out], searcher out, **explorer**; scout.

ex-pōnō, -ere, -posuī, -positus [ex, forth; pōnō, put, set], set forth, **explain**, point out.

ex-pūgnō, -āre, -āvī, -ātus [ex, out, to the end; pūgnō, fight], (fight to the end, and so) take by assault.

ex-sequor, -ī, -cūtus [ex, **out**, to the end; sequor, follow], **follow to the end**; **execute, maintain**.

exsĭlĭum, -ĭī, N. [exsul- (st. of **exsul**), exile], being an exile, banishment, **exile**.

ex-spectō, -āre, -āvī, -ātus [ex, forth, out; spectō, look], look for, look forward to, await, wait for; wait; wait to see.

ex-stĭnguō, -ere, -nxī, -nctus [ex, completely; stĭnguō, quench], quench completely; **extinguish**; annihilate.

ex-stō, **-āre** [ex, out; stō, STAnd], STAnd out, be conspicuous; be extant.

ex-struō, -ere, -strūxī, -strūctus [ex, from below, up; struō, build], heap up, raise, construct.

ex-sul, -ĭs, c., **exile**.

ex-sultō, -āre, -āvī, **-ātum** [ex, from below, up; saltō, leap, dance], leap up; revel, **exult**.

*exterus, -tera, -terum, adj. [comp. fm. **fr. ex**, out], on the *outer side, on the outside.* Superl., **extrēmus**, -a, -um, *last, remotest, extreme, farthest,* (in agreement w. subst.) *remotest part of.*

extermĭnō, -āre, -āvī, -ātus [ex, *out of, beyond;* terminus, *boundary* (through presumed adj. st.)], *drive beyond the boundaries, banish.*

ex-timēscō, -ĕre, **-muī** [ex, intens.; *timēscō, fear*], *fear* or *dread greatly.*

ex-torqueō, -ēre, -torsī, -tortus [ex, *from;* torqueō, *wrest*], *wrest from, take away forcibly, extort.*

extrā [abl. fem. of *exterus, used adv.*], **adv. and prep. w. acc.,** *beyond.*

extrēmus, see *exterus.

F.

fābŭla, -ae [√fā-, *say, tell*], (what is told, and so) *story; play.*

facies, -ē, F. [√fac-, *shine, appear;* cf. **fax**, *torch*], *appearance, face, visage, countenance.*

facile, adv. [n. acc. of facilis, *easy,* used adv.], *easily, readily.* Comp., **facĭlĭus**, *more easily, more readily.*

facĭlis, -e, adj. [√fac-, DO], (capable of being done, and so) *easy.*

facĭlĭtās, -ātis, F. [facili- (st. of facilis), *easy*], *ease; affability, courtesy.*

facĭlĭus, see facile.

facĭnus, -oris, N. [√fac-, DO], DEE**d**, *act;* misDEE**d**, *crime;* **mala facĭnora**, *acts of lawlessness.*

facĭō, -ere, fēcī, factus (for the pass., **fĭō**, fĭerī, factus is used) [√fac-, DO, *make*], DO, *make, prosecute,* **commit**, *perpetrate; cause, produce, bring to pass; grant, furnish, give; act,* DO; *render;* **aliquem certiōrem facere,** *to inform;* **iter facere,** *to march;* **vim facere,** *to resort to force;* **facere nōn possum quin,** *I cannot help.*

factĭō, -ōnis, F. [√fac-, DO,

make], DO*ing, making; party spirit; faction, division, political party.*

factum, -ī, N. [n. perf. part. of faciō, DO], DEED, *act, proceeding, exploit.*

facultās, -ātis, F. [faculi- (one fm. of the st. of facilis), *ready, apt*], **readiness**, *aptitude, capability; opportunity; abundance.*

fallō, -ere, fefelli, falsus [√fal-, *make* FALL, *trip, deceive*]**,** *deceive, disappoint.*

falsus, -a, -um [p. a. of fallō, *deceive*], *deceptive, false.*

falx, falcis, F., *hooked knife, pruning hook; hook* (implement used in sieges for pulling down walls).

fāma, -ae, F. [√fā-, *make known, say*], (what is said, and so) *common talk, report; good name, reputation.*

famĭlĭa, -ae, F. [famulo- (st. of famulus), *servant*], (collection of servants, and so) *slaves of a household; family* (descendants of a common ancestor); *ancestry;* **pater famĭlĭās** or **famĭlĭae,** *master of a house, head of a family.*

famĭlĭāris, -e, adj. [famĭlĭā- (st. of familia), *household*]**,** *pertaining to a household* or *family;* **rēs familĭāris**, *patrimony, property; intimate;* subst., *trusted friend.*

familĭārĭtās, -ātis, F. [familĭāri- (st. of familĭāris), *intimate*], *intimacy.*

Fannĭus, -ĭī, M., *Gajus Fannius Strabo* (son-in-law of Laelius, and one of the characters in Cicero's work on Friendship).

fās, N. def. [√fā-, *make known, say;* conn., therefore, with fāma], (the divine word or command, and so) *divine law;* translated adj., *right, lawful, proper.*

faveō, -ēre, fāvī, fautum, *favor.*

ferāx, -ācis, adj. [√fer-, BEAR], (apt to bear, and so) *productive, fertile.*

ferē, adv., *nearly, almost, about, substantially, for the most part, almost all; chiefly; generally.*

ferō, ferre, tulī, lātus [pres., √fer-, BEAR; perf., √tol-, *lift, bear;* perf. part., √(t)lā-, *bear*], BEAR, *carry, bring, contribute; endure; regard, consider;* **fertur**, *is said;* **ferendus** (gerundive), *sufferable.*

ferreus, -a, -um, adj. [ferro- (st. of ferrum), *iron*], *of iron; iron-hearted, unfeeling.*

ferus, -a, -um, adj., *wild, fierce.*

fessus, -a, -um, adj., *weary.*

festīnō, -āre, -āvī, -ātus [festīno- (st. of festīnus), *hasty*], *hasten.*

fidēs, -ēī, F. [√fid-, *trust*], *faith, trust, confidence;* **keeping, protection.**

fīdus, -a, **-um, adj.** [√fid-, *trust*], *trusty, faithful.*

figūra, -ae, F.[√fig-, *shape*], *shape.*

fīlia, -ae, F. [fem. of fīlius, *son*], *daughter.*

fīliola, -ae, F. [fem. of dim. fīliolus, *little son*], *little daughter.*

fīlius, -iī, M., *son;* in pl., also *children.*

fīniō, -īre, -īvī or -iī, -ītus [fīni- (st. of fīnis), *end*], *put an end to, limit, fix, determine; compute, reckon.*

fīnis, -is, M. (sometimes F. in sing.), *limit, boundary, frontier; end;* in pl., *land included within boundaries,* and so *territories, territory, estates.*

fīnitimus, -a, -um, adj. [fīni- (st. of fīnis), *limit*], *bordering on, adjacent, neighboring;* subst., **fīnitimī**, -ōrum, M., *neighbors, neighboring tribes.*

fīō, fierī (factus, see faciō), *become, be made, be done, be committed, be in progress, happen, take place;* **certior fierī,** *to* **be informed;** *fit, the result is.*

firmō, -āre, -āvī, -ātus [firmo- (st. of firmus), *firm*], *make firm, strengthen.*

firmus, -a, -um, adj., **firm,** *strong, stable, steadfast.*

flāgitium, -iī, N. [√flāg-, *burn*], *shameful act* (done in the heat of passion), *disgraceful act.*

flamma, -ae, F. [for *flagma, fr. √flag-, *burn*], *flame.*

flāveō, -ēre [flāvo- (st. of flāvus), *yellow*] *be yellow.*

fleō, -ēre, -ēvī, -ētus, *weep.*

flōreō, -ēre, -ruī [flōs- (st. of flōs), *flower* (-s- becomes -r- between two vowels)], *be in flower, blossom; flourish;* p. a. **flōrēns**, -entis, *flourishing.*

flūctus, -ūs, M. [√flūgu-, *flow*], *flowing; wave, billow.*

flūmen, -inis, N. [√flū(gu)-, *flow*], (*that which flows, and so*) *river.*

fōns, fontis, M., *spring, fountain.*

foris, adv. [abl. pl. used adv.], *out of* DOORS, *abroad.*

fors (nom.), **forte** (abl.), F. (used in these two cases only) [√fer-, BEAR, BRING], (*what brings itself, and so*) *chance.*

fortis, -e, adj., *brave.*

fortiter, adv. [forti- (st. **of** fortis), *brave*], *bravely, courageously, with bravery, with courage, with fortitude.*

fortitūdō, -inis, F. [forti- (st. of fortis), *brave*], *courage,* **fortitude.**

fortūna, -ae, F. [conn. w. fors, *chance*], **fortune;** *good* **fortune,** *success; misfortune.*

fortūnātus, -a, -um [p. a. of fortūnō, *make prosperous*], **fortunate.**

fossa, -ae, F. [fem. of perf. part. of fodiō, *dig*, used subst. (sc. terra)], *ditch, moat.*

fragmentum, -ī, N. [√frag-, BREAK], (*result of breaking,* and so) *fragment.*

frangō, -ere, frēgī, fractus [√frag-, BREAK], BREAK, *crush.*

frāter, -tris, M., BROTHER.

frequēns, -entis, adj., *crowded, in great numbers.*

frīgus, -oris, N., *cold, frost.*

frōns, frontis, F., BROW, *front.*
Frontō, -ōnis, M., *Marcus Cornelius* **Fronto** (celebrated orator, native of Cirta in Numidia, flourished in the second century A.D.).
frūctuōsus, -a, -um, adj., [frūctu- (st. of frūctus), *fruit*], *fruitful, productive.*
frūctus, -ūs, M. [√frūgu-, *enjoy*], (enjoyment, and so) *fruit, produce, profit, income.*
frūmentārius, -a, -um, adj. [frūmento- (st. of frūmentum), *grain*], *pertaining to grain;* **rēs frūmentāria,** *provisions.*
frūmentum, -ī, N. [√frū(gu)-, *enjoy*], (means of enjoyment, and so) *grain* (usu. harvested); in pl. *grain* (especially, standing grain).
fruor, -ī, frūctus [√fru(gu)-, *enjoy*], *derive enjoyment from, enjoy.*
frūstrā, adv. [conn. w. **fraus,** *deceit*], *in vain.*
fuga, -ae, F. [√fug-, *bend, turn aside, flee*], *flight.*
fugiō, -ere, fūgī [√fug-, *bend, turn aside, flee;* cognate w. Eng. BOW], *flee.*
fugō, -āre, -āvī, -ātus [fugā- (st. of fuga), *flight*], *put to flight.*
fugitīvus, -ī, M. [adj. used subst., fr. √fug-, *bend, turn aside, flee*], *fugitive, deserter.*
fūmus, -ī, M., *smoke.*
fundāmentum, -ī, N. [**funda-** (st. of fundō), BOTTOM, *make secure*], (means of making secure, and so) *foundation.*
fundō, -ere, fūdī, fūsus, *pour.*
fungor, -ī, fūnctus, *discharge, perform.*
fūnis, -is, M., *rope.*
fūnus, -eris, N. [said to be conn. w. fūmus, *smoke*, and having reference primarily to the burning of the body after death], *funeral, funeral rites.*
fūr, fūris, C. [conn. w. √fer-, BEAR], (one who carries off, and so) *thief.*

furor, -ōris, M. [√fur-, *rage*], *madness, insane folly, fury.*
fūrtim, adv. [acc. used adv.; conn. w. fūr, *thief*], *stealthily.*
fūrtum, -ī, N. [conn. w. fūr, *thief*], *theft.*

G.

Galba, -ae, M., *Servius Sulpicius* **Galba** (one of Caesar's lieutenants in Gaul).
galea, -ae, F., HELMET; see Fig. 3.
Gallī, -ōrum, M., *the Gauls* (inhabitants of Gaul; see Gallia).

Fig. 3.
Helmet of a Roman soldier, from the column of Trajan.

Gallia, -ae, F., *Gaul* (Transalpine Gaul comprised substantially modern France, the Netherlands, and Switzerland; Cisalpine Gaul comprised the valley of the Po in northern Italy).
Gallicus, -a, -um, adj., *Gallic, of the Gauls* (see Gallī and Gallia).
Gallus, -ī, M., *Gajus Sulpicius* **Gallus** (celebrated for his knowledge of Greek and astronomy; famous also as an orator; lived in the second century B.C.).
Gallus, -ī, M., *a Gaul* (see Gallia).
gaudium, -iī, N. [conn. w. gaudeō, *rejoice*], *joy.*
Genāva, -ae, F., *Geneva* (on Lake Geneva at its outlet into the Rhone).
gener, -erī, M., *son-in-law.*
gēns, gentis, F. [√gen-, *beget, give birth to*], *offspring, race, people,* NATION, *tribe.*
genus, -eris, N. [√gen-, *beget, give birth to*], *birth; stock, race, family;* KIND, *class, order, mode.*
Gergovia, -ae, F., *Gergovia* (town of the Arverni in Celtic Gaul).
Germānī, -ōrum, M., *the Germans.*
gerō, -ere, gessī, gestus [√ges-

gīgnō (-s- becomes -r-), *carry*], *carry, conduct, manage, transact, perform, do, carry on, wage;* in pass., *be in progress.*

gīgnō, -ere, genuī, genitus [√gn- (reduplicated) and gen-, *beget, give birth to*], *bring forth, bear.*

gladiātor, -ōris, M. [gladiā- (st. of *gladiō), *fight with the sword* (gladius)], (one who fights with the sword, and so) *gladiator.*

gladius, -ī, M., *sword* (straight and two-edged); see Fig. 4.

Fig. 4.
Sword of a Roman soldier, from the Museo Borbonico.

glōria, -ae, F., *glory, renown.*
glōrior, -ārī, -ātus [glōriā- (st. of glōria), *glory*], *glory, boast;* **idem glōriārī**, *to make the same boast;* **hōc glōriārī**, *to make this boast.*

gradus, -ūs, M., *step; stage.*
Graecia, -ae, F., *Greece.*
Graecus, -a, -um, adj., *Greek.*
grandis, -e, adj., *full-grown;* **quidam grandis nātū**, *a* [man] *advanced in years.*

grātia, -ae, F. [grāto- (st. of grātus), *pleasing*, **grateful**], *favor, friendship, credit, influence; good will, gratitude.*

grātulor, -ārī, -ātus [*grātulo- (st. of *grātulus, perhaps dim. of grātus), *somewhat pleasing*], *manifest pleasure, wish joy, congratulate.*

grātus, -a, -um [p. a. **fr. √grā-**, *hold dear, desire*], (held **dear**, desired, and so) *pleasant, agreeable, gratifying, acceptable, welcome; grateful; deserving of gratitude.*

gravis, -e, adj., *heavy; severe, hard, oppressive, unfortunate;* **gravior aetās**, *advanced age.*

graviter, adv. [gravi- (st. of gravis), **heavy**], *heavily; severely, harshly.*

gubernātor, -ōris, M. [gubernā- (st. of gubernō), *steer*], *steersman, pilot.*

H.

habeō, -ēre, -uī, -itus, *have, hold, keep;* (of confidence) *repose;* (of an address) *deliver; consider, esteem, regard, deem;* **grātiam habēre**, *to feel* or *cherish gratitude;* **habēre immūnitātem**, *to enjoy immunity.*

haesitō, -āre, -āvī, -ātum [intens. of haereō, *stick fast*], *be at a loss, hesitate.*

Hannibal, -alis, M., *Hannibal* (leader of the Carthaginians in the second Punic war, B.C. 218-201).

Hellēspontus, -ī, M., *the Hellespont* (mod. Dardanelles, strait connecting the sea of Marmora and the Aegean sea).

Helvētiī, -ōrum, M., *the Helvetii* or **Helvetians** (a tribe in the eastern part of Celtic Gaul occupying that part of modern Switzerland which lies between lakes Geneva and Constance).

hērēditās, -ātis, F. [hērēd- (st. of hērēs), *heir*], *heirship, inheritance.*

Hermēs or **Herma**, -ae, M., *Hermes-pillar* (a four-cornered post or pedestal terminating in a carved head, often that of the god Hermes; these were frequently to be found in Athens in streets and public places, and before private houses); see Fig. 5.

Fig. 5.
Hermes-pillar, from the capitol at Rome.

hīberna, -ōrum, N. [n. pl. of hibernus, *pertaining to winter*, used subst.; sc. **castra**], *winter-quarters.*

Hibērus, -ī, M., *the Ebro* (a river in Spain).

hic, haec, hoc, demonstr. pron., (used adj.) *this;* (used subst.) *this man,* etc., *he,* etc. (emphatic); hic ... ille: *the latter ... the former; of* (pertaining to) *the latter ... of* (pertaining to) *the former.*

hic, adv., *here; upon this, hereupon.*

hiemō, -āre, -āvī, -ātus [hiem- (st. of hiems), *winter*], *pass the winter, winter.*

hiems (hiemps), -emis, F., *winter.*

Hilōtae, -ārum, M., *Helots* (the servile class in Sparta).

Hispānia, -ae, F., *Spain.*

historia, -ae, F., *history.*

hodiē, adv. [abl. fm. of pron. st. ho-, *this;* abl. fm. of diēs, *day*], *to-day; at the present day.*

hodiernus, -a, -um, adj. [conn. w. hodiē, *to-day*], *of this day;* **hodiernus** diēs, *this day, to-day.*

homo, -inis, C. [conn. w. humus, *ground*], (son of earth, and so) *human being, man; fellow.*

honestō, -āre, -āvī, -ātus [honesto- (st. of honestus), *honorable*], *clothe with honor, adorn, dignify, embellish.*

honestus, -a, -um, adj. [conn w. honōs, *honor*], *honorable, worthy of honor.*

honōri-ficus, -a, -um, adj. [honōs- (st. of honōs), *honor;* √fac-, *make*], (making honor, and so) *honorable.*

honōs or honor, -ōris, M., *honor, dignity, estimation;* honōris causā, *out of compliment to, out of respect to.*

hōra, -ae, F., HOUR (the Romans divided the interval between sunrise and sunset into twelve parts called hours; accordingly, their hour did not have a fixed value, but varied in length according to the season).

hortor, -ārī, -ātus, *encourage, urge, exhort.*

hortus, -ī, M. (conn. w. cohors, q.v.], (enclosure, and so) GARDEN.

hospes, -itis, C., *host;* GUEST (whether friend or stranger).

hostis, -is, C., *stranger, foreigner; enemy* (especially a *public enemy* in contrast to inimīcus, a *private enemy*); in pl., *enemy, a hostile army.*

hūc, adv. [case fm. of pron. st. ho-, *this,* with demonstr. ending -c(e)], *to this place, to this point, hither.*

hūmānitās, -ātis, F. [hūmāno- (st. of hūmānus), *human; refined*], *humanity; refinement* (of manners, language, etc., resulting from a liberal education, and so) *accomplishments.*

hūmānus, -a, -um, adj. [conn. w. homo, *man*], *human; humane; refined, highly civilized.*

humilis, -e, adj. [humo- (st. of humus), *ground*], (pertaining to the ground, and so) *low; insignificant, weak.*

humus, -ī, F., *ground.*

I.

ibī, adv. [pron. st. i- (of is), *that,* w. loc. suff.], *in that place, there.*

ictus, -ūs, M. [√ic-, *hit*], *hitting; blow.*

idem, eadem, idem [is, *that,* w. demonstr. suff.], *the same;* trans. adv., *also, likewise, again.*

idōneus, -a, -um, adj., *suitable; convenient, accessible.*

īdūs, -uum, F., *the Ides* (one of the three points in the month from which the Romans reckoned; **the Ides** fell on the thirteenth except in March, May, July, and October, when they fell on the fifteenth).

igitur, conj. (usu. placed after the first word of the sent.), *then, therefore, accordingly.*

ignāvia, -ae, F. [ignāvo- (st. of ignāvus), *idle*], *idleness, sloth.*

ignis, -is, M., *fire.*

īgnōrō — **in-cendō** — 271

ignōrō, -āre, -āvī, -ātus [conn. w. ignārus, *ignorant*], *not* KNOW, *be ignorant of*.

ī-gnōscō, -ere, -gnōvī, -gnōtum [i(n)-, *not*; (g)nōscō, *take steps to* KNOW], (not inquire into, and so) *overlook, pardon*.

ille, illa, illud, demonstr. pron., (used subst.) *he, she, it*; (used adj.) *that; the well known, that . . . of old, of yore; the following*; hic . . . ille, *the latter . . . the former*; in pl., *those, they*; ille ferreus, *so iron-hearted*.

illō, adv. [case fm. of *ille, that*], *to that place, thither*.

imber, -bris, M., *rain, rainstorm*.

immānis, -e, adj., *monstrous, imMENse, huge*.

im-mātūrus, -a, -um, adj. [in-, *not*; mātūrus, *ripe, seasonable*], UNseasonable, *before one's time*.

immolō, -āre, -āvī, -ātus [in, upON; mola, *sacrificial* MEAL (through presumed adj. st.)], (sprinkle sacrificial meal on the victim to be sacrificed, and so) *sacrifice, immolate*.

im-mortālis, -e, adj. [in-, *not*; mortālis, *mortal*], *immortal*, UNdying, *perpetual*; translated adv., *forever*.

im-mūnis, -e, adj. [in-, *not*; mūnis, *under obligation*; cf. commūnis], *exempt*.

immūnitās, -ātis, F. [immūni- (st. of immūnis), *exempt*], *exemption, immunity*.

impedīmentum, -ī, N. [impedī- (st. of impediō), *hinder*], *hindrance, impediment*; in pl., *baggage*.

impediō, -īre, -īvī or -iī, -ītus [in-ped- (st. of pēs), *having the* FEET *entangled*], (cause one's feet to become entangled, and so) *impede, hinder, interfere with, prevent*.

im-pellō, -ere, -pulī, -pulsus [in, ON, against; pellō, *drive*], *drive* ON **or** against, *urge* ON, *impel*.

im-pendeō, -ēre [in, *over*; pendeō, *hang*], *hang over, impend, threaten*.

imperātor, -ōris, M. [imperā- (st. of imperō), *command*], *commander, general*.

im-perītus, -a, -um, adj. [in-, *not*; perītus, *experienced*], *inexperienced*, UNPRActised, UNskilled.

imperium, -iī, N. [conn. w. imperō, *command*], *order, command; power, direction, authority, control; persons in power; government*.

im-perō, -āre, -āvī, -ātus [in, withIN, *thoroughly*; parō, *prepare*], (lit., prepare thoroughly, work over, and so) *command, direct, govern; demand, make a requisition for*.

im-petrō, -āre, -āvī, -ātus [in, (by appeal) *to*; patrō, *bring to pass*], *bring to pass by entreaty, obtain a request*.

impetus, -ūs, M. [in-√pet-, *fly at, fall upON*], (falling upon, and so) *onset, attack*.

im-pius, -a, -um, adj. [in-, *not*; pius, *dutiful, reverent*], UNdutiful, *irreverent, impious, wicked*.

im-plōrō, -āre, -āvī, -ātus [in, *to*; plōrō, *cry out*], *cry out to, call upon, ask beseechingly, entreat, implore*.

im-pudēns, -entis, adj. [in-, *not*; pudēns, *modest*], *shameless*.

impulsor, -ōris, M. [in-√pol-, *push* ON], (one who pushes on, and so) *instigator, urger*; **impulsor esse**, *to urge*.

in, prep. w. acc. and abl. 1. w. acc.: INto, *to, towards, for*; IN *favor of*; against, *over*; 2. w. abl.: IN, ON, IN *the midst of*, amid, IN *the case of*: **in armīs**, UNder *arms*; **in lātitūdinem**, IN *width*; **in cōnspectum**, IN *sight*.

incendium, -iī, N. [in-√cand-, *set fire to*], *setting fire to; fire, conflagration*.

in-cendō, -ere, -cendī, -cēnsus [in, *to*; *cand- (√cand-), *set fire*], *set fire to, burn; fire, inflame*.

inceptum, -ī, n. [n. perf part. of incipiō, *begin*], (that which has been begun, and so) *attempt*, UN*dertaking*.

in-cidō, -ere, -cidī, -cāsus [in, upon; cadō, *fall*], *fall upon; happen, occur, arise*.

in-cipiō, -ere, -cēpī, -ceptus [in, upon; capiō, *lay hold*], (lay hold upon, and so) *begin*.

in-colō, -ere, -uī [in, IN; colō, *dwell*], *inhabit; dwell*.

incolumis, -e, adj., UN*injured*, UN*harmed*.

incommodum, -ī, n. [n. of adj. incommodus, *inconvenient*, used subst.], *inconvenience, disadvantage, injury, harm, disaster, defeat*.

in-crēdibilis, -e, adj. [in-, *not;* crēdibilis, *credible*], *incredible*.

in-crepitō, -āre, -āvī, -ātus [in, to, against; crepitō, *rattle much, make a loud noise*], *call out to; exclaim against, rebuke, chide*.

incursiō, -ōnis, f. [in-curr-(base in currō), *rush* IN or *against*], *incursion*, IN*road*.

in-cūsō, -āre, -āvī, -ātus [in, against; causa, *charge* (through presumed denom. vb. *causō; cf. causor)], *bring a charge against, find fault with, complain of, blame, upbraid*.

inde, adv., *from that place, thence; next in order*.

indicium, -iī, n. [indic- (st. of index), *he who* or *that which points out*], *pointing out, informing; information, testimony*.

in-dicō, -āre, -āvī, -ātus [in, towards; dicō, *make known*, and so *point*], *point out, disclose, reveal, betray*.

indigeō, -ēre, -uī [indigo- (st. of indigus), IN *want*], *be* IN *want of, need, stand* IN *need of*.

indignē, adv. [abl. **form of** indignus, UN*worthy*], UN*worthily,* UN*deservedly*.

in-dignus, -a, -um, adj [in-, *not;* dignus, *worthy*], UN*worthy*.

in-dūcō, -ere, -dūxī, -ductus [in, IN*to;* dūcō, *lead*], *lead* IN*to*.

indulgeō, -ēre, -sī, -tus, *indulge*.

induō, -ere, -uī, -ūtus [indu, ON; √u-, *clothe*], *put* ON.

industria, -ae, f., *industry*.

in-eō, -īre, -īvī or **-iī, -itus** [in, IN*to;* eō, *go*], *go* IN*to*, *enter; enter upon* or IN*to, begin, form*.

inermis, -e, adj. [in-, *without;* armo- (st. of arma, *arms*)], *without arms*, UN*armed*.

īnfāmia, -ae, f. [īnfāmi- (st. of īnfāmis), *disreputable*], *disrepute, dishonor, disgrace, infamy*.

īn-fēlix, -īcis, adj. [in-, *not;* fēlix, *happy*], UN*happy*.

īnferior, -ius, adj., comp. of īnferus, q. v.

in-ferō, īnferre, intulī, inlātus [in, prep., against; ferō, BEAR], (of war) *wage* or *carry* ON *against,* (of arms or standards) *carry* IN*to,* **carry** against; *inflict;* (w. in and acc.) *cast* IN*to;* **vim et manūs inferre,** *to lay violent hands upon*.

īnferus, -a, -um, adj., *below*. Comp., **īnferior, -ius,** *lower*. Superl., **īnfimus, -a, -um,** *lowest, lowest part of, at the bottom*.

īnfestus, -a, -um [p. a. of *īnfendō, *strike* or *thrust against;* cf. dēfendō, *strike* or *thrust off*], (dashed against, and so) *hostile, opposed;* **īnfestīs signīs cōnsistere,** *to come to a halt and assume the defensive*.

īnfimus, -a, -um, adj., superl. of īnferus, q. v.

īn-firmus, -a, -um, adj. [in-, *not;* firmus, *firm*], *weak, feeble, infirm*.

in-fluō, -ere, -xī, -xum [in, IN*to;* fluō, *flow*], *flow* IN*to, flow*.

ingenium, -iī, n. [in-√gen-, *beget* IN], (what is born in one, and so) *disposition; mind*.

ingēns, -entis, adj. [in-, *out of, beyond;* genti- (st. of gēns) KIN*d, class*], (beyond its kind, and so) *great* (in an exaggerated degree), *huge; a great quantity of*.

in-gredior, -ī, -gressus [in, INto; gradior, step], go INto, enter; walk.

in-iciō (pronounced: injiciō), -ere, -jēcī, -jectus [in, INto; jaciō, throw], throw INto, infuse, impart.

inimīcitia, -ae, F. [inimīco- (st. of inimīcus), hostile, UNfriendly], hostility, enmity.

in-imīcus, -a, -um, adj. [in-, not; amīcus, friendly], UNfriendly, hostile; subst., personal enemy (opp. hostis, public enemy), enemy.

iniquitās, -ātis, F. [iniquo- (st. of iniquus), UNjust], injustice.

in-iquus, -a, -um, adj. [in-, not; aequus, fair], UNfair; UNreasonable.

initium, -iī, N. [in-\i-, go INto, begin], beginning; first principles, elements.

injūria, -ae, F. [in-, not; jūs- (st. of jūs), right (-s- becomes -r-)], (violation of right, and so) injury, wrong, UNjust treatment, oppression; **injūriā,** wrongfully, UNjustly, without provocation.

in-lacrimō, -āre, -āvī, -ātum [in, at; lacrimō, shed TEARS], shed TEARS, weep.

in-liciō, -ere, -lexī, -lectus [in, INto; *laciō, lure], lure INto, entice, decoy, seduce.

inlustris, -e, adj., distinguished, illustrious, high, exalted.

in-nocēns, -entis, adj. [in-, not; nocēns, criminal, guilty], guiltless, innocent; subst., the innocent.

inopia, -ae, F. [inopi- (st. of **inops**), without resources], want; necessitous condition.

in prīmis, inprīmis, or **imprīmis,** (among the first, and so) especially, particularly.

inquam, def., I say; **inquit,** says he; said he.

insāniō, -īre, -īvī and -iī, -ītum [īnsāno- (st. of īnsānus), insane], be insane.

inscientia, -ae, F. [inscient- (st. of inscīēns), inexperienced], inexperience.

in-scrībō, -ere, -scrīpsī, -scrīptus [in, ON; scrībō, write], inscribe, entitle.

in-sequor, -ī, -cūtus [in, close upON; sequor, follow], follow close upON or after, pursue.

insigne, -is, N. [n. of adj. īnsignis, marked], distinguishing mark, badge.

insolenter, adv. [insolent- (st. of īnsolēns), insolent], insolently.

in-stituō, -ere, -uī, -ūtus [in, INto; statuō, place], (place into, and so) fix, establish, institute.

institūtum, -ī, N. [n. perf. part. of īnstituō, establish], (what is established, and so) institution, regulation, usage.

in-struō, -ere, -strūxī, -strūctus [in, INto; struō, build], build INto; draw up, arrange.

insula, -ae, F., island.

in-sum, inesse, īnfuī [in, IN; sum, be], be IN, belong to.

integer, -gra, -grum, adj. [in-√tag-, not touch], UNtouched, whole; **in integrum,** to a former condition.

integrō, -āre, -āvī, -ātus [integro- (st. of integer), whole], make whole, renew.

intel-legō, -ere, -lēxī, -lēctus [inter, between, INto; legō, see], see INto, UNDERstand, know; perceive, be aware.

in-tempestus, -a, -um, adj. [in-, not; *tempestus, seasonable], UNseasonable; **intempestā nocte,** at an UNseasonable hour of the NIGHT, late at NIGHT.

inter, adv. and prep. w. acc. [comp. fm. of in, IN], between, AMONG; **inter sē,** (according to the context) AMONG themselves, to one anOTHER, from one anOTHER, one anOTHER, with each OTHER, etc.

inter-cēdō, -ere, -cessī, -cessum [inter, between; cēdō, go], go between, intervene.

inter-clūdō, -ere, -sī, -sus [inter, between; claudō, shut],

shut off (by interposing something), *shut out, cut off*.

inter-dico, -ere, -dīxī, -dictus [inter, *between*; dīcō, *speak*], *forbid, prohibit, exclude*.

interdum, adv. [inter, *between*; dum, *while*], *sometimes, occasionally*.

intereā, adv. [inter, AMONG; acc. pl. n. ea (orig. eā), *these things*. cf. anteā w. foot-note], *meanwhile*.

inter-eō, -īre, -iī, -itum [inter, AMONG; eō, *go, be lost*], (be lost among other things, and so) *perish, become extinct*.

inter-ficiō, -ere, -fēcī, -fectus [inter, AMONG; faciō, *put, make go, cause to be lost*. cf. intereō], (cause to be lost among other things, and so) *dispatch, kill, put to death*.

interim, adv., *meanwhile*.

inter-imō, -ere, -ēmī, -ēmptus [inter, (out from) AMONG; emō, *take*], (take an object out from its surroundings, and so) *kill*.

interior, -ius, adj. [comp. of *interus], INNer; *the interior of*.

inter-mittō, -ere, -mīsī, -missus [inter, *between*, and so, IN *the midst*; mittō, *let go*], (leave off in the midst, and so) *interrupt, intermit; let pass, suffer to elapse*.

inter-pōnō, -ere, -posuī, -positus [inter, *between*; pōnō, *place*], *interpose*.

interpretor, -ārī, -ātus [interpret- (st. of interpres), *interpreter*], *explain, expound, interpret*.

inter-rogō, -āre, -āvī, -ātus [inter, *between* (the questioner and the person questioned); rogō, *ask*], *interrogate, question, ask*.

inter-sum, -esse, -fuī [inter, *between*; sum, *be*], BE *between*, **intervene**; *take part* IN, *have to do with*; *attend to, superintend*; impers., **interest**, *it concerns, it interests, it is important*.

intervallum, -ī, N. [inter, *between*, and so *with*IN; vāllum, *rampart*], (space within the rampart, i.e. between the rampart and the soldiers' tents, and so) *interval, distance*.

in-tueor, -ērī, -itus [in, *at*, ON; tueor, *look*], *look at, gaze* ON.

intus, adv. [in, IN], *with*IN.

in-ūtilis, -e, adj. [in-, *not*; ūtilis, *useful*], *useless*, UN*profitable*; *injurious*.

in-vādō, -ere, -vāsī [in, IN*to*; vādō, *go*], *go* IN*to*, *enter, invade, rush* IN, *fall upon, take possession*.

in-veniō, -īre, -vēnī, -ventus [in, *upon*; veniō, COME], COME *upon, find* (by accident; cf. reperiō, which often means 'find by searching').

inventor, -ōris, M. [in-√ven-, COME *upon, discover*], *discoverer, inventor, contriver*.

in-victus, -a, -um, adj. [in-, *not*; victus (perf. part. of vincō), *conquered*], UN*conquered; invincible*.

in-video, -ēre, -vīdī, -vīsus [in, *askance at*; videō, *look*], *look askance at; envy*.

invidia, -ae, F. [invido- (st. of invidus), *envious*], *envy; obloquy, odium, unpopularity*.

invītus, -a, -um, adj., UN*willing*.

ipse, ipsa, ipsum, demonstr. pron., *self, himself, herself, itself; mere, very, in person*.

īra, -ae, F., *anger, passion*.

īrācundia, -ae, F. [īrācundo- (st. of īrācundus), *passionate*], *passion*.

īrācundus, -a, -um, adj. [īrā- (st. of *īror), *be angry*], *passionate, choleric*.

īrāscor, -ī, īrātus [incept. fr. īrā- (st. of *īror), *be angry*], *give way to passion, be angry*; **īrātus**, -a, -um, p. a., *angry, in anger*.

ir-rumpō, -ere, -rūpī, -ruptus [in, IN*to*; rumpō, *burst*], *burst or rush* IN*to*.

is, ea, id, demonstr. pron., 1. adj., *this, that, such, of such a kind*; 2. subst., *this one, that one, he, she, it*; in pl., *these, those*,

iste **lac** 275

they; eō...quō, *by that...by which, the...the.*

iste, ista, istud, demonstr. pron., THAT *of yours,* THAT; (with contemptuous implication) THAT, THAT *one;* **ista vēritās,** THE *truth coming from you.*

ita, adv., *in such a way, so,* THUS; **ita...ut,** *so...as.*

Italia, -ae, F., *Italy.*

itaque, conj. [ita, *so;* -que, *and*], *and so,* THEREFORE.

item, adv. [conn. w. ita, *so*], *likewise.*

iter, itineris, N. [√i-, *go*], *journey, march, marching, passage, way, road, route, line of march;* **iter facere,** *to march*

iterum, adv., *again, a second time.*

J.

jaceō, -ēre, -cuī [intr. fin. conn. w. jaciō, *throw*], (be thrown, and so) *lie, lie prostrate.*

jaciō, -ere, jēcī, jactus, *throw, cast.*

jam, adv., *now; already; at once, forthwith; even.*

jānua, -ae, F., *street door, door.*

Juba, -ae, M., *Juba* (king of Numidia and opponent of Caesar).

jubeō, -ēre, jussī, jūssus, *order.*

jūcundus, -a, -um, adj. [conn. w. juvō, *help*], (helpful, and so) *pleasant, agreeable.*

jū-dex, -icis, C. [jūs- (st. of jūs), *what is binding;* √dic-, *point out*], (one who points out what is binding, i.e. justice, and so) *judge.*

jūdicium, -ī, N. [jūdic- (st. of jūdex), *judge*], *judgment, decision, sentence;* **in jūdicium vocāre,** *to summon before the court.*

jūdicō, -āre, -āvī, -ātus [jūdic- (st. of jūdex), *judge*], *judge; pronounce, proclaim; consider, deem, think.*

jugum, -ī, N. [√jug-, YOKE], YOKE; (mountain) *ridge.*

Jūliānus, -a, -um, adj. [Jūlio- (st. of Jūlius)], *Julian (i.e.,* belonging to Julius Caesar).

jūmentum, -ī, N. [√ju(g)-, YOKE], (that which is yoked, and so) *beast of burden.*

Juppiter, Jovis, M. [Jovi- (for Diovi-, st. of Diovis), *god of heaven;* pater, FATHER], *Jupiter* (supreme deity of the Romans).

Jūra, -ae, M., *the Jura mountains* (a chain extending from the Rhine to the Rhone and separating the Sequani from the Helvetii).

jūs, jūris, N. [√ju-, *bind,* conn. w. √jug-], (that which is binding, and so) *right, justice; authority; one's rights, redress;* in pl., *rights, authority;* **jūs dīcere,** *to pronounce judgment, to administer justice.*

jūsjūrandum, jūrisjūrandī, N. [jūs, *what is binding;* gerundive of jūrō, *swear*], *oath.*

jūssū, M. (in abl. sing. only) [fr. same root as jubeō, *order*], *at the bidding.*

jūstitia, -ae, F. [jūsto- (st. of jūstus), *just*], *justice.*

jūstus, -a, -um, adj. [jūs- (st. of jūs), *right*], *founded in right, just; regular, proper, due, usual.*

juventūs, -ūtis, F. [juven- (st. of juvenis), YOUNG], YOUTH.

juvō, -āre, jūvī, jūtus, *help, aid, assist, benefit.*

K.

Karthāgō, see Carthāgō.

L.

L., abbr. of **Lūcius,** -ī, M., *Lucius* (Roman praenōmen or first name).

Labiēnus, -ī, M., *Titus Attius Labienus* (Caesar's chief lieutenant in the Gallic war, 58–50 B.C.).

labor, -ōris, M. [√lab-, *lay hold of*], (laying hold of, and so) *labor, toil, exertion.*

lābor, -ī, lāpsus [√lāb-, *glide, fall*], *glide, fall, sink; err.*

labōrō, -āre, -āvī, -ātus [labor- (st. of labor), *labor*], *labor; struggle against odds.*

lac, lactis, N., *milk.*

Lacedaemōn, -ŏnis, F., *Lacedaemon* or *Sparta* (chief city of Laconia, in Peloponnesus).
Lacedaemŏnii, -ōrum, M., *Lacedaemonians* (inhabitants of Lacedaemon, q. v.).
lacertus, -ī, M., *upper arm, arm;* in pl., also *muscle, brawn.*
lăcessō, -ĕre, -īvī, -ītus, *challenge, irritate, attack.*
lacrima, -ae, F., TEAR.
lacus, -ūs, M., *lake.*
Laeca, -ae, M., *Marcus Porcius Laeca* (one of Catiline's accomplices in the conspiracy of 63 B.C.).
Laelius, -iī, M., *Gajus Laelius* (friend of Scipio Africanus the younger, and principal character in Cicero's work on Friendship; flourished in the latter half of the second century B.C.).
laetitia, -ae, F. [laeto- (st. of **laetus**), *joyful*], *joy.*
laetor, -ārī, -ātus [laeto- (st. of **laetus**), *joyful*], *be joyful, rejoice; rejoice at.*
lapis, -idis, M., *stone.*
largior, -īrī, -ītus [largo- (st. of **largus**), *abundant*], *bestow lavishly, be lavish of.*
lātē, adv. [abl. fm. of **latus,** *wide*], *widely;* **quam lātissimē,** *as widely* or *extensively as possible.*
Latīnus, -a, -um, adj., *Latin* (pertaining to Latium, q. v.).
lātitūdō, -inis, F. [lāto- (st. of **lātus**), *broad*], *breadth, extent.*
Latium, -iī, N., *Latium* (district in Italy containing the city Rome).
Latovici, -ōrum, M., *the Latovici* (German tribe, neighbors of the Helvetii).
lătrō, -ōnis, M., *robber.*
lătrōcinium, -iī, N. [conn. w. **latrōcinor,** *rob on the highway*], *robbery.*
lātus, -a, -um, adj., *broad, extensive.*
latus, -eris, N., *side, flank.*
laudō, -āre, -āvī, -ātus [laud- (st. of **laus**), *praise*], *commend, praise.*

laus, laudis, F., *praise, commendation; glory, distinction, renown.*
lēctor, -ōris, M. [vlĕg-, *read*], *reader.*
lēgātiō, -ōnis, F. [lēgā- (st. of **lēgō,** *depute*], *deputing; deputation, embassy.*
lēgātus, -ī, M. [perf. part. of **lēgō,** *depute*], (one commissioned or deputed, and so) *ambassador, envoy; lieutenant* (the lēgātī were experienced officers commanding separate divisions of the army under the general direction of the commander-in-chief; often in special exigencies they exercised independent command).
legiō, -ōnis, F. [vlĕg-, *pick, gather*], (a levy, and so) *legion* (a full legion in Caesar's time contained about 6000 men; the legion was divided into ten cohorts, each cohort into three maniples, and each maniple into two centuries).
legiōnārius, -a, -um, adj. [legiōn- (st. of **legiō**), *legion*], *pertaining to legions, legionary.*
lĕgō, -ĕre, lēgī, lēctus [vlĕg-, *pick, gather*], *gather; select; read.*
Lemannus, -ī, M., (ancient name of) *Lake Geneva.*
Lemnos or **Lemnus, -ī,** F., *Lemnos* or *Lemnus* (island in the northern part of the Aegean sea).
Lemovicēs, -um, M., *the Lemovices* (tribe in Celtic Gaul, west of the Arverni).
lēniō, -īre, -īvī or **-iī, -ītus** [lēni- (st. of **lēnis**), *soft*], *make soft, soothe.*
Lentulus, -ī, M., *Publius Cornelius Lentulus Sura* (one of Catiline's accomplices in the conspiracy of 63 B.C.).
leō, -ōnis, M., *lion.*
Lepidus, -ī, M., *Manius Aemilius Lepidus* (consul 66 B.C.).
levis, -e, adj., LIGHt, *slight.*
lĕvō, -āre, -āvī, -ātus [levi- (st. of **levis**), LIGHt], LIGHten, *relieve, release.*

lēx, lēgis, F., LAW.

libenter, adv. [libent- (st. of libēns), *willing*], *willingly, cheerfully*.

liber, -brī, M., *book, treatise, work*.

līber, -era, -erum, adj., *free, unrestricted*.

līberālis, -e, adj. [lībero- (st. of līber), *free*], *belonging to a freeman: liberal, lavish*.

līberāliter, adv. [līberāli- (st. of līberālis), *pertaining to a freeman*], (in a manner becoming a freeman, and so) *graciously, courteously*.

līberē, adv. [abl. fm. of līber, *free*], *freely, without constraint*.

līberī, -ōrum, M. [masc. pl. of adj. līber, *free*, used subst.], (the free members of the household in distinction from the slaves, and so) *children* (with reference to their parents; cf. puerī, *children* in general).

līberō, -āre, -āvī, -ātus [lībero- (st. of līber), *free*], *set free, free, liberate, relieve, release*.

lībertās, -ātis, F. [lībero- (st. of līber), *free*], *freedom, liberty*.

libet, -ēre -buit or -bitum est (older forms, lubet, etc., √lub-, *desire*; cognate w. English LOVE], *it is pleasing* or *agreeable; mihi libet, I am disposed*.

licet, -ēre, -cuit or -citum est [√lic-, *leave free* (through presumed adj.)], *it is permitted, it is lawful, one is at liberty, it is possible*.

Lingonēs, -um (acc. Lingonas), M., *the Lingones* (tribe in Celtic Gaul near the sources of the Marne and Meuse).

lingua, -ae, F., TONGUE; *language*.

Liscus, -ī, M., *Liscus* (prominent Aeduan of Caesar's time).

Litaviccus, -ī, M., *Litaviccus* (Aeduan of Caesar's time).

littera, -ae, F., *letter* (of the alphabet), *character*; in pl., *letter* (epistle), *dispatch, letters, dispatches; litterīs mandāre, to commit to writing*.

lītus, -oris, N., *shore* (of the sea; cf. rīpa, *bank of a river*).

locō, -āre, -āvī, -ātus [loco- (st. of locus), *place*], *place*.

locus, -ī, M.; in pl., (usu.) **loca**, -ōrum, N., (sometimes) **locī**, -ōrum, M., *place, spot, site, position; room; rank*.

longē, adv. [abl. fm. of longus, LONG], *far; by far; for a LONG time, LONG*.

longinquus, -a, -um, adj. [conn. w. longus], LONG, LONG-*continued*.

longitūdō, -inis, F. [longo- (st. of longus), LONG], LENG*th*.

longus, -a, -um, adj., LONG; nāvis longa, *ship of war*.

loquor, -ī, -cūtus [√loqu-, *sound, speak*], *speak*.

lūceō, -ēre, lūxī [conn. w. lūx, LIGH*t*], *be* LIGH*t, shine*.

lūdus, -ī, M., *game*.

lūgeō, -ēre, lūxī, *mourn, lament*.

lūmen, -inis, N. [√lū(c)-, *shine*], (that which shines, and so) LIGH*t*.

lūna, -ae, F. [√lū(c)-, *shine*], *moon*.

lūstrum, -ī. N. [√lou-, *wash*], *purificatory sacrifice*.

lūx, lūcis, F. [√lūc-, *shine*], LIGH*t*.

Lycus, -ī, M., *Lycus* (an Athenian, father of Thrasybulus; lived in the fifth century B.C.).

M.

M., abbr. of **Mārcus**, -ī, M. (Roman praenōmen or first name).

M', abbr. of **Mānius**, -iī, M. (Roman praenōmen or first name).

māchinātiō, -ōnis, F. [māchinā- (st. of māchinor), *devise*], (devising, and so) *mechanism; engine*.

māchinor, -ārī, -ātus [**māchinā-** (st. of māchina), *machine*], *invent, contrive, devise*.

magis, adv. [for *magius, n. acc. sing. comp. of adj. used adv.], MORE.

magister, -trī, M. [√mag-, *be great, be powerful*, w. double comp. suff.: -ls = -ius, and -ter], (he who is greater or more powerful, and so), *master*.

magistrātus, -ūs, M. [magistrā- (st. of *magistrō), *be master*], (being master, and so) *office of a magistrate, magistracy; magistrate*.

magnificus, -a, -um, adj. [māgno- (st. of magnus), *great;* √fac- do], (of great deeds, and so) *magnificent, glorious, splendid*.

magnitūdō, -inis, F. [magno- (st. of magnus), *great*], *greatness, size, bulk, extent, magnitude*.

magnus, -a, -um, adj. [√mag-, *be great*], *great, large;* **magnī** (gen. of value), *greatly, highly*. Comp., **mājor**, -us, *greater; older, elder;* pl. subst., **mājōrēs**, *ancestors;* **mājōrēs** nātū, *elders, old men*. Superl., **maximus**, -a, -um, *greatest;* quam maximus (with or without some form of possum), *greatest possible*.

mājor, -us, see magnus.

male, adv. [abl. fm. of malus, *bad*], *badly, ill*.

maleficium, -iī, N. [malefico- (st. of maleficus), *mischievous*], *mischief*.

mālō, mālle, māluī [mage (=magis), *rather;* volō, *wish*], *wish rather, choose rather, prefer*.

malus, -a, -um, adj., *bad, evil, mischievous, evil-minded; wretched, unfortunate;* subst., **malum**, -ī, N., *evil*. Comp., pējor, -us, *worse*. Superl., pessimus, -a, -um, *worst*.

mandātum, -ī, N. [n. perf. part. of mandō, *command*], *injunction, order, commission, message*.

mandō, -āre, -āvī, -ātus [manu- (st. of manus), *hand;* dō, *give* (through presumed adj. st.)], (put into one's hands, and so) *commit, intrust; order, command*.

māne, adv., *early in the morning*.

maneō, -ēre, mānsī, mānsum [√man-, *think*], (stand wrapt in thought, and so) *wait, remain, abide, continue;* manēre in, *to remain IN, to abide by*.

manus, -ūs, F., *hand; art; force, band;* in manibus, IN *preparation;* vim et manūs inferre, *to lay violent hands* UPON.

Mārcius, -iī, M., *Quintus Marcius Rex* (consul 68 B.C.).

mare, -is, N., *sea;* marī, *on the sea, by sea*.

maritimus, -a, -um, adj. [mari- (st. of mare), *sea*], *belonging to the sea, maritime*.

Mārs, Mārtis, M., *Mars* (Mars was originally a Roman agricultural divinity, but early came to be identified with the Greek god Ares; hence he is generally viewed as the god of war).

Massīva, -ae, M., *Massiva* (grandson of the Numidian king Masinissa; assassinated at the instigation of Jugurtha B.C. 108).

māter, -tris, F. [√mā-, *form, fashion, make*], MOTHER.

māteria, -ae, F. [māter, MOTHER], (mother-stuff, and so) *materials; timber*.

mātūrē, adv. [abl. fm. of māturus, *ripe*], *seasonably; speedily*.

mātūrō, -āre, -āvī, -ātus [mātūro- (st. of māturus), *ripe*], *ripen; hasten*.

mātūrus, -a, -um, adj.[conn. w. māne, *early in the morning*], *ripe*.

maximē, adv. [abl. fm. of maximus, *greatest*], *especially,* MOST *of all,* MOST.

maximus, -a, -um, see magnus.

mediocris, -e, adj. [conn. w. medius, MIDDle], MIDDling; *slight*.

medius, -a, -um, adj., MIDDle, MIDDle *part of, in the* MIDDle; per mediōs, *through the* MIDst *of them*.

mehercle or **mehercule** [mē, acc. pers. pron. w. vowel shortened (sc. juvēs); hercle or hercule, voc. of Herculēs], (Hercules, [help] me! and so) *by Hercules!*

melior, -ius, see bonus.
membrum, -ī, N., *limb*, *member*.
meminī, def. (only in perf. system, w. meaning of pres.) [√men-, *think*; cf. mēns], *think of, remember, cherish the memory of; mention, make mention of*.
memor, -oris, adj. [√mor- (reduplicated), *tarry over, brood*; conn. w. mora, *delay*], *mindful, thoughtful, recalling*.
memoria, -ae, F. [memori- (st. of memor), *mindful*], **remembrance**, *memory*; *time*; memoriae prōditum est, *the story* **runs** (lit., it has been handed **down** to memory).
memorō, -āre, -āvī, -ātus [memori- (st. of memor), *mindful*], (make mindful, **call** to mind, and so) *mention, recount*.
Menapiī, -ōrum, M., *the Menapii* (tribe in the northern part of Belgic Gaul).
mēns, mentis, F. [√men-, *think*], MIND, *the intellectual faculties; disposition; opinion; purpose, intention*.
mēnsis, -is, M. [conn. w. mētior, *measure*], (measure of time, and so) MONth.
mentior, -īrī, -ītus [menti- (st. of mēns), MIND (with special reference to the imagination)], (draw upon the imagination, invent, romance, and so) *lie, speak falsely*.
mercātor, -ōris, M. [mercā- (st. of mercor), *trade*], *trader, merchant*.
mercātūra, -ae, F. [mercā- (st. of mercor), *trade*], *trade, traffic, commerce*; in pl., *commercial transactions*.
mercēs, -ēdis, F. [conn. w. mercātor and mercātūra], *hire, pay*.
Mercurius, -iī, M. [conn. w. the foregoing words], *Mercury* (Roman god of commerce and gain; later identified with Greek god Hermes, and so viewed as herald and messenger of the gods, presider over roads, etc.).

mereor, -ērī, -itus, *deserve, merit*.
Messālla, -ae, M., *Messalla* (Messala).
-met (pron. suff. appended for emphasis to certain forms of the pers. and poss. prons.), *self*.
mētior, -īrī, mēnsus [conn. w. modus, MEAsure, and mēnsis, MONth], *measure, estimate, judge*.
metuō, -ēre, -uī, -ūtus (once) [metu- (st. of metus), *fear*], *fear*.
metus, -ūs, M., *fear, apprehension*.
meus, -a, -um, poss. pron., MY; meā interest, *it* **interests** ME, *it is of importance to* ME.
mīles, -itis, M., *soldier*.
mīlitāris, -e, adj. [mīlit- (st. of mīles), *soldier*], *pertaining to soldiers, military*; **rēs mīlitāris**, *the military art*.
mīlitia, -ae, F. [mīlit- (st. of mīles), *soldier*], *warfare, military service*; **mīlitiae**, *abroad, in the field*.
mīlle, in sing., indecl. adj., *thousand*; also in nom. **and acc.** sing. (w. part. gen.), subst., *thousand*: **mīlle passuum**, *a thousand* **paces**, *a mile*; in pl., milia (millia) (w. part. gen.), subst., *thousands*: **milia passuum** or **milia** (sc. passuum), *miles*.
Miltiadēs, **-is**, M., *Miltiades* (celebrated Athenian general; defeated the Persians in the battle **of** Marathon B.C. 490).
mina, -ae, F. [borrowed from **the** Greek], *mina* (sum of money equivalent to about $18).
Minerva, -ae, F., *Minerva* (goddess of wisdom, of the arts and sciences, of spinning and weaving, etc.).
minimus, -a, -um, see parvus.
minimē, adv. [abl. fm. of minimus, *least*], *least, least of all*.
minitor, -ārī, -ātus [intens. **of** minor, *threaten*; formed as if the perf. part. were minitus], *threaten, menace*.
minor, -us, see parvus.

minus, adv. [acc. n. sing. of minor], *less; not;* **minus valēre**, *not to be strong enough, to be too weak.*
minuō, -ere, -uī, -ūtus [conn. w. minor, *less*], *lessen, diminish; check, prevent;* (of disputes) *settle.*
mīrābilis, -e [mīrā- (st. of mīror), *wonder at*], *to be wondered at, wonderful.*
mīror, -ārī, -ātus [mīro- (st. of mīrus), *wonderful*], *wonder at, admire, wonder.*
mīrus, -a, -um, adj. [√(s)mī-, smi*le*], *wonderful, strange;* **mihī mīrum vidētur,** *I am at a loss to understand.*
miser, -era, -erum, adj., *wretched, unfortunate.*
misereor, -ērī, -eritus or -ertus [misero- (st. of miser), *wretched*], (be wretched in another's behalf, and so) *feel pity, pity, have compassion.*
miseret, -ēre, -eritum, impers. [misero- (st. of miser), *wretched*], *it distresses,* **it moves to pity;** **mē miseret,** *I pity, I am sorry for.*
misericordia, -ae, F. [misericordi-, (st. of misericors), *tender-hearted*], *tender-heartedness, compassion, pity.*
miseri-cors, -cordis, adj. [misero- (st. of miser), *wretched;* cordi- (st. of cor), heart], *tender-hearted, compassionate.*
miseror, -ārī, -ātus [misero- (st. of miser), *wretched*], *express pity for, lament, bewail.*
Mithridātēs, -is, M., *Mithridates* (king of Pontus and enemy of the Roman people; committed suicide 63 B.C.).
mītis, -e, adj., *mild.*
mittō, -ere, mīsī, missus, *send.*
modestē, adv. [abl. fm. of modestus, *temperate*], *temperately.*
modestus, -a, -um, adj. [conn. w. modus, measure], (measured, observant of due restraint, and so) *modest.*
modicus, -a, -um, adj. [modo- (st. of modus), measure], *moderate.*
modo, adv. [abl. of modus, measure, w. final vowel shortened], (by measure, *i.e.* not exceeding, and so) *only, merely, but; if only;* **nōn modo ... vērum etiam,** *not only ... but also.*
modus, -ī, M. [√mod-, measure], measure, *quantity, amount; manner, way, sort;* **hūjusce modī,** *of this sort, the following, as follows;* **ējusmodī,** *of such a kind, such;* **ad hunc modum,** *as follows;* **in servīlem modum,** *as in the case of slaves.*
molestus, -a, -um, adj. [conn. w. mōlēs, *mass, burden*], *burdensome, troublesome, annoying.*
molliō, -īre, -īvī and -iī, -ītus [molli- (st. of mollis), *soft*], *soften.*
mollis, -e, adj., *soft, pliant, yielding; feeble.*
mōmentum, -ī, N. [√mov-, *push*], (result of pushing, and so) *movement; weight, importance, moment.*
moneō, -ēre, -uī, -itus [√mon-, *think, cause to think*], remind, *warn.*
mōns, montis, M., *mountain.*
morbus, -ī, M. [√mor-, *waste away;* conn. w. morior and mors], *disease.*
Morinī, -ōrum, M., *the Morini* (tribe in Belgic Gaul near strait of Dover).
morior, morī (morīrī), mortuus [√mor-, *waste away;* conn. w. morbus and mors], *die.*
moror, -ārī, -ātus [morā- (st. of mora), *delay*], *delay, remain, linger.*
mors, -tis, F. [√mor-, *waste away;* conn. w. morior and morbus], *death.*
mortālis, -e, adj. [morti- (st. of mors), *death*], *pertaining to death, mortal;* subst., *human being, mortal, man.*
mortuus, -a, -um [p. a. of morior, *die*], *dead.*
mōs, mōris, M., *custom, wont, usage, practice;* in pl., *morals, character.*

moveō, -ēre, mōvī, mōtus [√mov-, *push* (through presumed adj. st.)], **move;** *excite, cause; affect, disturb,* **trouble;** *influence.*

mulier, -eris, F., *woman.*

multiplex, -icis, adj. [multo- (st. of multus), *much;* √plec-, FOLD], *maniFOLD;* **plausus multiplex,** *repeated outbursts of applause.*

multitūdō, -inis, F. [multo- (st. of multus), *much*], *great number, multitude; the people, the public.*

multō, -āre, -āvī, -ātus [multā- (st. of multa), *penalty, fine*], *punish, fine;* **aliquem pecūniā multāre,** *to fine one in a sum of money.*

multus, -a, -um, adj., *much;* in pl., *many;* **multum** (used adv.), *much, widely;* **multō** (w. comp.), *much, far;* **multā** nocte, *late at* NIGHT. Trans. adv., *frequently.* Comp., plūs, plūris, *more;* pl., plūrēs, plūra, *more than one,* and so *several.* Superl., **plūrimus, -a, -um,** *most, very much, very many, most numerous;* **plūrimum posse,** *to be most* or *very powerful, to be very influential.*

Mulvius, -a, -um, adj., *Mulvian* (bridge across the Tiber).

mundus, -ī, M., *universe, world.*

mūnīmentum, -ī, N. [mūnī- (st. of mūniō), *fortify*], *means of defence, fortification, rampart.*

mūniō, -īre, -īvī or -iī, -ītus [old fm., moeniō, fr. moeni- (st. of moenia, *walls*)], *build a wall;* *make secure, fortify.*

mūnītiō, -ōnis, F. [mūnī- (st. of mūniō), *fortify*], *fortification.*

mūnus, -eris, N., *office, function, duty; burden; service; gift.*

mūrus, -ī, M., *wall.*

mūtō, -āre, -āvī, -ātus [for *mōtō, intens. of moveō, *move;* fr. mōto-, st. of perf. part. mōtus], *change.*

N.

nam, conj. (stands at the beginning of the sentence), *for;* (in interrog. sentences expressing surprise or emotion) *but* or *pray.*

namque, conj. [nam, *for;* que, *and;* cf. etenim] (stronger than nam), *for indeed, for.*

nāscor, -ī, nātus [for *gnāscor, inceptive fr. √gnā-, *be born*], *be born; arise.*

nātālis, -e, adj. [nāto- (st. of nātus), *born*], *pertaining to one's birth;* **diēs nātālis,** *birthday.*

nātiō, -ōnis, F. [for *gnātiō, fr. √gnā-, *be born*], *being born, birth; race; nation, people, tribe.*

nātū (in abl. only), M. [for *gnātū, fr. √gnā-, *be born*], *by birth;* grandis nātū, *advanced in years.*

nātūra, -ae, F. [for *gnātūra, fr. √gnā-, *be born*], *nature, character;* nātūrā, *by nature, naturally.*

nātūrālis, -e, adj. [nātūrā- (st. of nātūra), *nature*], *belonging to nature, natural.*

nātus, -a, -um [perf. part. of nāscor, *be born*], *born.*

nāvālis, -e, adj. [nāvi- (st. of nāvis), *ship*], *belonging* or *pertaining to ships, naval.*

nāvigō, -āre, -āvī, -ātus [nāvi- (st. of nāvis), *ship;* √ag-, *drive* (through presumed adj. st.)], *sail.*

nāvis, -is, F., *ship;* **nāvis longa,** *ship-of-war, man-of-war;* see Fig. 6.

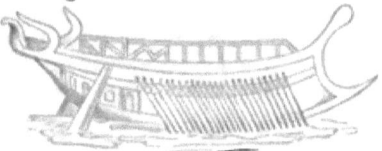

Fig. 6.
Nāvis longa, from a mosaic in a tomb near Puteoli.

nē, adv. (regular negative w. hort. **and** opt. subj.), *not;* (in final **clauses**) *that not, lest;* (w. verbs of fearing) *that* or *lest.*

nē ... quidem, *not even* (w. emphatic word **or words** between nē and quidem).

-ne, enclitic interrog. particle; it simply inquires, without implying what answer is expected. cf. nōnne **and** num.

Neāpolis, -is, F., *Naples* (NEWton).
nec, see neque.
necesse, n. adj. used in nom. and acc. sing., *necessary*.
neg-legō, -ere, -ēxī, -ēctus [nec, NOT; legō, *gather, heed*], *disregard, neglect; set at defiance.*
negō, -āre, -āvī, -ātus, *deny, say ... Not.*
negōtium, -iī, N. [nec, NOT; ōtium, *leisure*], *business, affair, matter, enterprise, undertaking.*
nēmō (in place of gen. nēminis, nūllīus is used; in place of abl. nēmine, nūllō, M. or **nūllā**, F. is used), C. [nē, NOT, NO ;* hemo (homo), *man*], NO one, *Nobody*.
neque or **nec**, conj. [nē (w. vowel shortened), NOT ; -que, *and*], *and* NOT, *Neither*, NOR ; **neque ... neque** or **nēc ... nec**, *Neither ... Nor*.
Nervii, -ōrum, M., *the Nervii* (tribe in Belgic Gaul between the Sambre and the Scheldt).
ne-sciō, -īre, -īvī or **-iī** [nē, NOT; sciō, *know*], NOT *know*.
neuter, -tra, -trum, adj. [nē, NOT; uter, *eiTHER*], NEITHER; in pl., neutrī, NEITHER *party.*
nēve or **neu**, conj. [nē, NOT; ve, *or*], *and* NOT, NOR, *and that* NOT (takes the place of neque in clauses expressing purpose, exhortation, and prohibition).
nex, necis, F. [√nec-, *destroy;* conn. w. noceō and **perniciēs**], *death* (by violence).
niger, -gra, -grum, adj., *black.*
nihil, N., def. (also **nihilum, -ī**, N., and **nīl**) [nē, NOT; hīlum, *trifle, the least thing*], *Nothing;* nihil (adv. acc.) NOT *at all;* nihil posse, *to be without any effective strength.*
nimis, adv., *too, excessively.*
nimius, -a, -um, adj. [conn. w. foregoing], *too much, excessive.*
nisi, conj. [nē, NOT ; sī, *if*], *if*

NOT, *unless, except;* **nihil nisi,** *Nothing but;* nisi **cum,** *until.*
nītor, -ī, nīsus or **nīxus,** *depend, rely.*
nōbilis, -e, adj. [√gnō-, KNOW], *capable or worthy of being* KNOWN ; *famous, celebrated, renowned ; high-born, noble;* subst., *nobleman, noble.*
nōbilitās, -ātis, F. [nōbili- (st. of nōbilis), *well* KNOWN], *fame; nobility, noble birth, rank ; nobles, the nobility.*
nōbilitō, -āre, -āvī, -ātus [nōbili- (st. of nōbilis), *famous*], *make famous.*
noceō, -ēre, -uī, -itum [√noc-, *destroy, injure* (through presumed adj. st.); conn. w. nex and perniciēs], *injure, damage, inflict injury.*
nocturnus, -a, -um, adj. [conn. w. noctū, *by* NIGHT], *pertaining to the* NIGHT, *nocturnal, posted by* NIGHT.
nōlō, nōlle, nōluī [nē, NOT; volō, *wish*], *be unwilling, decline ;* id nōlle, *to object to this.*
nōmen, -inis, N. [√gnō-, KNOW], (means of knowing, and so) NAME ; **nōmine**, *under the* NAME, *as, by way of.*
nōminātim, adv. [nōminā- (st. of nōminō), NAME], *by* NAME, *in detail.*
nōminō, -āre, -āvī, -ātus [nōmin- (st. of nōmen), NAME], NAME, *call.*
nōn, adv. [old forms, nocnum, noenu, fr. nē, NOT, and ūnum, ONE], NOT, NO.
nōnāgēsimus, -a, -um, ord. num. adj., NINETIETH.
nōndum, adv. [nōn, NOT; dum, *yet*], NOT *yet.*
nōnne [nōn, NOT; -ne, interrog. particle], interrog. particle introducing questions to which an affirmative answer is expected.
nōn nūllus or **nōnnūllus, -a, -um**, adj. [nōn, NOT; nūllus, NO], *some;* pl. subst., nōnnūllī, *some.*

nōn nunquam (numquam) or **nōnnunquam** (numquam), adv. [nōn, not; nunquam, never], sometimes.

nōnus, -a, -um, **ord.** num. adj. [conn. w. novem, nine], ninth.

Nōricus, -a, -um, adj., belonging to Noricum (a country lying between the Alps and the Danube) Norican.

nōscō, -ere, nōvī, nōtus [inceptive fr. √gnō-, know], become acquainted with; acknowledge; in perf., know.

noster, -tra, -trum, **poss.** pron. [nōs, we], our.

novem, num. **adj.** indecl., nine.

novō, -āre, **-āvī**, -ātus [novo-(st. of **novus**), new], make new, renew.

novus, -a, -um, adj., new, strange; superl., novissimus, hindmost, rear; novissimum agmen, rear; ab novissimis, in the rear.

nox, noctis, f. [√noc-, destroy, injure; conn. w. noceō], night; multā nocte, late at night.

noxa, -ae, f. [√noc-, destroy, injure; conn. w. noceō], offence, crime.

nūbō, -ere, nūpsī, nūptus, (of a bride) veil one's self (for the bridegroom), and so marry; nūptum (sup.) conlocāre, to give in marriage.

nūdō, -āre, **-āvī, -ātus** [nūdo-(st. of nūdus), **bare**], strip, lay bare.

nūdus, -a, -um, adj. [for *nugdus; cognate w. English naked], bare, destitute.

nūgātor, -ōris, m. [nūgā-(st. of nūgor), trifle], trifler.

nūllus, -a, -um, adj. [**nē**, not; fīlius, any], not any, no; annihilated; subst., no one.

num, interrog. particle **introducing** questions to which a neg. answer is expected; also (in dependent questions), whether.

Numantia, -ae, f., Numantia (town in Spain on the upper Douro, destroyed by Scipio Africanus the younger 133 b.c.).

nūmen, -inis, n. [√nū-, nod], (that which is expressed by a **nod**, and so) divine will or power.

numerus, -ī, m., number; account, estimation, rank.

numquam, see nunquam.

nunc, adv., now.

nunquam or **numquam**, adv. [nē, not; unquam, ever], never.

nūntiō, -āre, -āvī, -ātus [nūntio-(st. of nūntius), messenger], announce, report.

nūntius, -iī, m. [conn. w. novus, new], messenger; message, news; order, injunction.

nusquam, **adv.** [nē, not; usquam, anywhere], nowhere.

O.

ō, interj., O, Oh.

ob, prep. w. acc., in view **of**, on account of, for.

ob-dūcō, -ere, **-dūxī, ductus**[ob, towards, forward; dūcō, draw], draw forward, extend.

ob-iciō (pronounced: objiciō), -ere, **-jēcī**, -jectus [ob, before, against; jaciō, cast], cast before; set against, match.

oblītus, -a, -um [p. a. of oblīviscor, forget], forgetful.

oblīviscor, -ī, -lītus, forget, turn one's thoughts from.

obscūritās, -ātis, f. [obscūro-(st. of obscūrus), obscure], obscurity.

ob-secrō, -āre, -āvī, -ātus [ob, towards, before; sacrō, declare sacred], (appeal to one in the name of the gods, and so) beseech, implore.

ob-servō, -āre, -āvī, -ātus [ob, before; servō, keep], observe, mark, keep; respect, follow, comply with.

ob-ses, -idis, c. [ob, before; √sed-, sit], (one who sits or remains as a pledge, and so) hostage.

ob-sĭdĕō, -ēre, -sēdī, -sĕssus [ob, *before;* sedeō, SIT], *besiege.*

ob-stō, -āre, -stĭtī [ob, *against;* stō, STAnd], STAnd *against, oppose.*

ob-strŭō, -ere, -strūxī, -strūctus [ob, *against;* strŭō, *build*], *build against, barricade.*

ob-tĭnĕō, -ēre, -tĭnŭī, -tentus [ob, *against;* tenĕō, *hold*], *lay hold* OF; *hold; be in authority over; obtain.*

ob-tĭngō, -ere, -tĭgī [ob, *towards;* tangō, *touch*], *fall to one's lot.*

ob-truncō, -āre, -āvī, -ātus [ob, implying attack; truncō, *cut off*], *cut down, kill.*

obvĭam, adv. [ob, *towards, on;* via, WAY], *on the* WAY, *to meet;* **obviam īre** (w. dat.), *to go to meet, to resist.*

occāsĭō, -ōnis, F. [ob-√căd-, *fall towards*], (falling **towards** one, and so) *occasion, chance, opportunity.*

occāsus, -ūs, M. [ob-√căd-, *fall towards, sink down*], (sinking, and so) *setting.*

oc-cīdō, -ere, -cīdī, -cīsus [ob, *against;* caedō, *cut*], *kill, slay.*

occultē, adv. [abl. fm. of occultus, *secret*], *secretly.*

occultō, -āre, -āvī, -ātus [intens. of occulō, *cover up,* fr. occulto- (st. of perf. part.)], CONCEAL, *secrete.*

occultus, -a, -um [perf. part. of occulō, *cover up*], CONCEALed, *secret;* **in occultō**, IN *secret.*

occŭpō, -āre, -āvī, -ātus [ob-√cap-, *lay hold* OF (through presumed adj. st.)], *take possession* OF, *seize; occupy, employ.*

oc-currō, -ere, -currī (-cucurrī, rare), -cursum [ob, *towards;* currō, *run*], *run to meet; hasten to oppose; hasten*(againsttheenemy) *to the rescue* (of one's friends).

Ōcĕănus, -ī, M., *ocean.*

octingentī, -ae, -a, **num. adj.** [octin-, conn. w. octō, EIGHT; -gintī, conn. w. centum, HUNDred], EIGHT HUNDred.

octō, indecl. num. adj., EIGHT.

octōgēsĭmus, -a, -um, ord. num. adj., EIGHTI*eth.*

octōgintā, indecl. num. adj. [octō, EIGHT; -gin- represents (de)cem, TEN], EIGHTY.

ŏcŭlus, -ī, M. [fr. √oc-, *see* (through presumed subst.)], EYE.

ōdī, ōsus, def. (pres. system wanting), *hate, cherish hatred.*

ŏdĭum, -ĭī, N. [√od-, *hate;* conn. w. ōdī], *hatred; grudge.*

of-ferō, offerre, obtulī, oblātus [ob, *towards;* ferō, BEAR], *present, offer.*

officium, -ĭī, N. [base op- (in **opus**), *work, service;* √fac-, DO], *service, office, duty; sense of duty; obedience, allegiance.*

ōmen, -ĭnis, N., *omen.*

o-mittō, -ere, -mīsī, -missus [ob, *before, aside;* mittō, *let go*], *let go; disregard.*

omnīnō, adv. [abl. fm. conn. w. omnis], *altogether, in all, only, but; in general.*

omnis, -e, adj., *all, every.*

ŏnus, -eris, N., *burden, weight; ennui.*

ŏpēs, -um, F. (nom. sing. used only as name of goddess of Plenty), *means, resources, property, wealth, riches;* opis (gen. sing.), *aid, help, assistance.*

ŏpīnĭō, -ōnis, F. [conn. w. opīnor, *be of opinion*], *opinion, views, belief, impression; expectation; suspicion;* **celerius opīnīōne**, *more quickly than any one had supposed possible.*

ŏpĭtŭlor, -ārī, -ātus [opi- (st. of opis), *aid;* √tol-, *bear* (through *opitulus)], *bring aid, relieve.*

oportet, -ēre, -uit, impers., *it is proper, it is right, it behooves.*

oppĭdānus, -a, -um, adj. [oppido- (st. of oppidum), *town*], *belonging to the town;* subst., **oppĭdānī**, -ōrum, M., *inhabitants of the town, townspeople.*

oppĭdum, -ī, N., *town* (viewed as stronghold).

opportūnitās   **parum**   285

opportūnitās, -ātis, F. [opportūno- (st. of opportūnus), *convenient*], *convenience, favorableness; opportunity.*
opportūnus, -a, -um, adj., *convenient, fit,* **opportune.**
op-primō, -ere, -pressī, -pressus [ob, *against;* premō, **press**], *crush, overpower.*
op-pūgnō, -āre, -āvī, -ātus [ob, *against;* pūgnō, *fight*], *assault.*
optimus, see bonus.
[**Ops**], opis, F., see opēs.
opus, -eris, N., *work;* **undertaking**; in pl., *manufactures.*
opus, N., used as nom. and acc. only [same as foregoing], *need, necessity;* translated adj., *necessary.*
ōrātiō, -ōnis, F. [ōrā-, *speak*], *speaking, speech, language; address.*
ōrātor, -ōris, M. [ōrā-, *speak, plead*], *speaker,* **orator.**
orbis, -is, M., *circle,* **orb**; *compact mass.*
ōrdō, -inis, M., *row, rank; company.*
Orgetorīx, -īgis, M., **Orgetorix** (prominent Helvetian of Caesar's time).
orior, -īrī, ortus, *rise, spring up, take one's* **origin**, *begin; descend.*
ōrnāmentum, -ī, N. [ōrnā- (st. of ōrnō), *embellish*], (means of embellishing, and so) *mark of honor, distinction,* **ornament.**
ōrnō, -āre, -āvī, -ātus, *embellish, adorn, honor, distinguish.*
ōrō, -āre, -āvī, -ātus [ōs- (st. of ōs) (**-s-** becomes **-r-**), *mouth*], *entreat,* **beg**, *beseech.*
ortus, -ūs, M. [√or-, *rise;* conn. w. orior], *rising; origin.*
ōsculor, -ārī, -ātus [ōsculo- (**st.** of ōsculum), *a kiss*], *kiss.*
os-tendō, -ere, -tendī, -tentus [*obs = ob, *towards;* tendō, *stretch*], *point out,* **show**; *make known, declare, give to understand.*
ōstium, -ii, N. [conn. **w. ōs**, *mouth*], *entrance, door.*
ōtium, -iī, N., *leisure.*

P.
P., abbr. **of Pūblius**, -iī, M. (Roman praenōmen or first name).
paene, adv., *almost.*
paenitet, -ēre, -uit, impers. [conn. **w.** poena, **penalty**], **cause to repent;* mē paenitet, *I repent, I regret,* **I** *am dissatisfied.*
pāgus, -ī, M. [√pāg-, *make fast*], (place enclosed by fixed boundaries, and **so**) *district.*
palam, adv., *openly, publicly.*
Palātium, -iī, N., *the Palatine hill* (one of the seven hills on which Rome **was** built).
palūs, -ūdis, F., *swamp, marsh.*
pandō, -ere, pandī, pāssus, *stretch out, expand.*
pār, paris, adj., *equal; match for; of equal rank or consideration.*
parātus, -a, -um [p. a. of parō, *prepare*], *prepared, ready; eager.*
parcō, -ere, pepercī (parsī), SPARE.
parēns, -entis, C. [part. of pariō, *bring forth*, used subst.], **parent.**
pāreō, -ēre, pāruī [intr. form conn. w. tr. parō, *make ready*], (be ready, and so) *appear;* (appear in response to orders, and so) *obey.*
pariter, adv. [pari- (st. of pār), *equal*], *equally; at the same time.*
parō, -āre, -āvī, -ātus [tr. fm. conn. w. intr. pāreō, *be ready*], *make ready, prepare; procure, acquire.*
pars, partis, F. [√par-, *assign, make ready;* the same root is contained in parō and pāreō], (assignment, and so) **part**, POUTION, *share; side, direction, quarter.*
parti-ceps, -cipis, adj. [parti- (st. of pars), **part**; √cap-, *take*], *taking* **part**, *sharing;* **particeps** esse, *to come in* **for** *a share.*
partior, -īrī, **-ītus** [parti- (st. of pars), **part**], **part**, *divide, distribute.*
parum, adv. [acc. used adv.; parum (for *sparum) is conn. w.

parcō (for *sparcō), SPARE], *too little.*

parvulus, -a, -um, adj. [dim. fr. **parvo**- (st. of parvus), *small*], *very small, tiny;* ab **parvulis**, *from childhood.*

parvus, -a, -um, adj. [= *paurus (cf. nervus = *neurus); conn. w. **paucī**, FEW], *small, little, slight.* Comp., **minor**, -**us**, *less, smaller;* **minus**, used adv.: *less; not;* **minus valēre**, *not to be strong enough, to be too weak.* Superl., **minimus**, -a, -um, *very little, least.*

passus, -ūs, M. [√pat-, *spread, stretch;* conn. w. pateō], (stretching forth of the legs in walking, and so) *pace;* (as a measure of length) *five Roman feet* (a little less than five English feet).

pateō, -ēre, -uī [√pat-, *spread, stretch* (through presumed adj. st.)], *be open, lie open, extend.*

pater, -tris, M. [of uncertain origin], FATHER.

pater familiās or **paterfamiliās**, **patris familiās**, M. [pater, FATHER; familia, *household of slaves*], *master of a house, head of a household.*

patera, -ae, F. [conn. w. pateō, through √pat-, *spread*], *libation-saucer, sacrificial dish;* see Fig. 7.

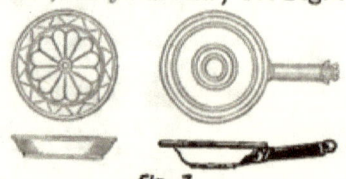

Fig. 7.
Front and side view of two paterae, one with handle, the other without. The illustrations are copies of bronze originals found at Pompeii.

patienter, adv. [patient- (st. of patiēns), *patient*], *patiently.*

patior, -ī, passus, *suffer; permit.*

patria, -ae, F. [fem. of patrius, *belonging to one's* FATHERS; sc. terra], *native country.*

paucī, -ae, -a, adj. (sing. very rare) [conn. w. parvus, *small,*

q. v.], FEW, *but* FEW; **pauca**, FEW *words, briefly;* **paucīs**, in a FEW *words, briefly.*

paulisper, adv., *for a little while, for a short time.*

paulus, -a, -um, adj. [dim. fr. *pauro- = parvo- (stem of parvus) *little*], *a little;* paulō, *by a little, a little.*

Paullus, -ī, M., 1. *Lucius Aemilius Paullus* (Roman consul, killed in the battle of Cannae 216 B.C.); 2. *Lucius Aemilius Paullus* (son of preceding, defeated Perses, king of Macedon, at Pydna 168 B.C.).

pāx, pācis, F. [√pāc-, *bind fast*], (that which binds fast, and so) *peace;* pāce tuā, *with your permission.*

peccō, -āre, -āvī, -ātum, *make a mistake, transgress, sin.*

pecūnia, -ae, F. [conn. w. pecū, *cattle*], (as cattle constituted the earliest form of wealth, therefore) *wealth, riches; money, a sum of money.*

pedes, -itis, M. [ped- (st. of pēs), FOOT], FOOT-*soldier.*

pedester, -tris, -tre, adj. [pedit- (st. of pedes), FOOT-*soldier*], *pertaining to* FOOT-*soldiers.*

peditātus, -ūs, M. [peditā- (st. of peditō) *go on* FOOT], (orig., going on foot, and so, used concretely) FOOT-*soldiers, infantry.*

pējor, -us, comp. of malus, q. v.

pellis, -is, F. [cognate w. English FELL], *skin; tent;* **sub pellibus**, *in camp.*

pellō, -ere, pepulī, pulsus, *beat; drive, expel; rout.*

pendō, -ere, pependī, pēnsus, *weigh; pay.*

pēnsum, -ī, N. [n. perf. part. of pendō, *weigh*], *something weighed; weight, consideration, importance;* **pēnsī habēre**, *to consider of importance.*

per, prep. w. acc., *through; by, by means of, through the instrumentality of;* **per sē**: *of himself,* *herself, itself* or *themselves; through his, her, its* or **their** *own exertions.*

per-cipiō, -ere, -cēpī, -ceptus [per, *completely;* capiō, *take*], **perceive,** *learn, understand; receive in one's own person, experience.*

per-discō, -ere, -didicī [per, *thoroughly;* discō, *learn*], **learn thoroughly,** *commit to memory.*

per-dō, -ere, -didī, **-ditus** [per, *through, away;* dō, **put**], *make away with, destroy,* **ruin.** The forms of pereō supply the pass.

per-dūcō, -ere. -dūxī, -ductus [per, *through;* dūcō, *lead*], *lead through, lead; carry, extend, conduct.*

peregrīnus, -a, -um, adj. [peregro- (st. of adv. peregrē, *abroad*)], **strange, foreign;** subst., *stranger, foreigner.*

per-eō, -īre, -iī [per, *through, away;* eō, *go, pass*], **perish,** *be destroyed;* **periit,** *is dead.*

per-facilis, -e, adj. [per, *very;* facilis, *easy*], *very easy;* **perfacile est,** *it is a very easy matter.*

per-ferō, -ferre, -tulī, -lātus [per, *through;* ferō, BEAR], BEAR *to the end, endure, submit to, sustain.*

per-ficiō, -ere, -fēcī, -fectus [per, *through;* faciō, **DO**], *carry through* or *out, accomplish; finish,* **bring** *to completion.*

per-fruor, -ī, **-frūctus** [per, *thoroughly;* fruor, **enjoy**], *enjoy fully.*

perfuga, -ae, M. [per-√fug-, *flee through* (the lines)], (one who flees through the lines, and so) *deserter.*

pergō, -ere, perrēxī, perrēctus [per, *through, on;* regō, *guide*], 1. tr. *proceed with;* 2. intr. *proceed.*

periclitor, -ārī, -ātus [intens, verb; conn. w. periculum, **trial**], *make trial of, try, test.*

periculōsus, -a, -um [periculo- (st. of periculum), **peril**], *full of peril, dangerous, perilous.*

periculum, -ī, N. [perī- (st. of *perior;* cf. experior and perītus), *try, test*], *trial;* **danger, peril,** *risk.*

perītus, -a, -um [p. a. of *perior (cf. experior), *try, test*], *tried, experienced, skillful.*

per-maneō, -ēre, -mānsī, **-mānsum** [per, *through;* maneō, **stay**], *stay through,* **remain,** *abide,* **continue;** *survive.*

per-misceō, -ēre, **-scuī, -mīstus** or **-mixtus** [per, **thoroughly;** misceō, **MIX**], *disturb,* **throw** *into confusion.*

per-mittō, -ere, -mīsī, -missus [per, **through;** mittō, *let go*] (orig., **let go** through), *intrust, commit.*

per-moveō, -ēre, -mōvī, -mōtus [per, *thoroughly;* moveō, **move**], *move deeply, influence, alarm.*

perniciēs, gen. -iī, -iēs, or -iē, F. [per-√nec-, *completely destroy*], *destruction, ruin.*

perniciōsus, -a, -um, adj. [perniciē- (st. of perniciēs), *destruction*], *destructive,* **ruinous, pernicious.**

per-rumpō, -ere, -rūpī, **-ruptus** [per, *through;* rumpō, **break**], *break* or *rush through.*

per-sequor, -ī, -cūtus [per, *persistently;* sequor, *follow*], *follow up; avenge.*

Persēs, -ae, M., *Perses* (last king of Macedonia, defeated by Lucius Aemilius Paullus at Pydna 168 B.C.).

per-solvō, -ere, -solvī, -solūtus [per, *completely;* solvō, *discharge*], *discharge fully, pay.*

per-spiciō, -ere, -spexī, -spectus [per, *through;* speciō, *look*], *examine; perceive, ascertain.*

per-suādeō, -ēre, -sī, -sus [per, *through, to the end;* suādeō, *urge*], **persuade,** *convince; inculcate.*

per-terreō, -ēre, -uī, -itus [per, *thoroughly;* terreō, *frighten*], *frighten thoroughly; paralyze with fear.*

per-tineō, -ēre, -uī [per, *through, to the end;* teneō (intr.), *continue*], EXTENd; TENd.

perturbātiō, -ōnis, F. [perturbā- (st. of perturbō), *throw into confusion*], *confusion, disquiet, perturbation.*

per-turbō, -āre, -āvī, -ātus [per, *greatly;* turbō, *disturb*], *throw into confusion, rout; disturb, disquiet, discompose, agitate.*

per-veniō, -īre, -vēnī, -ventum [per, *through, to the end;* veniō, COME], *arrive,* COME; (of money) *revert.*

pēs, pedis, M. [√ped-, *tread*], FOOT.

petō, -ere, -īvī or -iī, -ītus [√pet-, *fly at, fall*], *fall upon; make for, repair to; go to seek, go after, seek, ask for, beseech.*

pictor, -ōris, M. [√pĭg-, *paint*], *painter.*

pietās, -ātis, F. [pio- (st. of pius), *dutiful, reverential*], *dutiful or reverential conduct;* (with reference to the gods) *piety;* (with reference to parents) *filial respect.*

piget, -ēre, -uit, -itum, *it irks, it disgusts;* mē **piget**, *I loathe, I am disgusted.*

pīlum, -ī, N., *heavy javelin.*

pingō, -ere, pinxī, pictus [√pĭg-, *paint*], *paint.*

Pīsō, -ōnis, M., 1. *Lucius Calpurnius Piso* (lieutenant of Cassius 107 B.C.); 2. *Lucius Calpurnius Piso Caesonius* (grandson of the preceding and father-in-law of Caesar).

placeō, -ēre, -uī, -itus (p. a.) [conn. w. plācō, *reconcile*], *be pleasing;* impers., **placet**, *it pleases, it seems good, it is one's pleasure.*

placidus, -a, -um, adj. [conn. w. placeō, *be pleasing*], *calm, placid.*

plācō, -āre, -āvī, -ātus [conn. w. placeō, *be pleasing*], *reconcile; appease, propitiate.*

plānitiēs, gen. -ae, F. [plāno- (st. of plānus), *level*], *plain.*

plānus, -a, -um, adj., *level,* FLAt, *plane.*

plausus, -ūs, M. [base plaud- (in plaudō), *clap*], (clapping, and so) *applause.*

plēbēs, F., archaic form of plēbs, q. v.

plēbs, -is, F. [conn. w. plēnus, FULL, through √plē-, FILL], *the multitude, the common* PEOPLE, *commons, lower orders,* POPULace.

plēnus, -a, -um, adj. [√plē-, FILL], FULL.

plērumque, see plērusque.

plērusque, -raque, -rumque, adj. (usu. pl.) [conn. w. plēnus, FULL], *very many, most, the greater part;* adv., **plērumque**, *for the most part, commonly.*

plūrēs, pl. of plūs, q. v.

plūrimus, -a, -um, superl. of multus, q. v.

plūs, **plūris**, comp. of multus, q. v.

poena, -ae, F., *satisfaction; penalty, punishment;* **poenās dare**, *to give satisfaction,* and so *to suffer punishment.*

Poenī, -ōrum, M., *inhabitants of Carthage, Carthaginians* (see Carthāgō. The Carthaginians were descended from the Phoenicians; hence the name Poenī).

poēta, -ae, M. [borrowed from the Greek], *poet.*

pol-liceor, -ērī, -itus [por- (old prep.), *to, towards;* liceor, *make an offer*], PROMISE (voluntarily).

Pompējus, **Pompēī**, M., *Pompey* (celebrated conqueror of the pirates of the Mediterranean and of Mithridates; defeated by Caesar at the battle of Pharsalus 48 B.C.).

Pompējus, -a, -um, adj., *of Pompey, Pompeian* (see preceding).

pondus, -eris, N. [conn. w. pendō, *weigh*], *weight.*

pōnō, -ere, posuī, positus, *place, deposit;* (of a camp), *pitch.*

pōns, pontis, M., *bridge.*

populāris   **praemium**   289

populāris, -e, adj. [populo- (st. of populus), *people*], *belonging to the people, popular*.

populor, -ārī, -ātus, *lay waste, devastate*.

populus, -ī, M. [conn. w. plēbs and plēnus], *people*.

porta, -ae, F. [√por-, FARE, *go through*], *gate*.

portō, -āre, -āvī, -ātus [portā- (st. of porta), *gate*], *carry*.

portus, -ūs, M. [√por-, FARE, *go through*], *entrance; harbor*, **port**.

poscō, -ere, poposcī, *ask urgently for, demand*.

possessiō, -ōnis, F. [por- (old prep.),*BEFORE*; √sed-, SIT], (sitting before, and so) *possession,* **property**.

pos-sideō, **-ēre**, -sēdī, -sessus [por- (old prep.), BEFORE; sedeō, SIT], *hold, be master of,* **possess**.

possum, posse, potuī [potis, *able*; **sum**, *be*], *can, be able;* **plūrimum posse**, *to be the most powerful, to have the most power, to be very influential;* **nihil posse**, *to be without any effective strength;* **facere nōn possum quīn**, *I cannot help*.

post, adv. **and** prep. w. acc., 1. adv.: *afterwards, later, after;* **annō post,** *the year after* 2. prep. w. acc.: (of place) *behind, in the rear of, next to;* (of **time**) *after*.

posteā, adv. [post, *after;* acc. pl. n. eā (orig. eā), *these things;* **cf**. anteā], *afterwards*.

*posterus,-era,-erum,adj.[posti- (st. of post), *after*], *coming after, following;* subst., **posterī**, -ōrum, M., *posterity*. Comp., **posterior**, -ius, *later*. Superl., **postrēmus**, -a, -um, *last*.

postquam or postquam [post, *later;* quam, *than*], *after,* WHEN.

postrēmus, **-a**, -um, superl. of *posterus, q. v.

postulō, **-āre**, -āvī, -ātus [conn. w. poscō], *press earnestly, demand, claim, request*.

potēns, -entis [p. a. of verb

conn. w. possum, *be able*], *powerful*.

potentātus, -ūs, M. [potent- (st. of potēns), *powerful* (through presumed verb stem)], *political power*.

potentia, -ae, F. [potent- (st. of potēns), *powerful*], **political** *power, influence*.

potestās, -ātis, F. [potent- (st. of potēns), *powerful*], *power; sovereignty, majesty;* **possibility**.

potior, -īrī, -ītus [poti- (st. of potis), *able*], *become master of, get possession of, obtain; reduce to subjection*.

potius, adv. [n. sing. comp. of potis, *able*], **rather**.

praebeō, **-ēre**, -uī, -itus [= praehibeō, fr. **prae**, BEFORE; habeō, *hold*], *offer, produce,* FURNISH, *give ground* FOR.

prae-cēdō, -ere, -cessī, -cessus [prae, BEFORE; cēdō, *go*], *go* BEFORE, *precede; surpass, excel*.

praeceps, -cipitis, adj. [prae, BEFORE; caput, HEAD], HEAD FOREmost, HEADlong; *steep,* **precipitous**.

prae-cipiō, **-ere**, -cēpī, -ceptus [prae, BEFORE; capiō, *take*], *take* BEFOREhand; *instruct, order, direct*.

prae-clārus, -a, -um, adj. [prae, *exceedingly;* clārus, *illustrious*], *very illustrious, illustrious, glorious*.

praeda, -ae, F. [conn. w. prehendō, *seize*], *booty*.

prae-dīcō, -āre, -āvī, -ātus [prae, BEFORE, and so *publicly;* dīcō, *declare*], *proclaim, declare, maintain, avow*.

prae-ficiō, -ere, -fēcī, -fectus [prae, BEFORE; faciō, *make, put*], *appoint over, place in command*.

prae-mittō, -ere, -mīsī, -missus [prae, FORward; mittō, *send*], *send* FORward, **send in** *advance*.

praemium,-iī,N.[=*praeimium, fr. prae-√em-, *take* BEFORE (others)], (what **one** receives more

290   praescriptum   **prō-cūrō**

than or in preference to others, and so) *reward; privilege.*

praescrīptum, -ī, N. [n. perf. part. of praescrībō, *prescribe*], *dictate, order.*

praesidium, -iī, N. [prac-√sed-, sit before], (sitting before for protection, and so) *defence, protection, aid, support; guard, garrison.*

prae-stō, -āre, -itī, -ātus (once), -itus (once) [prae, before; stō, stand], (intr. w. dat. pers.) *excel, surpass;* (impers.) **praestat,** *it is better;* (tr.) *perform; exhibit, display.*

praestō, adv. [superl. fm. com. w. **prae,** before], (in the foremost place, and so) *at hand.*

prae-sum, -esse, -fuī [prae, before; sum, *be*], be *at the head of, have charge or command of,* be *invested with, preside over.*

praeter, adv. and prep. w. acc. [comp. form of prae, before], *beyond; besides; except.*

praetereā, adv. [praeter, besides; acc. pl. n. ea (orig. eā), *these things;* cf. anteā], *besides, moreover, too.*

praeter-mittō, -ere, -mīsī, -missus [praeter, *beyond, by;* mittō, *let go*], *let pass, omit, leave.*

praeteritus, -a, -um [p. a. of praetereō, *go by*], *past.*

praetor, -ōris, M. [= *praeitor, fr. prae-√ī-, *go* before], (one who goes before, and so) *leader;* **praetor** (Roman magistrate who administered justice).

precēs, -um, F. (usu. pl.), *entreaties, prayers.*

prēndō = prehendō, -ere, -hendī, -hēnsus, *grasp.*

premō, -ere, pressī, pressus, *press hard, beset, weigh down, burden, overpower, distress.*

pretium, -iī, N., *price.*

*****prex, *precis, F., see **precēs**.

pridiē, adv. [pri- = prae (loc.),

before]; loc. *or* abl. form of diēs, *day*], *the day* before.

prīmus, -a, -um, adj., superl. of prior, q. v.

prīn-ceps, -cipis, adj. [prīmo- (st. of prīmus), first; √cap-, *take*], (taking the first place, and so) foremost, *chief;* subst., foremost *man, leader, head.*

prīncipātus, -ūs, M. [prīncip- (st. of prīnceps), foremost (through presumed verb st.)], (being foremost, and so) foremost *place, supremacy presidency.*

prīncipium, -iī, N. [prīncip- (st. of prīnceps), foremost], *beginning.*

prior, prius, adj. [comp. of st. com. w. prae and prō], former. Superl., prīmus, -a, -um, first, foremost; (in agreement with subst., often) first *part of;* in prīmīs, *especially,. particularly;* adv., prīmum, first.

prīstinus, -a, -um, adj. [prīs- for priōs- (st. of prior), former], *belonging to* former *times,* former, *earlier, ancient, pristine.*

prius quam *or* **priusquam,** adv. [prius, *sooner;* quam, *than*], before, *until.*

prīvātus, -a, -um [p. a. of prīvō, *deprive*], *private;* subst., *private individual.*

prō, prep. w. abl., *in front of,* before; *in behalf of,* for; *in view of, considering; in the light of, as; in return* for.

probitās, -ātis, F. [probo- (st. of probus), *upright, good*], *uprightness, probity.*

probō, -āre, -āvī, -ātus [probo- (st. of probus), *good*], *esteem good, approve; recommend, make satisfactory* or *acceptable.*

prō-cēdō, -ere, -cessī, -cessum [prō, before; cēdō, *go*], *go forward, advance, proceed.*

Prōcillus, -ī, M., *Gajus Valerius Procillus* (a Gaul much trusted by Caesar).

prō-cūrō, -āre, -āvī, -ātus [prō,

in behalf of, FOR; cūrō, *take care*], *attend to*, *look after*, *conduct*, *superintend*.
prō-currō, -ere, -currī and -cucurrī, -cursum [prō, FOR*ward*; currō, *run*], *run* FOR*ward*.
prōditiō, -ōnis, F.[prō-√da-, *give up*, *betray*], *betrayal, treachery, treason*.
prōditor, -ōris, M. [prō-√da-, *give up, betray*], *betrayer, traitor*.
prō-dō, -ere, -didī, -ditus [prō, FOR*th*; dō, *give, put*], *give* or *put* FOR*th, make known, publish; give up, betray; hand down* (as by tradition); memoriae prōditum est, *the story runs* (lit., it has been handed down to memory).
proelior, -ārī, -ātus [proelio-(st. of proelium), *battle*], *engage in battle, fight*.
proelium, -iī, N., *battle, fighting*.
profectiō, -ōnis, F. [prō (w. vowel shortened)-√fac-, *make off*], (making off, and so) *setting out, departure*.
profectō, adv. [prō (w. vowel shortened), FOR; factō (abl. of factum), *accomplished fact*], *assuredly*.
pro-ficīscor, -ī, -fectus [prō (w. vowel shortened), FOR*th*, *off*; *faciscor (inceptive of faciō), *begin to make*], (begin to make off, and so) *set out, depart, proceed; proficiscī* in w. acc., *set out for, depart to join*.
pro-fiteor, -ērī, -fessus [prō (w. vowel shortened), FOR*th*, *openly*; fateor, *acknowledge*), *declare one's self, give in one's name*, **volunteer**.
pro-fugiō, -ere, -fūgī [prō (w. vowel shortened), FOR*th*; fugiō, *flee*], *flee* FOR*th*, *flee, run away*.
prō-gnātus, -a, -um, adj. [prō, FOR*th, from*; (g)nātus, *born*, perf. part. of nāscor], *born from, born, descended*.
pro-hibeō, -ēre, -uī, -itus [prō (w. vowel shortened), FOR*th, off*; habeō, *hold*], *keep off, exclude, cut off, restrain, prevent, impede; prohibit; defend*.
prō-iciō (pronounced: prōjiciō), -ere, -jēcī, -jectus [prō, FOR*th, off*; jaciō, *cast*], *cast off*.
prō-lātō, -āre, -āvī, -ātus [prō, FOR*ward*; *lātō (intens. fr. st. of lātus, perf. part. of ferō), *carry*], (carry forward, and so) *defer, postpone*.
prō-moveō, -ēre, -mōvī, -mōtus [prō, FOR*ward*; moveō, *move*], *move* FOR*ward*.
prope, adv. and prep. w. acc., *near*.
prōpēnsus, -a, -um [p. a. of prōpendeō, *hang* FOR*ward*], *inclined, disposed*.
propinquus, -a, -um, adj. [conn. w. prope, *near*], *near*; substs.: propinquus, -ī, M., *relative, kinsman*; propinqua, -ae, F., *female relative, kinswoman*.
propior, -ius, adj. [comp. of st. contained in prope, *near*], *nearer*. Superl., proximus, -a, -um, *nearest, next, neighboring*; proximā nocte, *last* NIGHT.
prō-pōnō, -ere, -posuī, -positus [prō, FOR*th*; pōnō, *put, set*], *set* FOR*th, display; make known, declare*.
proprius, -a, -um, adj., *one's own, peculiar to one's self, private, personal*.
propter, adv. and prep. w. acc. [comp. form of prope, *near*; cf. inter and practer], *close to; owing to, on account of*.
prō-pūgnō, -āre, -āvī, -ātus[prō, *in front*; pūgnō, *fight*], *rush out to fight, make a sortie*.
prō-pulsō, -āre, -āvī, -ātus[prō, FOR*th, off*; pulsō, *drive*], *ward off, repel, avert*.
prō-ripiō, -ere, -uī [prō, FOR*th*; rapiō, *seize, drag*], *drag* FOR*th*; w. sē, *rush* FOR*th*.
prō-videō, -ēre, -vīdī, -vīsus [prō, FOR*ward*; videō, *see*], *provide, have in view*.
prōvincia, -ae, F., *province*.

proximitās, -ātis, F. [proximo- (st. of proximus), *next*], *nearness; relationship.*
proximus, -a, -um, adj., superl. of propior, q. v.
proximē, adv. [abl. fm. of proximus, *nearest*], *last.*
prūdentia, -ae, F. [prūdent- (st. of prūdēns), *sagacious*], *sagacity, practical wisdom, prudence, skill.*
Ptolomaeus, see Ceraunus.
pūblicē, adv. [abl. fm. of pūblicus, *belonging to the state*], *in behalf of the state, from a public point of view, as a measure of state* POLicy.
pūblicus, -a, -um, adj. [= *populicus, fr. populo- (st. of populus), *people*], *belonging to the people or state, public, common;* **rēs pūblica,** *common weal; commonwealth;* **in pūblicō,** IN *public.*
pudet, -ēre, puduit *or* puditum est, *it shames;* **mē pudet,** *I am ashamed.*
pudīcitia, -ae, F. [pudīco- (st. of pudīcus), *modest*], *modesty; chastity.*
pudor, -ōris, M. [base pud- (in pudet), *shame*], *sense of shame, modesty.*
puella, -ae, F. [= *puerula (-udisappeared and -r- was assimilated to -l-) dim. fr. puero- (st. of puer) *child*], *female child, girl, little girl.*
puer, -erī, M., *child; boy.*
puerīlis, -e, adj. [puero- (st. of puer), *child, boy*], *boyish, youthful.*
pueritia, -ae, F. [puero- (st. of puer), *child*], *childhood, boyhood.*
pūgna, -ae, F., *fight.*
pūgnō, -āre, -āvī, -ātus [pugnā- (st. of **pūgna**), *fight*], *fight.*
pulcher, -chra, -chrum, adj., *beautiful; honorable, glorious.*
pulvis, -eris, M., *dust.*
pungō, -ere, pupugī, punctus [√pug-, *thrust*], *prick, sting;* **disquiet.*
pūniō, -īre, -īvī *or* -**iī, -ītus** [old form, poeniō, fr. poenā- (st. of poena), *punishment*], *inflict punishment on, punish.*
puppis, -is, F., *stern.*
pūrgō, -āre, -āvī, -ātus [= *pūrigō, fr. pūro- (st. of pūrus), *clean;* √ag-, *drive, make* (through presumed adj. st.)], *make clean, cleanse, purge; free from suspicion, exculpate.*
putō, -āre, -āvī, -ātus [puto- (st. of putus), *cleanseD*], *cleanse;* (of trees) *prune;* (of accounts) *clear up,* **settle;** *reckon; think, suppose.*

Q.

Q., abbr. of **Quintus, -ī,** M., *Quintus* (Roman praenōmen or first name).
quadrāgintā, indecl. num. adj. [quadrā-, conn. w. quattuor, FOUR; -gin- represents (de)cem, TEN], FORTY.
quadringentī, -ae, -a, num. adj. [fr. st. of quadrīnī, distr. num. adj., FOUR; -gentī, conn. w. centum, HUNDRed], FOUR HUNDRed.
quaerō, -ere, -sīvī *or* -**siī, -sītus,** *seek, search, strive to obtain; acquire; ask, ask for, seek to learn, inquire, make inquiry, inquire for.*
quaestiō, -ōnis, F. [base quaes- (in quaerō, orig. quaesō), *inquire*], *inquiring; investigation; examination by torture.*
quaestus, -ūs, M. [base quaes- (in quaerō, orig. quaesō), *acquire*], *acquiring, acquisition; gain.*
quālis, -e, interrog. and rel. adj. [pron. st. quo- seen in forms of quis and quī], 1. interrog., *of* WHAt *sort;* 2. rel., *of* WHICH *sort, as.*
quam, interrog. and rel. adv., HOW; (used to strengthen superlatives) **quam māximus,** *as great as possible, the greatest possible;* **quam lātissimē,** *as extensively as possible;* (in comparisons) *as, than.*
quam ob rem *or* **quamobrem,** interrog. and rel. adv., WHErefore, *for* WHICH *or* WHAt *reason.*

quamquam, conj. [quam, HOW; quam, HOW], (however, and so) *though, although; and yet.*

quamvīs, adv. and conj. [quam, HOW, *as;* vīs (volō), *you wish*], *as you* WILL; HOW*ever,* HOW*ever much, though, although, though ever so.*

quantus, -a, -um, interrog. and rel. adj. [pron. st. quo- seen in forms of quis and quī], 1. interrog., HOW *great,* HOW *much;* quantī (gen. of indef. value), *for* HOW *much.* 2. rel. (correlating with tantus) *as;* (w. tantus omitted) *as much as;* quantō ... tantō, *by* HOW *much ... by so much, the* ... THE.

quārē, interrog. and rel. adv. [abl. of quae rēs], WHY, WHERE*fore.*

quartus, -a, -um, ord. num. adj. [quattuor, FOUR], FOURTH.

quasi, adv. [quam, *as;* sī, *if*], *as if.*

quaternī, -ae, -a, distr. num. adj. [quattuor, FOUR], FOUR [from] *each.*

quattuor, indecl. num. adj., FOUR.

quattuordecim, indecl. num. adj. [quattuor, FOUR; decem, TEN], FOURTEEN.

-que, conj., *and.*

quem ad modum or quemadmodum, interrog. and rel. adv., *in* WHAT *or* WHICH *way.*

queror, -ī, questus, *complain.*

quī, quae, quod, interrog., rel., and indef. pron., 1. interrog. (used adj.) WHICH, WHAT. 2. rel., WHO, WHICH, WHAT, *that;* (w. ant. omitted) HE WHO, *those* WHO, *any* WHO, etc.; (at the beginning of a sentence, often) *this, these,* etc.; (= ut is, etc.) *in order that* HE, *that* HE, etc.; quō ... eō, *by* WHAT ... *by that, the ... the;* eō ... quō, *by that ... by* WHICH, *the ... the.* 3. (after sī and nē), indef., *any.*

quīcumque, quaecumque, quodcumque, indef. rel. pron. [quī, rel. pron.; -cumque, indef. suff.], WHOever, WHATever; *any* WHAT*ever.*

quidam, quaedam, quoddam and (subst.) **quiddam, indef. pron.** [quī, rel. pron.; -dam, pron. suff.], *a, a certain, some one.*

quidem, adv., *indeed;* nē ... quidem (with emphatic word or words between nē and quidem), *not even.*

quiēscō, -ere, -ēvī, -ētus (p. a.), *become quiet, go to rest, refrain from action.*

quiētus, -a, -um [p. a. of quiēscō, *be quiet*], *quiet, at rest.*

quīlibet, quaelibet, quodlibet and (subst.) quidlibet, indef. rel. pron. [quī, rel. pron.; libet, *it is pleasing*], *any you will, any* WHAT*ever.*

quīn, conj. [quī, abl. fm. of rel. pron. quī; nē, *not*], WHO ... *not, that, but that, so that* NOT, *from* or *without* (w. part.).

quīndecim, indecl. num. adj. [quīnque, FIVE; decem, TEN], FIFTEEN.

quīnī, -ae, -a, distr. num. adj. [quīnque, FIVE], FIVE *apiece.*

quīnquāgintā, indecl. num. adj. [quīnquā-, conn. w. quīnque, FIVE; -gin- represents (de)cem, TEN], FIFTY.

quīnque, indecl. num. adj., FIVE.

quīnquennium, -ī, N. [quīnquenni- (st. of quīnquennis), *of* FIVE *years*], *a period of* FIVE *years.*

quīntus, -a, -um, ord. num. adj. [quīnque, FIVE], FIFTH.

Quirītēs, -ium, M. [Curi- (st. of Curēs, town of the Sabines)], *Quirītes (i.e.,* inhabitants of Curēs. After the union of the Sabines with the Romans, the name *Quirītēs* was applied to the combined people when acting in a civil capacity; the name *Rōmānī*, on the other hand, was applied to them when acting in a military capacity); *fellow citizens.*

quis, quid, interrog. **and** indef. pron., 1. interrog., WHO, WHAT; (occasionally used adj.) WHAT; neut. sing. acc. **quid** (used adv.), WHY. 2. (after sī and nē) indef., *any one, any thing;* (occasionally used adj.) *any;* **sī quid,** *if anything, if at all.*

quispiam, quaepiam, quodpiam and (subst.) **quidpiam** *or* **quippiam,** indef. pron., *any one, any.*

quisquam, quicquam or **quidquam** (pl. and fem. sing. wanting), indef. pron. (used when a neg. is expressed or implied), *any one, any thing.*

quisque, quaeque, quodque and (subst.) **quicque** *or* **quidque,** indef. pron., *every one, each one, every, each;* **nōbilissimus quisque,** *all the nobility;* **antiquissimum quodque tempus,** *priority* (of occupation) *in each instance.*

quīvīs, quaevīs, quodvīs and (subst.) **quidvīs,** indef. pron. [**quī,** rel. pron.; **vīs** (volō), *you wish*], *any you please, any* WHATever*; any* one *you please, any one* WHATever.

quō, adv. [case fm. of pron. st. quo-], WHIther; (at the beginning of a sentence, often) *thither, there.*

quō, conj. [neut. abl. of rel. pron. **quī**] (= ut eō, usu. w. comp.), *that thereby, in order that, that.*

quoad, adv. [quō (w. vowel shortened), WHIther; **ad,** *to*], (how long, and so) *as long as; until.*

quod, conj. [neut. acc. of rel. pron. **quī**], *because, that.*

quōminus, cŏnj. [quō, neut. abl. of rel. pron. **quī;** minus, *less, not*], *that thereby the less, so that not, from* (w. part.).

quoniam, conj. [quom = cum, *since;* jam, *now*], *seeing that.*

quot, indecl. interrog. and rel. adj., HOW *many;* as.

quot annīs or **quotannīs** [quot, HOW *many, as many as;* annīs, abl. pl. of annus, *year*], (on as many years as there are, and so) *every year, annually.*

quotiēns, adv. [quot, HOW *many*], HOW *often,* HOW *many times; as often as.*

R.

ratiō, -ōnis, F., *account, computation; list, register; business matter, transaction; manner, way, method, procedure.*

ratis, -is, F., *float, raft.*

Raurīcī, -ōrum, M., *the Raurici* (tribe in Celtic Gaul, neighbors of the Helvetians).

recēns, -entis, adj., *recent.*

re-cipiō, -ere, -cēpī, -ceptus [re(d)-, *again, back;* capiō, *take*], *take back; receive;* **sē recipere,** *to betake one's self, return, flee for refuge, recover;* **sē inde recipere,** *to come off.*

re-citō, -āre, -āvī, -ātus [re(d)-, intensive; citō, *recite*], *recite.*

re-cōgnōscō, -ere, -gnōvī, -gnitus [re(d)-, *again;* cōgnōscō, *become acquainted with*], *recall to mind, review.*

recordor, -ārī, -ātus [re(d)-, *again;* cord- (st. of cor), HEART (through presumed adj. st.)], (take to heart, and so) *think over, reflect on, review, recall.*

rēctē, adv. [abl. fm. of rēctus, RIGHT], RIGHT*ly.*

rēctus, -a, -um [p. a. of regō], RIGHT, *fitting.*

re-cūsō, -āre, -āvī, -ātus [re(d)-, *against;* causa, *objection* (through denom. vb. *causō; cf. causor)], *make objection against, refuse;* **recūsāre dē,** *to make objection to, to object to.*

red-dō, -ere, -didī, -ditus [red-, *back;* dō, *give*], *give back, return, restore; accord, award, grant, pay.*

red-eō, -īre, -iī, -itum [red-, *back;* eō, *go*], *go* or *come back, return; come for settlement, come in the last resort.*

red-igō, -ere, -ēgī, -āctus [red-, back; agō, drive, bring], bring back, reduce.

red-imō, -ere, -ēmī, -ēmptus [red-, back; emō, buy], buy back, **redeem; contract** for, farm; purchase, procure.

red-integrō, -āre, -āvī, -ātus [red-, again; integrō, make whole], make whole again, renew.

re-dūcō, -ere, -dūxī, -ductus [re(d)-, back; dūcō, lead], lead **or** bring back.

re-ferciō, -īre, -sī, -tus [re(d)-, intens.; farciō, stuff, cram], fill full, crowd.

re-ferō, -ferre, rettulī, relātus [re(d)-, back; ferō, BEAR], BEAR, carry **or** BRING **back,** report; **referre ad senātum,** to lay a matter before the **senate.**

rē fert or rēfert, -ferre, -tulit, it matters, it **is** of importance.

re-fugiō, -ere, -fūgī [re(d)-, back; fugiō, flee], fleeback, **retreat.**

rēgālis, -e, adj. [rēg-(st. of rēx), king], pertaining to a king, royal.

regiō, -ōnis, F. [√reg-, guide, direct], direction; boundary-line; territory, **region;** province, district.

rēgius, -a, -um, adj. [rēg- (st. of rēx), king], pertaining to a king, royal, regal.

rēgnō, -āre, -āvī, -ātus [rēgno- (st. of rēgnum), sovereignty], exercise sovereignty, reign.

rēgnum, -ī, N. [√reg-, guide, direct], kingdom; sovereignty, **royal** power.

regō, -ere, rēxī, rēctus [√reg-, guide, direct], direct; rule, preside over.

re-laxō, -āre, -āvī, -ātus [re(d)-, intens.; laxō, loosen], **relax, unbend.**

religiō, -ōnis, F. [re(d)-√leg-, go over again, regard attentively], (regard for the gods, and so) religion; superstition, sacredness, **sanctity;** in. pl., religious matters, **religious** rites, matters pertaining to the worship of the gods.

re-linquō, -ere, -līquī, -lictus [re(d)-, back, behind; linquō, leave], leave behind, leave.

reliquus, -a, -um, adj. [re-√liqu-, leave behind], remaining, other, rest of; subst., the rest.

re-maneō, -ēre, -mānsī [re(d)-, back, behind; maneō, stay], stay behind, remain.

remedium, -iī, N., **remedy, means** of defence.

Rēmi, -ōrum, M., the Remi (tribe in Belgic Gaul on the Marne).

rēmigium, -iī, N. [rēmig- (st. of rēmex), ROWER], ROWING; OARS; rowers.

re-miniscor, -ī [re(d)-, again; *miniscor, **call to** MIND], recall to MIND.

re-mittō, -ere, -mīsī, -missus [re(d)-, back; mittō, send, let go], send or let go back; **relax,** enfeeble.

re-moveō, -ēre, -mōvī, -mōtus [re(d)-, back, away; moveō, move], remove, dismiss.

re-mūneror, -ārī, -ātus [re(d)-, back, in **return;** mūneror, bestow], recompense.

Remus, -ī, M., one of the Remi (see Rēmī), a **Reman.**

re-novō, -āre, -āvī, -ātus [re(d)-, again, novō, make NEW], reNEW.

re-nūntiō, -āre, -āvī, -ātus [re(d)-, back; nūntiō, bring word], bring back word, report.

re-pellō, -ere, reppulī, repulsus [re(d)-, back; pellō, drive], drive back.

repente, adv. [case fm. of repēns, sudden], suddenly.

repentinus, -a, -um [repent- (st. of repēns), sudden], sudden.

re-periō, -īre, repperī, repertus [re(d)-, again; pariō, procure], find, find out (by making inquiry) learn, ascertain, discover; invent, devise.

re-petō, -ere, -īvī **or** -iī, -ītus [re(d)-, again; petō, demand], demand back, demand; lay claim to.

re-prehendō, -ere, -hendī, -hēnsus [re(d)-, *back*; prehendō, *grasp, hold*], *hold back, check; disapprove, reprehend.*
re-primō, -ere, -pressī, -pressus [re(d)-, *back*; premō, *press*], *check, restrain, repress.*
repudiō, -āre, -āvī, -ātus [repudio- (st. of repudium), *rejection*], *reject.*
re-pūgnō, -āre, -āvī, -ātum [re(d)-, *back, against*; pūgnō, *fight*], *oppose, resist.*
re-quīrō, -ere, -sīvī *or* -siī, -sītus [re(d)-, *again*; quaerō, *seek*], *seek after, ask for, be in want of.*
rēs, gen. reī (rĕī, rĕ), F., *thing, affair, matter, subject, object, fact, circumstance, condition, movement, business, enterprise, it;* rēs mīlitāris, *the military art;* rēs frūmentāria, *corn, grain, provisions;* rēs pūblica: *common weal, public welfare; civil affairs, government; commonwealth, state;* summa rēs pūblica, *the highest interests of the commonwealth;* tōta rēs pūblica, *complete control of public affairs;* rēs familiāris, *private resources, patrimony, property;* in turbidīs rēbus, IN *distressed circumstances;* rēs dē, *proposition to.*
re-sistō, -ere, -stitī [re(d)-, *back, against*; sistō, STAnd], *resist.*
re-spondeō, -ēre, -spondī, -spōnsus [re(d)-, *in return*; spondeō, *promise*], (orig., present in return), *answer,* make *answer,* say *or tell in reply.*
respōnsum, -ī, N. [neut. perf. part. of respondeō, *answer*], *answer.*
re-stituō, -ere, -uī, -ūtus [re(d)-, *again*; statuō, *set up*], *restore*
re-tineō, -ēre, -uī, -tentus [re(d)-, *back*; teneō, *hold*], *hold fast, retain, detain, keep.*
re-vellō, -ere, -vellī, -volsus *or* -vulsus [re(d)-, *back, away;* vellō, *pluck, pull*], *pull away, tear away.*
reversiō, -ōnis, F. [re(d)-√vert-, *turn back*], *return.*
re-vertō, -ere, -vertī, -versus [re(d)-, *back;* vertō, *turn*], *turn back; return.*
re-vertor, -ī, -versus [re(d)-, *back;* *vertor, *turn*], *turn back; return.*
re-vocō, -āre, -āvī, -ātus [re(d)-, *back;* vocō, *call*], *recall, restore.*
rēx, rēgis, M. [√rĕg-, *guide, direct*], *king.*
Rhēnus, -ī, M., **Rhine** (river separating Gaul from Germany).
Rhodanus, -ī, M., **Rhone** (river in Gaul).
rīpa, -ae, F., *bank of a river.*
rōbur, -oris, N., *oak.*
rogō, -āre, -āvī, -ātus, *ask.*
Rōma, -ae, F., **Rome** (city on the Tiber in Italy).
Rōmānus, -a, -um, adj [Rōmā- (st. of Rōma), *Rome*], *belonging to* **Rome** (see Rōma), *Roman;* subst., Rōmāna, -ae, F., *Roman woman.*
Rōmānī, -ōrum, M., *Romans* (inhabitants of Rome; see Rōma).
rota, -ae, F., *wheel.*
ruber, -bra, -brum, adj. [√rub-, REDDen], RED.
Rūfus, -ī, M., *Lucius Vibullius Rufus* (adherent of Pompey).
ruīna, -ae, F. [conn. w. ruō, *fall violently*], *downfall, crash.*
rūmor, -ōris, M., (orig., noise, murmur, and so) *hearsay, rumor, report.*
rūpēs, -is, F. [√rŭp-, *break*], (broken, precipitous) *rock.*
rūrsus, adv. [= revorsus, perf. part. of revertō, *turn back*], *again.*
rūs, rūris, N., *the country* (opp. the city).

S.

Sabis, -is, M., *the Sabis* (mod. Sambre, river in Belgic Gaul).
Saburra, -ae, M., *Saburra* (lieutenant of Juba, king of Numidia).
sacrificium, -iī, N. [sacrifico- (st. of sacrificus), *sacrificial*], *sacrifice.*
sacrō, -āre, -āvī, -ātus [sacro- (st. of sacer), *sacred*], *declare sacred.*

saepe, adv [neut. acc. of *sacpis, crowded, frequent;* conn. w. saepēs, *hedge*], *often.*
saepe numerō or saepenumerō [saepe, *often;* numerō, *in number*], *oftentimes, again and again.*
saepēs, -is, F. [conn. w. saepe, q. v.], *hedge, fence.*
saeviō, -īre, -iī, -itum [saevo-(st. of saevus), *fierce, be fierce, rage*
sagittārius, -iī, M. [adj. used subst., fr. sagittā- (st. of sagitta), *arrow*], (one having to do with arrows, and so) *archer, bowman.*
salūs, -ūtis, F. [conn. w. salvus, **safe**], *safety.*
salūtāris, -e, adj. [salūt- (st. of salūs), *safety*], *pertaining to safety, salutary.*
salūtō, -āre, -āvī, -ātus [salūt- (st. of salūs), *safety*], *wish safety to, greet, pay one's respects to, salute.*
salvus, -a, -um, adj. [√sal- (akin to √ser- in servus), *protect, support*], *sound, unimpaired, safe, unharmed, preserved.*
sanciō, -īre, sanxī, **sānctus** (sancītus, once) [conn. w. sacer, *sacred*], *render sacred;* (of laws) *establish, ordain, enact.*
sānctus, -a, -um [p. a. of sanciō, q. v.], *sacred, inviolable.*
sānē, adv. [abl. fm. of sānus, *sound*], *indeed, by all means, for aught I care, if you will.*
sanguis, -inis, M., *blood* (flowing in the body).
Santonī, -ōrum, M., *the Santoni* (tribe in Celtic Gaul on the northern bank of the Garonne).
sapiēns, -entis, p. a. (of sapiō, *taste; discern*) *discerning, wise.*
Sardinia, -ae, F., *Sardinia* (island in the Mediterranean, west of Italy).
Sardiniēnsis, -e, adj. [Sardiniā- (st. of Sardinia), *Sardinia*], *of Sardinia, Sardinian* (see Sardinia).
sarmenta, -ōrum, N. (usu. pl.) [√sarp-, *lop, prune*], (what is lopped, and so) *light branches.*

sarmentum, see sarmenta.
satis, adv., *enough, sufficiently; very.*
satis faciō or satisfaciō, -ere, -fēcī, -factum [satis, *enough;* faciō, DO], *give satisfaction, make reparation.*
saxum, -ī, N., *stone* (large and rough).
Scaevola, -ae, M., *Quintus Mucius Scaevola* (augur and jurist of Cicero's time; he was a son-in-law of Laelius).
scelerātus, -a, -um [perf. part. of scelerō, *pollute*], *polluteD; accurseD.*
scelus, -eris, N., *crime.*
scientia, -ae, F. [scient- (st. of sciēns), *knowing*], *knowledge, skill.*
sciō, -īre, -īvī, -ītus, *know.*
Scīpiō, -ōnis, M., 1. *Publius Cornelius Scipio Africanus Major* (conqueror of Hannibal at Zama 202 B.C.). 2. *Publius Cornelius Scipio Africanus Minor* (destroyer of Carthage 146 B.C.).
scrībō, -ere, scrīpsī, scrīptus [√scrīb-, *dig,* GRAVE], (cut with a pointed instrument, grave, and so) *write.*
scūtum, -ī, N. [√scū-, *cover*], *an oblong shield* (the scūtum of the Roman legionaries was made of wood covered with leather; it was semi-cylindrical in shape, and was 4½ ft. long by 2½ ft. broad); see Fig. 8.

Fig. 8. Shield (scūtum) of the Roman infantry soldier, from the column of Trajan. The decoration represents a thunderbolt.

sē-cernō, -ere, -crēvī, -crētus [sē(d)-, *apart;* cernō, *separate*], *set apart,* **separate.**
secundus, -a, -um, adj. [= *sequendus, gerundive of sequor, follow*], *(following, and so) second; favorable.*

sed, conj., *but.*
sedeō, -ēre, sēdī, sessum, SIT.
sēdēs, -is, F. [√sed-, SIT; cf. sedeō], SEAT: *habitation, abode.*
Segusiāvī, -ōrum, M., *the Segusiavi* (tribe in Celtic Gaul on the Rhone).
sē-jungō, -ere, -jūnxī, -jūnctus [sē(d)-, *apart;* jungō, *join*], *disjoin, separate, sever.*
Seleucus, -ī, M., *Seleucus* (one of the ablest generals of Alexander the Great; murdered by Ptolemy Ceraunus 280 B.C.).
sēmen, -inis, N. [√se-, SOW], (that which is sown, and so) SEED; *origin, source.*
sēmentis, -is, F. [sēmen, SEED], sow*ing*
sēminārium, -iī, N. [adj. used subst., fr. sēmin- (st. of sēmen), SEED], (having to do with seed, and so) *nursery.*
semper, adv. [conn. w. Lat. similis and English SAME], *always.*
Semprōnia, -ae, F., *Sempronia* (wife of Decimus Junius Brutus; Sempronia was implicated in Catiline's conspiracy 63 B.C.).
senātor, -ōris, M. [conn. w. senex and senātus], *senator.*
senātus, -ūs, M. [conn. w. senex, *elder*], *council of elders, senate.*
senātūs cōnsultum or **senātūscōnsultum,** -ī, N., *decree of the senate.*
senectūs, -ūtis, F. [senec- (st. of senex), *old*], *old age.*
senex, senis, adj., *old, aged;* subst., *old man* or *woman.*
senīlis, -e, adj. [sen- (st. of senex), *old person*], *belonging to an old person, senile.*
Senonēs or **Sēnōnēs,** -um, M., *the Senones* (tribe in Celtic Gaul along the upper Seine).
sēnsus, -ūs, M. [base sent- (in sentiō), *become aware through the senses*], *sense-perception; sense.*
sententia, -ae, F. [conn. w. sen-
tiō, *think*], *opinion, view; vote;* ad sententiam redīre, *to come back to the main question;* in eam sententiam, *to this effect, of this purport.*
sentiō, -īre, sēnsī, sēnsus, *perceive, be aware; think.*
septem, indecl. num. adj., SEVEN.
septentriō, -ōnis, M.; also pl., **septentriōnēs,** -um, M. [septem, SEVEN; triōnēs, *ploughing oxen*], *the SEVEN prominent stars in the constellation Ursa Major or the Great Bear; the north.*
septimus, -a, -um, ord. num. adj. [septem, SEVEN], SEVEN*th.*
Sēquanī, -ōrum, M., *the Sequani* (tribe in Celtic Gaul enclosed by the Saône, the Rhone, and Mt. Jura); sing., **Sēquanus,** -ī, M., *a Sequanian.*
sequor, -ī, secūtus [√sequ-, *follow*], *follow, pursue.*
sermō, -ōnis, M. [√ser-, *connect*], (connected discourse, and so) *conversation, intercourse.*
servīlis, -e, adj. [servo- (st. of servus), *slave*], *pertaining to a slave, servile.*
serviō, -īre, -īvī and -iī, -ītum [servo- (st. of servus), *slave*], *be a slave, serve, submit to.*
servitūs, -ūtis, F. [servo- (st. of servus), *slave*], *slavery, servitude; serfdom, vassalage.*
servō, -āre, -āvī, -ātus [servo- (st. of servus), *protected;* see servus], *protect, preserve; keep, lay by.*
servus, -ī, M. [√ser- (akin to √sal- in salvus), *protect*], (a captive in war, not killed, but saved alive, and so) *slave.*
Sēstius, -iī, M., *Publius Sestius* (tribune of the people 57 B.C., and friend of Cicero).
sevērus, -a, -um, adj., *severe.*
sex, indecl. num. adj., SIX.
sexāgintā, indecl. num. adj. [sexā-, conn. w. sex, SIX; -gintā represents (de)cem, TEN], SIXTY.

Sextius, -iī, M., *Titus Sextius* (one of Caesar's lieutenants).

sextus, -a, -um, ord. num. adj. [sex, SIX], SIXTH; sextus decimus, SIXTEENTH.

sī, conj., *if;* sī quis, *if any one;* sī quī, *if any* (see quis and quī).

sīc, adv., *in such a way, so, in this way, thus; as follows; to such a degree;* ut ... sīc, *as ... so, although ... yet.*

sīcut and **sīcutī,** adv. [sīc, so; ut or utī, *as*], *just as, as.*

sīdus, -eris, N., *group of stars, constellation; star.*

significō, -āre, -āvī, -ātus [sīgnific-(st. of *signifex), *sign-making*], *show by signs, show, make evident.*

signum, -ī, N., *sign, signal;* in pl., *military standards;* signa ferre, *to advance against the enemy;* conversa signa inferre, *to face about and advance against the enemy;* infestīs signīs cōnsistere, *to come to a halt and assume the defensive;* see Fig. 9.

silva, -ae, F., *wood, forest.*

silvestris, -e, adj.[conn.w.silva, *wood*], *overgrown with wood, wooded.*

similis, -e, adj. [cognate w. SAME], *like.*

simul, adv [neut. fm. of similis, *like*], *at the* SAME *time;* simul atque, *as soon as.*

simulācrum, -ī, N. [simulā-(st. of simulō), *imitate*], *image.*

simulō, -āre, -āvī, -ātus [fr. st. of similis, *like,* seen in adv. simul], *imitate; pretend.*

sin, conj. [sī, *if;* nē, *Not*], *if however, but if.*

Fig. 9.
Military standards, from a medal. The middle figure represents the eagle, the standard of the legion; the two side figures represent the standards of cohorts.

sine, prep. w. abl. [sī, *if, in that case;* nē, Not], *without.*

singulī, -ae, -a, distr. num. adj., *one by one,* **single,** *individual, separate, several;* translated adv., *singly, individually;* in annōs singulōs, *each* or *every year.*

sinister, -tra, -trum, adj., *left.*

sī quidem or **sīquidem,** conj. [sī, *if;* quidem, *indeed*], *since indeed.*

sitis, -is, F., *thirst.*

sitiō, -īre, -īvī or -iī [siti- (st. of sitis), *thirst*], *thirst.*

situs, -ūs, M. [√si-, *put*], (putting or placing, and so) *position, situation.*

socer, -erī, M., *father-in-law.*

socius, -iī, M. [adj. used subst., fr. √soc-, *follow;* conn. w. sequor], *associate, confederate, ally.*

Sōcraticus, -a, -um, adj. [borrowed from the Greek], *belonging to Socrates* (celebrated Athenian philosopher; lived 468–399 B.C.); subst., *disciple of Socrates.*

sodālis, -is, C., *mate, comrade, intimate.*

sōl, sōlis, M., *sun.*

soleō, -ēre, -itus, *be accustomed, be wont.*

sōlitūdō, -inis, F. [sōlo- (st. of sōlus), *alone*], *solitude; deserted place* or *tract, desert, wilderness.*

sollicitō, -āre, -āvī, -ātus [sollicito- (st. of sollicitus), *agitated*], *stir up, agitate, urge, stimulate, incite; approach with corrupt overtures, corruptly solicit.*

Solōn (Solō), -ōnis, M., *Solon* (famous Athenian law-giver; his public career belongs to the first half of the sixth century B.C.).

solum, -ī, N., *ground, soil.*

sōlum, adv. [neut. of sōlus, *alone*], *only;* nōn sōlum, *Not only.*

sōlus, -a, -um, adj. *alone, only, sole.*

somnus, -ī, M. [for *sopnus, fr. √sop-, *sleep*], *sleep.*

somnium, -iī, N. [adj. used subst., fr. somno- (st. of somnus), *sleep*], (resulting from **sleep**, and so) *dream*.

spatium, -ĭī, N. [√spa-, SPAN, *stretch out*], *space; distance; time enough, time; interval, division, period*.

speciēs, gen. -ē, F. [√spec-, SPY], *seeing; appearance; show*.

spectāculum, -ī, N. [spectā- (st. of spectō), *look at*], *spectacle, sight*.

spectō, -āre, -āvī, -ātus [intens. of speciō, formed as if from a perf. part. *spectus], *look at; face, extend; regard, heed*.

spērō, -āre, -āvī, -ātus [conn. w. spēs, *hope*], *hope, look for*.

spēs, gen. -ēī (-ĕī), F., *hope; prospect; hopefulness;* in spem venīre, *to cherish or entertain hope*.

spīritus, -ūs, M. [conn. w. spīrō, *breathe*], *breath*.

spolium, -ĭī, N., usu. in pl., **spolia**, -ōrum, N., *spoils*.

sponte, abl. F. (only in gen. [spontis] and abl. sing.), *impulse;* sponte is regularly accompanied by a poss. pron.; as, tuā sponte, *of your own free will*.

statim, adv. [acc. fm. of st. stati-, fr. √sta-, STAND], *on the spot, forthwith*.

statiō, -ōnis, F. [√sta-, STAND], STANDing; *station, post;* in statiōne, ON *guard*.

Stator, -ōris, M. [√sta- (causative), *make* STAND], STAYer, *supporter* (epithet of Jupiter).

statuō, -ere, -uī, -ūtus [statu- (st. of status), STANDing, *position*], *put in position, set up, station; decide, determine, resolve*.

statūra, -ae, F. [√sta-, STAND], (standing, and so) *stature*.

stipendium, -ĭī, N. [= *stipipendium, fr. stipi- (st. of *stips), *contribution;* base pend- (in pendo), *pay*], (payment of a contribution, and so) *tribute, tribute money*.

stirps, -is, F., *stock, root; origin, source*.

stō, -āre, stetī [√sta-, STAND], STAND; *abide;* dēcrētō stāre, *acquiesce in a decision*.

strepitus, -ūs, M. [base strep- (in strepō), *make a noise*], *noise, din*.

studeō, -ēre, -uī, *be eager for, strive earnestly for, apply one's self to, devote special attention to, cultivate; exercise partiality*.

studiōsus, -a, -um, adj. [studio- (st. of studium), *zeal*], *full of zeal, zealous, earnest; eager* [for], *assiduous* [in], *fond* [of].

studium, -ĭī, N. [base stud- (in studeō), *be eager*], *eagerness, earnest desire, zeal, enthusiasm; devotion, attachment; pursuit.* In pl., *zealous efforts; studies, pursuits*.

suāsor, -ōris [√suād-, *make* SWEET, *urge, advise*], (one who advises, and so) *adviser;* suāsor esse, *to advise*.

sub, prep. w. acc. and abl., *under;* sub occāsum, *towards the setting*.

sub-dūcō, -ere, -dūxī, -ductus [sub, *from* under; dūcō, *draw*], *withdraw*.

sub-eō, -īre, -īvī or -ĭī, subitus [sub, *under;* eō, *go*], *go under, go close to, approach; come stealthily;* (w. acc.) *undergo, submit to*.

sub-igō, -ere, -ēgī, -āctus [sub, *under;* agō, *drive, force*], *constrain, impel, prompt*.

subitō, adv. [n. abl. of subitus, *sudden*], *suddenly*.

subitus, -a, -um [p. a. of subeō, *come stealthily*], *sudden*.

sublātus, -a, -um, perf. part., RAISED (see tollō).

submōtus, -a, -um [perf. part. of submoveō, *remove, drive back*], *driven back;* subst., **submōtī**, *those driven back*.

sub-sequor, -ī, -cūtus [sub, *close upon;* sequor, *follow*], *follow close upon, follow, succeed*.

subsidium, -ĭī, N. [sub-√sed-, SIT *in support of*], (sitting in reserve for support, and so) **support**, *aid, relief*.

sub-sistō, -ere, -stitī [sub, under; sistō, STA*nd* STI*ll*], *come to a halt, halt; maintain one's ground, with*STA*nd*.

sub-trahō, -ere, -xī, -ctus [sub, *from under;* trahō, *draw*], *withdraw, keep out of reach*.

sub-veniō, -īre, -vēnī, -ventum [sub, *under, to the support of;* veniō, COME], COME *to the support of*.

suc-cēdō, -ere, -cessī, -cessum [sub, *under, close upon;* cēdō, *go*], *follow close upon,* **succeed**.

suc-cendo, -ere, -cendī, -census [sub, *from below;* *cendō(√cand-), *set fire*], *set fire to* (from below).

Suēbī, -ōrum, M., *the* **Suebi** or **Swabians** (collective name of several German tribes; their king at the time of Caesar's first campaign in Gaul was Ariovistus).

Suēbus, -a, -um, adj., *pertaining to the Suebi, Swabian*.

Suessiōnēs, -um, M., *the* **Suessiones** (tribe in Belgic Gaul).

suffrāgium, -ī, N. [sub-√frāg-, BREAK *somewhat* or *partially*], (fragment used for voting, and so) *voting tablet;* *vote,* **suffrage**.

suī, gen.(nom. wanting), reflex pron., *of himself, herself, itself, themselves;* **inter sē**, see inter.

Sulla, -ae, M., *Lucius Cornelius Sulla* (famous Roman dictator 82–79 B.C.).

sum, esse, fuī [sum,√s-,*be* ; esse, √es-, *be;* fuī, √fu-, *grow, become*], BE (cognate w. √fu-), *exist, prevail, consist, live, remain*.

summa, -ae, F. [fem. of summus (sc. res), *highest*], *the main thing,* sum; *supreme control* or *direction;* **in summā**, IN *general*.

summōtus, see submōtus.

summus, -a, **-um**, adj., superl. of superus, q. v.

sūmō, -ere, sūmpsī, sūmptus [sub, *from under,* UP; emō, *take*], *take* UP, *take; assume, arrogate;* **sibi sūmere,***to take* UPON *one's self,*

to assume; **supplicium sūmere dē**, *to exact punishment from, to inflict punishment on*.

sūmptnōsus, -a, -um, adj. [sūmptu- (st. of sūmptus), *expense*], **expensive**, *costly*.

sūmptus, -ūs, M. [sūm- for sub-√em-, *take* UP (for some purpose, and so) **spend**], *expense;* in pl., *extravagance*.

superbia, -ae, F. [superbo- (**st.** of superbus), *proud*], *pride, arrogance*.

superior, -ius, **adj., comp.** of superus, q. v.

superō, -āre, **-āvī**, -ātus [supero- (st. of **superus**), *above*] (be above, and **so**) *be left* OVER, *remain, survive; surpass, exceed; beat, defeat,* OVER*come, conquer, vanquish;* **vitā superāre**, *outlive*.

superstitiō, -ōnis, F. [super-sta-, STA*nd* OVER], (standing over as in wonder, awe, etc., and so) *exaggerated fear of the gods,* **superstition**.

super-sum, -esse, -fuī [super, OVER; sum, *be*], BE *left, remain*.

superus, -a, -um, adj. [conn. w. sub, *from under,* UP], *above*. Comp., **superior**, -ius, *higher,* UP*per;* (of time) *preceding, former;* **superiōre nocte**, NIGHT *before last*. Superl., **summus**, -a, -um, *highest; greatest, chief; of the highest importance; supreme;* *extreme;* **summus mōns**, *the summit of the* **mountain**; **summus cruciātus**, *the severest punishment*.

sup-plex, -icis, adj. [sub, *under;* √plec-, FO*ld, bend*], (kneeling, and so) *suppliant;* translated adv., *in supplication*.

supplicātiō, -ōnis, F. [supplicā- (st. of supplicō), *kneel to,* **pray** *to*], (kneeling to, praying to, **and** so) *public supplication; thanksgiving*.

supplicium, -iī, N. [supplic- (st. of supplex), *suppliant*], (humiliation, and so) *punishment;* in pl., *sacrifice*.

sup-portō, -āre, -āvī, -ātus [sub, *from below*, UP *to;* portō, *convey*], *convey to a place, bring* UP.

suprā, adv. and prep. w. acc. [abl. fem. of superus, aBOVE], 1. adv., *aBOVE;* (of time) *before, previously.* 2. prep., *before.*

suspiciō, -ōnis, F. [conn. w suspiciō, *look askance at*], *suspicion; ground of suspicion;* **in suspiciōnem venīre,** *to be attended with suspicion, to be open to* **suspicion.**

sus-tĭneō, -ēre, -uī, -tentus [*subs, collateral fm. of sub, *from below*, UP; teneō, *hold*], *support, sustain; perform, discharge; rein in, check; withstand.*

suus, -a, -um, poss. pron., *his own, her own, its own, their own; his, her, its, their;* subst., **suī,** *his men.*

Syrācūsae, -ārum, F., *Syracuse* (city on the eastern coast of Sicily).

T.

T., abbr. of **Titus, -ī,** M., *Titus,* (Roman praenōmen or first name).

tābēscō, -ere, tābuī [inceptive fr. tābē- (st. of tābeō), *melt*], *begin to melt; pine away.*

tabula, -ae, F., *board, plank; writing tablet;* **tabula picta,** *painting.*

tabulātum, -ī, N. [neut. of tabulātus, *boarded*], *flooring, story.*

taceō, -ēre, -uī, -itus, *be silent; pass over in silence.*

taedet, -ēre, -duit or (rarely) **-sum est,** *it wearies;* **mē taedet,** *I am weary.*

talentum, -ī, N., *talent* (sum of money equivalent in value to about $1080).

tālis, -e, adj. [pron. st. to-, THAt; cf. quālis], *of THAt kind, of such a kind, such.*

tam, adv., *so;* **nōn tam,** *Not so,* NOt *so much.*

tamen, adv., *neverTHEless, yet, still, however, notwithstanding.*

tametsī, conj. [tamen, *neverTHEless;* etsī, *although*], *alTHough.*

tandem, adv., *at length;* (in exclam.) *pray.*

tantulus, -a, -um, adj. [dim. fr. tanto- (st. of tantus), *so great*], *so small, so slight.*

tantummodo, adv. [tantum, *so much, so far,* n. acc. of tantus; modo, *only*], *only, merely.*

tantus, -a, -um, adj. [pron. st. to-, THAt; cf. quantus], *so great, so much, so strong a, so important, such* (= *so great*); *so foul, so heinous, of such enormity;* **quantus ... tantus,** HOW *much ... so much,* and *so as much ... as;* **quantō ... tantō,** *by* HOW *much ... by so much, the ...* THE; *est* **tantī,** *it is worth while.*

tardō, -āre, -āvī, -ātus [tardo- (st. of tardus), *slow*], *make slow, retard, delay, hinder.*

tardus, -a, -um, adj., *slow, tardy.*

Tasgetius, -iī, M., *Tasgetius* (chief of the Carnutes in the time of Caesar).

taurus, -ī, M. [for *staurus; cognate w. English STEER], *bull.*

Taurus, -ī, M., *Taurus* (mountain range in Asia Minor).

tectum, -ī, N. [n. perf. part. of tegō, *cover*], *roof; dwelling.*

tegō, -ere, tēxī, tectus [√teg-, *cover;* cognate w. English THATCH and DECK], *cover.*

tēlum, -ī, N., *javelin; weapon.*

temerārius, -a, -um, adj. [F. st. contained in adv. temerē, *rashly*], *headstrong, rash, indiscreet.*

temperō, -āre, -āvī, -ātus [conn. w. tempus, (lit.) *portion*], *apportion duly;* (conduct one's self with due proportion, and so) *refrain, abstain;* (w. dat.) *restrain.*

tempestās, -ātis, F. [conn. w. tempus, *time*], *time; weather; storm.*

templum, -ī, N. [prob. for *temulum, dim. fr. √tem-, *cut,* through lost subst.], (orig. a space marked off by the augur's wand and consecrated, and so) *a consecrated place; temple.*

tempus, -oris, N. [√tem-, *cut*], (lit., a *section* or *portion*, and so) *a period of time, season, time.*

tendō, -ere, tetendī, tēnsus or tentus [√ten-, *stretch*], *stretch, stretch out, extend.*

tenebrae, -ārum, F., *darkness.*

teneō, -ēre, -uī [√ten-, *stretch*], *hold fast, hold, keep; occupy; detain;* (with **quōminus**) *restrain,* **prevent;** (culpā) **tenērī,** *to be controlled by, to be under the dominion of, to be subject to, to be chargeable with; enchain, hold spell-bound, paralyze;* (of wind) adversum tenēre, *to blow in the face of.*

tentō or **temptō,** -āre, -āvī, -ātus [intens. fr. tento- (st. of perf. part. of tendō, *stretch*)], *attempt, try to effect, test.*

tenus, prep. w. abl. (follows its word) [√ten-, *stretch*], *as far as.*

tergum, -ī, N., *back.*

ternī, -ae, -a, distr. num. adj. [tri- (st. of trēs) THREE], THREE and THREE, *in groups of* THREE, THREE *from* each, THREE *apiece,* THREE *each.*

terra, -ae, F. [for *tersa, fr. √ters-, *be dry;* conn. w. Lat. torreō, *parch,* and cognate w. English THIRST], *dry land, land, earth, ground;* **terrā,** *by land, on land; land, country;* in pl., *the earth* (as made up of various lands).

terreō, -ēre, -uī, -itus [for *terseō, √ters-, *tremble*], *frighten, terrify, alarm.*

terribilis, -e, adj. [conn. w. terreō, *frighten*], *frightful, terrible.*

terror, -ōris, M. [for *tersor, fr. √ters-, *tremble*], *fright, alarm, terror.*

tertius, -a, -um, ord. num. adj. [conn. w. trēs, THREE], THIRD.

testāmentum, -ī, N. [testā- (st. of testor), *bear witness*], (what is acknowledged before witnesses, and so) *will.*

testis, -is, C., *witness.*

theātrum, -ī, N. [borrowed from the Greek], *theatre.*

Thēbae, -ārum, F., *Thebes* (most important city of Boeotia).

Thrasybūlus, -ī, M., *Thrasybulus* (distinguished Athenian general; freed Athens from the yoke of the thirty tyrants 403 B.C.).

Thūȳs, Thūȳnis, M., *Thuys* (prince in Paphlagonia).

Tigurīnus pāgus, -ī, M., *Tigurine district* (one of the four divisions of the Helvetian country; its inhabitants were called Tigurīnī).

timeō, -ēre, -uī, *fear.*

timor, -ōris, M. [√tim-, *choke, be breathless;* coun. w. timeō], *fear, alarm; cowardice.*

Titūrius, -iī, M., *Quintus Titurius Sabinus* (one of Caesar's lieutenants in the Gallic war).

Titus, -ī, M., *Titus* (Roman praenōmen or first name).

tolerō, -āre, -āvī, -ātus [conn. w. tollō (√tol-), *raise*], *sustain.*

tollō, -ere, (sustulī), (sublātus) [√tol-, *lift, raise;* perf. and perf. part. borrowed from sustollō], *raise; remove, take away, break off; put an end to.*

Tolōsa, -ae, F., *Tolosa* (mod. Toulouse, city in the Roman province of Gaul).

tormentum, -ī, N. [√tor(qu)-, *twist, hurl*], (means of hurling, and so) *engine for hurling missiles; instrument of torture; torture.*

tōtus, -a, -um, adj., *whole, all, entire, complete, throughout.*

trā-dō, -ere, -didī, -ditus [trā(ns), *over;* dō, *give*], *surrender, deliver; intrust, impart.*

trā-dūcō, -ere, -dūxī, -ductus [trā(ns), *across;* dūcō, *lead*], *lead, convey* or *conduct across.*

tragoedia, -ae, F. [borrowed from the Greek], *tragedy.*

trahō, -ere, traxī, tractus, *draw, drag.*

trā-iciō (pronounced : trājiciō)

-ere, -jēcī, -jectus [trā(ns), *across;* jaciō, *throw*], *throw across, convey over.*

tranquillus, -a, -um, adj., *tranquil, undisturbed.*

trāns, prep. w. acc., *across.*

trāns-eō, -īre, -īvī or -iī, -itus [trans, *across;* eō, *go*], *go over or across, cross, pass over, pass; remove, migrate.*

trāns-ferō, -ferre, -tulī, -lātus [trāns, *over, across;* ferō, BEAR], BRI*ng over, transfer, transplant.*

trāns-fīgō, -ere, -fīxī, -fīxus [trāns, THR*ough;* fīgō, *fix, thrust*], *pierce.*

trāns-portō, -āre, -āvī, -ātus [trāns, *across;* portō, *convey*], *transport.*

trānsversus, -a, -um [perf. part. of trānsvertō, *turn across*], *transverse, cross.*

trecentī, -ae, -a, num. adj. [tri- (st. of trēs), THREE; st. of centum, HUND*red*], THREE HUND*red.*

trepidō, -āre, -āvī, -ātus [trepido- (st. of trepidus), *restless, alarmed*], *be in a state of trepidation or alarm.*

trēs, tria, num. adj., THREE.

Trēverī, -ōrum, M., *the Treveri* (tribe in Belgic Gaul in the lower valley of the Moselle).

tribūnus, -ī, M. [tribu- (st. of tribus), *tribe*], (orig., head of a tribe) *tribune;* tribūnus mīlitum, *military tribune* (there were six tribunes attached to each legion, and they commanded in turn, each two months at a time; they seldom led troops in battle, but were employed for the most part in routine administrative duties).

tribuō, -ere, -uī, -ūtus [tribu- (st. of tribus), *tribe*], (orig., assign to a tribe, and so) *assign, ascribe, award, allot, bestow, give, contribute, confer, render.*

tribūtum, -ī, N. [n. perf. part. of tribuō, *contribute*, used subst.], *tribute, tribute money.*

• **trīduum**, -ī, N. [trī-, conn. w.

trēs, THREE; -duum, conn. w. diēs, *day*], *space of* THREE *days.*

trīgintā, indecl. num. adj. [trī-, conn. w. trēs, THREE; -gin- represents (de)cem, TEN], THIRTY.

trīnī, -ae, -a, distr num. adj, used with substs. pl. in form, but sing. in meaning [conn. w. trēs, THREE], THREE.

trī-plex, -icis, adj. [tri- (st. of trēs), THREE; √plec-, FOL*d*], THREEFOL*d, triple.*

trīsticulus, -a, -um, adj. [dim. fr. trīsti- (st. of trīstis), *sorrowful*], *somewhat sorrowful.*

trīstis, -e, *sad, gloomy.*

trīstitia, -ae, F. [trīsti- (st. of trīstis), *sad*], *sadness.*

triumphus, -ī, M., *triumph.*

tū, tuī, pers. pron., THOU, *you.*

tuba, -ae, F., *a straight trumpet;* see Fig. 10.

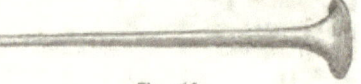

Fig. 10.
Tuba, from the arch of Titus.

Tuberō, -ōnis, M., *Lucius Tubero* (one of Pompey's lieutenants).

Tulingī, -ōrum, M., *the Tulingi* (German tribe on the Rhine, north of the Helvetii).

Tullius, -iī, M., *Marcus Tullius Cicero* (the famous Roman orator).

Tullus, -ī, M., *Lucius Vocatius Tullus* (consul 66 B.C.).

tum, adv., *at* THA*t time,* THEN; tum cum, *at* THE *time* WHEN, *at* THE *moment* WHEN.

tumulus, -ī, M. [dim. fr. √tu-, *swell* (through *tumus*)], (orig., *a little swelling*, and so) *rising ground, earth-mound; pile, heap.*

tumultus, -ūs, M. [tumulo- (st. of tumulus), *swelling*], *tumult* (especially used of an outbreak in Italy or Gaul).

turba, -ae, F. [conn. w. turma, *throng*], *uproar; crowd, multitude,* *mob*; **turba et conluviō**, *vile rabble*.

turbĭdus, -a, -um, adj. [turbā- (st. of turba), *uproar*], *disturbed; troubled, dangerous*.

turma, -ae, F. [conn. w. turba, *uproar*], *throng; squadron*.

turpis, -e, adj., *base, disgraceful, unbecoming, indecorous*.

turris, -is, F., *tower, turret*.

tūtus, -a, -um [p. a. of **tueor**, *protect*], (protected, and so) *safe, secure*.

tuus, -a, -um, poss. pron. [**conn.** w. tū, THOU], THY, *your*; tuā rēfert, *it concerns you, it is of importance to you*.

tyrannus, -ī, M. [borrowed from the Greek], *tyrant*.

U.

ubĭ, adv. [= *cubī = *quobī, loc. **fm. of** pron. st. quo-], 1. (of place) WHEre; WHErever. 2. (of time) WHEn; **ubĭ prīmum**, *as soon as*.

Ubii, -ōrum, M., *the Ubii* (a German people on the right bank of the Rhine).

ubīvis, adv. [ubī, WHEre; vīs (volō), *you* WILL], WHEre *you* WILL, *in any place* WHAtever.

ūllus, -a, -um, adj. (used where a negative is expressed or implied) [dim. fr. ūno- (**st. of** ūnus), ONE], (least one, **and so**) ANy at all, ANy; subst., ANy ONE.

ultĕrĭor, -ius, adj. [comp. of *ulter, *on the farther side*], *farther*. Superl., **ultĭmus**, -a, -um, *farthest, remotest*.

ultĭmus, -a, -um, superl. of ultĕrĭor, q. v.

ultrā, adv. and prep. w. acc. [abl. fem. of *ulter, *on the farther side*], *beyond*.

ultrō, adv. [case fm. of *ulter, *on the farther side*, used adv.], *to the farther side, beyond; without urging, of one's own motion, voluntarily, spontaneously*.

Umbrēnus, -ī, M., *Umbrenus* (freedman implicated in Catiline's conspiracy 63 B.C.).

umerus, -ī, M., *shoulder*.

umquam, see unquam.

'**ūnā**, adv. [abl. fem. of ūnus, ONE], *in company, together, in common, at the same time*.

ūndēvīcēsĭmus, -a, -um, ord. num. adj. [ūndēvīgintī, ONE *from* TWENTY or *nine*TEEN], *nine*TEEN*th*.

undĭque, adv., *on all sides, from all parts or quarters*.

ūnĭ-versus, -a, -um, adj. [ūno- (st. of ūnus), ONE; versus, perf. part. of vertō, *turn*], (all combined in one, **and so**) *all together, all in* A *body*.

unquam or umquam, adv. (generally used where a neg. is expressed or implied; cf. quisquam), *ever, at any time*.

ūnus, -a, -um, num. adj., ONE; A *single*, A; *the same*; alONE, ONly, *sole*. In pl., (usu.) alONE; (with substs. pl. in form, but sing. in sense) ONE.

urbānus, **-a**, **-um**, adj [urbi- (**st. of urbs**), *city*], *belonging to the city, in the city*.

urbs, -is, F., *city, town*.

ūrus, -ī, M., *the ure-ox*.

ūsūra, -ae, F. [base ūt- (in ūtor) *use*], *use, enjoyment*.

ūsus, -ūs, M. [base ūt- (in ūtor), *use*], *use; advantage; experience, skill, acquaintance; service; occasion, need, necessity;* ex ūsū, *expedient, advantageous;* ex ūsū, w. gen., *for the advantage*.

ut or utī, adv. and conj., HOW; *as, in proportion as;* ut ... sīc, *as ... so, although ... yet;* (w. perf. indic.) *as soon as*, WHEn; (in final clauses) *in order that, that;* (after verbs of fearing) *that not;* (in clauses of result) *so that, that*.

uter, utra, utrum, interrog. and indef. rel. pron. [= *cuter = *quoter, comp. fm. of pron. st. quo-; cf. English WHO and WHETHER],

1. interrog. *which (of two).* 2. indef. rel., *whichever* (*of* two).

uterque, utraque, utrumque, indef. pron. [uter; cf. quisque from quis], *each of two, both.*

Ŭtica, -ae, F., *Utica* (city in northern Africa, north of Carthage).

ūtĭlis, -e, adj. [base ūt- (in ūtor), *use*], *useful.*

ūtĭlĭtās, -ātis, F. [ūtĭli- (st. of ūtilis), *useful*], *usefulness, serviceableness, utility.*

utinam, adv [utī (w. vowel shortened), HOW; nam, *pray*], *O that! would that!*

ūtor, -ī, ūsus, *use, make use of, employ; enjoy.*

utrum, adv. [n. acc. of uter, *which of two*], WHETHER.

uxor, -ōris, F., *wife.*

V.

văcātĭō, -ōnis, F. [vacā- (st. of vacō), *be free*], (being free, and so) *exemption.*

văcō, -āre, -āvī, -ātum, *be empty; be free from; (of lands) lie unoccupied.*

văcŭus, -a, -um, adj. [base vac- (in vacō), *be empty*], *vacant, empty.*

vălĕō, -ēre, -uī, (fut. part.) valĭtūrus, *be strong* (physically), *be well; have power, be able; (in leave-taking) farewell;* minus valēre, *not to be strong enough, to be too weak.*

Vălerius, see Procillus.

vallum, -ī, N. [neut. of vallus, *stake*, used in collective sense], (collection of stakes, and so) **wall,** *rampart* (of earth surmounted by **a palisading of** sharpened stakes).

vānĭtās, -ātis, F. [vāno- (st. of vānus), *empty*], *emptiness; vanity.*

Vărus, -ī, M., *Publius Attius Varus* (praetor in Africa and adherent of Pompey).

vastō, -āre, -āvī, -ātus [vasto-

(st. of vastus), *unoccupied,* **waste**], *lay waste.*

vectīgal, -ālis, N. [neut. of vectīgālis (w. final -e lost)], (payment for carriage, and so) *tax; revenue.*

vectīgālis, -e, adj. [conn. w. vehō, *carry*], *pertaining to payment for carriage, pertaining to taxes or tribute; subject to tribute, tributary.*

vĕhĕmenter, adv. [vehement- (st. of vehemēns), *violent,* **vehement**], *violently, impetuously; strongly, powerfully, greatly, exceedingly, severely.*

vel, conj. [prob. imperat. of volō, *wish, choose*], (take your choice, and so) *or, or if you please;* vel ... vel, *either ... or.*

vēlōcĭter, adv. [vēlōci- (st. of vēlōx), *swift*], *swiftly, quickly.*

vēlōx, -ōcis, adj., *swift.*

vēnātĭō, -ōnis, F. [vēnā- (st. of vēnor), *hunt*], *hunting.*

vēn-dō, -ĕre, -dĭdī, -dĭtus (vēn-eō, -īre, -īvī or -iī, -ĭtum, is used as the pass.) [vēnum (acc. of place to which), *sale;* dō, *put*], (expose for sale, and so) *sell.*

Venetī, -ōrum, M., *the Veneti* (tribe in Celtic Gaul on the coast).

vĕnĭō, -īre, vēnī, ventum [vven-, COME], COME; in spem venire, *to cherish or entertain hope.*

ventus, -ī, M., WIND.

verbum, -ī, N. [vver-, *speak*], WORD; in pl., WORDS, *expressions.*

Vercingetorix, -ĭgis, M., *Vercingetorix* (prominent leader of the Gauls in the time of Caesar).

vērē, adv [abl. fm. of vērus, *true*], *truly, rightly.*

vĕreor, -ērī, -ĭtus [vver-, *be wary* (through presumed adj.)], *fear.*

vergō, -ĕre, *incline, slope,* **verge.**

vergobretus, -ī, M., *vergobretus, vergobret* (title of the chief magistrate of the Aedui).

vērĭtās, -ātis, F. [vēro- (st. of vērus), *true*], *truth.*

vērō, adv. [n. abl. of vērus, *true*], *in truth, indeed,* **verily,** *pray; but.*

versor **vinco** **307**

versor, -āri, -ātus [intens., fr. verso- (st. of perf part. of verto, turn)], busy one's self, occupy one's self, engage; **versāri in,** to be encompassed by, to expose one's self to.

versus, -ūs, M. [vvert-, turn], (lit., a turning [of the plow], and so) furrow; verse.

verto, -ere, -tī, -sus, turn.

vērum, adv. [n. acc. of vērus, true], (but in truth, and so) but; **vērum etiam,** but also.

vērus, -a, -um, adj., true; subst., **vērum,** -ī, N., the truth.

vescor, -ī, take food, eat, subsist.

Vesontiō, -ōnis, M., Vesontio (mod. Besançon, chief town of the Sequani in Celtic Gaul).

vesper, -erī and -eris, M., evening.

vester, -tra, -trum, poss. pron. [vōs, you], your (pl.).

vestigium, -ī, N. [conn. w. vestīgō, track, trace], footstep, track; place, spot; **in vestigiō,** on the spot, forthwith.

vestiō, -īre, -īvī or -iī, -ītus [vesti- (st. of vestis), clothing], clothe.

vestītus, -ūs, M. [vestī- (st. of vestiō), clothe], clothing.

vetus, -eris, adj., old; of long standing; **veteran;** former.

vexillum, -ī, N., red flag hoisted on the general's tent as a signal for battle; see Fig. 11.

via, -ae, F. [vveh-, move, carry; conn. w. vehō, carry], WAY, highWAY, road, street; journey, march; distance; method, WAY.

Fig. 11. Vexillum.

viātor, -ōris, M. [viā- (st. of viō), travel], traveller.

Vibullius, see Rufus.

vicēni, -ae, -a, distr. num. adj. [conn. w. viginti, TWENTY], TWENTY each, TWENTY.

vicēsimus, -a, -um, ord. num. adj. [viginti, TWENTY], TWENTI-eth; **vicēsimus sextus,** TWENTY-SIXTH.

victima, -ae, F. [vvig-, be strong, w. superl. suff. (the finest animals being selected for sacrifice)], victim for sacrifice, sacrifice.

victor, -ōris, M. [vvic-, conquer], victor; used adj., victorious.

victōria, -ae, F. [victōr- (st. of victor), victor], victory.

victus, -a, -um [perf. part. of vinco, vanquish], vanquisheD; subst. **victi,** -ōrum, M., the vanquisheD.

victus, -ūs, M. [vvigu-, live], (living, and so) sustenance, food, maintenance; **cōnsuētūdō victūs,** manner of living, mode of life.

vicus, -ī, M. [vvic-, settle; cf. the ending -WICK in English geographical names; as, WarWICK, BerWICK], village.

videō, -ēre, vidī, visus [vvid-, see (through presumed adj. st.)], see. In pass., be seen; seem; seem good.

vigeō, -ēre [vvig-, be strong (through presumed adj. st.); conn. w. vigil, aWAKE], be vigorous, thrive, be **in force.**

vigilia, -ae, F. [vigili- (st. of vigil), aWAKE], WAKEfulness; WATCH (the Romans divided the night, i.e. the interval from sunset to sunrise, into four equal parts called watches; hence the watch, like the hour, varied in length according to the season); in pl., WATCHmen.

vigilō, -āre, -āvī, -ātus [vigili- (st. of vigil), aWAKE], WATCH.

viginti, indecl. num. adj. [vī- (= dvī-), conn. w. duo, TWO; -ginrepresents(de)cem, TEN], TWENTY.

viginti quattuor, indecl. num. adj., TWENTY-FOUR.

viginti quinque, indecl. num. adj., TWENTY-FIVE.

vimen, -inis, N. [vvī-, plait], (that which is plaited, and so) withe, osier.

vincō, -ere, vici, victus [vvic-, conquer], vanquish, conquer.

vīnum, -ī, N., *wine*.
violō, -āre, -āvī, -ātus [conn. w. vīs, *strength, violence*], *injure, offer violence to*.
vir, virī, M., *man; husband*.
virgō, -inis, F., *virgin, maiden*.
virgulta, -ōrum, N. [virgulā- (st. of virgula), *twig*], *shrubbery, brushwood*.
virīlis, -e, adj. [viro- (st. of vir), *man*], *pertaining to a man, manly*.
virtūs, -ūtis, F. [viro- (st. of vir), *man*], *manliness, and so valor, virtue; merit, ability, preëminence; military talent*.
vīs, vīs; pl. vīrēs, vīrium, F. *strength, power, might, vigor, force; violence;* vim facere, *to use force, to resort to force;* vim et manūs inferre, *to lay violent hands upon*.
vīta, -ae, F. [√vī(gu)-, *live*], *life*.
vitiōsus, -a, -um, adj. [vitio- (st. of vitium), *fault*], *full of faults, faulty, defective; corrupt, vicious*.
vitium, -iī, N. [√vi-, *plait*, (through presumed *vitus)], (*a twist, and so) fault; vice*.
vītō, -āre, -āvī, -ātus, *seek to escape, avoid*.
vīvō, -ere, vīxī, (fut. part.) vīctūrus [√vī(g)u-, *live;* cogn. w. Eng. QUICK], *live, be alive;* vītam vīvere, *to pass one's life*.
vīvus, -a, -um, adj. [√vī(g)u-, *live*], *alive, living*.
vix, adv., *with difficulty, scarcely, barely*.
vocābulum, -ī, N. [vocā- (st. of vocō), *call*], (*that by which a thing is called, and so) name, designation; word*.
vocō, -āre, -āvī, -ātus [√voc-, *speak, call* (through presumed adj. st.)], *call, summon, convene, invite; call, name*.
Volcānus, -ī, M., **Vulcan** (*the fire god); fire*.
volō, velle, voluī [√vol-, WILL],

wish, desire; be WILL*ing;* sibī velle, *to mean;* vellem possem, WOU*L*d *that I could!*
voluntās, -ātis, F. [volunt-, earlier form of volent- (st. of volēns, pres. part. of volō, WILL)], WILL*ingness*, WILL, *wish*.
voluptās, -ātis, F. [volupi- (st. seen in adv. volup, *agreeably*); cf. facultas and simultas from sts. faculi- and simuli-], *pleasure; sensual gratification*.
Volusēnus, -ī, M., *Gajus Volusenus Quadratus* (military tribune in Caesar's army).
voveō, -ēre, vōvī, vōtus, *vow*.
vōx, vōcis, F. [√vōc-, *speak, call*], *voice; speech, utterance, outcry; expressions*.
vulgō, adv. [abl. of vulgus, *the multitude*], *commonly, generally, universally*.
vulgus, -ī, N. (sometimes M.), *the multitude, the common people, the public*.
vulnerō, -āre, -āvī, -ātus [vulnes- (st. of vulnus), *wound;* -s- of the stem becomes -r-], *wound, inflict wounds*.
vulnus, -eris, N., *wound*.
vultus, -ūs, M. [√vol-, WILL], (*manifestation of will through the countenance, and so) countenance, visage, aspect*.

X.

X, as an abbreviation, decem, TEN.
Xeno-phōn, -ōntis, M., *Xenophon* (Athenian historian and general, also disciple of Socrates; lived about 445–356 B.C.).
Xerxēs, -is, M., *Xerxes* (son of Darius Hystaspes and king of Persia; made an unsuccessful invasion of Greece; his land forces were defeated at Thermopylae and his fleet at Salamis 480 B.C.).

II. ENGLISH–LATIN VOCABULARY.

NOTE. — The numeral placed at the right of a verb designates the conjugation to which the verb belongs. The dash (—) is used to represent the leading word; thus (under 'able') 'be —' is to be read 'be able.'

a, usu. not translated; *ūnus, -a, -um*, adj.; *quīdam, quaedam, quoddam*.
  abandon, *dēsistō*[3] (w. abl.).
  abide, *stō*.[1]
  able, be —: *possum*; (= be strong enough) *valeō*.[2]
  about, *dē*, prep. w. abl.; w. numerals: *ad*, prep. w. acc.; *circiter*, adv.
  absent, be —, *absum*.
  absurd, *īnscītus, -a, -um*, adj.
  abundance, *cōpia, -ae*, F.; *facultās, -ātis*, F.; **in —**, *abundē*, adv.
  abuse, *abūtor*[3] (w. abl.).
  acceptable, *grātus, -a, -um*, adj.; *acceptus, -a, -um*, p. a.; **a thing —**, *grātum*, n. adj. used subst.
  access, *aditus, -ūs*, M.; **gain —**, *adeō*.[4]
  accomplish, *cōnficiō*[3]; *efficiō*.[3]
  accordingly, *igitur*, conj. (usu. placed after the first word).
  according, — to, sign of abl.; *ad*, prep. w. acc.
  account, on — of: *propter*, prep. w. acc.; *ob*, prep. w. acc.; **call to —**, *accūsō*.[1]
  acquire, *adipīscor, -ī, adeptus*.
  across, *trāns*, prep. w. acc.
  act, 1. subst., *factum, -ī*, N. 2. vb., *faciō*.[3]
  action, *manus, -ūs*, F.
  Adamastus, *Adamastus, -ī*, M.
  address, *ōrātiō, -ōnis*, F.
  adequate, less —, *minor, -us*, adj.
  adjacent, *fīnitimus, -a, -um*, **adj.**
  administer, *administrō*.[1]
  admonish, *moneō*.[2]
  admonition, to give this — above all others, *id ūnum monēre* (w. acc. pers.).
  adopt, *capiō*[3]; (= make use of) *ūtor*[3] (w. abl.).
  advance, *prōcēdō*[3]; (against the enemy) *signa ferō*; **send in —**, *praemittō*.[3]
  advantage, *commodum, -ī*, N.
  advantageous, *ūtilis, -e*, adj.
  adversary, *adversārius, -ī*, M.
  adverse, *adversus, -a, -um*, p. a.
  Aeduan, *Aeduus, -ī*, M.
  Aeduans or Aedui, *Aeduī, -ōrum*, M.
  affair, *rēs*, gen. *reī* (*reī, rē*), F.
  affect, *moveō*.[2]
  afford, *dō*.
  after, *post*, prep. w. acc.; *post*, adv.
  again, *rūrsus*, adv.; (= the same) *īdem, eadem, idem*, demonstr. pron.; **— and —**: *etiam atque etiam*; *saepenumerō*.
  against, *contrā*, prep. w. acc.; *in*, prep. w. acc.; (as translation of *ob-* or *in-*) sign of dat.
  age, old —, *senectūs, -ūtis*, F.
  Agesilaus, *Agēsilāus, -ī*, M.
  ago, long —, *jampridem*, adv.
  agreeable, *grātus, -a, -um*, adj.
  aid, *auxilium, -ī*, N.
  alarm, 1. subst., *timor, -ōris*, M. 2. vb., *commoveō*[2]; *permoveō*[2]; **in —**, *commōtus, -a, -um*, perf. part.
  Alcibiades, *Alcibiadēs, -is*, M.
  all, (without exception) *omnis, -e*, adj.; (when the object is viewed as a whole) *tōtus, -a, -um*, adj.; **at —**, *omnīnō*, adv.
  allegiance, *officium, -ī*, N.
  Allobroges, *Allobrogēs, -um*, M.

allow, *patior.*³
ally, *socius, -ī,* M.
almost, *paene,* **adv.**
also, *etiam,* conj.; (= and) *et,* conj.; (= likewise) *item,* adv.; (= the same) *īdem, eadem, idem,* demonstr. pron.; but —: *sed etiam; et.*
 although, *quamquam,* conj. (w. indic.); *cum,* conj. (w. subj.); *tametsī* (w. indic. and subj. like *sī*); sign of abl. abs.
 altogether, (= enough) *satis,* adv.
 always, *semper,* adv.
 amass, *comparō.*¹
 ambassador, *lēgātus, -ī,* M.
 amity, *amīcitia, -ae,* F.
 among, *apud,* prep. w. acc.; *inter,* prep. w. acc.; *in,* prep. w. abl.; — themselves, *inter sē.*
 ancestors, *mājōrēs, -um,* M.
 anchor, *ancora, -ae,* F.
 ancient, *prīstinus, -a, -um,* **adj.**
 and, *et,* conj. (connects expressions that are viewed independently of each other); *-que,* conj. (connects closely); (= and also, and to, with emphasis on the second member) *atque* (before vowels or consonants), *āc* (before consonants only), conj.; — not, *neque, nec,* conj.
 anger, in —, *īrātus, -a, -um,* p. a.
 angry, *īrātus, -a, -um,* p. a.
 animal, *animal, -ālis,* N.
 announce, *nūntiō.*¹
 annoying, *molestus, -a, -um,* adj.
 another, *alius, alia, aliud,* adj. and subst.; — (of two) *alter, -era, -erum,* adj. and subst.; one —, *alius . . . alius;* at one —, *inter sē;* from one —, *inter sē;* at one time . . . at another, *aliās . . . aliās.*
 answer, 1. vb., *respondeō*² (w. dat. pers.). 2. subst., *respōnsum, -ī,* N.; **make** —, *respondeō.*²
 anxiety, *cūra, -ae,* F.
 any, (in neg. and **conditional** sentences and interrog. **sentences implying** a neg.) *ūllus, -a, -um,* **indef. adj.**; (after *sī* or *nē*) *quī, qua*

or *quae, quod,* indef. adj.; (= some) *aliquī, aliqua, aliquod,* indef. adj.; — **whatever,** *quīvis, quaevis, quodvis,* indef. adj.
 anybody, anyone, (in neg. and **conditional** sentences and in interrog. sentences implying a negative) *quisquam,* indef. pron., also *ūllus* (used subst.); (after *sī* or *nē*) *quis,* indef. pron.
 anything, *quicquam* or *quidquam;* (after *sī* or *nē*) *quid.*
 apart, keep —, *distineō.*²
 apiece, sign of distr. num.; *in singulōs.*
 apply, *adhibeō.*²
 appoint, *creō.*¹
 apprehension, *metus, -ūs,* M.
 approach, 1. subst., *adventus, -ūs,* M. 2. vb., *appropinquō*¹ (w. dat. or *ad* w. acc.).
 approve, *probō.*¹
 approver, *approbātor, -ōris,* M.
 April, of —, *Aprīlis, -e,* adj.
 Aquitania, *Aquītānia, -ae,* F.
 Aquitanian, *Aquītānus, -a, -um,* adj.
 Aquitanians, *Aquītānī, -ōrum,* M.
 Arar, *Arar, -aris,* M.
 archer, *sagittārius, -ī,* M.
 Archias, *Archiās, -ae,* M.
 ardently, — **desire,** *exoptō.*¹
 Ariovistus, *Ariovistus, -ī,* M.
 arise, *orior*⁴ (w. some fms. of the 3d conjugation); (= arise together) *coörior.*⁴
 arm, *armō.*¹
 armor, *armātūra, -ae,* F.
 arms, *arma, -ōrum,* N.; **in** —, *armātus, -a, -um,* p. a.
 army, *exercitus, -ūs,* M. (generic term); *agmen, -inis,* N. (on the march); *aciēs,* gen. *-ē* and *-ēī,* F. (in order of battle).
 arouse, *incitō.*¹
 arrival, *adventus, -ūs,* M.
 arrive, *perveniō*⁴; to — at, *pervenīre ad.*
 arrogance, *adrogantia, -ae,* F.
 art, *ars, artis,* F.; (= work) *opus, -eris,* N.

Arverni, *Arvernī, -ōrum*, M.
as, *ut* or *utī*, adv.; *quemadmodum*, adv.; (= that which) *id quod*; (= inasmuch as) *quoniam*, conj.; (= since) *cum* (w. subj.), conj.; **just—**, *sīcut*, adv.; —**follows**, *sīc*, adv.; —**soon—**, *ubī prīmum, simul atque*; —**not** (in clauses of result) *quī nōn* or *ut nōn*; —**usual**, *ex cōnsuētūdine*; **so ... as, tam ... quam**; **to regard—**, *habēre prō* (w. abl.); **to serve—**, *esse* w. dat.; —**to** (= concerning) *dē*.
  ascend, *adscendō*.³
  ascent, *adscēnsus, -ūs*, M.
  ascertain, *cōgnōscō*.³
  ashamed, I am—, *mē pudet* (w. gen.).
  aside, lay or **put—**, *dēpōnō*.³
  ask, *rogō*¹ (**w.** two accs.); *quaerō*³ (**w.** acc. th., and abl. pers. w. *ex* or *ē, ab* or *ā,* or *dē*); **ask,— for**, *petō*³ (w. acc. th., and abl. pers. **w.** *ab* or *ā*).
  assault, 1. subst., *impetus, -ūs*, M. 2. vb., *oppūgnō*¹; **take by—**, *expūgnō*.¹
  assemble, 1. tr., *convocō*.¹ 2. intr., *conveniō*.⁴
  assembly, *concilium, -ī*, N.
  assent, to — to, *approbātor esse* (w. gen.).
  assert, *dīcō*.³
  assign, *attribuō*.³
  assistance, *auxilium, -ī*, N.
  associate, *socius, -ī*, M.
  assume, *sibī sūmō*.³
  asunder, keep —, *distineō*.²
  at, (= in) *in*, prep. w. abl.; [arrive] **at**, *ad*, prep. w. acc.; (= at the house of) *apud*, prep. w. acc.
  Athenian, *Athēniēnsis, -e*, adj.; **also** used subst.
  Athens, *Athēnae, -ārum*, F.
  attach, *adjungō*³ (w. acc. and dat.).
  attachment, *studium, -ī*, N.
  attack, 1. subst., *impetus, -ūs*, M.; *congressus, -ūs*, M. 2. vb., (= thrust at, rush at, aim at) *petō*³; (= provoke, challenge to

combat, irritate) *lacessō*³; (= approach with hostile intention) *adeō*.⁴
  attempt, *tentō*¹ or *temptō*¹; *cōnor*.¹
  attention, call one's — to (= remind forcibly), *commonefaciō*.³
  audacity, *audācia, -ae*, F.
  augment, *augeō*.²
  authority, *auctōritās, -ātis*, F.; (= right) *jūs, jūris*, N.; **sovereign —**, *rēgnum*; **supreme —**, *imperium, -ī*, N.; **to be in — over**, *obtinēre* (w. acc.).
  Autronius, *Autrōnius, -ī*, M.
  auxiliaries, *auxilia, -ōrum*, N.; *ālārū, -ōrum*, M.
  avail, *valeō*.²
  avert, *dēpellō*.³
  avoid, *vītō*.¹
  await, *exspectō*.¹
  award, *tribuō*.³
  aware, be — of, *sentiō*⁴; *sciō*.⁴
  away, — from, *ab* (before vowels and some consonants), *ā* (before consonants only).
  Axona, *Axona, -ae*, M.

B.

bad, (morally) *improbus, -a, -um*, adj.
back, *re(d)-*.
badge, *īnsigne, -is*, N.
baggage, *impedīmenta, -ōrum*, N.
band, *manus, -ūs*, F.
banishment, *exsilium, -ī*, N.
bank, (of a river) *rīpa, -ae*, F.
barbarian, *barbarus, -ī*, M.
barely, *vix*, adv.
barricade, *obstruō*³ (w. acc.).
base, *turpis, -e*, adj.
battle, *proelium, -ī*, N.; **carry on —**, *pūgnō*.¹
be, *sum*; — **in**, *īnsum* (w. dat.); — **away**, *absum*.
beak, *rōstrum, -ī*, N.
beat, *pellō*.³
beautiful, *pulcher, -chra, -chrum*, adj.
beauty, *forma, -ae*, F.
because, *quod* (w. indic.); *cum* (w. subj.).

become — **burn**

become, *fīō;* — firmly established, *inveterāscō, -ere, -āvī.*
becoming, it is —, *decet,*[2] impers.
beech, *fāgus, -ī,* F.
before, *ante,* prep. w. acc.; *antequam, priusquam,* conj.; (= preceding) *superior, -ius,* adj. comp.; (= already) *jam,* adv.; (= near) *apud,* prep. w. acc.; (= up to) *ad,* prep. w. acc.; — **one's time,** *immātūrus, -a, -um,* adj.; **on the day —,** *prīdiē,* adv.; **to lay the matter —,** *referre ad* (w. acc.).
beg, *petō*[3] (w. *ab* or *ā* and abl. pers.).
began, *coepī,* def.
begin, (= make a beginning) *initium faciō*[3]; (= enter) *ineō*[4] (w. acc.); — **at** (= rise from) *orior*[4] (w. *ab* and abl.); **to — battle,** *proelium committere.*
beginning, *initium, -iī,* N.
behalf, in — of, *prō,* prep. w. abl.
behavior, (= thing) *rēs,* F.
behind, leave —, *relinquō.*[3]
Belgians, *Belgae, -ārum,* M.
believe, *crēdō*[3] (w. dat. pers.); (= judge) *jūdicō.*[1]
Bellovaci, *Bellovacī, -ōrum,* M.
belonging, — to the town, *oppidānus, -a, -um,* adj.
bench, *subsellium, -iī,* N.
benefit, *beneficium, -iī,* N.
beseech, *petō*[3] (w. acc. th., and abl. pers. w. *ab* or *ā*).
best, *optimus, -a, -um,* adj. (superl. of *bonus*).
bestow, *dō.*
betake, to — one's self, *sē cōnferre.*
betoken, *dēsignō.*[1]
betray, (= surrender treacherously) *prōdō*[3]; (= point out) *indicō.*[1]
better, it is —, *praestat,* impers.
between, *inter,* prep. w. acc.; (= in) *in,* prep. w. abl.
bewail, *miseror.*[1]
beyond, *extrā,* prep. w. acc.; *suprā,* prep. w. acc.

bidding, at the —, *jūssū* (in abl. only).
bitter, — experience, *acerbitās, -ātis,* F.
blockade, *obsideō.*[2]
blood, *sanguis, -inis,* M.
bloodshed, *clādēs, -is,* F.
boast, *glōrior*[1]; **make a — of,** *glōrior*[1] (w. abl.); **to make the same —,** *idem glōriārī.*
body, *corpus, -oris,* N.
boldly, *audācter,* adv.; **more —,** *audācius,* adv. comp.
boldness, *audācia, -ae,* F.; **with —,** *audācter,* adv.; **with the greatest —,** superl. of *audācter.*
book, *liber, -brī,* M.
booty, *praeda, -ae,* F.
bordering, — on, *fīnitimus, -a, -um,* adj.
born, be —, *nāscor.*[3]
both, (= each of two) *uterque, utraque, utrumque,* pron.; **both ... and,** *et ... et.*
bound, *contineō.*[2]
boy, *puer, -erī,* M.
branches, light —, *virgulta, -ōrum,* N.
brave, *fortis, -e,* adj.
breadth, *lātitūdō, -inis,* F.
break, (= throw into disorder) *perturbō*[1]; **— through,** *perfringō*[3]; **— through** (=burst through) *perrumpō*[3]; **— into,** *irrumpō*[3] (w. acc.).
bribe, *largior.*[4]
bridge, *pōns, pontis,* M.
bring, *adferō;* (= lead to) *addūcō*[3]; (= lead across) *trādūcō*[3]; **— back,** *redūcō.*[3]
Britain, *Britannia, -ae,* F.
Britons, *Britannī, -ōrum,* M.
broad, *lātus, -a, -um,* adj.
brother, *frāter, -tris,* M.
Brundisium, *Brundisium, -iī,* N.
Brutus, *Brūtus, -ī,* M.
build, *aedificō*[1]; **— up,** *exstruō.*[3]
building, *aedificium, -iī,* N.
bulk, great —, *magnitūdō, -inis,* F.
burn, *exūrō, -ere, -ūssī, -ūstus;* *cremō,*[1] *ignī cremō.*[1]

burst, — into view, ērumpō³;
— **through,** perrumpō.³
business, negōtium, -iī, N.;
(= **care**) cūra, -ae, F.
but, sed, conj.; (somewhat stronger than sed) vērum; (introducing with emphasis a new thought, e.g. a supposed objection) at; (= indeed) vērō, adv.; (= unless) nisi, conj.; (= in all, altogether) omnīnō, adv.; (= except) praeter, prep. w. acc.; (= only) modo, adv.; nothing —, nihil nisi; no one —, **nēmō** nisi; but also or even : sed or vērum etiam; (correlating with et) et.
butcher, jugulō.¹
buy, emō³; — up, coemō.³
by, (denoting agency) ab (before vowels and some consonants), ā (before consonants only); (denoting means) sign of abl.; (= through) per, prep. w. acc.

C.

Caesar, Caesar, -aris, M.
Caeparius, Caepārius, -iī, M.
call, (= name) appellō¹; (= call together) convocō¹; — one's attention to (= remind forcibly), commonefaciō³; — to mind (for the purpose of reflecting on), recordor¹ (usu. w. acc.); — to **account,** accūsō.¹
    calm, tranquillus, -a, -um, adj.
    camp, castra, -ōrum, N.
    can, possum; (= may) licet,² impers. (w. dat.).
    capital, capitālis, -e, adj.
    capitol, capitōlium, -iī, N.
    Cappadocian, Cappadox, -ocis, M.
    captive, captīvus, -ī, M.
    Capua, Capua, -ae, F.
    care, cūra, -ae, F.; take —, cūrō.¹
    carry, portō¹; — on, gerō³; — off (= lead away) abdūcō,³ dēdūcō³; — on battle, pūgnō¹; to — on war against, bellum īnferre (w. dat.); to — one's arms into, **arma** īnferre (w. dat.).

Carthage, Carthāgō, -inis, F.
Carthaginians, Poenī, -ōrum, M.
case, in the — **of,** in, prep. w. abl.
Cassandra, Cassandra, -ae, F.
Cassius, Cassius, -iī, M.; with —, Cassiānus, -a, -um, adj.
cast, mittō³; — **down,** dēmittō.³
Casticus, Casticus, -ī, M
catch, — sight of, cōnspiciō.³
Catiline, Catilīna, -ae, M.
Cato, Catō, -ōnis, M.
Caturiges, Caturigēs, **-um,** M.
cattle, pecus, -oris, N.
cause, 1. subst., causa, **-ae,** F. 2. vb., faciō³; efficiō.³
cavalry, 1. subst., equitātus, -ūs, M.; equitēs, **-um,** M. (pl. of eques, horseman). **2. adj.,** equester, -tris, -tre, adj.
cease, dēsistō³; fīnem faciō.³
Celts (Kelts), Celtae, -ārum, M.
centurion, centuriō, -ōnis, M.
Ceraunus, Ceraunus, -ī, M.
certain, a —, **a** — **man,** quīdam, quaedam, quoddam and (subst.) quiddam.
Cethegus, Cethēgus, -ī, M.
change, — **the direction of,** convertō.³
chariot-man (i.e. one who fights from a chariot), essedārius, -iī, M.
    charioteer, aurīga, -ae, M.
    cheap, vīlis, -e, adj.
    cheese, cāseus, -ī, M.
    cherish, — **the memory of,** meminī, def.; — **hatred,** ōdī, def.
    chief, 1. subst., prīnceps, -ipis, M. 2. adj., māximus, -a, -um, adj. (superl. of māgnus).
    chiefly, plērumque, adv.
    child, puer, -erī, M.
    children (in general) puerī, -ōrum, M.; (with reference to their parents) līberī, -ōrum, M.
choose, — **rather,** mālō.
Cicero, Cicerō, -ōnis, M.
Cimbri, Cimbrī, -ōrum, M.
Cimon, Cīmōn, -ōnis, M.
Cingetorix, Cingetorīx, -igis, M.
circuit, circuitus, -ūs, M.

circuitous, by a — path, *in circuitū*.
citizen, *cīvis, -is*, C.
city, *urbs, -is*, F.; in the — (= belonging to the city), *urbānus, -a, -um*, adj.
civil, *cīvīlis, -e*, adj.
claim, have a —, *oportet*,² impers. (w. acc. and infin.); lay — to, *repetō*.³
class, *genus, -eris*, N.
Claudius, *Claudius, -ī*, M.
clear, (= make vacant) *vacuēfaciō*³; make —, *explānō*¹; it is altogether —, *satis cōnstat*, impers.
climb, *adscendō*.³
Clodia, *Clōdia, -ae*, F.
close, at — quarters, *comminus*, adv.
clothe, *vestiō*.⁴
clothing, *vestītus, -ūs*, M.
coast, *ōra, -ae*, F.; sea —, *ōra maritima*.
cohort, *cohors, -tis*, F.
collect, *cōgō*³; *conligō*³; *comparō*.¹
come, *veniō*⁴; (= arrive) *perveniō*⁴; — upon, *occurrō*³ (w. dat.); — out, *ēgredior*³; — back, *redeō*⁴; to — off, *sē inde recipere*; to — up to, *accēdere ad* (w. acc.); to — up with, *venīre ad* (w. acc.).
command, 1. subst., *mandātum, -ī*, N.; (military) *imperium, -ī*, N. 2. vb., *imperō*¹; be in — of, *praesum* (w. dat.); place in — of, *praeficiō*³ (w. acc. pers. and dat. th.).
commander, *imperātor, -ōris*, M.
commend, (= praise) *laudō*.¹
commit, (of an injury) *faciō*³; (of crime) *admittō*³; (= intrust): *permittō*³ (w. acc. and dat.); *commendō*¹ (w. acc. and dat.).
common, *commūnis, -e*, adj.
commonwealth, *rēs pūblica, reī pūblicae*, F.
community, *cīvitās, -ātis*, F.
company, *concilium, -ī*, N.
compare, *comparō*¹ (w. acc., and dat. or *cum* w. abl.).

compassion, have — on, *misereor*² (w. gen.).
compel, *cōgō*.³
comrade, *comes, -itis*, C.
concerns, it —, *interest*, impers.
concerning, *dē*, prep. w. abl.
condemn, *damnō*¹ (w. gen. of charge or penalty); *condemnō*¹ (w. gen. of charge or penalty); *multō*¹ (w. acc. and abl.); to — to death, *capitis damnāre*.
condition, (= thing) *rēs*, F.
conduct, (= manage) *gerō*³; — across, *trādūcō*.³
confer, *agō*.³
conference, *conloquium, -ī*, N.; have a —, *conloquor*.³
confidence, *fidēs, -ēī (-ĕī, -ē)*, F.
confident, — expectation, *fīdūcia, -ae*, F.
confines, *fīnēs, -ium*, M. (pl. of *fīnis*).
conflagration, *incendium, -ī*, N.
confusion, *tumultus, -ūs*, M.
conquer, *vincō*.³
conqueror, come off —, *superior discēdō*.³
conscious, *cōnscius, -a, -um*, adj. (w. gen. th.; w. or without dat. pers.).
conscript, *cōnscrīptus, -a, -um*, p. a.
consent, withhold — (= [be] unwilling), *invītus, -a, -um*, adj.
consider, (= hold, regard) *habeō*² (w. two accs. in act.); (= ponder) *reputō*.¹
consign, *mandō*¹ (w. acc. and dat.).
consist, — in, *sum* (w. *in* and abl.).
conspiracy, *conjūrātiō, -ōnis*, F.
conspire, *cōnsentiō*.⁴
constitution, *jūs, jūris*, N.
constrain, *cōgō*.³
consul, *cōnsul, -is*, M.
consulship, in the — of, *cōnsul* (abl. abs. w. name of pers.).
consult, *cōnsulō*³ (w. acc.); — for, — the interests of, *cōnsulō*³ (w. dat.).
consume (by fire), *cremō*.¹

**contempt, ** *contemptus, -ūs,* M.
**contend, ** *contendō*³ (w. *cum* and abl.); *certō*¹ (w. *cum* and abl.).
**contentedly, ** *aequō animō.*
**contention, ** *contentiō, -ōnis,* F.
**continue, ** *maneō.*²
contradictory, ** *contrārius,* **-a, -um, adj.
**contribute, ** *cōnferō.*
control, ** (supreme) *imperium,* **-iī, N.
**convene, ** (= call) *vocō.*¹
**convey, ** (in a body) *comportō*¹; — across, *trādūcō.*³
convict, ** *convincō, -ere, -vīcī, -victus* (w. gen. **of the crime).
**convince, ** *persuādeō*² (w. dat. pers.).
   Corinth, ** *Corinthus,* **-ī, F.
corner, ** *angulus,* **-ī, M.
Cotta, ** *Cotta,* **-ae, M.
council, ** *concilium,* **-iī, N.
**country, ** (= native country) *patria, -ae,* F.; (= land) *ager, -grī,* M.; (= territories) *fīnēs, -ium,* M. (pl. of *fīnis*); (opp. city) *rūs, rūris,* N.; (= commonwealth) *rēs pūblica, reī pūblicae;* native —, *patria, -ae,* F.; — districts, *agrī, -ōrum,* M. (pl. of *ager*); in the —, *rūrī* (loc.).
**countrymen, ** *cīvēs, -ium* (pl. of *cīvis*); *cīvitās, -ātis,* F.
courage, ** *animus,* **-ī, M.; full of —, *animōsus, -a, -um,* adj.
**course, ** (= plans, measures, proceedings) *cōnsilia, -ōrum,* N. (pl. of *cōnsilium*); shameless —, *audācia, -ae,* F.
**cover, ** *tegō.*³
covetous, ** *appetēns,* **-entis, p. a. (w. gen.).
**cowardice, ** *timor, -ōris,* M.
**craft, ** *ratiō, -ōnis,* F.
Crassus, ** *Crassus,* **-ī, M.
**creature, ** living —, *animal, -ālis,* N.
   **Crete, ** *Crēta, -ae,* F.
**crew, ** that —, *istī, -ōrum,* M.
**crime, ** *scelus, -eris,* N.; (= daring, lawless crime) *facinus, -oris,* N.
**criticize, ** (adversely) *accūsō.*¹

**cross, ** *trānseō.*⁴
**crown, **(as, with glory)*honōrō.*¹
**cruel, ** *crūdēlis, -e,* adj.
**crush, ** (= break in pieces) *frangō;* (= overpower) *opprimō.*³
**custody, ** *custōdia, -ae,* F.
**custom, ** *mōs, mōris,* M.
**cut, ** — off, *excipiō*³; — off, (from supplies) *prohibeō*² (w. acc. and abl.).
Cyrus, ** *Cȳrus,* **-ī, M.

D.

**daily, ** *cottīdiānus, -a, -um,* adj.
**damage, ** *noceō*² (w. dat.).
danger, ** *perīculum,* **-ī, N.
**dangerous, ** *perīculōsus, -a, -um,* adj.
**dare, ** *audeō.*²
dart, ** *tēlum,* **-ī, N.
**daughter, ** *fīlia, -ae,* F.
**day, ** *diēs,* gen. *-ēī (-ēī, -ē),* M. (sometimes F. in sing.); on the — before, on the preceding —, *prīdiē,* adv.
dear, ** *cārus, -a, -um,* **adj.; how —, *quantī* (gen. of indef. value).
death, ** *mors, mortis,* F.; (as a penalty for crime) *caput, -itis,* N.; put **to —, *necō*¹; to condemn to —, *capitis damnāre.*
**deceive, ** *fallō.*³
**decide, ** *cōnstituō.*³
**Decii, ** *Deciī, -ōrum,* M.
decision, ** *jūdicium,* **-iī, N.
**declare, ** *dēclārō*¹; *prōnūntiō*¹; (= set forth) *prōpōnō*³; (of war) *indīcō.*³
**decline, ** (= be unwilling) *nōlō.*
**decree, ** *cēnseō.*²
**deem, ** *jūdicō*¹ (w. two accs. in act.).
**deep, ** *altus, -a, -um,* p. a.
**deeply, ** — move, *permoveō.*²
**defeat, ** 1. subst., *adversum proelium.* 2. vb., *superō.*¹
**defend, ** *dēfendō.*³
defence, ** *praesidium,* **-iī, N.; means of —, *remedium,* **-iī,** N.
**defiance, ** set at —, *neglegō.*³
**delay, ** *moror.*¹
**deliberate, ** *dēliberō.*¹

deliver, (of an address) *habeō*.²

demand, *poscō*³; (= claim, demand as a right) *postulō*¹ (w. acc. th., and abl. pers. w. *ab*, *ā*); (= command, order) *imperō*¹ (w. acc. th. and dat. pers.).

Demaratus, *Dēmarātus*, *-ī*, M.

denarius, *dēnārius*, *-iī*, M.

dense, *dēnsus*, *-a*, *-um*, adj.

deny, *negō*.¹

depart, *exeō*⁴; *dēcēdō*³; *sēcēdō*³; (= set out) *proficiscor*³; — to join, *proficiscor*³ *in* (w. acc.).

departure, *profectiō*, *-ōnis*, F.

depredation, *maleficium*, *-iī*, N.; *injūria*, *-ae*, F.

deprive, (= wrest from) *ēripiō*³ (w. acc. th. and dat. pers.).

descend, (of birth) *orior*.⁴

description, (= kind) *genus*, *-eris*, N.

desert, (= be wanting, fail) *dēsum*.

deserter, *perfuga*, *-ae*, M.

deserve, *mereor*²; to — well of, *merērī dē*.

design, *cōnsilium*, *-iī*, N.

desire, 1. subst., *voluntās*, *-ātis*, F. 2. vb., (of voluntary desire, i.e. desire prompted by the will) *volō*; (of involuntary desire, i.e. natural inclination) *cupiō*³; — ardently, *exoptō*.¹

desirous, *studiōsus*, *-a*, *-um*, adj. (w. gen.).

desperately, (= sharply, vigorously) *ācriter*, adv.

despise, *dēspiciō*.³

destitute, *nūdus*, *-a*, *-um*, adj. (w. abl.).

destroy, (= annihilate) *dēleō*²; (= squander, ruin) *perdō*³ (*pereō* is used for the pass.); (= break through) *perfringō*³; (= cut down, e.g. a bridge) *interscindō*, *-ere*, *-scidī*, *-scissus*.

destruction, *perniciēs*, gen., *-iī*, *-iēs* or *-iē*, F.; (= downfall) *obitus*, *-ūs*, M.

destructive, *perniciōsus*, *-a*, *-um*, adj.

detail, in —, *singulātim*, adv.

deter, *dēterreō*²; to — from, *dēterrēre quōminus* (w. subj.).

determine, (= fix, establish) *cōnstituō*.³

devote, — one's self, *serviō*⁴ (w. dat.).

devoted, — to, *dīligēns*, *-entis*, adj. (w. gen.).

devotion, *studium*, *-iī*, N.

dictates, *praescrīptum*, *-ī*, N.

die, *morior*, *morī* (*morīrī*), *mortuus*; *ēmorior*.

differ, *differō*, *differre* (the meaning *differ* appears to be confined to the pres. system); to — from one another, *inter sē differre*.

difficult, *difficilis*, *-e*, adj.

difficulty, with —, *aegrē* adv.; (= scarcely) *vix*; with the utmost —, *aegerrimē*, adv. (superl. of *aegrē*).

difficulties, *angustiae*, *-ārum*, F.

digest, *dīgerō*, *-ere*, *-gessī*, *-gestus*.

dignity, priestly —, *sacerdōtium*, *-iī*, N.

diligence, *dīligentia*, *-ae*, F.

diminutive, — stature, *brevitās*, *-ātis*, F.

Dionysius, *Dionȳsius*, *-iī*, M.

direct, (= order) *imperō*¹ (w. dat.).

direction, (= part) *pars*, *partis*, F.; (= supreme control) *imperium*, *-iī*, N.; change the — of, *convertō*.³

disaffection, *aliēnātiō*, *-ōnis*, F.

disagreement, *dissēnsiō*, *-ōnis*, F.

disapprove, *reprehendō*.³

disaster, *calamitās*, *-ātis*, F.

discharge, *fungor*³ (w. abl.).

discipline, *disciplīna*, *-ae*, F.

discuss, *disserō*³ (w. *dē* and abl.); *agō*³ (w. *dē* and abl. th., and *cum* w. abl. pers.).

dish, sacrificial —, *patera*, *-ae*, F.

dismiss, *dīmittō*³; (= lay aside) *dēpōnō*.³

dispatch, *mittō*.³

**display, ** ostendō.³
dispose, — of (= sell), vēndō⁸ (vēneō is used as the pass.).
**disposed, ** cupidus, -a, -um, adj. (w. gen.); **favorably —, ** amīcus, -a, -um, adj.; **be not disposed, ** nōlō.
**disposition, ** animus, -ī, M.; **favorable —, ** voluntās, -ātis, F.
**dispute, ** contrōversia, -ae, F.
**disquiet, ** perturbō¹; commoveō.²
**disquieting, ** molestus, -a, -um, adj.
**disregard, ** neglegō⁸; (= despise) contemnō, -ere, -tempsī, -temptus.
**dissatisfied, I am —, ** mē paenitet, impers. (w. gen.).
**dissension, ** dissēnsiō, -ōnis, F.
**distance, ** intervāllum, -ī, N.; **to a —, ** procul, adv.; **at a — from, ** longē ā.
**distant, be —, ** absum.
**distress, ** premō.³
**distribute, ** distribuō.³
**district, ** pāgus, -ī, M.; (= territory, domain), ager, -grī, M.; (= quarter, region) regiō, -ōnis, F.; **country —s, ** agrī, -ōrum, M.
**disturb, ** perturbō.¹
**ditch, ** fossa, -ae, F.
**Divico, ** Divicō, -ōnis, M.
**divine, ** dīvīnus, -a, -um, adj.
**Divitiacus, ** Divitiacus, -ī, M.
**divulge, ** ēnūntiō.¹
**do, ** faciō⁸; agō⁸; **have to — with, ** pertineō² (w. ad and acc.); **— away with, ** tollō.³
**done, be —, ** fīō.
**doubt, ** dubitō¹; **there is no —, ** nōn est dubium (w. quīn and subj.).
**doubtful, ** dubius, -a, -um, adj.
**doubtless, ** profectō, adv.
**down, cast —, ** dēmittō⁸; **to lay — arms, ** ab armīs discēdere.
**drag, ** trahō.³
draw, (of a sword) ēdūcō⁸; (= draw apart) distrahō³; **— near, ** appropinquō¹ (w. dat. or ad w. acc.); **— up, ** īnstruō.³
**dream, ** 1. subst., somnium, -iī, N.; vb., somniō.¹

**drink, ** bibō, -ere, bibī.
**drive, ** agō⁸; (= cast out) ēiciō⁸; (= drive in a body) compellō⁸; **— out, ** expellō.⁸
**drug, ** medicāmentum, -ī, N.
**Dumnorix, ** Dumnorix, -īgis, M.
**dust, ** pulvis, -eris, M.
**duty, ** officium, -iī, N.
**dwell, ** incolō.³
**dwelling, ** tectum, -ī, N.; — **place, ** domicilium, -iī, N.

E.

**each, — one, ** quisque, quaeque, quodque (adj.) and quicque or quidque (subst.), indef. pron.; (of two) uterque, -traque, -trumque, pron.; **with — other, ** inter sē (sēsē).
**eager, ** alacer, -cris, -cre, adj.
**eagerly, ** intentus, -a, -um, p. a. (in agreement w. subst.).
**earlier, ** prīstinus, -a, -um, adj.
**early, ** (= ancient) antīquus, -a, -um, adj.
earnest, ** studiōsus, -a, -um, adj (w. gen.**).
**earnestly, press —, ** postulō¹ (w. acc. th. and abl. pers. w. ab. ā.)
**earth, — mound, ** tumulus, -ī, M.
easily, ** facile, adv.; (= at random) temerē, adv.; **very — (after a neg.), satis commodē, adv.
**east, ** (= rising sun) sōl oriēns, sōlis orientis, M.
**easy, very —, ** perfacilis, -e, adj.
**Ebro, ** Hibērus, -ī, M.
**effect, to — a purpose, ** rem efficere, rem obtinēre.
**effects, their —, ** n. pl. of suus, -a, -um, poss. pron.
**effectually, ** facile, adv.
effort, ** opera, -ae, F.; **to bestow, — operam dare (w. ut and subj.).
**eight, ** octō, indecl. num. adj.
**eighteenth, ** duodēvīcēsimus, -a, -um or octāvus decimus, -a, -um, ord. num. adj.
**eighty, ** octōgintā, indecl. num. adj.

either ... or, (when an alternative is offered) *vel ... vel;* (when one excludes the other) *aut ... aut;* **not ... either ... or**, *neque ... neque, nec ... nec.*
elect, *dēsīgnātus, -ī*, masc. p. a.
embankment, *agger, -is*, M.
embarked, — on, *impositus, -a, -um*, perf. part. of *impōnō* (w. in and acc.).
embassy, *lēgātiō, -ōnis*, F.
empty, (= make vacant) *vacuēfaciō.*³
encamp, *cōnsīdō.*³
end, *fīnis, -is*, M. (sometimes F. in sing.).
endeavor, *cōnor*¹*;* **to — to force** (= to attempt by force), *per vim tentāre.*
endeavors, *cōnāta, -ōrum*, N.
endure, *ferō; patior.*³
enemy, (personal) *inimīcus, -ī*, M.; (public) *hostis, -is*, C.; (= a hostile army) *hostēs, -ium*, pl. (usu., but also) *hostis, -is*, M., sing.
energy, *vīs, vīs*, F.; **with —**, *ācriter*, adv.; **with the greatest —**, superl. of *ācriter.*
engage, to — in battle, *proelium committere.*
engagement, (= battle) *proelium, -ī*, N.; **to come to an —**, *proeliō dēcertāre;* **to open an —**, *proelium committere.*
engine, *māchinātiō, -ōnis*, F.
enjoy, *fruor*³ (w. abl.); (= make use of) *ūtor*³ (w. abl.).
enmity, *inimīcitia, -ae*, F.
enough, *satis*, adv.; **well —**, *commodē*, adv.
ensue, *sequor.*³
enterprise, (= thing) *rēs*, gen. *reī (reī, rē)*, F.; (= business) *negōtium, -ī*, N.
entire, *tōtus, -a, -um*, adj.
entreat, *ōrō.*¹
entreaties, *precēs, -um*, F. pl.
envoy, *lēgātus, -ī*, M.
envy, 1. subst., *invidia, -ae*, F. 2. vb., *invideō*² (w. dat.).
Epaminondas, *Epamīnōndās, -ae*, M.

Eporedorix, *Eporedorix, -igis*, M.
equal, *pār, paris*, adj.; *aequus, -a, -um*, adj.; (= same) *idem, eadem, idem*, demonstr. pron.
equally, *juxtā*, adv.
equanimity, *aequus animus.*
erect, *ērigō*³*;* (of a tower) *excitō.*¹
error, *peccātum, -ī*, N.
escape, *effugiō*³*;* (= flee) *fugiō.*³
especially, *maximē*, adv.
establish, *cōnfirmō.*¹
established, become firmly —, *inveterāscō, -ere, -āvī.*
esteem, (= consider) *habeō.*²
eternal, *aeternus, -a, -um*, adj.
even, *etiam*, conj.; **— to**, *jam ad* (w. acc.); **but —**, *sed etiam,* **vērum** *etiam;* **not —**, *nē ... quidem* (w. the emphatic word or words between *nē* and *quidem*); **— though**, *etiamsī* (w. indic. and subj., like *sī;* the indic. is more common).
ever, *unquam* or *umquam*, adv.
every, **omnis, -e**, adj.; **—, — one**, *quisque, quaeque, quodque* (adj.), and *quicque* or *quidque* (subst.), indef. pron.
every thing, *omnia* (n. pl. of *omnis, -e*, adj.); *cūncta* (n. pl. of *cūnctus, -a, -um*, adj.).
evident, make —, *significō*¹*;* **it is —**, *appāret.*²
exceed, *superō.*¹
excel, *praestō*¹ (w. dat.); *superō*¹ (w. acc.); *praecēdō*³ (w. acc.).
except, *praeter*, adv. and prep. w. acc.; (= unless) *nisi*, conj.
excessive, *nimius, -a, -um*, adj
exchange, to —, *inter sē dare.*
exclaim, *conclāmō.*¹
exculpate, *pūrgō.*¹
execute, *administrō.*¹
exercise, (= apply) *adhibeō*²*;* **— partiality**, *studeō.*²
exhort, *cohortor.*¹
exile, *exsilium, -ī*, N.
expectation, *opīniō, -ōnis*, F.; **confident —**, *fīdūcia, -ae*, F.

expel, *expellō*³; (= drive) *pellō*³; (= cast out) *ēiciō*.³
expense, *sūmptus, -ūs*, M.
experience, 1. subst., *ūsus, -ūs*, M.; **bitter —**, *acerbitās, -ātis*, F. 2. vb. (= receive) *accipiō*.³
experienced, *perītus, -a, -um*, p. a. (w. gen.).
explain, (= set forth) *expōnō*.³
explanation, say by way of —, *explānō*.¹
expression, *vōx, vōcis*, F.
extend, 1. intr., *exeō*⁴; (= lie open) *pateō*²; (= look) *spectō*.¹ 2. tr. (= construct) *perdūcō*.³
extensive, *lātus, -a, -um*, adj.
extreme, *extrēmus, -a, -um*, adj. (superl.).
eye, *oculus, -ī*, M.
eyes, in my —, *mihi* (dat. ref.).

F.

Fabius, *Fabius, -ī*, M.
face, in the — of, *contrā*, prep. w. acc.
fact, (= thing) *rēs*, gen. *rēī* (*reī, rē*), F.; **in point of —**, *rē* (abl. of *rēs*).
Faesulae, *Faesulae, -ārum*, F.
fail, 1. intr., *dēsum*. 2. tr. and intr., *dēficiō*.³ 3. tr., *dēserō*.³
faint-hearted = of feeble courage; see **feeble** and **courage**.
faithful, *fīdus, -a, -um*, adj.
fall, (of javelins) *accidō*³; (= fall together, fall with a crash) *corruō*; **— upon**, (= chance upon) *incidō*³ (w. *in* and acc.).
family, (= stock, race) *genus, -eris*, N.
famous, (= that) *ille, illa, illud*, demonstr. pron.
fancy, *arbitror*.¹
Fannius, *Fannius, -ī*, M.
far, *longē*, adv.; **by —**, *longē*, adv.; **too —**, *longius*, adv. (comp. of *longē*).
farm, *redimō*.³
farther, *ulterior, -ius*, adj.
fast, make —, *dēstinō*.¹
father, *pater, -tris*, M.; *genitor, -ōris*, M.

father-in-law, *socer, -erī*, M.
fault, *culpa, -ae*, F.
favor, *faveō*² (w. dat.).
favorable, (= good) *bonus, -a, -um*, adj.; **— disposition**, *voluntās, -ātis*, F.
favorableness, *opportūnitās, -ātis*, F.
favorably, — disposed, *amīcus, -a, -um*, adj.
fear, 1. subst., *metus, -ūs*, M.; *timor, -ōris*, M. 2. vb., *timeō*²; *metuō*³; *vereor*²; **paralyze with —**, *perterreō*.²
fearing (pres. part.), *veritus, -a, -um* (perf. part. of *vereor*).
feeble, *īnfīrmus, -a, -um*, adj.
fellow, **— citizen**, *cīvis, -is*, C.
fertile, *ferāx, -ācis*, adj.
few, *paucī, -ae, -a*, adj.; **a — words**, *pauca, -ōrum*, N.
field, *ager, -grī*, M.
fifteen, *quīndecim*, indecl. num. adj.
fifty, *quīnquāgintā*, indecl. num. adj.
fight, 1. subst., *pūgna, -ae*, F. 2. vb., *pūgnō*¹; *cōnflīgō*.³
fighting, *pūgna, -ae*, F.; (= battle) *proelium, -ī*, N.
figure, (= body) *corpus, -oris*, N.
fill, *compleō*²; (= fill full, crowd) *referciō*.⁴
find, (by search or inquiry) *reperiō*⁴; **— out**, (= trace out) *investīgō*.⁴
finish, *cōnficiō*.³
fir, *abiēs, -etis*, F.
fire, *īgnis, -is*, M.
firmly, become — established, *inveterāscō, -ere, -āvī*.
first, *prīmus, -a, -um*, adj.; *prīmum*, adv.; **for the — time**, *prīmum*, adv.; **at —**, *prīmō*, adv.
five, *quīnque*, indecl. num. adj.; **in groups of —**, *quīnī, -ae, -a*, distr. num. adj.
five hundred, *quīngentī, -ae, -a*, num. adj.
fix, (= value, appraise) *aestimō*.¹
flattery, *adsentātiō, -ōnis*, F.
flee, *fugiō*³; (= flee forth) *pro-*

fleet

*fugiō*³; (= flee back) *refugiō*³; to — for refuge, *sē recipere*.
fleet, *classis, -is,* F.
flight, *fuga, -ae,* F.
float, *ratis, -is,* F.
flock, *concurrō*.³
flow, (= flow into) *influō*³ (w. *in* and acc.).
follow, *sequor*³; (= follow close upon) *insequor*³ (w. acc.).
following, **posterus, -era, -erum,* adj.; (= that about to be mentioned) *ille, illa, illud,* demonstr. pron.; (= of this sort) *hūjusce modī*.
follows, as —, *hīc, haec, hōc,* demonstr. pron.; *sīc,* adv.; **substantially as —,** *hūjusce modī*.
folly, (= infatuation, madness) *dēmentia, -ae,* F.; (= absence of reason) *āmentia, -ae,* F.; **insane —,** *furor, -ōris,* M.
fond, — of, *studiōsus, -a, -um,* adj. (w. gen.); (= desirous of) *cupidus, -a, -um,* adj. (w. gen.).
food, *cibus, -ī,* M.
foot, *pēs, pedis,* M.
foot-soldier, *pedes, -itis,* M.
for, *nam,* conj. (begins the sentence or clause); *enim,* conj. (follows the first word or closely associated words); (= from) *dē,* prep. w. abl.: as, *quā dē causā,* **for what reason;** (= in behalf of) *prō,* prep. w. abl.; (= towards) *ergā,* prep. w. acc.; (= during) **sign of** acc. of duration of time; (= concerning) *dē,* prep. w. abl.; (= into) *in,* prep. w. acc.: as, **to depart for,** *proficiscī in;* (expressing purpose) *ad,* prep. w. acc. (of gerund or gerundive); (expressing adaptation w. *idōneus*) *ad,* prep. w. acc., also dat.; (= on account of) *ob,* prep. w. acc.
forage, *frūmentor*.¹
force, (= strength, violence) *vīs, vīs,* F.; (= armed force, band) *manus, -ūs,* F.; (= a multitude) *multitūdō, -inis,* F.; **to endeavor to —,** *per vim tentāre*.

friendly

forced, (= the greatest possible) *quam maximus, -a, -um,* adj.
forces, *cōpiae, -ārum,* F.
foremost, *princeps, -ipis,* adj.; **— man,** *princeps, -ipis,* M.; **— place,** *principātus, -ūs,* M.; **to be —,** *plūrimum valēre*.
foresee, *praevideō*.²
foreshadow, *canō, -ere, cecinī*.
forest, *silva, -ae,* F.
forever, *perpetuō,* adv.
forget, *oblīviscor*³ (w. gen., or [w. neut. pron.] acc.).
form, *faciō*³; **(of a design)** *capiō*³; **to —** (= to collect themselves), *sē conligere*.
former, *vetus, -eris,* adj.; **the —,** *ille, illa, illud,* demonstr. pron.
forsake, (= withdraw from) *discēdō*³ (w. *ab* and abl.); (= lay aside) *dēpōnō*.³
forth, set —, *prōpōnō*.³
fortify, *mūniō*.⁴
fortunate, *fortūnātus, -a, -um,* p. a.
fortune, *fortūna, -ae,* F.
forty, *quadrāgintā,* indecl. num. adj.
forward, go —, *exeō*⁴; **move —,** *prōmoveō*.²
founded, — in right, *jūstus, -a, -um,* adj.
four, *quattuor,* indecl. num. adj.; **— each,** *quaternī, -ae, -a,* distr. num. adj.
fourteenth, *quartus decimus, -a, -um* or *decimus et quartus, -a, -um,* ord. num. adj.
fourth, *quartus, -a, -um,* ord. num. adj.
fraught, — with danger, *perīculōsus, -a, -um,* adj.
free, *līber, -era, -erum,* adj.; **— from,** *vacuus, -a, -um* (w. *ab* or *ā* and abl.); **— from suspicion,** *pūrgātus, -a, -um,* p. a.; **— town,** *mūnicipium, -ī,* N.; vb., *līberō*.¹
freedom, *lībertās, -ātis,* F.
frequent, *crēber, -bra, -brum,* adj.
friend, *amīcus, -ī,* M.
friendly, *amīcus, -a, -um,* adj.

friendship **ground** 321

friendship, *amīcitia, -ae,* F.; (= favor) *grātia, -ae,* F.
from, *dē,* prep. w. abl.; (= away from) *ab* (before vowels and some consonants), *ā* (before consonants only), *abs* (sometimes before *tē*), prep. w. abl.; (= out of) *ex, ē,* prep. w. abl.; (after verbs of hindering) *quōmĭnus, nē,* (also, when there is a neg. expressed or implied w. the vb.) *quīn*(w. subj.).
front, in — of, *prō,* prep. w. abl.
frost, *frīgus, -oris,* N.
fruit, *frūctus, -ūs,* M.
full, *plēnus, -a, -um,* adj. (w. gen.); **— of courage,** *animōsus, -a, -um,* adj.
Furius, *Fūrius, -ī,* M.
furnished, — with saddles, *ephippiātus, -a, -um,* adj.
further, (= furthermore) *autem,* conj. (placed not at the beginning of the sentence, but after one or more words); (= oftener, more) *saepius,* adv.
future, *futūrus, -a, -um,* p. a.; **the —,** *futūra, -ōrum,* N.; **at some — time,** *aliquandō,* adv.

G.

Gabinius, *Gabīnius, -ī,* M.
gain, — access, *adeō.*⁴
Gajus, *C.* (abbr. of *Gājus, Gāī,* M.).
Galba, *Galba, -ae,* M.
Gallic, *Gallicus, -a, -um,* adj.
game, *ferīna carō (ferīnus, -a, -um,* of wild animals; *carō, carnis,* F., flesh).
garrison, *praesidium, -ī,* N.
gate, *porta, -ae,* F.
gather, — themselves, *congregō*¹ (in pass.).
Gaul, *Gallia, -ae,* F.
Gauls, *Gallī, -ōrum,* M.; **of the —,** *Gallicus, -a, -um,* adj.
gaze, — on, *intueor*² (w. acc.).
general, *commūnis, -e,* adj.; (= military commander) *imperātor, -ōris,* M.; **in —,** *omnīnō,* adv.

generally, — speaking, *plērumque,* adv.; **it is — understood,** *cōnstat,* impers.
generosity, *beneficium, -ī,* N.
Geneva, *Genāva, -ae,* F.; **lake —,** *lacus Lemannus, -ī,* M.
Germans, *Germānī, -ōrum,* M.
get, — together, *cōnferō.*
girl, *puella, -ae,* F.
give, *dō;* (= deliver) *trādō*³; **to — battle,** *proelium committere.*
glance, — at, *adspiciō.*³
glorious, *praeclārus, -a, -um,* adj.
glory, *glōria, -ae,* F.
go, *eō*⁴; (= set out) *proficiscor*³; (= go apart) *sēcēdō*³; **go, — away,** *abeō*⁴; **go, — out:** *exeō*⁴; *ēgredior*³; **— away** (= go out), *exeō*⁴; **— forward,** *exeō*⁴; **— over,** *trānseō.*⁴
god, *deus, -ī,* M.
good, *bonus, -a, -um,* adj.; **— will,** *grātia, -ae,* F.; **it seems —,** *placet,*² impers. (w. dat.)
govern, *imperō*¹ (w. dat.).
gradually, *paulātim,* adv.
grain, (= harvested grain) *frūmentum, -ī,* N.; (= standing grain) *frūmenta, -ōrum,* N.; *rēs frūmentāria.*
grandfather, *avus, -ī,* M.
grant, *dō.*
gratifying, *grātus, -a, -um,* adj.
great, *magnus, -a, -um,* adj.; **how —,** *quantus, -a, -um,* adj.; **so —,** *tantus, -a, -um,* adj.; **in — numbers** (= crowded), *frequēns, -entis,* adj.; **a — many,** *complūrēs, -a (-ia),* adj.
greatest, *maximus, -a, -um,* adj. (superl. of *magnus*); *summus, -a, -um,* adj. (superl. of *superus*); **— possible,** *quam maximus* (w. or without the proper fm. of *possum*).
grievous, *gravis, -e,* adj.
ground, *humus, -ī,* F.; (= earth) *terra, -ae,* F., **rising —,** *tumulus, -ī,* M.; **— of suspicion,** *suspīciō, -ōnis,* F.; **maintain one's —,** *subsistō*³; **to give — for,** *praebeō.*²

groups, in — of five, *quīnī, -ae, -a*, distr. num. adj.; **in — of six, sēnī**, *-ae, -a*, distr. num. adj.
guard, *custōs, -ōdis*, C.; (= garrison) *praesidium, -ī*, N.; **be on one's —**, *caveō*.²

H.

habitation, *sēdēs, -is*, F.
Hamilcar, *Hamilcar, -aris*, M.
hand, *manus, -ūs*, F.; **at —**, *praestō*, adv.
Hannibal, *Hannibal, -alis*, M.
happen, *accidō*³; (= become, be done) *fīō*.
happy, *beātus, -a, -um*, p. a.
harass, *premō*³; *exagitō*.¹
haste, make —, *contendō*.³
hasten, *mātūrō*¹; *contendō*³; *properō*.¹
hate, *ōdī*, def.
hatred, cherish —, *ōdī*, def.
have, *habeō*²; *sum* (w. dat. of possession); **— to do with**, *pertineō*² (w. *ad* and acc.).
he, (= that man) *ille*; (weaker than *ille*) *is*; (emphatic, = himself) *ipse*; (in indir. disc. referring to principal subject) *sē*; omitted when implied in the ending of the vb.
head, *caput, -itis*, N.; (= chief man) *princeps, -ipis*, M.
headlong, *praeceps, -ipitis*, adj.
headstrong, *temerārius, -a, -um*, adj.
health, *valētūdō, -inis*, F.
hear, *audiō*⁴; (= hear from a distance or hear distinctly) *exaudiō*⁴; (= receive by communication from others) *accipiō*.³
heaven, *caelum, -ī*, N.
heavily, *graviter*, adv.
height, *altitūdō, -inis*, F.
heinous, so —, *tantus, -a, -um*, adj.
help, *auxilium, -ī*, N.; **I cannot —**, *facere nōn possum* (w. *quīn* and subj.).
Helvetians, *Helvētiī, -ōrum*, M.
Helvetii, *Helvētiī, -ōrum*, M.
hem, — in, *contineō*² (w. acc.).

hence, *hinc*, adv.
Hercules, by —, *mehercule*.
here, be —, *adsum*.
herself, (reflex.) *sē*.
hesitate, *dubitō*.¹
Hesperia, *Hesperia, -ae*, F.
high, *altus, -a, -um*, p. a.; (= great) *māgnus, -a, -um*, adj.
higher, *superior, -ius*, adj. (comp. of *superus*).
highest, *summus, -a, -um*, adj.; (superl. of *superus*); **at the — possible price**, *quam plūrimō*.
highly, *māgnī* (gen. of indef. value).
hill, *collis, -is*, M.
himself, (reflex.) *sē*; (emphatic) *ipse* (alone or in apposition w. the reflex. *sē*).
hinder, *impediō*.⁴
hire, *condūcō*.³
his, *ejus* (gen. of *is*); (referring to the subject) *suus, -a, -um*, poss. pron.; **— own**, *suus, -a, -um*, poss. pron.; omitted when the context shows who is meant.
hither, *citerior, -ius*, adj.
hold, *teneō*²; *obtineō*²; **— off**, *abstineō*²; (= regard, consider) *habeō*.²
home, *domus, -ūs*, F.; **at —**, *domī*; **from —**, *domō*.
honor, *honor, -ōris*, M.; **personal —**, *modestia, -ae*, F.
honorable, *honestus, -a, -um*, adj.
hope, *spēs, -ēī (-eī)*, F.
horse, *equus, -ī*, M.; (= horsemen) *equitēs, -um*, M.
horseman, *eques, -itis*, M.
hostage, *obses, -idis*, C.
hostile, *inimīcus, -a, -um*, adj.
hour, *hōra, -ae*, F.
house, *domus, -ūs*, F.; **at the — of**, *apud*, prep. w. acc.
how, *quam*, adv.; **— great**, *quantus, -a, -um*, adj.; **— much**, *quantus, -a, -um*, adj.; **— dear**, *quantī* (gen. indef. value); **— long**: *quam diū*, adv.; (= how far) *quousque*, adv.
however, *quamvīs*, adv.; (= nevertheless) *tamen*, conj.

hundred   **intercessor**   323

hundred, *centum,* indecl. num. adj.; **two —,** *ducenti, -ae, -a,* num. adj.; **three —,** *trecenti, -ae, -a,* num. adj.; **six —,** *sescenti, -ae, -a,* num. adj.
    hundredth, *centesimus, -a, -um,* ord. num. adj.

I.

I, *ego, meī,* pers. pron.
Iccius, *Iccius, -ī,* M.
idleness, *ignāvia, -ae,* F.
if, *sī*; **— not,** *sī nōn*; **— not** (= unless) *nisi*; **— only,** *dum,* conj. (w. subj.).
ignominiously, *turpiter,* adv.
ill, *aeger, -gra, -grum,* adj.
illustrious, *clārus, -a, -um,* adj.; *amplus,* **-a, -um,** adj.
imagine, (= think) *existimō.*¹
immortal, *immortālis, -e,* adj.
impede, *impediō*⁴; **to — the army's march,** *itinere exercitum prohibēre.*
implore, *obsecrō*¹; *implōrō.*¹
import, *importō*¹; *inferō.*
importance, of the highest —, *summus, -a, -um,* adj. (superl. of *superus*); **it is of — :** *interest,* impers.
important, it is —: *interest; refert, -ferre, -tulit.*
in, *in,* prep. w. abl.; (after a superl.) sign of the gen.; (= into) *in,* prep. w. acc.: **in breadth, in width,** *in lātitūdinem*; **in length,** *in longitūdinem*; **to be —,** *inesse* (w. dat.); **to vie —,** *certāre dē* (w. abl.); **— the rear,** *ā novissimō agmine, ab novissimīs*; **— my eyes,** *mihi* (dat. ref.); **— that he,** *quī* (= *cum is*) w. subj.
inasmuch, — as, *quoniam,* conj.; sign of abl. abs. denoting cause.
incident, *rēs,* gen. *reī* (*reī, rē*), F.
inclination, to restrain one's — to, *sibi temperāre quīn* (w. subj.).
increase, *amplificō*¹; *augeō.*²

incur, *adeō*⁴ (w. acc.).
indeed, *quidem* (follows the word that it emphasizes), adv.; (introducing a corroborative or a parenthetical clause) *etenim,* conj.
indignity, *contumēlia, -ae,* F.
indulge, *indulgeō*² (w. dat.).
industry, *industria, -ae,* F.
inexperience, *īnscientia, -ae,* F.
infamy, *īnfāmia, -ae,* F.
infantry, *cōpiae pedestrēs* (*pedester, -tris, -tre,* adj.).
inflict, *sūmō*³; **to — punishment on:** *supplicium sūmere dē* (w. abl.); *vindicāre in* (w. acc.).
influence, *auctōritās, -ātis,* F.; (arising from good will) *grātia, -ae,* F.; **of great —,** *potēns, -entis,* adj.; **to have very little —,** *minimum posse*; **to have very great —,** *largiter posse.*
inform, *certiōrem faciō*³; **be informed,** *certior fīō*; **thoroughly —,** *ēdoceō*² (w. two accs. in act.).
infuse, *īnferō* (w. acc. th. and dat. pers.).
inhabit, *incolō*³ (w. acc.).
inhabitants, (= people) *hominēs, -um,* M.
injure, *noceō*² (w. dat.).
injury, *injūria, -ae,* F.; **without risk of —,** *sine fraude.*
innocent, *innocēns, -entis,* adj.
inquire, *quaerō*³ (w. acc. th., and abl. pers. w. *ab, dē,* or *ex*).
inquiry, make —, *quaerō.*³
insane, — folly, *furor, -ōris,* M.
institution, *īnstitūtum, -ī,* N.
instruction, (= commission, injunction) *mandātum, -ī,* N.
intellect, *ingenium, -ī,* N.
intelligence, receive — of, *cōgnōscō*³ (w. *dē* and abl.).
intend, *esse in animō* (w. dat. pers.).
intention, it is one's —, *alicui est in animō.*
intercession, at the — of, *dēprecātor, -ōris,* M. (abl. abs.).
intercessor, *dēprecātor, -ōris,* M.

**interval, *intervallum*, -ī, N.;
place at intervals, *dispōnō*[3]
intervene, *intercēdō*.[3]
intimacy, *ūsus, -ūs*, M.
into, *in*, prep. w. acc.
intrust,** *mandō*[1]*; trādō*.[3]
inured, — to, *patiēns, -entis*, p. a. (w. gen.).
iron-hearted, so —, *ille ferreus* (*-a, -um*).
issue, to bring to a successful —, *bene gerere*.
it, *is, ea, id*, pron.; omitted if implied in the ending of the verb or understood from the context.
Italy, *Ītalia, -ae*, F.
its, (referring to the subject) *suus, -a, -um*, poss. pron.
itself, (intens.) *ipse, ipsa, ipsum*, demonstr. pron.

J.

January, of —, *Jānuārius, -a, -um*, adj.
join, *jungō, -ere, jūnxī, jūnctus*; **to — battle,** *proelium committere*; **depart to —,** *proficiscor*[3] (w. *in* and acc.).
Juba, *Juba, -ae*, M.
judge, *jūdex, -icis*, C.
judgment, pass — upon, *sentiō*[4] (w. *dē* and abl.).
jugerum, *jugerum, -ī*, N.; in pl., *jugera, -um*, N.
Jugurtha, *Jugurtha, -ae*, M.
Julian, *Jūliānus, -a, -um*, adj.
Jupiter, *Juppiter, Jovis*, M.
Jura, *Jūra, -ae*, M.
just, *jūstus, -a, -um*, adj.

K.

Kalends, *Kalendae, -ārum*, F.
keep, *teneō*[2]; (= keep together, confine) *contineō*[2]; **— back,** *teneō*[2]; **— apart, — asunder,** *distineō*[2]; **— one's word,** *fidem servō*[1]
keeping, *fidēs*, gen., *-ēī* (*-eī, -ē*), F.
kill, *interficiō*[3]; (by cutting or striking down) *occīdō*.[3]
kind, (= sort) *genus, -eris*, N.

king, *rēx, rēgis*, M.
kingdom, *rēgnum, -ī*, N.
kinsmen, *cōnsanguineī, -ōrum*, M.
knight, *eques, -itis*, M.
know, *sciō*[4]; (= understand) *intellegō*[3]; not —: *ignōrō*[1]; *nesciō*.[4]
known, *nōtus, -a, -um*, p. a.; *cōgnitus, -a, -um*, p. a.; **make —,** *ostendō*.[3]

L.

Labienus, *Labiēnus, -ī*, M.
Lacedaemon, *Lacedaemōn, -onis*, F.
lack, *egeō*[2] (w. gen. or abl.).
Laeca, *Laeca, -ae*, M.
lake, *lacus, -ūs*, M.
land, *ager, -grī*, M.; **by —,** *terrā*.
language, *lingua, -ae*, F.; (= phraseology) *ōrātiō, -ōnis*, F.
large, *māgnus, -a, -um*, adj.; *amplus, -a, -um*, adj.; **so —,** *tantus, -a, -um*, adj.
last, (= nearest, as in 'last night') *proximus, -a, -um*, adj.; (= remotest) *extrēmus, -a, -um*, adj.
lasting, *perpetuus, -a, -um*, adj.
latter, *hīc, haec, hōc*, demonstr. pron.
lavish, *profūsus, -a, -um*, p. a.
law, *lēx, lēgis*, F.
lawful, it is —, *licet*,[2] impers. (w. dat. pers.).
lay, — claim to, *repetō*[3]; **to — down arms,** *ab armīs discēdere*; **— waste,** *vastō*[1]; **— aside,** *dēpōnō*[3]; **to — the matter before,** *referre ad*.
lead, *dūcō*[3]; **— across,** *trādūcō*[3] (may take two accs.); **— out,** *ēdūcō*[3]; **— away,** *abdūcō*[3]; **— against,** *addūcō*[3] (w. *ad* and acc.).
leader, *dux, ducis*, C.; (= foremost man) *prīnceps, -ipis*, M.
league, unite in a sworn —, *conjūrō*.[1]
learn, *discō*[3]; (= become acquainted with) *cōgnōscō*[3]; (= find out by search or inquiry) *reperiō*[4]; (by looking at, examining) *perspiciō*.[3]

least, — of all, *minimē*, adv.
leave, *relinquō*³; **— behind,** *relinquō*.³
left, *sinister, -tra, -trum,* adj.; **on the —,** *sinister;* **be —,** *supersum*.
legion, *legiō, -ōnis,* F.
length, in —, *in longitūdinem*.
less, *minor, -us,* adj.; (adv.) *minus*.
lest, *nē* (w. subj.).
let, — loose, *ēmittō*.³
letter, *epistula, -ae,* F.
level, *coaequō*.¹
liberty, one is at —, *licet*² (w. dat. and inf. or *ut* w. subj.).
lie, — prostrate, *jaceō*.²
lieutenant, *lēgātus, -ī,* M.
life, *vīta, -ae,* F.; (with ref. to its several stages, as boyhood, youth, etc.) *aetās, -ātis,* F.; (= [manner of] living) *victus, -ūs,* M.
light, (subst.) *lūx, lūcis,* F.; (adj.) *levis, -e;* **to make — of,** *parvī pendere* (w. acc.).
lightning, strike by —, *dē caelō percutiō, -ere, -cussī, -cussus*.
line, (= line of battle) *aciēs,* gen. *-ē* and *-ēī,* F.; **— of march,** *iter, itineris,* N.
lip, *labrum, -ī,* N.
list, *ratiō, -ōnis,* F.
listen, *audiō*.⁴
little, *parvus, -a, -um,* adj.; **very —,** *minimus, -a, -um,* adj.; *minimē,* adv.; **a —** (= by a little) *paulō*.
live, *vīvō*.³
living, — creature, *animal, -ālis,* N.
long, *longus, -a, -um,* adj.; (= for a long time) *diū,* adv., *longē,* adv.; **how —,** *quam diū,* adv.; (= how far) *quousque,* adv.; **— ago,** *jamprīdem,* adv.
longer, (= for a longer time) *diūtius,* adv., *longius,* adv.
look, (= look at) *adspiciō*³; **— for,** *exspectō*.¹
loose, let —, *ēmittō*.³
lose, *āmittō*.³
loss, *dētrīmentum, -ī,* N.; **to risk the — of,** *āmittere*.

lot, (= fortune) *fortūna, -ae,* F.; (= condition) *condiciō, -ōnis,* F.
love, 1. subst., *amor, -ōris,* M. **2.** vb., *amō*¹; (= esteem highly) *dīligō*.³
low, *humilis, -e,* adj.
lower, *īnferior, -ius,* adj.
Lucius, *Lūcius, -iī,* M., abbr. *L.*
luxury, *luxuria, -ae,* F.
Lycomedes, *Lycomēdēs, -is,* M.
Lysander, *Lysander, -drī,* M.

M.

made, be —, *fīō*.
magistracy, *magistrātus, -ūs,* M.
maiden, *virgō, -inis,* F.
main, — question, *sententia, -ae,* F.
maintain, (of one's rights) *exsequor*³; **— one's position,** *cōnsistō*³; **— one's ground,** (= withstand) *subsistō*³; **the fight was maintained,** *pūgnātum est*.
majority, *major pars*.
make, *faciō*³; (= render) *efficiō*³; (= choose, **elect,** appoint) *creō*¹; **(of a** speech) *habeō*²; **— for,** *petō*³; **— out** (of a list) *cōnficiō*.³
man, (= human being, and so including woman) *homo, -inis,* C.; (= an adult male person; opp. *mulier,* woman) *vir, virī,* M.; (= man of noble qualities) *vir, virī,* M.
manage, *administrō*.¹
Manilius, *Mānīlius, -iī,* M.
maniple, *manipulus, -ī,* M.
Manlius, *Manlius, -iī,* M.
many, *multī, -ae, -a,* adj.; **a great —, very —,** *complūrēs, -a* (*-ia*), gen. *-ium,* adj.; **so —,** *tot,* indecl. adj.; **so — things,** *ita multa*.
Marcellus, *Mārcellus, -ī,* M.
march, 1. subst., *iter, itineris,* N.; **line of —,** *iter, itineris,* N. **2.** vb., *iter faciō*.³
marches, (= frontiers) *fīnēs, -ium,* M.
marching, *iter, itineris,* N.

Marcus, *Mārcus*, -ī, M., abbr. *M.*
maritime, *maritimus, -a, -um,* adj.
Marius, *Marius, -ī,* M.
mark, — out, *mētor.*[1]
marriage, to give in —: *nūptum* (sup.) *dare; conlocō*[1] (w. or without *nūptum*).
marry, (of the woman) *nūbō*[3]; see also marriage.
Marseilles, from —, *Massiliēnsis, -e,* adj.
marsh, *palūs, -ūdis,* F.
mass, — meeting, *cōntiō, -ōnis,* F.
massacre, *caedēs, -is,* F.
Massiva, *Massiva, -ae,* M.
master, *magister, -trī,* M.; *dominus, -ī,* M.
match, to be a — for, *pār* (gen. *paris*) *esse; —* **against,** *obiciō*[3] (w. acc. **and dat.**).
matter, (= **thing**) *rēs,* gen. *reī* (*reī, rē*), F.
matters, it —, *interest, rē fert* or *rēfert;* (subst.) *rēs, rērum,* F.
me, to — (= in my estimation), *apud mē.*
mean, to —, *sibi velle* (see *volō*).
means, (= resources) *facultātēs, -um,* F. (pl.); **— of defence,** *remedium, -ī,* N.; **by no —,** *minimē,* adv.
meantime, (of an event extending through the interval) *intereā,* adv.; (of an event occurring within the interval) *interim,* **adv.**
meanwhile, *interim,* adv.; *intereā,* adv. See also meantime.
measure, (= thing) *rēs,* gen. *reī* (*reī, rē*), F.
Medea, *Mēdēa, -ae,* F.
meet, to —, (w. vbs. of motion) *obviam,* adv.
meeting, mass —, *cōntiō, -ōnis,* F.
memory, *memoria, -ae,* F.; **cherish the — of,** *meminī,* def.
men, (w. poss. pron.) omitted: as, **our —,** *nostrī, -ōrum,* M.
merchant, *mercātor, -ōris,* M.
mere, *ipse, ipsa, ipsum,* demonstr. pron.

merely, *sōlum,* adv.
messenger, *nūntius, -ī,* M.
Messalla, *Messālla, -ae,* M.
mid, — summer, *media aestās* (*-ātis,* F.).
middle, — of, *medius, -a, -um,* adj.
midst, *medius, -a, -um,* adj.; **through the — of them,** *per mediōs.*
mile, *mīlle passūs; mīlle passuum.*
miles, *mīlia* (*mīllia*) *passuum; mīlia* (sc. *passuum*).
military, *mīlitāris, -e,* **adj.**; **— tribune,** *tribūnus mīlitum.*
milk, *lac, lactis,* N.
mind, *animus, -ī,* M.; *ingenium, -ī,* N.; *mēns, mentis,* F.; (= purpose, intention) *mēns, mentis,* F.; **call to —,** *recordor*[1] (usu. w. acc.); **recall to —,** *reminiscor, -ī* (w. gen.; also w. acc.). When *reminiscor* and *recordor* are distinguished, the former means 'recall to mind,' the latter 'reflect on' or 'review.'
mindful, *memor, -oris,* **adj.** (w. gen.).
mischief, *maleficium, -ī,* N.
misery, *malum, -ī,* N.
misfortune, *fortūna, -ae,* F. (the *misfortune* is here implied in the context).
miss, *dēsīderō.*[1]
mistakes, make —, *peccō*[1]; **to make the same —,** *eadem peccāre.*
mob, *multitūdō, -inis,* F.
mock, *ēlūdō, -ere, -sī, -sus.*
mode, *cōnsuētūdō, -inis,* F.; (= kind) *genus, -eris,* N.
modestly, *modestē,* adv.
moment, (= time) *tempus, -oris,* N.; **at the — when,** *tum cum;* **for the —,** *jam,* adv.
moon, *lūna, -ae,* F.
Moor, *Maurus, -ī,* M.
Moorish, *Maurus, -a, -um,* adj.
morally, — bad, *improbus, -a, -um,* adj.
morals, *mōrēs, -um,* M. (pl.).
more, *magis,* adv.; (of quan-

tity) *plūs*, comp. adj. used subst. (w. part. gen.); (frequently w. expressions of number) *amplius*, adv.
 Morini, *Morinī, -ōrum*, M.
 mortification, *dolor, -ōris*, M.
 most, — **people**, *plērīque*, adj. used subst.
 mother, *māter, -tris*, F.
 mound, **earth** —, *tumulus, -ī*, M.
 mount, *mōns, montis*, M.
 mountain, *mōns, montis*, M.
 move, *moveō*² ; — **forward**, *prōmoveō*² ; — **deeply**, *permoveō*² ; **to** — **on**, *pergere hinc*.
 movement, (= thing) *rēs*, gen. *reī (reī, rē)*, F.
 much, *multus, -a, -um*, adj. ; **very** —, *plūrimus, -a, -um*, adj. ; (adv. = by much) *multō* ; **how** —, *quantus, -a, -um*, adj.
 multitude, *multitūdō, -inis*, F.
 music, *mūsicē, -ēs*, F.
 my, *meus, -a, -um*, poss. pron. ; — **own**, *meus* ; **it is** — **pleasure**, *mihī placet* ; **for** — **part**, *equidem*, adv.
 myself, oblique case of *ego*, *meī*, pers. pron.

N.

 name, *nōmen, -inis*, N.
 named, (= by name) *nōmine*.
 Nantuates, *Nantuātēs, -um*, M.
 Naples, *Neāpolis, -is*, F.
 naturally, *nātūrā* (abl.).
 nature, *nātūra, -ae*, F.
 near, *ad*, prep. w. acc.
 nearest, *proximus, -a, -um*, adj.
 nearly, *ferē*, adv.
 necessary, *opus*, N., used as nom. and acc. only (w. dat. pers. and abl. th.).
 need, *opus*, N. (see foregoing word); (vb.) *indigeō*² (w. gen. or abl.).
 neglect, *neglegō*.³
 neighbors, *fīnitimī, -ōrum*, M. (adj. used subst.).
 neighboring, *fīnitimus, -a, -um*, adj. ; (= nearest) *proximus, -a, -um*, adj.

 neither, *neque, nec*, conj. ; — **party**, *neutrī, -ōrum*, M.
 Nero, *Nerō, -ōnis*, M.
 Nervii, *Nerviī, -ōrum*, M.
 never, *nunquam* or *numquam*, adv.
 nevertheless, *tamen*, conj.
 new, *novus, -a, -um*, adj.
 next, *proximus, -a, -um*, adj.
 night, *nox, noctis*, F.
 night-fall, (= first part of the night) *prīma nox* (**gen.** *noctis*, F.).
 ninth, *nōnus, -a, -um*, ord. num. adj.
 no, *nūllus, -a, -um*, adj. ; (emphatic) *nēmō* (used adj.) ; (= not) *nōn*, adv. ; — **one**: *nēmō* (see *nēmō* in Latin-English vocabulary) ; *nūllus, -īus* (adj. used subst.) ; — **one but**, *nēmō nisī* ; **by** — **means**, *minimē*, adv. (superl.).
 nobility, *nōbilitās, -ātis*, F.
 noble, *nōbilis, -e*, adj. ; subst., *nōbilis, -is*, M.
 nor, *neque, nec*, conj.
 north, *septentriō, -ōnis*, M.
 north-east, see '**north**' and '**east**.'
 not, *nōn*, adv. ; *haud*, adv. (usu. w. adverbs; also w. *sciō*) ; (= less) *minus*, adv. ; (in questions implying an affirmative answer) *nōnne*, interrog. particle ; **and** —, *neque, nec*, conj. ; **that** —, **not** (in final, hortatory, imperat., and optative clauses) *nē* ; **that** — **any**, **that no** (in final and imperat. clauses), *nē quī, qua* or *quae, quod*, indef. adj. ; **not** . . . **either** . . . **or**, *neque* . . . *neque*.
 note, *animadvertō*.³
 nothing, *nihil* or *nīl*, N., def. ; *nūlla rēs* ; — **but**, *nihil nisi*.
 now, *nunc*, adv. ; *jam*, adv.
 Numantia, *Numantia, -ae*, F.
 number, *numerus, -ī*, M.
 numbers, **great** —, *māgnae cōpiae (-ārum)*, F. ; **in great** —, *frequēns, -entis*, adj.
 numerous, *crēber, -bra, -brum*, adj.
 Numidians, *Numidae, -ārum*, M.

O.

O, oh, *ō,* interj.

obedience, yield —, *pāreō, -ēre, -uī.*

obey, *pāreō*[2] (w. dat.).

object', *recūsō*[1]*; to — to, recūsāre dē* (w. abl.).

ob'ject, *rēs,* gen. *rĕī* (*rēī, rē*), F.

obscurity, *obscūritās, -ātis,* F.

observe, *animadvertō.*[3]

obtain, *obtineō*[2] (w. acc.); (= prepare) *comparō*[1]; (= obtain possession of) *potior*[4] (w. abl.; also w. gen.); **— a request,** *impetrō.*[1]

occur, *accidō*[3]*; fīō.*

Octodurus, *Octŏdūrus, -ī,* M.

odds, struggle against —, *labōrō.*[1]

Oedipus, *Oedĭpŭs, -odis* or *-ī,* M.

of, sign of gen.; (= about, concerning) *dē,* prep. w. abl.; (= from) *ab, ā, ex, ē, dē,* preps. w. abl.; **out —,** *ex, ē,* prep. w. abl.

off, to come —, *sē inde recipere;* **to come — conqueror,** *superior discēdere;* **carry —,** *abdūcō*[3]*;* **cut —:** *excipiō*[3]*;* (from supplies) *prohĭbeō*[2] (w. acc. and abl.); **ward — from,** *prōpulsō*[1] (w. *ab, ā* and abl.); **hold —,** *abstineō.*[2]

offence, *rēs,* gen. *rĕī* (*rēī, rē*), F.

offer, — resistance, *resistō.*[3]

office, (= duty, function) *mūnus, -eris,* N.

often, *saepe,* adv.

oftentimes, *saepenumerō,* adv.

old, *vetus, -eris,* adj.; **— man,** *senex, senis,* M.

old age, *senectūs, -ūtis,* F.

on, in, prep. w. abl.; (designating the point from which) *ab, ā, ex, ē,* preps. w. abl.; (= concerning) *dē,* prep. w. abl.; (= against) *in,* prep. w. acc.; (= from this place) *hinc,* adv.; **On!** *agite* (imperat.); (in expressions of time) sign of abl. of time.

once, *quondam,* adv.; **at — (= at one time)** *ūnō tempore.*

one, *ūnus, -a, -um,* num adj.; (of two) *alter, -era, -erum;* (w. substs. pl. in form, but sing. in meaning) *ūnī, -ae, -a* (pl. of *ūnus*); **— by —,** *singŭlī, -ae, -a,* distr num. adj.; **this — thing,** *id ūnum;* **one ... another,** *alius ... alius;* **at one time ... at another,** *aliās ... aliās.*

one's self, *suī, sibī, sē* (*sēsē*), reflexive pron.; **devote —,** *serviō*[4] (w. dat.).

only, (= altogether, in all) *omnīnō,* adv.; **if —,** *dum,* conj (w. subj.); **the — one,** *ūnus, -a, -um,* num. adj.; **not only ... but also,** *et ... et, nōn modo* or *nōn sōlum ... sed etiam* or *vērum etiam;* **and not only ... but also,** *neque sōlum ... sed etiam.*

onset, *impetus, -ūs,* M.

open, *laxō*[1]*;* **to — an engagement,** *proelium committere.*

openly, *apertē,* adv.

opinion, *sententia, -ae,* F.; *opiniō, -ōnis,* F.

opportune, *opportūnus, -a, -um,* adj.

opportunity, *occāsiō, -ōnis,* F.; *facultās, -ātis,* F.

opposed, *dīversus, -a, -um,* adj.

or, *aut,* conj.; **either ... or:** (when a choice is offered) *vel ... vel;* (when one excludes the other) *aut ... aut;* **not ... either ... or,** *neque ... neque.*

orator, *ōrātor, -ōris,* M.

order, 1. subst., *imperium, -ī,* N. 2. vb., *jubeō* (w. infin.). 3. conj., **in — to:** *ut* (w. subj.); (w. comp.) *quō* (w. subj.).

Orgetorix, *Orgetorix, -ĭgis,* M.

other, *alius, -a, -ud,* adj. and subst.; **some ... others,** *pars ... aliī;* (= the rest of) *cēterī, -ae, -a,* adj.(usu. pl.); **with each —,** *inter sē;* **some ... the others,** *alteri ... alterī;* **others',** *aliēnus, -a, -um,* adj.

ought, *dēbeō*[2]*; oportet,*[2] impers. (w. acc. and infin. as subject; also w. subj. clause).

our, — own, *noster, -tra, -trum,* poss. pron.; **— men, — party,** *nostrī, -ōrum,* M.

out   **Pompey**   329

out, — of, *ex, -ē*, prep. w. abl.
outcry, *vōx, vōcis,* F.
outstretch, *pandō.*³
over, see 'go' or 'step.'
overcome, — with terror, *perterreō.*²
overlook, *condōnō.*¹
overwhelm, *opprimō.*³
owing, — to, *propter,* **prep. w.** acc.
own, his —, their —, *suus, -a, -um,* poss. pron.; our —, *noster, -tra, -trum,* poss. **pron.**; my —, *meus, -a, -um,* poss. **pron.**

P.

pace, *passus, -ūs,* M.
pain, *dolor, -ōris,* M.
pains, *opera, -ae,* F.
panic, there is a —, *trepidātur.*
paralyze, — with fear, *perterreō.*²
pardon, *ignōscō.*³
parent, *parēns, -entis,* C.
Parmenio, *Parmeniō, -ōnis,* M.
part, *pars, partis,* F.; for my —, *equidem,* adv.; take — in, *intersum* (w. dat.).
partiality, exercise —, *studeō.*²
party, *pars, partis,* F.; our —, *nostrī, -ōrum,* M.
pass, *effluō, -ere, -xī;* — judgment upon, *sentiō*⁴ (w. dē and abl.); — round, *circumferō;* — through, *trānseō.*⁴
passage, *iter, itineris,* N.
passion, give way to —, *īrāscor.*³
passionate, *īrācundus, -a, -um,* adj.
past, the —, *praeterita, -ōrum,* N., p. a. used subst.
path, by a circuitous —, *in circuitū.*
patience, *patientia, -ae,* F.
patrimony, *rēs familiāris,* adj.
patriotism, *amor patriae.*
pay, — respects to, *salūtō.*¹
peace, *pāx, pācis,* F.
Pelusium, *Pēlūsium, -ī,* N.
penalty, *poena, -ae,* F.; (= fine) *līs, lītis,* F.

penetrate, — to, *adeō*⁴ (w. ad and acc.).
penetrating, *ācer, -cris, -cre,* adj.
people, *populus, -ī,* M.; common —, *plēbs, -is,* F.; most —, *plērīque,* M. pl. adj. used subst.
perceive, *animum advertō* or *animadvertō*³ (w. acc.); *perspiciō.*³
perform, *praestō*¹ (w. acc.).
peril, *perīculum, -ī,* N.
perilous, *perīculōsus, -a, -um,* adj.
period, *tempus, -oris,* N.
permit, *patior.*³
permitted, it is —, *licet,*² impers. (w. dat. pers.).
pernicious, *perniciōsus, -a, -um,* adj.
persevere, — in, *cōnfīrmō.*¹
personally, he, they, etc. —, proper form of *ipse.*
persons, these same —, *īdem* (masc. pl.), demonstr. pron.
persuade, *persuādeō*² (w. dat. pers.).
Picene, *Picēnus, -a, -um,* adj.
pile, *līgnum, -ī,* N.
pilot, *gubernātor, -ōris,* M.
Piso, *Pīsō, -ōnis,* M.
pitch, *pōnō.*³
pitiable, *miser, -era, -erum,* adj.
pity, *misereor*² (w. gen.).
place, 1. subst., *locus, -ī,* M.; in pl. (usually) *loca, -ōrum,* N.; in that —, *ibī,* adv.; to some —, *aliquō,* adv.; take —, *fīō.* 2. vb., *pōnō*³; *conlocō.*¹
plan, *cōnsilium, -ī,* N.
pleasant, *grātus, -a, -um,* adj.
please, *dēlectō*¹; (= wish, choose) *volō.*
pleasure, it is one's —, *placet,*² impers. (w. dat. pers.).
point, to that —, *eō,* adv.; in — of fact, *rē;* to make a — of, *dare operam ut* (w. **subj.**); — out, *expōnō.*³
policy, *cōnsilium, -ī,* N.
political, — power, *potentia, -ae,* F.
Pompey, *Pompējus, Pompeī,* M.

Pontus, *Pontus, -i*, M.
poor, *pauper, -eris*, adj.
popular, (= acceptable) *acceptus, -a, -um*, p. a.
population, *hominum numerus, -i*, M.
position, (= place) *locus, -i*, M.; take —, maintain one's —, *consisto*.[3]
possess, *possideo*.[2]
possession, *possessio, -onis*, F.; obtain — of, *potior*[4] (w. abl.; also w. gen.); take — of, seize, *occupo*[1] (w. acc.).
possible, possibly, (w. superl.) *quam*, adv. (w. or without proper fm. of *possum*); it is —, (= it is permitted) *licet*,[2] impers. (w. dat. pers.).
post, *constituo*[3]; **be posted**, *consisto*.[3]
posterity, *posteri, -orum*, M. (adj. used subst.).
poverty, *inopia, -ae*, F.
power, *potestas, -atis*, F.
powerful, *potens, -entis*, adj.; to be very —, *largiter posse*.
practice, *consuetudo, -inis*, F.; (= training) *exercitatio, -onis*, F.
praetor, *praetor, -oris*, M.
praise, *laudo*.[1]
pray (exclam.), *tandem*, adv
precautions, take special —, *magnopere* **praecaveo** (*-ere, -cavi, -cautus*).
preceding, *superior, -ius*, adj. comp.; on the — day, *pridie*, adv.
prefer, *antepono*[3] (w. acc. and dat.); (= wish rather) *malo*.
preoccupation, *cogitatio, -onis*, F.
prepare, *paro*.[1]
presence, *praesentia, -ae*, F.
present, *praesens, -entis*, adj.; the —, *praesentia, -ium*, neut. pl. adj. used subst.; be —, **adsum**.
preserve, *conservo*.[1]
preserved, *salvus, -a, -um*, adj.
press, — earnestly, *postulo*[1] (w. acc. th., and abl. pers. w. *ab, a*).

prevail, — upon, *persuadeo*[2] (w. dat. pers.).
prevent, *prohibeo*.[2]
price, at the highest possible —, *quam plurimo*.
priestly, — dignity, *sacerdotium, -ii*, N.
principle, recognized —, *jus, juris*, N.
private, — citizen, *privatus, -i*, M. (p. a. used subst.); — resources, *res familiaris*.
Procillus, *Procillus, -i*, M.
proclaim, (= declare, pronounce) *judico*.[1]
produce, *fructus, -us*, M.
progress, be in —, *fio*.
promise, *polliceor*.[2]
proper, it is —, *oportet*,[2] impers.
prophetess, prophet, *vates, -is*, C.
prospect, *spes*, gen. *spei* (*ei*), F.
prosperous, *florens, -entis*, p. a.
prostrate, lie —, *jaceo*.[2]
protect, *munio*[4]; *circummunio*[4]; — from, *prohibeo*[2] (w. *ab* and *abl.*).
protection, *praesidium, -ii*, N.
provide, *provideo*.[2]
provided, *dum, dummodo* (w. subj.).
province, *provincia, -ae*, F.
provisions, *res frumentaria*.
provocation, without —, *injuria*.
public, *publicus, -a, -um*, adj.; — enemy, *hostis, -is*, C.
punish, *punio*.[4]
punishment, *supplicium, -ii*, N.; (= expiation or penalty) *poena, -ae*, F.
pupil, *discipulus, -i*, M.
purificatory, — sacrifice, *lustrum, -i*, N.
purpose, *mens, mentis*, F.; (= wish) *voluntas, -atis*, F.; for the — of, *causa* (w. gen. preceding); (= thing) *res*, gen. *rei* (*rei, re*), F.
pursue, *sequor*.[3]
put, — aside, *depono*[3]; — to death, *neco*[1]; — to flight, *in fugam conicio*.[3]

quantity   remiss   331

Q.

quantity, a great — of, *ingēns, -entis,* adj.
quarter, (= part, direction) *pars, partis,* F.
quarters, winter —, *hīberna, -ōrum,* N.; **at close —,** *comminus,* adv.
quest, go in — of, *petō.*[3]
question, main —, *sententia, -ae,* F.
quickly, *celeriter,* adv.
quiet, be —, *quiēscō.*[3]
quietly, *modestē,* **adv.**
quite, *plānē,* **adv.**

R.

race, *genus, -eris,* N.; (= people) *populus, -ī,* M.
raid, to make a — on, *sē ēicere* (w. *in* and acc.).
raise, *exstruō.*[3]
rampart, *vāllum, -ī,* N.
rank, *ōrdō, -inis,* M.; (= nobility) *nōbilitās, -ātis,* F.; **of high —,** *nōbilis, -e,* adj.
rapidly, *strēnuē,* adv.
rate, at any —, *certē,* adv.
rather, (w. an adj.) sign of comp.; **choose —,** *mālō.*
reach, *ēvādō, -ere, -sī, -sus* (w. *in* and acc.).
readily, *facile,* adv.
rear, *novissimum agmen, -inis,* N.; **in the —:** *ab novissimīs;* *ā novissimō agmine.*
reason, *causa, -ae,* F.; **for what —,** *quā dē causā.*
recall, — to mind, *reminiscor, -ī* (w. gen.; also w. acc.); (= withdraw) *dēdūcō.*[3]
recalling, (= mindful of) *memor, -oris,* adj. (w. gen.).
receive, *accipiō*[3]; (= take) *capiō.*[3]
recent, *recēns, -entis,* adj.
recklessly, *temerē,* adv.
recklessness, *audācia, -ae,* F.
recognized, — principle, *jūs, jūris,* N.
recollection, *animus, -ī,* M.
recompense, *remūneror.*[1]

recount, *memorō*[1]; **commemorō.**[1]
recourse, have — to, *dēscendō*[3] (w. *ad* and acc.); *dēclīnō*[1] (w. *ad* and acc.).
recover, to — (intr.), *sē recipere;* (from illness) *convalēscō, -ere, -uī.*
redoubt, *castellum, -ī,* N.
reduce, *redigō.*[3]
reënforcement, *subsidium, -ī,* N.
reference, make — to, *referō* (w. *ad* and acc.).
reflect, — on, *recordor*[1] (usu. w. acc.).
refrain, — from, *temperō* (w. *ab* and abl.).
refuge, to flee for —, *sē recipere.*
refuse, *recūsō*[1]; **to — to :** *recūsāre quōminus* or *quīn* (w. subj.); also *recūsāre* w. infin.; **to — to pay,** *recūsāre dē* (w. abl.).
regard, (= consider) *habeō*[2]; (= respect, heed) *spectō*[1]; **have — for,** *cōnsulō*[3] (w. **dat.**).
region, *regiō, -ōnis,* F.
regret, *paenitet,*[2] impers. (w. **acc.** pers. and gen. th.).
reject, *repudiō.*[1]
release, *līberō*[1] (w. acc. and abl.).
relief, *subsidium, -ī,* N.
relieve, (= succor) *sublevō*[1] (w. acc.); (= set free) *līberō.*[1]
remain, *maneō*[2]; (= stay behind) *remaneō*[2]; (= stay through) *permaneō*[2]; (= be) *sum.*
remaining, *reliquus, -a, -um,* adj.
Reman, *Rēmus, -ī,* M.
remarkable, (= great) *māgnus, -a, -um,* adj.
remember, *meminī,* def. (w. gen.; also w. acc.); *memoriā teneō.*[2]
remembrance, *memoria, -ae,* F.
Remi, *Rēmī, -ōrum,* M.
remind, *admoneō*[2] (w. acc. pers. and gen. th.; also abl. th. **w.** *dē*).
remiss, be —, *dēsum.*

remotest, — part **of,** *extrēmus, -a, -um,* adj.
remove, *removeō*[2]; (= move to a distance) *āmoveō*[2]; (= do away with, destroy) *tollō.*[3]
render, *efficiō*[3]; (= bring) *ferō.*
renew, *renovō.*[1]
renown, of the highest —, *clārissimus, -a, -um,* adj.
reparation, make —, *satisfaciō*[3] (w. dat.).
repel, *dēfendō.*[3]
repent, *paenitet,*[2] impers. (w. acc. pers. and gen. th.).
reply, tell in —, *respondeō.*[2]
report, *nūntiō*[1]; (= divulge) *ēnūntiō*[1]; (= bring back word) *renūntiō.*[1]
reprobate, *improbus, -a, -um,* adj.
reputation, *opīniō, -ōnis,* F.
request, obtain a —, *impetrō.*[1]
require, *egeō*[2] (w. gen. or abl.).
requisition, make a — for, *imperō*[1] (w. acc. and dat.).
rescue, *ēripiō.*[3]
resist, *resistō.*[3]
resistance, offer —, *resistō.*[3]
resolve, *cōnstituō.*[3]
resources, *opēs, -um,* F.; (= private resources) *rēs familiāris.*
respect, *spectō*[1]; *observō.*[1]
respects, pay — to, *salūtō.*[1]
respond, *respondeō.*[2]
rest, the **— of,** *reliquus, -a, -um,* adj.; the —: *reliquī, -ōrum,* masc. adj. used subst.; *cēterī, -ōrum,* masc. adj. used subst.; set at —, *compōnō*[3]; (vb.) *requiēscō, -ere, -ēvī, -ētus* (adj.).
restore, *reddō*[3]; *restituō.*[3]
restrain, to — one's inclination, *sibi temperāre quīn* (w. subj.).
result, the — is, *fit (fīō).*
results, it —, *fit (fīō).*
retain, *retineō.*[2]
retard, *tardō.*[1]
return, 1. intr., *revertō*[3]; *revertor*[3]; *redeō.*[4] 2. tr., *reddō.*[3]
revenue, *vectīgal, -ālis,* N.
review, *recordor*[1] (usu. w. acc.); *recōgnōscō.*[3]

revile, *carpō.*[3]
revolt, — from, *dēscīscō*[3] (w. *ab* or *ā* and abl.).
reward, *praemium, -ī,* N.
Rhine, *Rhēnus, -ī,* M.
Rhone, *Rhodanus, -ī,* M.
riches, *dīvitiae, -ārum,* F.
ridge, *jugum, -ī,* N.
right, *dexter, -tra, -trum,* also *-tera, -terum,* adj.
ripe, *mātūrus, -a, -um,* adj.
rise, *orior*[4] (w. some fms. of the 3d conjugation).
rising, *ortus, -ūs,* M.; — ground, *tumulus, -ī,* M.
risk, *perīculum, -ī,* N.; — the loss of, *āmittō*[3]; without — of injury, *sine fraude.*
river, *flūmen, -inis,* N.
road, *iter, itineris,* N.; (= the travelled road) *via, -ae,* F.
rob, *exspoliō*[1] (w. acc. and abl.).
rock, *rūpēs, -is,* F.
Roman, *Rōmānus, -a, -um,* adj.
Romans, *Rōmānī, -ōrum,* M.
Rome, *Rōma, -ae,* F.
room, *locus, -ī,* M.
rough, *asper, -era, -erum,* adj.
round, pass —, *circumferō.*
rout, (= drive before one's self) *prōpellō, -ere, -pulī, -pulsus;* (= throw into confusion) *perturbō.*[1]
route, *iter, itineris,* N.
royal, *rēgius, -a, -um,* adj.
rugged, *asper, -era, -erum,* adj.
ruinous, *perniciōsus, -a, -um,* adj.
rule, *regō.*[3]
rush, make a —, *concurrō.*[3]

S.

Sabinus, *Sabīnus, -ī,* M.
sacrifice, 1. subst., *supplicia, -ōrum,* N.; purificatory —, *lūstrum, -ī,* N. 2. vb., (of victims) *immolō*[1]; (= lose) *āmittō.*[3]
sacrificial, — dish, *patera, -ae,* F.
sad, *tristis, -e,* adj.
saddles, furnished with —, *ephippiātus, -a, -um,* adj.

sadly — shut — 333

sadly, (= sad) *tristis, -e*, adj.
safe, *salvus, -a, -um*, adj.
safety, *salūs, -ūtis*, F.
sail, *nāvigō*.¹
sailor, *nauta, -ae*, M.
sake, for the — of, *causā* (w. gen. preceding).
Sambre, *Sabis, -is*, M. (acc. *-im;* abl. *-ī*).
same, *īdem, eadem, idem*, demonstr. pron.; **these — persons,** *idem* (pl. masc.); **at the — time**, *simul*, adv.
Santones, *Santonēs, -um*, M.
sate, *expleō*.²
satisfaction, give —, *satisfaciō*³ (w. dat.).
satisfy, *expleō*.²
savage, *barbarus, -a, -um*, adj.
say, *dīcō*³; **says he**, *inquit* (placed after one or more words of a direct quotation); **— not**, *negō*.¹
Scipio, *Scīpiō, -ōnis*, M.
sea, *mare, -is*, N.; (w. ref. to the surface) *aequor, -oris*, N.; by **—;** *mari;* (adj.) *maritimus, -a, -um*.
search, *quaerō*.³
season, winter —, *brūma, -ae*, F.
second, *secundus, -a, -um*, adj.; a **— time**, *iterum*, adv.
secondly, *deinde*, adv.
secret, in —, *occultō*, adv.
secure, *mūniō*⁴; **make —**, *mūniō*⁴; **strive to —**, *appetō*.³
see, *videō*²; *cernō*³; (= descry) *cōnspiciō*³; (= provide or see to) *prōvideō*.²
seek, *petō*³; **— after**, *appetō*.³
seem, *videor*.²
seems, it — good, *placet*,² impers.
Seguslavi, *Segūslāvī, -ōrum*, M.
seize, (= grasp firmly) *comprehendō*³; (= take away) *dētrahō*³ (w. acc. th. and dat. pers.); (= take possession of) *occupō*.¹
select, *dēligō*.³
Sena, *Sēna, -ae*, F.
senate, *senātus, -ūs*, M.

senator, *senātor, -ōris*, M.
send, *mittō*³; **— forward, — in advance**, *praemittō*³; **— back**, *remittō*³; **— for**, *arcessō*.³
separate, *dīvidō*³; *sēcernō*.³
Sequani, *Sēquani, -ōrum*, M.
Sequanian, *Sēquanus, -a, -um*, adj.
serve, to — as, *esse* (w. dat.).
service, *beneficium, -ī*, N.
services, *opera, -ae*, F.
serviceable, *idōneus, -a, -um*, adj.
Servius, *Servius, -ī*, M.
set, — up, *cōnstituō*³; **— out**, *proficiscor*³; **— forth**, *prōpōnō*³; **— at rest**, *compōnō*.³
setting, *occāsus, -ūs*, M.
settle, (of disputes) *compōnō*.³
sever, — themselves, pass. of *discernō, -ere, -crēvī, -crētus*.
several, *complūrēs, -a (-ia)*, gen. *-ium*, adj.
severe, *gravis, -e*, adj.
severely, *graviter*, adv.; *vehementer*, adv.
shake, **concutiō**, **-ere**, **-cussī, -cussus**.
shameless, — course, *audācia, -ae*, F.
shames, it —, *pudet*² (w. acc. pers. and gen. th.).
shape, *figūra, -ae*, F.
shave, *rādō, -ere, -sī, -sus*.
she, *ea* (fem. of *is*); omitted when implied in the context.
shed, *vīnea, -ae*, F.
shield, *scūtum, -ī*, N.
ship, *nāvis, -is*, F.; **— of war**, *nāvis longa*.
shipwreck, *naufragium, -ī*, N.
shore, (of the sea) *lītus, -oris*, N.
short, *brevis, -e*, adj.
shortest, *proximus, -a, -um*, adj.
shouting, *clāmor, -ōris*, M.
show, *ostendō*³; *doceō*.²
shrink, — from, *dēprecor*.¹
shudder, — at, *perhorrēscō, -ere, -horruī*.
shut, — up, *clausus, -a, -um*, p. a.

sick, *aeger*, *-gra*, *-grum*, adj.
side, *latus*, *-eris*, N.; (= part) *pars, partis*, F.
sight, *conspectus*, *-ūs*, M.; (= eyes) *oculi*, *-ōrum*, M.; catch — of, *conspiciō*.³
signal, *signum*, *-ī*, N.
Silanus, *Sīlānus*, *-ī*, M.
similar, *similis*, *-e*, adj.
since, *quoniam*, conj.; *cum*, conj. (w. subj.).
single, *singuli*, *-ae*, *-a*, distr. num. adj.; a —, *ūnus*, *-a*, *-um*, num. adj.
site, *locus*, *-ī*, M.
six, *sex*, indecl. num. adj.
sixty, *sexāgintā*, indecl. num. adj.
skilled, *perītus*, *-a*, *-um*, p. a. (w. gen.).
skillful, *perītus*, *-a*, *-um*, p. a. (w. gen.).
skin, *pellis*, *-is*, F.
slaughter, *caedēs*, *-is*, F.
slave, *servus*, *-ī*, M.
slavery, *servitūs*, *-ūtis*, F.
slaves, *familia*, *-ae*, F.; *servitium*, *-iī*, N. (in sing. or pl.).
slay, *occīdō*.³
sleep, (= rest) *requiēscō*, *-ere*, *-ēvi*, *-ētus* (adj.).
slight, *parvus*, *-a*, *-um*, adj.; *mediocris*, *-e*, adj.
sloping, *dēclīvis*, *-e*, adj.
small, *parvus*, *-a*, *-um*, adj.; (= low) *humilis*, *-e*, adj.
smaller, *minor*, *-us*, adj.
smoke, *fūmus*, *-ī*, M.
so, *sīc*, adv.; *ita*, adv.; *tam*, adv.; and —, *itaque*, conj.; so ... that, *sīc* or *ita* ... *utī* or *ut* (w. subj.); so ... as, *tam* ... *quam*.
soil, *ager*, *-grī*, M.
soldier, *miles*, *-itis*, M.; common —, *miles*, *-itis*, M.; foot —, *pedes*, *-itis*, M.
solicit, *postulō*.¹
solicitude, kind —, *voluntās*, *-ātis*, F.
solitude, *sōlitūdō*, *-inis*, F.
some, *aliquī*, *aliqua*, *aliquod*, indef. adj. pron.; — one, — thing, *aliquis, aliquid*, indef. pron.; some (pl.), *aliquī, quīdam*; some ... others, *aliī* or *pars* ... *aliī*; some ... the others (the whole number being made up of two parties), *alterī* ... **alterī**; to — place, *aliquō*, adv.
son, *fīlius*, *-iī*, M.
son-in-law, *gener*, *-erī*, M.
soon, as — as, *simul atque*, *ubī primum*.
sooner, *celerius*, adv.; *mātūrius*, adv.
sorry, I am —, *mē miseret*,² impers. (w. gen.).
sort, of such a —, *ējus modī*.
source, (= head) *caput*, *-itis*, N.
sovereign, — power, — authority, *regnum*, *-ī*, N.
space, *spatium*, *-iī*, N.
spare, 1. vb., *parcō*³ (w. dat.). 2. adj., *exiguus*, *-a*, *-um*.
speak, *loquor*³; *dīcō*.³
speaking, generally —, *plērumque*, adv.
special, (= specially) *magnopere*, adv.
speed, *celeritās*, *-ātis*, F.
speedily, *celeriter*, adv.
speedy, *celer*, *-eris*, *-ere*, adj.
spend, — the winter, *hiemō*.¹
spirit, *animus*, *-ī*, M.
spiritless, *iners*, *-ertis*, adj.
spring, *vēr*, *vēris*, N.
Spurius, *Spurius*, *-iī*, M., abbr. *Sp*.
squander, *profundō*, *-ere*, *-fūdī*, *-fūsus*.
stable, *firmus*, *-a*, *-um*.
stage, *gradus*, *-ūs*, M.
stand, (= keep erect) *stō*¹; stand, make a —, *cōnsistō*³; — by, *adsum* (w. dat.).
standards, *signa*, *-ōrum*, N.
state, *cīvitās*, *-ātis*, F.; *rēs pūblica*, *reī pūblicae*, F.
Statilius, *Statilius*, *-iī*, M.
station, *cōnstituō*³; *conlocō*.¹
stature, *statūra*, *-ae*, F.; diminutive —, *brevitās*, *-ātis*, F.
steadfastness, *cōnstantia*, *-ae*, F.

stealthily, *furtim*, adv.
steep, (= high) *altus, -a, -um,* p. a.
steer, *gubernō.*[1]
step, — **over,** *trānsgredior, -ī, -gressus* (w. acc.).
stern, *puppis, -is,* F.
still, (= nevertheless) *tamen,* conj
stimulate, *excitō.*[1]
stone, *saxum, -ī,* N.
stores, *cōpiae, -ārum,* F.
storm, *tempestās, -ātis,* F.
story, *tabulātum, -ī,* N.
strange, *mīrus, -a, -um,* adj.; (= new) *novus, -a, -um,* adj.
stratagem, *cōnsilium, -ī,* N.
strengthen, *corrōborō.*[1]
stretch, *tendō.*[3]
strife, (of political parties) *studium, -ī,* N.
strike, (by lightning) *percutiō, -ere, -cussī, -cussus.*
strive, — **to secure,** *appetō.*[3]
strong, so — **a,** *tantus, -a, -um,* adj.
struggle, 1. subst., *contentiō, -ōnis,* F. 2. vb., — **against odds,** *labōrō.*[1]
subject, *rēs,* gen. *rĕī (reī, rē),* F.; (= tributary) *stīpendiārius, -a, -um,* adj.
submit, *serviō*[4] (w. dat.); — **to:** *patior*[3]; *subeō*[4] (w. acc.).
subsist, *vescor*[3] (w. abl.).
substantially, (= almost) *ferē,* adv.; — **as follows,** *hūjusce modī.*
successful, *secundus, -a, -um,* adj; **bring to a** — **issue,** *bene gerō.*[3]
succession, in —, *continuus, -a, -um,* adj.
successive, *continuus, -a, -um,* adj.
such, *tālis, -e,* adj.; *is, ea, id,* demonstr. pron.; **of** — **a sort,** *ējus modī*; (= so great) *tantus, -a, -um,* adj.
sudden, *repentīnus, -a, -um,* adj.
suddenly, *subitō,* adv.; *repente,* adv.

Suebi, *Suēbī, -ōrum,* M.
Suessiones, *Suessiōnēs, -um,* M.
suffer, *patior.*[3]
sufferable, *ferendus, -a, -um* (ger. of *ferō*).
sufficient, *satis* (w. part. gen.); — **time,** *spatium, -ī,* N.
suitable, *idōneus, -a, -um,* adj. (w. *ad* and acc., or w. dat.; also w. rel. clause containing subj.).
Sulla, *Sulla, -ae,* M.; **of** —, *Sullānus, -a, -um,* adj.
sum, *summa, -ae,* F.
summer, *aestās, -ātis,* F.; **mid** —, *media aestās.*
summit, *summus, -a, -um,* adj.
summon, *ēvocō.*[1]
sun, *sōl, sōlis,* M.
sunrise, *ortus sōlis* (*ortus, -ūs,* M.).
sunset, *sōlis occāsus, -ūs,* M.
supplication, in —, *supplex, -icis,* adj.
supplies, *commeātus, -ūs,* M.
supply, *cōpia, -ae,* F.
support, send to the — **of,** *submittō*[3] (w. dat. pers.); **come to the** — **of,** *subveniō*[4] (w. dat.).
suppose, (ironical) *crēdō*[3]; (= believe) *crēdō*[3]; (= think) *existimō*[1]; (= judge) *jūdicō.*[1]
supremacy, *prīncipātus, -ūs,* M.
supreme, — **authority,** *imperium, -ī,* N.
surpass, *superō.*[1]
surrender, *trādō*[3]; *dēdō.*[3]
surround, *circumstō.*[1]
suspicion, (= opinion) *opīniō, -ōnis,* F.; **ground of** —, *suspīciō, -ōnis,* F.; **free from** —, *pūrgātus, -a, -um,* p. a.
sustain, *sustineō*[2]; *tolerō.*[1]
Swabians, *Suēbī, -ōrum,* M.
sway, *imperium, -ī,* N.
swear, *jūrō.*[1]
swift, *celer, -eris, -ere,* adj.; *vēlōx, -ōcis,* adj.
swiftness, *celeritās, -ātis,* F.
sword, *gladius, -ī,* M.; *ferrum, -ī,* N.
sworn, unite in a — **league,** *conjūrō.*[1]

T.

take, *capiō*[3]; (= lead out) *ēdūcō*[3]; — from or away, *adimō*[3] or *ēripiō*[3] (w. acc. **th.** and dat. pers.).
 talent, *talentum*, -ī, N.
 talk, — of, *dīcō*.[3]
   Tarquinii, *Tarquiniī*, -*ōrum*, M.
 task, take to —: *incūsō*[1] (w acc.); *accūsō*[1] (w. acc.).
 teach, *doceō*[2] (w. two accs.).
 teacher, *magister*, -*trī*, M.; *praeceptor*, -*ōris*, M.
 tear, *lacrima*, -*ae*, F.
 tell, — in reply, *respondeō*.[2]
 tempest, *tempestās*, -*ātis*, F.
 temple, *templum*, -ī, N.
 ten, *decem*, indecl. num. adj.; — **each,** *dēnī*, -*ae*, -*a*, distr. num. adj.
 tenth, *decimus*, -*a*, -*um*, ord. num. adj.
 territory, *fīnēs*, -*ium*, M.
 terror, overcome with —, *perterreō*.[2]
   Teucri, *Teucrī*, -*ōrum*, M.
 than, *quam*.
 thanks, *grātiae*, -*ārum*, F.
 that, *ille*, -*a*, -*ud*, demonstr. pron.; (weaker than *ille*) *is*, *ea*, *id*, demonstr. pron.; (= that of yours) *iste*, -*a*, -*ud*, demonstr. pron.; (stronger than *iste*) *iste tuus*; (contemptuous)*iste*,-*a*,-*ud*; — **one,** *ille*; (= who or which) *quī*, *quae*, *quod*, rel. pron.; (in final clauses): *ut*, *utī* (w. subj.); (w. comp.) *quō* (w. subj.); — not, *nē* (w. subj.); (in clauses of result) *ut*, *utī* (w. subj.); (after neg. expressions or interrog. expressions implying a neg.) *quīn* (w. subj.); (after verbs of fearing) *nē* (w. subj.); would —, *utinam* (w. opt. subj.); **in — the,** *quī* (= *cum is*) w. subj.
   the ... the, *quō* ... *eō*.
   Thebes, *Thēbae*, -*ārum*, F.
 their, (referring to the subject) — own, *suus*, -*a*, -*um*, poss. pron.; (= of them, of these) *eōrum*, *eārum* (gen. pl. of *is*); omitted when readily understood from the context.
 them, (pers. pron.) proper fm. of *is*, *ea*, *id*.
 themselves, (reflex.) *suī*, *sibī*, *sē* or *sēsē*; (intens.) *ipsī*, -*ae*, -*a*.
 then, (of time) *tum*, adv.; (= secondly) *deinde* (pronounced: de'inde), adv.; (of inference or transition) *igitur*, conj. (usu. follows the first word of the sent.).
 thence, *inde*, adv.
 there, *ibī*, adv.; (= thither) *eō* or *illō*, adv.
 therefore, *quā rē*; *proinde* (pronounced: pro'inde), adv.
 these, pl. of *hīc*, *haec*, *hōc*; (weaker) pl. of *is*, *ea*, *id*; — **things,** *haec*; **these ... those,** *hī ... illī*.
 they, (emphatic, = they themselves), *ipsī*.
 thing, *rēs*, gen. *rēī* (*reī*, *rē*), F.; **this one —,** *id ūnum*.
 think, *putō*[1]; (of a personal opinion) *opīnor*[1]; (= reckon, consider) *exīstimō*[1]; (= ponder, reflect on) *cōgitō*[1]; (= feel, be sensible of) *sentiō*[4]; (= judge) *jūdicō*[1]; (of an official opinion, as of a senator) *cēnseō*.[2]
 third, *tertius*, -*a*, -*um*, ord. num. adj.
 thirst, *sitis*, -*is*, F.
 thirteenth, (of a month) *Īdūs*, -*uum*, F.
 thirty, *trīgintā*, indecl. num. adj.
 this, *hīc*, *haec*, *hōc*, demonstr. pron.; (weaker than *hīc*) *is*, *ea*, *id*, demonstr. pron.; (= which) *quī*, *quae*, *quod*, rel. pron.; — **man,** *hīc*; — **one thing,** *id ūnum*.
 thither, *eō*, adv.
 thoroughly, — inform, — train, *ēdoceō*[2] (w. two accs.).
 those, pl. of *ille*; (= those of yours) pl. of *iste*; (contemptuous) pl. of *iste*; (ant. of rel.) pl. of *is*; [those] **who,** *quī*; **these ... those,** *hī ... illī*.

though, *quamvis* (w. subj.); *licet* (w. subj.); **even —,** *etiamsi* (w. indic. and subj. like *si*; the indic. is more common).

thought, take — for, *cōnsulō*[3] (w. dat.).

thousand, *mille*, indecl. **adj.**; also *mille* (as nom. and acc. sing.), subst. (w. part. gen.); in pl., *mīlia* or *mīllia*, subst. (w. part. gen.).

threaten, *minitor*[1] (w. dat. pers. and abl. or **acc.** th.).

three, *trēs, tria*, num. adj.; (w. substs. pl. in form, but sing. in meaning) *trīnī,* **-ae,** *-a.*

through, *per*, prep. w. acc.

throughout, *tōtus, -a, -um,* adj.

throw, (= throw to, **as of a** javelin) *adiciō, -ere, -jēcī, -jectus*; **— away,** *ēmittō*[3]; **— away (of on opportunity)** *āmittō.*[3]

thus, *ita*, adv.

tides, *maritimī aestūs.*

Tigurine, *Tigurīnus, -a, -um,* adj.

timber, *māteria, -ae,* F.

time, *tempus, -oris,* N.; (= season) *tempestās, -ātis,* F.; **at any —, at some —,** *aliquandō*, adv.; **at the same —,** *simul,* adv.; **at that —,** *tum,* adv.; **up to this —,** *adhūc,* adv.; **at one time ... at another,** *aliās ... aliās.*

tithes, *decimae, -ārum,* F.

Titurius, *Titūrius, -ī,* M.

Titus, *Titus, -ī,* M., abbr. *T.*

to, sign of dat.; (w. expressions of motion) *ad*, prep. w. acc.; (= into) *in*, prep. w. acc.; (expressing purpose) *ut* or (w. comp.) *quō* w. subj.

together, (= in company) *ūnā*, adv.; **— with,** *ūnā cum* (w. abl.); (= in succession) *continuus, -a, -um,* adj.; **come —,** *conveniō*[4]; **get —** (tr.), *cōnferō*; **call —,** *convocō*[1]; **to join —** (tr.), *inter sē jungere.*

toil, *labor, -ōris,* M.

too, (before an adj.) sign of comp.; (= also) *etiam*; (= excessively) *nimis,* adv.

topmost, *summus, -a, -um,* adj.

Torquatus, *Torquātus, -ī,* M.

total, sum —, *summa omnium.*

Toulouse, *Tolōsa, -ae,* F.

towards, *ergā*, prep. w. acc.; (= into or against) *in*, prep. w. acc.; **— the setting,** *sub occāsum.*

tower, *turris, -is,* F.

town, *oppidum, -ī,* N.; **free —,** *mūnicipium, -ī,* N.; **belonging to the —,** *oppidānus, -a, -um,* adj.

trader, *mercātor, -ōris,* M.

train, *exerceō.*[2]

transport, *trānsportō.*[1]

treat, *agō.*[3]

Treveri, *Trēverī, -ōrum,* M.

trial, *perīculum, -ī,* N.; **without —,** *indemnātus, -a, -um,* adj.

tribune, *tribūnus, -ī,* M.

tributary, *vectīgālis, -e,* adj.

tribute, *stīpendium, -ī,* N.

troops, *cōpiae, -ārum,* F.

trouble, *molestia, -ae,* F.

Troy, *Trōja, -ae,* F.

true, *vērus, -a, -um,* adj.

truly, *vērē,* adv.

trumpet, *tuba, -ae,* F.

truth, *vēritās, -ātis,* **F.**

try, *tentō*[1] or *temptō.*[1]

tumult, *tumultus, -ūs,* M.

twelfth, *duodecimus, -a, -um,* ord. num. adj.

twelve, *duodecim,* indecl. num. adj.

twenty, *vigintī,* indecl. num. adj.; **— sixth,** *sextus et vīcēsimus* or *vīcēsimus sextus, -a, -um,* ord. num. adj.

two, *duo, duae, duo,* num adj.; (w. substs. pl. in form, but sing. in meaning) *bīnī, -ae, -a,* distr. num. adj.; **— each, — and —,** *bīnī, -ae, -a,* distr. num. adj.

tyrant, *tyrannus, -ī,* M.

U.

Ubii, *Ubiī, -ōrum,* M.

unable, be —, *nōn possum.*

unacquainted, — with, *ignārus, -a, -um* (w. gen.).

under, (w. vb. of rest) *sub*, prep. w. abl.; (w. vb. of motion)

338 **understand**

sub, prep. w. acc.; — **arms,** *in armīs.*
  understand, *intellegō.*³
  understood, it is generally —, *cōnstat.*¹
  undertake, *suscipiō, -ere, -cēpī, -ceptus;* (= prepare) *parō.*¹
  undertaking, (= work) *opus, -eris,* N.
  unfair, *inīquus, -a, -um,* adj.
  unfavorable, *aliēnus, -a, -um,* adj.
  unfortunate, *miser, -era, -erum,* adj.
  unharmed, *incolumis, -e,* adj.
  uninjured, *incolumis, -e,* adj.
  uninterrupted, *continuus, -a, -um,* adj.
  unite, *conjungō*³ (w. acc. and dat. or *cum* w. abl.).
  unjustly, *injūstē,* adv.
  unless, *nisi,* conj.
  unmoved, *firmus, -a, -um,* adj.
  unparalleled, *singulāris, -e,* adj.
  unreasonable, *inīquus, -a, -um,* adj.
  unsuccessful, *adversus, -a, -um,* p. a.
  until, (= up to) *ad,* prep. w. acc.; *dum, quoad,* conj.; (= before) *antequam, priusquam,* adv.
  unwilling, *invītus, -a, -um,* adj.; be —, *nōlō.*
  up, see **verb or other** prominent word of the phrase.
  upbraid, *incūsō*¹ (w. acc.).
  upon, see **verb or** other prominent word of the phrase.
  upper, *superior, -ius,* adj.
  urge, *hortor*¹; — **to,** *hortor*¹ (w. *ut* and subj.); — **on,** *impellō.*³
  use, *ūtor*³ (w. abl.); (= be wont) so *leō*²; **to — force,** *vim facere.*
  useful, (= for use) *ūsuī.*
  usual, as —, *ex cōnsuētūdine.*
  Utica, *Utica, -ae,* F.
  utmost, sign **of** superl.
  utterly, sign of superl.

V.

Vaga, *Vaga, -ae,* F.
vain, in —, *nēquīquam,* adv.

ward

valor, *virtūs, -ūtis,* F.
value, *existimō.*¹
vanity, *vānitās, -ātis,* F.
Venelli, *Venellī, -ōrum,* M.
Venetia, *Venetia, -ae,* F.
Veneti, *Venetī, -ōrum,* M.
venture, *audeō.*²
Veragri, *Veragrī, -ōrum,* M.
Verbigene, *Verbigēnus, -a, -um,* adj.
verily, *vērō,* adv.
very, sign of superl.; (= self) *ipse, -a, -um,* demonstr. pron.; — **easily,** (after a neg.) *satis commodē;* — **first,** *prīmus statim.*
Vesontio, *Vesontiō, -ōnis,* M.
veteran, *mīles vetus* (*-eris,* adj.).
vice, *vitium, -iī,* N.
victor, *victor, -ōris,* M.
victory, *victōria, -ae,* F.
vie, *certō.*¹
view, in — of, *prae,* prep. w. abl.; **have in —,** *prōvideō*²; **burst into —,** *ērumpō.*³
vigor, *vīs, vīs,* F.
village, *vīcus, -ī,* M.
violence, *vīs, vīs,* F.
violent, *saevus, -a, -um,* adj.
virtue, *virtūs, -ūtis,* F.
visit, — with, *adficiō*³ (w. acc. and abl.).
Volusenus, *Volusēnus, -ī,* M.
vote, 1. vb., *dēcernō.*³ 2. subst., *cōnsilium, -iī,* N.
voyage, make a —, *nāvigō.*¹

W.

wage, — against, *īnferō* (w. acc. and dat.).
wagon, *carrus, -ī.* M.
wait, — for, *exspectō.*¹
wall, (generic term) *mūrus, -ī,* M.; (= rampart about a camp) *vāllum, -ī,* N.
want, (= wish) *volō.*
wanting, be —, *dēsum.*
war, *bellum, -ī,* N.; **ship of —,** *nāvis longa;* **to make — on,** *bellum facere* (w. dat.).
ward, — off from, *prōpulsō*¹ (w. *ab* or *ā* and abl.).

warlike — words

warlike, *bellicōsus, -a, -um,* adj.
warn, *moneō.*[2]
waste, lay —, *vastō.*[1]
watchmen, *vigiliae, -ārum,* F.
water, *aqua, -ae,* F.
way, give — to passion, *īrāscor*[3]; **be on one's —,** *pergō*[3]; **in what —,** *quem ad modum.*
we, *nōs, nostrī* and *nostrūm,* pers. pron.
wealth, *dīvitiae, -ārum,* F.
weary, *fessus, -a, -um,* p. a. (w. abl.); **I am —,** *mē taedet,*[2] impers., w. gen.
weep, *fleō.*[2]
welfare, *rēs,* gen. *reī (reī, rē),* F.
well, *bene,* adv.; **— enough,** *commodē,* adv.
what, (interrog.) *quī, quae, quod* (adj.) and *quid* (subst.); (= of what sort) *quālis, -e,* interrog. and rel. adj.; (= that which) *id quod.*
whatever, any —, *quīvis, quaevis, quodvis* and (subst.) *quidvis,* indef. pron.
when, *ubĭ, postquam, posteā quam, ut* (w. indic., usu. the perf. or hist. pres.); *cum.*
whenever, *cum* (w. indic.).
where, *ubĭ,* interrog. and rel adv.
wherefore, *quam ob rem.*
whether, *num,* interrog. particle; *-ne,* interrog. particle.
which, *quī, quae, quod,* rel. and interrog. pron.
while, *dum,* conj.
who, *quī* (M.), *quae* (F.), rel. pron.; *quis,* interrog. pron.
whoever, whatever, *quīcumque, quaecumque, quodcumque,* indef. rel. pron.; **— you please,** *quīlibet, quaelibet, quodlibet,* and (subst.) *quidlibet,* indef. pron.
whole, *tōtus, -a, -um,* adj.; (= all joined or massed together) *cūnctus, -a, -um,* adj.
why, *cūr,* adv.; (= for what reason) *quā dē causā; quid* (n. acc. used adv.).
wide, *lātus, -a, -um,* adj.

widely, *lātē,* **adv.; more —,** *lātius,* adv.
width, *lātitūdō, -inis,* F.
wife, *conjunx, -jugis,* F.
wild, *ferus, -a, -um,* adj.
will, good —, *grātia, -ae,* F.
willing, be not —, *nōlō.*
wine, *vīnum, -ī,* N.
wing, (of an army) *cornū, -ūs,* N.
winter, *hiems (hiemps), -emis,* F.; **— quarters,** *hīberna, -ōrum,* N.; **spend the —,** *hiemō.*[1]
wish, *volō; cupiō*[8]; **— well to,** *cupiō*[3] (w. dat.); **— rather,** *mālō.*
with, *cum,* prep. w. abl. (w. the abl. of pers. and rel. prons., *cum* is appended; as, *tēcum, quibuscum*); (in an expression of manner in which the subst. is limited by an adj.) sign of the abl.; **— each other,** *inter sē (sēsē);* **have to do —,** *pertineō*[2] (w. *ad* and acc.).
withdraw, 1. intr., *discēdō*[3]; *dēcēdō*[3]; *excēdō*[3]; (less often) *concēdō.*[3] **2. tr.,** *subdūcō*[3]; (= lead out) *ēdūcō.*[3]
withhold, — consent, (= [be] unwilling), *invītus, -a, -um,* adj.
within, sign of **abl.** of time within which.
without, *sine,* prep. w. abl.; (w. participial noun after neg. expressions) *quīn* (w. subj.); **— trial,** *indemnātus, -a, -um,* adj.; **— provocation,** *injūriā* (abl. of manner).
withstand, *sustineō*[2] (w. acc.).
witness, (= eye witness) *arbiter, -trī,* M.; (one who attests) *testis, -is,* C.
woman, *mulier, -eris,* F.
wonder, — at, *mīror.*[1]
wonderful, *mīrus, -a, -um,* adj.; (= to be wondered at) *mīrābilis, -e,* adj.
wont, *mōs, mōris,* M.
wood, *silva, -ae,* F.
word, to keep one's —, *fidem servāre.*
words, a few —, *pauca, -ōrum,* neut. pl. adj. used subst.

work, *opus, -eris,* N.
worst, *pessimus, -a, -um,* adj.
worthy, *dignus, -a, -um,* adj. (w. abl.; also w. rel. clause w. subj.).
would, — that, *utinam* (w. opt. subj.).
wound, *vulnero.*[1]
wrest, *eripio*[3] (w. acc. th. and dat. pers.).
wretched, *miser, -era, -erum,* adj.
write, *scribo.*[3]
wrong, *injuria, -ae,* F.

X.

Xenophon, *Xenophon, -ontis,* M.

Y.

year, *annus, -i,* M.; **the — after,** *anno post.*
yet, (= nevertheless) *tamen,* conj.; **and —,** *quamquam,* conj.; **not —,** *nondum,* adv.

yield, — obedience, *pareo.*[2]
yoke, *jugum, -i,* N.
yonder, (= that) *ille, illa, illud,* demonstr. pron.
you, (sing.) *tu, tui;* (pl.) *vos,* gen. *vestri* and *vestrum,* pers. pron.; **to —,** (= thither where you are) *istuc* (accent the last syllable), adv.
your, (sing.) *tuus, -a, -um;* (pl.) *vester, -tra, -trum,* poss. pron.; (contemptuous) *iste, ista, istud.*
yours, that of —, *iste tuus.*
yourself, *tui, tibi, te,* pers. pron. used reflex.
yourselves, *vos* (pl. of *tu* used reflex.).
youth, *adulescentia, -ae,* F.; (= young person) *adulescens, -entis,* C.

Z.

Zama, the people of —, *Zamenses, -ium,* M.
zeal, *studium, -ii,* N.

www.ingramcontent.com/pod-product-compliance
Lightning Source LLC
Chambersburg PA
CBHW030306240426
43673CB00040B/1077